Teaching High School
Social Studies

HARPER'S SERIES ON TEACHING

Under the Editorship of
ERNEST E. BAYLES

Teaching
High School
Social Studies

Problems in Reflective Thinking
and Social Understanding

Maurice P. Hunt
Social Science Division
Fresno State College

Lawrence E. Metcalf
College of Education
University of Illinois

HARPER & ROW, PUBLISHERS

New York, Evanston, and London

TEACHING HIGH SCHOOL SOCIAL STUDIES
Problems in Reflective Thinking and Social Understanding

Library of Congress catalog card number: 55–10940

CONTENTS

EDITOR'S FOREWORD vii

PREFACE ix

Part One
The Problem of Method

1. ALTERNATIVE THEORIES OF LEARNING AND THE DEMOCRATIC IDEAL

2. LEARNING AS DEVELOPMENT OF INSIGHT 23

3. THE REFLECTIVE METHOD 50

4. THE REFLECTIVE METHOD (CONTINUED) 65

5. VALUES AND REFLECTION 89

6. TECHNIQUES FOR STIMULATING REFLECTION 108

7. CLIMATE MAKING AS A PART OF METHOD 130

8. DISCUSSION AS A TOOL OF REFLECTIVE LEARNING 157

Part Two
The Problem of Content

9. THE TRADITIONAL CONCEPT OF CONTENT 191

10. A PROPOSAL FOR SELECTION OF CONTENT IN THE SOCIAL STUDIES 214

11. THE CLOSED AREAS: ECONOMICS 233

12. THE CLOSED AREAS: RACE AND MINORITY-GROUP RELATIONS 250

13. THE CLOSED AREAS: SOCIAL CLASS 270

14. THE CLOSED AREAS: SEX, COURTSHIP, AND MARRIAGE 287

Contents

15. THE CLOSED AREAS: RELIGION AND MORALITY   305

16. THE CLOSED AREAS: NATIONALISM, PATRIOTISM, AND
NATIONAL INSTITUTIONS   323

Part Three
Special Problems

17. ADAPTING REFLECTIVE METHOD TO THE STANDARD SOCIAL-
STUDIES SUBJECTS   343

18. MATERIALS OF INSTRUCTION IN THE SOCIAL STUDIES   368

19. EVALUATING THE RESULTS OF REFLECTIVELY ORIENTED
TEACHING   396

20. BUILDING AND MAINTAINING ACADEMIC FREEDOM IN THE HIGH
SCHOOL   431

INDEX OF NAMES   457

INDEX OF SUBJECTS   461

EDITOR'S FOREWORD

It is hard to do justice to this book without having it read like an advertiser's blurb, yet merit deserves recognition. If a social-studies teacher is to do the kind of work which his position demands and at the same time retain that position, he must build his procedures on the solid bedrock of genuinely democratic principles. This is true, to a degree, of all teachers, but those in the social studies are particularly exposed to pressures and attacks by anti-democratic forces.

Since this book is thoroughly grounded in democratic theory and is, in addition, abundantly illustrated by detailed, practical examples, it has what is necessary to supply real and far-reaching assistance not only to beginning teachers but to experienced ones as well. Moreover, much of the discussion is of such general value that the book can well be used in general-methods courses or even in philosophy of education. It is a product of discerning minds and is beautifully written—clear, forceful, cogent, stylistically excellent, logical, scholarly. If much of the current educational discussion of thinking and problem solving had been written in light of what is in the following pages, it would be tremendously improved. I know of no treatment of reflective teaching which equals it. Moreover, in my final examination of page proof, much as I tried I found it almost impossible to skim or skip; everything in the book is important, even the final and distinctly unusual chapter on academic freedom. A well chosen, pertinent bibliography accompanies each chapter.

Ernest E. Bayles

PREFACE

This book is addressed chiefly to prospective, beginning, and experienced teachers of secondary-school social studies. Although intended as a textbook in methods of teaching the social studies, the book gives considerable attention to general education and its content.

Unlike many methods books, this one has a definite theoretical orientation, and an approach to teaching consistent with that theory is explicitly elaborated throughout the text. It is the authors' belief that the foremost purpose of social-studies instruction in the secondary school should be reflective examination of value conflicts now besetting American culture. The recommended method of learning is reflective study of problems, and the recommended content of the social studies consists of the data which render understandable to high-school students the major conflicts of our time.

The most important *technical* problem facing social-studies teachers is taken to be the stimulation and guidance of reflection. This technical task can be mastered only by teachers who possess an adequate theory of education; therefore, the authors reject an eclectic, bag-of-tricks approach to methods instruction.

The first two chapters develop a theory of learning based upon pragmatic philosophy and field psychology. The implications for social-studies instruction of these two areas of intellectual investigation are made explicit. In the authors' view, research in learning and the implications of a democratic philosophy point straight to reflective thinking as the most productive and democratic method of instruction. A research worker is able to discover knowledge only to the extent that he is able to reflect carefully and precisely upon the problems in his discipline. Likewise, a learner in school must think reflectively in order to develop the best possible insights into the nature of his social environment.

Chapters 3 and 4 give particular attention to the process of reflective thinking. Topics treated in these chapters include the differences between non-reflective and reflective approaches to problem solving, the contribu-

ix

tions of semantics to reflective method, the characteristics of hypotheses, the nature and role of evidence, and the logic of the testing process. These chapters are included on the assumption that, unless teachers understand clearly the difference between good and bad thinking, they are not likely to be successful in promoting conceptual learning.

It is generally agreed that the social studies are normative (evaluative) in much of their content. Even factual content sometimes has meaning only in terms of value interpretations. Therefore, in Chapter 5 the authors treat the problem of values. Reflective thinking is a term which embodies the fundamental meaning of scientific method, and one of the most pervasive issues in American culture is whether the methods of science can serve as a guide to the good life. In Chapter 5 the authors try to show how reflection may help one to choose wisely among competing and contradictory values. It is their belief that reflective thinking is a method of inquiry which can, within certain prescribed limits, help confused and strife-torn individuals solve their moral difficulties.

Having presented the theory of reflective method in the first five chapters, the authors turn to certain practical problems of instruction in Chapters 6, 7, and 8. Chapter 6 discusses the various technical difficulties involved in use of reflective methodology. Techniques of instruction are treated in considerable detail. In Chapter 7, recognition is given to the fact that many persons regard the reflective approach as overly intellectualistic and neglectful of man's emotional make-up. It is shown in this chapter how teachers may create in their classrooms an atmosphere emotionally favorable to reflection. Chapter 8 treats the discussion "method" and relates various problems in discussion to different steps or phases of reflection. This "how-to-do-it" chapter is illustrated with excerpts drawn from classroom discussions.

Part II is entirely devoted to problems of content. The first two chapters discuss curriculum organization and the question of what content is most appropriate to our proposed theory of teaching. A rationale for a new type of core is developed, but the authors also argue that teachers of conventional high-school subjects can use reflective thinking as a means for teaching social understanding.

Chapters 11–16 present the results of a cultural analysis which seeks to expose the belief patterns of Americans. On the basis of recent studies of

American culture the authors identify some of the conflicts in each of six "closed areas." A closed area is defined as a segment of culture which traditionally has been largely closed to reflective examination, and within which many superstitions and rationalizations may be identified. These closed areas and their contradictions are, the authors believe, the chief sources of social tension today. One cannot understand today's society and its problems unless one explores fully and freely the dominant and conflicting beliefs in each of our closed areas.

Chapters 11–16 not only list and discuss some of our most disturbing conflicts but also present data which shed light on the origin and meaning of these conflicts. Discussion questions for high-school students are included, in the hope that they may suggest to teachers ways to use cultural conflicts as starting points in instruction. At all times teachers are cautioned not to believe that conflicts described in these chapters are the only ones worthy of reflective study in the high school. Also teachers are warned against assuming that students are necessarily aware of the conflicts described and enumerated.

Part III deals with some of the special problems of a teacher who employs the reflective method as a road to social understanding. Chapter 17 shows how teachers of conventional textbook-oriented subjects may use reflective thinking as a method of teaching. The use of textbooks, workbooks, and other standard materials is discussed for each of the commonly offered social-science courses. Chapter 18 discusses materials of instruction. Chapter 19 discusses problems in evaluation peculiar to teachers who stress reflective thinking and social understanding. Chapter 20 discusses academic freedom, and how teachers may protect from minority attack the students' freedom to study in areas of controversy.

Although the present book is of special interest to those who teach courses in the teaching of secondary-school social studies, the authors believe that it should have appeal to other groups. In treating basic issues in psychology, philosophy, and social science, and in treating ideological conflicts in a way not heretofore attempted, the book should be of interest to all of the following:

Teachers of educational sociology (because of its treatment of American thought patterns in Chapters 11–16).

Teachers of speech (because of its treatment of emotional climate-making

and of discussion techniques, and its identification of controversial issues,
in Chapters 7–8 and 11–16).

Teachers of educational psychology (because of its treatment of learning
theory and of the nature of reflective thinking, and its identification of
typical intrapersonal conflicts of youth, in Chapters 1–5 and 11–16).

Guidance counselors (because of its treatment of typical emotional conflicts of youth).

Anyone charged with developing programs of general education, whether
in high school or college, whether in social sciences or humanities.

Acknowledgments

The authors are indebted to many persons both living and dead. Throughout the book, the influence of the thinking of John Dewey will be evident
to readers. An immense debt is also owed the late Boyd H. Bode, with
whom both authors were privileged to take courses. The imprint of H.
Gordon Hullfish's thinking will also be visible, particularly in the authors'
interpretation of moral conflicts as representing choices between competing
goods. Alan Griffin helped the authors see the significance of contradictions
in belief in the "closed areas" as starting points for the teaching process in
the social studies.

The influence and direct help of Professor Ernest E. Bayles have been of
incalculable value. He read carefully the entire manuscript and through his
suggestions it was greatly improved. Morris L. Bigge also read parts of the
manuscript and gave invaluable help. William C. Beatty, Jr., gave appre-
ciated assistance by criticizing Chapters 12–14. Thomas M. Brigham offered
suggestions for treating material in Chapter 7. We wish to thank the following publishers for permission to quote material in Chapter 19: Educational
Testing Service for Problem III, Logical Reasoning Test, Form A; Harper &
Brothers for test exercises drawn from *Appraising and Recording Student
Progress* by Eugene Smith and Ralph W. Tyler; Houghton Mifflin Company
for the test items drawn from *The Construction and Use of Achievement
Examinations* by Herbert E. Hawkes, E. F. Lindquist, and C. R. Mann.
We wish to thank both the Philosophy of Education Society and the maga-
zine, *Educational Theory*, for permission to quote in full the Society's state-
ment of intellectual freedom, which appears in Chapter 20.

Preface

Deep appreciation goes to our wives, Mabel and Barbara, who helped to prepare the manuscript for publication. The authors, of course, take full responsibility for whatever shortcomings the book possesses.

M. P. H.
L. E. M.

June, 1955

PART ONE

The Problem of Method

Chapter 1

Alternative Theories of Learning and the Democratic Ideal

VIEWED broadly, Chapter 1 examines the role of education in a democracy. It is assumed that this role is the transmission to new generations of democratic ideals, but that this function will not be fulfilled except as students learn to think critically about issues which are central to our democratic society. Specifically, the chapter explores certain characteristics of American culture which produce conflicts for individuals and pervasive social tensions. Further, it scrutinizes two fundamentally different approaches to education, issuing from different conceptions of how students learn, and shows the bearing of these approaches on individual and social problems.

The Function of Education in a Democracy

EDUCATION AS TRANSMISSION OF CULTURAL HERITAGE [1]

In every culture, education is regarded as the transmission from one generation to another of that part of the culture which is considered of ongoing value. Although a culture has material as well as nonmaterial aspects, it is chiefly the nonmaterial with which education is concerned: attitudes, beliefs, knowledge, values, ideas, myths, skills, techniques, and habits. Education, then, is that process by which the young are helped to develop or acquire the ideational and symbolic equipment and physical skills believed necessary by adults to carry on the chosen way of life.

---

[1] The authors use the term *culture* in its sociological sense of a "way of life." The culture of a people includes their material achievements (tools, buildings, artifacts, etc.), social institutions, symbol systems, customs, beliefs, and attitudes.

Simply to say that education is the transmission of the cultural heritage, however, leaves many questions unanswered. The present book finds its justification and its chief problem in the fact that transmission of culture can take many forms and that the appropriate form depends upon the nature of existing culture as well as upon the kind of culture which people envision for the future.

Great uncertainty has developed in the United States over the kind of education we should have. Some of our most hotly debated issues relate to the curriculums and methods of teaching in our public schools. One reason why Americans find it difficult to agree on what the schools should be doing is that many of us do not understand our culture, and neither can we agree on what would constitute cultural improvement. Many Americans at the mid-point of the twentieth century even seem to favor educational practices which would eventually destroy those very aspects of the culture which they prize most highly. Like moths impelled by their tropisms to fly into a flame, they seem bent on destroying the very things they cherish.

SOME FEATURES OF THE AMERICAN CULTURE WHICH BEAR ON THE PROBLEMS OF EDUCATION

Certain aspects of American culture are especially relevant to social-studies education. We shall discuss two such features. One is the presence of conflict on a wide scale, a characteristic of most societies at our stage of history. But compared with many other cultures, our own is particularly conflict ridden, and for good reasons. Settled by peoples of diverse origins and outlooks, the United States has been, ever since its founding, the scene of competing political, economic, and social beliefs. Furthermore, the rate of industrialization itself tends to generate conflict. It speeds change, with a result that from generation to generation beliefs undergo marked alteration. Industrialization creates gulfs between children and parents, parents and grandparents. It also tends to fragmentize society into highly specialized occupational groupings, each with its own point of view and its peculiar interests.

There are two levels of conflict. *Interpersonal* conflict arises when individuals or groups hold beliefs sharply opposed to those of other individuals or groups. We often refer to conflicts on this level as "controversial issues." Persons on each side of an interpersonal conflict, or dispute, may be quite consistent in their own outlooks, even though in sharp disagreement with the opposing position. In our culture such conflict arises between capital

4

and labor, among social classes, among racial, religious, and ethnic groups, among age groups, and sometimes between the sexes.

Interpersonal conflict tends to become internalized within the personalities of individuals so that they are at war with themselves. Caught in a culture in which interpersonal conflict is always present, they often accept as true and good *both* sides of many issues, thus incorporating cultural conflicts into their own personalities. When individuals become aware of their own incompatibilities of outlook, the resulting internal struggle may be referred to as *intrapersonal* conflict. Although the content of an intrapersonal conflict may be no different from that of an interpersonal conflict, it may exact a greater toll because it can lead to disintegration of personality.

Intrapersonal conflict often takes a particular form, as follows: We have a great number of norms, or standards, to which individuals are expected to accede: success, friendliness, honesty, sexual purity, and a certain degree of gentility. Unfortunately, biological drives or culturally imposed barriers prevent many persons from achieving these goals. The culturally imposed barriers include physical and social conditions which make it difficult to achieve goals—as in the case of the ideal of economic success, which obviously not everyone can achieve. They also include existence of contradictory or conflicting goals, which logically can never be achieved by the same person at the same time. For example, money and friends are major goals in today's culture. But it is not unusual to find that the more money one makes the fewer friends he has. As one cynic—or perhaps realist—has put it: "The higher you go, the colder it gets." Persons in our culture are often driven in their behavior to violate their own beliefs. Plagued with conflict of this kind, they tend to become increasingly uncertain as to what to believe and value.

Conflict *per se* is not necessarily harmful. In fact, it stimulates individuals to expenditure of effort. Thought itself may be stimulated by conflict. One writer suggests that "Every sort of conflict may be useful if it is not too intense." [2] Conflict becomes burdensome to individuals when they can no longer make normal progress toward resolving it; and it becomes dangerous to a culture only when solutions do not keep pace with generation of new issues. Some students of culture feel that at present the United States is overburdened with conflict. For example, we are told that "It is doubtful

[2] Mandel Sherman, *Mental Hygiene and Education,* Longmans, Green & Company, 1936, p. 150.

5

. . . if other societies have such a large number of persons who are unable to measure up to basic role expectations as is the case in our society." [3]

Another feature of American culture which prospective teachers should understand is the presence of *closed areas*—areas of belief and behavior which are largely closed to rational thought. In these areas people usually react to problems blindly and emotionally. Closed areas are saturated with prejudices and taboos. In our culture, irrational responses commonly occur in the areas of morality and religion, sex, race and minority-group relations, social class, nationalism and patriotism, economics, and politics.

Our closed areas change from one historical period to another. For example, sex is now much more open to reflective study than it was fifty years ago, whereas comparative socioeconomic ideologies (including the issue of communism) is more nearly closed to rational examination than even a decade ago. At any given time some of the areas named above will be much more tightly closed to reflection than will others; and all have their open aspects—facets which are relatively free of prejudiced thinking.

Our closed areas today exist as islands of totalitarian thought and practice in the midst of a culture which is straining in democratic directions. The term *totalitarian* is appropriate here because the behavior of the American people with respect to their closed areas is akin to the behavior of the peoples of totalitarian states. That is, each closed area has a set of sanctioned (albeit often irrational or inconsistent) beliefs which we try to inculcate in the young through indoctrination and propaganda; people are not taught to rely for answers on independent reflection but on the authority of tradition, the church, or political leaders. And severe pressure—both social and legal—may be placed on persons who adopt beliefs or behavior contrary to those sanctioned.

Perhaps the chief difference between totalitarian cultures and our own is that in the former virtually *all* controversial fields are closed—and closed uniformly and consistently. In a culture with democratic inclinations fewer areas are closed to open discussion, and in certain places—as in the universities—there may be none closed at all. It is perhaps the freedom of inquiry of our universities which differentiates us most sharply from totalitarian nations.

It is hardly surprising that our sharpest intrapersonal conflicts occur in closed areas. Conflicts in areas of belief such as sex, religion, and race are

[3] Francis E. Merrill and H. Wentworth Eldredge, *Culture and Society,* Prentice-Hall, Inc., 1952, p. 182.

6

not only common but often sufficiently intense to cause severe emotional disturbance. In areas open to free reflection, conflicts are frankly faced and resolved—if not easily, at least without undue tension. But in closed areas every problem is likely to be troublesome because of the difficulty of examining it.

During the past two decades it has been widely recognized among social scientists and mental hygienists that discrepancies in a culture may have an eroding effect on the mental health of its members. We are told that "A well-integrated culture will presumably not produce as many maladjusted personalities as a disintegrated one. Cultures that are full of glaring contradictions will produce more than their share of personality difficulties." [4] A similar view is stated by Horney: ". . . We recognize that neuroses are generated not only by incidental individual experiences, but also by the specific cultural conditions under which we live." [5] Some authorities feel that, since certain conflicts are central to our culture and tend to be reflected in most personalities, there is a common neurotic type expressive of the times. [6]

It would be an overstatement, of course, to say that in modern America most persons who feel conflict become neurotic. Neurotic symptoms occur only in cases where a conflict is unusually intense or where, because of repression or other factors, an individual cannot face a conflict and deal with it rationally. But where serious mental disturbance does result, moral problems of an unfortunate sort are generated. A typical "moral" problem in our culture results from feelings of guilt or remorse over failure to attain goals sanctioned by the culture. And, as one authority puts it, "This feeling of guilt is the only one which most people experience as a moral problem, while the genuine moral problem, that of realizing one's potentialities, is lost from sight." [7]

The existence of closed areas has resulted in uncritical transmission of values from one generation to another. It was inevitable that this practice could not continue indefinitely, because the rise of science and spread of the scientific spirit, coupled with the growth of democracy, were bound to

[4] *Ibid.*, p. 180.
[5] Karen Horney, *The Neurotic Personality of Our Time*, W. W. Norton & Company, 1937, p. viii. See also Franz Alexander, *Our Age of Unreason*, J. B. Lippincott Company, 1942, chap. 7.
[6] Horney, *op. cit.*, pp. 284 ff.
[7] Erich Fromm, "Individual and Social Origins of Neurosis," *Personality in Nature, Society and Culture* (Clyde Kluckhohn and Henry Murray, eds.), p. 411.

bring under critical scrutiny all traditional beliefs and values. The inconsistency of beliefs within the closed areas, as well as their common tendency to conflict with facts established by modern scientific disciplines such as medicine, psychiatry, and the social sciences, meant that increasingly beliefs in these areas would come under attack. Such attack against old values has proceeded steadily since the rise of modern science and has reached new peaks in the twentieth century. It has had temporary setbacks, to be sure, and there will be more. Present attempts in the United States to label subversive any criticism of traditional values are one example of such. These temporary setbacks only serve to foster moral uncertainty and confusion.

But the process of extending the method of scientific inquiry into the closed areas seems likely to continue. Old, uncritically accepted values will lose much of their force. And, although the culture is sure to develop new standards, it may be that new, more critical attitudes will prevail, even toward newly developed norms. In short, there may in the future be fewer closed areas—which is the same as saying that as a people we shall have become more reflective.

To reach this condition, however, involves a great deal of stress and strain. The birth of a more open-minded approach to issues in closed areas is not easy. Many persons feel that they can find security only in destroying freedom of thought and returning to an authoritarian pattern of living.

The Resolution of Conflicts in Authoritarian as Opposed to Democratic Cultures

Let us further explore the idea of education as transmission of culture. It has been pointed out that the method by which culture is transmitted from one generation to another differs from society to society, and that a particular culture calls for particular educational practices. We shall now illustrate this generalization by examining how education functions in two contrasting types of culture.

Education in a Modern Totalitarian State. An educational system designed to serve the needs of dictatorship will differ fundamentally from an educational system designed to serve the best interests of a democracy. One of the most significant facts of dictatorship, from the standpoint of education, is the existence of a body of doctrine which functions as a national ideology. This group of beliefs is likely to be fairly consistent internally and to pervade all areas of the culture. Its central ideas are relatively unchanging over long periods of time, whether they revolve around racial supremacy or around the beliefs of Marx and Lenin.

The function of education in a dictatorship is conceived to be the uncritical transmission of this official belief-structure. The subject matter of education is thus predetermined and essentially the same in every school. The method of instruction is likewise uniform; it is the method of prescription and indoctrination. The "correct" beliefs are taught by withholding and slanting evidence. Doubt and reflection are rigorously excluded from classrooms, because in a dictatorship these are the truly subversive influences.

The Soviet Union of today furnishes an excellent example of the practice of education in a dictatorship. At first, Soviet educators borrowed ideas freely from the progressive-education movement in the United States and for a time it looked as if the Soviet school system might come to emphasize free and independent thought. But the Russian rulers soon decided that, given their aims, such emphasis would be fatal. A school system which permitted doubt and inquiry would soon undermine the official dogmas on which the state was built. It is reported that Shatsky, the leading Russian "progressive," escaped liquidation in the early 1930's only by committing suicide. The Soviet system now stresses indoctrination and prescription, drill and rote memorization.

In any culture, schools must take some stand with respect to how conflict is to be treated in classrooms. In a dictatorship, schools try to minimize both interpersonal and intrapersonal conflict by teaching an official ideology and by allowing students, in so far as possible, to perceive only one side of questions which in a democracy would be regarded as highly controversial. In short, school authorities hope that suppression of free intellectual inquiry will reduce conflict to an innocuous level. Even so, in a dictatorship some conflicts are bound to appear, for many of the same reasons that they appear in our own culture. When interpersonal conflicts arise, attempts are made to remove them from sight through use of propaganda and terror. If either interpersonal or intrapersonal conflict appears in classrooms, teachers have no alternative but to tell students what to believe and to try to gain assent through use of rewards and punishments.

In summary, in dictatorships a foremost task of education is *uncritical* transmission of sanctioned features of the culture, achieved by suppressing intelligence and by dealing forcefully with controversy wherever it threatens to unsettle the social order.

Education in a Democratically Inclined Culture. Although a democratic culture does not have an official ideology in the sense that a dictatorship has, it is assumed that, if a democratic society is to survive, there will be general agreement among its members as to its central values. While peripheral values may remain in flux, a democracy is in peril if its citizens cannot agree on an operational meaning of core values such as the dignity and worth of individuals, the method of intelligence, and political freedom. If such agreement is impossible, conflicts between individuals and groups and disintegration of personalities are likely to reach unmanageable proportions.

Some students of American culture feel that it is approaching a state of possible breakdown and disintegration because of growing inability to agree on central values. It is thought that, in addition to conflict normally attached to disputes over peripheral values, conflict is developing over fundamental ends. We are ceasing to be a community, as this term is used by sociologists.[8]

An urgent task of education in a democracy is to help members of society find consensus in their central values. This role of education is no less essential in democratic than in nondemocratic societies. But in democracies the task is perhaps more difficult. To say that "The schools of America should teach children the American heritage," or that, whatever is meant by the American heritage, it should be taught to the young as something absolutely true and good, is an oversimplification. Any school in the United States which tries to transmit the cultural heritage uncritically, in the same manner in which officially supported beliefs are transmitted to the young in a dictatorship, finds itself in a paradoxical position. *There is not one heritage in the United States; there are many heritages.* The competing traditions that have always been characteristic of American culture have been accentuated by an accelerated rate of change during the past century. Uncritical transmission of all of them can do little but compound confusion and intensify conflict.

A challenge before American education is to help the American people find consensus on the meaning of democracy—but in ways consistent with the requirements of democratic culture. The means which are used are of crucial importance because they determine whether society shall move in

[8] See Joseph K. Hart, *Education in the Humane Community*, Harper & Brothers, 1951, chaps. 1 and 2; also W. O. Stanley, *Education and Social Integration*, Teachers College, Columbia University, 1953.

authoritarian or democratic directions. Consensus building is synonymous with resolution of conflict. To achieve consensus there must be general agreement among individuals as well as inner harmony of individual personalities. An apt term for describing the unique task of education in a democracy is "creative resolution of conflict." By this we mean achievement by disputing persons and by individuals suffering inner turmoil of "third alternatives," that is, new positions which, although perhaps to some degree compromises of competing outlooks, also include genuinely new values which effectively erase conflict and place life on a level of deeper insight. It is assumed that creative resolution of conflict can occur only in an atmosphere which is reflective and in which ego defenses are reduced to a minimum.

In summary, we may say that the chief role of education in a democracy is intelligent or critical transmission of cultural heritages, during the course of which disagreements among individuals and incompatibilities in personal outlook are exposed and resolved creatively.

Theories of Learning and Their Implications for Classroom Practice

Whether a teacher believes that education can and should foster creative resolution of conflict in closed areas of culture depends in part on his theory of learning. A great deal of confusion and uncertainty exists among teachers as to just how learning proceeds. A root source of confusion lies in the fact that the *products* of learning are several in number and appear on the surface to differ greatly from each other. They include sensory-motor skills (as walking), perceptual-motor skills (as typing from copy), memorized information (as "Columbus discovered America in 1492"), concepts (as an understanding of the principles of democratic living), tastes (as a preference for blondes), and problem-solving ability (as a capacity to analyze arguments relating to protective tariffs in order to select an intelligent course of action).

Theories of learning which have so far emerged seem to explain certain of these products of learning more adequately than others. One explanation is that psychologists have given more attention in their experimentation to those products of learning—particularly motor skills and memorized information—which lend themselves most readily to laboratory study. Concentration of study on a few learning products, to the exclusion of the rest, has resulted in theoretical explanations which are limited in usefulness. A brief

11

review of the development of learning theory over the past century makes this point evident.

HISTORICAL DEVELOPMENT OF LEARNING THEORY

A theory of learning which gained wide acceptance in the nineteenth century has come to be known as *associationism*. "Associationism is the doctrine that we connect things in memory, in thought, and in all mental life, simply because they were connected in our original experience with them; and since our first encounters with things are by means of our senses, the associationist maintains that all the complexity of mental life is reducible to sense impressions, the elementary components of consciousness, as connected in experience." [9] Although associationism dates back as far as Aristotle, Thomas Brown (writing in the early nineteenth century) gave it its first modern development. He devised the celebrated "secondary laws of association," which have a decidedly modern ring: the principles of (1) duration, (2) liveliness, (3) frequency, and (4) recency. Alexander Bain (writing in the middle of the nineteenth century) developed associationist theory further. He tied learning closely to physiological responses, believing that feelings of pleasure and pain are responsible for most learning. He suggested that learning begins with random movements and proceeds through retention of acts which bring pleasure and elimination of acts which bring pain; the new response is fixed through repetition. [10]

The rise of the doctrine of evolution introduced the principle of heredity to explain individual differences. Organs and functions were explained in terms of survival value—that is, physiology and behavior were thought to undergo continuous modification in such a way as to promote adaptation of the organism to its environment. Behavior which did not contribute to survival was abandoned and behavior which did have survival value was reinforced. These ideas made untenable the older associationist theory. Herbert Spencer did more, perhaps, than anyone else to apply the evolutionist point of view to psychology.

In the early twentieth century a movement in psychology known as *behaviorism* developed. Behaviorists defined human behavior in terms of physical and chemical processes. The human organism was regarded as a mechanism, without purpose, behaving in certain ways because of the laws

[9] Gardner Murphy, *Historical Introduction to Modern Psychology*, Harcourt, Brace & Company, 1949, p. 26. The following four pages follow Murphy's analysis.
[10] *Ibid.*, pp. 60, 105–106.

of chemistry and physics. Behavioristic psychologists were not concerned with problems of consciousness, feeling, mental states, purposes, and values. Behaviorists ignored the existence of learning which involved purely mental processes and constructs (ideational learning). Watson in the United States denied that mental phenomena are susceptible to scientific study and, like Pavlov, tried to explain behavior as a product of conditioned responses. In behaviorist thinking, a conditioned response was established as a result of repeated association with a given stimulus. Such responses were thought to be established as "pathways" developed in the nervous system through lowered synaptic resistance.

Murphy tells us that "In place of the classical doctrine of the association of ideas, behaviorism substitutes the conception of an ordered series of *motor* responses. The center of gravity is moved, so to speak, from the cortex to the periphery." [11]

This quotation requires explanation. The older associationist psychology recognized the existence of ideas having their origin (or place of residence) in brain centers (particularly the cortex). Learning occurred as a result of associations of ideas. In contrast, behaviorists came to think of learning as motor (rather than ideational) responses to stimuli. They thought the origin of motor responses to be nerve centers outside the cortex—i.e., the "periphery" of the nervous system.

Thorndike was a leading exponent of a related point of view. His name is associated with a stimulus-response (S-R bond) theory of learning. S-R bond or connectionist psychology, although not advocating the same neurological basis for learning as early behaviorism, appears to interpret learning in essentially the same way. Connectionists assume that, through repetition, responses "connect" with stimuli and tend to repeat themselves whenever the same stimuli are encountered. The term *conditioned response* may likewise be used to refer to the basic unit of learning as S-R theorists interpret it.

In spite of the apparent difference between associationist and behaviorist-connectionist psychologies, there are significant similarities. Most of the early laws of association (such as recency, frequency, intensity, and the effects of rewards and punishments) were adopted by connectionists, but stated now in terms of stimulus-response relationships. In other words, the same factors which were believed to fix mental associations under the older

[11] *Ibid.*, p. 265.

theory of learning were now seen as fixing stimulus-response connections under the new.

According to Murphy, behaviorism (in which he includes connectionism) may be labeled a new form of associationism. He says, "It is . . . not very difficult to bring conditioning into line with the classical associationist view that rewards and punishments, pleasures and pains, act in some way to reinforce some acts and to inhibit others. . . ." [12] And at another point Murphy says, "If there is more emphasis upon behavioral phenomena, and less emphasis on mental connections in the classical sense, in the learning experiments of the present century, one must still admit that it is associationism with which one is concerned. . . ." [13]

Modern connectionist and associationist theories of learning are similar in fundamental respects. Both say that the basic unit of learning is the conditioned response. For both, habit formation is acquisition of automatically repetitive and unvarying responses. Learning which follows the principles of associationism (in which we include connectionism) is considered largely *thoughtless* and *without understanding*. It involves fixing responses in a more or less mechanical fashion. It emphasizes drill and memorization and relies for motivation chiefly upon rewards and punishments. From here on we shall call this general interpretation of learning *associationism*.

Present Tendencies in Learning Theory

The most recent major movement in psychology is known as *field* psychology. Field psychology incorporates many of the insights of earlier Gestalt, or configurational, psychology. Although using a different terminology and in some of its aspects making different metaphysical assumptions, field psychology is markedly similar to the pragmatic psychologies of John Dewey and Boyd H. Bode. Its significance for our present discussion lies largely in the fact that it has focused attention once more on "ideational" learning. Instead of viewing learning as the connecting of formerly unrelated stimuli and responses, field theorists see learning as the discovery of meaning in a perceptual field—commonly called *insight*. Tested insights lead to generalizations which enable a learner to behave intelligently in similar confronting situations of the future.

Within the framework of field psychology, learning is always accompanied by *understanding* or *grasp of meaning*. This is true of all types of

[12] *Ibid.*, p. 273.
[13] *Ibid.*, p. 269.

learning, whether habits, skills, attitudes, or knowledge. Although most field theorists would not maintain that all learning stems only from problematic situations, they give much more attention to problem solving as a form of learning than do associationist psychologists. According to field theorists, problems are solved by bringing to bear meanings (insights) gained in previous learning situations. But in the process the earlier meanings are enlarged and refined, so that the learner achieves a reconstruction of his conceptual pattern. We shall refer to learning of this type as *conceptual* or *reflective* learning.

It should be noted that field psychology, particularly as elaborated by Boyd H. Bode and in some of the later writings of Kurt Lewin, implies metaphysical assumptions which are fundamentally different from those of modern associationism. Whereas field psychology may exhibit pragmatic philosophic tendencies, associationism appears to reflect a philosophy of realism.[14]

Field psychology has scarcely taken psychologists of the United States by storm. On the other hand, it has attracted a considerable following and has made its mark where not fully accepted. In many cases, according to Murphy, behavior study has evolved to a point where it has "a theoretical flavor not very far removed from that of Gestalt psychology, while differing from it fundamentally in the exclusion of reference to the organism's inner world of insights and purposes." [15] In spite of the tendency of the two positions to merge somewhat, Murphy says, ". . . it is generally fairly easy to classify students of learning into two main groups, those accepting the associationist tradition and those rejecting it, in favor of some Gestalt-like principle. . . ." [16]

It is not reasonable to assume, however, that the proponents of these opposed learning theories have reached a balance of power in the United States. The polarity among contemporary learning theories is obvious, but associationism still appears to have the better of it. As Murphy points out, ". . . The dependence of contemporary work upon classical associationism on the one hand, and objective connection-forming on the other, can be easily brought out by almost any examples that might be chosen." [17] "If one

[14] Morris L. Bigge, "The Harmonies and Conflicts of Principles of Topological and Vector Psychology with the Tenets of Three Educational Philosophies," unpublished doctoral dissertation, University of Kansas, Lawrence, 1951, chaps. 7 and 8.
[15] Murphy, *op. cit.*, p. 281.
[16] *Ibid.*
[17] *Ibid.*, p. 271.

had to summarize the main trend as it now exists in the middle of the century, it would almost certainly have to be to the effect that despite huge and continuous protests of strong and active personalities, the conceptions of Spencer and Bain a hundred years ago remain dominant." [18]

At present, experimental evidence is adduced to support both associationist and Gestalt explanations of learning. In selecting its data each school of thought has apparently preferred to focus on certain of the products of learning to the exclusion of others. Associationists have devoted their studies to those forms of learning which can best be explained as association and connection-forming—i.e., learning of motor skills and memorization of verbal patterns. Field theorists have given most of their attention to learning of a more thoughtful sort—i.e., conceptualization and problem solving.

One of the most significant things we know about learning, however, is that we may control learning experiences in such a way as to emphasize one or more of the products of learning and deëmphasize others. That is, situations may be arranged so that the chief product of learning will be motor skills, or verbal associations, or concepts. This does not mean, of course, that any one of these can be taught in isolation from the others. Learning is all of one piece. Even the learning of an apparently mechanical motor skill will be accompanied by some change in a student's values and conceptual pattern. But the *emphasis* can be thrown toward one or the other, *particularly in subjects like the social studies.* In social-studies classes we may promote learning which is primarily thoughtless or learning which is primarily thoughtful. The tools for each are in our hands.

IMPLICATIONS FOR EDUCATION OF UNCERTAINTY OVER LEARNING

At the present time teachers' colleges give relatively little attention to issues connected with theory of learning. In his general psychology course a prospective teacher is likely to encounter two or three chapters on learning in an already overcrowded textbook. Generally speaking, these chapters stress associationist principles. Educational psychology courses may or may not deal explicitly with learning theory. There is some tendency among textbooks in this field to stress practical classroom application of assumed psychological principles rather than learning theory as such. A majority of books do have at least one chapter, however, on theory of learning.

Of approximately twenty textbooks in educational psychology examined

[18] *Ibid.,* p. 283.

by the authors, a majority are eclectic in the sense that they describe both associationist and field theories of learning, generally without showing clear preference for either. Furthermore, they mix and confuse the two outlooks, as when field terminology is used in connection with a basically associationist outlook. Only one book appears to be consistently associationist in viewpoint.[19] Several others, although somewhat eclectic, lean toward associationism.[20] One book is consistently field oriented,[21] and several lean rather strongly in this direction.[22]

Eclecticism of textbooks is explained by present uncertainty over the nature of learning and by lack of recognition that philosophical premises of field and associationist psychologies are incompatible. Teachers should clearly understand that teaching dominated by associationist principles gives results different from teaching dominated by field principles. Nevertheless, only a few textbooks suggest that it makes any difference to the learner whether teaching is dominated by associationist or by field principles.[23] And only two suggest that it makes any difference to the future of democracy whether learning is relatively mechanical or stresses reflection.[24] Furthermore, none of the books examined gives an adequate account of just how a person might organize his teaching so as to emphasize deliberately one or the other of these positions. Some books attempt it, but suffer from an absence of sufficiently concrete directives.

In many of their education courses prospective teachers encounter the philosophy of John Dewey, which implies a field psychology. Although these courses do suggest classroom practices designed to produce conceptualization and problem-solving ability, they seldom make explicit a theory of learning.[25] But students of education who take seriously the theory of

[19] Edwin R. Guthrie and Francis F. Powers, *Educational Psychology*, Ronald Press Company, 1950.

[20] Examples are Herbert Sorenson, *Psychology in Education*, McGraw-Hill Book Company, 1948, and William Clark Trow, *Educational Psychology*, Houghton Mifflin Company, 1950.

[21] George W. Hartmann, *Educational Psychology*, American Book Company, 1941.

[22] Examples are Asahel D. Woodruff, *The Psychology of Teaching*, Longmans, Green & Company, 1951, and Howard L. Kingsley, *The Nature and Conditions of Learning*, Prentice-Hall, Inc., 1946.

[23] Examples are Lawrence Cole and William F. Bruce, *Educational Psychology*, World Book Company, 1950, and Henry Beaumont and Freeman G. Macomber, *Psychological Factors in Education*, McGraw-Hill Book Company, 1949.

[24] Woodruff, *op. cit.*, and Cole and Bruce, *op. cit.*

[25] G. Lester Anderson in his introduction to *Learning and Instruction* (Forty-Ninth Yearbook of the National Society for the Study of Education), University of Chicago Press, 1950, says few teaching methods books are built on a theory of learning or even bear any relation to one.

17

learning implied in their education courses are likely to emerge with a smattering of field theory superimposed on a smattering of associationism gained in their psychology courses. The result is almost certain to be confusion and a tendency toward inconsistency.

However, it is doubtful whether a typical student of education learns during his four or five years in college that a theory of learning is important to a teacher. It is doubtful whether he learns that there are more or less contradictory explanations of learning, each resting on different assumptions about human nature and each having its own distinctive educational and social implications. It is doubtful whether his grounding in theory of learning is sufficient ever to make much difference in his teaching.

Suppose a teacher does not understand the educational and social implications of alternative definitions of learning. What will be the effect on his classroom practices? Some of the consequences are logically deducible, as follows:

1. We could not expect classroom teaching to be dominated by visible purpose. Where teachers are not motivated by a clearly understood theory of learning, we would expect their teaching to appear aimless. Aimlessness is not the same as planlessness. Teachers without conscious purpose could still follow elaborate plans. These plans could even be prefaced by statements of purpose and still lack real point. Such plans would give themselves away as soon as one got past the initial statements of purpose; not being rooted in an understanding of learning theory, the procedures called for would probably not bear much relationship to the stated purposes. Like some insurance policies, everything would be all right until one got to the fine print. Purposelessness also does not imply lack of activity. We may imagine classes in which everyone worked diligently—breathlessly even— toward an end which escaped both teachers and students.

2. We could expect students to be engaged in busywork much of the time. By busywork is meant the pursuit of tasks which are not clearly related to purpose. Busywork is the inevitable result of teaching which is not consciously purposeful. There would be textbook recitation in which arbitrary learnings were required, current-events periods in which students read news reports they did not understand, films which were irrelevant to anything else the class was studying, and workbook assignments given for the purpose of keeping students quiet while at their desks.

3. We could expect emphasis on *techniques* to dominate much of classroom practice. By a technique we mean a practice having to do with skill

in performance. A technique is supposed to foster smoothness and efficiency of execution. A technical emphasis in education means that teachers give a great deal of attention to what has sometimes been called "method," without corresponding attention to purpose. Put another way, teachers devote much time to developing a "bag of tricks."

No matter what conception of learning dominated teaching, firm mastery of technique would be desirable. But in a situation where no clearly formulated learning theory dominates teaching an inordinate emphasis on technique sometimes fills the vacuum. Teachers who lack a clear sense of purpose make a fetish of tricks of execution. One type of content serves as well as another as a medium on which to practice their techniques.

It is important to observe in this connection that through study of technique no one could ever find a purpose for teaching. Technique alone could never tell a teacher what he wanted to do or where he wanted to go. In the absence of clearly conceived purposes, techniques—no matter how polished —merely serve to keep students busy.

4. Whether by conscious intent or not, we could expect teachers to stress repetitive drill in their classes. An associationist outlook has historically favored this approach. It has called for memorization of verbal associations relatively low in meaning (the so-called textbook-recitation method as traditionally conceived). Most present-day teachers have been schooled in this sort of environment on elementary, high-school, and college levels.

Under the traditional approach, teachers concentrate on teaching a number of verbal associations usually referred to as "right answers." Students are taught, for example, to say that Columbus discovered America in 1492, that Andrew Jackson invented the spoils system, that slavery was a major cause of the Civil War, and that the first colonists came to America to escape religious persecution. These responses are retained until they have served their purpose at examination time and are then discarded by most students. It would be difficult for any teacher to break from this established pattern unless he had a clear understanding of the learning alternatives which exist and of their consequences to learners and to society.

5. We could expect social-studies education to ignore value conflicts of the culture. Uninfluenced by a clear conception of learning theory, a teacher encountering a conflict in the classroom would lack the necessary methodology for dealing with it. He could fall back on an indoctrinative approach, which is implied in theories of associative learning. But he might have been sufficiently influenced by his education courses to find this method of han-

dling controversy unpalatable. He could, of course, try letting students "hash over" problems in a highly permissive atmosphere; but without teacher guidance based on an understanding of how students learn conceptually his class would not be likely to resolve its value differences.

The upshot would almost certainly be that, lacking a satisfactory way of dealing with controversial issues, he would simply stop trying. He would stick to the content in textbook, workbook, and course outline (which is usually as noncontroversial as it is humanly possible to get). To the extent that he did allow controversial issues to enter the thinking of his students, he would try to confine them to peripheral rather than to central issues.

6. We could expect attempts to be "progressive" to meet with failure. In some teachers' colleges and university departments of education a good deal of pressure is put on teachers nowadays to adopt the leading recommendations of figures such as John Dewey and Boyd H. Bode. Since anyone who does not try to practice these ideas is thought old-fashioned, most teachers do seriously try—at least to some degree.

But if teachers were not well grounded in field theory of learning, their attempts to develop a problem-centered curriculum, to create a truly democratic atmosphere, to stress thinking and study of controversial issues would degenerate into rote-memory work. Such teachers would have difficulty seeing the real point of many potentially constructive measures and so would have little chance of extricating students when the new practices floundered in aimless confusion.

The Issue Drawn

The issue posed in this chapter may be sharpened by reviewing briefly what has been said. Two features of the American culture should be understood by every teacher of the social studies: the widespread presence of conflict and the existence of areas largely closed to rational inquiry. These two aspects of the culture are closely related. In closed areas, conflicts are more intense and more difficult to resolve than in areas relatively open to scientific inquiry.

The decisive differences between modern totalitarian and democratic cultures lie in the methods of handling conflict and in the relative number of areas closed to rational thought. Again, these two are related. A culture which is consistently democratic resolves conflict in all areas reflectively, whereas a totalitarian culture tries to suppress conflict and to preserve its many closed areas.

Alternative Theories of Learning and the Democratic Ideal

The present is a time of moral crisis in that large numbers of persons in some nominally democratic nations have come to question certain ideas traditionally associated with democracy. They are afraid of their own creed. This fear shows primarily in a tendency to reject the method of critical inquiry in the realm of social affairs. There seems instead to be a growing disposition to flee to some sort of authoritarian principle in areas of pressing conflict.

The schools are implicated in this crisis. In any society the schools serve as an arena in which typical methods of handling conflict are perfected and demonstrated. In a democracy the schools must remain a sanctuary for creative resolution of conflict, which in turn requires the practice of critical inquiry in a democratic environment.

How well the schools discharge their function of perfecting and demonstrating the method of democracy depends in large part on how well teachers understand the learning alternatives. These alternatives, as they have developed historically, are (1) emphasis on the learning of skills, habits, and memorized relationships, according to the principle of repetitive drill, and (2) emphasis on conceptualization and reflection, and insightful learning of skills and habits, as implied in the newer Gestalt theories of learning and the psychology of Dewey and Bode. At present, there is question as to whether teachers are being taught the nature and implications of the learning alternatives in our teachers' colleges and university departments of education, to the point, at least, where they see clearly the issue involved.

Stated in its barest form the issue is this: Learning which involves primarily the acquisition of non-thoughtful responses is not consistent with the needs of democratic citizenship. Learning in the associationist tradition is more suited to the requirements of a totalitarian state, where closed areas are held inviolate and conflicts are erased or suppressed through an education based on prescription and indoctrination. The alternative is much greater emphasis on developing higher thought processes, with all that this implies for reflective examination of critical social issues.

DISCUSSION QUESTIONS AND EXERCISES

1. It is generally assumed that communism is a major threat to the survival of democratic values. If this assumption is correct, how do you explain the fact that reflective study of communism is widely feared in the American culture? What assumptions are made by those who appear to feel that the more suc-

cessful we are in keeping communism a "closed area" the more likely it is that democracy will survive?

2. Would there be any closed areas in a fully democratic culture? Would the ideas of democracy in themselves constitute a closed area in the sense that people would be discouraged from critical study of them? Does an absence of closed areas mean an absence of fixed values?

3. How do you react to the assumption that most Americans are more or less confused over what to believe and value in areas of moral controversy? Do you agree with those who feel that modern America is in the midst of a great moral crisis? Is it possible that every culture at each stage of its history has been regarded by some persons as undergoing a moral crisis?

4. Discuss critically the idea that teaching which follows associationist premises is less appropriate to a democratic civilization than teaching which follows the premises of field psychologies. Could teaching be undemocratic in effect, even though teachers were deeply committed to democracy?

5. Compile a list of subjects which in your community cannot be freely discussed and studied. Ask some representative persons if they agree with your list. In what ways have attitudes toward closed areas changed during your lifetime?

REFERENCES

For further information about education in a totalitarian culture, see the following titles: Gregor A. Ziemer, *Education for Death* (Oxford University Press, 1941); George S. Counts and Nucia Lodge, *The Country of the Blind* (Houghton Mifflin, 1949); B. P. Yesipov and N. K. Gonharov, *I Want to Be Like Stalin* (Day, 1947); and John Scott, *Behind the Urals* (Houghton Mifflin, 1942), particularly Part II, Chapter X, and Part VIII, Chapter II.

For discussion of the nature of democracy and of democratic education, see John Dewey, *Democracy and Education* (Macmillan, 1937); Boyd H. Bode, *Democracy as a Way of Life* (Macmillan, 1937); Alan F. Griffin, *Freedom—American Style* (Holt, 1940); and T. V. Smith and E. C. Lindeman, *The Democratic Way of Life* (Mentor Books, 1951).

For criticism of progressive education gone wrong, see Boyd H. Bode, *Progressive Education at the Crossroads* (Newson, 1938), and John Dewey, *Experience and Education* (Macmillan, 1952).

Perhaps the best introduction to alternatives in learning theory is Boyd H. Bode, *Conflicting Psychologies of Learning* (Heath, 1929). This book is thought by many to be superior to Bode's later treatment of the same subject in *How We Learn*. Also recommended is Gardner Murphy, *Historical Introduction to Modern Psychology* (Harcourt, Brace, 1949).

Chapter 2

Learning as Development of Insight

IT IS usually assumed that, when persons learn, physical change occurs within the nervous system. Unfortunately, although there has been much speculation on the subject, very little is known for sure about the physical bases of learning. Particularly baffling have been the problems of explaining in physical terms the phenomenon of memory and the capacity of living organisms to abstract and generalize from experience.[1]

On the other hand, a large quantity of data has been accumulated on the ideational, emotional, and motor aspects of learning behavior. That the meaning of this evidence is not entirely clear is attested by the fact that we continue to have rival "schools of thought" regarding the learning process— as indicated in Chapter 1. The authors take the position that learning may best be described in field terms. We believe not only that a field interpretation is more in accordance with present experimental data than is associationism but also that the teaching and learning emphases which it implies harmonize with a democratic outlook. The present chapter is designed to describe as simply as possible basic aspects of a field interpretation of learning and to show some of their implications for teaching the social studies.

The Perceptual Basis of Learning

It is convenient to begin a description of the field point of view with an analysis of perception. Not only is all learning rooted in perception, but recent experiments in perception appear to support field assumptions.

[1] E. D. Adrian, *The Physical Background of Perception*, Oxford University Press, 1947, chap. 6.

Our understanding of our environment, hence our capacity to learn, is based upon interpretation of what comes to us through our senses. That part of ourselves and our environment of which we are directly aware is our "perceptual field." Experimentation during recent years suggests that perceptions are not literal descriptions of an environment. There is an element of creation in each act of perception. A given percept is a product of at least three factors: (1) the influence of a person's past experience; (2) a person's purposes at the time of perception; and (3) the object or process in the environment toward which perception is directed. In short, we tend to "see" in each new situation what we are in the habit of seeing and what we want to see, as well as what is "really there." These subjective factors tend to operate even when a person looks at something as impersonal as a geometrical design.[2]

Since what each person sees is not independent of his background of experience and his purposes, it is obvious that no two persons ever see anything exactly alike. Although they may give identical labels to what they see, its *meaning* for each of them is different. "When we behold a tree, we see it in the light of all our tree experience. The plainsman sees one thing, the woodsman another. No two people see precisely the same thing, and in no individual case does perception actually correspond with the tree. It is an interpretation made by the individual in the light of his experiences and purposes."[3]

Although most of our interpretations of the physical features of our everyday world may be presumed to be relatively accurate, when we move into areas where intense purpose and strong emotional sets characterize behavior, perception becomes increasingly undependable. In closed areas, for example, we tend to be governed by habit and desire rather than by "the facts." Confronted with complex evidence, we tend to select that which will support beliefs to which we are attached. A member of the National Association of Manufacturers sees a labor leader in a certain light; a friend of the labor leader sees him in an entirely different light. Both are observing the same man, but to each he has a fundamentally different meaning. Teachers of the social studies dare not forget that students have preformed beliefs and attitudes concerning social issues which cause them to make highly subjective and, from the standpoint of a social scientist, often inac-

[2] Earl C. Kelley, *Education for What Is Real,* Harper & Brothers, 1947, pp. 27–28.
[3] Earl C. Kelley and Marie I. Rasey, *Education and the Nature of Man,* Harper & Brothers, 1952, p. 32.

curate interpretations of factual data. They may, in fact, find it quite impossible to perceive (i.e., admit as evidence) facts which to a teacher seem plain beyond possibility of question. Ways of coping with this problem will be discussed in Chapter 7.

Content of courses in social studies consists of "facts"—the facts of history, geography, civics, economics, and sociology. It was once assumed that "a fact is a fact" and therefore has the same meaning for everybody. A statement such as "Columbus discovered America in 1492" was thought to have the same meaning for students as for a teacher. We now know that this is not the case. Not only will any item of information in the social studies mean different things to students and to teacher; it also will not mean the same to any two students. This is true because no two individuals, whether teachers or students, have the same purposes or the same fund of experience. Furthermore, the meaning which a fact has for a given student changes as his own experiences and purposes change.

Although in a given situation the perceptual fields of two individuals can never be precisely the same, we get along because the perceptions of most of us most of the time have a common operational meaning. But sometimes at crucial moments communication fails and rational behavior disappears because the worlds of individuals diverge to create an impassable gulf.

Learning as Development of Insight

Let us now see what happens when a person learns. Learning is an interactive process between an individual and his environment. Let us begin with some concrete illustrations: George, age 17, wants a date with Mary. Mary refuses repeated requests. Finally one of George's friends tells him that he will have more luck with girls if he "dresses up a bit." Without knowing it, he has been ridiculed for infrequent haircuts, a dirty neck, and long fingernails. George goes to work on his appearance, asks Mary once more, and is accepted. He has learned that, so far as success with girls is concerned, it pays to be clean and neat.

Let us try another illustration. Ever since seeing a movie depicting the life of a lumberjack, Henry has wanted to make lumbering his lifework. He takes a course in economic geography and discovers in his textbook a chapter on the lumbering industry. He reads that lumberjacks must arise at five in the morning, must work twelve hours a day, are sometimes crushed by logs, and seldom can marry. He is now less sure that he wants to be a lumberjack, for he has learned that the life is not an easy one.

25

Next, let us see how a motor skill may be learned. William wants to learn how to fly-cast. He takes the rod his uncle has given him to his back yard and begins practicing. He finds that every time he pitches his backcast forward his line, leader, and fly strike him in the back of the neck or head. Sometimes they wrap around his neck. He keeps trying, rather aimlessly varying stance and arm motion. Suddenly he realizes that on the swing he is pointing the tip of his rod inward. He concentrates on keeping it vertical and his next cast is a success. He has learned that one must swing his rod in a vertical arc if he is to control his cast.

These illustrations have common elements. In each case the learner has a *goal* in mind. He has a reason for wanting to learn. Some aspect of his social or physical environment must be interpreted and dealt with if the goal is to be reached. In each case the learner is successful in "sizing up" the social and physical environment in relation to his goal, so that he "sees" a way of coping with it. This "seeing" we call *insight*. If the insight itself is not a generalization, the learner derives a generalization from it. That is, he infers that the insight will work in similar situations in the future.

NATURE AND ROLE OF LEARNING GOALS

Goal-seeking behavior is a part of every situation which produces learning. This does not mean that every insight is consciously sought. One may catch an insight by chance when not seeking it; but we assume that such insights are seen in relation to a purpose—otherwise they would not be caught. Goals may be primarily intellectual or may emphasize physical and emotional needs. For example, a desire to satisfy intellectual curiosity or to reconcile contradictory beliefs may lead to vigorous attempts to learn. A person may spend a lifetime trying to learn how to decipher inscriptions on ancient tombs or trying to reconcile religious and scientific outlooks on life. Or he may devote immense effort to learning how to get along with people, how to perform capably in a given occupation, or how to lower his golf score.

Goal setting is not naturally characterized by laziness. When individuals set their own learning goals, they tend to set goals which require genuine effort for their attainment. Ambitious goal setting may occur in a classroom, as when a student becomes intellectually engaged with a problem which he feels as a challenge. But all too often in classrooms students do not appear to have developed impelling learning goals, presumably because they have not come to share the learning goals which teachers have in mind for them.

The problem of motivation is chiefly one of getting students to see the pertinence of classroom study to goals which they care about. This should not be taken to mean that teachers cannot successfully introduce learning goals with which students would otherwise be unfamiliar. It does mean that, whatever learning goal is introduced, it must be one which students will come to feel as important and challenging.

NATURE AND ROLE OF A CONFRONTING SITUATION

A confronting situation may be regarded as a person's physical and social environment, including his own physiological organism. It is at any given time a person's "outer world"—what is "out there" in contradistinction to his "world of insight," or self. A confronting situation is assumed to have onto-logical existence, more or less independent of a viewer's perception.

One is always in the process of interpreting confronting situations, and interpretation is affected not only by what is "out there" but also by one's past experiences, goals, and expectations. This is in line with what was said earlier: a perceptual field is always to some degree "created" and will vary markedly among persons in similar confronting situations.

If a confronting situation is unclear—that is, in any way puzzling or con-fusing—a person tries to "make sense" out of it. The speed and overt appear-ance of a given act of learning depends on how easily this is accomplished. If a confronting situation is comprehensible, a possible solution may be seen quickly, perhaps at a glance. If it is highly puzzling, a learner has no alternative but to act according to whatever hunches may come to him. Until the boy learning to fly-cast saw what was wrong with his perform-ance, he kept varying his swing, trying one move and another somewhat arbitrarily. When animals are placed in incomprehensible situations (such as mazes), they exhibit conspicuously this same tendency to try rather blindly one behavior after another.

NATURE AND ROLE OF INSIGHT

We have defined insight as a sensed course of action with reference to a goal and a confronting situation; it is a sensed or imagined "way through" or "answer." This definition must be distinguished from a more common one accepted by most laymen. We often hear it said that someone is a man of "insight"—perhaps of "great insight." This usage assumes that insight is "wisdom." A person of insight, in this sense, is one who knows a lot and knows it well. His solutions to problems are the correct solutions. In contrast, our use of the term *insight* does not imply either wisdom or its absence. Insights may be true or false, may reflect wisdom or not. An aim of education is to help students progressively improve the quality of their insights. We assume that the improvement of insights comes chiefly from subjecting them to reflective tests.

It seems probable that insights are "caught" before words come to express them, and that in some learning situations insights never lead to verbal formulations. They may remain merely a "sense of pattern," particularly when learning is primarily motor. A person may improve his golf swing by getting the "feel" of it without necessarily being able to describe just how he has changed his procedure.

Other insights may be formulated verbally. *Hypotheses* are insights of this type. A hypothesis is a statement of an anticipated solution to a problem, so phrased as to be verifiable. Implicit in it is an if-then relationship. For example, George may hypothesize, "Mary is more likely to date a boy who is neat and clean than one who is not." But if this idea is to be acted upon, it should be converted to an if-then statement, as follows: "If I become more clean and neat, then Mary may give me a date." The language requirements of hypotheses, as well as means for verifying them, will be considered in detail in Chapter 4. Hypotheses are the insights with which social-studies teachers are most concerned.

It is important to understand that insights are always a learner's. They may, of course, become his through adoption. In the first two of the illustrations on pages 25 and 26, the learner gained an insight because it was suggested to him, in one case by students, in the other by a textbook. Neither example contradicts what we are saying here. To get the point of an insight, a learner must see it in relation to his own problem. He must be able to "fit it in." He must understand its significance—for him. A teacher cannot give an insight to a student as we serve a person meat on a platter.

We have indicated that persons tend to generalize their insights. Each of the three examples given on pages 25 and 26 includes a generalized statement of the idea gained (see the last sentence of each example). When a person gains an insight, he is likely to assume that it may work in similar situations in the future. Suppose, for example, that studying a particular situation, I hypothesize, "Jerry became a shoplifter because he felt unwanted by his parents." If this hypothesis stands the test in Jerry's case, then I am likely to reason further, "Boys who feel unwanted at home may become thieves." Of course, this generalization is *suggested* and not *war-*

ranted by the single case. Before generalizations become reliable it is usually necessary that they rest on a number of specific insights, all suggesting the same conclusion. That is, dependable generalizations are usually products of considerable experience. Further, they tend to change and develop with the course of experience, evolving continuously in the direction of greater usefulness as tools.

A tested generalization is assumed to be valid in any future confronting situation similar to the situations in which it was tested. Tested generalizations have the character of *rules, principles,* or *laws.* Syntactically, generalizations may be said to be if-then-always statements: *If* we take a given action, *then* the probability is high that a given consequence will follow. The term *always* refers to syntactical form only; it does not mean that generalizations are taken to be true in an absolutistic sense. We wish to emphasize the probability character of any generalization. Although, to behave with foresight, we must assume that our generalizations have predictive value, the predictions are to some degree always based on faith. Even in the most exact sciences, laws are now regarded only as probabilities.

If-then-always generalizations, like other if-then statements, may be expressed in present-tense declarative sentences. For example, when a person says, "An increase in the quantity of money is likely to produce a rise in prices," he may mean exactly the same as if he said, "If the quantity of money in circulation is increased, prices are likely to rise." A literal if-then statement tends to suggest operations to be performed, and therefore throws emphasis upon experimental tests.

We say that a person who has developed an insight into a generalization has *conceptualized.* A generalization which forms a part of one's cognitive structure, "a rule to live by," is a *concept.* A concept is either a theory or a law, depending on how well established it is. A given act of learning will have no future use unless it is conceptualized. It is the acquisition of concepts which permits transfer of learning (or, as we often say, transfer of training).

THE TESTING OF INSIGHTS

Until insights have been tested, learning is not dependable. There are two basic ways in which a learner may test an insight. First, he may check it against the results of experience. If it harmonizes all known data, this fact may be construed as support. It may not, however, be interpreted as proof that an insight is finally or ultimately true. There are inherent difficulties in this sort of test, stemming from the fact that each person is unique and therefore interprets previous experience differently. Hence, what one person construes as support for an insight may be thought by another to cast doubt on it. Tests based wholly on referring a hypothesis to the "established facts" are highly subjective and are not always easily communicable from one person to another.

An experimental test is more significant. The aim of an experimental test is to see whether, when an insight is acted on, the predicated results occur. The if-then relationship implied in the insight sets the course of the action. Since the pattern of action and its consequences may be described and similar courses of action tried by other persons, an experimental test is often easily communicable to others. This is not to say that we may not communicate our procedure when we refer a hypothesis to the previous facts of experience, but only that experimental tests, by and large, *are more objectively communicable*. An experimental test constitutes an operational definition of insight. It is the method preferred by science today, although scientific workers commonly use both historical and experimental tests, checking the results of one against the other.

When from a given insight we can deduce successfully the data of past experience and unknown data which prove to be verifiable through experiment, we have dependable knowledge. Such an insight is true. A person's accumulation of tested insights is his store of knowledge.

It may be useful at this point to distinguish between intelligence and wisdom. Intelligence refers to acting with foresight or insight—with regard for the future. An intelligent act is one designed to achieve a given end. Wisdom, on the other hand, stems from possession of a store of tested insights or concepts. Wisdom refers to achievement; it is a product of experience. The insights of a wise individual are more likely than those of the unwise to eventuate in the predicted results. Thus a person may be intelligent and unwise, but he could not be wise and unintelligent. A person without much natural brilliance, however, might in time acquire a good deal of wisdom.

The Learning of Attitudes and Values

We have suggested that development of neuromuscular skills, as well as of knowledge, is based on changes in insight. We have implied that all learning is insightful. We have taken the general position expressed by

Bode when he says, "Learning . . . combines thinking, skill, information, and appreciation in a single unitary process. . . ." [4] We shall now pursue this theme further with special reference to the learning of attitudes and values.

Let us first define these terms. Every action we take and every thought we have is accompanied by a "feeling tone." Feeling tones may be favorable or unfavorable or perhaps both. A feeling tone which persistently accompanies a given thought or action may be referred to as an *attitude*. In other words, an attitude is an emotional set which makes us want to act in a certain way when confronted by situations of a particular type. A standard dictionary definition of an attitude is "a disposition with regard to a person or thing." In the quotation above, Bode includes attitudes under the term *appreciation*.

A *value* we take to be an attitude which has been clarified or "intellectualized," i.e., which has been subjected to reflective scrutiny and as a result is better understood and better grounded. A value reflects a tested insight whereas an attitude reflects an untested one. In a sense, a value may be said to be more "wise" than an attitude. This definition of value differs sharply from one which is commonly given. Many persons regard a value as any idea, thing, or process in the environment toward which one has an emotional attachment. According to this definition, attitudes refer to the way in which we regard the things we value; that is, our attitude is favorable toward something on which we place value, unfavorable toward something we dislike. This approach has the disadvantage of failing to make a clear distinction between attitudes and values. It permits the interchangeable use of the terms and makes pointless the retaining of both of them. We take it that this distinction can be established only by regarding values as tested or clarified attitudes. A person's "attitudes and values" include all his preferences, his likes and dislikes, *both* those which he has never reflected upon and those which he has. His behavior is motivated by his attitudes and values; we assume that every action has behind it an emotional preference.

Since the term *belief* may best be understood in relation to the terms *attitude* and *value*, we shall define it here. One of the best definitions of belief has been developed by Krech and Crutchfield: "A belief is an enduring organization of perceptions and cognitions about some aspect of the

[4] Boyd H. Bode, *How We Learn*, D. C. Heath, 1940, p. 249.

individual's world."[5] A person's structure of beliefs may include assertions about matters of fact, assertions which state preferences, and assertions of faith. This definition of belief is broader than the popular one, which limits beliefs largely to matters of faith.

Beliefs are distinguished from attitudes and values in that the former are regarded as the cognitive aspect of consciousness and the latter as the motivational aspect. However, beliefs and attitudes are never detached from one another. And although a belief may be attitudinally neutral, beliefs are always products of intellectual processes which are motivated by attitudes.

Let us now return to the question of how learning may produce changes in attitudes and values. We assume that every attitude and value is associated with some knowledge or fancied knowledge of its holder. As Krech and Crutchfield indicate, "All attitudes incorporate relevant beliefs about the object of the attitude. . . ."[6] Thus, if a person has a high regard for Anglo-Saxons (a favorable attitude toward them), we may assume that his attitude rests upon presumed knowledge such as that Anglo-Saxons are more intelligent, more moral, or more industrious than other groups.

The way to change attitudes, then, (and values), is to change the knowledge or purported knowledge which gave rise to them. We assume that a change in knowledge inevitably produces change in attitudes or values. But if so, how is one to explain the fact that very often individuals do accept new knowledge but at the same time retain old attitudes (and the behaviors to which they give rise)? For example, a person may come to understand that Negroes, in their intellectual, physical, and moral capacities, do not differ significantly from Anglo-Saxons but continue to behave as if he considered them inferior. Such apparent discrepancies between knowledge and attitudes may be explained by the assumption that, although new insights have been achieved, the old insights remain a part of the person's intellectual equipment. Within his thought processes are now two groups of incompatible insights, each with its own cluster of attitudes and behaviors. In the illustration just given, the insights supporting discriminatory behavior evidently retain the stronger pull; they thus tend to "overrule" the new insights (knowledge) which have been gained. Discrepancies of this sort may be explained as inconsistency, which may or may not be seen by the inconsistent person. If it is seen, he will presumably feel such incon-

[5] David Krech and Richard S. Crutchfield, *Theory and Problems of Social Psychology,* McGraw-Hill Book Company, 1948, pp. 150–151.
[6] *Ibid.,* p. 152.

sistency as a problem, and the elimination of it may become a learning goal.

If attitudinal change automatically accompanies change in insight, what is involved in the building of values? We take it that people acquire values through consciously examining or testing attitudes. A person is unlikely to examine his attitudes consciously and critically unless they cause trouble. Only when they appear inadequate is he willing to take a look at them, as, for example, when they come into conflict in such a way as to make him feel a problem. In Chapter 5 we shall examine this process in more detail and illustrate it in operation.

Insights as Tools: The Problem of Transfer

A theory of transfer is implicit in the theory of learning which we are advancing. Viewed historically, the theory of transfer most compatible with the theory of learning stated herein is that of Charles H. Judd. Judd asserted that transfer is a function of generalization. If a student generalizes a learning experience by subsuming it under a rule or principle, then carry-over to future and somewhat different situations is possible. Judd's conception is now regarded as inadequate by some because he neglected the role of insight and purpose in learning. He assumed that, if a confronting situation is favorable, transfer is automatic. Yet there is no reason to suppose that transfer will occur unless a student has sufficient insight to see how he may serve his goal by applying in the confronting situation some known principle.[7]

There are two broad types of situation in which transfer operates. The first consists of situations in which reflection is not necessary; the second, situations in which it is.

Let us imagine a situation identical in all significant respects with earlier situations in which a rule or principle was discovered and tested. For example, a student has learned that if a merchant stages a succession of going-out-of-business sales there is good reason to suspect that his "sale-priced" items are not real bargains. Any time in the future that this student finds a merchant who conducts several such sales, he will, without particular reflection, apply the rule he has learned and govern his behavior accordingly. Of course, if such a procedure is to be wise, the student should ascertain beyond question that the circumstances are essentially the same as those

[7] Ernest E. Bayles, *The Theory and Practice of Teaching*, Harper & Brothers, 1950, pp. 96–98.

under which he validated the rule. If this requires investigation, then we cannot refer to the situation as non-reflective.

Fortunately, many types of situations occur repeatedly in essentially similar form. The meaning of such situations has become sufficiently stabilized to be taken for granted; we say that the situation and its meaning occur simultaneously. For example, a motorist enters a busy thoroughfare from a side road. This situation means "danger," and it calls forth without reflection the rule "Stop, look both ways before proceeding," together with appropriate action. It is relatively standardized situations of this sort which make habits possible. A habit is nothing more than skillfully executed application of a rule (often involving motor behavior) in a situation wherein invocation of the rule will help a person achieve a goal. Habits are not to be regarded as automatic or blindly and compulsively repetitive. They are precise adjustments to situations which call for them, adjustments which may never have been made before. They are products of tested insight; if a changed situation requires revised insight, then actions change accordingly. Habits at any given time are functions of the psychological field in which they occur and are thus firmly rooted in the requirements of the present.

A tendency to reflect is itself a habit. Given a situation in which reflection provides the quickest and easiest way to achieve a goal, if a person has previously gained insights as to the role and method of reflection, he will reflect without stopping to debate whether he should. The habit of reflection is undoubtedly the most valuable habit which students can be helped to develop.

If a goal can be reached successfully without reflection, an individual will not stop to reflect. He will reach the goal in the easiest and most direct way which he senses or sees. Application without modification of tested insights in order to reach a goal is the part of wisdom, provided this is actually the easiest way to reach the goal. But if the confronting situation is dissimilar at crucial points from the situations in which an insight was originally tested and found good, it is highly unwise to apply the old insight.

How may a stock of tested insights or concepts serve as a basis for new insights in dissimilar situations? Let us assume that a student who feels strongly committed to a free-enterprise system becomes aware for the first time of the intended role of fair-trade laws in preventing retail price competition. He is puzzled because he does not see how a belief in fair-trade laws harmonizes with a belief in free competition. His learning goal is to understand why persons who claim allegiance to free enterprise at the same time support retail price maintenance.

This rather complex problem cannot be solved without recourse to a number of previously verified insights. In order to keep our illustration simple, let us examine only one of the dozens of possible hypotheses which might be adduced to explain the apparent contradiction. Suppose the student thinks of this explanation: *Retail price maintenance laws do not effectively prevent free pricing.* The question is, how did he get this idea? Let us grant that it is original to him. Even so, there must be a particular conceptual background on which to draw; otherwise he would not be able to imagine such an explanation. Perhaps he has had experiences with merchants in which they have evaded legal price maintenance by granting discounts or generous trade-in allowances. He has generalized these experiences, assuming that it is a rule of doing business to grant such price concessions. Perhaps he has also had experiences with mail-order houses whose products were not fair-traded but yet were generally available. To him, *merchants are persons who evade fair-trade laws* or *persons to whose merchandise fair-trade laws do not apply.* We see, therefore, how it was possible for him to achieve the insight stated above. (The reader should not assume that the insight given in the illustration is necessarily a good one.)

Transfer occurred in this learning situation because the student was able to combine the generalized results of experience, a desire to solve a problem, and the necessary insight to see how his conception of merchants suggested a possible answer.

John Dewey has referred to thinking as the reconstruction of experience. The foregoing illustration shows how this may occur. If the student, upon testing the insight, decides it is a poor one, his conception of what merchants do will change. If he finds support for the insight in his tests, his present conception of merchants will be fortified and expanded. Merchants will now be *persons who prevent fair trade from stifling competition.*

The Continuity of Learning

The first learning of an infant, while we take it to be insightful, involves considerable fumbling. But as conceptualization progresses, the amount of fumbling decreases. As a child's store of concepts increases, the comprehensibility of his world also increases. The older an individual, the more his learning may build on insights previously achieved. By the time adulthood is reached, problems are often solved quickly and smoothly by drawing upon tested insights for ideas.

Hence, learning is normally to be regarded as a chain affair—one insight leading to another, the latter leading to still another, and so on, *ad infinitum*. In the examples given on pages 25–26, we may assume that learning began with certain preconceived—but relatively inaccurate or unfruitful—ideas about how to win a girl, working conditions in the lumbering industry, and the technique of fly-casting.

In view of the discussion in earlier parts of the chapter, this assumption may seem quite obvious. Less obvious, perhaps, are its implications for teaching the social studies. The idea of learning as continuity suggests that a teacher who wishes to help students gain insights must begin with insights which they now have, with the attitudes, beliefs, and knowledges which they bring to their classrooms. Students can learn how their beliefs and knowledges may be inadequate as means for attaining worth-while learning goals, to see ways in which their attitudes, beliefs, and knowledges may be confused, contradictory, and poorly grounded. They are thereby motivated to reëxamine their cognitive structures, in which process they will presumably enlarge and refine their conceptual equipment. Later chapters on techniques will show specifically how this process may be motivated and guided.

It is necessary that we emphasize how important it is for the teaching-learning process to move learners to ever higher levels of insight. A single act of thought may begin with reconsideration of a particular belief or item of knowledge; it may end with affirmation or rejection of this same belief or knowledge. But in the learning process additional data are evaluated; new facts come to the attention of the learner. His store of tested beliefs expands. He "knows more," in the sense both of possessing additional quantities of conceptual material and of gaining greater depth of understanding. Bayles has this same idea in mind when he says that teaching should begin with a child's *world of insight* and should seek progressive expansion of that world in the direction of encompassing a child's *world of effect*. The world of effect is that part of his environment which impinges on him. It includes not only the local environment but also certain aspects of world and national scenes. It takes in all aspects of the environment which a child needs to understand in order to live with maximum intelligence.[8]

Unfortunately, social-studies teachers in the past have often disregarded a child's world of insight and tried to begin his education with study of a world of effect which to him was remote if not entirely incomprehensible.

[8] *Ibid.*, p. 119.

36

They have tried to begin with materials which students felt to be completely unrelated, or but insignificantly related, to their current beliefs, values, attitudes, and habits. This is one reason why learning has often been inconsequential.

The Role of Facts in Learning

We have noted that insight leads to generalization. Unless generalization occurs, insight can have little transfer value. Learning which cannot function in making a person's behavior wiser is futile. It should therefore be clear that teaching, if it is not to be a waste of effort, must lead to generalization.

Discrete or single insights or items of information (concretions, as opposed to abstractions) do not by themselves have meaning or usefulness. It can mean little to a student to memorize a statement such as "Aaron Burr killed Alexander Hamilton in a duel," unless its connection with some *general principle* or *rule* is made explicit. A fact can function in thought only when it comes to have evidential character—that is, the quality of supporting or casting doubt upon some general idea. This, of course, is what conceptualization means—encompassing specifics in the general. We may say that an aim of social-studies education is to help students acquire a store of tested social theory, or body of principles, which is relevant to contemporary social issues and beliefs.

Any assertion which cannot be made to function evidentially in testing an insight or its implied general rule may be called an *arbitrary statement* or an *arbitrary association*. The word *arbitrary* is apt because it implies sentences which are largely functionless or meaningless. They lack the character of data or evidence. This means that they must remain largely isolated, set apart, and discontinuous from the world of today and its problems.

There is no question, of course, but that such statements may be learned. We know that students do learn them, often great numbers of them. If it serves the purposes of a student to memorize arbitrary associations he can do so, provided they make some sense to him. We add the final qualification because experimentation suggests that it is impossible for a person to commit nonsense syllables to memory unless he can see pattern of some sort in them. Likewise, a sentence probably cannot be memorized successfully unless it conveys some feel of relationship. "Robespierre was an important figure in the French Revolution" may be committed to memory if a student understands vaguely the meaning of some of the words and gets a nebulous sense of Robespierre as a man in a revolution.

It is probable that learning even of the foregoing sort produces change in insights, but not the insights which teachers intend to communicate. Arbitrary associations may gain meaning after they are memorized, but their meaning is likely to lie in their being seen as instrumentalities by which to "pass tests," "win diplomas," or gain some other goal unrelated to possible literal meaning of the statements themselves. Teachers assume that students who memorize "Robespierre was an important figure in the French Revolution" are learning something about Robespierre and the French Revolution; but they may be learning only how to pass a test, how to gain praise and social status, or—perhaps—how to function successfully in a radio or TV quiz show. Of course, if he remembers them, a person may later discover in memorized statements connotations not originally seen.

It is relevant at this point to discuss what may be called the *background fallacy*. Teachers commonly assume that students must acquire background information before they are ready to think or conceptualize. They conceive of mind as a kind of container, into which discrete facts may be poured to be stored. When needed at some later time as grounds for generalization, these facts may be sorted quickly and appropriate ones extracted from the container. In short, it is assumed that one may learn facts at one time and generalize from them at another.

The nature of mental functioning would seem to prohibit much of such behavior. Facts memorized for future purposes tend to remain in thought as isolated items. Their meaning is minimal; they point to little else. They are held in mind for extrinsic purposes, such as passing tests. When they have served their purposes, they are quickly forgotten. All research in this matter indicates that, when isolated facts or irrelevant generalizations are memorized in order to serve goals unrelated to their intellectual content, retention is poor and transfer practically nil.

The only usable—and therefore worth-while—"background" consists of if-then-always generalizations. Of course, these are validated only through examination of factual data, which tend to be remembered with the generalizations they support. They are remembered because they were instrumental in conceptualization—that is, because they functioned as data or evidence. One does not learn facts at one time and generalize from them at another; instead, he learns data and generalizations simultaneously. Facts can function as data only as one thinks about them. Facts are taught meaningfully only if they are *used while being taught,* or *taught through use.*

The foregoing ideas are of great significance to teachers of the social studies because, as the social-studies curriculum is now constituted, much of its content is irrelevant to any conceivable if-then-always generalizations which students might make. Much textbook space is devoted to descriptive matter consisting largely of detached or isolated facts. If the facts do bear on generalizations of any sort, the generalizations are likely to encompass matters which are difficult, if not impossible, to relate to present attitudes, beliefs, and knowledge of students. Students are not likely to formulate meaningful if-then-always generalizations unless they encounter in their studies substantial quantities of factual detail which can function as the data of goal-related thought.

Although much of the content of all the standard secondary social studies presents difficulties in learning because of the frequency of arbitrary associations, history presents perhaps the greatest difficulty. Although we shall discuss in Chapters 9 and 17 some of the special problems involved in teaching history, it is significant at this point to recall that typical history textbooks consist mainly of descriptive or narrative material. From the standpoint of students, description of the past tends to remain on the level of arbitrary associations. As usually selected, much of the content of history is irrelevant to any conceivable generalization or idea which a student could see as instrumental to a learning goal (except goals such as passing the course).

It is true that history textbooks often have statements which some historians call generalizations. These are either conditional (if-then) or declarative sentences with *past-tense verbs.* Examples are: "Unless American soldiers fought like Indians, the redmen usually defeated them," and "Businessmen who became government officials commonly instigated anti-labor policies." As we use the terms here, past-tense generalizations are not to be regarded as true generalizations. The latter are always *timeless* in quality— they refer to past, present, and future. A past-tense generalization, even if incorporated in one's cognitive structure, does not of itself have transfer value and is therefore not a concept as we have defined it. *Past-tense generalizations, like solitary facts, can function in conceptualization only as they are related evidentially to present-tense (if-then-always) generalizations.*

Perhaps the role of historical data, as well as the instructional task of history teachers, may be made clearer by analyzing briefly the role of experience in learning. It is not past events *per se* which affect present behavior but, as Kurt Lewin has said, the "psychological past." Present behavior is affected by past experience *if* such experience has made the present perceptual field look different from what it otherwise would. It is the *contemporary* meaning of objects which determines our behavior toward them. The past is crucially important, but only as it affects our thinking about the present. An event in one's past is insignificant unless it entered into one's experience at the time he encountered it and changed the way he now sees his environment. In short, it is the insights one gains, and the enhancement of wisdom which comes from them, that afford a measure of the value of experience.

One may say that what is important in life is the "living past"—living, because it is still with us. It is integrally incorporated in our present outlook. Now, one might look back into his past and get meaning out of some event which had little meaning when it occurred. But meaning accrues to events of a person's past only as he sees how to incorporate them into his present outlook.

Obviously a great amount of the history of the human race does bear on possible present-tense generalizations (that is, present outlooks), including those which serve the natural interests of students. It is only necessary that the potential relevance of historical data to such generalizations be shown. For example, historical data can support or cast doubt upon many rules or principles of human behavior. Furthermore, ancient history may be as productive of fruitful content as modern; world history may be as useful as American. Probably certain events of the fourth century B.C. are more relevant to several large issues today than most of the "news" reported in current-events classes. The task of a teacher of history is to bring history into the experience of youngsters; and this may be done only as youngsters are helped to use historical facts as data in the purposeful testing of ideas.

Many students do a good deal of conceptualization in learning situations where teachers have no awareness of the need of factual content to function as the data of thought. This is not a demonstration of the falsity of any theory of learning. It may be explained as one recognizes that many students can and do incorporate facts into their thinking in ways not understood by teachers. In short, students learn in some situations in spite of textbooks and teachers, rather than because of them, and the mental processes by which they learn may be quite different from those which teachers assume to occur. But when this happens it is because of either fortuitous circumstances or the exceptional brightness of students.

To summarize, there is only one role which facts can play in meaningful learning: to function as evidence, or data, in conceptualization. If they do not, they may perhaps be memorized and retained for a while, but their meaning and future usefulness will be slight.

The Role of Problem Solving in Learning

We have described the learning of concepts as a process by which a person in an unclear confronting situation seeks interpretations of the situation which will enable him to clarify it and thereby reach his goal. These interpretations are insights; when generalized, we label them concepts. The interaction of learner and environment occurring during conceptualization is what we mean by an experience. It is a transforming process in which both environment and learner change—environment, because it acquires new meaning, and learner, because he acquires new rules by which to cope with future situations.

Some writers assume that conceptualization is motivated only by *problems* or, as we sometimes say, *problematic situations*. They define a problem as an unclear or unstructured (i.e., puzzling) confronting situation which appears to a learner as an obstacle to smooth achievement of his goals. Dewey, for example, says that achievement of insights (or, as he puts it in the following quotation, the forming of judgments) occurs only when a learning situation is of this character. "Unless there is something doubtful, the situation is read off at a glance; it is taken in on sight; *i.e.*, there is merely perception, recognition, not judgment. . . . But if it suggests, however vaguely, different meanings, rival possible interpretations, there is some *point at issue*, some *matter at stake*. Doubt takes the form of . . . controversy within the mind. Different sides compete for a conclusion in their favor. . . . Every judgment proceeds from some such situation." [9]

Perhaps most learning theorists of today would not accept Dewey's thesis that conceptualization occurs only in a situation which presents rival meanings. A perceptual field may be structured by insights even though a learner is not in doubt about its meaning. It is only necessary that an insight be understood as an interpretation of a confronting situation which will assist a learner in better achieving a goal. Suppose, for example, that a group of students wants to find out more about how people in their city live. To be

[9] John Dewey, *How We Think,* D. C. Heath & Company, 1933, p. 121.

41

receptive to information they do not have to have this as a clearly formulated goal or to be steadily aware of it as a goal. Now suppose that, on a
given day, even though these students feel satisfied with their knowledge
at the time, their teacher reports to them that twenty-seven babies starved
to death in the city during the previous year. The assertion may immediately appear goal-related, in the sense that students recognize it as information which helps them understand their community better. Assume also
that students take the assertion at face value; they have no reason to doubt
their teacher and the statement is not incompatible with present beliefs.
They adopt the statement as an insight, smoothly and unhesitatingly.

Situations of this general type seem—at least on the surface—to differ
from the situation described by Dewey. There is no element of doubt prior
to conceptualization. The confronting situation is in one respect inade-
quately structured: it has significant features of which students are unaware. Yet until they become aware of the "missing information," they see
nothing unclear or puzzling in the confronting situation. They are not
aware of a problem.

Such situations probably confront us regularly. There are many types of
information of which we are unaware and which we therefore feel no need
of knowing; but as soon as they come to our attention we see instantly how
they will serve a purpose.

We may not say, however, that learning of the foregoing sort is entirely
thoughtless. It is likely to include evaluation of a sort. Students may tend to
accept a statement which comes from an authoritative source, but they
may, at least in slight degree, debate with themselves whether a particular
statement is trustworthy, whether a previously unquestioned source is still
reliable. Further, there is the task of "fitting in" the statement, of seeing its
relationship to current goals. Its pertinence may be suggested almost instantly, yet some mental effort obviously is involved. Simply to see that
knowledge of how many babies starve to death in a year helps one understand his community requires relating of two previously unrelated matters.
The question we raise is whether, although thought may be but barely
recognizable, conceptualization ever occurs without some mental effort.

We shall not try here to answer the question of whether conceptualization is impossible outside of problematic situations. We believe it will be
generally agreed that, whether or not conceptualization goes forward in
situations which are unproblematic and thoughtless, some instances of
conceptualization require much more thinking than do others. Incorpora-

tion into our cognitive structure of if-then-always generalizations may occur in ways which consume so little thought that for practical purposes they are thoughtless; or such learning may require long and sustained intellectual effort.

How may we evaluate conceptualization which, on the surface, appears largely unproblematic and thus unreflective? One thought which comes immediately is that insights—hence concepts—acquired thoughtlessly are necessarily uncritical. They have come, unquestioned, from a source which learners see as authoritative. Of course, if their source is questioned, perhaps the learning situation is not unproblematic. For example, if students doubt a teacher's word, they have created a "forked-path" situation: Is teacher's word to be accepted or not? The answer requires thought. But if there is no apparent doubt, if an insight is accepted on faith, then it is uncritical—in essence, authoritarian.

If conceptualization remains generally on a relatively thoughtless or uncritical level, we question the pertinence of such learning to the needs of a democratic society. It does not foster intellectual independence. In many everyday situations it matters little whether conceptualization is motivated by felt problems. We would not maintain, for example, that democracy will fail to survive if youngsters generally gain their understanding of garden fences and humming birds in situations with no clearly recognizable problem. On the other hand, we would question whether democracy can survive for long if most youngsters gain their understanding of social issues in situations which lack problematic elements. Teaching in the social studies which ignores the use of felt problems as the motives of learning cannot but result in uncritical transmission of our cultural heritage with all this implies for intensification of conflict. Such teaching does not provide students with practice in, or understandings capable of, identifying and resolving contradictions among beliefs and attitudes.

We assume that learning which is achieved in problematic situations is commonly better understood, longer remembered, and more functional than insights which are adopted uncritically from authority. Further, we assume that, provided problems are not so formidable as to produce neurotic responses, the more keenly a problem is felt the better will be the quality of learning which results. As noted early in the chapter, facts tend to be differently understood by teachers and by students. Because each individual has a unique background and unique purposes, he interprets data in unique ways. A problem of teaching is to help students come progressively to "see"

43

facts of the social studies as they are "seen" by professional social scientists. In our theory of learning, the more problematical a learning situation is for students, the more likely are the facts as they come to see them to resemble the facts as teachers and professional social scientists see them. Only through rigorous intellectual effort may the "worlds" of students and of trained adults be brought closer together.

In short, a goal of social-studies teachers, if learning is to have maximum quality, is to help students experience problematic situations of the general nature described by Dewey—situations which are puzzling, uncertain, doubtful. These have alternative solutions or no solutions at all; they are "forked-path" or "no-path" situations. Feeling consciously blocked, students are impelled to "think their way through" if their goals are to be achieved.

What is often termed problem-centered instruction in the social studies is not problem centered at all. The learning "problems" commonly presented in many social-studies textbooks, courses of study, and unit plans are problems only to the person preparing the curricular material—if to him. It is not unusual to see "problems for the student" such as these:

To learn about the public utility companies of your community.
To see how many articles devoted to farming and rural life appear in the local newspaper.
To find out how many ways there are to send money from one city to another.
To find out what instructions are given to Boy Scouts for the protection of forests.
To learn more facts about life insurance.
To determine the advantages and disadvantages of good roads.[10]

As stated, it is unlikely that any of these would be a problem for students. A problem is personal and intimate, and can never be transferred directly from one person to another simply by telling the latter that it exists. Each problem "belongs" to someone. This is not to say that many persons may not share the same problem; they often do. But each person in the group must feel the problem to be of significance to him personally as well as to the others; otherwise, no problem exists for him. Problems vary in intensity, of course—some create but a mild tickle whereas others cause an impelling itch.

"Problems" of the sort listed above are evidence of misunderstanding of what a problem is. A problem can appear only when a student feels thwarted in achieving a purpose that he cares about. The tendency in education to label the most non-problematic activities and projects "problems" is in

[10] These "problems" are based upon an actual list which came to the writers' attention a few years ago.

44

part due to the associationist tradition in psychology and education. The true nature of problem solving and of learning-problems was never well understood by older associationist psychologists.

The intensity of felt problems rises sharply as beliefs and attitudes of students become involved. *The most effectual learning emerges from situations where cherished beliefs or attitudes are felt to be at stake.* In such situations the principle of continuity of learning is always operative. It is this type of situation which the authors recommend as most desirable for learning in the social studies, and it is toward achievement and exploitation of this type of situation that most of the remainder of this book is directed. The recommended chronological progress of conceptualization may be diagramed as follows, and this schematization, since it portrays learning typical of the most effectual teaching in the social studies, will be assumed throughout the book.

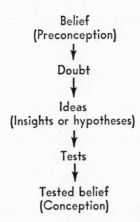

It is essential, at this point, to show the bearing of intrapersonal conflicts on the type of learning situation we are proposing. An intrapersonal conflict, as defined in Chapter 1, is a sensed incompatibility of outlook which places an individual in disagreement with himself. A person may feel a problem without experiencing intrapersonal conflict, as when he is merely puzzled or doubtful. But the appearance of conflict is normally regarded as a problem for persons experiencing it. There seems to be a drive toward harmony in human nature, once disharmony is recognized as such. Awareness of inconsistency or of inner conflict makes persons feel uncomfortable; it thus creates its own learning goal.[11]

[11] Max Wertheimer, *Productive Thinking*, Harper & Brothers, 1945, pp. 198–200.

That the urge for consistency does not appear more often may be explained by the fact that much inconsistency has not been discovered to be such by inconsistent persons. Myrdal has provided an explanation of why this is so. According to him, valuations exist at differing levels of generality. Our central beliefs and values, which include what Myrdal labels the American Creed, represent the more general valuations. For example, many Americans tend to value equality—but at a high level of abstraction. On the other hand, some of the same persons practice racial segregation. But their beliefs concerning segregation are on a more specific, or less general, level. This explains why Americans so often profess high ideals but regularly violate them in practice. Specific practices often remain intellectually unrelated to ideals. Stereotypes, conventions, and compartmentalizations help us to ignore these inconsistencies. Myrdal maintains, however, that the spread of knowledge, changed material conditions stemming from changed technology, and growing interdependence of society are exposing such inconsistencies to more and more persons. As inconsistencies are revealed, people tend to seek new equilibriums in their valuations. Myrdal believes that these new equilibriums normally embrace the more general, or abstract, valuations.[12]

But not always. Once a person has come to feel intrapersonal conflict involving an ideal and a specific behavior, he may resolve the conflict by rejecting the ideal. One who favors equality and segregation and who comes to see them as inconsistent may reject equality. We assume that democratic-reflective study of such issues is more likely than unreflective study to resolve them in the direction of fuller commitment to traditional democratic ideals. Our position advocates reflective reconstruction of beliefs as a means of clarifying and preserving the central ideals of democracy; it is in a large sense, therefore, a "conservative" outlook. It is conservative in a further sense: Awareness of inconsistency without opportunity for reflective resolution theoretically might eventuate in accumulation of unmanageable and frustrating conflicts, which, in turn, might produce violent social disturbances. Myrdal, for example, sees reflective resolution of conflict as an antidote to revolutionary impulses.

Our position has significant implications for the problem of mental health in our society. Chapter 1 noted that, when individuals hold contradictory

---

This view also appears frequently in the literature of psychiatry and mental hygiene. Myrdal, cited below, develops the same point.

[12] Gunnar Myrdal, Richard Sterner, and Arnold Rose, *An American Dilemma; The Negro Problem and Modern Democracy*, Harper & Brothers, 1944, Vol. I, pp. 75–77; Vol. II, pp. 1031–1034.

beliefs and attitudes, neurotic conflict may result. A reflectively oriented social-studies curriculum which focuses on a study of the pervasive ideological or moral issues of the culture should have the effect of preventing absorption of unrecognized conflicts and should also give students basic habits helpful in resolving conflicts which are recognized. Although we do not maintain that social-studies teachers should try to play the role of psychiatrists, we feel strongly that reflective study of closed areas in our schools would have a "preventive-hygiene" effect and over the long run would reduce our many national schizophrenias.

We feel these generalizations to be warranted: The learning problems capable of producing maximum motivation, maximum learning, and maximum transfer grow out of awareness of intrapersonal conflict in the closed areas. Further, reflective study of such conflict, more than any other type of study, holds promise of improving the mental health of individuals, of producing commitment to democratic ideals, and of leading to orderly and peaceful social change. This view will be elaborated more fully in later chapters; its curricular implications will be explored in Chapter 10.

Intrapersonal conflict may not always be present in areas in which teachers deem conceptualization desirable. Learning may then be kept problematic by creating in the minds of students genuine doubt or puzzlement. Questions which ask students to explain what, in terms of their present concepts, is unexplainable may create true problematic situations. Until mechanical teaching and learning have discouraged them, youngsters have an abundance of natural curiosity about their environments. For example, we have known relatively immature youngsters to become highly interested in trying to answer questions such as, If millions of persons in India are starving, how may we explain their refusal to kill cattle for food? and, How may we explain the fact that in some places Eskimos have wastefully destroyed the natural resources on which their own lives depend? Of course, such questions will not produce thought if the principle of continuity of learning is violated; there must be, in the conceptual structure of students, belief or knowledge which can provide a basis for hypothesization.

Because they have not yet become vitally interested in ideological issues, junior-high students often may best be motivated by confrontation with puzzling aspects of their environment. Even junior-high students, however, usually have budding interests in ideological issues. We may promote such interests by raising questions about matters of belief. For example, it is common in the United States to require study of the Federal Constitution

47

in the seventh or eighth grade, as a part of either civics or American history. Teachers have difficulty making study of the Constitution meaningful at this grade level. Learning is often mechanical and lifeless.

However, suppose a teacher opens a discussion of the First Amendment with a description of attempts to have comic books censored, or of present policies with regard to television or motion-picture censorship, or perhaps of restrictions placed on freedom of students to study controversial subjects. Then suppose he asks, "Do you feel that comic-book censorship violates the First Amendment?" or "Are restrictions on the freedom of students to study controversial issues unconstitutional?" or, in case of the Fifth Amendment, "What is meant when some senators use the expression, Fifth-Amendment Communist?" Even among junior-high students approaches of this type are likely to generate interest in conflicts in beliefs and attitudes.

For students of the senior high school we recommend that, in so far as possible, all social-studies learning be approached through the medium of contradictory beliefs, attitudes, and values. Theoretical bases for this outlook will be developed more fully in Chapters 5 and 10, and appropriate teaching techniques will be described in detail in Chapters 6–8 and 17. We shall say here only that, given ingenuity of teaching, probably all socially important issues confronting Americans may be approached through reflective analysis of those beliefs and attitudes which high-school students have acquired from out-of-school environments. It is generally possible to help students expand their world of insight to encompass more nearly their world of effect through the study of ideological questions.

The next logical step in developing our outlook toward the function, methods, and content of social-studies education is to describe with precision what is meant by the reflective process. Chapters 3 and 4 will be devoted to this task.

DISCUSSION QUESTIONS AND EXERCISES

1. Why is an understanding of perception usually considered essential to an understanding of learning? Is all learning based on acts of perception?
2. In the sentence "George is a man of insight," what is meant by the term *insight?* Does this use of the term differ from its use in the present chapter?
3. What is the significance in human history of general ideas (if-then-always generalizations)? Can knowledge ever have any functional value except as it is translated into generalizations? How may the human capacity to generalize be abused?
4. Is it possible for a student to go through high school and college, perhaps with

high marks, without significantly improving the quality or quantity of his concepts? If this is possible, is such a person what is meant by the expression *educated fool?*

5. Is there a place for drill and memorization in classroom learning? Could there be any learning without memorizing? Does the meaning of the terms *drill* and *memorization* shift according to one's theory of learning?
6. Is it possible to devise objectives and methods of teaching history apart from consideration of a theory of learning? If you are familiar with Arthur E. Bestor's book *Educational Wastelands,* would you say that Dr. Bestor makes assumptions about the nature of learning? What are they?
7. React to this statement: "The first task of a teacher is to motivate students." Do you agree or disagree? How might different theories of learning make different assumptions about the nature of motivation? What theory of motivation is implicit in field psychology?

REFERENCES

For treatments of learning theory which are in harmony with field psychology, see John Dewey, *Experience and Education* (Macmillan, 1952), Boyd H. Bode, *Conflicting Psychologies of Learning* (Heath, 1929), J. W. Tilton, *An Educational Psychology of Learning* (Macmillan, 1951), and Ernest E. Bayles, *The Theory and Practice of Teaching* (Harper, 1950).

The following three articles are also recommended: Ernest E. Bayles, "The Idea of Learning as Insight," *Educational Theory,* April, 1952; Martin Levit, "On the Psychology and Philosophy of Concept Formation," *Educational Theory,* July, 1954; and Morris L. Bigge, "A Relativistic Approach to the Learning Aspect of Educational Psychology," *Educational Theory,* July, 1954. Dr. Bigge is working toward an integration of the theoretical positions of Bode and Kurt Lewin.

Students interested in the implications for learning theory of recent experiments in perception should read Earl C. Kelley, *Education for What Is Real* (Harper, 1947), or Earl C. Kelley and Marie I. Rasey, *Education and the Nature of Man* (Harper, 1952).

A standard reference in comparative theory of learning is Ernest R. Hilgard, *Theories of Learning* (Appleton-Century-Crofts, 1948). Also useful to students is the Forty-First Yearbook of the National Society for the Study of Education, Part II, *The Psychology of Learning* (1942).

Chapter 3

The Reflective Method

WE SHALL use the method of comparison in establishing our definition of reflection. That is, various non-reflective approaches to problem solving will be described in an effort to make more clear the unique aspects of reflection as a method of inquiry. Chapter 4 will pursue the analysis further by discussing certain technical features of the reflective handling of problems.

Some Unconstructive Behaviors in Problematic Situations

Faced with a baffling confronting situation, a person may attempt to bring all his intellectual resources to bear on the problem. On the other hand, he may adopt one or more of a variety of evading reactions. These never actually solve problems; they may enable a person to live with his problems in a state of uneasy equilibrium. Such behaviors are usually classified as neurotic. Some possible behaviors in problematic situations, as classified and labeled by mental hygienists, are represented schematically in the following diagram:

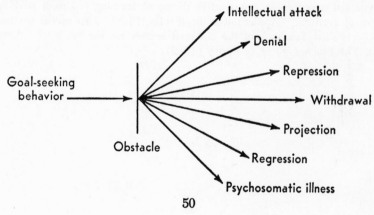

Intellectual attack will be discussed in the following section. *Denial* refe
to behavior which ignores a problem. When a person practices denial, l
pretends—often without full awareness of what he is doing—that no prol
lem exists. He may ignore facts which could create one side of a conflic
He may hold incompatible beliefs which cause confused and inconsisten
behavior yet refuse to recognize that fact. *Repression* is a psychological
mechanism by which a person buries problems beneath the level of consciousness. Feeling a problem keenly, knowing that he has emotional conflicts, he still may not dare to examine them openly and freely. One who
conceals his problems in this fashion risks injury to mental health. Redl and
Wattenberg are of the opinion that repressed conflict is the most frequent
source of neurotic behavior.[1]

Withdrawal may refer to physical retreat from a baffling confronting
situation, but more often applies to intellectual retirement. A person who
denies to himself the existence of a problem does not try to run away because he sees nothing to run from; a person who recognizes a problem and
chooses not to try to live with it may see no alternative but to flee. A person
who "flees" intellectually is given to daydreams and fantasies; he loses
touch with the worlds of normal individuals. *Projection* involves placing
blame on someone else for one's own inability to cope with a problem. This
form of behavior is sometimes called scapegoating. A person who ascribes
to others his own inadequacies tends to be highly critical or contemptuous
of others, and sometimes hostile. Projection may lead to delusions of persecution (paranoia). *Regression* is another form of fleeing behavior—retreat
from a problem by emotional and intellectual return to an earlier stage of
development when the problem was not present. Persons who regress develop emotional characteristics typical of childhood. Although severe regression is characteristic of certain forms of insanity, virtually everyone
shows mild forms of regression on occasion.

Psychosomatic illness expresses itself in such forms as migraine head-
aches, allergies, peptic ulcers, and high blood pressure. It has been estimated that, on the average, 75 percent of the clientele of one of the largest
general hospitals in the United States suffer from psychoneurotic symptoms
of some sort; the most conservative estimates place the percentage of psy-
chosomatically ill at 40 percent of all ill persons.[2] Psychologists have iden-

[1] Fritz Redl and William Wattenberg, *Mental Hygiene in Teaching*, Harcourt, Brace
& Company, 1951, p. 54.
[2] Herbert A. Carroll, *Mental Hygiene, the Dynamics of Adjustment*, Prentice-Hall,
Inc., 1951, p. 7.

tified a number of other neurotic behaviors associated with inability to solve problems constructively.[3]

In connection with a given problem, a person may behave to some degree in each of the ways named. Behaviors are not usually unmixed. What we have labeled an intellectual attack may be combined with rather strongly emotional behavior. Whether behavior emphasizes intellectual or emotional components, or whether it involves one emotional form rather than another, depends on the nature of the problem and of the previous learnings of the individual. Conflicts in closed areas are more likely to produce highly emotional and irrational reactions than are conflicts in other areas. Conspicuously aberrant behavior is unlikely to occur except in cases where a conflict poses a pressing problem and at the same time cannot be solved by any method which the individual is able to use. It is reasonable to assume that educational experiences in school can be arranged so as to produce fruitful intellectual responses more often than they would otherwise occur.

Some Forms of Intellectual Attack

So far, we have distinguished a group of evading, unproductive types of behavior from what we have chosen to call "intellectual attack." By the latter term we have meant any handling of a problem which involves deliberate intellectual grappling designed to solve the problem constructively. However, one may operate with design—even with great mental effort—and not exhibit much wisdom. One may habitually *think* about problems without arriving at right answers. An intellectual method may be judged only by its results. Some widely used methods of thinking have proved either too unreliable or insufficient in themselves to afford good solutions to problems. It is necessary, therefore, to distinguish one type of intellectual attack from another.

Chapter 2 proposed that an insight is adequate if it proves successful as a plan of action (or a rule to live by). An insight is likely to prove valuable in proportion as it harmonizes all available data. By the same token, tested insights, or concepts, are useful as guides to future behavior in proportion as they encompass and add consistency to as many data as possible. The critical test of a person's insights is whether they provide him with a set of beliefs about himself in relation to his social and physical environment which are extensive in scope, dependable in action, and compatible with

---

[3] For fuller analysis of the disorganizing behaviors described above, and others not treated here, see Redl and Wattenberg, *op. cit.*, chap. 3.

one another. The particular kind of thought most likely to lead to such a pattern of beliefs we shall refer to as reflection, or scientific method.

As suggested above, problem solving may take different forms. Some of the possible forms of intellectual attack are shown in the accompanying diagram. In proportion as problem-solving methods are unscientific, they are likely to result in beliefs which are incomplete, unreliable as guides, and inconsistent with each other. From the standpoint of producing dependable and useful knowledge, as well as the harmony of outlook which is essential to mental health, teachers need to help students solve problems on an increasingly reflective (i.e., scientific) plane.

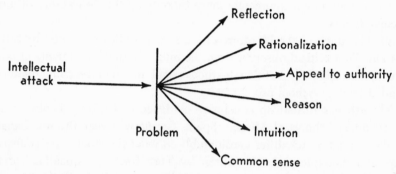

On the assumption that the method of reflection can be better understood by drawing contrasts, we shall describe in more detail each of the non-reflective (or semi-reflective) intellectual methods indicated in the diagram.

RATIONALIZATION

Rationalization is the attempt to defend a cherished belief by an unconscious distortion or slanting of evidence. Rationalization makes use of facts, but of only part of those available. Rationalization is inventing "good reasons" for what we are already determined to believe. The widespread tendency toward rationalization in our society should surprise no one. In a culture which places considerable emphasis on rationality and science, persons feel obligated to make their beliefs, values, and attitudes appear reasonable to others.

Reflective thinking is very different from rationalization, but teachers who say that they value thinking in their students often mean rationalization rather than reflection. Although almost everyone says that he is in favor of thinking, there seems to be considerable suspicion of those who think reflectively about social issues. Many teachers like reflection in the social studies only if there is some advance guarantee that thinkers will not reach unpopular conclusions. No physicist could make such a guarantee and we would be distressed if he tried. Rather, we say to the physicist: "Seek out the truth and let the chips fall where they may."

In economics, on the other hand, people sometimes say that students should study the evils of monopoly in order that they may better appreciate the virtues of free competition. Such an approach to the teaching of economics prejudges the truth of a hypothesis. Applied to the teaching of physics it would mean that students would study a wave theory of light in order that they might appreciate more thoroughly the desirability of a corpuscular theory.

Probably much of the literature of the social studies is colored by rationalization. To a critical observer even the most "factual" treatments of issues often appear slanted, both in textbooks and in other teaching materials intended for high-school use.

Walworth has turned up conclusive evidence that history books used in the secondary schools of Mexico, Spain, Germany, Great Britain, Canada, and the United States differ considerably in what the "facts" are conceived to be. For example, a book written by Toro for the "education" of the Mexican student treats the annexation of Texas as follows: ". . . The partisans of the South looked toward us to increase their territory, make new slave states out of it, and strengthen their domination; and they resolutely determined to acquire Texas, counting upon the aid of President Jackson, an unscrupulous man who, as a proprietor of slaves, was personally interested in the matter and resorted to every sort of means, even the most immoral, to accomplish his ends. . . ." [4] High-school students of the United States may read the more "enlightening" pages of Faulkner and Kepner and learn that "It was hardly to be expected that these aggressive Anglo-Saxon frontiersmen could long dwell in peace under the control of a people representing a very different civilization, and under a weak and inefficient government continually changing as one revolution succeeded another." [5]

No doubt teachers in Mexico, like teachers in the United States, feel that they are teaching the facts and that the learning of such facts will help students to think about their problems. Yet both textbooks cannot be completely right. Both may be completely or partly wrong. Moreover, much of

[4] Arthur Walworth, *School Histories at War*, Harvard University Press, 1938, p. 40.
[5] *Ibid.*, p. 41.

the content in both books is neither true nor false, as it deals with values rather than beliefs. The statement that Jackson was an *unscrupulous* man is as nonfactual as the statement that the government in Mexico was *weak* and *inefficient*.

A teacher who values reflection above rationalization would make it possible for students to learn that Mexican and American textbooks do not agree on all the facts. This demonstration of contradiction might cause doubt of certain established beliefs, but resolving the uncertainty thus created would further students' conceptual learning.

APPEAL TO AUTHORITY

Search for authoritative opinion is closely related to rationalization. Reliance on authority is a legitimate and necessary aid to reflection provided the authorities on whose opinions we rely have themselves depended on reflection in reaching their opinions. The next chapter will suggest criteria for judging the reliability of authorities. Unfortunately, we often choose to recognize only those authorities whose opinions support our own foregone conclusions, in which case reliance on authority becomes a form of rationalization. For well over a century students of economics in the United States and western Europe habitually turned for authoritative opinion to the writings of Adam Smith, Thomas R. Malthus, and David Ricardo. Students of radical persuasion turned to the writings of Karl Marx. In retrospect, we may wonder how much of the thinking of these eighteenth- and nineteenth-century students was rationalization.

The most common source of authority in public schools is, of course, textbooks. Utterances of textbook writers are regarded by most students as final truths, which is hardly surprising in view of our tendency to elevate textbooks to a central position in our educational system. But since textbooks in the social studies are to a large degree interpretive and evaluative rather than factual, it should be obvious that reliance on a particular text easily becomes a form of rationalization.

Often the appeal to authority attempts to uncover the dictates of a divine or supernatural giver of truth. For example, at the conclusion of the Spanish-American War President McKinley had to decide whether to take the Philippines as part of the spoils. Of his method of problem solving Charles and Mary Beard say:

> The intellectual and moral methods by which he resolved his perplexity the President later explained. . . . "I walked the floor of the White House night after

55

night," he said, "and I am not ashamed to tell you, gentlemen, that I went down on my knees and prayed Almighty God for light and guidance more than one night. And one night late it came to me in this way—I don't know how it was, but it came— . . . . There was nothing left for us to do but to take them all, and to educate the Filipinos, and uplift and civilize and Christianize them. . . ." [6]

This is not the only time, of course, that divine authority has been used as a justification for a given course of social action. Of hundreds of possible examples, we cite one more. Abolitionists of both North and South prior to the Civil War attacked slavery with the claim that it was immoral in the sight of God. Southern apologists were equally certain that slavery was divinely sanctioned. In 1858 a Southern member of Congress exclaimed, "We learn from the Holy Scriptures that Abraham and many wise and good men of that day not only held slaves but exercised acts of ownership over them; and that God Himself, after he had rescued the children of Israel from the house of bondage, sanctioned and recognized slavery both in principle and practice." [7]

USE OF REASON

The terms *reason* and *thinking* are often used interchangeably. Persons reach "reasoned conclusions" or "behave rationally." The popular meaning of reason is sometimes very close to the meaning of scientific method. But there is a difference. Strictly defined, reasoning is the process of deducing conclusions from given premises. It is therefore not the whole of the reflective, or scientific, method. A reflective approach includes reliance upon empirical evidence as well as upon logic.

The formal use of reason as a road to truth dates back to early Greek civilization. Aristotle originated the classical laws of logic and invented the syllogism as a purported reasoning device. His influence held sway for many centuries. Today the Aristotelian tradition may be observed among the rational humanists, who include persons such as Robert Hutchins, Mortimer Adler, and B. I. Bell. The Great Books Movement, as a guide to curriculum making, seems generally to be based on the assumption that reason, rather than scientific reflection, is the best single road to the nature of truth and morality.

What is wrong with reason? A conclusion based on reasoning alone can never be any better than the premises on which it rests. If the premises are

[6] Charles A. Beard and Mary R. Beard, *Rise of American Civilization*, The Macmillan Company, 1930, Vol. II, pp. 375–376.
[7] *Ibid.*, Vol. I, p. 705.

false, then the conclusions will be false even though the logic is impeccable. And those who prefer to rely on pure reason have disdain for the experimentation and observation which would be necessary in most cases to check the truth of their premises. The difference between scientific and Aristotelian methods is exemplified in the comment of a distinguished professor who told his students shortly after Galileo had invented the telescope and found spots on the sun, "You need not be troubled. I have read Aristotle from cover to cover three times, and he nowhere mentions sun spots, so that there is no truth to the idea." [8]

A number of modern writers have developed the idea that many human problems exist as a consequence of the Aristotelian tradition. This tradition is well expressed in the three laws of Aristotle:

(a) A is A.
(b) Everything but A is non-A.
(c) Nothing is both A and non-A.

Reasoning which starts from these laws has an either-or quality. *Either-or reasoning* (sometimes called *two-valued orientation*) occurs when we are able to see only two choices in a complex situation. It causes us to see the world and ourselves only in black and white. One may wonder, for example, whether his life has been a success. He can always find some evidence that it has been and some evidence that it has not. The laws of Aristotle prevent him from concluding that his life has been both a success and a failure. Instead, he is impelled to conclude that it has been *either* a success *or* a failure.[9]

INTUITION

For some problems it has been recommended that we rely upon intuition. Women are supposed to have a well-developed capacity for intuition and men are supposed to be frequent victims of it. What people mean by intuition is not always clear. A good operational definition would be "hunch." A hunch is a hypothesis based on vague or fragmentary evidence.

But those who recommend that we solve problems intuitively seem to have in mind something other than hunches or hypotheses. Faced with a problem, one may have several hunches. Which should he choose? A choice

[8] Quoted by Fred Hechinger, "Progressive Education Versus 'Spectatoritis,'" *The Reporter*, August 5, 1952, p. 36.
[9] For an excellent treatment of this subject see Wendell Johnson, *People in Quandaries*, Harper & Brothers, 1946, pp. 6–10.

may be made reflectively, but it is maintained that some problems cannot be solved reflectively and that intuition is a necessary alternative. It would seem that a form of self-deception akin to rationalization may be at work here. Usually the claim that one has been intuitive is made *after* the event, not before. A man who breaks his leg in the afternoon may report that he had had a feeling that morning that disaster was in store for him. His claim to intuitive judgment would be more plausible if he had expressed his premonition before the disaster took place. It may be that an intuition is a good guess and that bad guesses are never reported as intuition but are simply forgotten.

Stuart Chase has a somewhat different conception of intuition; he calls it a "loose term for a half-conscious blend of many minute observations. A good outfielder starting to run at the crack of the bat is an example of superlative intuition." [10] Evidently, this outfielder would not be able to teach his skill to another outfielder. He does not know how he does what he is doing; he just does it. But surely some outfielders could teach their skill to others if they became more conscious of their "blended and minute" observations.

In any event, a baseball coach does more than recommend to his outfielders that they play their positions intuitively. Minute observations are broken down reflectively and outfielders are taught to judge a fly ball by the crack of the bat, the direction of the wind, the pitching of the ball, and the hitting habits of the batter. Apparently any merely intuitive operation could never be taught to anyone else because no one can describe in objective terms what happens during an act of intuition.

We find that an intuitive thinker has no publicly available data, that he has tested no hypotheses, that he is unable to pinpoint his procedures, and that he may be blissfully ignorant of having made any assumptions. Verification of his conclusions is impossible, for the entire process is so hidden and private that no one can even be sure what it is that exists, or even that it exists.

COMMON SENSE

John Dewey has made a distinction between empirical thinking and scientific thinking. Empirical thinking is based purely on sensory data, particularly of a superficial or limited sort.[11] Empirical thinking is a basis for

[10] Stuart Chase, *The Proper Study of Mankind,* Harper & Brothers, 1948, p. 9.
[11] Empirical has a somewhat different meaning in much modern writing, namely,

much that we call common sense. It is common sense, for example, to believe that the earth is flat and that the sun revolves around the earth. This is the way it *looks* to the ordinary person.

Common sense often reflects the fallacy of *post hoc, ergo propter hoc* ("after this, therefore on account of it"). Events are given a cause-effect interpretation simply because they are consecutive. For example, a swimming pool is opened to all races. A riot takes place. It is empirically concluded that the second event was caused by the first. This conclusion seems to be a matter of common sense, but its unscientific nature is apparent when one notes that there may have been present some other causal factor not evident to the casual or untrained observer. In contrast, the reflective or scientific method would look for minute and specific connections between one event and the other. Occasionally, of course, the noting of empirical relationships leads to discovery of a scientific truth, but just as often empiricism results in erroneous conclusions.

It would require many volumes to catalogue all the mistaken beliefs which have seemed a matter of common sense to those who held them. The early common-sense beliefs in alchemy, magic, and witchcraft may seem crude and indefensible today, but many of our present-day common-sense beliefs are based on just as little evidence. The beliefs that a protective tariff can increase our standard of living and that wage increases are the root cause of price inflation are cases in point.

The Method of Reflection

There is no essential difference between reflection, as the term is used in this book, and the scientific approach. The term *scientific* does carry a connotation which is less suited to our purposes than is the connotation of *reflective.* "Science" implies white-gowned technicians, microscopes and telescopes, chemical tables, and cyclotrons. It suggests precise measurements, use of mathematics, a large amount of esoteric wizardry, and neglect of moral values.

"Reflection" refers to the essential but non-gadgetlike features of the scientific method, to an attitude of mind and a generalized set of operations with which we may approach all problems whether physical or social in nature. Dewey gave us a classic definition of reflection when he called it

---

factual, in the sense of correspondence to data disclosed through observation or experiment. It is a broad term referring to all data procured through the senses and does not have the unfavorable connotation that it seems to have in Dewey's writing.

the "active, persistent, and careful consideration of any belief or supposed form of knowledge in the light of the grounds that support it and the further conclusions to which it tends. . . ." [12]

THE REFLECTIVE METHOD AND A COMPLETE ACT OF THOUGHT COMPARED

On page 45 a complete act of thought, as instigated by a problematic situation, was diagramed and analyzed. An act of thought was seen to progress from established belief, to doubt, to ideas, to testing of ideas, to verified belief or conclusion.

We may compare the process of thought with the steps of the scientific method, which we take to be as follows:

1. Recognition and definition of a problem. This is usually an outgrowth of a sensed discrepancy in known data.
2. Formulation of hypotheses.
3. Elaboration of logical implications of hypotheses. This includes deducing observations which have already been made—so that hypotheses may be checked against present knowledge; and deducing observations which have not already been made—so that hypotheses may be tested through experimentation.
4. Testing of hypotheses. This involves attempts to verify consequences deduced under step 3, in terms of data of previous experience and data procured in experimental tests.
5. Drawing of conclusions. This involves acceptance, modification, or rejection of hypotheses.

Yet there is more to an adequate description of the scientific or reflective method than to a description of an act of thought in the elemental terms offered in Chapter 2. The reflective method carries with it a set of rules, or axioms, which must be observed scrupulously or the method fails. We may say, therefore, that the reflective method is the complete act of thought as described on page 45, *with certain safeguards attached.* These are the conditions which long experience with the method has shown must be fulfilled if it is to produce adequate conclusions.

RULES OF THE REFLECTIVE METHOD

The rules or axioms governing the reflective method include the following:

1. Whenever one belief or conclusion is accepted in preference to an-

[12] John Dewey, *How We Think,* D. C. Heath & Company, 1933, p. 9.

other, it is presumed that reasons exist for its acceptance. The grounds for acceptance may be scant, but so long as they are better than the grounds any competing belief can offer, they justify its acceptance.

2. Conclusions are always made provisionally. All knowledge is assumed to be relative, in the sense that no question is closed to reëxamination provided a reason to reëxamine it develops. This does not mean that one may not establish laws or principles which are assumed to be valid indefinitely. Such laws are not absolutes so long as there is a willingness to reopen the question of their validity.

3. Conclusions are consistent with each other. Contradictory beliefs can never be true at the same time and under the same conditions. This does not mean that one may not switch from one belief to another which is incompatible with it. Changing one's mind is not an example of inconsistency; a person is inconsistent only when he holds two opposites at once, and under the same assumed conditions.

4. All pertinent evidence is scrutinized before conclusions are drawn. An investigator looks at all facts then available, no matter how unpalatable some of them may seem. There is never a slanting, ignoring, or distortion of data to prove a point. Taboos and ungovernable prejudices do not mix with a reflective approach.

5. The ultimate authority for any conclusion is to be found in natural phenomena, as revealed by observation and experimentation. The subject matter of reflection is always rooted in nature.

6. All operations must be performed openly and in a fashion which will enable others to repeat the same procedures. Each act of reflection must be able to supply its own recipe, so to speak. Stated in another way, the methods of an investigator must be subject to operational description. We also use the term *publicly verifiable* to describe the methods and data of reflection.[13]

For the purpose of clarity, the foregoing "rules" have been treated out of relationship to one another. Further, they have referred to method alone, and method cannot be fully defined except in relation to expected results. It is necessary, therefore, to carry our analysis another step forward, by developing a point suggested earlier in the chapter (pages 52–53).

The purpose of the rules associated with the scientific outlook is to make

[13] Rules of the reflective or scientific method may be listed from numerous sources. Five of the above rules were derived from Felix Kaufman, *Methodology of the Social Sciences*, Oxford University Press, 1944, pp. 39–40. See also Max C. Otto, "Scientific Humanism," *The Antioch Review*, Dec., 1943, p. 532.

for "good thinking," which, in the final test, may be judged *only against its results*. The presumed purpose of any act of thought, or of any application of scientific or reflective methodology, is to achieve tested beliefs which are worth more to a person than the beliefs he previously held. But when are they "worth more"? They are worth more as they come to encompass more data. As this happens, we presume not only that one's stock of beliefs expands but also that individual beliefs become more "accurate" in the sense that they become more reliable as guides to action. Their reliability is a function of how well they explain the characteristics of the learner's environment. A person's beliefs are also worth more as they come to be more consistent, more compatible, with one another. Inconsistent beliefs are worthless as guides to action because they lead to "riding off in several directions at once." They lead only to confused behavior. And as we have seen, sensed inconsistency also leads to emotional discomfort and perhaps to neurotic behaviors.

We may summarize the foregoing position: A method is successfully reflective in proportion as it leads to adequacy and harmony of outlook in light of obtainable data.[14] The reflective method, as we have defined it, is more likely than any non-reflective method to achieve this end.

How the Reflective Method Differs from Nonscientific Modes of Thought

Rationalization avoids use of all pertinent evidence; or it slants or distorts it. Rationalization also implies a dogmatic clinging to judgments made unreflectively. The reflective investigator may *hope* that his hypotheses will prove correct, but he never allows hope to overrule cold facts. No one can predict in advance of reflection what its results will be. Reflection begins when someone does not know what to believe about some question. He tests hypotheses in order to achieve verified belief. If he knew his conclusions in advance, there would be no need for reflective thought. The decisive difference between the two methods on this point, perhaps, is that a person who rationalizes wants, and assumes for himself, an advance guarantee that his conclusions will be thus and so. A reflective individual needs no such guarantee.

Reflection may rely on authority, but a person following the reflective method is always critical of authorities and careful to ascertain the basis of

---

[14] Cf. Ernest E. Bayles' principles of *adequacy* and *harmony, The Theory and Practice of Teaching*, Harper & Brothers, 1950, pp. 107–109.

conclusions drawn by them. He tries to determine whether the authorities themselves were dominated in their inquiry by the rules of the reflective method, and if he finds they were not, he has little use for their opinions. A reflective individual also relies only on secular authorities in connection with the problems he is trying to attack scientifically.

Reasoning—i.e., the deduction of conclusions from premises—is a legitimate part of the reflective method, but only a part of it. In reflection, "self-evident" premises are always suspect. No conclusion is regarded as final until it has been verified against data from nature. The decisive difference here lies in the refusal of those using the reflective method to accept premises as true without investigation of empirical data. Rationalists do not believe this to be necessary.

Intuition differs from reflection in part because it is more mysterious and hidden. We cannot verify another person's intuition because it is impossible for anyone to repeat the steps he has gone through. In reflection, when we doubt that a problem has been solved reflectively, certain lines of inquiry are open. We may ask the "thinker" to state his problem more exactly, to clarify his hypotheses, to give his assumptions, his sources of data, and the procedures by which he collected and weighed his data. We may identify assumptions and data which he has overlooked. If he values the reflective process, he welcomes this kind of inquiry.

The method of common sense has features resembling the reflective method in that it makes use of data of the senses and combines observation with theorization (i.e., generalization). Undoubtedly many of man's fundamental discoveries (like the use of fire, the wheel, and the development of agriculture) arose through operation of something very much like what we now label common sense. The chief—and crucial—difference between the common-sense method and reflection is in the tendency of those who rely on the former to be satisfied with superficial examination of data and to jump to hasty conclusions. There is also a dogmatic quality to common-sense conclusions which is unbecoming to a truly reflective approach.

DISCUSSION QUESTIONS AND EXERCISES

1. How old is our present conception of scientific method? Were the ancient Greeks scientific in a modern sense? Has our conception of scientific method changed since Isaac Newton's time? How? Is it likely to change in the future?
2. In what sense, if any, is one intellectual method (such as reflection) superior to another? Is there any way that such superiority can be proved? Would the "proof" have to take into consideration the purpose which a method is to serve?

3. If reflection has the virtues claimed for it, why would everyone not want habitually to be reflective? How do you explain the widespread opposition to reflective investigation in certain areas of human life? Is such opposition based on understanding or lack of understanding of the possible outcomes of a reflective approach?
4. Can you describe and illustrate non-reflective methods other than those treated in Chapter 3?
5. Bergen Evans, in *The Natural History of Nonsense*, catalogues a large number of mistaken beliefs. After acquainting yourself with some of these, try to decide what kind of intellectual processes produced them. Are all popular superstitions adopted unreflectively?
6. Is there any guarantee that reflection will produce beliefs which are relatively consistent and which embrace all available and obtainable data? Is there any reason to suppose that non-reflective methods would not serve this end just as well?

REFERENCES

Probably the most readable introduction to the nature of scientific method is Chapters 1–2 of Stuart Chase, *The Proper Study of Mankind* (Harper, 1948). A combination of readability and philosophic depth may be found in James B. Conant, *Modern Science and Modern Man* (Columbia University Press, 1952). George A. Lundberg, *Can Science Save Us?* (Longmans, Green, 1947), provides a lucid analysis of the meaning of modern science and defends the idea that social problems can be solved scientifically.

Rewarding but more difficult is Max C. Otto, *The Human Enterprise* (Appleton-Century-Crofts, 1940), Chapters 8–9. For advanced students the following are recommended: Erwin Schrodinger, *Science and the Human Temperament* (Norton, 1935); John Dewey, *How We Think* (Heath, 1933), and, by the same author, *Logic: The Theory of Inquiry* (Holt, 1938); and Felix Kaufman, *Methodology of the Social Sciences* (Oxford University Press, 1944).

Books which deal specifically with the structure of the thinking process include: James Harvey Robinson, *The Mind in the Making* (Harper, 1921), Chapter 2; Boyd H. Bode, *Fundamentals of Education* (Macmillan, 1928), Chapter 6; Max Wertheimer, *Productive Thinking* (Harper, 1945); and Dewey, *How We Think*.

Students will find stimulating the interpretation of science developed by scientific philosophers of the school of thought known as logical positivism. Both readable and provocative are the following: Anatol Rapoport, *Science and the Goals of Man* (Harper, 1950); Philipp Frank, *Relativity: A Richer Truth* (Beacon, 1950), and, by the same author, *Modern Science and Its Philosophy* (Harvard University Press, 1950). Excellent, but more difficult to read, is Hans Reichenbach, *The Rise of Scientific Philosophy* (University of California Press, 1951).

Chapter 4

The Reflective Method (Continued)

Chapter 3 sought to define the reflective method by describing it in general terms and comparing it with several widely used non-reflective methods. The present chapter explores more fully certain aspects of the reflective method. We shall examine certain language difficulties involved in the stating of problems and the formulation of hypotheses. We shall discuss the testing of hypotheses, in this connection giving attention to what is sometimes referred to as "rules of evidence."

Language and the Reflective Method

If one examines the operations included in the reflective, or scientific, handling of problems (as stated on page 60), it is clear that much of the method involves working with statements or propositions. Problems must be stated, hypotheses formulated, and these hypotheses tested with evidence—which in turn consists of statements describing the results of observations. The results which reflection is uniquely capable of producing depend, among other things, on the conventions adopted for the use of language. As Johnson observes, "The language of science is the better part of the method of science." [1]

It was once assumed that thinking conforms to laws of reason and logic which are common to all mankind and an implicit part of mental life, *preceding* language. That is, even though using a different language, a Choctaw, Hottentot, and Englishman, it was supposed, would think in the same way. Thus any logical idea could be translated without damage into any language. However, this assumption has been rejected by semanticists and

[1] Wendell Johnson, *People in Quandaries*, Harper & Brothers, 1946, p. 50.

other students of scientific methodology. It is now widely believed that the language forms which a person uses influence the kinds of problems he considers important, his manner of stating problems, his choice of testing procedures, and the outcome of inquiry. What each person sees as being "real" and his interpretation of it depend in part on his language habits.[2]

A cardinal principle for the use of language in reflection is that all terms and expressions must be meaningful. We may define a socially meaningful term or statement as one which may be tested or verified, publicly, by persons other than the user.

Only to the extent that those who hear a statement agree as to the specific conditions or observations required for ascertaining its validity can the question of its validity have meaning. And the extent to which they do agree in this sense is, of course, an indication of the extent to which the statement is clear or meaningful. If a statement is such that those who hear it do not agree at all as to how it might be verified or refuted, the statement may be "beautiful" or "eloquent," or grammatically irreproachable, but it is also, and above all, nonsense.[3]

The present chapter will keep in the forefront the assumption that only when language is used meaningfully is reflection possible. This assumption will be implicit in later chapters, and classroom practices which it implies will be described in chapters treating techniques of teaching. Chapter 8, on classroom discussion, will give particular attention to methods of averting confusion which results from ambiguous use of language.

Meaningful Statement of Problems

We suggested in Chapter 2 that a problem is a sensed difficulty—a feeling of confusion, bafflement, or inconsistency issuing from inability to proceed quickly and smoothly to a goal. Before a social-studies class can reflectively examine common problems they must be stated explicitly. Statements which express felt problems should, in so far as possible, communicate the same thought or idea to all members of the group; they should also suggest or imply methods by which the problem may be studied, or at the very least make possible the formulation of such methods.

It is essential to recognize that some kinds of problems can be stated meaningfully and others cannot. Unless a problem can be stated meaningfully, it is a waste of time to try to explore it very far. Of course, to discover

[2] Stuart Chase, "How Language Shapes Our Thoughts," *Harper's Magazine*, April, 1954, p. 78. For a fuller treatment of this thesis, see Stuart Chase and Marian Tyler Chase, *Power of Words*, Harcourt, Brace and Company, 1954.

[3] Wendell Johnson, *op. cit.*, pp. 51–52.

that a particular problem cannot be stated meaningfully has educational value. Attempts to state meaningless problems in meaningful language are enlightening. Since problems are very often expressed as questions, what we are saying here is that some questions are answerable, some unanswerable, and trying to answer the unanswerable may help students to appreciate why some questions cannot be answered.

Certain types of problems, or questions, may not be treated reflectively because of the nature of their subject matter. If the operations needed to solve them are outside the scope of shared human experiences, they are not susceptible to reflection. For example, questions which require information about the "nature of reality" outside of man—such as the "basic substance or essence" of the universe, whether the universe is dominated by purpose, and identification of "first causes"—would appear to be unanswerable by scientific inquiry. The same is true of questions concerning the nature of God, heaven and hell, and divine moral law. In short, if inquiry is confined to reflection as we have defined it, most questions associated with traditional philosophy and theology are unanswerable. This does not mean that reflection cannot be used to explore the differences in methodology implied by problems of this sort and problems which may be handled scientifically.

Although problems of the foregoing kind are not commonly treated in social-studies classrooms, questions are often raised by students (or teachers) which are unanswerable because their content is outside the range of possible human experience. We have known classes to debate questions such as "What would the course of history have been if Lincoln had not been assassinated?" "Will the world be a better place in which to live in 2000 A.D.?" "Do all people in the world dream when they sleep?" It is true that evidence of a sort may be obtainable in the case of some such questions, but their answers hinge primarily on evidence which is unknown and cannot be known, either because it does not exist or because procuring it would require studies beyond the scope of scientific inquiry.

Another type of unmanageable problem common to social-studies classes is that which seeks to discover fixed rules, principles, or laws. By "fixed," we are referring not to principles which are generally valid as guides to behavior and thus of ongoing usefulness but to principles which are regarded as unchanging or absolute.

Questions sometimes raised in social-studies classrooms are on this order: What are *the* principles of economics? What laws govern the behavior of groups? What is permanent and universal in human nature? What form of

67

government is better than any other? What is final moral truth? Such questions usually or often imply a search for absolutes.

We do not mean, of course, that students of the social studies are not to seek useful generalizations; this is a primary aim of learning. And when judged adequate, such generalizations may be regarded as true. It is better to phrase questions, however, so they do not imply a search for ultimates. It is quite legitimate to ask questions like the following: At present in the United States, what appears to be the most usual relationship between the quantity of money and the general price level? What behaviors do anthropologists now feel are common to most human cultures? Are there any moral rules which, if followed, would allow a maximum of individual growth under modern conditions of life? Such questions lead to answers which encourage further investigation.

A person may be aware of a problem potentially susceptible to scientific inquiry, but fail to phrase it meaningfully. This difficulty is very common in discussions of social affairs. Johnson illustrates the point as follows: He received a letter from the president of a woman's club asking him to help answer the question, "Will democracy defeat religion?" As stated, this question was meaningless because it was unlimited as to time and because no attempt had been made to define democracy, defeat, or religion. Johnson suggested that a more meaningful question would have been, "Do persons who attend town meetings in our town attend church less often than those who don't?" [4]

We assume that problems involving questions of value—what is good or bad, right or wrong, moral or immoral—may be handled reflectively, but only in a special way. Chapter 5 will discuss the study of values as a part of social-studies education and will further explore methodological problems related to the testing of values.

Hypotheses as Verifiable Statements

As scientific method is now conceived, any statement which is meant to serve as a hypothesis must be verifiable—that is, subject to the test of empirical evidence. When used in this connection, the term *verifiable* means *testable*—capable of being shown either true or false. The verifiability of a statement hinges on both its content and the way in which it is phrased.

In so far as possible, a hypothesis must be so worded that it conveys approximately the same meaning to each party to an investigation. Of

[4] *Ibid.*, pp. 53–54.

course, a statement can never mean exactly the same to all members of a group because, to some degree, its meaning for each person stems from his own unique experiences and purposes. On the other hand, through careful handling of content and phraseology, we may approach a commonness of meaning. This shared meaning is essential in order that thought may be communicated from one person to another, one person's effort may be a check on that of another, and there may be some consensus of findings.

Our task in the present section, therefore, is to analyze some common causes of ambiguity in statements, and to establish guides for producing more fruitful hypotheses.

Some Causes of Ambiguity in Statements

Although the two bear a relationship to each other, clarity of meaning is not necessarily a function of grammatical correctness. If a student says, "Men is smarter than women," we know approximately what he means (unless "smarter" gives us trouble). However, grammatical sloppiness may interfere with communication of meaning. Ambiguity is often the result of improper use of connectives, cramming two or more ideas into a clause or simple sentence, failing to complete a sentence, and including in a single sentence incongruous or contradictory statements. Slang and colloquialism may likewise produce ambiguity.

Words which have an indefinite meaning and which each listener interprets to suit himself are called weasel words. In the following sentences weasel words are italicized: "I am in favor of reducing taxes, but not *too much.*" (How much is "too much"?) "If elected, I will maintain the *right balance* between conservatism and liberalism." (What is the "right balance"?) "You must have *faith* as you grapple with the most *important* problems of your life." (In this sentence, what do "faith" and "important" mean?) Political speeches and commencement addresses usually are studded with weasel words and are thus ambiguous.

Intended hypotheses are often couched in figurative language. A figure of speech is a word, phrase, or sentence which is used outside its usual or literal meaning. It is language used in ways not sanctioned by a dictionary. Figures include metaphors, similes, analogies, exaggeration and understatement, coined words, and puns. Unless all members of a class have a common understanding of the figures used, figurative language is likely to cause confusion.[5]

[5] For a fuller discussion of the pitfalls of metaphor, see F. A. Philbrick, *Understanding English: An Introduction to Semantics,* The Macmillan Company, 1942, chaps. 8–11.

Statements which contain high-order abstractions usually require very careful definition before they can serve as hypotheses. Although the value of careful definition has often been stressed, we find that the task of definition is often approached in inefficient or fruitless ways. It is not enough for a social-studies teacher to refer students to a dictionary for the meaning of abstract concepts in social science. Nor are the typical short definitions offered by teachers during recitation or discussion adequate.

Definitions profit from examples or illustrations, or from reference to objects or processes which may be experienced by students. But if a class is studying copper mining, bringing a sample of copper ore to class for students to observe, touch, and smell is not enough to constitute a full definition of copper ore. Its *use* in the economy, its effects on people's lives, must also be understood.

Of the various kinds of definition, the one of greatest significance in scientific methodology is the *operational definition.* An operational definition describes an object or process *in use.* In the physical sciences, operational definitions are like recipes—they describe operations involved in experiencing a concept. Thus, a generalization such as Boyle's law is "defined" by describing the laboratory operations necessary to demonstrate it.[6] Operational definitions of terms and concepts in social science may follow the same procedure. For example, the law of demand might be defined by describing the nature of research which would be required to demonstrate the law. On the other hand, a description of how individuals behave who are obeying the law of demand is also an operational definition. Again, capitalism may be defined operationally by telling how persons in a capitalistic society live, particularly those whose behavior is most effective in giving the society its capitalistic character. Such a definition would be even more effective if students could be placed in situations where they would have personal experience with private ownership, market operations, investment, and production for personal gain.[7]

Judgments of Fact and Judgments of Value

In classifying statements as verifiable or unverifiable, it has been common

[6] For an excellent exposition of the significance of operational definitions in science, see Percy W. Bridgman, *The Logic of Modern Physics,* The Macmillan Company, 1927.

[7] For further reading on the subject of definitions, see Anatol Rapoport, *Science and the Goals of Man,* Harper & Brothers, 1950, chap. 7. In the light of later discussion in the present chapter, students may wish to reflect on Rapoport's contention that all value judgments are operationally meaningless.

to make a distinction between *judgments of fact* and *judgments of value.*[8]
Properly defined, these terms have pedagogical value. We shall first give
conventional definitions for them and then show what appears to be a
necessary qualification if they are to have maximum usefulness.

Judgments of fact (fact judgments) are statements which describe relationships between things. They are objective; i.e., they have assumed
referents in nature. The grounds for a judgment of fact always lie in observations or experiments. They are testable with public evidence; that is, any
investigator may verify them (assuming, of course, that he has whatever
special training is necessary). Examples of judgments of fact are: "Women,
on the average, live longer than men," and "The price of corn is $1.10 a
bushel."

A judgment of fact may or may not be true. Its distinctive quality depends not on its being true but on the supposition that its truth can be
checked objectively. For example, the statement "Bigamy is legal in South
Carolina" is a judgment of fact but untrue. After it has been checked and
confirmed a judgment of fact becomes a *fact*.

Whether a statement is a judgment of fact hinges not on whether the
judgment can be verified at the time it is made but on the type of subject
matter with which it deals. For example, although mankind may never have
the evidence to verify it, a proposition like "Some form of animal life exists
on the planet Mars" is a judgment of fact. A proposition like "The adoption
of socialism in a country leads eventually to loss of political freedom" deals
with objective cause-and-effect relationships and is thus theoretically verifiable. But the terms are difficult to define and the data involved are complex and susceptible to widely differing interpretations. Competent and
impartial investigators might never agree on an answer. But the proposition
is still a judgment of fact.

Semanticists use the term *judgment of value* (or value judgment) to refer
to a statement which is not now subject to the test of observation or experiment. A value judgment is thought unsusceptible to reflective verification
not because evidence is complex or lacking but because its subject matter
is now beyond the scope of scientific investigation. A value judgment expresses an attitude or value. Since it expresses personal preference or taste,
it may not be adjudged true or false (except in so far as its implied value
is instrumental to the achievement of other values—see Chapter 5). A value
judgment tells us something about its holder but not about the world
around him.

[8] *Ibid.*, chap. 2.

We may usually identify value judgments by the presence of one or more *value terms*. A value term denotes the quality of the preference which the utterer intends to express. In the sentence "Marilyn is a beautiful woman," the value term is *beautiful*. Commonly encountered value terms are *good* and *bad, right* and *wrong, naughty* and *nice, decent* and *indecent, moral* and *immoral*.

We sometimes refer to statements which contain the words *should* or *ought* as *policy statements*. Examples are: "Everyone should go to church on Sunday," or "Women ought to wear higher necklines than they do." The first of these statements means the same as "It is good for people to go to church on Sunday," and the second, "It would be good for women to wear higher necklines." Policy statements are thus a form of value judgment. However, we must pay careful attention to the use of the term *should* before classifying a statement containing it. It may refer only to simple possibility and not to moral judgment, as when we say, "I should be able to meet the 6:30 train."

It is often argued that only judgments of fact may serve as hypotheses in any investigation which purports to be scientific. A preference, it is held, can never be shown to be true or false on the basis of public evidence. We accept this supposition as correct, but only after we have qualified the definitions given above.

Careful analysis suggests that the distinction commonly made between judgments of fact and judgments of value is an oversimplification. The usual distinction conveys the notion that judgments of fact are divorced from acts of evaluation; that they are merely true or false descriptions of a physical reality outside a speaker—objective, exact, and dependable; and that judgments of value refer to nothing of substance. That is, the notion is conveyed that fact judgments refer to what is "real," value judgments to what is "unreal." If this were the case, value judgments would have no place in inquiry. The foregoing connotation is quite misleading. It is also misleading to suppose that any such hard-and-fast distinction may be made between statements.

In one sense, all statements are evaluative. If one person says to another, "You are a thief," he is employing a judgment of fact, but it is obvious that he is also expressing a value; he dislikes the person spoken to. But even relatively neutral statements reflect acts of valuation. Suppose a person says, "Marilyn wears a size 4 shoe." This is a judgment of fact. But why was it said? Clearly, the speaker feels that knowledge concerning Marilyn's shoe

72

size is important. He has chosen to focus attention on this, rather than on some alternative interest. The very fact that he is interested gives a clue to some one or more of his values. It seems likely that all thought involves the making of valuations—the continuous selection of what is important in relation to one's ends.

Let us now examine the situation with respect to judgments which contain value terms, as defined on pages 71–72. Are such statements always unverifiable? Probably not, as the following example will show. Suppose we are working with the statement "Mexicans are good agricultural workers." If this statement reflects a like or dislike for Mexican agricultural workers, it is clearly a value judgment. But in "good" we commonly include qualities such as skill, willingness to work, and reliability, which can be described operationally—that is, in terms of observable behaviors. The same thing would apply if "good" were taken to mean moral; one might describe a series of specific behaviors which he defines as moral. In either case, one could, on the basis of factual data, either affirm or deny the statement. Furthermore, since everyone else who accepts our definitions may check our investigations, the statement is publicly verifiable.

The same would be true with "Marilyn is a beautiful woman." If beautiful is defined in terms of specific and measurable qualities, such as having certain curves in certain places, it is possible to say with assurance that Marilyn either is or is not beautiful. It is also evident that whoever says Marilyn is beautiful *likes* the way she looks.

Obviously, some value terms are more difficult than others to define operationally. For example, suppose a person says, "This pie is delicious." "Delicious" refers to a group of highly subjective judgments the grounds for which are difficult to communicate. If deliciousness can be defined in terms of measurable qualities—sweetness, tartness, juiciness, or tenderness —then it is possible to judge the statement objectively. A judgment affirming the deliciousness of pie is fundamentally no different from one affirming the goodness of an agricultural worker or the beauty of a woman. But since we may identify widely shared cultural standards for good work and for feminine beauty, it may be somewhat easier to secure general agreement as to what is meant by these values than as to what is meant by delicious pie.

The last sentence above holds the clue to determining whether a statement can function as a hypothesis in reflection. Apparently any statement whose truth may be tested by scientific means, any statement which may be shown through public tests to be true or false, may function as a hypothesis. From such a statement we may deduce possible tests. It is not the presence of particular types of words which determines the role of a proposition in thought, but rather whether the proposition may be defined meaningfully (that is, operationally) in a way acceptable to all investigators.

The verifiability of many statements, particularly those which express attitudes, appears to hinge on whether *general agreement* on the meaning of all terms may be secured. If all persons engaged in a coöperative investigation can agree as to the measurable qualities implied by a value term, then a statement containing such a term may be tested with a possibility of agreement as to outcome.

An indispensable feature of scientific method is its openness or communicability. Since we assume that for inquiry to be scientific all operations performed may be repeated by others, there must be agreement on the meaning of terms. In the social sciences to a much greater degree than in the physical sciences such agreement is difficult to attain.

Rather than trying to apply to statements a rigid two-way classification which distinguishes sharply between fact judgments and value judgments, it is more realistic to think of statements as falling on a continuum, at one extreme of which are those having a common operational definition and at the other those expressing preferences too individualized and subjective to permit shared definitions. It should be remembered, however, that whether a given statement falls toward one end or the other of the continuum depends on the shared meanings of the persons engaged in investigation. A statement which is easily defined by one group may stymie another. We may express our manner of describing statements as follows:

Fact-Value Continuum

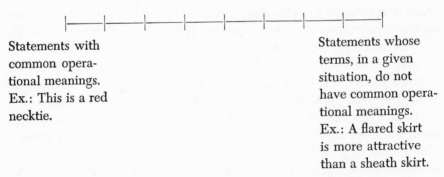

| Statements with common operational meanings. Ex.: This is a red necktie. | Statements whose terms, in a given situation, do not have common operational meanings. Ex.: A flared skirt is more attractive than a sheath skirt. |

Statements which fall toward the right end of the scale usually do so because of the presence of value terms with highly subjective meanings. In the example, *attractive* would probably present serious difficulties in definition. Used as hypotheses or as "factual evidence," such statements create unmanageable problems in investigation.

The question of whether value judgments may be operationally defined and thus serve as hypotheses is not the same as the question of whether values may be shown to be true or false apart from their instrumental use. The latter question will be explored in Chapter 5.

In the present book, by judgment of fact we shall mean statements about observable and measurable qualities, from which we may derive if-then relationships open to scientific tests. Such a statement may and usually does imply something about the speaker's values. By value judgments we shall mean attitudinal statements which contain a very strong element of personal preference, and which it is difficult to define operationally to the satisfaction of most persons investigating them.

The Nature of Evidence

Hypotheses are tested by determining how well they explain data deduced from them. If one wishes to discover whether men are more intelligent than women, he deduces if-then propositions, such as "If men are more intelligent than women, then they should make higher average scores on intelligence tests." This deduction may be tested by referring to studies made in the past or by arranging new studies. These studies provide factual data which either support or cast doubt on the hypothesis. What is the nature of factual data used in tests of this sort?

Facts, as we use the term, are not objects or processes in the environment. They are statements which represent tested insights. Facts have a creative aspect; they never mean exactly the same to any two individuals. However, if they are acquired reflectively and state matters which are relatively simple to investigate, then they may have approximately the same meaning for large numbers of individuals. One aim of education is to accomplish this commonness of meaning.

Factual evidence is taken to mean statements which have a high probability of being true and which are relevant to determining the truth of a hypothesis. In connection with the illustration given above, the following statement would be pertinent evidence: "The average IQ score of a representative sample of women is 103; the average score of men, 99." For most persons who understand what is involved in intelligence testing, including its inadequacies, this statement is likely to have approximately similar meanings. To serve adequately as evidence in problem solving, statements must have the same general qualities as hypotheses; they must by their nature be verifiable. They are cast in declarative-sentence form, they may be defined operationally, and they are phrased as unambiguously as possible.

It is important to understand that hypothetical and factual propositions tend to be interchangeable. Hypotheses become facts as they are tested reflectively and fact judgments revert to hypotheses whenever their truth is questioned. However, the relationship between hypotheses and facts is more complex than the foregoing sentence suggests. In a given problem, a statement may not be capable of adequate verification and yet function as evidence because at that time there is *somewhat* more warrant for accepting it than for accepting the hypothesis under test. In other words, in a given problem we use statements of which we are *more sure* to test statements of which we are *less sure*. Perhaps this will not appear to some as a satisfactory situation, but, given the nature of scientific truth-getting, it is the best we can do.

This principle has application for our daily living. Although a person who tries to live reflectively usually withholds action until he has had a chance to think about it, he does not wait until the "data are all in." It is never possible to know when the data are all in, but in social affairs action is always necessary. If a person acts in terms of the best evaluation he can make of currently obtainable data, he behaves reflectively. Reasons for pursuing one line of behavior may be only slightly better than those for pursuing another; but if we are wise, we follow the behavior which commands the most support.

Students in social-studies classes may make use of factual data drawn from a variety of sources. We broadly classify such data as (1) data of remembered experience and (2) data procured through student observation or experimentation. The first may be regarded as historical data, the second as contemporary data.

Data of remembered experiences may come from students themselves. The principle of continuity of learning suggests that, if conceptualization is to occur, each learning problem will be rooted in present tested insights of students. That is, for every problem studied, students will have a background in experience from which to draw. Some problems may be solved without evidence beyond what a group of students can recall from their own experiences. In such cases, students pool information and interpret remembered facts in accordance with requirements of the problem. Many problems involving school, home, and community affairs are handled in this manner.

Students may find it useful to examine the remembered experience of other persons—teachers, parents, and other community adults. To this end they may solicit information through polls or interviews, or they may invite resource persons into the classroom.

However, a word of warning is needed at this point. Although personal experience is often a valuable source of evidence, we must make certain that what is adduced from experience is dependable evidence. It is common for persons to romanticize, falsify, and misinterpret their own experiences, this despite the best of intentions. Before personal experience is admissible as evidence it requires rigorous interpretation. Teachers must be prepared to ask, "Did it really happen that way?" "Is this your personal interpretation, and would others regard it differently?" and "How conclusive is an experience of this sort?"

Another source of remembered experience is documents—books, magazines, pamphlets, and newspapers. Chapter 18, on materials of instruction, lists and evaluates many sources of documentary evidence. Needless to say, documentary evidence must undergo the same careful scrutiny as remembered experiences.[9]

The second broad class of data, facts procured through current observation or experiment, represents "new" data. They have not been in existence before. The use of research, in the sense of creating new data, is not now common among social-studies classes. However, in some places students have conducted community surveys of one sort and another, or pursued other limited types of research, and there is a growing interest in vitalizing social-studies instruction through student-conducted research. The Citizenship Education Project, sponsored by Teachers College, Columbia University, has been instrumental in promoting types of community activities and projects which in some cases are of a research character. Social-studies teachers should be grounded in research techniques in the social sciences.

Whether data are drawn from remembered experience or from tests of

[9] For an excellent brief treatment of problems involved in validating documentary evidence see Henry Johnson, *Teaching of History in Elementary and Secondary Schools,* The Macmillan Company. (The 1915 and 1925 editions are preferable to the 1940 edition.)

the present, much of the time students of the social studies will have to rely to some degree on the opinions of authorities. It is essential, therefore, that we examine the role of authorities in the social sciences. Most of the time, we use facts verified by someone else, taking his word for it that the statements are actually true. Individuals do not have time or opportunity to investigate directly many of the problems in which they are interested; even if they did, they would still have to rely heavily on observations or experiments of others. The most carefully compiled statistics represent personal judgments made by investigators; they rest on a foundation of human fallibility.

In the case of questions which have been settled to the satisfaction of most investigators, we may accept the facts disclosed with a great deal of confidence. Though never to be taken as conclusive, consensus of competent investigators is one of our best indications of truth. However, many issues in the realm of social affairs have not been settled in such a definite way. The most respected authorities are likely to disagree as to which insights are most reliable in the areas of economics, politics, sex, religion, and race.

Some of the problems involved in using expert opinion in the social sciences are well illustrated within the field of economics. This field is split into a number of "schools of thought" (neoclassicists, institutionalists, socialists, underconsumptionists, and Keynesians, to name a few), and the opinions of members of one school may differ drastically from those of members of another. To the great confusion of the unsophisticated, this difference in opinion may occur in connection with fundamental issues. Nevertheless, there are many propositions in economics on the truth or falsity of which most economists agree.

Before a class places reliance on the pronouncements of any supposed authority, they should ask and try to answer questions such as these:

Is he recognized as an authority by other experts in the field in which he speaks?

Is he in substantial agreement with other authorities in his field?

Does he base his opinion on evidence gained from the reflective method?

Is his own social and economic status unrelated to the disputed issue? (I.e., does he have any personal reasons for being prejudiced?)

Is he likely to be free from bias on other counts—e.g., is he free from marked religious, racial, class, or other prejudices? [10]

[10] For a more thorough treatment of the role of authorities in investigation see Rapoport, *op. cit.*, chap. 5.

Unfortunately, pseudo authorities are very common in our society. There is no question on which most newspaper columnists and radio and television commentators are not willing and eager to make confident pronouncements. Many politicians, preachers, professors, and businessmen seem equally disposed to make dogmatic assertions about social issues. These persons let their publicly expressed opinions range freely over the fields of economics, history, political science, sociology, psychology, anthropology, and philosophy even though most of them have but little, if any, scientific training in these fields. Often they have axes to grind—as when a power-company executive gives the "inside story" of TVA, or a labor leader expresses convictions on the economic effects of various wage policies.

Not only must teachers and students guard against pseudo authorities, but they must use great care in interpreting responsible experts. One of the most common errors in interpretation is quoting a person out of context. The meaning of a sentence or paragraph can usually be fully understood only in relation to what has gone before or what comes after. As Beardsley points out, "You can make the Bible say, 'There is no God,' if, in quoting, you omit the first part of the sentence. . . ."[11]

The Use of Evidence

The testing process may not be understood apart from its general aim, which is not to reach certainty, not to search for absolute proofs, but to find corroborating or damaging cases. The aim of testing is to provide support, rather than conclusive verification, for a hypothesis.

A hypothesis is supported when facts which are deduced from it correspond to facts observed in investigation. If any observed fact contradicts any fact as deduced from a hypothesis, then we must question the validity of the hypothesis or rephrase it to allow for exceptions. In short, a given hypothesis must harmonize all pertinent observed facts if it is to be of maximum value. The object of the remainder of the chapter is to show in more detail what is involved in the testing process and what are some of its pitfalls.[12]

Making Deductions

We have already observed that hypotheses are declarative sentences which state matters of fact, and that the first step in testing a hypothesis is

[11] Monroe C. Beardsley, *Thinking Straight: A Guide for Readers and Writers,* Prentice-Hall, Inc., 1950, p. 35.

[12] In this connection, students may wish to read Edwin R. Burtt, *Right Thinking,* Harper & Brothers, 1946, Part III.

to deduce if-then statements from it. Let us first examine what is involved in making such deductions and what makes some deductions better than others. We may best do this by an illustration, as follows:

Problem: What are some possible explanations of the present rise in the rate of juvenile delinquency in the United States?

Hypothesis: The increasing use of automobiles by teen-agers in the United States contributes to the rise in the rate of delinquency.

Deduction: If the use of autos contributes to delinquency, then we should find more auto users among delinquents than among non-delinquents.

There are certain things to be noted concerning this deduction. First, we should examine its form. The "if-clause" (antecedent) is a brief statement of the hypothesis itself. The "then-clause" (consequent) states a fact which should be true if the hypothesis is true. A deduction is a good one if the truth of the then-clause is warranted by the truth of the if-clause. In other words, if the if-clause is true, the then-clause is necessarily true also. In the foregoing example this would appear to be the case. The then-clause follows directly and logically from the if-clause. Clearly, a positive correlation between the rate of use of automobiles and the rate of delinquency would be highly significant in judging the truth of the hypothesis.

However, even given a positive correlation between automobile use and delinquency, we would not be entitled to conclude that the use of autos *caused* the delinquent behavior. Correlations do not necessarily denote causation; they may be accidental, or they may result from some third factor. In the above instance a third factor might be producing simultaneously both delinquency and high use of autos. To circumvent this possible flaw in reasoning, we might make another test, such as this:

Hypothesis: The positive relation between the rate of delinquency and the rate of use of autos is an indication that the latter is causing the former.

Deduction: If the use of autos is a cause of delinquent behavior, then we should find no significant differences between users and nonusers of autos, except the use of autos itself.

We are still not out of the woods. Our deduction might be shown false by the uncovering of some significant third variable, such as indulgence by parents. Thus indulgence rather than use of autos might be responsible for increase in the delinquency rate. But the rise in delinquency might be a product of *both* indulgence *and* the use of autos. This possibility suggests, among other things, that we should explore as many hypotheses as we can in connection with any problem, since a given result often has multiple causes.

One must be very cautious about inferring causes and effects. We can determine whether the relationship of two events indicates actual causation only by asking and successfully answering questions like these:

Could any causes be operating other than the observed ones?

Could the observed effects be stemming from causes other than the apparent ones?

Could the apparent causes be only partly responsible for the observed effects?

Could the apparent effects be only partly a result of the observed causes?

Social affairs in particular usually have multiple causes and effects. Many persons blamed Herbert Hoover for the crash of 1929 and the ensuing depression. But how could one man cause a depression? We undoubtedly oversimplify to try to explain depressions in terms of any single cause. The same may be said of wars, even though some people have tried to place the sole responsibility on munitions manufacturers, high protective tariffs, or the machinations of the enemy.

Given the hypothesis with which we began, let us examine another possible deduction:

Deduction: If the use of autos contributes to delinquency, then we should find more delinquents among upper-class than among lower-class youth.

This deduction is less useful than the first because it contains an unstated inference, namely, that upper-class youth are more likely to use autos than lower-class youth. This may be a good inference, but it should be tested on its own merits and not concealed. The experience of the authors suggests that students very often make deductions which, because they contain one or more concealed inferences, do not go to the heart of a problem. Such deductions have an illogical character; the then-clause does not logically follow from the if-clause, and affirmative support of the former does not constitute support of the latter.

Another type of faulty deduction is exemplified by the following:

Deduction: If the use of autos contributes to delinquency, then we should find more auto users among students who fail to pay their debts than among those who pay on time.

This illustration, far-fetched as it may seem, represents a frequent cause of inadequate deductions: confusion about the meaning of a term. Here delinquent is interpreted to mean "failure to pay debts on time." Now this is one meaning of the term, but it is not the meaning intended by those who framed the problem. If the meaning of a hypothesis is misinterpreted, then we may expect the deduced consequences to be illogical or irrelevant. Thus, semantic confusion may be a source of faulty deductions.

Consider also the following:

Deduction: If the use of autos contributes to delinquency, then we should find more auto users among delinquents than among non-delinquents in the student body at Central High School.

This deduction is faulty because its antecedent is more general than its consequent. That is, the if-clause implies a relationship operating throughout the United States (see the statement of the hypothesis), whereas the then-clause refers to a relationship among a limited group which may or may not be representative of delinquents the nation over. If the if-clause is true in the foregoing deduction, of course the then-clause should be true also. But if the then-clause is found to be true, it does not furnish a very strong ground for believing that the if-clause (hypothesis) is true. Since what we are trying to determine is the truth of the if-clause, such a deduction may not be of much use. Central High School may indeed be a microcosm of the nation, but if this is the assumption, it has not been clearly stated. A deduction of this sort raises questions about sampling procedure, which will be discussed later. As a general rule, the then-clause of a deduction should refer to the same situation or group of cases to which the if-clause refers.

The results of inquiry are no better than the quality of deductions made from hypotheses. Teachers should help students understand the significance of the deductive process and how weak deductions lead to weak conclusions. Students should learn to guard against such sources of trouble as then-clauses which contain concealed inferences, then-clauses which misinterpret the hypothesis, and then-clauses which would provide fewer data than needed to support the hypothesis.

The Supporting of Hypotheses

The next step in our analysis of testing procedure is to examine more closely what constitutes adequate grounds or support for a hypothesis. When is a person warranted in concluding that a given hypothesis is reliable? Let us continue with the same illustration used above:

Hypothesis: The increasing use of automobiles by teen-agers in the United States contributes to the rise in the rate of delinquency.

Deduction: If the use of autos contributes to delinquency, then we should find more auto users among delinquents than among non-delinquents.

To test this hypothesis, it is necessary to conduct the investigation implied in the deduction. Students will need to study the rate of auto use among delinquents and among non-delinquents and compare the two groups. The question arises, How many cases need to be studied before the hypothesis can be considered affirmed?

In the illustration as given, it would appear that the hypothesis refers to all teen-agers in the United States. Such a hypothesis thus requires some limitation of coverage if it is to be supported. Progressive degrees of limitation are suggested:

The increasing use of automobiles by teen-agers in California contributes to the rising rate of delinquency in that state.

The increasing use of automobiles by teen-agers in Meadville contributes to the rising rate of delinquency in that city.

The increasing use of automobiles by teen-agers in Central High School contributes to the rising rate of delinquency among the student body of Central.

A hypothesis should be limited to statement of an idea which we may reasonably hope to support. Of the limited hypotheses above, perhaps the last might be supported by examining *all* pertinent cases. It might even be possible to examine all cases of delinquency in Meadville. It would be much more difficult to study all cases of delinquency in California and probably impossible to study all cases in the United States. Clearly, generalizations which are relatively unlimited in number of cases embraced may be supported only by using sampling procedures. If it can be shown that the youth of Meadville are representative of the youth of the entire nation, then support of the hypothesis as limited to Meadville would provide grounds for inferring the truth about the national situation.

We may restate this point as follows: If a hypothesis is to be supported, then all cases embraced in it should be studied, or, if that is impossible, a representative sample may be studied. But with the latter approach, the results of investigation are no better than the quality of the sample.

(Of course, we do not wish to imply that students studying delinquency should limit their study to the cases in Central High School or in Meadville. It might be worth something to make a survey of one's local community. But it would be worth a good deal more to read what has been written about delinquency on a state- or nation-wide basis. Most of the time, then, the most fruitful research for social-studies students is not surveys of the local community but research from books which treat problems in their full breadth and depth. And this implies much use of historical data.)

Since sampling technique is fundamental to many investigations in the social sciences, we shall examine it in more detail. One way of choosing cases for study is to use *random selection*. For example, suppose we have on cards the names of all the people in a city, one name to a card. We shuffle the cards thoroughly and draw out the number desired—as in a lottery. If the master group is absolutely homogeneous—i.e., if all individuals are identical—then only one case constitutes an adequate sample. The more heterogeneous the master group, the larger the sample required if it is to be truly representative.

If the master group is relatively heterogeneous, we may draw items from it at regular intervals. That is, instead of shuffling, we arrange the master group according to some predetermined pattern (depending on what we want to find out) and then pull, say, every tenth card, or interview every fifth family.

Proportional selection involves first examining all cases and noting the composition of the whole with respect to all significant factors. To illustrate, suppose we want to conduct a poll of voting intentions in Precinct 20. We must first decide which factors are important in causing people to vote as they do, such as age, economic status, and party affiliation. Then we must determine just what proportions of voters are in each age group, in each economic class, and in each party. The sample is then deliberately chosen so that it will have the same distribution of ages, incomes, and party members as the total population of the precinct.

Proportional selection is good sampling technique whenever it is possible to determine accurately the typicalities of the master group. When these are known, increasing the size of the sample does not always increase its representativeness. A sample of a thousand cases or so may accurately represent a total population of millions.

There are no rules of thumb as to how large a sample must be to be representative. It depends on the nature of the master group and the manner of selection. But there is an empirical test which shows well enough whether a sample is adequate: select several samples by the same method and compare them. If they differ very much, they are not representative.

An understanding of sampling technique will be of use to social-studies students undertaking community surveys or any other type of investigation which requires sampling procedures. However, this is not the primary use which such understanding will have. Much more often it will be of value in helping teacher and students to judge the validity of conclusions proffered them by authorities. For the most part, social-studies students are "research consumers" rather than "research producers." But critical use of the research of others depends on ability to appraise its reliability. An understanding of sampling technique helps students guard against over-generalization in any situation where reflection is in process. Students (and sometimes teachers) often make sweeping generalizations from only one or two cases—even when dealing with items as heterogeneous as human beings. An elementary knowledge of sampling should help them evaluate the worth of a generalization based on one case.

Of course, the broader the scope of a generalization, the more useful it will be. On the other hand, it will be useful only if it is truthful—that is, reliable as a predictive tool. There is a dilemma here for which no very satisfactory solution exists. As a practical matter, we simply do the best we can. Experience with one or a few cases may suggest a generalization, but usually we would not want to place much trust in it.

Generalizations suggested by scanty evidence should be regarded as *trial generalizations*. These retain the status of hypotheses. As additional supporting cases become available, we gain confidence in such generalizations, and in time they may come to be regarded as highly reliable tools. But no generalization ever entirely loses its trial character; it is always tentative in the sense that it is open to reëxamination. Generalizations tend to evolve with experience.

Decision as to the number of cases necessary to support a hypothesis is only one of the decisions which must be made in determining its adequacy. We must also consider how well the hypothesis *orders* the evidence. We seek insights which will explain all obtainable data. Data framed by adequate insights have an appearance of coherence and consistency.

Hypotheses which will not order all the data may be phrased to allow for exceptions. For example, we may say:

> In most cases, the increasing use of automobiles by teen-agers in the United States contributes to the rise in rate of delinquency.

If we are trying to support the hypothesis as now worded, then some exceptions do not destroy it. It can withstand the finding of some communities in which there is a negative correlation between the use of autos and the delinquency rate. If there is a positive correlation in a large majority of communities examined, the hypothesis is sufficiently supported. Generalizations which admit of exceptions are naturally to be regarded as less reliable predictive instruments than those for which no exceptions have so far been found. Generalizations supported by a majority of cases do help us establish a probability, or a tendency. It is better to have such generalizations than none at all.

What are we to conclude if data are contradictory or incoherent? What if we find that in one community studied there is a strong positive correlation between use of autos and delinquency, in another community a strong negative correlation, and in another community no significant correlation at all? If this is the situation, we must discard the hypothesis entirely. A hypothesis is useful only if it brings order to the obtainable data—perhaps not perfect order, but a large measure of order. Ideally, a hypothesis should order all obtainable data—should explain the data as they exist. The data should all point clearly in the direction of the hypothesis. There should be no data which we do not understand, no data which do not "fit." In short, hypotheses, if they are to have maximum reliability, should harmonize all the relevant facts. So long as a hypothesis fails to explain, or harmonize, all obtainable data, we should continue to search for a better one. At any given time we make use of the most adequate hypotheses which we can achieve, but we continually reconstruct them as we gain new insight.

Because of the interrelatedness of all aspects of human life (as well as of all nature), there is serious question as to whether we may ever adequately support any hypothesis *singly*. That is, to construct a single hypothesis, such as "The increasing use of automobiles by teen-agers in the United States contributes to the rise in the national rate of delinquency," and to confine testing operations to this hypothesis in the hope of finding an important cause of juvenile delinquency is an undertaking of limited usefulness.

Any given hypothesis gains support as other hypotheses which might be made concerning the problem are tested and discarded. Before a hypothesis such as that given above may become maximally reliable, it is necessary to have examined all other hypotheses which might reasonably be made about the causes of delinquency in the United States. Furthermore, it may be necessary to examine hypotheses concerning causes of crime generally, causes of personality maladjustment, and motivations of the lawmakers who established our definitions of delinquency.

The Reflective Method

We are saying that life is an integral whole and knowledge of life must therefore form an integral whole. Although for convenience investigation must go forward on narrow fronts, none of these fronts dares ignore what is going forward on other fronts. This is as true in the physical as in the social sciences. Any particular problem of a social nature becomes increasingly susceptible to solution as we bring to bear on it knowledge from all relevant disciplines—the social sciences, psychology and psychiatry, biology, and medicine.[13]

DISCUSSION QUESTIONS AND EXERCISES

1. What is the meaning of the term *meaning?* Can you define meaning operationally? Is the meaning of a word found within the word itself?
2. Can you define operationally the following words? Truth, liberty, justice, love, freedom, peace, kindness, morality, honesty. (Add to this list as you wish.)
3. List five questions which because of their intellectual content are unanswerable. List five questions which you believe are answerable through reflective inquiry.
4. When may a proposition be regarded as true? When may it be regarded as untrue? What do you mean when you use the expression *scientific truth?* Is there more than one kind of truth? Once discovered, does truth ever change?
5. See how many value judgments (or statements relatively near the value pole of the fact-value continuum) you can find in a news report; a social-studies textbook; a professional journal; a political speech.
6. Of what value is the distinction between fact judgments and value judgments? What role does such a distinction play in reflective investigation? Would it be possible for a person who does not understand this distinction to behave reflectively?
7. Is it possible for a single individual to behave reflectively, even though he cannot define his terms or describe his procedures? Must reflection always be communicable to others and thus open to public verification?
8. List five current social problems, such as might be experienced by anyone living in our culture. In the case of each, carefully phrase a hypothesis which, if verified, would increase our understanding of the problem. Make certain your hypotheses are phrased so as to be verifiable.

REFERENCES

Books which treat problems of semantics and the role in reflection of semantic understanding include: Wendell Johnson, *People in Quandaries* (Harper, 1946);

---

[13] For the advanced student, the analysis of this problem given by Otto Neurath, *Foundations of the Social Sciences* (International Encyclopedia of Unified Science, Vol. II, No. 1), University of Chicago Press, 1944, may prove rewarding. See also Philipp Frank, *Relativity: A Richer Truth*, The Beacon Press, 1950, chap. 7.

S. I. Hayakawa, *Language in Thought and Action* (Harcourt, Brace, 1949); and Anatol Rapoport, *Science and the Goals of Man* (Harper, 1950).

Books concerned with practices of straight thinking include: Edwin A. Burtt, *Right Thinking* (Harper, 1946); Harold A. Larrabee, *Reliable Knowledge* (Houghton Mifflin, 1945); and Robert H. Thouless, *How to Think Straight* (Simon & Schuster, 1950).

The more technical aspects of investigation in the social sciences are treated in the following: Russell L. Ackoff, *The Design of Research Techniques* (University of Chicago Press, 1953); Wilson Gee, *Social Science Research Methods* (Appleton-Century-Crofts, 1950); William J. Goode and Paul K. Hatt, *Methods in Social Research* (McGraw-Hill, 1952); and George A. Lundberg, *Social Research* (Longmans, Green, 1946).

Yet to be fully developed is a social-science methodology which consistently reflects the relativistic philosophies of persons such as John Dewey and Boyd Bode. Perhaps closest to achieving this is Kurt Lewin, and mature students may wish to read his *Field Theory in the Social Sciences* (Harper, 1951). Also rewarding for advanced students is Felix Kaufman, *Methodology of the Social Sciences* (Oxford University Press, 1944).

Chapter 5

Values and Reflection

Adolescent Youth and the Problem of Values

A FEW years ago Bruce R. Raup and a group of associates published a book in which certain novel and provocative proposals for public education were outlined.[1] American society, they said, "reveals fault lines in its moral structure."[2] There is great confusion and uncertainty over ends or objectives, with the result that the formulation of practical policy is hesitant, confused, and inconsistent in outcome.

Our schools, according to these authors, have stressed fact finding to the exclusion of the study of values, producing thereby a pseudo neutrality with respect to moral issues. Schools could perform a greater service if students were helped to understand their own values and those of the social group by resolving value conflicts in the classroom. Education should prepare them to handle events of "deep personal crisis," should help them—working democratically and coöperatively—to formulate policies in areas of experience vital to them. These should be primarily the closed areas, as this term is used in the present book. "The school program should consist predominantly of situations which demand for their resolution the deliberative making of policies wherein differing points of view meet and the characters of the participants are at once both socialized and objectified by the experience."[3]

---

[1] *The Improvement of Practical Intelligence*, Harper & Brothers, 1950.

[2] The term *moral*, as used in the present book, does not mean moral in the narrow, popular sense of "orthodox sexual behavior." Moral decisions are any decisions which have implications for the welfare of others (including even a decision on the part of a steel company to raise prices). Moral decisions always involve values; they represent the selection of one value (or end) over some competing value.

[3] Raup and others, *op. cit.*, p. 275.

These authors argue that the central content of the curriculum should be comparative moral systems and ideals, and that the central activity of education should be deliberative examination of conflicts of a moral sort. The schools' chief concern should be the study of *ideologies* (that is, systems of social objectives or values). Curriculum innovations—such as broad fields, fused courses, cores, activities and experience programs—have achieved little to date because they fail to focus on questions of policy at the level of moral conflict. We have tinkered with the curriculum without changing in any essential way what has gone on in the classroom.

According to Raup and his associates, we need in education a new orientation, a complete shift of viewpoint with respect to what is important, a redefinition of the purposes of education. All of which does not necessarily mean changing the formal structure of the curriculum.

The Improvement of Practical Intelligence is without doubt a profound contribution to educational thought. Our brief review scarcely begins to reveal its significance, since the heart of the book is devoted to consideration of a methodology for policy decisions. The present book accepts a large part of the Raup thesis and builds on it, although on certain questions —as will be noted later—we must take issue with *The Improvement of Practical Intelligence*. We make note of the book here chiefly as a means of setting the stage for the analysis to follow.

Adolescent Youth and the Problem of Moral Choice

That a need exists for greater attention to problems of value in the classroom is supported not only by the philosophical arguments of Raup and his collaborators but also by data from the fields of mental hygiene and adolescent psychology. We shall review some of these data briefly.

Our data suggest that moral decisions are more critical and difficult during adolescence than at any other period in life. Adults have learned a sophisticated approach to moral decision (that is, the ability to slur moral issues or to "ride two horses at once"). But a sophisticated approach is likely to be distasteful to adolescents, who tend to be idealistic and often shocked by inconsistencies.

Margaret Mead has familiarized students of personality with the notion that American culture is more disturbing to adolescent youth than is the Samoan, and probably many another, culture.[4] Our culture generates many tensions which are not inherent in puberty itself. One reason for this situa-

[4] *Coming of Age in Samoa*, William Morrow & Company, 1928.

tion is *discontinuity* in standards applied to childhood and adulthood. Our culture has a special set of behavioral rules for children. In addition to expecting children to conform to publicly proclaimed values of the most respectable people—such as honesty, patriotism, respect for property, and modesty—we also expect them to follow standards which apply only to children. For example, we expect them to be sexually innocent, to be obedient and dependent, and to remain out of contact with all of the cruder and more vulgar aspects of life: criminal behavior, profanity, dirty talk, selfishness, gambling, use of intoxicants and tobacco. We also try to protect children from major stresses and strains of life—e.g., knowledge of death, mortal illness, and great suffering.[5]

At adolescence, youth are rather suddenly confronted with a need to undergo a fairly complete conversion job. As two authorities tell us, "The main task of adolescence is to become an adult." [6] Adolescents have reached a point where they can no longer be shielded from the crudities and vicissitudes of adult life. They must begin acquainting themselves with the adult values and behavior from which they have been kept. Furthermore, they must in various ways begin imitating adult behavior. This would be inevitable in any case, but the adolescent peer culture of our society places a premium on "acting grown up." It provides numerous devices for proving manhood and womanhood.

Adults often fail to recognize the extent to which adolescent youth must learn to reject the values and practices of childhood and in their place substitute values and practices which may be quite incompatible with the earlier ones. In addition to the strain naturally involved in shelving one set of values and adopting another, the adult values to be adopted present a special problem in our culture because of their often confused and illogical nature. The incongruity (and often hypocrisy) of some adult ways is more evident to adolescents than to adults; they come at adolescents rather starkly, whereas adults have lived with them so long that they take them for granted. It may be easy for a practiced adult to turn values on and off as needed like hot and cold water from a tap, but such a skill may be painful in the learning. Redl and Wattenberg tell us:

Acts about which he was expected to feel guilty while a child are now permitted,

[5] Ruth Benedict, "Continuities and Discontinuities in Cultural Conditioning," in *Personality in Nature, Society and Culture* (Clyde Kluckhohn and Henry A. Murray, eds.), Alfred A. Knopf, Inc., 1949, chap. 30.

[6] Fritz Redl and William Wattenberg, *Mental Hygiene in Teaching,* Harcourt, Brace and Company, 1951, p. 80.

even expected, of him. . . . Conflict arises where adults still cling to the more childhood-designed demands. . . . Older boys and girls face a variety of new situations in which they are forced to judge for themselves, often without direct help from old heads. Here we find them using their newly mastered command of such abstractions as "justice," "fair play," and "morality." These abstractions have now come to have real meaning, as answers to questions on standardized intelligence tests show. Unfortunately, the adult world rarely measures up to the new ideals in their pristine purity. This introduces another source of conflict. . . .[7]

Since neuroses usually do not come to the attention of authorities and there is no means of reporting them, we lack adequate data on the degree to which conflicts of adolescence produce serious emotional disturbance. We do know that *dementia praecox* (schizophrenia) shows a marked upturn in late adolescence and reaches its peak of incidence in the twenties.[8] There is also some reason to suppose that the problem of adjustment is more difficult for highly intelligent children than for the dull because the former are more sensitive to conflicts in belief.[9]

In tackling the problem of adjusting to adult standards, adolescents inevitably find the closed areas the most troublesome. It is in these fields that youth find the adult ideology the most confusing, and adult authority the most irrational and oppressive. It is here that they must cope with unreasonableness and emotional response from adults whenever they seek help. For this reason they may be reluctant to seek help at all.

The most critical problem of youth, therefore, is the finding of a workable set of standards in the closed areas. This is not to say that youth do not have problems other than the essentially moral ones we are describing here. They do, of course. But it seems likely that problems of belief and value are the most difficult to solve, and that such problems are most likely to produce personality disturbances. In helping youth to find their way through the ideological maze with which they are confronted we are helping future generations of adults to tackle more intelligently the great social issues of our times.

Moral Uncertainty of the Present Era

It has already been pointed out (Chapter 1) that the present stage of history is one of great moral uncertainty and confusion. We are faced with

[7] *Ibid.*, pp. 92–93.

[8] Carney Landis and James D. Page, *Modern Society and Mental Disease*, Farrar & Rinehart, 1938, p. 163.

[9] Mandel Sherman, *Mental Hygiene and Education*, Longmans, Green & Company, 1936, p. 141.

numerous conflicts in values, some of which threaten to tear democratic society apart.

For example, in the United States we want to preserve our cherished civil liberties but we also want to be secure from possible subversion. We want to retain a free-enterprise system but we also value certain economic ends which only government can give us. We want to preserve the family but we want to give married couples freedom, if the going gets rough, to dissolve their marriage. We want to practice economy in government but we want the services which only government can provide. We want to extend democracy but we want the right to exclude from our company those whom we dislike. We want to give everyone maximum opportunity for mental health and good adjustment but we want to maintain our traditional value of sexual asceticism.

It seems clear that the greatest problems of the day are problems of value, or moral choice. The technical problems are minor by comparison.

The Challenge to the School

If public schools are to meet both the personal and the social needs of youth, as well as needs of the nation at large, they cannot escape responsibility for moral education of youth. Many persons recognize this, and pressure is being placed on schools to confront this problem. Unfortunately, the pressure often arises from a background of misunderstanding concerning the nature of moral behavior in our culture and methods by which moral behavior can be taught. Therefore, it is essential for a prospective teacher to clarify these matters in his own mind. The remainder of the chapter will be devoted to a consideration of the nature of moral choice, methods of moral choice, and how schools can best help students learn to choose values reflectively.

The Nature of Moral Choice

Almost daily people are called upon to make moral decisions. It is generally assumed that morality is a matter of learning the difference between right and wrong and always practicing the former. School people sometimes list desirable traits of character—such as honesty, loyalty, kindness, coöperation, independence, self-reliance, spirituality, respect, and dignity—and tell students to incorporate these traits in their personalities. Conversely, school people are likely to point out to children that no worthy individual ever deliberately chooses to be dishonest, disloyal, unkind, uncoöperative, dependent, materialistic, disrespectful, or undignified. Parents and church leaders also spend a good deal of time trying to get children to distinguish right from wrong.

Actually, school, church, and home probably overestimate the difficulty involved in teaching children to distinguish good from bad behavior. Most children learn the cultural attitudes toward good and bad at a comparatively early age. Not only that; it also seems likely that most children want to be good, to do the right thing, just as do most adults.

If the difficult decisions of life involved only choices between good and evil, where would be the problem? Who would deliberately choose evil? Unfortunately, moral choice is not this simple. It never involves merely distinguishing between right and wrong. *For a person making a choice, moral decision requires distinguishing between two or more good things.* It is when at least two desired courses of action come into conflict that moral choice becomes necessary.

For example, we try to teach children to be both honest and kind. Let us suppose that Mr. and Mrs. Brown and their small son have been invited to dinner by the Joneses. Mrs. Jones asks the son, Johnny, how he likes the soup. Johnny, if he is honest, says that it is the worst he has ever tasted. This is anything but a kind answer, and is very likely an answer which none of the adults want Johnny to make. If Johnny has been "well taught" in his attitudes toward honesty and kindness he can hardly know what to say without first reflecting on his problem. Should he be honest or kind, and how is he to determine which to be?

Many adults would solve Johnny's problem by adding sophistication to the list of desirable traits. If Johnny has been taught to be sophisticated rather than honest and kind, he will know what to do in this situation. He will murmur something trite and perhaps unintelligible, and hope that he is not offered a second serving.

Adults experience the same difficulty as children in making moral choices. The story is told of a secretary who sought advice from the editor of a lovelorn column in a local newspaper. The secretary wrote that she was working for a man for whom she had developed strong feelings of loyalty. He had raised her salary several times, provided liberal vacations, furnished good working conditions, and even helped to finance the medical care of her aged mother. The secretary, in sharing many of her employer's business secrets, had learned that he was embezzling large sums of money from the corporation. She wanted to know whether she should be loyal and keep quiet, or be honest and report his crime to the police authorities. The columnist advised her that a moral person is always both honest *and* loyal!

The usual procedure for a person in this kind of situation is to decide in some way what he wants to do, then rationalize his decision by describing it as either honest or loyal. He will never rationalize it as either dishonest or disloyal. A moral training which uncritically inculcates both honesty and loyalty tends to produce in a learner self-deception rather than moral responsibility.

This kind of confused and contradictory thinking will always exist in the area of values so long as we teach that moral problems involve choices between good and evil rather than between two or more goods. The felt moral problems of our culture arise when people find it desirable to follow two cherished but incompatible ends at the same time.

That typical moral problems of youth involve choices among competing goods is supported by a recent study of beliefs and behavior in sixteen-year-old boys and girls.[10] Havighurst and Taba report that the adolescent peer culture places great value on social participation, group loyalty, and individual achievement and responsibility. The group studied also accepted the traditional middle-class values of a midwestern community—respectability, thrift, responsibility, self-reliance, and good manners. Adults could hardly find fault with the predominant values of the youth culture of this community. High-school students seemed committed to the ends most revered in our society.

But the study also revealed clearly the kinds of conflicts in which persons in our culture become embroiled. Loyalty to one's friends is a universally respected value. And this was one of the most cherished values of the sixteen-year-olds. But being loyal to the group seemed to require following the pattern of behavior generally practiced in the group, minding one's business about what others did, avoiding criticism of one's friends, and refusing to condone such criticism on the part of others. In many cases, members of the peer culture were violating some one or more of the traditional moral standards, but other members felt obligated to protect them in this behavior. They were thus caught in a conflict between two loyalties—one to the peer culture and one to the adults of the community who were trying to enforce the conventional mores. Two good ends were at stake, not a good and a bad end. (This was true also of those who were violating orthodox

[10] Robert J. Havighurst and Hilda Taba, *Adolescent Character and Personality,* John Wiley & Sons, 1949.

behavioral patterns: through their actions they were seeking prestige, adventure, and proofs of manhood—all widely desired and accepted ends in our society.)

Since students had never been taught the nature of moral choice, it is hardly surprising that a great deal of confusion and self-deception was evident among them. Test results showed that when they were confronted with a value conflict they tended to choose courses of action which violated the abstract principles in which they believed. Not more than one-third of those examined seemed able to apply their abstract beliefs about morality in concrete situations. Furthermore, the reputation of a student seemed to have little to do with his understanding of moral principles or his ability to apply them in specific situations. Reputation seemed based on the adoption and consistent application of certain overt behavioral forms which included coöperation with teachers, regular church attendance, and verbal (and vocal) espousal of traditional middle-class moral standards. The students who seemed most confused, and most likely to follow expedient rather than consistent courses of action, were those with social ambitions. Social climbers usually adopted a virtuous pose in conduct without corresponding conviction.

The Method of Moral Choice

Reflection of an evaluative nature consists of operations which can be performed with value judgments. Our problem here is to determine the manner in which value judgments can be tested. Much of the present analysis follows that to be found in *An Introduction to Reflective Thinking*.[11]

A person is likely to have very little success if he tries directly to compare competing values. As we have seen, value judgments tend to differ from judgments of fact; they cannot be shown to be true or false in the same sense that judgments of fact can. This is but another way of saying that traditional science does not furnish ends of behavior but confines itself to means.

The foregoing assumption requires qualification. If a person accepts the method of science as an appropriate means of truth getting, he must also accept a culture pattern which permits the scientific method to work. In short, if he values science, he is obligated to value certain specific social behaviors. The scientific method is not "neutral" with respect to social ends. Rapoport suggests that commitment to the scientific method implies com-

[11] Columbia Associates in Philosophy, *An Introduction to Reflective Thinking*, Houghton Mifflin Company, 1923, chap. 9.

mitment to freedom of inquiry, the democratization of knowledge, and freedom of the individual.[12] Frank says that, according to his experiences in Nazi Germany, persons trained in the exact sciences but rarely adopt fascism as a social philosophy. By and large, they are strongly committed to a democratic outlook.[13] It seems highly probable that science (or reflection), as we have defined it, can produce maximal results only in a democratic culture. Scientific method implies the social ends of democracy—even if in its direct operation it remains a means or instrument.

In a given situation a value judgment is not verifiable in the same sense that a fact judgment is. With reference to a particular problem, reflection cannot tell us whether a value is true or false in itself. Perhaps, then, values are entirely beyond the scope of the reflective method, and we had better turn to nonscientific methods when we work with problems in evaluation. Not at all. Reflection plays an important and necessary role in connection with the process of evaluation, even though the process is not reflective in all its steps.

We have seen that moral problems arise when attitudes or values come into conflict. The need for selection of one value in preference to another may arise on a group level (as when a group must agree on ends in order to carry out some common function) or on an individual level (as when a person experiences a conflict in attitudes or values). In at least one sense it is impractical to distinguish interpersonal and intrapersonal levels of conflict, because group decisions can be made only after individuals in the group come to feel the conflict on an intrapersonal level and resolve it on that level. (It may be helpful at this point to review the discussion of conflict on pages 4–6.)

In any case, unless autocratic or coercive methods are to be used, conflict in values can be resolved in only one way. Groups (or individuals) must, for the purpose of the occasion, accept without question some third value. As the Columbia Associates point out, "In any given process of evaluation, some preferred end must remain unquestioned."[14] This unquestioned end is then used as a point of reference for judging competing values. Each conflicting value is regarded as a potential instrumentality for achieving the accepted goal and is judged according to whether it would lead toward the goal.

Because at any given time people value certain things more highly than

[12] Anatol Rapoport, *Science and the Goals of Man,* Harper & Brothers, 1950, p. 224.
[13] Philipp Frank, *Relativism: A Richer Truth,* The Beacon Press, 1950, pp. 107–109.
[14] Columbia Associates, *op. cit.,* p. 220.

others, a group or individual is usually able to adopt for the moment some undisputed value as a point of reference. Normally we arrange our values in a kind of hierarchical order. This does not mean that there is any eternal scale on which values are ranged from "high" to "low" but only that our previous experiences plus the configuration of the confronting situation lead us at the time to hold some values more dear than others. In another situation we might place our values in an entirely different order in the hierarchy. For example, much of the time most of us would place physical survival at the top; but there are occasions when we might place the survival of a loved one or service to an ideal above life itself.

Whether a questioned value may serve as an instrument for helping achieve a value which for the moment is accepted without question can be determined only by carefully examining the *consequences* of acting in terms of both of the conflicting values. "If we are to decide reflectively, when goods are compared with other goods, we cannot attempt to choose between them until all of the consequences that will flow from their acceptance, and all of the other values which are implied in them, have been carefully developed so far as lies in our power." [15] Going back to the problem of Johnny and his soup, Johnny might face the problem reflectively by trying to predict the consequences of his behavior before he selects a course of action. Would telling the truth in this situation antagonize the Joneses? Or would they pass it off as a joke? Would a truthful response result in better cooking in the future, or is the situation hopeless in this respect?

It should be noted that moral choice involves an examination of the consequences of a projected act not only to oneself but also to others. Unless the feelings and interests of others are held on a par with one's own, evaluation becomes purely egocentric and opportunistic.

There is a difference between saying that one should not tell the truth to the Joneses, and saying that if one tells the truth feelings will be hurt. The first statement is evaluative in form (a value judgment) and is neither true nor false. The second is a judgment of fact. It is a true-false statement and can be tested with reference to publicly verifiable data. *The exploration of consequences of acting on a given value always entails the formulation and testing of judgments of fact.* At this point in evaluation the scientific method can and should operate to the full. Unless it does, evaluation becomes wholly unreflective.

It may be objected that the casting and testing of hypotheses which show

[15] *Ibid.,* p. 216.

causal relationships between disputed values and some third, undisputed value does not tell us whether the undisputed value is good or true. Suppose Johnny decides that he wants his immediate behavior to be instrumental in improving the quality of Mrs. Jones's cooking, rather than in getting for himself a reputation for politeness. How is he to be sure that he has selected the correct long-range goal? Does adopting as his highest value a concern for his own eating pleasure represent the best, or most moral, solution to the problem?

The practical answer is that unless Johnny has reason to question appetite as a criterion, he may as well accept it without worry. In problems of an evaluative nature, it seems sensible for one to regard for the time being the unquestioned value as an absolute (but for the time being only!). Unless some values are regarded as fixed points of reference, we shall never be able to make decisions where other values are at stake.

But if anything happens to make the unquestioned value appear of doubtful worth, then a new problem has arisen which is essentially similar to the first. Again two values are in conflict, and again the conflict can be resolved only by testing each in relation to some further value which is not in doubt. "It is obvious that the unquestioned ends which are accepted as the outcome of the process of elaboration are but preferences, in the sense that they are assumed to be good without further proof. When two men conflict upon these preferences, there can be but one way of reaching agreement. These preferences must themselves be subjected to elaboration and clarification, until it is made plain that the acceptance of one or the other will bring with it some still further good upon which the two disputants can agree." [16]

Suppose a value conflict cannot be resolved by referring each conflicting value to an agreed-on third value? Might not an individual faced with a moral problem be unable to settle it reflectively because he is not sure what his ultimate ends in that situation are? Or might not a group find it impossible to agree on an end to which an immediate conflict may be referred? The Columbia Associates tell us, "If two men could reach no agreement whatsoever upon any thing that both considered good, then, of course, it would be impossible to choose reflectively between their proposals; the final choice would needs be based upon their irrational preferences for one of the alternatives." [17] However, even though situations of conflicting values

[16] *Ibid.*, p. 218.
[17] *Ibid.*, p. 219.

are characteristic of our culture, in almost any such situation a third value can be found which is acceptable to all, even if it is necessary to settle on some abstract end such as justice, democracy, coöperation, or happiness. Of course, where the long-range goal adopted is relatively abstract, it may be difficult to see clearly the connections between the immediately disputed values and the accepted one. In such problems the tracing of connections may involve a great deal of time and perhaps controversy.

We finally arrive at the question, If the reflective method cannot tell us whether, in any final sense, values are true or false, then what can it tell us about values which is worth knowing? The use of reflection can profoundly affect the quality of our value structure. Specifically, it can help us understand better what our values are. It can help us clarify our ends in our own thinking. The result will be greater consistency in values and greater ability to apply abstract values in concrete situations. A great deal of the present confusion and uncertainty concerning values might be erased with the more widespread cultivation of an ability to assess values in terms of consequences.

We shall next see how the process of evaluation relates to an act of thought, as described on page 45. We may represent the process of evaluation schematically as follows:

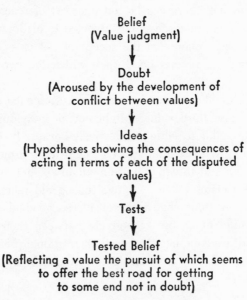

Belief
(Value judgment)
↓
Doubt
(Aroused by the development of
conflict between values)
↓
Ideas
(Hypotheses showing the consequences of
acting in terms of each of the disputed
values)
↓
Tests
↓
Tested Belief
(Reflecting a value the pursuit of which seems
to offer the best road for getting
to some end not in doubt)

Values and Reflection

An act of evaluative thought bears the same outward form as an act of thought which is confined to the testing of judgments of fact. The logic of evaluation, however, is quite different at certain of its stages from the logic of scientific reflection. An act of thought of a wholly reflective nature confines itself at all stages to manipulation of judgments of fact. In contrast, an act of evaluative thought shifts from operations with value judgments to operations with judgments of fact, then back again.

Furthermore, a person cannot deduce one form of judgment from the other in the sense in which he can deduce one fact judgment from another, as when he says, "If such-and-such is true, then so-and-so must also be true." At the point where doubt (that is, conflict) arises, a thinker moves from disputed value judgments to hypotheses by asking, "What are the possible consequences of acting on each of these disputed values?" or more simply, "*Why* might one hold either of these disputed beliefs?" In the classroom, the "why" question is often the best means of getting students to formulate judgments of fact for further study.

In each of the following cases (illustrative of a number of possible fact judgments) a "why" question might help a class move from a controversial value judgment to the ensuing judgment of fact.

Value judgment: I would rather have a man than a woman for a boss.
Judgment of fact: If employers are men, then employees will coöperate more fully than if employers are women. (*Or,* Men employers get more coöperation from their employees than women employers.)
Value judgment: There ought to be a law against the use of tobacco.
Judgment of fact: If people would quit using tobacco, they would live longer on the average. (*Or,* The use of tobacco shortens the life span of persons using it.)
Value judgment: We ought to restore free enterprise in this country as soon as possible.
Judgment of fact: If we restore more freedom of enterprise, then the per capita real wage will increase. (*Or,* A free-enterprise system produces a higher per capita real wage than socialism.)

If its meaning can be clarified sufficiently, the judgment of fact elicited in each case may function as a hypothesis. It should be noted that hypotheses used in evaluation may (but do not necessarily) take the form of if-then statements. As suggested in the examples above, such if-then statements can be recast as declarative sentences. Hypotheses suggested by doubted values tend to have the if-then form because they show the possible instrumental character of one value in relation to another—"If I act on value A, then I shall achieve value B."

101

In problems of evaluation, the testing of hypotheses proceeds in the same manner as described in Chapter 4. A series of "facts" is deduced from hypotheses and observations are made or experiments performed to see if, indeed, these are facts. Since this is a reflective, or scientific, procedure, the rules of evidence must be observed as scrupulously as in any other scientific problem. Furthermore, the exploration of the objective consequences of acting in a given way may involve lengthy and painstaking study, with much recourse to factual data.

The final step is inaugurated by raising questions such as "Which consequences are preferable among those we have examined?" or, better, "Which of the consequences we have examined seems most consistent with values which our social group is willing to accept?" It may be discovered, of course, that the problem is not concluded at this point. The group may not be able to agree on any of the explored consequences, in which case they cannot settle the original controversy. If the consequences examined lead to values which, when clearly seen, are not generally acceptable, then new value conflicts appear which can be resolved only through the exploration of their consequences. Thus, what begins as study of a single conflict may evolve into study of a second or third conflict, or even more (see page 99).

But an act of evaluation will come to a conclusion at any time that a group (or individual) can settle on some one consequence as being preferable to others. This concluding step represents the selection of a third, unquestioned value—the fixed point of reference which was discussed on pages 97–99.

All of this may seem unnecessarily technical. Just what is its significance to classroom teachers? Since a part of evaluation is the testing of judgments of fact, it is necessary for teachers to insure that, during discussions of values, students actually move from discussion of values to discussion of fact judgments. Discussions about values often become mired because of failure to recognize this point. Students will never get anywhere with a discussion of a conflict in values if they by-pass one of the necessary aspects of evaluation—a study of values in their factual bearings. Evaluative thought must make steady and abundant use of publicly verifiable evidence. In order to bring judgments of fact into the open, teachers must be alert to the need for asking students persistently *why* they value what they do.

Actually, the hardest and most time-consuming feature of evaluation is likely to be the objective exploration of consequences, the testing of hypotheses. This may involve extended units of work which include discussions, research periods, and use of community resources.

The final step, that of selecting consequences which will be agreeable to the group, involves not reflection as we have defined it but deliberation. It requires students to check consequences against the values they hold, and to come to some sort of agreement with respect to common values. It requires a search for consensus, and members of a group may employ persuasion and emotional appeal at this point. Students are most likely to succeed in reaching consensus if they are encouraged to talk freely about values in a permissive atmosphere.

Proposals for classroom procedure found in the present book differ from those in *The Improvement of Practical Intelligence* in degree if not in substance. Raup and collaborators minimize the role of examination of factual judgments as part of the process of evaluation. They emphasize the emotive, non-reflective features of value choice. The present book stresses the role of reflective testing of hypotheses as part of evaluation. Probably securing group consensus on a referential value—a value accepted for the moment as fixed and against which the values in conflict may be judged—is less difficult than the job of tracing the objective consequences of the conflicting values. As a practical matter, settling on long-range ends, or ultimate values, may not be extremely difficult because of widespread acceptance in our culture of numerous abstract values—such as coöperation, justice, democracy, truth, and happiness. Although in a given problem such abstract concepts may themselves come into conflict with each other, a group is likely to find, without lengthy dispute, at least one mutually acceptable end. The central task in any problem of evaluation remains the discovery of what the agreed-upon abstract end means in terms of concrete behavior. And this can be made only by tracing objective consequences of values which are means to achievement of the abstract end, so that their instrumental character will be clear to all. Therefore, the immediate and major job of each problem in evaluation must always be the exploration of objective, cause-and-effect relationships between values of immediate concern and those of longer-range concern.

How Teachers May Best Approach Moral Education

There is probably only one way of teaching moral behavior. It is not indoctrination of uncritical attitudes toward conventional moral standards, but rather teaching a *method of choice* to be used when confronted with conflicts in attitudes and values. We cannot teach moral behavior except as we confront students with conflicting values and encourage them to work out independent and reflective solutions to the conflicts. Students should be given chances to study a wide range of value conflicts, including those of immediate personal import as well as those which affect the culture at large.

ROLES OF PERMISSIVISM AND REFLECTION

We develop values and achieve solutions to moral problems through our own efforts. Although outside forces may stimulate and guide us, moral behavior always represents growth from within. Students can develop an understanding of what is meant by reflective evaluation only as they are given opportunities to pursue their own problems in an atmosphere of intellectual freedom.

Schools must provide permissive environments for students, then, in which they are encouraged to study value conflicts. Permissiveness can be abused, and can result in chaos rather than learning. The nature of a situation which is healthily permissive will be discussed in Chapter 7. The only point we need make here is that students must feel free to follow reflection wherever it may lead them. If conclusions are predetermined, moral problems, like problems of fact, can never be solved intelligently.

As we have seen, the most common method of teaching moral behavior is for adults to decide which forms of behavior are "good" or "right" and to teach these unreflectively to children. Teaching usually consists of telling or showing children what is right and wrong, and rewarding them when they do right and punishing them when they do wrong. Much emphasis is also placed on "setting a good example"—doing in front of children as many "good" things as possible and never doing "bad." Community members put great pressure on teachers to serve as moral examples.

Such teaching is largely futile because it ignores the nature of moral problems. It assumes that moral choice is always a question of choosing good and rejecting evil. When we develop in students deeply entrenched attitudes or build strong but unreasoning commitments to certain values, we may only be intensifying the conflicts which are bound to occur. When children face conflicts of good versus good they become confused and insecure. If their moral education has neglected to give them a method of moral choice, they are unable to face a conflict intelligently. It is impossible to overemphasize that morality cannot be taught satisfactorily by either precept or exemplariness.

104

Many experienced teachers are aware of this fact. Their battle scars are reminders that youth resent being told that "this is wrong" or "this is right." If they think it is directed at them, youth heartily dislike moralizing and preaching. This is not because they want to be immoral, but because many of them are wiser than we think. They realize full well that memorizing a group of platitudes will not help them with the real problems of life.

Hampering Effect of the Associationist Tradition

In the past, schools have probably played a relatively minor role in helping youth learn a method of intelligent moral decision. They have generally either disregarded problems of moral decision or tried to teach uncritically a series of "right" answers. Their preoccupation with moral education of this sort is an inevitable result of the associationist tradition in learning.

Associationist learning stresses acquisition of motor responses and memorization of more or less arbitrary associations. Wherever associationist principles dominate teaching, students are expected to memorize formulas for goodness and to learn a series of proper attitudes. In learning situations of this type they cannot be expected to develop values which they understand. They cannot develop ideals capable of application when problems of moral choice arise. In short, their moral behavior must remain blind, confused, and contradictory.

Distinctive Role of Schools in Moral Education

That our schools face a challenge with respect to moral education was pointed out earlier. Strong pressures are now being put on administrators and teachers to introduce more intensive programs of moral education. But most proposals for increasing the volume or effectiveness of moral instruction seem to imply that schools should use more forceful and persistent methods of teaching values uncritically. Furthermore, proposals usually imply a need for inculcating a particular conception of right and wrong—the American middle-class conception. We cannot debate the merits of middle-class standards here; the error of the proposal is not so much in whose standards are to be inculcated as in the fact that unreflective inculcation of some sort is intended. The validity of the associationist conception of learning, as well as of an authoritarian moral structure, is assumed. Adoption of such proposals would probably result in expansion and solidification of closed areas of culture and make conflict more intense and more difficult to resolve.

105

In spite of the deficiencies of most of these proposals, our schools remain one of our best potential agencies for moral education. As Raup and associates point out, their resources for moral education have never really been exploited. In public schools it is possible to establish an arena for reflective examination of moral issues, to provide a degree of permissiveness and an impartial, yet skilled, form of guidance not elsewhere available.

DISCUSSION QUESTIONS AND EXERCISES

1. It is common practice to reward a child when he does "right things" and to punish him when he does "wrong things." In what ways, if any, does this practice help him to become a moral being? In what ways does it not?
2. Discuss the following proposition: "Science can ascertain truth but it cannot ascertain goodness." Is it necessary for a scientist to define truth before looking for it? If he could define goodness, could he then use his method as a means for ascertaining it?
3. Do you believe that a person who reflects on a conflict between good and good is likely to choose that course of action which is immediately most pleasurable? (This kind of choice has been condemned as expedient.) Can any program in moral education reduce the likelihood of expedient behavior?
4. Give some examples of conflicts between good and good on the level of national and international policy. For example, is there a conflict between our valuing of free trade and our valuing of full employment? Between our valuing of full employment and our valuing of a balanced budget?
5. Discuss the proposition "No one can know the difference between right and wrong except as he examines conflicts between good and good."
6. Would a program in moral education which succeeds in indoctrinating a core of values constitute a solution to the moral problems of the American people?

REFERENCES

For data on the moral conflicts of youth, students should read the book by Havighurst and Taba cited in this chapter. Also good is August B. Hollingshead, *Elmtown's Youth* (Wiley, 1949). Fritz Redl and William Wattenberg, *Mental Hygiene in Teaching* (Harcourt, Brace, 1951), contains a good analysis of the nature of conflict among youth.

Moral conflicts of the culture and their implications for teaching are treated effectively in William O. Stanley, *Education and Social Integration* (Teachers College, Columbia University, 1953), George Counts, *Education and American Civilization* (Teachers College, Columbia University, 1952), and The Association for Supervision and Curriculum Development, *Growing Up in an Anxious Age* (1952).

Very good short introductions to the theory of valuation are provided in Harold A. Larrabee, *Reliable Knowledge* (Houghton Mifflin, 1945), Chapter 17, and

Columbia Associates in Philosophy, *An Introduction to Reflective Thinking* (Houghton Mifflin, 1923), Chapter 9. Also useful is Edwin A. Burtt, *Right Thinking* (Harper, 1946), Part IV. For advanced students, John Dewey's *Human Nature and Conduct* (Holt, 1922) is a richly rewarding treatment of ethics and morality. An advanced and difficult treatment of valuation is presented in John Dewey's *Theory of Valuation* (Vol. II, No. 4 of the *International Encyclopaedia of Unified Science*, Chicago, 1939).

Chapter 6

Techniques for Stimulating Reflection

The Difference Between Method and Technique

SELDOM does literature of education clearly distinguish method from technique. In fact, the two terms are often used interchangeably. As used in this book, *method* refers to a basic mode of investigation. In large part, we take methodological questions to be questions of epistemology, or of *the means of coming to know*. Chapter 3 described several different methods of problem solving; Chapter 4 treated in more detail one of these, the method of reflection.

Technique, on the other hand, refers to the particular way in which method is applied. *Technique* is a narrower term than *method*; it makes no direct reference to epistemology. It is concerned only with smooth and efficient operation of whatever approach to truth seeking we may choose to employ. Any of a number of techniques might be equally useful in connection with any of the methods described in Chapter 3. A certain method, however, might require the development of special techniques, or might find certain techniques more useful than others. In scientific investigation, commonly used techniques include case study, sampling procedure, controlled experiment, and historical study. The fact that these techniques are in use does not necessarily mean that the method is scientific. Whether it is scientific depends on *how* the techniques are used. It should be noted, however, that techniques developed in the theoretical sciences presume that reflection is the only dependable route to knowing.

Teaching has its special techniques: discussion, lecture, supervised study, recitation, projects, panels, sociodramas, and the like. Unlike scientific disciplines, pedagogy has often ignored or retreated from the presumption that reflection is preferable to non-reflection.

To know that a particular teacher is using one or more techniques tells us little about his basic methodology. Any of the common instructional techniques can be made to serve the purposes of rote or meaningful learning or of any of the broad approaches to truth seeking—such as rationalization, common sense, intuition, and reflection. It is necessary to watch the operation of techniques over a period of time and evaluate their cumulative effect before one can tell for sure what approach to truth or what level of learning is being achieved.

Most techniques of investigation in the physical sciences—mathematical procedures, precise methods of measurement, and controlled experimentation—cannot be widely used in a social-studies classroom. But at certain points in classroom procedure, particularly in connection with student projects and research periods, students may make case studies, surveys, historical analyses, and, in some instances, controlled experiments. In general, teaching technique in the social studies is addressed to helping students evaluate and use in the thinking process evidence which has already been uncovered by skilled investigators who have made use of the basic techniques of science. Nevertheless, for individual students there may be a large element of discovery in learning, just as there is for experts doing frontier research.

Techniques can, and often do, promote largely authoritarian and non-reflective learning. Or they can promote various kinds of problem solving, including those which are reflective. A purpose of the present book is to show how techniques may be made to increase the amount and improve the quality of reflection among pupils. It is not intended so much to show *which* techniques are to be used as *how* they are to be used. Reflective teaching is less a matter of selecting a particular technique than of knowing how to use any of a variety of techniques so as to promote reflection. There are lectures and lectures, discussions and discussions. Our chief interest here is in exploring differences between lectures and discussions which produce reflection and those which do not. It means little merely to say that techniques should "arouse interest," be "informal," or be "progressive."

A BASIC PHILOSOPHY MORE IMPORTANT THAN TECHNIQUE

It is unsound to divorce theory and practice. Pure technique, being blind and purposeless, is pointless, if not dangerous. At best it is a waste of time.

There is nothing in a technique *per se* to give its user a sense of direction. By learning techniques alone one cannot arrive at a guiding theory or philosophy. But the reverse is not true. If a person already has a guiding philosophy and if he has a reasonably fertile imagination, he can devise suitable techniques for implementing his philosophy.

In professional fields where technicians must be trained it is being increasingly recognized that philosophy (or theory) must have priority over techniques, or at least must accompany them. Rogers comments on the training of counselors: "Our concern has shifted from counselor technique to counselor attitude and philosophy, with a new recognition of the importance of technique on a more sophisticated level. . . . We have proven in our own experience Kurt Lewin's oft-quoted statement that 'Nothing is so practical as a good theory.'"[1] He further says that once a counselor has achieved an orientation which stresses the worth of each person, he does not have much difficulty in learning the client-centered techniques which implement this view. More than that, if someone with a different philosophy tries to use techniques which Rogers has developed, he is doomed to fail. He will inevitably use the techniques in ways which pervert their original purpose; he will slant and distort them so that they reflect his own philosophy, whatever that may be. Although Rogers does not say so, we may assume that, if a counselor has not achieved a philosophy *of any kind*, his techniques will produce no results other than bewilderment.

A teaching-methods course which stresses techniques might be useful for a student who brings to it a well-developed philosophy of education, including a theory of learning. For a student without this background, a teaching-methods course is likely to be a waste of time, unless it is designed to teach theory at the same time that it teaches technique. The same is true of observation, participation, and practice-teaching experiences. An ideal situation is undoubtedly one in which prospective teachers receive abundant philosophical and theoretical training and at the same time are given instruction in practical implementation of the theory under study. The study of techniques then serves to define *operationally* one or more theoretical positions.

The Elements of Reflective Procedure

If learning is to be reflective, each act of a teacher should be fashioned

[1] Carl B. Rogers, *Client-Centered Therapy*, Houghton Mifflin Company, 1951, pp. 14–15.

to encourage and help students to move through one or more of the steps involved in an act of reflective thought. This statement can easily be misunderstood. It is not to be assumed that the pattern of reflection is rigid. The steps of an act of thought are to be regarded as phases which are indispensable but not necessarily followed in 1-2-3 order or, in a particular problem, given equal emphasis. In short, an act of thought has a fluid character. In it we may usually observe hesitation, repetition, forward jumps, and doubling back. However this may be, thought is necessarily structured, and an effectual teacher will be aware of how each of his actions contributes to one or more of its necessary elements.

Probably the most fruitful way of approaching the problem of selecting techniques—and more important, of using them correctly—is to show first the matters for which a teacher must be responsible: (1) helping students to feel and clarify problems and (2) arranging an emotional and intellectual environment in which students may freely explore problems, but with due respect for methodological rules. When viewed as part of a series of steps, as described below, these broad responsibilities will be better understood. Techniques may be evaluated in terms of how well they contribute to performance of one or more of these steps.

We have said that teachers have certain responsibilities. We should now like to add, "teachers, or whoever is performing the functions of leadership in the reflective process." This qualification is necessary because a student or group of students might well have responsibility for the steps we are to list. In so far as possible, democratic teachers will encourage students to assume these responsibilities. In Chapter 7 the whole question of the role of teachers as leaders of reflection will be examined in detail.

Specific responsibilities of teachers in fostering reflective learning we take to be as follows:

1. Teachers familiarize themselves with present knowledge, understandings, and beliefs of students. In educational circles one often hears the injunction, "Teachers should start where their pupils are," which reflects the principle of continuity of learning. Unfortunately, teachers neglect this principle; particularly do they ignore points of conflict and confusion in the beliefs and values of their students. According to the theory underlying the present book, student beliefs and values are raw materials of reflective learning. Therefore, teachers need the most comprehensive and accurate picture they can get of their students' attitudes and beliefs. They may get this picture by directly studying students, by observing behavior and listen-

111

ing to what students say. The permissive type of discussion is a good technique for bringing beliefs to the surface. Teachers may also analyze written assignments, use pencil-and-paper tests, or interview students. If all these techniques are used and the results cross-checked, a more accurate picture is likely to be gained than if only one or two are used.

Studies of student beliefs indicate that students are strongly influenced by community ideology.[2] Therefore, teachers may make promising inferences about student beliefs by studying the belief-and-value pattern of the community as revealed in editorials in local newspapers, letters to editors, speeches by community members, church sermons, and in what is said at union meetings, meetings of service clubs, and community forums. Of course, most teachers do this regularly, but seldom as deliberate observers and students of community ideology.

And, just as students tend to reflect in their own beliefs those of their community, so do individual communities reflect those of region or nation. It is therefore helpful for teachers of the social studies to read reports of the various community studies which have been conducted by teams of psychologists, sociologists, and anthropologists. These studies are the most reliable sources of data we have on beliefs and values of different social classes of the United States. Much that they tell can be applied to any American community of comparable size, age, and ethnic composition.[3]

The teacher may also study national or regional public-opinion polls whenever they deal with issues of general significance, and platforms, programs, and public pronouncements of national and regional organizations (e.g., political parties, labor unions, veterans' and patriotic associations, and businessmen's organizations). Chapters 11–16 of the present book sur-

[2] See Robert J. Havighurst and Hilda Taba, *Adolescent Character and Personality,* John Wiley & Sons, 1949, or August B. Hollingshead, *Elmtown's Youth,* John Wiley & Sons, 1949, which reports on the same community. Also, a series of informal studies of student belief in the field of economics, conducted among college sophomores by one of the authors of this book, suggests that the beliefs of students in this area closely parallel national economic ideology as suggested by sociological studies.

[3] Examples of useful community studies are: John Dollard, *Caste and Class in a Southern Town,* Yale University Press, 1937; Geoffrey Gorer, *The American People: A Study in National Character,* W. W. Norton & Company, 1948; Alfred Winslow Jones, *Life, Liberty and Property,* J. B. Lippincott Company, 1941; Robert S. and Helen Merrell Lynd, *Middletown in Transition,* Harcourt, Brace & Company, 1937; Celia Stendler Burns, *Children of Brasstown,* University of Illinois Press, 1949; W. Lloyd Warner and associates, *Democracy in Jonesville,* Harper & Brothers, 1949; W. Lloyd Warner and associates, the "Yankee City" series, Yale University Press; James West, *Plainville, U.S.A.,* Columbia University Press, 1945.

vey points of confusion in American ideology, as revealed by psychological and sociological research.

Teachers may find it useful to compile a written record of beliefs which they find to be held by their students. Each statement of belief could be put on a card and the cards filed under general categories. Such a file should show conflicts, inconsistencies, and points of confusion in belief. It may be wise not to associate particular beliefs with particular students.

2. Another step, or function, of teachers (or whoever may assume the role of leader of reflection) is selection of a belief or a value for study. In traditional classrooms, selection of content is usually thought to be a prerogative of teachers (or, more often, of textbook writers). Under a reflective approach to learning, teachers may continue to be arbiters with regard to what content is to be included in a course although, if the reflective method is to work, they must learn to select beliefs for study with careful regard to present conceptual development of students (which should be clear if step 1 above has been taken seriously). They must take cognizance of what can be made problematic to students.

Whatever the technique used in selecting beliefs for study, the following criteria may be helpful to teachers and students in making the selection:

a. The belief selected should be capable of being related to some important social issue, or should serve as a stepping stone to later examination of beliefs related to critical social issues.

b. Priority should go to beliefs related to sharply controversial issues, to beliefs held on the level of sheer prejudice, to beliefs which reflect confusion and uncertainty, and to contradictory belief-pairs (conflicts) held by students or community adults, or suggested in text materials.

c. The belief selected should be held by a substantial proportion of students in either its positive or negative form, or both, or in a related form. It does not matter whether students accept or reject it, so long as they have some feeling about it.

d. The belief selected should be one which, in the judgment of the teacher, will lend itself to fruitful study—that is, a belief which the teacher is prepared to handle and one for which a worth-while amount of understandable factual data is available to students.

3. If reflection is to get started at all, the person who leads reflection must also see that students *feel* a problem. Failure here automatically destroys whatever opportunity may have existed to stimulate sustained and energetic reflection.

As suggested previously, a person may feel a problem when his present conceptual equipment is incapable of interpreting a confronting situation. Problems are characterized by the generation of tension and development of new behaviors. These behaviors may include an intellectual attack on the problem (reflective or otherwise) or a variety of emotional responses of an evading character, as listed on page 50. The most urgent problems will result when students become aware of evidence which questions some cherished belief or value. Simply being confronted with facts which to others seem contrary to the belief in question will not in itself make a student feel a problem; he may not accept the facts as evidence. (The way in which a person's past experiences may distort his present perceptual field and make it difficult for him to see facts as evidence will be dealt with in the next chapter.)

This step involves both the clarification and the creation of problems. Clarification means helping students better understand problems which they already feel. Clarification comes through talking to others about the problem and through learning to describe the problem clearly (perhaps with the help of others). For example, if a student feels a conflict but is not able to describe it intelligibly either to himself or to others, obviously the nature of the conflict is unclear to him. By delving into it he may become able to describe it in such a way that it can become a subject of further study. Even though a student feels that he understands a given problem very well, it is usually possible to help him understand it still better.

Many of the problems treated in a problem-centered approach to teaching should be those of which students are aware, however confusedly, before classroom study is undertaken. This will inevitably be the case whenever a classroom situation is sufficiently permissive to allow students to select for themselves the conflicts in belief, or the confusions, which they want to study.

However, we assume that the obligations of social-studies teachers have not been fulfilled with only a clarification and study of problems already felt. The conceptual structure of every individual is always a ground for latent or potential problems. That is, all of us at any given time espouse beliefs which are mutually contradictory, or accept beliefs incompatible with our behavior—and do this without awareness of conflict. The reason is simply that we have not as yet been confronted with any situation which has thrown the discrepancies into relief. Whenever the inconsistency become evident to us, a problem will become felt.

Techniques for Stimulating Reflection

A teacher, or other leader of reflection, should assume responsibility for exposing as many latent or potential conflicts as possible. This involves not merely clarifying problems but also "creating" them—in the sense that, where previously there was no awareness of conflict or feeling of discomfort, a teacher deliberately tries to bring a conflict to light and to make students feel uncomfortable enough to try to resolve the conflict reflectively. In short, a teacher's job is to get students into "an intellectual jam." This position may be rejected by some. It may be argued that it is better to "let sleeping dogs lie." Such an argument, however, denies validity to the idea of preventive therapy which is generally accepted in the fields of medicine, mental hygiene, and social work. If a problem seems fairly certain to develop later, perhaps in a situation wherein a person will not have sympathetic or professional help, the sensible course would seem to be to expose it earlier, when it can be dealt with wisely. A teacher may be thought of as a surgeon, who gets people into immediate trouble so that they may avoid more serious trouble later.

How should teachers "create" problems for students? There is first the task of creating an emotional atmosphere or climate which is conducive to open-mindedness. Students must be helped to become receptive to evidence which may, for the time being, make them feel uncomfortable. Emotional climate-making is a topic in itself and is the subject of the next chapter. We shall say no more about it here.

Creating problems for students is essentially a matter of confronting them with highly convincing negative evidence. Such evidence should be forceful—that is, easily understood, factual, and, on the surface, decisive. Quoted opinions are usually not the most forceful kind of evidence; nor are high-order generalizations if introduced by themselves. Relatively concrete evidence is called for—evidence which can be translated into quantitative terms ("the facts and figures," as we sometimes say). As a rule, evidence introduced into a teaching situation for the express purpose of creating a problem for students is deliberately sharpened by the teacher in order as clearly as possible to contradict or corroborate the belief in question.

A cherished belief or value may also be shaken by helping students see ways in which their behavior or other beliefs contradict it. Awareness of inconsistency similar to that produced when a student is presented with new evidence from an outside source may thus be developed. The basic technique to be used in exposing inconsistency and confusion in belief is asking questions. Teachers learn to ask probing questions and to stay with an issue long enough to bring to light students' thought processes.

Often a contradiction in conceptual patterns can be exposed by a questioning device known as the *subject-matter switch*. A subject-matter switch is performed when we generalize, or reduce to principle, a particular belief, then demonstrate how a further belief is incompatible with the principle and, consequently, with the first belief. For example, a student expresses the belief that "Relief payments should be kept low; otherwise recipients would never bother to look for jobs." The teacher then seeks agreement on the principle that "Poverty is the best incentive a man can have for working." If the student agrees, the teacher then places the principle in a different context (i.e., gives it a different subject matter) with a question like "If this is true, then would it not be well to prevent inheritance of wealth by the rich?" The student, who also believes that "Any limitation on accumulation of property would destroy incentive," is thus placed in a position which forces some kind of revision (if he attempts to extricate himself) of one or both of the contradictory beliefs.

4. As soon as doubt and a desire to reduce it begin motivating students, the next logical step in thought is development of alternatives to the beliefs which have come to seem inadequate. This step may be described as the casting, clarifying, and defining of hypotheses. Alternatives to the idea in question may emerge from a student's own thinking or may be suggested by others. Class discussion in which a number of competing ideas are expressed is often a good source of testable statements. A teacher may suggest hypotheses by saying, "Here are some possible solutions which have been suggested by others," or "Here are some ideas which have occurred to persons who have studied this issue."

Once ideas for testing are before a class, they must be rephrased where necessary to clarify meaning. By questioning and discussion, the teacher encourages students to remove as much ambiguity as possible. The class reworks the statement until it conforms to the requirements of a hypothesis, as given on pages 68–75.

If the problem originated in a conflict of values, the class will arrive at statements suitable for hypotheses only after answering a question such as "Why do people hold this belief?" "Why" questions following expression of value judgments may bring judgments of fact which can be tested. (The reader may want to review pages 101–103.)

Clarifying and defining hypotheses is often a lengthy procedure, but it is

116

absolutely necessary if thought is to go forward at all. One of the most common reasons why discussions deteriorate is that a group tries to discuss a proposition which, because of the presence of value terms, ambiguity, or vague meaning, is not suitable for reflective testing.

5. The next task is to encourage students to test the hypotheses which have been developed. Since this process was treated in Chapter 4, we shall do no more than review it briefly here. Testing consists of deducing consequences from hypotheses and making observations designed to show whether any of the hypotheses harmonize the available and obtainable data. The purpose of testing is not to prove hypotheses true or false in any final sense, but to demonstrate their relative adequacy or inadequacy as predictive tools. Although the search is never for final affirmative proof, it should be noted that tentative affirmation may often be possible and that definite proof of the inadequacy of a belief is very common in classrooms.

The function of a teacher includes acquainting students with the nature of reflection, but it is not his function to dominate testing procedure to a point where students feel obligated to accept his personal selection and interpretation of evidence. Whatever the degree of permissiveness up to this point, permissiveness must now prevail if the interests of reflection are to be served effectually. The foregoing sentences should not be misunderstood. Under reflective procedure, the only defensible criteria for selecting data are relevance and representativeness. When we urge permissiveness, we are not advocating that students be "turned loose" to disregard these criteria as they please. It is essential that the teacher help them to understand the proper bases for selection of data under reflective procedure, and to see when they are violating these bases.

In connection with the last point, a teacher must take care lest the search for evidence degenerate into a search for positive (supporting) or negative (damaging) cases only. The search must be for all cases obtainable, be they pro or con.

If the pooled experience of students is capable of providing all pertinent evidence which is then available and obtainable, the testing of hypotheses may be completed through class discussions alone. Otherwise, testing operations will require not only discussions but also research of some sort— perusal of documentary materials, trips, surveys, and polls.

6. The final step of reflective problem solving is drawing conclusions. A teacher's responsibility for this is essentially the same as for step 5. A teacher is obligated to help students understand the generalized rules by

which decisions are made and to check all decisions offered against these rules. If there is general agreement as to the rules of reflection, then, since it is a public process, we may expect a minimum of failure to reach consensus. It is assumed, however, that conclusions reached by students will be their own. If a teacher does his best to help them understand the requirements of reflection, and his best to help them check their conclusions against these requirements, he can do no more. In the final analysis, the environment of conclusion making must be permissive, not in the sense that the teacher does not participate, but in the sense that he does not use his authority to dominate decisions.

We have already treated the scientific criterion for judging conclusions. To restate briefly, hypotheses are accepted or rejected on the basis of whether they explain all available and obtainable data. That is to say, a conclusion will be considered satisfactory only if it represents a conceptual pattern which takes into account (or from which can be logically deduced) all available data and from which can be logically deduced new data which can then be sought and will, if found, serve as further verification.

If the foregoing principle is understood by students, they can evaluate a teacher's proposals just as a teacher who understands the principle can evaluate theirs. In short, we can have a give-and-take situation in which each person (including the teacher) is free and obligated to make proposals and criticize proposals made by others. In such an environment students and teachers will frequently find it desirable to reëxamine previously accepted conclusions. It is not inappropriate for a teacher, by virtue of his greater knowledge, to acquaint students with conclusions which have been reached by social scientists or other experts. However, such conclusions must be evaluated on their merits, with all the cautions concerning the use of authorities which were suggested in Chapter 4.

Techniques Which May Be Used to Promote Reflection

On page 111 it was suggested that a given technique may be judged by whether it contributes at some point to one or more of the steps of a complete act of thought. If it does, then is it possible to identify any technique as better than others for producing reflection? And is it possible to recognize techniques which have special value in furthering a particular step in an act of thought? The answer seems to be that, although reflection does not depend on any single technique, some techniques are more likely to encourage reflection. And some are more applicable than others to a given stage in thought. But the leader of reflection must never forget that the significance of any technique *is not the technique* per se *but how it is used;* and how it is used depends upon the purposes of the teacher. For example, a teacher interested in promoting reflection might make use of informal discussion. But informal discussion, unless used with conscious purpose, may not produce reflection at all. It may produce only noise. Another teacher might rely on informal discussion as his predominant technique but get no reflection because he is not trying to do so, or does not understand how an informal discussion must be managed if it is to produce thinking.

In the above treatment of the elements of reflective procedure a number of specific teaching techniques were mentioned in order to make more clear the nature of a teacher's responsibility. In the section to follow, each technique will be discussed with reference to its potential usefulness in stimulating reflection and with reference to the manner in which it must be used if it is to produce a maximum of reflection.

Techniques may be classified as either *directed* or *undirected*. Directed techniques are those which place teachers in a central position in the teaching-learning process. They require a maximum of activity and responsibility on the part of teachers and a minimum on the part of students. Undirected techniques require a minimum of activity and responsibility from teachers and a maximum from students. This classification is one of convenience; obviously techniques may be placed on a continuum ranging from relatively directed to relatively undirected. Most fall somewhere between the two extremes.

Techniques may also be regarded as *authoritarian* or *permissive*. This is a useful distinction but not suitable for a general classification. Probably any technique which we are about to describe may be used in authoritarian -or permissive fashion. Authoritarianism and permissivism are not functions of a technique *per se* but of how it is used. When used for authoritarian ends techniques serve to stamp a teacher's thought processes on the minds of his students, allowing him to dominate his group intellectually. Permissive techniques, on the other hand, encourage intellectual independence among students. They stimulate reflection and free the mind. Directed techniques, if so used, may be permissive. Undirected techniques might conceivably serve authoritarian ends, as when students ostensibly are allowed great freedom in selecting learning projects but, in their reading, are given materials which are slanted to support a teacher's personal convictions.

Teaching High School Social Studies

Investigatory Techniques of Teachers

The job of teachers, outside of actual classroom teaching situations, has generally been thought to consist of reading to "keep up," making lesson plans, making and scoring tests, making study guides, and supervising extracurricular activities. But although a teacher may do all these things under a reflective approach to teaching, he must do more if he is to succeed.

Just as a psychiatrist needs to know all he can about the mental processes of a patient, so a teacher needs to know all he can about the mental processes of his students, even though he plans to establish relatively undirected learning situations in which students function largely as free and independent agents. Reasons for the need to be familiar with the conceptual structure of students were suggested in the section on teacher responsibilities.

One of the functions of a teacher, as we have seen, is to assist in testing operations by acquainting students with publications and other community resources from which data pertinent to the beliefs in question may be drawn. This involves something more than just "keeping up," in the usual sense. Many routine publications in a field—new text and reference books, research monographs, professional journals—contain some data pertinent to the belief conflicts and value conflicts of students. In addition, a teacher needs to read widely in popular and semipopular periodicals and newspapers—with the intent of procuring information and ideas of a sort useful in testing beliefs. Note-taking is an essential part of this activity; so is development of clipping files.

In this process, a teacher must guard against selecting data which support only his own point of view. Investigation of the sort we are discussing here is similar in nature to the investigation a scientific worker might conduct in order to test a hypothesis, except that the hypotheses which a teacher has in mind are suggested by student conflicts, and data collected will be simple enough for students to understand. We do not imply that students should not be encouraged to find their own sources of data. But when they become concerned with problems for which there are no local sources of information, students are completely thwarted unless they use their teachers as resources.

A third type of investigation comes under the heading of evaluation. Since evaluation will be treated in a separate chapter, we need only say here that it is properly an investigatory function of teachers, requiring numerous special techniques of formal and informal nature. But it is also a function of students. So far as students themselves are concerned, self-evaluation is by far the most meaningful kind.

TRANSMITTING OR TELLING TECHNIQUES

These include any means by which a teacher directly transmits ideas or information to his group. He may "tell" them through lectures and demonstrations, or by reading to them. Audio-visual presentations also may be classified under this general heading.

First, let us consider the lecture. Lectures appear to be in disrepute among professors of education, many of whom lecture for hours each semester on the evils of the lecture system. To the extent that lectures are condoned at all, it is urged that they remain infrequent, short, informal, and interesting. Yet, if instruction is approached with the aim of promoting reflection, the criterion for judging a lecture is not its frequency, its length, its informality, or even whether it is entertaining. The test is whether the lecture does, in fact, stimulate or contribute to reflection.

It is true that the attention span of typical high-school students is not very great, and that they are capable of being stimulated by a lecture for a shorter length of time than are college students or adults. On the other hand, if the issues are vital to them, their attention span lengthens. A rule of thumb for lectures in high school might be to limit them to fifteen or twenty minutes in length, except that if they do not produce thought this is much too long and if they do it may be too short.

There are two points in reflection where lecturing (or telling) may be highly fruitful. One is at the point where a teacher is trying to help students clarify or feel a problem (he may need to present negative evidence, which is often best done through telling) or where he wishes to describe some situation in which values are in conflict, in hope that students will feel involved because of analogous situations in their own lives.

The other point where telling may be appropriate is while testing hypotheses. When a teacher has access to evidence not available to students, he may wish to give facts from his own experience or from his reading. He may wish to review books, articles, or monographs which would be too difficult for students to read. Or he may wish to present a guest speaker, or play a radio talk he has recorded.

The most deadening kind of lecture is one which gives students "the answers." Under the reflective approach this is not a function of teachers or group leaders. Instead lectures should raise problems or communicate

121

pertinent evidence. Lectures should always leave students with "something to think about."

Another category of transmitting or telling techniques is audio-visual presentations. Audio-visual materials include models, specimens, exhibits, field trips, motion pictures, still pictures, radio programs, recordings, charts, graphs, and maps. It is usually assumed that these materials bring more reality and concreteness to experience than can written or spoken words. Their use, however, leaves much to be desired. They may be used as an end in themselves, as when a film arrives and the principal announces an assembly "to look at pictures." Presented thus, films are often irrelevant to anything classes are doing; and they are shown without preparation or follow-up. Their chief justification is that teachers are given a much-needed chance to have a smoke.

In other cases, audio-visual materials may be used just as textbooks are used in traditional schools. They also may have no problematic content and may lead to question-and-answer recitations of a most sterile sort. Or audio-visual materials may be technically poor—films may be dim, recordings scratchy, and maps difficult to interpret.

Most textbooks on audio-visual education and courses taught on the subject stress the necessity of a film's "fitting in"—that is, being related to content in the unit under study. Emphasis is also placed on preparatory activities, by both teacher and students, and on follow-up activities, including evaluation. Yet all these procedures are described as sets of mechanical steps. Taken in themselves, there is nothing about them to produce reflection. Students who are studying China may see a film on the life of a Chinese peasant. But does it contain anything to challenge beliefs which students now hold, to raise questions, or to communicate evidence pertinent to a problem confronting students? If not, it may be a pleasant interlude in a student's day but it is scarcely of educational worth. Again, suppose a teacher conducts an elaborate preparation, including study questions and preliminary discussions. None of this in itself produces thought; whether reflection results depends on why and how it is done. Presumably, a teacher who understands value conflicts real to students could introduce a movie before it is shown so that its *evidential* quality will be clear. He might try through discussion to identify controversial beliefs to which a film is relevant. Or, in follow-up activities, questions might be raised as to what general ideas the film suggests and whether it tends to support or negate them.

As with lectures, audio-visual aids may be very effective in raising questions in students' minds. Aids which dramatize value conflicts may well serve to introduce or clarify a problem. Audio-visual aids may also be employed to present evidence and, like lectures, to acquaint students with proposed solutions to problems, provided such solutions are regarded as a challenge and not as something which they are obligated to accept.

Audio-visual aids may help a student to feel greater involvement in a problem. They may generate more emotional steam, more motivation, than most other devices. If this emotional energy is focused in the direction of reflective resolution of a problem, it may be very useful to teachers.

Unfortunately, the content of most audio-visual aids now available is unsuited to reflective learning of the sort most needed in high-school social studies. Relatively few aids now being sold bear on controversial subjects. Relatively few touch the closed areas. Those which do tend to be propagandistic. Some of the documentary films produced by the federal government during the late 1930's remain among the most provocative. The paucity of suitable audio-visual materials suggests that a teacher may do better at times by producing his own or, still better, having students produce them. A teacher can record radio programs or have students do so. He can take pictures—either movies or colored slides—of slum areas, picket lines, government power dams. He can make extensive use of a blackboard. He can make, or let students make, bulletin-board displays.

One of the authors had occasion to participate a few years ago in a graduate seminar on the living conditions of migrant agricultural labor in the San Joaquin Valley of California. One student was able to get from the files of a local newspaper a series of photographs showing dilapidated shacks, filthy privies, and hungry-eyed children. These pictures had more impact on the group than any amount of telling could have had. Only an actual trip to a labor camp would have been more effective. Beliefs which were challenged by this evidence include notions such as these:

No one ever goes hungry in the United States.
Most people get only what is coming to them.
The lower classes are usually happier than anybody else.

Another type of transmitting-telling technique is the demonstration, conducted by teacher or students. One of the authors has seen the following examples in classrooms:

How Galileo demonstrated the behavior of falling bodies. (Had a bearing on meaning of scientific method, the contrast between experimental and authoritarian methods of getting truth.)

How the Chinese eat with chopsticks. (Had a bearing on culture differences, "The American way is the only efficient or sensible way," etc.)

The position in which a cotton picker works, and the hand movements necessary in manual cotton picking. (Had an evidential bearing on an argument class had had as to whether agricultural labor is "hard work," whether it requires a high degree of skill, whether it is underpaid, etc.)

Arithmetical processes with and without the use of zero. (To support idea that Moslems made fundamental contributions to Western culture, which in turn has evidential bearing on ethnocentric belief that "Everything which is good in modern life is a product of Christian-Hebraic culture.")

THE USE OF QUESTIONING

Historically, questioning has been one of the most popular means of instruction in the social studies. As traditionally used, it is a part of textbook-recitation technique. Students are assigned material to read in a textbook and are asked questions about it. Teachers may ask questions in class, put questions on the blackboard, mimeograph and distribute sheets of questions, or ask students to answer questions appearing in a textbook or workbook. As Horn suggests, question-and-answer recitation is common "even where instruction is labeled to indicate other patterns of teaching." [4]

Question-and-answer recitation has been subjected to abundant criticism. Schutte, for example, says ". . . If a pure question and answer method—and nothing else—is used in the classroom, we probably might as well dispense with the teacher. Someone could work out a series of questions and have them mimeographed. A janitor could distribute them to the pupils at the beginning of the period and later gather the answers, which could then be scored by someone else." [5] As commonly used, question-and-answer recitation is probably relatively ineffective in promoting reflection. It usually requires the recall of more or less unrelated factual materials. This technique may help students to memorize content. But mere memorization of facts is education in the associationist tradition; it is not consistent with the needs of reflection and conceptualization.

However, questioning technique does have a necessary role in the stimulation and guidance of reflection. Questions may be used to inaugurate and push forward each step of an act of thought. Questioning is a natural technique for clarifying and creating problems. With questions like the following a teacher may help students to probe present beliefs and values.

[4] Ernest Horn, *Methods of Instruction in the Social Studies*, Charles Scribner's Sons, 1938, p. 338.
[5] T. H. Schutte, *Teaching the Social Studies on the Secondary Level*, Prentice-Hall, Inc., 1942, p. 336.

"Why do you say that?"

"Do you agree or disagree and why?"

"If you believe such-and-such, then how can you believe so-and-so?"

"Is such-and-such behavior (or belief) consistent with so-and-so behavior (or belief)?"

"What would you do in a case like this?"

"How do you explain this fact?"

When dealing with value judgments, hypotheses suitable for reflective study may be brought into the open by questions such as these:

"Why do you believe that?"

"Why would you do that?"

"Why do you think that so many people in our community believe so-and-so?"

"If you did that, what might the results be?"

"Can you define that statement operationally?"

Once judgments of fact have been stated, their clarification and definition may be furthered by asking:

"What does this statement mean?"

"What other way could you say it?"

"Can you give an example or illustration of this?"

"How would you define this word?"

The testing of hypotheses selected for study may be inaugurated and carried forward by questions such as:

"How could we prove or disprove a statement like this?"

"How can we get facts which will answer this?"

"How reliable are such data?"

"What do these facts mean?"

And the drawing of conclusions may be instigated through queries like:

"What can you conclude from a study of these data?"

"Which consequences (of acting on disputed values) do you prefer?"

These "thought questions" are not intended to elicit *only* the recall of a date, a name, a town, or a battle. They are probably the only kinds of questions with which teachers should bother. The use of questioning technique to instigate and to propel problem-solving discussions to conclusion will be treated further in Chapter 8.

TEACHER LED DISCUSSION

Very often what teachers label "discussion" is nothing more than question-and-answer recitation, perhaps of the most routine variety. True discussion is a form of group inquiry, in which questions are freely raised and answered. Discussion may range in degree of central control from that which is closely dominated by a teacher to that in which a teacher plays a minimum role.

In the literature of teaching methods, discussion is usually treated as a largely mechanical process. "Tricks" which may be used by a teacher to keep a class orderly during discussion are usually described. Also considered important are the amount of control to be exercised by a teacher, procedural rules, and physical conditions of the classroom. Although these are important points, focusing on them evades the main issue, which is whether discussion is actually getting anywhere. Unless a causal connection exists between what occurs during discussion and the steps of an act of thought, discussion is probably producing confusion (or killing time) rather than instigating reflection. At any given point during its course a discussion should be clarifying or exposing a problem, suggesting and refining hypotheses, or testing hypotheses.

UNDIRECTED DISCUSSION

This is an informal, loosely organized exchange of views during which the teacher keeps largely in the background. Although similar to a "bull session," it serves purposes not served by an out-of-class bull session.

As often conducted, however, undirected discussion is in fact a bull session. Instead of using such discussion as a basic technique of reflection, teachers do not *use* it at all. They simply allow it to occur, possibly for want of something better. Undirected discussion can serve as a climate-making device (see Chapter 7). It can reveal to teachers more about the beliefs and values of students, and when so used it may properly be classified as an investigatory technique of teachers. Students may clarify or raise problems during undirected discussion. Whether such discussion can be a medium for organized investigation of problems depends on maturity and size of class and its understanding of techniques of group inquiry. In most cases undirected discussion is not a good tool for producing a complete act of thought.

PROJECT AND ACTIVITY TECHNIQUE

Student "projects" or "activities" are learning experiences carried on more or less independently by students. A project may be undertaken by an individual or by a committee. It usually involves some kind of assembly and manipulation of materials requiring actual physical movement and leading to an outcome which is "practical" in the sense that there is something visible to show for it. Because projects involve physical activity they often are regarded as being necessarily "progressive" and therefore desirable. Examples of projects are:

Keeping a notebook
Making a map
Drawing a picture or cartoon
Building a model
Writing an essay
Making a book report
Making a survey of some community problem
Taking an opinion poll
Writing and giving a short play
Making collections and preparing exhibits
Giving a report on a current event
Doing the exercises in a workbook
Making diagrams, charts, graphs, tables
Making a series of lantern slides
Writing a letter to a congressman

Projects may be highly directed. When a teacher assigns projects and tells students exactly how to perform them, the technique is fully teacher-dominated. But a project *can* be relatively undirected, more so than any technique except permissive discussion. This will be the case if it grows out of a student's thinking and is freely planned and executed by him. Projects of one sort or another represent the basic investigatory technique of students.

As projects commonly operate, it is doubtful whether they produce much reflection. Project work is popular because of its "progressive" flavor and also perhaps because it is an effective way of keeping students occupied with little effort from a teacher. One often sees notebooks, workbooks, scrapbooks, gaily colored posters, maps, and exhibits which have been carefully prepared by students but which are meaningless if judged from the viewpoint of reflective learning. Unless a teacher has a clear sense of purpose, projects easily degenerate into busywork.

Even when used with conscious purpose, projects are probably often meant as an *aid* to memorization of cut-and-dried content. That is, they reflect an associationist conception of learning. It is erroneously assumed

127

that, if a student combines bodily activity with the act of memorization, he will be able to memorize faster and retain the material longer.

To function as an instrument of reflection, projects must at all times be regarded as an investigatory technique. They correspond to research periods of scientists and professional scholars. Through projects, students read, search for relevant radio programs, study the community, or talk with people, for the purpose of locating data which will be useful in solving a problem.

Project technique, more than most others, enables a teacher to gear learning situations to individual differences, particularly if projects are conducted within a permissive framework. For example, a class may be divided into committees roughly in accordance with ability. Groups of brighter students may conduct investigations which would be beyond the capacity of duller students. They might read and report on mature books and articles, or study radio and TV programs which handle their materials on an adult level. Special knowledge may be a basis for projects, as when two or three students with a knowledge of photography are assigned to take pictures of something which the entire class cannot visit. Project assignments may also reflect opportunity, as when the only student in a class who has visited the TVA region reports his experiences.

Projects are often an excellent means of presenting evidence to a group. Perhaps committees or individuals have gathered data which they feel will be useful to the rest of the group. They may report these data through use of charts, graphs, diagrams, or posters, or through written or oral reports, or through displays or collections (as of photographs).

DISCUSSION QUESTIONS AND EXERCISES

1. Comment on the following statement: "There are many methods of teaching, each of which is valuable in its place." Do you agree or disagree? What assumptions about the meaning of method are implied?
2. List the techniques of teaching which you remember having experienced as a student. What were the most commonly used techniques of your (a) elementary, (b) secondary, and (c) college education? Which techniques were most effective in inducing you to reflect? Which were least effective?
3. React to the following statement, made by a high-school principal: "I try to hire teachers on the basis of personality. A teacher who is pleasant and coöperative, and who gets along well with students and colleagues, is bound to be a success." What is the role of a teacher's personality? Is it more important than mastery of a theory of teaching?

4. Procedures described in Chapter 6 are treated in relation to the requirements of a reflective approach to teaching. Discuss how such techniques would need to be used in order to further some one or more of the non-reflective intellectual methods described in Chapter 3.
5. Review the general nature of a subject-matter switch (page 116). Devise as many subject-matter switches as you can, confining them to subject matter in areas of ideological conflict.
6. Plan a short lecture which you feel would be likely to motivate reflection about some issue. Deliver to your methods class and discuss its effectiveness in accomplishing what you intended.
7. Prepare a dozen or so questions (for discussion or study) about issues with which you think members of the class are familiar. Make them as thought provoking as you can. Discuss with the class their potential effectiveness.

REFERENCES

A number of books treat techniques (usually labeled "methods") of teaching the social studies. Perhaps most effective in treating technique in relation to a philosophic position are the following: Ernest Horn, *Methods of Instruction in the Social Studies* (Scribner, 1937); I. James Quillen and Lavone A. Hanna, *Education for Social Competence* (Scott, Foresman, 1948); and Henry Johnson, *Teaching of History* (Macmillan, 1915).

Students will also find of value any of the general methods texts in the teaching of the social studies. These include Arthur C. and David H. Bining, *Teaching the Social Studies in Secondary Schools* (McGraw-Hill, 1952); Maurice P. Moffatt, *Social Studies Instruction* (Prentice-Hall, 1950); C. D. Samford and Eugene Cottle, *Social Studies in the Secondary School* (McGraw-Hill, 1952); and Edgar B. Wesley, *Teaching Social Studies in High Schools* (Heath, 1950).

Certain of the books written to apply to the teaching of all school subjects are of great usefulness to social-studies teachers. Especially recommended is Ernest E. Bayles, *Theory and Practice of Teaching* (Harper, 1950). Also of value are Ray H. Simpson, *Improving Teaching-Learning Processes* (Longmans, Green, 1953) and Kimball Wiles, *Teaching for Better Schools* (Prentice-Hall, 1952).

Chapter 7

Climate Making as a Part of Method

A TEACHER'S success in inducing reflective learning in connection with critical social issues hinges on how open-minded students can become. The chief aim of the present chapter is to explore ways in which learners can be made receptive to points of view that are more scientific than the common run.

For this purpose we shall draw rather heavily from experience in fields outside formal education. Specifically, we shall survey briefly some findings from psychiatry which bear on the problem of reducing emotional blocks to learning. We shall also examine the area of study known as "democratic group leadership" in an attempt to see what an understanding of the dynamics of democratic adult groups may reveal concerning classroom practice. It should be noted at the outset that we make no attempt to apply directly to classroom practice the procedures which have been developed for use in therapeutic or normal adult groups. Many of these procedures are inapplicable in school classes. However, experience in these fields does suggest important clues for making learning in the social studies more reflective, functional, and permanent.

Resolution of Conflict from a Psychoanalytic Point of View

Psychotherapists differ in their interpretation of causes of emotional conflict. Freudians attribute conflict to a combination of instinctive drives and early childhood experiences. Non-Freudians are more inclined to emphasize a patient's present environment as a source of conflict. Therapists likewise differ in their approach to treatment, one group assuming that therapy should expose and help a patient reinterpret early experiences in life, and

130

another that therapy should focus on changing a patient's contemporary life situation. Another source of disagreement is in the question of how directive a counselor should be during counseling sessions. Still another issue relates to whether, in treating certain forms of mental illness, individual or group therapy is the more valuable. Because they are particularly pertinent to the problem of the present chapter, we shall explore briefly the last two of the issues mentioned.

DIRECTIVE VERSUS NON-DIRECTIVE THERAPY

In the language of psychotherapy, the issue posed here is between directive and non-directive (or patient-centered) therapy. What is probably the first attempt at careful description and defense of a non-directive approach to therapy was made by Rogers.[1]

We can best describe non-directive therapy through comparisons and contrasts. Rogers suggests that virtually all historical approaches to psychotherapy place a therapist in an authoritarian position with reference to a patient. These approaches assume that a counselor can and should determine a socially accepted goal for a patient and help him rearrange his personality structure or his life situation so that he can achieve this goal. A patient may be told what to believe and do by subtle and indirect methods, but told he is nevertheless.

Non-directive therapy avoids substituting a therapist's purposes for a patient's. A warm and permissive atmosphere is created in which a patient feels perfectly free to talk about his problems. The counselor accepts, recognizes, and clarifies feelings expressed by the patient, who talks his way through his problems, moving successively from a phase of "blowing off steam" to a phase of better self-understanding and heightened capacity for reflective handling of his own problems. Although non-directive therapy places more emphasis upon emotional adjustment than do some other approaches, it is assumed that an *outcome of therapy will be reflectively achieved insight*. The responsibility for this outcome is placed squarely on patients; whatever decisions they make are theirs alone.

We shall confine ourselves to one further point: In contrast to Freudian approaches to the theory of neurosis, non-directive therapy assumes that, rather than being largely internal and psychic, conflicts have a large cultural component. That is, they are mostly a result of one's present relationship with his environment: they grow from "some new cultural demand

[1] Carl Rogers, *Counseling and Psychotherapy*, Houghton Mifflin Company, 1942,

131

which opposes individual need." [2] This appears to be saying much the same as is said elsewhere in the present book: that most emotional conflicts are a result of a person's internalizing, or incorporating within the self, discrepancies of his surrounding culture (i.e., conflicting beliefs and behaviors).

A non-directive approach to psychotherapy has important implications for teaching. Although a teacher should not be "non-directive" in the sense described by Rogers, the idea of encouraging individuals (including students) to formulate their own purposes and solve their own problems in the presence of an adult who, rather than dictating, merely gives encouragement, has broad significance for group management in a democratic society. Limitations of the Rogerian outlook for school use will be treated later in the chapter.

INDIVIDUAL AND GROUP COUNSELING AND BEHAVIORAL CHANGE

Psychological counseling which acquaints a patient with "the facts" concerning his situation may fail to produce logically implied changes in behavior. For example, Rogers says, "It has come to be recognized that we do not change the client's behavior very effectively simply by giving him an intellectual picture of its patterning, no matter how accurate." [3] Change in knowledge leads to the adoption of new values. But if a situation rewards old values, they will continue to dominate the new. When this is the case, behavior reflects the old values and remains unchanged.

One reason a counselor may not succeed in bringing about significant changes in behavior is that the behavior of every individual is firmly rooted in the persons with whom he associates. That is, actions of a patient are largely controlled by groups to which he belongs and can be changed only as behavior of the groups themselves changes. [4]

One of the basic drives of human life is for security. The chief means of achieving security is through membership in a group. When a person feels that he has a place in a group, that he "fits in," that he is wanted, he feels secure. As Lewin points out, "The social climate in which a child lives is for the child as important as the air it breathes. The group to which a child belongs is the ground on which he stands. His relation to the group and his status in it are the most important factors for his feeling of security or in-

[2] *Ibid.*, p. 54.
[3] *Ibid.*, p. 27.
[4] As used in the present chapter, *group* is taken to mean two or more persons *in psychological interaction* with each other. Related terms are *in-group, primary group,* and *face-to-face group.*

security." [5] One achieves membership in a group by conforming, at least to a degree, to the mores of the group. To be accepted in a group of thieves, one must act like a thief; to be accepted in a group of saints, one must act like a saint.

This is not to say that an individual is completely subject to group control. He may develop beliefs and values which are novel to a group and may get them accepted by others in the group. With widening acceptance, the new beliefs and values become effective in controlling group behavior. The extent to which an individual can project his own unique personality into group life, and change a group thereby, depends on the situation (e.g., whether the group is itself democratic and the extent to which the larger culture outside the group is hostile or friendly to the changes) and on his own capacity for persuasion. A modern sociologist is likely to regard the process of interaction itself as the basic social datum; every group is constantly shaping individuals in it and simultaneously is being shaped by them.

Even though interaction is always present, we cannot imagine large changes occurring in individuals out of relationship to their primary group associations. A psychotherapist is constantly aware of the fact that there is little he can do to help a patient reorganize his personality *as an individual.* Such reorganization as may occur must fit exigencies posed by a patient's associations—the various needs and pressures, often highly subtle and complex, which grow out of the fact of group membership itself. This is particularly the case where values are concerned, and even more particularly, values in closed areas.

During World War II, experiments in group psychotherapy were undertaken out of necessity. There were not enough therapists or facilities for individual counseling. The results of counseling with groups of patients were often gratifying. Now, in certain situations group therapy is seen as having advantages over individual therapy.[6] The reason appears to lie in the previously mentioned supposition that it is easier for an individual to change his values and behavior if other persons with whom he is in intimate contact are also changing.

There is disagreement as to whether in group therapy the therapeutic effect comes primarily from the relationship of each member to the thera-

[5] Kurt Lewin, *Resolving Social Conflicts,* Harper & Brothers, 1948, p. 82.
[6] See Leon Gorlow and others, *The Nature of Nondirective Group Psychotherapy,* Teachers College, Columbia University, 1952, p. 8.

pist or from relationships of members to each other, but the latter interpretation seems to be growing in popularity. In some instances a patient can express himself more freely in a small face-to-face group than in individual relationship to a counselor, perhaps because he feels less alone, the group gives him courage, and other members have established precedents for speaking frankly. Through the give-and-take of free discussion some persons may come to see their own problems better than through individual counseling situations. As one writer suggests, "Patients can accept censure, suggestions, interpretation and guidance from each other with less disturbance and hostility than from the therapist." [7]

A group situation may also stimulate one to deal openly and creatively with his own conflicts. Foulkes summarizes this possible therapeutic effect of a group: ". . . Lectures, exhortations, sympathy, pity, advice, medicaments, explanations, encouragement, all can help a little, but they can not move the patient out of his fortress of entanglement. In the long run, they can only help him to entrench himself deeper in it. . . . If he is, however, brought into a situation, which he himself is continuously helping to create, to shape, he is forced to come out into the open with his own reactions and their contradictions." [8] Whether a patient benefits more from group than from individual therapy depends in large part on the nature of his illness. Group therapy is regarded as of limited usefulness for the mentally unbalanced and probably for extreme neurotics. The nearer a patient is to normality, the more effective group therapy is likely to be. Its greatest value may be, as Hobbs points out, "in the neglected field of therapy for the normal person with debilitating situational conflicts. . . ." [9]

What is the significance to classroom teachers of clinical experience in individual and group psychotherapy? The hypothesis is suggested that a wide range of personally felt problems may be handled successfully among normal persons, including adolescent youth, with resultant permanent changes in outlook and behavior, if they are encouraged to air problems freely in the give-and-take atmosphere of a face-to-face group. Although this general idea is not new, modern psychiatric practice offers clues as to the most effectual managerial techniques for such learning situations.

[7] S. R. Slavson, quoted in *ibid.*, p. 10.
[8] S. H. Foulkes, *Introduction to Group-Analytic Psychotherapy*, William Heinemann Medical Books, Ltd., 1948, p. 70.
[9] Nicholas Hobbs, "Group-Centered Psychotherapy," chap. 7 in Carl Rogers, *Client-Centered Psychotherapy*, Houghton Mifflin Company, 1951.

Climate Making as a Part of Method

The Democratic Group-Leadership Movement

Related to the development of group psychotherapy is the democratic group-leadership movement. This movement embraces a body of experiments and practices with normal adult and youth groups. Its aim is to translate a democratic philosophy into action on a group level and to compare the learning and behavioral results of democratic groups with those of nondemocratic groups. An understanding of the dynamics of groups is valuable to a social-studies teacher. In the concluding section of the chapter, we shall make applications, and also show why, because of differences in aims and competence of most adult groups involved in experimentation, certain aspects of the management of adult groups are not transferable to classroom situations.

The democratic group-leadership movement is rooted in a democratic social-political philosophy dating in the United States from the Jeffersonian period, and from earlier than that in Europe. The modern concept of group work seems to combine our traditional democratic philosophy with an understanding of group psychology which in human affairs is relatively recent.

In a large sense, the democratic group-leadership movement is a counterpart, for normal groups, of group psychotherapy for abnormal. Although there is disagreement as to just how directive a leader can be and still remain "democratic," democratic group leadership appears to be an application of some of the principles of non-directive group therapy. It is to be expected, therefore, that among the contributors to our understanding of group process we find the names of numerous psychiatrists and psychologists. As Haiman points out, modern methods of group leadership "find their origin in the work of Sigmund Freud and follow the patterns of the psychiatric tradition which has flowered since his time." [10] Because there are significant relationships between the concepts of psychiatric medicine and of leadership of normal groups, psychiatrists have transplanted their philosophy and methods to normal group situations.

Although the contribution of psychologists and psychiatrists to an understanding of group dynamics has been great, it is perhaps no more significant than that of experts in management-worker relations. Of studies along this line, perhaps the most notable were those conducted by staff members of the Harvard Graduate School of Business—F. J. Roethlisberger, W. J. Dick-

[10] Franklin S. Haiman, *Group Leadership and Democratic Action*, Houghton Mifflin Company, 1951, p. 39. This reference is one of the best general treatments of the subject and the following pages draw heavily from it.

son, and colleagues at the Hawthorne Works (Chicago) of the Western Electric Company between 1927 and 1932.

It was found from these studies that labor contentment and efficiency rose when workers were (1) organized in teams which felt a sense of common purpose, and (2) made participants in an interview system where they could talk freely about whatever they wished.

Among other experiments conducted with self-governing adult groups is the famous Peckham Experiment,[11] involving the work of the Pioneer Health Centre of Peckham, England. This health center was established to give family groups a program of mental and physical preventive therapy. In the main, the extensive program is run by members themselves without centralized direction. Marked—sometimes revolutionary—changes in the apparent values and behaviors of many members are noted by skilled observers.

It is from experiences and experiments such as have been described above that we have gained much of our knowledge of group dynamics. New concepts have developed as to how a democratic group functions and the role of a leader in it. It has become clear also that the idea of a democratic group, as developed in the democratic group-leadership movement, is very similar to the idea of a therapeutic group, as developed in the field of group psychotherapy.

The Nature of a Democratic Group

Democracy is a philosophic concept. We define democracy as a social arrangement in which all members of a group share equally in determining which freedoms and restraints shall apply. It is presumed that, in general, freedoms and restraints shall apply with the same force to all. But democracy must allow for the granting of special powers for special purposes (as in the case of its executive officers). If we think of democracy as a system of *equally limited* freedom, characterized by shared decisions regarding which specific rules are to prevail, then we have a simple criterion for distinguishing democracy from other social arrangements. A social system may provide *unlimited* freedoms, in which case it is called anarchy. Or it may provide *unequally limited* freedoms, in which case it is called autocracy.

A democratic group is self-governing. But it must provide for situations where disagreement occurs. Ideally, democratic decisions are by consensus

[11] See I. H. Pearse and Lucy H. Crocker, *The Peckham Experiment,* George Allen & Unwin, 1943.

—that is, mutually agreeable decisions reached through discussion and compromise. Then, by common consent action is taken. If consensus is not possible, a democratic group votes. Each person has an equal vote, and a majority vote wins. Votes are taken to facilitate action, not to enforce belief.

Successful and permanent operation of democracy seems to require that a group maintain certain conditions which, although not a part of the central idea of democracy, contribute to its functioning. For example, if participation is to be full and free, a group must establish an accepting atmosphere—an atmosphere in which every member is considered important and has his opinions guaranteed a hearing. Participation implies reasonable freedom of communication, and freedom of speech and thought. If any single individual or minority group gains disproportionate control over agencies of communication and opinion, the society has lost equality of participation in decision making.

It would also seem that, if a democratic society is to survive over time, a majority of its members must learn to make reflective decisions where socially important questions are involved. A democratic society assumes competence on the part of its members; any different assumption would lead to distrust and rejection of the principle of equal participation. We assume that without wise leadership no society can solve its problems and endure. In a democracy wise leadership is a function of wise citizenship. If a democracy is to survive, then its members must take steps to insure that the principle of reflection is employed as widely as possible in making choices of group concern. Among other things, this means that a democracy should always be in the process of reducing the number and extent of its closed areas.

THE ROLE OF DEMOCRATIC LEADERSHIP

Behavior of a group is influenced significantly by its leaders. Particularly if a group is immature, its overall emotional and intellectual climate and its direction and extent of growth depend largely on the conduct of its leadership. As a group matures, it becomes less dependent on particular leaders. It develops capacity to produce leaders from its own ranks and reject and select leaders according to need.

The role of democratic leadership is *to help a group realize its own potentialities for growth.* Such a statement becomes meaningful only when "growth" is defined in operational terms. One attempt at definition seeks to specify a number of "dimensions" of group growth,[12] including the following:

1. Progress toward fuller intercommunication among members. This includes growing acceptance and understanding by members of mechanics of language, with particular reference to meaning.

2. Progress toward viewing objectively the functioning of the group. This includes ability of all members to make and accept interpretations about member and group functioning and ability to collect and use pertinent information about itself.

3. Progress toward developing shared responsibilities. This includes growth toward a sharing of leadership functions, participation in setting goals, and coöperation in achievement of goals.

4. Progress toward developing group cohesion. Cohesion should be adequate to permit assimilation of new ideas without group disintegration, assimilation of new members in a way to strengthen rather than disrupt the group, holding to long-range goals when a situation requires, and making constructive use of internal conflicts.

5. Progress toward developing ability to inform itself, to think straight, and to make creative decisions about problems. This includes learning to make full use of the contribution potential of all members, to discover and utilize appropriate resource materials and persons, and to detect and correct fallacies in group thinking.

What specific functions does a democratic leader perform if a group is to move in these directions? He may execute or administer, serve as judge or arbiter, be an advocate (or shaper of opinion), or render expert advice. He may also play the role of discussion leader. Although a discussion leader may on occasion assume any of the above roles, his function is distinctively different from and more inclusive than any of them. He helps a group to achieve self-growth. Or, as one writer puts it, he tries to "release the creative talents of the members of a group, help them solve their own problems, and reach their own decisions." [13] Functions and techniques of discussion leadership will be treated in detail in Chapter 8.

SOME SIGNIFICANT EXPERIMENTS WITH GROUPS

Of significance to social-studies teachers are experiments in group climate conducted at the Iowa Child Welfare Research Station by Ronald Lippitt

---

[12] National Training Laboratory in Group Development, *Report of the Second Summer Laboratory*, Washington, D.C., Department of Adult Education, 1948, pp. 113–114.
[13] Franklin S. Haiman, *op. cit.*, p. 71.

and Ralph K. White.[14] In this study matched groups of eleven-year-old boys were subjected to variations in leadership and resulting behavior was noted. Leadership conformed to three contrasting patterns, defined as authoritarian, laissez-faire, and democratic.

Authoritarian leaders determined activities and procedures for their groups, decided which children should work together, and remained aloof except to issue orders. The pattern was one of arbitrariness and highly centralized direction. Laissez-faire leaders played a generally passive role. They explained what materials were available, gave information when asked, but made no suggestions unless absolutely necessary. The children were "on their own." Democratic leaders actively encouraged and assisted in group decisions. With the leaders' help, democratic groups formulated their own goals and plans of action. Although not helping with actual work, democratic leaders tried to be group members in spirit. In the democratic groups boys were allowed to select their own workmates and to divide responsibility as they saw fit.

Responses appeared to be significantly different in the three groups. Under authoritarian leadership two distinct reactions were noted. In most cases, authoritarian-led groups responded to leadership apathetically. They showed little hostility toward leaders; rather, they became highly dependent, displaying little capacity for initiating group action. Although when a leader was present their productivity was higher than that of other groups, in the absence of a leader they accomplished very little. When a group showed resentment toward authoritarian leadership, there was evidence of accumulated irritability and aggressive impulses. When an opportunity presented itself, these impulses were usually vented toward fellow club members (scapegoating). Authoritarian groups shifted to democratic leadership underwent a period of horseplay and disorganization but eventually learned to work productively.

Members of laissez-faire groups were characterized by much more of a tendency to be friendly and confiding, and to be dependent on each other for social recognition. They showed a greater willingness, also, to extend recognition to each other (less tendency to project inner resentments at fellow group members). But laissez-faire groups gave evidence of insecurity. For example, they asked repeatedly for help and after the experiment expressed dissatisfaction with their leadership.

[14] See Ronald Lippitt and Ralph K. White, "An Experimental Study of Leadership and Group Life," *Readings in Social Psychology* (Theodore M. Newcomb and Eugene L. Hartley, eds.), Henry Holt & Company, 1947, pp. 315–330.

Democratic groups rated higher than autocratic in evidence of a friendly and confiding atmosphere and in number of group-minded suggestions. Like members of laissez-faire groups, democratic group members seemed able to extend mutual recognition to each other. Democratic groups were also conspicuously different from authoritarian in showing a smaller number of leader-dependent actions. They showed more initiative, more ability to solve their own problems and to do constructive work in the absence of a leader. In fact, constructive effort was almost as great in the absence of a leader as in his presence. Interestingly, laissez-faire groups accomplished more when the leader was absent than when he was present.

A conclusion drawn from these experiments was that the adult-leader role is a "very strong determiner of the pattern of social interaction and emotional development of the group." It was felt that authoritarian and laissez-faire leadership both inhibited "psychological freedom," which might be interpreted to mean tendencies such as emotional comfort, creativity, and initiative.[15]

Perhaps the greatest significance of these experiments for our purposes rests in the light they throw on behavioral outcomes of three possible types of leadership situations. For example, work habits learned under democratic leadership, more than habits learned under authoritarian leadership, may have significant carry-over into situations where an adult leader is not present. That is, learning in a democratic group "cuts deeper." However, results of these experiments should not be regarded as conclusive or as suggesting characteristics of "basic human nature." They involved groups having rather special purposes and boys who were products of a culture which prides itself in being democratic. It would have been surprising if these boys had not preferred and functioned better under democratic leadership.

Another group of experiments pertaining to our general theme include those in food use made during World War II, likewise conducted at the Child Welfare Research Station of the University of Iowa. In this case, the effects of lecture and group discussion on behavior were compared. Three adult groups of housewives were lectured on nutritional value and contribution to war effort of wider use of beef hearts, sweetbreads, and kidneys. Three other groups discussed the problem of getting "housewives in general" to make greater use of these foods and as groups resolved to make use of them in their own families. A resource person who could supply recipes and other information was available to each discussion group.

[15] *Ibid.*, p. 329.

Of the women listening to the lecture, only 3 percent who had never before served the meats served one of them. Of the women in the discussion groups, 32 percent who had never before served the meats served one of them. Apparently discussion followed by group decision was much more effective than lectures in producing behavioral change. Experiments designed to increase home consumption of milk showed similar results.[16]

Lewin also cites experiments designed to test the relative effectiveness of individual instruction compared with group discussion and decision. In this case, a number of mothers received individual instruction on medically approved practices of feeding infants. Other mothers were formed in groups, received instructions, and then were given an opportunity for discussion and group decision. In this experiment, discussion and group resolve were found to be much more effective than individual instruction in producing behavioral change. We are reminded of experience in group psychotherapy, cited earlier, which indicated that group situations may sometimes be more effective than individual counseling in producing changes in beliefs and behavior.

Lewin concludes that, if group discussion and decision are to produce significant change, leadership must be democratic. It must avoid high-pressure methods and be sensitive to resistance to change. The burden of decision must be placed on group members themselves. Change is likely to be greater, too, if a goal is set on which consensus is possible; majority rule is less effective because minority members who are outvoted sometimes deliberately resist the decision. An object in achieving change is not to apply pressure from outside but to remove counterforces within individuals. Such removal seems to occur best in permissive group situations.

It was also found that less resistance is encountered if subjects are asked to discuss a problem as it relates to other persons—e.g., "How might it be possible to induce the housewives of the nation to use more milk?" Then they do not feel that their own habits are being selected as objects of criticism. This approach reduces resistance to a serious consideration of opposing practices. As is evidenced by their own changed behaviors, group members seldom fail to apply the problem to their own situations.

We shall describe one other experiment which appears significant for social-studies teachers. Shaw reports an experiment conducted among graduate students at Columbia University in which students tackled problems

[16] For a description and interpretation of these experiments and those described below, see Kurt Lewin, "Group Decision and Social Change," *Readings in Social Psychology*, Henry Holt & Company, 1947, pp. 330–344.

individually and in groups.[17] In each instance, it was found that small groups of students, working coöperatively on problems, attained a much higher proportion of correct answers than the same number of students working individually. Also, groups were able to solve problems coöperatively which were too difficult for students working individually to solve. Investigators attributed the results to a tendency of members of a group to criticize and cross-check suggestions raised within the group.

In all the experiments cited, the groups employed were essentially democratic in structure and function, as we have defined this term (see pp. 136–138). The implication is that in our culture a face-to-face group which is democratically structured permits its members to achieve greater ideological and behavioral change, and more permanent change, than any other acceptable organization for learning. Also, if we may generalize from rather scanty data, members of such groups tend to be more productive intellectually and to show more wisdom than individuals working alone. Further, they exhibit better "mental health"—as this term is conventionally defined —than members of either authoritarian or laissez-faire groups.

Classroom Teachers as Democratic Leaders and Climate Makers

In order to understand the task of teachers as it relates to the problem of creating open-mindedness and willingness to change beliefs and behaviors, we need to examine in detail how emotional blocking can prevent such changes. Only as a teacher understands the process of blocking and the manner in which it manifests itself can he take steps for its removal.

FAILURE OF PERCEPTION AS A CAUSE OF "CLOSED MINDS"

In just what way does blocking interfere with reflection? It might be supposed that, no matter how strong one's emotional attachment to a belief, if he is confronted with facts which seem clearly to question it, then question it he must. Any other course would appear highly unreasonable. Yet a normally intelligent and perfectly sane person may appear blind to evidence which others find thoroughly convincing.

Such behavior is not to be interpreted as willful irrationality. We agree with Wertheimer when he says that human beings have a "willingness to face problems straight, a readiness to follow them up courageously and

---

[17] Marjorie Shaw, "A Comparison of Individual and Small Groups in the Rational Solution of Complex Problems," *Readings in Social Psychology*, pp. 304–315.

sincerely, a desire for improvement, in contrast with arbitrary, wilful, or slavish attitudes." [18] What occurs, as a result of emotional blocking, apparently, is *failure of perception, which is not understood by the person involved and which without help he cannot prevent or overcome.*

What is failure of perception? Answering this question raises complex technical as well as philosophical issues. At any given moment of consciousness a person has a "perceptual field." It is that part of his physical and psychological environment of which through his senses he is directly aware.

There is disagreement as to whether a person can perceive directly with his senses the physical, social, and psychological surroundings which are assumed to exist. Philosophical realists assume that he can. The position taken in this book is essentially that of field theory, which maintains that a person takes the data of sense experience and *imposes on them* pattern, order, and meaning. This imposed pattern is what we mean by insight. Insights are dependent not only on the nature of the environment, or confronting situation, but also on the influence of past experience and one's purposes at the time. Thus, in a given situation we cannot expect the insights of any two persons to be identical. Nor can we assume that for an individual any reality exists except the insights which he has achieved.

The literature of psychotherapy defines failure of perception as "loss of contact with reality." The goal of therapy is the reëstablishment of accurate perception, or the reëstablishment of contact with reality. What does this terminology mean? In the present book, when we say that perception is accurate, or that a person is in touch with reality, we mean that his beliefs are accurate guides to action. That is, they have been or can be verified experimentally or experientially. They are consistent with the verified data of past experience (*facts* as we use the term here) or they produce the consequences which a person anticipates when he acts on them. This is what we expect of any scientific theory.

When we say that a person is suffering from a failure of perception, we mean either that his beliefs are inconsistent with one another or that deductions made from them do not check with the data of observation. Now it is true that a person who is out of touch with reality may deduce consequences from a proposition and make observations to see if the anticipated events occur. But he is likely to make faulty deductions and faulty observations; that is, he is likely to claim the occurrence of events which a dis-

[18] Max Wertheimer, *Productive Thinking*, Harper & Brothers, 1945, p. 198.

interested public cannot detect, or deny the occurrence of events which, to others, clearly happen.

Ideally, perception brings events of one's physical, social, and psychological environment into a person's consciousness with a minimum of distortion. But in normal life it is probable that most persons frequently perceive events which others do not and fail to perceive those which others do, or exaggerate or minimize the significance of events which they see. Rationalization, as defined in Chapter 3, is a matter of creating or disregarding facts in order to support a foregone conclusion. Most of the time it is quite unconscious; in fact, when we become conscious that we are reading into a field what we want to see there instead of what might enable us to make more accurate predictions, we tend to become uncomfortable.

A person is especially likely to experience a failure of perception when he is under heavy emotional pressure. If he feels insecure or frightened, particularly with respect to the integrity of his own personality, he tries to read into the perceptual field whatever immediately appears most likely to restore his security. In other words, if he feels that a cherished belief is under attack, he will read the facts of perception in such a way as to protect and preserve the belief.

Failures in perception are most likely to occur in the closed areas of belief and value. Here a person simply *does not see facts as data.* To him they remain as an insignificant—and perhaps entirely undifferentiated—part of his perceptual field, bearing no relevance to the issue under consideration. Consequently the facts do not change his thinking or behavior. We can hardly expect a person to incorporate data into his thinking when he remains unaware of their presence or significance. As Lewin says, "Since action is ruled by perception, a change in conduct presupposes that new facts and values are perceived." [19] Simply telling a person that data are there is often futile. If his perception does not permit him to see them, we must approach the problem in such a way as to remove the distorting factors.

We have not yet distinguished clearly the role of perceptual failure in blocking changes in behavior. Failure of perception may prevent changes in insight. But very often changes in insight appear to occur, without the changes in values (and their corresponding behaviors) which we would expect to result. When this is the case, it would follow from the theory of learning presented in Chapter 2 that other, competing insights remain

[19] Kurt Lewin, *Resolving Social Conflicts,* p. 63.

which furnish warrant for the old values. In short, we assume that all values and related behaviors issue logically from insights, and the former will not change unless the latter change also. But a person may hold to competing and contradictory insights (with corresponding contradictory values and attraction toward contradictory behaviors). In this case, the insights, attitudes, and behaviors which seem most attractive at the time remain dominant.

With the foregoing interpretation we may explain a phenomenon which was noted earlier in the chapter: namely, that a person may appear to accept a new set of facts, opposed to what he has heretofore accepted, without *observable* changes in behavior (see p. 132). If we understand that an individual in such situations is dominated by one of two competing cognitive structures and corresponding behavioral sets, then it is clear that he is a victim of inconsistency, either recognized or unrecognized. Failure of perception in this case is a failure to recognize the inconsistency.

Once a person is aware of inconsistency, we assume that he will take steps to change one of the two competing outlooks (and its corresponding behavioral pull). If he has a strong emotional need, however, to follow his old (and, to disinterested observers, perhaps less wise) pattern of behavior, he is likely to try to minimize the conflict, to try to live with it, or to escape through some neurotic response. However this may be, it should be apparent that failure to adjust overt behavior to what seems to be a change in insight is a problem of inconsistency and pedagogically must be treated so. In a democratic school, such incompatibilities are studied reflectively.

What are the conditions under which perception achieves maximum accuracy? How can we set the stage so that a person will most easily adopt new outlooks or see his inconsistencies?

In so far as experimental evidence allows an answer, it appears that the first requirement is a *non-threatening* emotional atmosphere. We referred to this need for accepting, non-menacing atmospheres earlier in the chapter as we discussed experience with psychotherapy and work with normal groups. What are the specific conditions of a non-threatening climate? A *threat*, as the term is used here, is anything said or done by others which *appears to a learner* to jeopardize his present beliefs. It is the equivalent of an anticipated attack on the self. A normal individual wants to maintain a feeling of consistency and adequacy in his beliefs and values, which feeling is what we mean when we refer to integration or integrity of personality. A person's knowledges and values may be shot through with inconsistency and confusion, but if the person is not aware of this, he may continue to feel integrated. If he does feel that someone is trying to destroy his integrity of self, he is likely to resist. Rogers describes this problem very well: "Experience which, if assimilated, would involve a change in the organization of self tends to be resisted through denial or distortion of symbolization. The structure and organization of self appears to become more rigid under threat; to relax its boundaries when completely free from threat. Experience which is perceived as inconsistent with the self can only be assimilated if the current organization of the self is relaxed and expanded to include it." [20]

For a climate to seem non-threatening, it is necessary for a subject to feel that no one is trying to judge him. He needs to feel completely accepted. He is particularly likely to resist criticism if it comes from someone he regards as having arbitrary power and authority over him. He needs to feel complete freedom to express his opinions without danger of censure, no matter how ill formed or unorthodox they may be.

The type of climate in which a person feels so secure that he dares entertain evidence contrary to present knowledge and values seems best achieved in a small, face-to-face group in which warmth and permissiveness have been deliberately cultivated. Some techniques which a teacher may use in creating such a situation, and in leading a class to change its views and behavior, will be discussed in the following section and further illustrated in Chapter 8.

CLASSROOM TECHNIQUES FOR ASSISTING CONCEPTUAL AND BEHAVIORAL CHANGE

Reducing Threat and Promoting Open-Mindedness. We have suggested that a student feels threat to his ego if he regards his beliefs as under fire. The intensity of threat depends on its source, its power, and the valuation placed on beliefs which are in jeopardy. Unless threat can be largely eliminated, a student is not likely to entertain evidence contrary to present beliefs or, when facts warrant, to change his mind. Several techniques are available for keeping a sense of threat to a minimum.

One rule is that a teacher should treat student opinions with respect. This does not necessarily mean that a teacher expresses approval; but he avoids ridicule or sarcasm, or any expressions which might be so interpreted by students. He does not cast aspersions on the intelligence or motives of students who render serious opinions. Opinions offered in good faith are

[20] *Client-Centered Therapy*, p. 390.

taken for what they are—the best insights which students have been able to achieve up to then.

On occasion, as during relatively undirected discussion preceding serious study of an issue, it may be advisable for a teacher to give students plenty of opportunity to express the very beliefs which he hopes later to bring under question. It may even help for a teacher to express considerable sympathy with these ideas—for the time being to "go along." Lewin, for example, recommends that a group leader may get farther by letting members of a group freely express the very values which he hopes to change because "a feeling of complete freedom and a heightened group identification are frequently more important at a particular stage of re-education than learning not to break specific rules." [21]

When a teacher wishes to challenge an opinion expressed by a student, he should do it in such a way that conflict is internalized. That is, the student is made to feel the conflict within his own personality. He may not feel a problem, or at least not the problem which the learning situation demands, if he sees the conflict merely as a contest between him and someone else. For this reason a teacher should not argue with a student. Arguments between students also are usually fruitless. When a teacher desires to contest the opinion of a student, he may best handle it something like this: "You have an opinion, and I think I understand and appreciate your reasons. But there are contrary opinions which are widely held in this country. I wonder if there is any merit in a point of view such as . . . ?" The student is thus asked to entertain, not an opinion of the teacher or a classmate, but simply an opinion which "some persons" hold. Experiments cited by Lewin and noted earlier in the chapter suggest that, when a group is presented with a problem to discuss, beliefs and behaviors contrary to those accepted by group members are more likely to be seriously entertained and later adopted if the problem is discussed with reference to persons other than themselves, at least in early phases of discussion.

Another means of inducing students to internalize conflict is to arrange the learning situation so that facts "speak for themselves." Other things being equal, facts—especially if impersonal, sharply relevant, and simple enough to be easily grasped—are more likely than expressions of opinion to break through an emotional barrier. This is particularly true if the facts are coming to a student in life situations. It may then only be necessary to remind a student of their relevance and their bearing on a problem. For

[21] *Resolving Social Conflicts*, p. 68.

example, a trip to a slum may speak eloquently against the notion that everyone is adequately housed, or the witnessing of a congressional investigation over TV may show quite convincingly that traditional American principles of fair play are not always employed. Lewin has suggested that "An individual will believe facts he himself has discovered in the same way he believes in himself or in his group." [22]

In most instances it probably pays to minimize, or at least not encourage, expressions of personal opinion in social-studies classrooms. Issues may be handled as issues and propositions discussed on their merits. The learning enterprise should focus on raising questions about what will come of acting in accordance with a given proposition or hypothesis. An opinion may be converted to a proposition by saying, "Here is an opinion which is before the class. Let us take it as a proposition to be tested. If it is true, what consequences may we deduce from it?" If propositions are relevant to beliefs of students, then students often make their own connections. Even though beliefs are not studied directly, significant revisions may come. It is necessary, of course, that students do see connections; if emotional blocking prevents this, steps must be taken to expand perception. Perhaps only mentioning the connections will be enough; perhaps patient effort will be needed further to reduce emotional barriers.

Encouraging Group Decision. A student is more likely to drop prejudices, revise his moral values, or make almost any other type of significant change if he is a member of a group *which is making the same change together*. Assuming that a teacher does all he can to produce a non-threatening climate, what can be done to form a class into a true in-group, a "team," so to speak, and help them, as a team, to change basic outlooks?

Although significant learning may occur in discussion groups formed of strangers, learning in areas of strong prejudice (such as in the closed areas) seems more likely to occur in groups characterized by friendships and some degree of mutual intimacy. There may be sound pedagogical advantages in helping students become well acquainted with each other, whether simply through classroom informality or by deliberately fostering out-of-school contacts.

Cliques, self-contained groupings based on religious or social class affiliations, racial groupings, or associations based on academic achievement may develop within any school and be reflected in a single classroom. Such groupings may entirely omit certain students, who in turn become social

[22] *Ibid.*

isolates. With development of subgroups of this sort, especially if chauvinistic attitudes are involved, a class may become badly split and team spirit difficult to achieve. If observation or use of sociometric devices suggests to a teacher that an unhealthy social situation exists in his classroom, he should take steps to alleviate it.[23]

In establishing group feeling, there are possible advantages to be gained from group study and group projects. When this sort of thing is attempted, it is usually necessary to divide a class into small groups and to see that the same students do not always work together. A committee system can ordinarily be made to work fairly well for gathering information. Whether it can be made to function in reflective evaluation of data and the productive solution of problems depends on the maturity of students and their familiarity with the rules of reflection. Generally, a teacher must be central to reflective deliberation if it is to be productive.

Encouragement of full and free communication among members will heighten the cohesiveness of a group. If students understand each other, they will almost inevitably work together better as a group. A teacher should urge and help students to state opinions and propositions meaningfully. He should discourage use of emotive language, particularly when students are inclined to direct personal jibes at each other. He should make certain that every member has a chance to be heard and is correctly interpreted.

A teacher's personality may contribute much to group spirit. A teacher can add warmth to a classroom by smiling frequently and keeping a weather eye open for jokes which will appeal to students. He should cultivate a friendly interest in everybody and demonstrate it by expressions of concern over student problems and a knowledge of affairs in which students are involved.

Although important, these suggestions concerning the development of "groupness" are peripheral to the problem. In a given learning situation, group spirit probably hinges primarily on whether all members of a class feel personally involved in the problem under study. If motivation to study a problem is high, a common interest exists which transcends lack of acquaintance, clique interests, or personal antagonisms. In the final analysis, whether group spirit is achieved at the point where it is needed—where a

[23] One of the most useful references on means of analyzing the social structure of groups and techniques to use in establishing greater cohesiveness is Helen Hall Jennings, *Sociometry in Group Relations: A Work Guide for Teachers*, American Council on Education, 1949.

problem is to be studied and beliefs are to be changed—depends largely on a teacher's skill in focusing effort on a common goal.

No matter how great their internal rapport, groups do not change beliefs automatically. As we have observed, the most effectual situation for producing group change appears to be a democratically led discussion. For purposes of the present analysis, probably the most important aspect of discussion (or other modes of study) designed to change basic attitudes is that it have the quality of freely permitting self-learning. (This should not be taken to mean absence of directedness.) We have already noted, in our discussion of threatening situations, that students resist outside pressure to change opinions. As Lewin has indicated, the object in achieving change is not to apply pressure from outside but to remove counterforces within the individual.[24] Although a teacher can and usually must help in the removal of these counterforces, students must perform the actual removal. If they can independently explore a problem, feeling no authoritarian pressure from above to explore it in a particular way or emerge with particular conclusions, they are much more likely than otherwise to undergo real and permanent changes in conceptual and behavioral patterns. They need to be encouraged to use investigatory techniques of their own, to explore by themselves provocative readings, trips, interviews, radio and TV programs, and the like. A teacher's role here is to suggest possible directions of exploration and to help students evaluate facts which are exposed.

For maximum change, permissive discussion of problems should culminate in group decisions. That is, in addition to discussing and studying a problem, students as a group should consider what conclusions are warranted, what these conclusions mean to them, and what if anything they intend to do about them. Students need to communicate their views to each other, so that intentions of each are known to all. If it is evident to individuals that most members of a group have revised their outlooks and expect to change their behavior in stated ways, then members who are reluctant to change because of long-standing attachment to certain beliefs may find change easier. This should not be interpreted to mean that a group or its leader should pressure individual members to accept conformity. We are referring to changes which individuals see the logic of making but find difficult because of opposing forces. The opposing forces are often social pressures exerted by peer culture, community mores, or parental dictates.

[24] Kurt Lewin, "Group Decision and Social Change," in *Readings in Social Psychology,* p. 342.

These may be combatted more successfully if a student feels that others intend to combat them with him.

Ideally, group decision should represent consensus. Proposed changes in belief normally should be kept within the bounds of what is possible for all. If a group is in agreement on the rules of reflective methodology, if it confines its learning operations to the testing of propositions which may be defined operationally, and if the threat-removing techniques employed by a teacher are sufficient so that without serious inhibitions all students are able to examine pertinent facts, then at least some degree of consensus is likely. This point of view assumes that for many problems there will, at a given time, be a "best" answer, in the sense that one hypothesis, more than any other, will adequately harmonize data deduced from it. This is a denial of the common belief that "every problem has two sides" and the further implication that "one opinion is as good as another." Of course, if consensus based on reflection is impossible, no attempt should be made by a teacher to force it.

A Teacher's Role in a Democratic Classroom

Within a democratic framework there is room for disagreement as to the amount of centralized direction which is required. According to definitions previously suggested, a democratic group is distinctively different from a laissez-faire or authoritarian group. It would seem as unreasonable to try to establish these as completely hard-and-fast categories as any other differentiated concepts. A democratic group might, under certain circumstances, operate with a minimum of centralized leadership and appear to approach the laissez-faire extreme. On the other hand, it might delegate to particular persons positions of such authority as to appear to approach the authoritarian norm. (The former extreme might be illustrated in a small adult study group, the latter in a democratic nation which, during a war, grants extraordinary powers to its executive branch.)

We would place a non-directive discussion group, as defined by Rogers and others, near the laissez-faire end of our scale. We would hesitate, however, to place such a group outside the democratic framework. Although under certain circumstances it may resemble anarchy (which is not necessarily the same as chaos), a non-directive group may also produce firm leadership from within its own ranks and formulate and pursue purposes with dispatch and efficiency. When non-direction is employed with an immature group, however, such an outcome is doubtful.

151

We would place an ordinary classroom, as dominated by a textbook-recitation procedure and arbitrary decision-making by a teacher, near the authoritarian end of the scale. This is not to suggest that, if a teacher has certain types of authority over students, a teaching-learning situation necessarily violates democratic practice. We shall try to show how such authority may be compatible with democracy. Many classrooms, however, gravitate in structure and pattern of leadership toward the concept of an authoritarian group, as defined in experiments by Lippitt and White.

It is not enough simply to say that in a classroom a democratic pattern is preferable. Democracy in a classroom and democracy in adult discussion or psychotherapeutic groups ordinarily take different forms. In examining the form of democracy in a classroom the following points are pertinent:

1. Although it gives us valuable clues with respect to the dynamics of emotion, experience with therapeutic groups is not fully applicable in classrooms. A typical group of students is composed chiefly of normal persons. The conceptual structure of an ordinary student is often inadequate in the sense that it is a poor guide to behavior—owing to erroneous, incomplete, and contradictory concepts. But concepts of a typical student are certainly not so inaccurate as to be largely unusable, as is the case with insane persons or incapacitated neurotics. Conflicts may be troublesome for ordinary high-school and college students and emotional disturbance may become conspicuous at times, but we do not expect to find deep neuroses. Basically, then, persons with whom a teacher deals are different from those with whom a professional therapist deals.

This difference, between normality and abnormality, immediately suggests some differences in the job of a leader. Emotional blocking which might prevent reflection is probably much easier to remove in a normal group than in an abnormal group. A psychotherapist working with abnormals must usually use extreme and time-consuming methods in order to relieve repression to a point where insights can become reliable predictive tools. Furthermore, a private counseling session or a small discussion group of disturbed adults led by a psychiatrist represents a situation where more drastic means for relieving inhibition may be used. The mores of our culture do not tolerate in school classrooms the freedom of expression which can be permitted in a true therapeutic group. Whenever catharsis requires that a person talk freely about deep personal issues which would seem shocking or embarrassing to others, the case is one not for a teacher but for a trained therapist. One major difference, then, between a social-studies class and a therapeutic group is that the former will be less free to delve deeply into personal problems, less free to tolerate extreme and shocking expressions of opinion.

Thus it is both possible and desirable in a classroom to place more emphasis on intellectual experience and less upon catharsis than is done in a therapeutic group. It seems preferable to think of the expression of emotion—of catharsis—as a *tool* for achieving conceptualization rather than as an end in itself. What we want in a social-studies classroom is an increase in amount and an improvement in quality of thinking. Emotional release is to be encouraged only as it helps to achieve reflection.

In the literature of client-centered psychotherapy we find the opinion that, if a patient is placed in a non-threatening, accepting climate and allowed to talk freely about his problems, he will by himself gain more adequate insights. In a social-studies classroom, however, a good psychological climate and free discussion are not usually enough to produce accurate insight *because of the difference in learning goals and type of problems discussed.* In a social-studies classroom many of the problems treated involve complex social issues and complicated and extensive evidence. Many of the data required to work with them successfully are unknown to students. Although relatively undirected discussion may be desirable to get issues into the open, to expose data from the prior experience of pupils, and to reduce repression, it is not enough. If students do not know what a tariff is, for example, such discussion will not make them more intelligent about tariff issues. A teacher must be in charge to lead discussion, inject criticism, suggest research, and in general head the learning enterprise.

2. How far can we go in applying to a social-studies classroom principles of democratic leadership as developed through experiences of the democratic group-leadership movement? First, a classroom can and should be fully as democratic as any adult group. There are impelling reasons: School may be the only part of a child's environment where he has a chance to experience by living it the meaning of democracy. All too often he experiences authoritarian practices in home, church, and part-time employment. Not that a person must necessarily be able to live democratically in order to learn to appreciate democracy; it is conceivable that while in a concentration camp a person could learn to appreciate democracy deeply. But probably a child is more likely to understand and value democracy through direct experience with it than in any other way.

Once having stated the necessity for democracy in classrooms, we must make certain qualifications. In a democratic society every member has an equal share in determining the goals and behavioral rules of the society, an equal share in deciding which freedoms and restraints are to apply. But this democratic principle applies only to the larger group (i.e., the entire society), which may limit the jurisdiction of its own subgroupings in any way it pleases. For example, jurisdiction over certain matters is left to adults, under the assumption that children are not competent to decide some things. Within the limits of their jurisdiction, students should have the same right of equal participation in decision making as adults.

Let us explore further the question of jurisdiction. Adults have seen fit in various ways to limit the overt behavior of children. For example, children are not permitted to destroy property, to flout community mores, or to loaf through school (when it can be helped). The adult community holds teachers responsible for seeing that the actions of children conform to these rules. In this sense a teacher is a representative, or agent, of the larger community. Although a democratic teacher will encourage his students to discuss problems of behavior, independently formulate rules which are reasonably compatible with those of the larger community, and obey them voluntarily, he must retain the right to overrule students if necessary. On some questions a teacher's vote must remain a majority vote. But only where matters of action or overt behavior are concerned. It is presumed that in a democratic school freedom of thought among students is not restricted; students have exactly the same freedom as adult groups. However, even this statement requires qualification.

We have assumed that, if a democratic society is to govern itself wisely, the principle of reflection will be a necessary adjunct of democratic life. We have assumed further that, if a democratic society is to live into the future, the principle of reflection must be extended into all problem areas which seriously threaten democracy. Now not all adult members of a democratic society will agree that these needs exist. Many persons may reject reflection and the critical study of certain areas of controversy. But probably a majority of adult Americans do uphold the principle of reflection and the necessity of free and critical thought in all areas of general social concern. If this is the case, then teachers may be regarded as agents of the larger community in acquainting students with the rules of accurate thinking and in encouraging them to think seriously about the most troublesome issues. Even when a local community objects to such practices, a teacher's responsibility to the larger group would seem to obligate him, in so far as he is able, to select methodology and content which are reflective and socially important.

Students in a self-governing classroom might select learning experiences capable of making effective citizens of them; but again they might not. Whether or not students want to think, a teacher must be an instigator of thought. If they want to, the job is easier; if they don't, a teacher has to arouse the desire to think. Whether or not students want to study critical social issues, a teacher must see that, to the best of their ability, they do.

The obligations of leaders in adult democratic groups are no different from the obligations of teachers. But because of their greater competence all members of an adult group are to some degree presumably capable of assuming leadership roles. Although in given cases they may not be, members of adult groups are often somewhat acquainted with reflective problem solving and in a position to decide wisely which problems they should pursue. Student groups, on the other hand, are less mature, less cognizant of the meaning of reflection, less aware of troublesome issues in the culture. By and large, therefore, teachers must play a more dominant role than leaders of adult groups.

DISCUSSION QUESTIONS AND EXERCISES

1. Do you know persons who have made noticeable shifts in their fundamental beliefs as a result of classroom experiences? Can you identify changes which you yourself have made? Under what circumstances have you observed such shifts?
2. Does a democratic culture, more than any other, provide conditions which make for open-mindedness and mental flexibility? If so, is this an asset or a liability?
3. Have you known of situations where students reëxamined and perhaps revised basic beliefs under the direction of a tyrannical teacher? If so, does such behavior contradict the hypotheses advanced in Chapter 7? Could a teacher be autocratic and permissive at the same time?
4. If a democratic group is the most effective instrument for promoting change in basic outlooks, how do you explain the drastic changes in outlook achieved by Hitler, using methods of propaganda and coercion?
5. Could many of the guidance functions now performed by counselors be performed better in group situations? Does the key responsibility for guidance fall on classroom teachers? What is meant by the expression, "Education is guidance"?
6. Does a search for consensus in a group imply a totalitarian outlook? Can consensus ever be achieved without putting pressure on individuals to conform? Is majority vote a more democratic practice than seeking consensus?

REFERENCES

One of the most provocative treatments of how a teacher or group leader may reduce resistance to new insights among group members is Nathaniel Cantor, *The Dynamics of Learning* (Foster & Stewart, 1946). See also, by the same author, *Learning Through Discussion* (Human Relations for Industry, 1951). Also recommended is Carl Rogers, *Client-Centered Therapy* (Houghton Mifflin, 1951), Chapters 8–9.

More than anyone else, Kurt Lewin has contributed to our theoretical understanding of reëducation through groups. Most pertinent to the theme of Chapter 7 are his *Resolving Social Conflicts* (Harper, 1948) and "Group Decision and Social Change," in *Readings in Social Psychology* (Holt, 1947).

Students who wish a general treatment of the group dynamics movement may read Franklin S. Haiman, *Group Leadership and Democratic Action* (Houghton Mifflin, 1951). Specific applications to classroom teaching situations may be found in Kimball Wiles, *Teaching for Better Schools* (Prentice-Hall, 1952). One of the most useful references on means of analyzing the social structure of groups and techniques for establishing greater group cohesiveness is Helen Hall Jennings, *Sociometry in Group Relations* (American Council on Education, 1949).

Those interested in industrial experiments relating to group behavior will find rewarding Elton Mayo, *Human Problems of an Industrial Civilization* (Macmillan, 1933), T. N. Whitehead, *The Industrial Worker* (Harvard University Press, 1938), or F. J. Roethlisberger and W. J. Dickson, *Management and the Worker* (Harvard University Press, 1941).

A stimulating discussion of the need for directed learning is Boyd H. Bode, *Progressive Education at the Crossroads* (Newson, 1938). Bode forcefully rejects laissez faire in education in favor of a directed, but democratic, pattern.

Chapter 8

Discussion as a Tool of Reflective Learning

Types and Values of Discussion

DISCUSSIONS, like techniques in general, may be classified as *directed* or *undirected,* depending on how much responsibility a teacher takes for guidance. Or they may be *authoritarian* or *permissive,* depending on the degree to which a teacher tries to stamp the group with his own thought processes. It is assumed here that a teacher will always try to maintain at least minimal permissiveness, as suggested and described in Chapter 7. For our purposes, the most useful classification is that based on degree of directedness, and the present chapter will be devoted to explanation and illustration of undirected and directed discussions as tools of conceptual learning.

Since the aim assumed for discussion is conceptual learning and since the kind of conceptualization we wish in the social studies emerges from situations which appear to students to be problematic, the chief interest of the present chapter will be on *problem-solving discussion,* which in the main is necessarily directed discussion. First, however, we shall consider undirected discussion since, although this form is not likely to lead to much conceptualization, it can play a significant preparatory role in the learning process.

UNDIRECTED DISCUSSION

Undirected discussion is informal and loosely organized exchange of views in which no systematic attempt is made to reach conclusions—or, in fact, to follow any predetermined direction. In order to get students to talk freely, the teacher deliberately imposes as few restraints as possible. Undirected discussion is similar to an out-of-class bull session.

Such discussion may serve very worth-while purposes. It requires a student to formulate his own opinions and to watch how they fare in a give-and-take situation. It requires him to listen to the opinions of others. All of this should help an individual student to become more aware of what he believes, and to identify common points of dispute and agreement within the group. It may make him more tolerant of divergent or unorthodox views. Undirected discussion also serves a climate-making function in that it "warms up" a class by making students feel at ease and encouraging backward students to talk. It may also—and this is most important—help a teacher to identify the real problems of students, or to discover unexamined beliefs (prejudices) which can later be brought under question in such a way as to create problems. Undirected discussion may therefore be of great value in helping a teacher plan and lead more organized discussion later.

By and large, classroom discussions tend to be relatively undirected in the sense that no organizational pattern is evident. They are likely to wander, and seldom produce grounded conclusions. Prevalence of this sort of discussion probably results from the fact that, although at times it is difficult to control, little planning is required on the part of teachers or students. Since few teachers understand the potential values of undirected discussion, the largely undirected discussions they conduct may serve no good purpose at all.

But even when used deliberately and purposefully, undirected discussion has conspicuous limitations. It may expose students' problems, but it can do little toward solving problems which require methodical examination of evidence. It may prepare the soil for reflection, but it is hardly capable in itself of supporting sustained reflection. It may create a situation which encourages participation, but it is not designed to lead to continuously constructive effort. The all-but-exclusive emphasis in schoolrooms on relatively undirected discussion or variations of it has led to the charge that typical classroom discussion is a mere "pooling of ignorance." A teacher must know when to permit undirected discussion and when to discourage it.

PROBLEM-SOLVING DISCUSSION

Problem-solving discussion is perhaps indicated when a class needs to reach a decision, form a policy, establish a program, or take some other step in the face of difficulty more or less common to the whole group. It is distinguished from undirected discussion in being a disciplined, sharply pointed form of group thinking. It always has the purpose of moving thought forward. Unless students emerge with increased understanding of issues they confront, it fails to advance its purpose.

The essential task of problem-solving discussion is reflective testing of a hypothesis under the established rules of scientific method. A problem-solving group selects a hypothesis for testing, defines it, determines what kind of evidence is needed to test it, seeks and examines evidence, and comes to some conclusion. Discussion may be led by one person or by all or several members of a group sharing the functions of leadership. These functions include establishing climatic and other conditions for group reflection and helping the group move through the steps of a complete act of thought—or as far in this direction as possible.

Although when writing about the subject one may establish neat classifications, it is much more difficult in practice to lead discussion so that it will appear to an observer to fit into one of the established categories. The terms *undirected* and *problem solving*, as applied to discussions, are relative. Undirected discussion tends spontaneously at various points to develop some of the structure of a problem-solving discussion. And the latter at times may appear undirected. Thus, many discussions fall somewhere between the two types, or alternate from one to the other.

Participants in a problem-solving discussion are limited in the extent and nature of the techniques of inquiry which they can use. For example, they can only mentally perform experiments during discussion proper. They can examine the results of observations and experiments made by others, however, and can plan to do individual or group research during recesses in discussion, deferring decisions until further evidence is before them.

Besides learning the attitudes and skills of reflective method, students may also be expected to gain control of substantial quantities of factual data relevant to problems which concern them. There is reason to believe that factual content acquired in this way is remembered longer, and applied more readily and meaningfully, than that learned through recitation or individual study. Students will also, it is hoped, develop disposition and ability to work closely with others in solving problems of group interest, and move nearer to agreement on basic issues or at least understand better the source of their differences. Achievement of these aims naturally presupposes reasonable skill on the part of a teacher in directing discussion and in encouraging development of discussion skills in students.

Although they may be more apparent than real, problem-solving discussion has certain limitations. Just as serious reflection in an individual may lead into blind alleys and have its periods of frustration and despair, so may coöperative reflection also experience periods of retreat and bewilderment. Discussion may therefore appear to be a time-consuming technique. However, if well led, it is probably one of the most efficient techniques for producing conceptualization. And if we are interested in results which are permanent and functional, discussion is probably one of the most efficient means of teaching informational content.

Discussion gives best results in small groups. To secure the benefits of discussion in very large groups (say, 100 or more) special techniques are required: the panel, round table, or symposium. In most instances, teachers work with groups of forty or less and need not make use of large-group techniques unless they have special reasons for doing so.

The physical requirements of a small-group discussion are simple and can be met in most classrooms. In an ideal situation, students sit around a large table or draw their chairs into a circle. The teacher is at a focal point, but not separated from students by platform, desk, or speaker's stand. If this arrangement is not possible, students may be seated with reasonable compactness near the front of a classroom and the teacher may sit, stand, or move slowly around the room. The purpose of physical arrangement is to promote an informal, friendly atmosphere—one in which all that is said may be readily heard and in which the "total" person speaking may be easily observed.

Some Responsibilities of Leadership

As suggested in Chapter 7, the modern view is that a teacher does not have a monopoly on tasks of leadership. There are certain leadership functions which must be performed if a discussion is to remain for long on a problem-solving level, and it does not matter who performs them, so long as they are performed satisfactorily. It is a teacher's responsibility to see that they are carried out but not necessarily to monopolize their performance himself. Probably the more widely the functions of leadership are distributed the better. This should not be taken to mean that a discussion profits from an absence of direction; it means only that furnishing directedness may often be the coöperative task of several persons. Obviously, a group consisting of young students or students who have had little experience in problem-solving discussion will require more direction from a teacher than other groups.

The remainder of this section deals with a number of the functions of leadership and, wherever it seems profitable, illustrates the conduct of these functions by means of verbatim excerpts from classroom discussions. These transcripts are not supposed to represent perfection in leadership technique; they are meant to be suggestive only.

ESTABLISHING PROCEDURAL RULES

If possible, rules of procedure should be made democratically. That is, class members should be encouraged to initiate and help enforce their own rules. A classroom situation naturally determines the rules. In general, large classes call for stricter application of rules than do smaller groups, and students who are accustomed to discussion can operate under more lenient rules than novices. Procedural rules should never be regarded as ends, but rather as tools. They should be freely modified as a situation demands. Some commonly observed rules follow:

1. Before he speaks, each student gains recognition from the teacher. At times, of course, it may be stifling to require every pupil to first address the teacher; but unless this rule is followed noisy confusion often develops.

2. Students speak one at a time. In spite of a teacher's best efforts, during a heated discussion students will break this and the preceding rule. But a group should learn to accept the rule as the best means of respecting the right of each to be fairly heard.

3. Students gain recognition by raising a hand. Also, as soon as a student is given the floor, all hands go down. The student who is talking deserves the best possible conditions in which to make his point; a roomful of waving arms is a discourtesy.

4. When more than one student wants the floor, a teacher gives preference to a student who has not yet spoken; or if all have spoken, to the student who in the past has said least.

5. A teacher spreads discussion around as much as possible. Any time they show the slightest inclination to speak, he encourages students who are usually silent to talk. He expresses appreciation for the contributions, no matter how feeble, of timid students. He is always careful not to give the appearance of favoring one student, or one group of students, over the rest.

6. A teacher may establish a time limit for individual comments, or a limit on the number of times a single student is allowed to speak. This rule may be needed to prevent a few from monopolizing discussion.

7. The teacher makes sure that students remain impersonal in their re-

marks. Statements such as "That is just stupid . . ." or "Coming from you, I'm not surprised," have no place in discussion.

Establishing and Maintaining a Warmly Permissive Emotional Climate

For good psychological reasons, it is essential that a teacher manage discussion so that students feel relaxed, in a good mood, and free from threat. A distinctive function of discussion is that, properly conducted, it is one of the best tools for inducing permanent changes in beliefs and values. But, as suggested in Chapter 7, most persons find it possible to change their fundamental thought habits only in a permissive emotional climate. Discussion excerpts below illustrate some of the points made in Chapter 7.

In the following two examples the teacher tries to insure that students feel their views are respected.

RUTH: Well—I don't really know much about this subject—maybe I'd better just keep still—

TEACHER: I'm sure we would all like to hear your opinion.

RUTH: I don't think it's fair that we should be partial to industry over agriculture in our tariff rates. That is, industry enjoys a high degree of protection. It wouldn't be fair to lower the tariff on farm goods and keep it on—say—autos.

TEACHER: A good point, a very good point. Your idea is that if we were going to lower tariffs, we ought to lower them equally on agricultural and industrial products.

HAROLD: Well, you know what people always say—it's even in the textbooks— kids should honor and respect their parents. In a way, I believe that but I think parents ought to honor and respect kids, too, and not do some of the things they do.

TEACHER: That sounds like a perfectly reasonable point to me.

HAROLD: Yeah, but as soon as a guy like me says that some parents deserve to be hated and disobeyed—then people start thinking there is something wrong with you.

TEACHER: I should think that generally when a boy or girl hates his parents he has some reason—maybe a pretty good one.

Often a teacher needs to introduce in class opinions contrary to what his students hold. Such opinions should be presented not as personal viewpoints but as positions which are held by some persons, as outlooks common in our society. The following examples illustrate how one teacher tried to introduce fresh opinions and facts without generating resistance among students.

162

Discussion as a Tool of Reflective Learning

TEACHER: You have suggested several possible policies that the government might follow with respect to taxation—but no one has suggested that taxes ought generally to be raised.

JOHN: Who would want taxes raised, anyway?

TEACHER: Maybe it's an idea we ought to explore.

RALPH: Do you think taxes ought to be raised? Or are you kidding somebody?

TEACHER: I wasn't advocating raising taxes. I simply mean that there are some persons who do and that there is a definite school of thought along that line. I thought you might be interested in the line of reasoning of a person who favors higher taxes.

JACK: Well, I don't see why the Western states shouldn't have control of the public land within their boundaries. Local people ought to know how to use it better than a bunch of Washington bureaucrats.

JOE: I never could figure out how the federal government could legally hold title to millions of acres of land in the West anyhow.

MARY: Isn't the whole idea of public lands—well, like socialism in some way?

TEACHER: I think for the moment it might be better to avoid trying to pin labels on it. Wouldn't it be better first to get some of the arguments, pro and con, out into the open?

JOE: My dad's a cattleman and all I've been hearing for years is arguments. And they all add up to one thing.

TEACHER: Would you be willing to grant that there is an argument on the other side—in favor of the present system of federal control?

JACK: Someone must believe it, or things would change.

TEACHER: I'm no expert on this and right now I wouldn't express an opinion one way or another. But there is a line of reasoning which you read fairly often, and unless you know what it is you can't defend your own view intelligently. Some persons who prefer federal ownership and control of public lands do so because they question the competence of most state governments to exercise control wisely. Is there anyone who will volunteer to read a magazine article which came out recently on this subject?

In a permissive classroom, students themselves always carry a large measure of responsibility for their own thinking. That is, they make their own decisions and expect to be asked to defend them. The following excerpts illustrate how a teacher may encourage students to think for themselves.

KAREN: (to teacher) Well, offhand, as things are right now, wouldn't you say there is a need for military preparedness?

TEACHER: I'd rather not try to answer that. Class, Karen is raising a question about our need for military preparedness. How about it? What do the rest of you think?

CHARLES: On this election I'm caught right in the middle. Dad's for the Democratic candidate and mother's for the Republican.

TEACHER: And whom are you supporting?

CHARLES: I just can't decide—I think a person ought to vote for the man, not the party. Which do you think is the better man?

TEACHER: Even if I wanted to try to help you decide, I couldn't until you told us what you mean by "better"—what is it you want in a President?

CHARLES: Well, that's not easy. You make a problem out of it. I suppose honesty might be one thing.

TEACHER: Okay. Why don't you make a list of the qualities you think the candidate should have and then try to see which man fits best?

CHARLES: If I make a list, then will you give me your opinion as to which candidate I ought to support?

TEACHER: I'm afraid not. You will have to decide. But I can help you find what biographical material there is on each candidate.

Just as a student has a right to be heard, he also has a right not to talk if he doesn't want to. Many teachers have found that it is better not to ask questions of designated students, particularly if a question is one which delves deeply into touchy areas of belief. One point of view is that if students want to talk they will volunteer and if they do not want to talk—but are required to—they will give minimal answers. That is, the answers will be sufficiently ambiguous or noncommittal to prevent the student's being exposed to later attack. The teacher is aware of this problem in the following illustrations.

HAROLD: (who has been showing signs of interest but seems reluctant to talk) There are some things—like in connection with the family problems we've been talking about—that you can't tell people.

TEACHER: That's true. If you have a specific case in mind, then use your own judgment about whether you want to mention it.

HAROLD: Well, it fits in but it's sort of personal.

TEACHER: Okay, use your own judgment—you are among friends, you know.

TEACHER: I want to ask several people in the class their opinions of the statement which is written on the board. But I want to repeat that no one needs to feel obligated to answer just in order to seem coöperative. Some of you may not want to say anything at all, and some may want to wait a while until some of the others have had their say. In other words, I'm not interested in putting someone on a spot. James, your name is the one I pulled out of the hat first, so to speak. What is your opinion, if you care to give one?

JAMES: I don't think I have any.

TEACHER: That's all right—maybe you'll get one later and if you do, feel free to express it. How about you, Helen?

164

HELEN: Well, I'm no expert on taxation—
TEACHER: (*laughing*) None of us here is. You're among equals.
HELEN: Well, I'll try.

Humor and good will are indispensable in helping to create a permissive atmosphere. A student is helped to be himself by such displays of warmth. He is helped to eliminate tensions and hostilities. The exchange below modified the tone of a discussion which had lacked warmth:

MELVIN: (following an explanation of some of the details of a plan for Universal Military Training) Some of the things usually associated with the military would be eliminated. In fact, many additional safeguards as to health and morals and the effects of military association would be eliminated or reduced under the type of plan they have in mind.
TEACHER: You mean that they would try to keep the young men away from women, liquor, gambling, and that sort of thing? (laughter)
MELVIN: Well, yes, I'm only quoting. They even have it figured out how many chaplains they would need and plan to locate training centers away from communities which have an—ah—unsavory reputation. (laughter)
TEACHER: I don't think the young men will want to go. (laughter)

FACILITATING COMMUNICATION

Students must be helped to make themselves understood. Sometimes this requires only that a class be asked to be more attentive to what a student is saying or that a contributor be asked to speak louder. More often it involves problems of semantics, of clarification of intended meaning. Communication will be treated in three of its aspects, as follows:

1. Insuring that individuals are heard. Whenever a teacher suspects that some in a class have not heard a statement, he should ask the contributor to repeat it in a louder tone of voice, or he himself should repeat it. Sometimes it is well to investigate how much is being heard by asking, "Did everyone hear what was just said?" Sometimes a teacher can induce shy students to talk louder by standing on the far side of the room from them.

2. Helping to reduce ambiguity. Probably the major cause of faulty communication is ambiguity. This in turn stems from inadequate language skills or a haziness of thought processes. One means of counteracting muddiness is to ask for examples or illustrations.

JANICE: Well, there are all these cases of creeping socialism, as it has been called. Trying to reduce everyone to a common level of wealth, or maybe poverty. That's what I'm talking about—
TEACHER: Can you give an example of creeping socialism?

JANICE: Well, there must be lots of examples—the TVA has been cited—I don't really know—

TEACHER: Do you have in mind activities of the federal government—or state and local governments?

JANICE: I think the threat must come mostly from the federal government.

TEACHER: Then is the TVA as good an example as you can think of? If so, can you tell the class something about the TVA—what sort of organization it is?

Sometimes a student uses an unintended word or phrase which confuses his entire statement. Questioning designed to draw a student out further, to get him to rephrase or repeat, may help, as in this illustration:

GEORGE: I remember one argument of one senator about the excess profits tax— that it should be spread out and cut down—I remember he said, I think—from 20 to 10 or 5 percent and apply it to all industries, instead of 20 percent on some products and none on others.

TEACHER: I don't exactly understand that because the maximum rate under the present excess profits tax is a lot higher than that, and it applies impartially to all firms earning over a certain level of profit.

GEORGE: Well, this senator, as I recall, wanted it spread out more to correspond to our national heritage of taxation—taxes for the all instead of the few, or something—I don't remember. I'm pretty balled up myself. Taxation, in his opinion, should cover food to some extent. I remember his mentioning bread, milk, or something that should have a 5 percent excise tax—

TEACHER: Oh, are you talking about excise taxes?

GEORGE: Yes, excise.

TEACHER: You had us a little confused there—I understood you to say excess profits—

GEORGE: I guess that was a mistake—I meant excise.

Sometimes the easiest means of reducing ambiguity is for a teacher to repeat in clearer language what a student is trying to say, if he can infer what the student is driving at.

GEORGE: One reason I'm opposed to Universal Military Training is because of the effect it would have on the minds of the young men of the country—the army has an outlook which is—well, okay maybe for the army, but to build it up in everybody—

RALPH: I question whether UMT would give everyone who went through it a military outlook on things. A lot of people think it just doesn't carry through. Men that have been in the service—if we take the bunch which went through the last war—when they got out not many had any hankering to start fighting again.

GEORGE: I was thinking of regimentation of thought—not war as a good or bad thing. For example, the tendency of the American people to think every which way, to go around in a circle and off in all directions. The tendency of the army to create a relationship between doing certain things and not doing certain things—respecting higher authority, the aristocrat—more so than the elected authority—that type of thing.

TEACHER: Oh, then you don't mean, George, that UMT would teach aggressiveness—you mean perhaps it would promote the development in civilian life of a caste system, a group who are habitually willing to obey and a group accustomed to commanding—like the Prussian social structure perhaps?

GEORGE: That's right.

3. Helping to overcome concealment. Communication may be hindered because a student hesitates to say what he really has in mind. A thought is lurking in the back of his head of which perhaps he is a little afraid, or which he does not quite understand, so he tries to phrase his comments so as to conceal what is actually there. Often such hidden thoughts include ideas which the student fears are extreme, unpopular in his community, or so lacking in grounds as to be open to attack. He may welcome a chance to examine these ideas critically if he can be helped to do it somewhat painlessly.

Sometimes a teacher can infer what a student is really thinking and state it himself, thus helping a student clarify his own ideas.

MARJORIE: The trouble with most parents is, they are old fogeys. They don't understand how the world has changed.

TEACHER: What do you mean, Marjorie?

MARJORIE: Well, they don't want you to do anything. It's always "don't do this" or "don't do that."

TEACHER: What, for example?

MARJORIE: Well, like going out on a date. They want to know all about the boy—his pedigree for ten generations. (laughter) And if they find anything wrong—and usually they do—they make you stay home.

TEACHER: Do you think high-school students should be allowed to choose their own associates?

MARJORIE: Sure, why not?

TEACHER: Do you think high-school girls should be free to go out with older men—say men of 30 or 40?

MARJORIE: (pause) Well, I guess a lot of people frown on that sort of thing.

TEACHER: But, if students are going to be really free to pick their own associates, then they should be free to run around with anyone they please—no matter what age—

MARJORIE: If I said yes to that—well, I know what people would think—

TEACHER: (laughing) Well, do you stand by your principle of freedom or don't you?

MARJORIE: I might as well be honest—sure I do—but that doesn't mean I'm planning to start dating married men.
TEACHER: But you feel you have a right?
MARJORIE: Yes.

ASSISTING TOWARD SOLUTION OF A PROBLEM

A group needs to be helped to conclude successfully each stage in the process of thought without serious log jams or bottlenecks and to move on to the next stage. A problem-solving discussion has direction and moves— even if sometimes by a circuitous route—toward some sort of conclusion. Some ways in which a leader can assist a group are described and illustrated below. In the next section we shall describe and illustrate in more detail how each step of a problem-solving discussion may be handled.

1. Orienting a group in the nature and purpose of problem-solving discussion. Sometime in each course a social-studies teacher should encourage discussion on the subject of discussion itself, in order to clarify the nature of reflective method, show how reflection may be served by discussion, show the logical pattern of problem-solving discussion, and treat problems of technique required for effective discussion. In most cases, such critical examination should be held early in a course; but with immature students it may be delayed until after the group has had considerable experience in dealing reflectively with content. But in every discussion—no matter how seasoned a group may be—it is always appropriate to raise questions about matters of methodology if thinking would be furthered thereby. The following excerpt illustrates a departure from the formal theme for the purpose of examining basic methodology:

WILLARD: I think I learn more in classes where the teacher lectures and gives definite assignments.
TEACHER: How do the rest of you feel about that?
JAMES: Well—this isn't meant as a criticism of this class—but it seems to me that we often go round and round. Sometimes I can't tell what I've gained from it.
TEACHER: Have our discussions been worthwhile? Has the class learned anything of value from them?
ELAINE: I think it has done me some good just to hear the opinions of other people.
WILLARD: But all you do hear is opinion. I want something more definite than that.
TEACHER: If our discussions have sounded like mere airing of opinion, something must be wrong. There should be some other ends that can be served by

discussion if it's done right. What do you think we ought to aim for when we discuss?

2. Guarding against superficiality and promoting critical-mindedness. Unless taught otherwise, secondary-school students are likely to be highly uncritical. But critical-mindedness is an essential of successful reflection. Closely related to lack of a critical faculty is the tendency to study issues superficially. Students actually may resist digging beneath the surface as a result of repressions, laziness, or habits acquired in previous courses. It is always legitimate for a teacher to press students for evidence whenever they come forth with sweeping generalizations or dubious facts. And whenever an opportunity presents itself a teacher should ask questions designed to expose inconsistency, conflict, or faulty logic, and questions that are probing enough to prevent discussion from confining itself to surface or peripheral matters. Of course, he should not become so much of a gadfly that students become hostile, discouraged, or withdrawn. Questioning should be good humored and tactful and should not go so far as to undermine essential permissiveness.

In the following excerpt a teacher tried to raise questions about an assertion of fact made by a student and in the process achieved a much deeper analysis than would have occurred if the teacher had remained passive.

RAMON: I don't see how we could get by without a protective tariff, that is, not unless we are willing to equalize our standard of living with other parts of the world. And I don't think the people in our nation are ready or willing to do that.

TEACHER: What do you mean by equalizing the standard of living?

RAMON: Well, putting everyone on the same level.

TEACHER: You mean everyone having the same real income—the same buying power?

RAMON: I guess that's it—the same number of cars and radios per capita, the same number of bathtubs, and that sort of thing.

TEACHER: Is it all right if we pursue this question a little farther—it interests me. What is the basis of a worker's income—that is, what determines how much he earns?

RAMON: His wages? Well, if he belongs to a union he is likely to get more. And the more profits an employer makes, the more he can afford to pay.

TEACHER: Maybe we can approach the question better if we try another way. A century ago a factory worker in the United States was lucky to make ten dollars a week; today factory workers average about seventeen or eighteen dollars a day. How do you explain that?

HAROLD: Price inflation probably has something to do with it. And like Ramon said, unions.

TEACHER: But does the average factory worker live better today than he did a century ago? More cars and radios, more bathtubs, better homes and the like?

HAROLD: Oh, sure.

TEACHER: Do you think all of the gain has been due to unions—all the gain in standard of living, I mean?

ELAINE: I think our ability to produce more has a lot to do with it—each worker now turns out a lot more in a day. Because we have better machines than they did then. And mass-production industries.

TEACHER: Elaine is saying that the average worker lives better now than he did a century ago because he is more productive. Is productivity a basis for wages—does the amount a worker can turn out have something to do with what his employer can pay him—and what his standard of living will be?

HAROLD: Naturally. Where is this leading us?

TEACHER: Well, is the labor force of every nation equally productive? I mean, does the average American worker produce as much as, say, the average Chinese worker? What about that, Ramon?

RAMON: I would say the American is much more productive. What has this got to do with the tariff?

TEACHER: I'll try to tie it in. Would you say that eliminating tariffs—pursuing a policy of free trade—would make the Chinese worker as productive as the American?

RAMON: Well—I don't know—I don't see why it would.

ELAINE: I think I get your point—there would still be different levels of productivity under free trade, therefore the people of the most productive nations would continue living better than the rest. Free trade couldn't equalize our standard of living with other parts of the world like Ramon said.

We shall illustrate one other means of helping to induce critical mindedness—getting qualifications attached to overly broad generalizations.

RAMON: Well, I guess I'm one of those reactionaries who believes that you can't change human nature.

TEACHER: I don't know whether holding that belief makes you a reactionary. If so, I would guess that you have lots of company. I would be interested in knowing just what you mean, though, when you say that you can't change human nature.

RAMON: Well, I mean that people are basically the same now as they were as far back as we have any records—as far back as the ancient Egyptians, for example.

TEACHER: Do you mean people have the same customs now?

RAMON: No, not the same customs—oh, I guess some customs haven't changed much.

TEACHER: Do you mean people have the same beliefs today as they had in ancient Egypt—about politics, economics, religion, sex, and so on?

RAMON: No, I don't mean that—you can't say that people haven't changed. But there are some things that don't change.

TEACHER: For example?

RAMON: People have always been and always will be basically selfish. And they still fight wars.

TEACHER: Then you would say that there are a few drives or motives that remain the same?

RAMON: Yes.

TEACHER: Would you say man has changed in more ways than he has remained the same, or remained the same in more ways than he has changed?

RAMON: Well, you've got me there. I suppose I will have to take back part of it. It wasn't a very careful statement.

3. Keeping students on the subject. A teacher should try to hold his group to the point of the discussion, although at times a wise teacher will decide that the point should be changed in midstream. Closely related to this problem is the need to prevent members of a group from obstructing emerging lines of thought with trivial or facetious remarks. Below is an example of how a teacher may prevent discussion from moving in irrelevant directions.

AL: Aren't we giving too much of a superman quality to the atom bomb and too little importance to old-fashioned infantry? I don't think the infantry will ever be replaced, even if only for mopping up operations—

GEORGE: My brother was in Japan and he talked with Japanese people around Hiroshima and also some who lived in Tokyo. Their worst fear—even after the atom bombing—was incendiary bombs.

AL: Our tendency to overrate new weapons is one reason why I'm in favor of UMT. We need a large, well-trained army of foot soldiers—

GEORGE: Can someone explain the principle of the H-bomb? I know the details are all secret, but the general idea has been published I think—can you?

TEACHER: That is a good question—but I am wondering if trying to answer it wouldn't be sidetracking us from the topic of discussion, which is UMT. The effectiveness of the H-bomb is, of course, important to us—but probably not the scientific principles. How about seeing me after class—I can explain all I know in a few minutes.

4. Keeping discussion unified so that form and direction will be clear. Discussions can easily become loosely jointed, if not dismembered. A few tangents, a few repetitions, and a group becomes confused. Points of confusion are usually sensed and sometimes openly revealed by questions such as "Where are we?" A teacher may keep confused wandering to a minimum by (a) making free use of the blackboard, (b) introducing at strategic

points brief summaries and reviews, and (c) reminding the group of the object of the discussion.

TEACHER: So far in our discussion of Universal Military Training, we have talked about its cost, its possible effect on young men, and whether there is a genuine military threat to the United States from enemy nations. Are there any other big questions which would have to be answered in order for a person to take an intelligent stand either for or against UMT?

TEACHER: Do you have the feeling that we are going around in circles, that we need some way to pull the discussion together and see where we are, and decide where we want to go? We began with the question of whether the federal government or private power companies ought to develop Hell's Canyon. Now we are on the government farm program. Did we talk about Hell's Canyon to the point where you feel the significant facts and the chief competing opinions got out in the open? Did we reach a point where you would want to draw any conclusions, or is it still hanging?

Leading a Group Through the Steps of a Complete Act of Thought

As was pointed out in Chapter 6, it is assumed that all legitimate teaching techniques operate to move students through one or more of the steps of a complete act of thought, in accordance with the requirements of scientific methodology. Thus, problem-solving discussion begins by raising questions about established beliefs, and, if enough doubt appears to justify further exploration, moves a group through the formulation and testing of hypotheses and the drawing of conclusions. Very often problem-solving discussion must be combined with other techniques, particularly research activities, if it is to be of maximum fruitfulness.

More specifically, a problem-solving discussion may be regarded as including these steps, though not necessarily in this order:

Step 1: Selecting and introducing the discussion topic.
Step 2: Clarifying and defining the problem.
Step 3: Developing and refining hypotheses.
Step 4: Testing hypotheses.
Step 5: Drawing conclusions.

STEP 1: SELECTING AND INTRODUCING THE TOPIC

Criteria for selection of topics for study presented in Chapter 6 included the suggestions that beliefs which are to be reflectively examined in classrooms should relate to social issues of wide concern, should have controversial aspects, should be held by a considerable proportion of students, and should, in the judgment of the teacher, lend themselves to fruitful study. We shall focus our main attention here on the mechanics of introducing topics which have already been chosen.

The first task of discussion is to confront students with statements which correspond to or bear an evidential relationship to their own beliefs or knowledge. These statements are the discussion "topic" and getting them before students is what we mean by "introducing the topic." The statements correspond to the established beliefs or preconceptions of step 1 of a complete act of thought as described on page 45.

There are two basic procedures for placing before students propositions (or questions) for discussion. One is to get students to make statements about their own beliefs or purported knowledge, as in the following examples:

TEACHER: Tom, as I recall, you had something to say about this question the other day—can you repeat it?

TOM: Well—I think I said that, if we went on a free trade basis we would have another recession—or I guess you would call it a depression—like we had starting in 1929.

TEACHER: That is your considered judgment—that a business depression would follow any general removal of tariffs?

TOM: That's right.

TEACHER: Nancy, without wanting to put you on a spot, I am wondering if you could state your opinion on whether morality is correlated with religious faith —that is, whether people who hold definite religious beliefs are more likely than nonbelievers to follow our conventional moral codes?

NANCY: I understand the question all right. Actually, I've never known many people who were non-religious— Oh, I guess quite a few people I know aren't really deeply religious—it's on the surface pretty much—but at least they claim a religion.

TEACHER: Maybe I'd better rephrase the question. Do you think people who seem deeply religious lead more moral lives, in the conventional sense, than those who take their religion pretty much for granted?

NANCY: Well—I don't know—I think the deeply religious person is more likely to conform to some of the standards that the churches talk about—like not drinking or gambling. I don't know whether what they say is immoral really is or not. For example, I think I approve of social drinking, at least my parents do it.

TEACHER: Would you say then that a deeply religious person is more likely to conform to conventional middle-class moral standards than a person who is only mildly religious?

NANCY: Yes, I think I would go along with that—so long as you'll let me make room for some exceptions.

In the two illustrations, the teacher has succeeded in getting statements of belief before the group. These particular beliefs may or may not be widely shared in the group, and it is evident that in the latter instance the student expressing the belief does not feel very deeply committed to it. In both cases, fruitful discussion of the belief may be possible, provided most other students in the class also have beliefs (including, we might hope, contrary ones) about the same subject.

A second basic procedure for confronting students with statements of belief is to introduce them from outside. Material introduced from the outside will be meaningless unless it is somehow related to previous experiences of students; that is, they must have beliefs of some sort about the material. Psychologically, the role of material introduced from outside is to bring students to recall and formulate more clearly what they already know and believe. Discussion of such material, although on the surface it may appear to be devoted only to testing propositions suggested by the material itself, will have the effect of making students reëxamine and perhaps revise or add to their own beliefs, provided, of course, that the material is relevant.

There are certain advantages to using materials introduced from outside as springboards to discussion. If statements of belief analyzed in class are —in appearance—those of outsiders, then a less threatening emotional climate results. Students do not see their own ideas as under direct attack and can thus remain more relaxed and perceptive. Of course, unless students do make their own connections and view their own notions more critically, the discussion will not have accomplished an educational purpose. A teacher can often tell what is going on in the minds of students by listening to what they say or observing the level of interest which develops.

If a problem-solving discussion is to be instigated through materials introduced from outside, introduction of the subject may, on the surface, seem quite conventional. Students may be asked to read something, to bring reports, to watch a movie, or simply to pay attention while the teacher reads or describes some situation. Any of the conventional sources of content may be used—textbooks, films, clippings, speakers, and trips—provided the content presented contains ideas, facts, or expressions of belief which can be related evidentially to the present beliefs of students. Techniques of presenting such materials may also appear similar to those of conventional subject-centered teaching, except that through questioning or explanation the teacher makes certain that students see clearly the propositions stated or implicit in the materials. The following may demonstrate this point:

TEACHER: Class, I have with me yesterday evening's edition of the comic strip "Blondie." How many of you have read it?
MARGE: Oh, is that where Blondie came home with the new hats?
TEACHER: Yes, how many of you saw that? (Several hands go up) Since some of you missed it, I'll read it. (The gist of the strip is that Blondie has spent a lot of money for foolish-looking hats while Dagwood, who supplies the cash, feels persecuted)
TEACHER: (after reading) What big point, or idea, do you think the cartoonist is trying to communicate?
MARGE: Well, to me the comic strip means that men don't always appreciate women's ideas of style the way they should. Personally, I think Blondie had a right to buy those hats.
TOM: I can't accept that interpretation at all. I think the cartoonist is trying to say that women are slaves to style and that they don't spend money wisely.

STEP 2: CLARIFYING AND DEFINING THE PROBLEM

This step involves getting clearly in mind what the problem is—that is, what it is that is blocking fuller understanding. A danger in discussion is that students will not come to feel involved in a problem—that the problem is only in the mind of the teacher. Step 2 tries to surround with doubt the beliefs or purported knowledge introduced in step 1; or it tries to expose incompatibilities or conflict in students' conceptual patterns. The function of discussion leadership in step 2 is—through questioning or other techniques—to expose inadequacies in the beliefs and knowledge of students, to help students see how their beliefs may be confused, contradictory, or ungrounded. Questioning seeks to make these inadequacies explicit—to define them so clearly that, if it seems desirable, they can be written on the blackboard. A teacher's intention is to raise doubts of the general form "If the one thing is true, how can the other be true also?" If he is successful in revealing to students discrepancies in their thinking, questions such as these will inevitably enter their minds: "Where is the flaw in my thinking?" "What is the right (or a better) answer to this?" and "How can I find out?"

The following example shows how a teacher may reveal inconsistencies through questioning:

TEACHER: (who has just read to the class a story in *Time* magazine about a son in an old, aristocratic New England family—the Stantons—who has been disinherited because of marrying a girl from the slums) What do you think of this story?

ANNE: I guess something like that could happen only in New England.

RUTH: Why not in San Francisco? We have a high society crowd out here that think they are just as important as the upper crust in Boston—

BILL: Going back to the story, I don't think his parents had any right to cut him off from the family fortune—I thought this was a free country—that anybody had a right to marry anyone he wanted to. If I decided I wanted to marry a migrant farm laborer living in a tent—well—no one had better try to stop me.

TEACHER: Do you girls share Bill's feeling that the young man in the story should be allowed to marry anyone he pleases, no matter what her social rank?

EILEEN: I think so. I think it is none of his parents' business.

ANNE: Oh, naturally his parents would be interested—but I think he had the right.

RUTH: I agree—some rich man's son might propose to me sometime. (laughter)

TEACHER: Let's carry this a little farther. From your answers, I take it that most of you don't think much of the idea of some people setting themselves up as better than others—the social arrangement you have when some people are "high society" and feel they are above the common crowd.

EILEEN: Doesn't the Declaration of Independence say everyone is equal? That's a principle of democracy.

TEACHER: Do you take that to mean that they are socially equal, equal in ability, or what?

EILEEN: Well, to me it means equal opportunity for everybody to do what he wants and live a happy life—but I think it means social equality too.

RALPH: I'm not upper crust, but then I don't come from the lower-lower class either. I try to treat everybody alike—no matter which side of the tracks they come from.

TEACHER: Then do all of you go along with the idea that any kind of social discrimination is bad—that we shouldn't have social barriers or social classes based on the feeling that some people are better than others? ("Yes's" and nods indicate general assent)

TEACHER: You have me really interested now. May I ask you some questions along a slightly different line? You may not see right away how it ties in, but I think you will later. How many of you expect to go to college? (A majority hold up hands) All right, fine. Eileen, you say you are going to college—I am wondering if you will be interested in joining a sorority then—if you will agree to go in.

EILEEN: Well, I don't know just what you are thinking of. I probably wouldn't have the money.

TEACHER: Let's assume you could afford it—I know they are often expensive. If you could afford it, and were invited, would you join a sorority?

EILEEN: Well, I don't know for sure—it's quite a long way off. But probably.

TEACHER: How about the rest of you girls? Ruth? Anne? Sarah? (Most girls answer a qualified yes—if they are asked, if it doesn't cost too much, etc.)

TEACHER: Why would you want to join a sorority? Can you tell us, Eileen?

EILEEN: That's a hard question (laughs). I guess it's just the thing to do—it's part of going to college.

TEACHER: There must be a more definite reason than that.

EILEEN: If you were asked, and could afford to join and didn't, then people would think you were a little strange—stand-offish or something.

SARAH: Well, if you go to State—that's a pretty big place—I think you'd feel a little more like somebody, if you joined a sorority.

TEACHER: Oh? What do you mean "You'd feel a little more like somebody?"

SARAH: Well—I don't know exactly—it's hard to explain. I guess you'd feel a little more important.

RUTH: I think maybe Sarah means that people would sort of look down on you if you didn't belong—

TEACHER: What people?

RUTH: Oh—other students—the important students on the campus—the leaders—you know, those who are officers in organizations.

TEACHER: And maybe sorority girls too—would they look down on you if you remained outside a sorority?

EILEEN: I suppose they might—

TEACHER: And, if you joined a sorority, would you look down on girls who didn't get in?

EILEEN: Well—I might feel sorry for them. I wouldn't really look down.

TEACHER: Let me ask this question: Do most of you feel that a sorority or fraternity is a means by which some students try to raise themselves in the eyes of their fellow students?

ANNE: I think so. One means.

TEACHER: Suppose I changed the wording of the question, and said, "Is joining a sorority or fraternity a means of raising your social position?"

EILEEN: I don't like the word *social position*. That sounds like society again.

ROGER: If a person raises himself in the eyes of his associates, then doesn't he have a higher social position?

TEACHER: Eileen, your use of the term *society* interests me. You mean society people, like the Stanton family in the *Time* magazine story?

EILEEN: Well, yes, I guess so.

TEACHER: Do you ever read the society page in the newspaper?

EILEEN: Sometimes. Mother always reads it before anything else.

TEACHER: Have you ever read about the affairs of sororities on the society page —about their parties and what the girls wear and that sort of thing?

EILEEN: Why, yes.

TEACHER: Could that be one reason girls join sororities—to get their pictures and names in the society pages?

ROGER: May I say something? You girls say you are opposed to social class, social discrimination, and things like that. You think it's awful if old man Stanton gets mad at his son for marrying someone who's socially below him. But sororities do the same thing—I know because I have a cousin who's in one and she now thinks she's top of the heap—

177

ANNE: I think maybe we've been trapped—you (looks at teacher) deliberately maneuvered us into that—some of us anyway. I think what you are trying to get across is that a lot of sorority girls are trying to accomplish the same thing through their sororities that Mr. Stanton was trying to do when he disinherited his son.

TEACHER: I wasn't trying to trap you. I only wanted you to think about it and see for yourselves.

EILEEN: I guess I will be a different kind of sorority girl—if I ever join one.

TEACHER: Maybe some of you would want to take back what you said about social equality—maybe it isn't always a good idea.

ROGER: I think practically everybody—especially girls—would be snobs if they had half a chance—it's human nature.

EILEEN: Why does Roger pick on the women? Men are just as bad.

RUTH: I wonder—maybe we all violate the idea of equality every day.

In the following example, the teacher tries to expose through questioning a contradiction in the editorial policies of a newspaper. Because he is using outside materials of an impersonal nature, rather than the stated beliefs of students, he can expose the conflict more quickly and directly. Less caution is needed, because students are less likely to feel their personal beliefs are in public jeopardy.

TEACHER: Chapter 19 of your textbook—which you are assigned for tomorrow—discusses the Department of the Interior, and in connection with that the work of the Federal Bureau of Reclamation. I want to start your thinking about some of the issues involved by reading two editorials which I clipped from the local paper. The first has to do with the generation and sale of electricity in federal projects. (Teacher reads from editorial, which begins as follows: "The cost of federal irrigation water would be prohibitive in most areas if not for income from the sale of government-generated power. The power features of Reclamaton projects have to date made the projects feasible for water users. To argue, as Senator —— has, that Reclamation should sell its power at cost to private utilities, and that in future projects Reclamation ought to stay out of the power business entirely, is to argue against the very future of the West. The Senator's contention that such projects are socialistic is matched only in absurdity by some of his other arguments. . . . Etc.")

TEACHER: What do you make of this editorial? What is the writer saying?

TOM: It seems clear enough—he thinks the Reclamation Bureau ought to keep on generating power and selling it at a profit. And applying the profits on the cost of the project.

TEACHER: Does the editorial writer think government generation of power is an example of socialism?

VERNON: He says—as I interpret it—that Senator —— is crazy—or words to that effect—for using the term *socialism*.

TEACHER: Well, I want to read you an editorial from the same paper—not the

178

same issue, but one which came out about a week later. This editorial is about a different subject—it seems—the present labor government in Britain. (The editorial starts as follows: "It is now the expressed intention of the labor government to nationalize British steel. Thus, one of Britain's most important manufacturing industries seems destined to go the way of coal, electricity, communication and transportation, and all the other industries that have felt the socialistic ax. How long will it take the labor government, we wonder, to realize the disastrous consequences of government ownership. . . . Etc.")

TEACHER: Now, what would you say the attitude of the writer is toward the nationalization of industry?

ANNE: He obviously doesn't think much of it in England—he's very bitter I would say—

ARNOLD: I would say he doesn't think much of it anywhere.

TEACHER: What, exactly, do you persons understand by the term *nationalization?*

TOM: I think it means the government taking over and operating business— doesn't the editorial say socialism and nationalization are the same—that is, nationalization leads to socialism?

TEACHER: All right. Let's say it means the socializing of industry. Industry is socialized when it comes under government ownership. Now, I want you to compare these two editorials, to consider them side by side. Do you see any inconsistency—anything which doesn't seem to jibe?

VERNON: Will you read the first one again—or part of it? (Teacher rereads editorial) Well, it seems to me that one editorial attacks government ownership and the other one praises it.

RALPH: But they are talking about government ownership in different fields— steel and electric power.

TEACHER: Would you say that when the government goes into the electric power business that is socialism?

TOM: It depends on how the government does it—if it benefits all the people, it isn't socialism.

TEACHER: Then you would say that Shasta Dam is not an example of socialism?

TOM: Well, it was built for all of us—it was authorized by a democratically elected Congress.

VERNON: Tom has already said that when the government takes over an industry, that is socialism. I don't see any difference between government ownership here and any place else.

TEACHER: You mean it's all socialism—by definition?

VERNON: Sure.

TEACHER: Getting back to the editorials—how many of you think that the writer —if it was the same man—was contradicting himself when he said one time that government electric power in the United States is not socialism, but government steel in England is?

TOM: Maybe there's a contradiction—but I wouldn't want to call Shasta Dam socialism—then I would have to be against it. (laughter)

TEACHER: Do you feel that perhaps some people in this country think that government ownership of industry in a foreign nation is socialism, but that when it happens here it is merely economic progress?

TOM: Just what is socialism, anyway? Everyone seems to think it's so bad, but, if Reclamation Projects are socialism—well, I don't know. I'm all confused, I guess.

STEP 3: DEVELOPING AND REFINING HYPOTHESES

This step is initiated by asking students general questions such as "Do you have any ideas which explain this discrepancy?" "Can you think of any solutions?" or "What are some possible answers?"

It is necessary to illustrate two procedures which are associated with step 3. One illustration will be of procedures used in moving from judgments of value which are at issue to judgments of fact capable of serving as hypotheses. The other will show how a group may refine judgments of fact in an effort to remove ambiguity and make their operational meaning clear. If step 2 deals only with judgments of fact, then step 3 will normally confine itself to their refinement. That is, the initial statements of belief brought under inquiry *become* the hypotheses of step 3. Step 3 involves the formulation of new ideas only when the judgments treated in step 2 are normative in content and not susceptible to the direct test of empirical data.

TEACHER: Yesterday we were discussing the pros and cons of drinking. I think you were concerned mainly with teen-age drinking. I gathered that a number of you were somewhat on the fence—you still hadn't made up your minds one way or another. Just what were some of the issues that came up?

MURIEL: Spud was arguing—I don't know if he meant it—that it's okay for anyone who is a senior in high school to do social drinking—with his parents maybe —like a glass of wine before dinner, or a cocktail in the evening.

TEACHER: Was there any opposition to Spud's opinion?

SPUD: Several people—Marion was one—thought that nobody, young or old— anyplace or anytime—should ever drink anything alcoholic. I suppose she might except vanilla extract when it's used in cooking—

TEACHER: Was the issue, then, between social drinking and total abstinence? I thought maybe some of you were concerned with drinking in still a different situation—

DAN: We were talking about the drinking high-school kids do on dates and at parties—or at games. I don't think we got very far into the morals of that.

TEACHER: Well, then, we have represented in class the opinion that no one should take alcoholic beverages in any situation. Let's get that idea down first. (Writes this on blackboard) And didn't someone also say yesterday that it's okay for adults to drink—persons over 21—but not for teen-agers?

MURIEL: Yes, that point was made. I think it was Anne.

Discussion as a Tool of Reflective Learning

TEACHER: (Writes statement on board) These two opinions both state that it is wrong for teen-agers to drink. Now what were some of the ideas on the other side?

SPUD: Put down mine—that social drinking done temperately and with adult supervision ought to be accepted.

TEACHER: (Writes: Supervised social drinking among high-school youth is proper.) Is there anyone who approves the idea that unsupervised drinking is okay—at parties or on dates?

LOWELL: I know some kids who do it—quite a few in fact. They talk older people into buying the stuff for them.

TEACHER: Do you approve it?

LOWELL: Well, that's a hard question. Probably not—but a lot of pressure is put on you sometimes. It's hard not to go along with the crowd.

TEACHER: Shall I put this down anyway, as a possible position one might take? If none of you accept it, there must be some teen-agers who do. (Writes)

TEACHER: Well, shall we begin with the first of these beliefs—people should not drink under any circumstances? What are some reasons for holding this belief? Marion, you ought to have first chance.

MARION: Well, I think drinking is wrong—immoral.

TEACHER: Is that saying in different words the same thing we have down—or at least not going much beyond it? I think we would be interested in some of the reasons *why* a person might think it's immoral.

MARION: Well—that's what my parents have always said. They don't drink.

TEACHER: Hm-m-m. Maybe you can tell us why your parents hold their opinion.

MARION: Well—they talk about it at home. I guess mother would say that most broken homes are caused by drink, and when a person starts he can't stop. She has a brother—well, I'd better not talk about that. (laughter)

TEACHER: Shall I write down these two reasons for not drinking, then? Drinking leads to broken homes and anyone who drinks at all is likely to become an excessive drinker?

MARION: That about sums it up, I guess.

TEACHER: Are these statements which we could show to be true or false?

MURIEL: I should think so. Wasn't there something in the textbook about drinking and the divorce rate?

Sometimes it is not possible to find reasons for holding value judgments which are both judgments of fact and susceptible to reflective testing. In this case, discussion may end with the conclusion, "These values cannot be supported by intellectual means; they are a matter of faith alone."

The following illustration shows the equally important, and even more difficult and painstaking, job of refining judgments of fact in the direction of usable hypotheses.

TEACHER: We have on the board the proposition "The excess profits tax stifles business initiative." Is the meaning of this statement clear enough so that you are ready to begin talking about its truth or falsity?

ANDY: It isn't clear to me. I know in general how the excess profits tax works—we have already talked about that. But that word *stifle* bothers me.

JAMES: I should think it might mean stop or shut off.

ROBERT: Then you would have to throw the statement out. Business hasn't been stopped or shut off—that sounds like destroyed—by the excess profits tax.

ELAINE: Well, maybe we could define it to mean simply slowed down.

TEACHER: Slowed down in relation to what?

ELAINE: Well, in relation, say, to what is possible.

TEACHER: Then could we define stifle in this case to mean slowed below the maximum possible amount of initiative? (Teacher rewrites statement.)

ANDY: That is certainly a more cautious statement—it's a lot clearer. But I doubt if it's true.

AL: Let's try to get the proposition worded right before deciding whether it is true. I don't know for sure what business initiative means.

TEACHER: A good point. Does anyone want to try to define it?

JAMES: Well, it means a willingness to go ahead.

TEACHER: To go ahead? Is that clear to everyone?

AL: What does he mean by go ahead? It seems to me that taking risks is a better term.

TEACHER: Then you would want to say, The excess profits tax reduces willingness to take risks below what it would be without the tax?

ELAINE: I don't like the use of the term *willingness,* but I'm not sure why.

TOM: I don't see how you could measure anything like willingness—we are trying to get a statement which we can prove one way or another.

ELAINE: How about this—suppose we said, The excess profits tax slows down the rate of expansion of business below the maximum possible rate. Willingness to take risks produces expansion, but expansion is something you can talk about more objectively.

TEACHER: Would you go along with a little simpler statement, say, When an excess profits tax is in effect, business expands more slowly than at other times?

STEP 4: TESTING HYPOTHESES

A teacher's first move in connection with step 4 usually is to ask, "How can we go about deciding whether this idea—or solution—is a good one?" or "What kind of information do we need and where can we get it?" Questions like these place responsibility on students for determining methods of testing. This helps them visualize better the procedure they are following, helps them develop a more critical outlook toward use of evidence, and helps to train them in the full use of the problem-solving method.

Of course, there may be no means of testing the hypothesis, as would be the case if a class were dealing with the statement "There are other planets in the universe which support life similar to that on earth." Or the available evidence may be so complex or so difficult for students to comprehend that testing is impossible. When no tests can be devised, discussion will end without fulfillment of step 4. In this case, again, a group may discover that the only conclusion it can draw is that no conclusion is possible.

The following illustration shows how one group of students approached step 4.

TEACHER: Here is the proposition before us: When an excess profits tax is in effect, business expands more slowly than at other times. How are you going to test it? What sort of data would you need?

HAROLD: You could check the rate of expansion of business during the years in which the excess profits tax has been in effect and you could compare that with rates of expansion before that time.

JAMES: I don't think your results would be very dependable. There are too many things which might enter in to throw it off—like wars, for example.

TEACHER: How could war affect it?

JAMES: If you have an excess profits tax only during a war, then business might be expanding pretty rapidly due to government spending and the pressure of war necessity. The rate might be higher than in peacetime, but how would you know that the rate would not have been still higher without an excess profits tax?

HAROLD: I know the approach has its weaknesses—but it might give you some clue.

GEORGE: There is a lot of literature on both sides—I don't know just what all the arguments are, but probably some of the literature discusses the tax in relation to the rate of business expansion—or maybe it talks about incentive.

ELAINE: If the literature does nothing but argue about the effect of the tax on incentive—or initiative—that won't help much. That's dealing with personal motives and not necessarily behavior.

GEORGE: Well, I never really got finished. I was going to say that we might try to get hold of some pamphlets—publications of, say, the CIO on the one hand and the NAM on the other.

JAMES: Or you could read the *Wall Street Journal*.

GEORGE: The literature could be analyzed for whatever it's worth.

RALPH: Somebody told me a long time ago that the surest way to find out something is to go and ask someone. If you want to know if this tax slows down business, the most direct way—of course, it would take time and people—would be to ask a number of business leaders themselves. Ask them, "Do you have any plans for expansion that you are holding up because of the excess profits tax?"

TEACHER: You could organize a committee here in class—is that it—and they could go down town and talk with some businessmen?

RALPH: On the local scene: Yes—

JAMES: If you do, take along a good supply of salt. (laughter)

RALPH: What I first had in mind was to write letters to some national business leaders and—

ANDY: Yes, and I know exactly what all of them will say. They will say, "Yes, it has stifled my business—I'm not expanding because of it." I'll venture to say that very few would tell the truth.

RALPH: Well, the excess profits tax—as I understand it—doesn't affect very many corporations at all in the United States.

ANDY: I still don't see how that would make your results any more objective. They all damn it because they're opposed in principle—they just assume that an excess profits tax is automatically a damper on production.

TEACHER: Does anyone else have a suggestion for testing the proposition before us?

ROGER: Have any other countries tried an excess profits tax similar to ours? If so, we might be able to get information on how it worked, whether it curtailed industrial expansion—or whether economists thought it did.

HAROLD: That suggests something else—why not look into some textbooks on taxation—something written by an objective tax expert—if there are any. I'd like to know what an economist would say.

TEACHER: Any other ideas? (pause) Then how would you like to handle this? Which of the things suggested do you want to try, and how should we organize ourselves?

The above illustration is of a situation where the pooled experiences of a group are not sufficient to test a hypothesis. In the following example, a group pools its present information on a subject and finds that a reasonably adequate conclusion is possible on the basis of it.

TEACHER: So advertising much of the time is not entirely honest, you feel? What kind of support do you have for such an idea?

BETH: Well, I was at a drive-in last night and there was some advertising on the screen before the show—it showed a car that was running on regular gas going up a hill and the motor made an awful noise—like a death rattle. Then it showed the same car pulling up the grade with ethyl gas in the tank and you could hardly hear the motor it was so quiet.

TEACHER: Was that dishonest advertising?

BETH: My dad is a garageman and he says that, unless you have an extra high-compression motor, regular gas is better for your car than ethyl. I don't know why—I don't know anything about cars—but I think he said the motor stays cleaner with regular.

ROD: What about power? I'll bet you get more power with ethyl—

BETH: I don't think so—I've heard dad mention that too.

TEACHER: Just what did the advertising claim—did it claim that ethyl kept your motor cleaner—or had more power?

BETH: Come to think of it, it didn't say so directly. But it sure implied that.

Discussion as a Tool of Reflective Learning

TEACHER: Does anyone have any more examples of what you think is dishonest advertising?

MAYNARD: I read an article in a magazine that said chlorophyll has no medical value—it doesn't stop bad breath, it doesn't keep your teeth from rotting out, or anything else that the ads say. People have been eating chlorophyll for millions of years—everytime they eat green plants.

MARGE: I saw a funny cartoon about that—a farmer was planning to give his cows chlorophyll to keep their breath sweet—and here they were standing knee deep in grass.

TEACHER: Is the manufactured chlorophyll—the kind which comes in medicines and cosmetics—the same chemically as when it occurs in nature? What I'm getting at is that maybe the two forms don't have the same effect on you.

MAYNARD: I suppose that could be true—but the article I read didn't say anything about it.

RUPERT: What magazine was that in—was it a pro-business magazine or an anti-business magazine?

MAYNARD: Well—I don't remember for sure where I saw it—I think it was *Reader's Digest*.

TEACHER: Martha, you had your hand up a moment ago.

MARTHA: I think one of the best examples of misleading advertising is in the cigarette ads. They advertise that a particular brand won't irritate your throat or make you cough. But doctors say that there is no way to keep any tobacco from having an irritating effect.

STEP 5: DRAWING CONCLUSIONS

Some pitfalls in the use of evidence may be avoided if a teacher is familiar with rules of evidence and criteria of a good conclusion as described in Chapter 4. Although it is assumed here that permissiveness is to be observed in the sense that students are allowed full intellectual independence in examining evidence and drawing conclusions, it is also assumed that a teacher should ask questions and make recommendations intended to prevent superficiality of thought. A teacher is obligated to prevent students from overlooking important evidence or neglecting established rules of evidence in drawing conclusions. Groups of younger children and groups inexperienced in problem-solving methods require more help and criticism than those accustomed to the discussion methods described here.

A conclusion of an act of thought may be only a restatement of an idea brought before the group at the start; what was presented at the start as established knowledge remains established knowledge. It is now seen in a different light—better grounded and more fully understood—and has therefore shifted in status from a preconception to a conception (but will function as a preconception in the next act of thought in which it is involved). In other instances a conclusion modifies an original statement or preconception, often in the direction of greater precision and clarity of statement or in the addition of qualifications. In still other cases a conclusion will affirm an entirely new idea—perhaps something quite contradictory to the original belief.

In the following illustration, a class achieved consensus on one point but remained in disagreement on others:

TEACHER: I wonder if it would be possible for us to draw any conclusions at this point—sum up your thinking if it has jelled at all.

ROGER: It seems to me that we have been moving steadily toward agreement on one point—and that is, that there should be a general lowering of tariffs, in order to stimulate imports and build up dollar balances abroad.

ROBERT: No one has maintained that the United States should continue its gifts in dollars and goods to foreign nations indefinitely, and yet I think it is generally felt that the only way this can be avoided is to help these nations pay their own way. They can do that only by increasing their exports to this country.

TEACHER: Is it the consensus, then, that there should be a general lowering of tariffs? (Nods indicate agreement. Teacher writes this on the board) All right. Is there any general agreement as to how much they should be lowered—is it a general abolition of the protective principle itself that we want?

JAMES: Absolutely not. I maintain—and I think there are two or three who agree —that tariffs should remain protective on most products. We might except a few—those that are not particularly important to us but mean a lot to the economies of certain other countries—like lace making, garlic, or handmade rugs.

TEACHER: Okay—we still have our protectionist group. (Writes this conclusion on the board) Any freetraders?

ANDY: I don't think anyone has argued for free trade, although I was pushing in that direction at the beginning of our discussion. I think that now I would favor a tariff for revenue only on most items, but would approve tariffs on the products of essential war industries—like synthetic rubber—if the industry can't compete in foreign markets without tariffs.

TEACHER: Have any other positions emerged from the discussion?

Note that two of the conclusions were carefully qualified. As a result of discussion, students who had advocated without qualification the protective principle had become willing to accept less protection than at present and to exclude one category of items entirely. Freetraders had modified their original stand to permit protective tariffs on essential war industries and to allow for low and income-producing duties generally. Note also that conclusions are in the form of value judgments or policy statements. No proof was adduced for the belief that tariffs should be lowered, but the discussion did apparently help students see that, in order to achieve one of their values (a preference for Europe's paying its own way), it would be necessary to lower tariffs.

The following illustration shows even more clearly how conclusions in the form of value judgments may be formed, and how a teacher through questioning may help students see just what they are doing as they move from value judgments to judgments of fact and back again.

MARIAN: The conclusion that I've reached as a result of our discussion is that our present treatment of criminals is all wrong.

TEACHER: Oh, why did you reach this conclusion?

MARIAN: Because of the figures we had showing how many minor and one-time offenders who serve prison terms become big-time criminals after they are released. They are taught to commit the big offenses—and how to go about it—by the criminals they come in contact with in prison.

TEACHER: Then the reason you feel our present method of dealing with criminals is bad is because you think it makes more criminals—multiplies the problem?

MARIAN: That's right.

TEACHER: There is an assumption there—what is it you are assuming?

MARIAN: Oh—well—I don't know—

JOHN: Isn't she assuming that it's bad to make more criminals?

MARIAN: Yes, of course—I thought that was obvious.

TEACHER: Perhaps, but I want to make sure you know exactly what you are doing. You want minor criminals to be reformed rather than turning into big-time crooks and habitual offenders—and you see prison reform as one means to this end. Could you prove that your chief aim here is good—are there any facts, I mean, which would prove it?

MARIAN: That we ought to try to reduce crime? Well, I guess that's only an opinion—but is there anyone who questions it?

HARRY: There are a lot of people who make a living out of crime—the bigger and oftener the crime, the better—so far as they are concerned. I'll bet they wouldn't agree with you.

MARIAN: Are you people trying to get me to say I favor more crime?

TEACHER: No—I only wanted to show that our desire to reduce crime is one of our values—although certainly a very widely held one. You can't prove it true or false the way you can a statement about conditions in a prison or the effect of prison life on a man's behavior. That doesn't mean it isn't a good value, of course.

DISCUSSION QUESTIONS AND EXERCISES

1. Studies which have been made of class time spent in different activities suggest that in the social studies relatively little time is given to problem-solving

discussion. Some reasons commonly given by teachers for not engaging in discussion more often include:

a. Discussion is an inefficient means of learning.

b. Discussions tend to fail because students lack the necessary informational background.

c. It is difficult to prevent discussions from becoming disorganized and heading off at tangents.

d. It is difficult to control students during discussion.

Evaluate each of these arguments.

2. Recalling discussions in which you have been a participant, what would you say were their chief inadequacies? How would you rate them from the standpoint of learning effectiveness? What rules or cautions would you suggest in order to eliminate the chief weaknesses which you have observed?

3. Select a topic which you judge to be suitable for problem-solving discussion in a senior high school and develop a plan for leading a discussion on this topic. Make your plan as concrete as possible, including key questions which you would ask and anticipated responses of students.

REFERENCES

For suggestions on leading relatively undirected discussions and help on how to keep any discussion permissive, see Nathaniel Cantor, *Learning Through Discussion* (Human Relations for Industry, 1951), and, by the same author, *The Dynamics of Learning* (Foster & Stewart, 1946). See also Carl Rogers, *Client-Centered Therapy* (Houghton Mifflin, 1951), Chapters 8–9.

There are a number of textbooks designed for college courses in discussion. Students will find worth-while material in any of the following: Albert C. Baird, *Discussion: Principles and Types* (McGraw-Hill, 1943); Henry L. Ewbank and J. Jeffrey Auer, *Discussion and Debate* (Appleton-Century-Crofts, 1951); James H. McBurney and Kenneth G. Hance, *Discussion in Human Affairs* (Harper, 1950); Alan Nichols, *Discussion and Debate* (Harcourt, Brace, 1941); and Russel H. Wagner and Carroll C. Arnold, *Handbook of Group Discussion* (Houghton Mifflin, 1950).

PART TWO

The Problem of Content

Chapter 9

The Traditional Conception of Content

The Content of the Social Sciences

THE most common social-studies curriculum today consists of the traditional social-studies courses of history, civics, geography, economics, sociology, and the somewhat more recently added "problems of democracy." As of the school year 1948–49, approximately 44 percent of all junior- and senior high-school students were enrolled in a full- or half-year course in history, 20 percent in civics and American government, 13.3 percent in geography, 4.1 percent in problems of democracy, 3.7 percent in economics, and 2.7 percent in sociology.[1]

The content of all the popular secondary social-studies courses (except perhaps community civics and problems of democracy) is largely drawn from the corresponding scholarly discipline of the university. Secondary-school history courses take their pattern from the discipline of history as developed by university historians, and secondary government courses take their pattern from the university discipline of political science. Even such secondary courses as problems of democracy and community civics draw heavily from the college fields of sociology, economics, and political science.[2] In many instances, particularly in the field of history, the difference between a typical high-school text and its college counterpart is chiefly a

[1] *Offerings and Enrollments in High School Subjects* (Biennial Survey of Education in the United States, 1948–49), Federal Security Agency, Office of Education. U.S. Government Printing Office, 1951, chap. 5.

[2] It is true that there is a class of rather amorphous courses known simply as "social studies" which do not take their pattern from the scholarly social-science disciplines. These courses are more characteristic of the elementary than of the secondary school; secondary courses in "social studies" will receive comment later in the chapter.

191

matter of vocabulary level and thoroughness of treatment; the basic kinds of subject matter and the sequence of topics remains much the same.

The first task of the present chapter is to scrutinize the social-science disciplines themselves. Next will come discussion of some of the problems involved in translating the content of these fields into school subjects, and some of the changes in emphasis which have been tried in recent years. Finally, the traditional content of the secondary social studies will be evaluated in terms of its overall worth and significance in the education of youth.

THE SOCIAL-SCIENCE FIELDS

The social sciences are those fields of inquiry—presumably "scientific"—which deal with the social behavior of man. The aim of a social scientist is to gain such insights into human behavior as will make possible its prediction in specified situations. Prediction may be confined to groups (men in the "mass") or extended to individuals. Although it is generally assumed that both are possible, the former appears much easier than the latter. In any case, it is *laws (however tentative) of human behavior which social scientists are seeking.*[3]

Traditional social-science fields have sometimes appeared to slight man himself in favor of study of physical environment or institutional forms in their most impersonal aspects. Economics, for example, has sought to describe economic laws as if they were akin to the law of gravity. Economists have insisted, it is true, that all their conceptual efforts rest on certain premises about human nature; but, since some of these premises are not acceptable to modern psychologists, we may question whether economics, in certain of its investigations, is behaving as a social science at all. Geography, as will be shown more fully in Chapter 17, often deals with aspects of climate, terrain, soil, and the like, which could scarcely throw much light on laws of human behavior. Many geographers have apparently never decided whether they are geologists or social scientists.

It has been customary to classify the following fields as social sciences: (1) history, (2) political science, (3) geography, (4) economics, (5) sociology, and (6) cultural anthropology. A few persons have regarded philosophy and ethics as social sciences. This traditional enumeration does not enjoy the almost universal acceptance which it had a few decades ago.

As newer outlooks have developed concerning the role and methodology

---

[3] I.e., relatively dependable if-then-always generalizations.

of the social sciences, there have been shifts in thinking about what fields should be included and the respective functions of each. Those branches of psychology which study social behavior (usually called social psychology) are now included. Psychiatry, because of new light it has shed on behavior of individuals and nature of culture, is coming into the picture as a social science, or at least as an important accessory. Mathematics and logic are still the accessory disciplines they have always been, but a new and important accessory discipline, semantics, has been added.

The relative status of the social-science fields is also changing. The core of modern social science will probably soon consist of the fields of cultural anthropology, sociology, psychology, and psychiatry. There seems to be a growing conviction among many social scientists that the most pressing need is to find out more about man himself—more about the laws of individual and social behavior—and that this can best be done through study of the interaction between individuals and culture. As Robert S. Lynd points out, it is essential that social scientists begin thinking of the basic datum of social science as "involving the interaction of these two basic factors: the dynamic biological organism carrying his version of the culture in the form of learned habit-structures, interacting with the culture as presented by the similarly dynamic culture-versions carried by the people about him." [4] This trend in thinking points inevitably toward much greater use of cultural and psychological data.

It is now felt that the attempt to maintain separate fields of inquiry is sometimes artificial and a handicap to vital research. There is a growing tendency to believe that the centers of organization of the social sciences should be, not the traditional subject disciplines, but broad problem areas, such as race or class tensions, relations between the sexes, and delinquency and crime. Studies centered around any of these areas (commonly called "area studies") employ teams of social scientists representing all the social-science fields but drawing more heavily on social psychology, sociology, anthropology, and psychiatry. The core fields seem to be melting and blending into one another to such an extent that they promise to lose their individuality. This is not to say that each field will lose every distinctive function; psychiatry, for example, will probably continue to focus its major effort on individual psychotherapy. But it seems certain that many workers in each core field will devote most of their time to interdisciplinary research,

---

[4] Robert S. Lynd, *Knowledge for What?* Princeton University Press, 1940, p. 166.

and the task of integration out of which a body of knowledge will develop will represent a fusion of the four areas.

What will happen to areas such as economics, political science, and geography is hard to say. Possibly these fields will eventually be incorporated into the core fields, except perhaps for certain narrow areas of specialization which perform indispensable functions—such as those areas of economics devoted to national income studies, the mechanics of foreign trade, and technical aspects of banking. But even these might produce more fruitful results if they made greater use of data from the core fields. Incorporation of the traditional social-science fields into the new core of anthropology, sociology, social psychology, and psychiatry will be resisted by many economists, political scientists, and geographers, who seem intent on keeping their separate identities. In fact, the mere suggestion that a field be "incorporated" into another is enough to give many a scholar the shudders.

History was deliberately omitted from the above discussion because it presents a special set of problems. There is undoubtedly a shift of outlook concerning the role of history which is of great significance—especially since history as a school subject is the most popular of the social studies. The problem of history deserves so much attention that the following section is devoted exclusively to it.

The Special Status of History

History, it is now often contended, is not a true social science at all. Stuart Chase, after polling a great many social scientists, concludes that it should be regarded as an accessory discipline. "History," he says, "deals with events which have gone into limbo . . . and can never hope to measure living phenomena or use the full scientific method." [5] Another social scientist, Robert S. Lynd, says, "There probably never was another era when 'the appeal to history,' uncorrected by the multiple new variants in the situation, meant less." [6] This argument deserves fuller exploration.

In Chapter 2 and in the pages on the teaching of history in Chapter 17 the point of view is presented that reflective thought seeks always to reach valid "if-then-always" generalizations. These are of the nature of rules or principles. Their role is to predict and control, and, applied in problematic situations, to suggest new hypotheses. Learning of such generalizations makes transfer of training possible. The aim of all scientific inquiry is to

[5] Stuart Chase, *The Proper Study of Mankind*, Harper & Brothers, 1948, p. 48.
[6] *Op. cit.*, p. 131.

achieve tested generalizations of this sort. This is what we mean by theory building.

To the extent that historians generalize, they do so usually in the *past tense;* e.g., "Large corporations were able to exert an unhealthy influence in politics," or "The tariff enabled American manufacturers to raise their own prices." Some historians, who pride themselves on being scientific, scrupulously avoid any sort of theorizing. And probably many historians would argue that historical writing must continue to avoid theoretical (i.e., if-then-always) generalizations if it is to remain scientific.

Such an argument seems to miss the fact that "being scientific" is *always* theorizing. That is what science is about: to construct ever better theoretical generalizations for use as predictive tools. Mere description, no matter how accurate, is not science. History as a field of inquiry *is not a science except in so far as historians use their understanding of past events to develop if-then-always generalizations.*[7]

But a historian is behind the eight ball as he faces this problem. There probably are not many generalizations about human behavior (social theory) which can be supported dependably with historical evidence alone. That is, one cannot prove much with history. One reason for this is the complexity and indefiniteness of historical evidence; a person can prove almost anything he wishes with it, which means he cannot really "prove" anything with certainty. History thus lends itself to rationalization. Another reason is that situations under which human behavior may be studied change constantly. The total field or ground against which it could be studied in 1855 was vastly different from the environment of 1955. Therefore, whatever social theories a historian may suggest need to be verified against evidence of the present. Contemporary observation and experimentation, as provided by nonhistorical social sciences, is needed as a final test. Lewin describes the essential difference between the methodologies of history and the nonhistorical social sciences as follows:

> To determine the properties of a present situation . . . one can follow two different procedures: One may base one's statement on conclusions from history . . . , or one may use diagnostic *tests of the present.*
>
> To use a simple example: I wish to know whether the floor of the attic is sufficiently strong to carry a certain weight. I might try to gain this knowledge by finding out what material was used when the house was built ten years ago. As I get reliable reports that good material has been used, and that the architect was

[7] Nor is it likely that historical content can be learned conceptually by students except as it can be made to suggest if-then-always generalizations. See pp. 37–38.

a dependable man, I might conclude that the load probably would be safe. If I can find the original blueprints, I might be able to do some exact figuring and feel still more safe.

Of course, there is always a chance that the workmen have actually not followed the blueprints, or that insects have weakened the woodwork, or that some rebuilding has been done during the last ten years. Therefore, I might decide to avoid these uncertain conclusions from past data and to determine the present strength of the floor by testing its strength now. Such a diagnostic test will not yield data which are absolutely certain; how reliable they are depends upon the quality of the available test and the carefulness of testing. However, the value of a present test is, from the point of view of methodology, superior to that of . . . [a historical test].[8]

Lewin goes on to suggest that two steps must logically be included in any historical test: (1) An investigator must determine what the past situation was—often no easy feat—and (2) he must show that nothing unknown has interfered in the meantime—that the theoretical generalization derived from the analysis of historical events is as true today as in the time that suggested it. The latter task is usually even more hazardous than the first.

This is not meant to suggest that a historical approach has no value. Rather it is intended to show difficulties involved in giving the field of history true scientific stature. Admittedly, there are obstacles to be faced by the nonhistorical social sciences as well, but they are of another sort. As a school subject capable of helping students acquire tested social theory, history may be less useful than the other social studies, unless it is regarded primarily as a source of hypotheses to be checked against data from nonhistorical social sciences. As a source of hypotheses, rather than proofs, it may be richly rewarding, if taught with that purpose in mind. (For further analysis of history as a school subject, see Chapter 17.)

THE HABIT OF SPECIALIZATION

The description of the state of the social sciences given earlier in the chapter could be highly misleading. It will be recalled that a tendency toward integration was emphasized. But as yet the separate fields are very much alive and kicking. In fact, the most characteristic trend right now is not toward integration but exactly the reverse: toward disintegration, or dissociation. Thus the social sciences *are being pulled in two opposite directions.*

The centrifugal pull is associated with the drift toward specialization.

[8] Kurt Lewin, *Field Theory in Social Science*, Harper & Brothers, 1951, pp. 48–50.

The Traditional Conception of Content

Each of the social sciences is now a field of specialization—an area of investigation which focuses on a small segment of human experience and studies that segment until a vast amount of detail has been unearthed. Most social scientists today are specialists—that is, experts in some more or less narrow phase of history, economics, political science, or other social-science field.

As each of the social sciences grows in content, it divides into subfields. The field of economics, as an example, consists of a number of separate subjects: money and banking, foreign trade, transportation, labor relations, business cycles, and the structure of industry. Likewise, history has divided into the history of various countries and of various time periods; there is also economic history, intellectual history, social history, religious history, diplomatic history, and so on.

Subfields are naturally more specialized than parent fields. As more subfields emerge, and as subfields divide into still further subfields, specialization is likely to increase. The point to which it already has gone may be illustrated by the titles of some recent doctoral theses:

The modal personality structure of the Tuscarora Indians, as revealed by the Rorschach Test.
The rise of Duluth as an ore port, 1901–15; an economic study.
The Stokely-Van Camp Company, 1898–1950: a business history.
Some factors affecting the quantity and quality of eggs marketed by certain producers.
The Port of New York, 1800–1810: the foreign trade and business community.
The part played by the pirates of Kwangtung and Kwangsi Provinces in the Taiping Insurrection.
The political implications of the trial of P. Clodius, 61 B.C.
Max Emanuel of Bavaria as a patron of the arts.
The growth and development of the Democratic party in Virginia since 1890.
An analysis of the functioning of the adoption process in Allegheny County, Pennsylvania.
Geography of settlement and land use in Alachus County, Florida.

As specialization increases, each field develops its own special concepts and vocabulary. Communication between fields becomes more and more difficult. A political scientist finds it hard to understand an economist; an economist finds it hard to understand a sociologist. Worse than that, a specialist in one field may not understand another specialist in the same field: an economist who specializes in tax theory may find it difficult to understand an economist who specializes in statistical measurement of business cycles. In fact, although almost everyone concerned is loath to admit it, one entire branch of economics—econometrics, or mathematical economics—remains largely unintelligible to most economists outside this special field.

Specialization reaches a point of diminishing returns when it begins to interfere with effective research and teaching. The reaction to overspecialization is increased attention to interdisciplinary research and to school courses which seek to integrate the social-science disciplines. We should not infer that there is anything wrong with specialization *per se*—specialists and specialism are absolutely essential. What we now increasingly recognize is the need for better communication and more pooling of effort among specialists, and a reduction of effort which is of trivial social significance.

Traditional Emphasis upon Content Rather Than Method

Another characteristic of some of the social-science fields—and especially older fields such as history, geography, political science, and economics—is the inordinate stress on content to the neglect of methodology. The word *science*, in its most general sense, is usually defined as a method, although it may also be regarded as an accumulation of content which has been verified scientifically. When persons refer to *a science*, they usually think of a systematically organized body of knowledge or content dealing with a particular subject rather than of the method which made the content available. They even think of certain fields—history is perhaps the most conspicuous example—as consisting of bodies of knowledge which are relatively fixed and static.

The tendency to turn away from problems of method has several unfortunate consequences. Although there has been a growth of vast bodies of formal content, the usefulness and validity of much of this content are seriously to be doubted. Many social scientists have substituted speculation for empirical investigation. Many weighty textbooks in the fields of history, geography, and economics never mention the methodological assumptions of the authors. These books often contain a curious mixture of fact, speculation, and value judgment, all of which is offered to unwary students as fact.

Stuart Chase has distinguished between social scientist $_1$ and social scientist $_2$. The first verifies content through use of scientific methodology; the second likes to speculate rather freely about social problems; he frames hypotheses and does not worry about proofs. This might be a fruitful procedure if hypotheses were not presented as conclusions. "Much of the material classified as 'social science' in the universities and the textbooks has not been arrived at by the scientific method. Its exponents have not cut loose from the older problem-solving methods of intuition, authority, and pure logic. The Royal Society has sent out no expeditions. The material may be interesting, stimulating, and educational in the scholastic sense, but it is not conclusive." [9]

There is growing but belated recognition among many social scientists— even in fields such as history and economics—that steady proliferation of content achieved through methods of questionable scientific worth is not useful. As a result of the reaction against speculative content, certain of the social sciences—particularly the younger ones—retain strong emphasis on methodology as well as on accumulation of formal content.

The formally organized content of the social sciences serves as a depository or storehouse of knowledge. It represents a large segment of the experience of mankind, organized in such a way as to be passed from one generation to another, as well as to be used by contemporary social scientists. As such it is not to be derided, provided its verification was as scientific as possible. Fred C. Hood has written about the values of classified knowledge in the following terms: ". . . Without classification there could be no inquiry, or what we call intelligence. One of the most prolific sources of confusion is lack of clarity with respect to *what it means to be one of a specified class or kind.* Knowledge of what the nature of a particular thing must be in order to be a member of a certain class is the only basis for determining the value of that thing as evidence of something else." [10]

But the usefulness of data furnished by social scientists is often circumscribed by failure to give proper attention to scientific methods of verification and by the way they are organized. Organization of the social sciences into traditional fields such as history, economics, and political science is both arbitrary and artificial and undoubtedly erects barriers to effective use of social knowledge in solving problems; it also constitutes a barrier to students' acquiring an understanding of social problems.

Traditional Content of Social-Studies Instruction

Since most secondary social-studies courses continue to be built around a textbook, we can best gain insight into the nature of conventionally taught

[9] Stuart Chase, *op. cit.*, pp. 38–39.
[10] Fred C. Hood, "Developing the Ability to Assess the Results of Thinking," *University of Illinois Bulletin,* February, 1949, p. 34.

content by examining the subject matter of textbooks. To understand why subject matter of certain types continues to be stressed, it is helpful to understand first why textbooks get written. Without question, many social scientists who write textbooks do so because of a new idea which they feel is a contribution to teaching—perhaps a new selection or organization of content, or new ways of explaining or illustrating. In any case, they write out of a sense of dedication and service.

But obviously there are other motives. Publication of a textbook advances a man professionally. It may also be an important extra source of income. If the latter consideration did not motivate the authors of textbooks, it would still be a pressing motive of publishing houses. It is evident that textbooks must be written with saleability in mind. But the saleability of a textbook, like that of a brand of whiskey, is compounded of exactly the right blend of traditional and novel content, adorned with an attractive package. Although a college text may have considerable novel content and still sell, content selection for high-school texts is governed largely by tradition, and for good reasons.

Before a high-school textbook can find a sale it must be approved by school board members, local school executives, and classroom teachers. It is also fairly common for pressure groups outside of school to insist on taking a hand in selection of textbooks. Each group has definite reasons for wanting to retain traditional patterns.

School board members, for the most part, have not been exposed to recent developments in the social sciences. They are almost invariably highly conservative in their attitude toward selection of textbook content. Veterans' organizations, patriotic societies, church groups, and the like are also certain to take a very conservative position regarding textbook content. These groups assume responsibility for guarding young minds from "subversive" influences, and feel they can do this by insisting that textbooks remain pretty much as they were in the good old days. Novel content of almost any sort is likely to be "suspect."

Principals and teachers are not likely to urge drastic changes in textbooks. They remember the content of their college courses in history, geography, political science, economics, and sociology. These college courses are models to them. A typical teacher or principal may accept a book more novel than would please a typical school board member; but he will still prefer books which do not depart much from traditional patterns.

Teachers and principals have further reasons for this preference. For each of their courses they have usually developed course outlines, lesson plans, and lists of teaching materials which were suggested by textbooks in use when they were compiled. A new text which departed radically from the old would render unusable many of these teaching materials.

Thus in most subjects, and particularly in history, one can identify a "standard" content which is perpetuated from one generation of textbooks to another with little variation. To demonstrate this in one subject field, the present authors analyzed a number of widely used high-school textbooks in United States history. The following list includes only part of the topics which seem to be universally treated in these books:

The Story of Pocahontas	Lewis and Clark Expedition
The Mayflower Compact	Battle of Fallen Timbers
King Philip's War	Tripolitan War
Braddock's Defeat	*Chesapeake* and *Leopard*
Adventures of Daniel Boone	Fulton's Folly
Boston Massacre	The Alamo
Boston Tea Party	Fifty-four Forty or Fight
Paul Revere's Ride	The Forty-Niners
Battle of Bunker Hill	Perry's Mission
Death of Nathan Hale	Underground Railroad
Treason of Benedict Arnold	The Pony Express
Winter at Valley Forge	*Monitor* and *Merrimac*
Citizen Genêt	Custer's Last Stand
XYZ Affair	Rough Riders

THE "NEW TEXTBOOK"

Although the content of textbooks in the most widely taught high-school social studies remains highly traditional, no one can deny that textbooks have changed a great deal in the past few decades. Just what is the nature of the "new textbook"? First, it has gained remarkably in visual attractiveness. High quality of paper and printing, artistry of arrangement, abundance and quality of pictures, charts, and maps—all these give modern books an eye appeal unknown a few generations ago. Second, readability undoubtedly has also increased, partly through the use of larger type, better spacing, and more pictures and charts, and partly because of vocabulary studies that have shown which words students of a given grade can understand. Third, the work of a teacher has been made easier by incorporation of "study aids." Teachers no longer need to decide for themselves what to do with a textbook; all they need do now is turn to the end of each chapter for lists of study questions and suggested activities.

Textbooks have been modernized in form; they have been "dressed up." But what textbooks *say* today does not depart fundamentally from what they have been saying for decades. They still tend to be built upon the "standard" facts of history, political science, geography, and other established social-science fields.

High-School and College Textbooks Compared

In spite of similarities between college and high-school texts, there are important differences. First, there is a time lag between adoption of new content on the college level and its adoption in high school. A study of the economic content of a selected group of high-school texts, conducted by one of the authors, showed that it usually takes a minimum of from ten to fifteen years for big new ideas in the field of economics to get from college to high-school books.[11] As measured by college standards, high-school texts in the social studies are often obsolete by a decade or so.

Writers of high-school texts are, on the whole, much more likely than writers of college texts to avoid controversial issues, or any sort of unorthodox thought. A high-school textbook in sociology, for example, is not likely to treat problems of the family as frankly as will its college counterpart. One in history will deëmphasize or omit those facts of history which are not entirely favorable to the United States (although history books are rather more honest now than they were thirty or forty years ago). A typical high-school book, more than a college book, may cater to ethnocentrism, nationalism, and traditional middle-class mores.

High-school texts are also more likely than are college texts to show defects of scholarship: to present sweeping generalizations with little consideration for factual evidence, to offer doctrinaire and dogmatic arguments, and to advance inconsistent conclusions. The investigator cited above gained the impression, for instance, that, without being fully aware of what they were doing, textbook authors had drawn from a number of different sources, representing incompatible schools of thought in economics. There

[11] Maurice P. Hunt, "The Teaching of Economics in the American High School," unpublished doctoral dissertation, The Ohio State University, 1948, pp. 269–277. The Keynesian theoretical system is perhaps the biggest innovation in economic thought of the twentieth century. Keynes *General Theory* was published in 1936. By 1940, Keynesian economics had become a subject of widespread discussion and, if not accepted, was mentioned by most authors of college textbooks. Of twenty-seven high-school textbooks (all bearing economic content) published between 1940 and 1947, only three mentioned the Keynesian explanation of economic fluctuations.

was some tendency to support a given position in one chapter, and in the next chapter a position in flat contradiction to the first (see pp. 345–346).

In spite of these defects, range in quality is very great. A few secondary social-studies textbooks are excellent; they are scholarly, yet lucid enough for students to understand, and they contain large amounts of content which is rather steadily relevant to significant social issues and ideas. Everything considered, social-studies textbooks of today probably show a net gain in quality over those of two or three decades ago. Two tendencies which are barely discernible at present may reverse this trend. One is an apparent tendency to oversimplify issues in order to make books "easier," and the other is a tendency to intensify nationalistic and ethnocentric slants which to some degree have always been evident, and to take a highly conservative position with respect to most social and economic problems.

ASSUMPTIONS GOVERNING SELECTION OF CONTENT FOR HIGH-SCHOOL SOCIAL-STUDIES TEXTBOOKS

Implicit in a traditional view of what is proper content for high-school social studies are certain assumptions. A list of some of the more obvious follows:

1. Suitable content for social-studies instruction can be chosen in advance of the development of a specific learning situation.

2. The most suitable content for high-school social studies consists of bodies of systematically organized subject matter.

3. Suitable content for high-school social studies can be drawn from the established social-science fields (such as history, economics, and political science).

4. There is a best, or most logical, organization of the content of any subject field. In general, this organization is the one which seems best to a majority of experts in the field.

5. The typical high-school student can profit from memorization of bodies of systematically organized knowledge, drawn from the social-science fields.

6. The value of content is unrelated to whether the student wants to learn it or sees any use for it.

7. The content of a field of study is more significant than the method by which it is taught. The important thing is for a student to "learn" what is presented to him.

8. It is not necessary that content be functional when it is learned; its

chief purpose is to provide background for future acts of thought which will concern unpredictable problems and occur at unpremeditated times.

Some Questionable Attempts to Modernize the Content of Social-Studies Instruction

So far, we have emphasized the traditional character of the content of most social-studies textbooks. Many persons would question the significance of this emphasis in the belief that, although textbooks remain widely used, they are now supplemented with a variety of outside materials. What the textbooks contain may now be of little importance as guides to course content.

It is true that in recent years fresh materials have been introduced. But it is doubtful if most attempts to supplement the textbook have led to significant change in the time-honored concepts of what types of content are most appropriate. Even when teachers use the newer teaching materials, courses tend for the most part *to be about the same things they have been about for a long time.* To demonstrate this, we shall describe four innovations which have had considerable impact on social-studies instruction: (1) the teaching-aids movement, (2) the current-events movement, (3) the unit-teaching movement, and (4) the integration movement.

THE TEACHING-AIDS MOVEMENT

The teaching-aids movement stems from a belief that printed words are not necessarily the best medium for communicating content to students. Teachers rely increasingly on visual and auditory aids—movies, radio programs, television, and the like. Instead of letting students read about rice-growing in Burma, we now show them a sound-motion picture of it; instead of letting them read the text of a speech by Mr. Churchill, we now play them a recording.

There is no question but that use of visual and auditory devices sometimes increases the efficiency of learning. If content is presented in this way, students may learn more and learn it faster. But—and this is the important point—the content, although presented more attractively, is generally not much different from what was learned under the older approach, which relied exclusively on a textbook.

This fact is perfectly illustrated by available films, pictures, and recordings in United States history. They take incidents which have traditionally been depicted in school history books and make them more exciting by presenting them with greater realism and drama. Whatever their values may be, audio-visual aids have done little to change the type of content stressed in high-school social studies.

THE CURRENT-EVENTS MOVEMENT

The current-events movement is a product of a belief that proper content of social-studies education is not limited to what has been discovered about the past; it should include, in addition, facts which are in the process of emerging. It is now customary in most social-studies classes for a teacher to suspend textbook study for one class period a week and have discussion and reports on the news.

So far as it goes, the current-events movement has introduced fresh content into the curriculum. It is open to criticism, however, because of its tendency to focus on the trivial, to emphasize reporting of news rather than analysis and interpretation, and its failure to link study of current events with the remainder of a course.

The point we are most concerned with here, however, is that artificial imposition of a class period a week of current-events instruction does not in any way change the remainder of a course, which is likely to remain highly traditional in content. History courses remain "standard history," even when supplemented periodically with a daily newspaper. A few talented teachers may be able to weave together the current scene and textbook content in meaningful fashion, but many social-studies teachers do not even try.

THE UNIT-TEACHING MOVEMENT

The unit movement covers a variety of schemes for organizing and selecting content. There is much confusion and inconsistency in the literature of education concerning the meaning of units, topics, problems, activities, and projects. Sometimes these terms are used interchangeably. Without conspicuous success, one book on the teaching of the social studies devotes nine pages to an attempt to distinguish between a problem and a project.[12] This confusion over terms brings to mind the following widely quoted story:

. . . Twenty-five years ago . . . when a hen was set by a primary class in a school that was under the dominance of the problem method, setting the hen was a "problem." In a few years setting a hen was a "project." Still later it was an

[12] T. H. Schutte, *Teaching the Social Studies on the Secondary School Level*, Prentice-Hall, Inc., 1942, pp. 351–359.

"activity," a "unit of work," a "center of interest," or an "enterprise." At the moment this paragraph is written, setting a hen is most commonly called an activity; yet the purposes of the children, the interest accompanying the enterprise, and the enlargement of knowledge and insight are essentially the same under all of these terminologies.[13]

Before a student can assimilate any content, it must be divided (or classified) in such a way that he may focus on a portion of manageable size—and a portion, furthermore,. which has some pertinence to the task at hand. A manageable block of content, chosen to fit the learning needs of the moment, may be termed a *unit*. This is all that most teachers mean when they use the term. Units which call for a considerable amount of independent activity on the part of a student may be called *projects*, and units which pose unanswered questions may be called *problems*.

If one accepts a problem-solving approach to teaching, most attempts to distinguish between units, problems, projects, and activities become quite pointless. Either a given piece of content functions as a problem or it functions as nothing at all save grist for memorization of arbitrary associations.

Use of these terms not only misleads the innocent but also obscures basic issues. Blocks of content which are highly traditional may be called "units," "projects," or "problems." Textbooks of the most conventional sort may substitute the word *unit* for the word *chapter* and lead teachers and students to think they are getting something new. Activities suggested at chapter ends are called "problems," even though there is nothing even remotely problematic about them. And some of the printed unit plans in the social studies represent selections of content which are just as traditional as those in textbooks. The practice of calling old subjects by new names has given the impression that schools are more progressive than they used to be. It is perhaps poetic justice that many schools are under criticism from a public which does not realize that, in most academic subjects, "progressivism" has had little effect on the content that is taught.

The Integration Movement

On its lowest level, integration is an attempt to correlate subjects—that is, teach separate subjects in such a way that they supplement or complement one another. In any school where no teacher knows, or cares, what any other teacher is doing even this is a radical step. A slightly more revolutionary move is the combining of two or more formerly separate subjects. Even

[13] Ernest Horn, *Methods of Instruction in the Social Studies*, Charles Scribner's Sons, 1937, pp. 413–414.

in schools with an otherwise conventional curricular structure it is not unusual to combine history and geography or history and government.

If two or more formerly independent subjects are fused, and the class period is lengthened, the new subject is commonly called a "core." Writers in the field of curriculum establish other requirements for a core, but as it works out in practice only the above-mentioned conditions need be met for the result to be designated "core." In 1948–49, about 3.6 percent of all students in grades 7–12 in the United States were enrolled in some core.[14]

The core represents a laudable attempt to introduce a fresh organizing principle into the subject matter of secondary schools. In fact, the integration of specialized fields is essential in any true problem-solving approach to teaching. Some core teachers are undoubtedly able to carry it off, and make of the core something approaching what educational theorists intend by it. But probably most leading theorists of the core movement would not dignify many present "cores" with the name.

Here is an extreme example of how far cores may depart from the theoretical conception. The authors have observed several "cores" in which the two- or three-hour period was divided into shorter periods by the teacher in charge, and the various subjects included in the core were taught separately, using a thoroughly traditional approach, including traditional textbooks. That is, in a two-hour period there may be 45 minutes devoted solidly to standard United States history, 45 minutes to formal grammar, 10 minutes to spelling, and 20 minutes to remedial reading (or arithmetic). No attempt is made to integrate these subjects—and better so, since they have few logical ties with each other. The effect is much worse when a teacher does try to blend several logically unrelated subjects simply for the sake of "integration."

Although integration has become fashionable in modern schools, it can scarcely be conducted effectively until teachers in charge of core classes come to understand their real point and can be trained for this sort of job. In Chapter 10 more will be said on the general problem of integration.

Weaknesses and Strengths of the Traditional Conception of Content in the Social Studies

The arguments most often given for retaining the traditional separate subjects of history, government, geography, economics, and the like, appear to assume an associationist theory of learning. Certain virtues are claimed

[14] *Offerings and Enrollments in High School Subjects,* chap. 5.

for learning—even if only on the level of simple memorization—the accumulated experience of the race as embodied in the traditional social-studies subjects. Although these arguments do not reject conceptualization as an aim of education, they do assume either that it is unimportant or that it will occur spontaneously in the minds of students as they memorize required content.

Perhaps the chief argument for maintaining conventional content is that, if conscientiously committed to memory, it gives a student necessary background for future acts of thought. It is held that a large store of potentially useful knowledge, acquired while in school by memory and held in readiness, will make intelligent behavior possible when problems arise later. Since no one can anticipate all or even most of the problems he will face, everyone should memorize as wide a range of content as possible. One item of content is just as relevant as any other, since relevance is judged against unknown uses.

Another argument maintains that everyone should share the common culture, as represented by accumulation of knowledge in the various scholarly disciplines, including the social sciences (but particularly the social sciences of long standing—history, geography, and government). The result is supposed to be *cultural cohesiveness.* Perhaps many who subscribe to this position assume that learning can best promote cultural unity if it is reflective; but clearly many others who hold to this aim of education feel that facts and ideas which are merely committed to memory are as useful as those which students have thought about.

The immediate and most cogent reason for retaining traditional subjects is that *they are there.* Long accumulation and the unceasing efforts of textbook writers to distill this accumulation into usable form have produced a group of definitely organized school subjects. They are known and accepted by adults in the community. Teachers have been trained in them. Students are familiar with the labels given them. The easiest course for everybody concerned is to stick with the known. The unknown is always a little frightening, if not indeed suspect. But even if it were not, there would be the problem of procuring and organizing new content to supplant old. Many teachers who would like to attempt fundamental reorganization in the social studies are frustrated by the amount of work involved.

ARGUMENTS FOR TRADITIONAL CONTENT EVALUATED

The first argument (that memorizing as much as possible of the traditional social-studies subjects supplies students with background for future intelligent behavior) may be judged in the light of our knowledge of how persons learn. If the interpretation of learning given in Chapter 2 is valid, this argument is not.

But the argument has strengths when applied in special cases. Every psychologist and every practicing teacher knows how great is the range of ability in students. A certain proportion—usually a small minority—is "academically minded." These are generally students from homes in which intellectual interests are paramount. They do well on "intelligence tests" and make A's in their academic courses—English, mathematics, science, history, and the like. There is reason to believe that the upper 5 or 10 percent of students may profit from traditional subjects taught "straight." Not much is known about how learning in a bright child differs from that in a dull one. A bright child does acquire more facts in a conventional program of study and remembers them longer. What is not well understood is the *qualitative* difference in learning between the two. Probably a bright child experiences many of the facts he encounters in a different way—conceptualizes on his own, unaided by teacher or textbook writer. In short, he relates standard facts of a subject to general ideas (to the extent to which it can be done); then uses these ideas in future problematic situations. A bright student, we know, is more likely to "mull over" what he finds in a textbook or reading reference—to try to "fit it in" to what he already knows (i.e., his present stock of generalizations). He searches actively for meaning.

Not only do average and below-average children learn less quantitatively but their learning is probably qualitatively inferior. They conceptualize less; that is, the facts they memorize tend to remain isolated. Facts come to them as arbitrary associations and remain so. The argument that standard facts of the social studies, if committed to memory, will serve as a background for future thought is probably erroneous except when applied to exceptionally able students and has weaknesses even then. It assumes that bright students will profit more from a traditional subject-centered approach than they would from a problem-centered approach. Although we may readily grant that a few bright students do enjoy and unquestionably profit from the mastery of a systematically organized body of knowledge, it would be very difficult to substantiate the above assumption. Possibly such students are benefited most if given an opportunity to delve into scholarly fields as deeply as they wish but at the same time encouraged and helped to use this material in problematic situations.

The second argument in favor of traditional social-studies subjects (that they give people common knowledge and values which produce a social cohesiveness, a group spirit, difficult if not impossible to achieve otherwise) also has both weaknesses and strengths. It is difficult to see how memorization by students of a common body of facts will help to bind people together if the facts are neither understood nor remembered, as is so commonly the case now. On the other hand, a set of widely shared working principles —the "rules" achieved through conceptualization—may effectively bind together that portion of a population which achieves conceptualization through contact with traditional social-studies subjects. It may be that the brightest 10 percent—or so—of a population is to a degree welded together in this manner.

The same reasoning applies where moral values are concerned. Moral ideals are probably learned (to the point of influencing behavior) only when a student has an opportunity to resolve reflectively conflicts in values. Moral rules are effective guides to behavior only when understood, not when held blindly in the form of mere verbal associations. A student is not likely to learn honesty simply by reading and reciting the story of George Washington and the cherry tree (especially since the story itself is dishonest), or patriotism by reading Nathan Hale's famous last words, or courage by memorizing Captain James Lawrence's immortal statement, "Don't give up the ship."

Let us now examine the last of the arguments given: that in most situations the only practical course is to hew fairly close to traditional content of the social studies because of the training of teachers, their work loads, and preference of administrators and community adults. Since most "integrated" courses appear to employ conventional types of content, their existence does not disprove that traditional content is the only practical content.

The argument is weak in that it infers that something which has not been tried is necessarily impractical. It is also weak in that it seems to reject *first moves* toward reorganization, even though first moves would appear feasible in a relatively traditional atmosphere.

Although a fundamental overhauling of the content of the social studies has not been tried on a widespread scale in this country, the present book assumes that *to some degree* such an overhauling is possible. It also assumes that an overhauling is desirable in any situation where a teacher knows what he is doing and where there is enough acceptance of the move so that general opposition will not develop. It is not suggested that fundamental overhauling is desirable in every situation.

Under what circumstances may it be best to remain basically with tra-

210

ditional courses and course content? If (1) a teacher has had no training or experience in any other curricular organization; (2) students have had no previous contact with anything but subject-centered courses; (3) a community strenuously objects to anything but the traditional subject-centered courses; (4) a teacher has a heavy work load—say, five classes daily of forty students each, and several required extracurricular and community obligations—in any of these cases, a definite course framework (as provided by a textbook and definite course boundaries) may impose less strain and insecurity on teacher and students than more flexible, integrated courses. We know that, if teacher and students feel reasonably comfortable, if stress and strain are at a minimum, more reflection can take place. Thus in some situations more conceptualization may occur from reorganizing and amplifying traditional content *in small ways* than from turning courses upside down.

In any case, *quality* of teaching is of fundamental importance. It is possible that in recent years revamping the curriculum has been overemphasized in relation to the act of teaching itself. Effectiveness of instruction probably depends more upon personality, intelligence, and skill of a teacher than upon particular curricular structures.

Quality of teaching *can* be very high in a traditional textbook- and subject-oriented school. Whether it is or not depends largely on *what use* the teacher makes of textbooks and *how he organizes his own courses* within the conventional framework of history, geography, civics, and the like. In Chapter 17 we shall demonstrate how a traditional textbook course can be enriched and vitalized.

The remaining chapters in Part II are devoted to examining the theoretical requirements of content which will have maximum usefulness in reflective learning, and to an examination of the areas of culture most likely to reveal fruitful problems and content for reflection.

DISCUSSION QUESTIONS AND EXERCISES

1. What are some possible outcomes of simultaneous operation of trends toward both specialization and integration in the social sciences? Write a short essay on "What is ahead for the social sciences?"
2. How much of a case could be developed for classifying as social sciences the following subjects? Human biology, medicine, psychiatry, ethics, literature, philosophy.

3. Can you see flaws in the analysis of Chapter 9 pertaining to the role of history? If history is not a social science, what is it?

4. How do you explain the dominance of history as a high-school social study? How do you interpret the fact that history is much more likely to be a required subject than, say, economics or sociology?

5. How do you explain the fact that most college textbooks in social science include no mention of the methodological assumptions of their authors? Does this suggest that the authors are unconcerned with methodology? Does it suggest that authors believe students already understand their methodological assumptions?

6. It has been argued that it is dull, not bright, students who profit most from a traditional subject-centered curriculum and memory-level learning. The contention is that, since dull students are incapable of reflection, a problem-centered program is impractical for them. Evaluate this argument carefully.

7. Many persons will disagree with the propositions advanced in Chapter 9 concerning present content of social-studies subjects. For students who wish to perform research on this question, the following is suggested: Select several high-school social-studies textbooks in the fields of history, civics (government), and geography. Include under each both recent titles and titles in use in the middle 1930's. Seek evidence pertinent to these propositions:

   a. In a given field, there is a body of standard content which is included in most textbooks.

   b. Except for considerable compression and simplification, much content of high-school texts resembles that of their college counterparts.

   c. In spite of changes in such aspects as organization, reading ease, format, and pictorial materials, the content treated has not changed significantly in twenty years.

REFERENCES

For readable and provocative treatments of the status and role of the social sciences in American civilization, see Stuart Chase, *The Proper Study of Mankind* (Harper, 1948), and Clyde Kluckhohn, *Mirror for Man* (Whittlesey House, 1949). The latter deals specifically with anthropology as a possible organizational core for the efforts of social scientists. Although recommended for mature students only, the classic study of the nature and role of the social sciences is Robert E. Lynd's *Knowledge for What?* (Princeton University Press, 1940).

Students who wish a short treatment of social studies in the secondary curriculum may read Edgar B. Wesley, *Teaching Social Studies in High Schools* (Heath, 1950), Chapters 2, 5–6. For a historical treatment see Henry Johnson, *An Introduction to the History of Social Sciences in Schools* (Scribner, 1932). Although the book is outdated, students will still find worth reading Charles A. Beard's *The Nature of the Social Sciences* (Scribner, 1934).

Those interested in textbooks may wish to read Bessie Pierce, *Civic Attitudes in American School Textbooks* (University of Chicago Press, 1930), and Arthur

Walworth, *School Histories at War* (Harvard University Press, 1938). A glowing account of modern textbooks is given in *Textbooks in Education,* published in 1949 by the American Textbook Publishers Institute.

Perhaps the best criticism of assumptions now underlying the selection of content is Earl C. Kelley, *Education for What Is Real* (Harper, 1947).

Chapter 10

A Proposal for Selection of Content in the Social Studies

Content as the Data of Reflection

INSTEAD of restricting our conception of the content of learning to pre-determined, formally organized bodies of knowledge, we may think of content as the subject matter which functions in the thinking process. *The content of learning may be regarded as the data of acts of reflective thought.*

The content of reflection—in contrast to the content of history, political science, geography, and so on—includes every relevant aspect of the mental and physical environment in which a given act of thought occurs, everything a thinker brings to bear on a problem. Prominent among the resources applied to any act of reflection are general ideas (if-then-always generalizations) which may be either judgments of fact or judgments of value. These generalizations supply the assumptions, the hypotheses, and to a degree the factual data of an act of thought. They represent the previous experience of a learner, as captured in his conceptual structure. An act of thought also makes use of concrete sensory data (observations) which are either recalled from past experience or obtained through new experiences implied by the problem. In short, the content of a given act of thought includes one's own personal resources plus pertinent data from the social and physical environment.

A given act of thought also employs facts, values, and assumptions about the nature of thought itself. A person may not be aware of the methodo-logical assumptions he is making; he may not realize that if he thinks reflectively he is selecting an approach to knowing which is fundamentally different from other approaches he might have selected. Nevertheless, whether explicit or not, whenever thought is undertaken such assumptions operate. This fact suggests an idea of crucial importance: a comparative study of methodologies should be an important part of any course in social studies.

Any act of thought involves *selection* of resources. A thinker can use only those mental, cultural, and physical resources which are pertinent to solution of the problem at hand—and no other. He must be able to distinguish what is relevant from what is not. He must learn to keep irrelevant resources in the background lest they clog the mind and impede thought.

Content assumes an *emergent* character. From the standpoint of a learner, it comes into existence as it is needed; it does not have a life independent of his own. During an act of thought, a learner searches for usable data. The data which he locates and uses were not data before that time. The factual materials from which he draws data may, it is true, have functioned as data for a great many other persons. But to an individual learner, factual materials are nothing until their function in thought is seen. In a very real sense, knowledge does not exist before learning begins.

Some Educational Implications of Viewing Content as the Data of Reflection

What does our proposed revision of outlook mean in practice? It suggests that a prominent part of the content of each learning problem will consist of items from the conceptual backgrounds of students: knowledges, values, and habits which have been acquired in former experience. As new problems arise, this conceptual equipment comes into play in new ways. At various places in Part I we discussed how necessary it is that teachers understand the conceptual equipment which students bring with them to a classroom. This aspect of the content of any given learning problem is fully as important as content which comes to a student from outside himself.

When a student views learning materials proffered from outside—as through a teacher's lecture—he sees as content only that part which is sharply pertinent to his learning problem. Content functions as *data* or *evidence*, or it is not to be regarded as the content of learning. Unless it functions literally as data, it is mere stuff—irrelevant, useless. Now what happens if we try to apply such a criterion to the traditional content of high-school social studies? It is quite probable that, whatever the problem under scrutiny, some traditional subject matter of the social studies will be serviceable; but it is also probable that much needed content will not be available through the traditional subjects (or will be inaccessible) and must be sought.

Thus traditional organization tends to provide materials which are irrelevant and to deny use of those which might be pertinent. At first glance, it might seem that, if we adopt the idea that the proper content of social-studies education is the data of thought, we have rejected all possibility of planning courses or of preparing teaching materials in advance of actual learning situations. However, even though the particular problems which a class will study may not always be predicted with certainty, and even though, when a problem has been selected, all needed data cannot be ascertained in advance, there are principles for partially solving this dilemma which will be treated later.

DIFFICULTIES IN VIEWING CONTENT AS DATA OF REFLECTION

It is not easy to think of content as the data of thought. For one thing, the entire weight of tradition is against it. We have always regarded the content of education as the products of prior thinking; students learn the conclusions of others. It is therefore quite out of pattern to view the content of learning as beliefs and evidence which evolve continuously and change with every change of learning situation. Yet this is precisely what content is *psychologically*, and, if most modern views of the nature of learning are correct, content can be nothing else.

Second, not enough is known about the psychological process of thinking and memory. As was indicated in Chapter 2, the exact mechanism of reflection is not yet well understood by psychologists. Therefore, any attempt to define the content of education as the content of thinking is bound to be somewhat unsatisfactory. But despite present limited knowledge, some such attempt must be made if schools are to make progress in promoting conceptual learning.

Third, the education which teachers typically receive tends to separate method and content. This problem is of such critical importance that it requires examination in some detail.

INSEPARABILITY OF METHOD AND CONTENT

The curriculum of teachers' colleges and university departments of education is usually separated into two parts: (1) subject-matter courses, in which prospective teachers are taught "content," and (2) methods courses, in which prospective teachers are taught something called "teaching methods." This distinction might be a useful convenience if everyone recognized its basically fictional character. As it is, the distinction does great damage because almost everyone takes it literally.

The task of selecting and organizing content is methodology in its intellectual and pedagogical sense. The right selection and organization of content virtually guarantees that reflection will occur among those who are exposed to it. If content is properly selected and organized, the technique of presentation is not likely to be so bad as to prevent reflection. Conversely, the smoothest and most efficient use of technique cannot produce reflection if content is irrelevant, trivial, unintelligible, or otherwise inappropriate.

Therefore, the statement that a method of teaching is wrong ought to mean that the content is wrong, and the statement that content is wrong ought to mean that it cannot advance the use of a desired intellectual method. A realistic discussion of what constitutes desirable content ought to show how that content is going to function in a learning situation, just as a realistic discussion of a particular intellectual method ought to reveal the kinds of content most appropriate to it.

If the inseparability of method and content is understood by all, then it should be fairly easy to appreciate the significance of the idea that the content of education should be regarded as including only the data of thought. For this is the same as saying that content, if it is meaningful and useful, must be related to an intellectual method appropriate to it. When we say that the content of learning is the data of reflection we are saying, in a different context, that no content has meaning apart from the method by which it is verified and used.

Individual Needs Versus Social Needs: A False Issue

It was suggested earlier that viewing the content of learning as the data of reflection, rather than as predetermined collections of facts, poses difficult problems for teachers and textbook writers; it seems to exclude the possibility of selecting subject matter in advance of the reflective acts in which it is to be used. A way around this dilemma would appear to be a frankly problem-centered approach, in which teaching materials are selected—and textbooks written—so as to incorporate data which are relevant to existing or potential problems of students. Such content may be regarded as problem centered; it has the general characteristic of presenting contrasting or conflicting ideas and factual data pertinent to them.

There still remains the question: Which problems are to be selected for study? We have suggested elsewhere that problems should be selected in such a way that they will involve beliefs which are widely held by students and which have broad social significance. This principle, although useful, does not without further clarification move us entirely out of the woods. High-school students have acquired hundreds, if not thousands, of beliefs about matters which might be judged socially important. Limitations of time and energy make it impossible to raise for reflective examination propositions corresponding to all of them.

The fact that many beliefs can never be challenged is less disturbing if, in the process of testing some beliefs, students have conceptualized a method of problem solving which they can apply widely. As suggested earlier, a study of reflective methodology *per se* should make up an important part of the social-studies curriculum.

Does this mean that so long as students can be taught a general methodology it does not make much difference what specific subjects they study? Undoubtedly, if the sole aim of a teacher is to get reflection along with some conceptual understanding of the reflective process, one item of subject matter (so long as it conforms to the general requirements of reflective content) may serve as well as another. If a teacher's only aim is this, his students may do as well by concentrating on the study of football plays as by concentrating on, say, the behavior of Congress.

However, most persons believe that some ideas and issues of American culture are in greater need of reflective scrutiny in our schools than are others. This view demands some discussion of the whole notion of *need* and the controversy which surrounds this term.

EDUCATION AS BASED ON NEEDS OF CHILDREN

Almost everyone agrees that public education should in some way take cognizance of the needs of children and youth. But not everyone agrees on what children need or on just how education should deal with needs, even if they could be determined. One group of progressives has insisted that no one can know the needs of a child better than the child himself. According to this group, children should be encouraged to tell about the problems that they feel right now, and school programs should be adjusted to deal with them.

Other groups feel that, although schools should not ignore immediate felt needs of pupils, other needs, of which children and youth are largely unaware, should be served by the curriculum in whatever ways adults deem best. For example, children have a need (which often they do not recognize) to prepare for various aspects of adult life, and only adults are likely to understand such a need. Children also need (which they seldom understand or appreciate) to become wise citizens. This need must be met if the standards of the social group are to be served.

EDUCATION AS BASED ON NEEDS OF SOCIETY

We may identify another position, which tends to disregard, or at least offer a different interpretation of, needs of children as a criterion for selecting content: Educationists should look first at the social order before trying to construct curriculums. They should seek to identify the most pressing societal needs and then see that children are so educated as to meet them.

For example, it might be ascertained that the nation has failed badly in relation to some goal which is generally acceptable. Democratic principles may be in process of violation. Economic difficulties or the specter of war may confront us. Youth should study these problems and should be taught the necessary knowledges and skills which will enable them, as adults, to reduce them.

This general point of view is not much different from the modification of the outlook first stated in the foregoing section, to the effect that although the needs of children and youth should be the basis for curriculum building, adults are best able to determine what these needs are. The focus is somewhat different, however; the one position focuses on students, the other on the social order.

EDUCATION AS BASED ON PERSONAL AND SOCIETAL NEED

There is a third position which reconciles the two approaches described above. If one accepts the culture concept of sociologists and anthropologists, it follows that an individual personality is always a product of its surrounding culture. Without culture (in the sociological sense of a total way of life) a human being is devoid of personality—and, one might add, of needs. According to the culture concept, the personality of each individual is simply an extension of the beliefs, customs, attitudes, needs, values, and habits of the group in which he lives. This does not mean that there is no such thing as individuality, but that even the most rugged of individualists derives the greater part of his personality from his social environment.

The aspirations and frustrations of any individual are likely, therefore, to resemble closely those of numerous other members of the same culture, or subculture. Personally felt problems will have a large element of commonness and be closely related to pervasive social conditions because they are a result of *problem-generating features of the culture.* Emotional conflicts among individuals, for example, develop from discrepancies and inconsistencies in the surrounding social situation. A culture which was integrated in its central values, or which possessed a satisfactory means for dealing with inconsistencies, would not produce personalities torn asunder with emotional conflicts.

Acceptance of this third position enables one to avoid certain dilemmas involved in acceptance of either of the other two positions. Curriculum planners often develop two lists of problems, one "personal" and the other "social," implying that social problems are not personal and that personal problems are not social. Yet it should be apparent that a problem of any kind is always personal in the sense that it is held by a person, or persons, and that every personally held problem has social consequences. A person who is unemployed, unable to support himself and his family, and looking for work certainly has a personal problem. But the fact that he is unemployed stems from a social problem and in turn produces certain social effects; and the way he solves his problem will have still other effects.

Likewise, a person who is expected to study unemployment as a social problem will not be motivated to do so except as he comes to feel personally that this social problem is his problem. Not that he must become unemployed in order to feel the problem of unemployment. As a matter of fact, the most objective and highly motivated studies of unemployment have been made by employed persons. But he must be able to identify himself with the unemployed person. He must have enough imagination to see how the unemployment of any person tends to affect his own income, cost of living, job opportunities, chances for war or peace, and so on.

Professor Louis E. Raths and his associates at New York University,[1] on the basis of exploratory research with elementary-school children, have postulated eight basic needs of children in the American culture: (1) the need to belong, (2) the need for a sense of achievement, (3) the need for economic security, (4) the need to be free from fear and aggression, (5) the need for love and affection, (6) the need to be free from intense feelings of guilt, (7) the need to share in decisions, and (8) the need to under-

[1] Louis E. Raths, *An Application to Education of the Needs Theory,* Bronxville, New York, 1949.

stand society, its problems, issues, beliefs, and values. Raths has elaborated the hypothesis that children who are unable to meet all of these needs tend to adopt defensive mechanisms such as those described on pp. 50–51.

Raths is of the opinion that these eight needs are not innate but are learned from the culture. He also has evidence that the culture often thwarts the very needs which it builds into individuals. For example, people learn to value a feeling of belonging but they also learn values of caste and class, which stand in the way of everyone's having a feeling of belonging. They learn to want a sense of achievement, but many of the accepted means for meeting this need produce intense feelings of guilt.

This analysis also illuminates the fact that means and ends are so continuous with one another that the actual meaning of any need is found in the means for achieving it. Thus it is unrealistic to categorize needs as social and biological. The need for food, for example, is usually considered biological, but a moment's reflection will show that this need has no meaning until food is defined. In some cultures a plate of fried grasshoppers would meet the need for food whereas a broiled steak would be more acceptable in the American culture.

For many Americans of the middle class, meeting the need for a sense of achievement means keeping up with the Joneses. This may conflict with other important needs and values. Such conflict is nowhere better illustrated than in the area of social class in the American culture. Although Americans typically believe that social climbers are contemptible, they also believe it desirable for a person to improve himself. Self-improvement usually means that a person tries to advance to the social class next above him. The culture is so structured that an individual is likely to experience frustration whether he succeeds or fails in his efforts at social climbing.

The frustration associated with failure is too obvious to need elaboration. Not so obvious is the frustration of success. The person who successfully rises into the social class above that of his parents and close friends sometimes becomes ashamed of his origins. His new associates may talk and dress differently from the way his parents, other relatives, and old friends do. He may feel that his new friends and old friends have little in common. He may arrange matters so that the two groups are not likely to meet. Whatever he does, he is open to feelings of guilt. His conflict is basically between a desire to improve himself and a desire to be loyal to his parents. The fact that the culture approves personal advancement does not change the fact that the culture also expects him to love, respect, and honor his parents.

Cultural analysis of personality and the problem of needs makes it clear that *there is a large class of problems which in content are at the same time both individual and societal.* Any problem of this class will be felt personally by large numbers of individuals; it will also correspond to one or more broad social issues. Education concerned with these serves at the same time the needs of individual students and the larger social group, and meets both felt and imputed needs. This does not mean that the content of education is never imposed, for an individual often fails to see a relationship between his frustrations and the broader social maladjustments in which they are rooted.

UNRECOGNIZED CULTURAL CONFLICTS

According to the cultural approach, the term *need* is a value term in the sense that the culture (1) values the absence of certain frustrations and (2) cherishes certain means for reducing frustration. The larger American culture, for example, does not condone a person's meeting his need to achieve by robbing as many banks as he can. Because needs are cultural in their origin and social in their meaning there is no escape from the practice of imposition in education. Much trouble today arises from the fact that the culture through its schools imposes conflicting values upon individuals with the result that many persons do not know what they need.

In the United States today there are many problems which cause great emotional disturbance in individuals in spite of, or perhaps because of, the fact that they are but dimly sensed or understood. Persons with such problems know that there is something wrong with their lives. They feel unhappy, lonely, frightened, or insecure and yet cannot tell why. Some of this confusion is plainly due to the fact that the culture tends to obscure and conceal from them the sources of their difficulties.

Since personal problems which are rooted in unrecognized cultural conflicts cannot be effectively verbalized by troubled individuals, certain psychoanalysts have turned to a study of culture as they seek to clarify the role of the unconscious in the neurotic lives of their patients. In their therapy they recognize that an untrained individual finds it difficult to analyze the culture objectively; he takes the culture for granted, assuming that because it is so familiar to him its structure must be logical, right, and natural. Cultural anthropologists and psychiatrists know better; they know that the culture may generate severe conflicts, which are understood but dimly, if at all, by persons suffering them.

In the future, curriculum making probably will rely heavily on data supplied by sociologists, anthropologists, psychologists, and psychiatrists. A number of professional educators are already working closely with scientists in these fields. The field of psychology has, of course, been an adjunct of education for more than half a century, but in the main its contribution has not been of the kind here suggested. Only recently have psychologists become interested in discrepancies of the culture as a source of intrapersonal conflict.

A Recommended Approach to Selection of Subject Matter in the Social Studies

We are now ready to suggest a purpose for social-studies education which takes into account both method and content: *The foremost aim of instruction in high-school social studies is to help students examine reflectively issues in the closed areas of American culture.*[2]

According to this statement of purpose, teaching materials should be drawn from a selection of conflicting propositions in such controversial areas as race and minority group relations, social class, economics, sex, courtship and marriage, religion and morality, and national and patriotic beliefs, plus a wide range of relevant data to be used in testing them. Many of these propositions will be derived from, or correspond to, the values, beliefs, and attitudes of high-school students. One might say, therefore, that in any given learning situation teaching materials should be drawn from (1) broadly social and highly controversial issues of the culture; (2) knowledges, values, and attitudes of students; and (3) relevant data of the social sciences.

One reason why social-studies education should focus on issues in closed areas is that it is here that personally felt problems (particularly intrapersonal conflicts) tend to intersect with pervasive and troublesome cultural issues. To study such problems provides a way of meeting both individual and social needs, by reducing the amount and intensity of intrapersonal conflict and by making such conflict more manageable as it arises. It is to be hoped that society will thus gradually achieve a clearer sense of direction, more harmony and cohesiveness, and fuller realization of the democratic ideal.

[2] Readers who wish to review the definition of closed areas should reread pp. 6–7.

Many objections will be raised to the above statement of purpose, method, and content. Some persons will argue that, if a policy of reflective learning is to be pursued at all, it should be followed only in connection with problems unaffected by strong emotional blockings; that further attempts to study closed areas in the schoolroom not only will inflict on teachers the wrath of organized interest groups in the community but, because the same taboos operate in the minds of students as in the minds of parents, will necessarily be unsuccessful. It is thought that students, like their parents, believe what they want to believe—particularly in the closed areas—and that attempts to produce reflection will not overcome this habit.

The task of getting students themselves to reflect in highly controversial matters has at least been made easier by knowledge gained from experience in psychiatry and group dynamics (see Chapter 7). Opposition of interest groups in communities to reflection in the classroom is another matter, and will be treated in Chapter 20. Our concern now is to examine whether a teacher may reasonably expect success (i.e., to produce reflection and help students achieve more harmonious and adequate beliefs), if he focuses his instruction on closed areas. Assuming that the proper emotional climate has been achieved, there are at least two reasons why a teacher can expect success.

First, it is impossible to induce serious reflection in students unless they can be made to *feel* a problem. Reflection is hard and often painful work. Unless a fairly pressing or enticing reason has emerged, very few persons will willingly engage upon it. It is in the closed areas that the great controversies, perplexities, and doubts of adolescent youth occur. A skillful teacher should be able to produce a higher level of motivation through study of issues in closed areas than through study of almost anything else. It is true that beliefs in closed areas are deeply cherished and that this may produce a serious barrier to reflection, but by the same token a teacher can usually create a reason for reflection by showing how one cherished belief is incompatible with an equally prized one.

Second, young people are reputedly more flexible and open-minded than adults. There are no closed areas at all in the outlook of a very small child. It is education, both formal and informal, which gradually closes certain areas of living to rational discussion. This process of closing the mind of a child takes time, but a considerable amount of closure has been accomplished by the time he reaches high school. However, the high-school period is also a time when youth begin to wonder about some of the beliefs they have learned to take for granted. Intellectual interests of many young persons reach their peak. Serious doubts develop as it is noted that adults do not always practice taboos which they have taught children to embrace. Faith in the omniscience of adults is shaken and one may note a general tendency to rebel against parental authority. Given the storm, the stress, the uncertainty, and the rebelliousness of this period, a serious threat to social stability results from any educational program which fails to take advantage of the motives for reflective study which develop at this time.

Many adults fear that tender young minds will not be able to understand the more serious controversies of life. Actually, the so-called tender young minds are more likely than adult minds to profit from reflective study of deeply controversial issues. If it is postponed until adulthood, such study is likely never to occur.

The fear that youth will accept "wrong" beliefs if they open their minds to new ideas is actually only a fear that they will accept different beliefs. This is not necessarily the outcome. Reflection may fortify or it may undermine conventional beliefs. There are no prior guarantees as to what conclusions it will produce, but a great many conventional beliefs can emerge from reflective scrutiny more strongly accepted than before. The aim of reflection is never to destroy a belief, but to evaluate it in light of the best evidence and logic. Reflection can only guarantee the emergence of beliefs which are relatively more adequate and harmonious than the ones young persons normally hold.

Curriculum Organization for a Reflective Approach to Learning

STANDARD SUBJECTS AS BURDENED WITH IRRELEVANT CONTENT

It was indicated in Chapter 9 and again in the present chapter that much of the subject matter of the standard social studies is irrelevant to problem solving in areas of ideological controversy. Learning materials are relevant when they can set and clarify problems for students or move them toward conclusions, preferably in the form of generalizations which have predictive value. If materials are unrelated, or cannot be related, to any imaginable values, beliefs, or attitudes of students, it will be difficult and probably impossible for them to supply content for reflection. This does not mean that a student must have an attitude toward the tariff—for example—in order to learn reflectively about the tariff. He may have an attitude toward something else—say, the cost of living—which can be clarified by his introduction to scholarly studies of the tariff.

Inclusion in the standard subjects of irrelevant material is not in itself an argument against a curriculum of separately organized subjects. We might retain our history, geography, and civics courses and, by proper revision of the subject matter in each, create courses far more provocative and useful than anything we now have. There is another respect, however, in which a curriculum of separately organized courses is less than ideal.

Life Problems and Subject-Matter Boundaries

The content of any act of thought is likely to cut across traditional subject-matter boundaries. Life problems of students almost invariably extend across more than one field of inquiry, unlike textbook problems of history, political science, economics, or any other social-science subject. If any issue of broad social import is to be understood, probably it can best be done through study of data from several of the social sciences and perhaps a number of other fields as well.

For example, problems of race cut across the fields of politics, economics, religion, biology, psychology, and probably others. Unless he can draw from all relevant sources and integrate pertinent facts into a single, meaningful picture, no one can hope to deal effectively with problems of race or with virtually any other social and personal problem.

In commenting on the curricular consequences of a separate-subject organization, Professor Harold C. Hand has said:

In consequence of this conflict of inner logic—i.e., the inner logic of real-life-problem-solving vs. the inner logic of standard subjects which at best admits of but incidental attention to such problems—efforts to "functionalize" the traditional high school subjects invariably and inevitably result in asking the teacher simultaneously to serve two contrarily-oriented masters. That this is frustrating in the extreme, there can be little doubt—as any number of intelligent and conscientious teachers will testify. What is more important, the traditional master almost invariably wins out in this unhappy and unequal struggle—to the educational neglect of society and youth, as we have demonstrated. If the course is labeled "English" or "social studies" or any other name identified with a recognized body of more or less standard subject matter, the teacher is conscience-stricken unless he gets across at least a respectable minimum of whatever this subject matter may be. This he usually does regardless of the fate of the problems with which he is also supposed to be dealing. But this neglect of problems also induces feelings of guilt, it must be recognized. What this adds up to is scarcely a recipe for good mental health.[3]

[3] B. Othanel Smith, William O. Stanley, Kenneth D. Benne, Archibald W. Anderson (eds.), *Readings in the Social Aspects of Education*, Interstate Press, 1951, pp. 387–388.

A *Proposal for Selection of Content in the Social Studies*

THE LOGIC AND PLAN OF THE CORE CURRICULUM

The core curriculum, or course in "common learnings," has been proposed as a solution to this conflict. Although many of the standard school subjects are retained for purposes of specialization, the most important offering of the curriculum focuses deliberately on problems of living. A block of time, two or more hours, is reserved for their study, and teachers responsible for this are freed from other subject-matter commitments. Experience to date suggests that teachers working with a core curriculum have not always understood the pedagogical implications of a reflective approach to learning. Teachers who are free to organize a core along lines most congenial to a reflective approach may be helped by the following suggestions: A core should be problem centered, and organized on the basis of a series of contradictions in belief in closed areas of the culture which we might expect to be shared by most students. Work should be organized in a sequence of blocks, one on the study of discrepancies in our racial ideology, another concerned with discrepancies in our beliefs about government and politics, another with discrepancies in our economic thinking, and so on. Ideally, all the closed areas would be covered in such a core, although probably not in any one year. In fact, it might be advisable to limit a single year to exploration of no more than two or three broad problem areas.

Although a core of this sort would inevitably "integrate" the social studies and embrace data from fields such as literature, science, mathematics, and perhaps medicine, it would not integrate simply for the sake of integration. The focus would always be *on a problem and what is needed to study it*. Irrelevant material would be rigorously excluded. The study of a particular issue might be regarded as a "unit of work," provided *unit* is defined broadly to refer to the experiences related to reflective study of an issue.

ACHIEVING A "CORE APPROACH" IN SUBJECT-CENTERED COURSES

Some teachers have revised their traditional courses in an attempt to make them serve better the needs of reflection. One teacher who had been teaching literature for thirteen years was assigned in his fourteenth year to a class in eighth-grade geography. Since he knew very little geography, he found it convenient to cover the textbook page by page in traditional recitation style. However, it soon became evident to the teacher that only a few of his students understood what was covered, and that student interest was lagging.

He solved this problem by sharing it with his students. Exploring with them the problem of making the course more worth while, he discovered that they were much interested in understanding conflicts between the United States and the Soviet Union. He and the class agreed that some knowledge of geography would help them to understand these conflicts, also that knowledge other than the "purely geographical" would be essential. It was decided to make a rather thorough study of conflicts between the two nations and to utilize geography only as needed.

As study developed, students learned relevant history, economics, philosophy, political science, and geography. They also acquired skill in letter writing, public speaking, interviewing, chart and map interpretation, and simple statistics. The course ceased to look like geography. The casual visitor would have thought he was observing a class in contemporary problems. A geography class altered in this way may acquire many characteristics of a core. In fact, it may achieve a more fruitful integration of data than a "core" taught by a less understanding teacher.

Chapter 17 will deal on a how-to-do-it level with means for teaching broadly certain traditional social-studies subjects so that maximum reflection may be achieved.

The Role of Social Analysis in the Selection of Content

It was suggested earlier in the present chapter that curriculum making will eventually rely heavily on data supplied by social scientists, particularly in the fields of sociology, anthropology, psychology, and psychiatry. With respect to education, the role of scientists in these fields will be to uncover and describe cultural contradictions and to discover the extent to which these have been incorporated in individuals as felt conflicts or as unconscious disharmonies in outlook. This type of information is as indispensable to a teacher of separately organized social-studies subjects as it is to teachers of core or other openly problem-centered approaches.

Unfortunately, the task of gathering and organizing this kind of information has been neglected. However, a teacher does not face an impossible task in social analysis when he tries to develop some catalogue of cultural inconsistencies. Many more or less adequate studies of belief have been made, sources of which include (1) public-opinion polls (such as the Gallup Poll); (2) community studies, as conducted by sociologists and anthropologists, which include means of sampling public opinion (such as the Middletown or Yankee City studies); (3) clinical experience of psychiatrists, psychologists, and social workers (as reported, say, by Karen Horney in *The Neurotic Personality of Our Time*); (4) studies of belief in special areas (as reported in Alfred Winslow Jones' *Life, Liberty, and Property*); and (5) the opinions of trained observers of the social scene based on observations of behavior, conversations with people, and study of documentary sources (as Harold Laski's *The American Democracy*).

Chapters 11–16 list some of the more apparent contradictions in American belief and behavior in certain of the closed areas. These chapters should be regarded as tentative and exploratory. They are offered for what they are: an initial attempt to catalogue certain American beliefs and values, and to indicate the meaning of the contradictions revealed by showing the historical origins and present motives for them. No such listing can be fully adequate for several reasons. First, sources available at present, although varying greatly in accuracy of conclusions, rely on techniques for discovering beliefs which need further refinement. Perhaps least adequate are public-opinion polls, and for this reason we have placed chief reliance on studies which have employed more intensive techniques of investigation. Second, the American culture changes with such rapidity that any study of beliefs risks obsolescence within a few years after it is made. Of necessity, we have drawn data from studies which are now several years old; however adequate at the time the studies were made, their conclusions may no longer be valid. For example, American attitudes toward civil liberties appear to have shifted considerably since World War II. American attitudes toward sex underwent significant change during the 1920's.

Third, most studies do not adequately depict the important differences in belief between regions, races, ethnic and religious groups, age groups, and the two sexes. For example, an average person of the Tennessee Valley is likely to be less alarmed about "creeping socialism" (of the TVA variety) than is an average person of, say, Iowa. Some of our sociological studies have been made of what were regarded as "typical communities"; but in a very real sense there are no typical communities. Further, the United States is class structured, and basic outlooks of the different classes vary in fundamental aspects. Research designed to show these differences has been conducted, particularly by a group of sociologists associated with W. Lloyd Warner. Our own cataloguing of beliefs and values emphasizes those of the middle class, first, because limitations of space do not permit full analysis in terms of class differences, and second, because we are, by and large, a middle-class people. Middle-class mores and attitudes tend increasingly to permeate the entire culture.

Each of the chapters from 11 through 16 is organized around what we have regarded as a closed area of culture. In Chapter 1, a closed area was defined as an area of belief and behavior characterized by a relatively large amount of irrationality, prejudice, inconsistency, confusion, and taboo. In closed areas reflective treatment of problems has largely been excluded. The areas treated in Chapters 11–16 are as follows:

1. Economics. Although this area is "open" to most professional economists and to many laymen, there is a popular lay economic ideology which is fraught with great confusion and inconsistency and is influenced by certain taboos which make rational thought difficult. Some of the commonly used terms—such as *socialism*—are freighted with emotion.

2. Race and minority-group relations. This area is becoming increasingly open to reflective inquiry and in some parts of the country could scarcely be termed a closed area. But in the South objective study of Negro-white relations, though not impossible, is still difficult, and in other places beliefs about Indians, Mexicans, Armenians, Jews, or Poles are confused and inconsistent.

3. Social class. This problem area is neatly ignored as a result of the widespread belief, "There are no social classes in America." Although objective study of class behavior is not regarded as sinful, it does make many persons uncomfortable. That social class is truly a closed area is demonstrated by the fact that people generally are highly inconsistent in their beliefs and behavior regarding class phenomena, and that our "success" ideology produces conflicts not understood by persons who regard themselves as "failures."

4. Sex, courtship, and marriage. This area is much more open to inquiry than it was even a decade ago. Sex education—of a sort—is now fairly common in public schools. But it usually does not encourage the critical analysis of our sex ideology, which is full of contradictions and which may well produce more intrapersonal conflict than belief patterns in any other area.

5. Religion and morality. It is generally felt that although one may be able to talk to a man rationally about any other subject, one cannot do so about his religion; this is personal and sacred. Yet religious beliefs are probably no more closed to rational inquiry than beliefs about free enterprise and communism, patriotism, certain aspects of sex, and miscegenation. Questions of morality, apart from religion and sex, although always having religious implications, are somewhat more open to reflective inquiry.

6. Nationalism and patriotism. Many persons feel that it is unpatriotic

to question traditional beliefs in this area (even when they are demonstrated to be inconsistent). Yet the area is characterized by many contradictions between belief and behavior, and between commonly held beliefs and the requirements of national survival.

There are, of course, other closed areas besides these. Our beliefs about crime and punishment, about education, and about many aspects of politics are also often confused and contradictory. Space limitations not only confine the present book to treatment of six areas but also circumscribe treatment of each area. It is hoped that teachers will acquire ability to extend the analysis for their own purposes and for their own school classes.

Included for illustrative purposes are sample questions which might be used to instigate serious study of a contradiction in belief. They are intended to be thought-provoking rather than leading or loaded. However, no question is thought-provoking in an abstract sense. The effects of any question depend on the context in which it is raised. Some of the most "thoughtful" questions can be leading or loaded when raised in an inappropriate context. Much of the effect of any question depends upon a teacher's intent in raising it.

DISCUSSION QUESTIONS AND EXERCISES

1. Stuart Chase has said, "The culture concept of the anthropologists and sociologists is coming to be regarded as the foundation stone of the social sciences" (*Proper Study of Mankind,* p. 59). Why is the culture concept so regarded? Do you feel its significance is overrated? What other applications might it have in education in addition to that which is explored in Chapter 10?

2. If one accepts the idea that, in any learning situation, the only content worth including is that which can function evidentially in reflection, how should a textbook writer pursue his task? Devise a plan for a textbook which would reflect the foregoing assumption.

3. Would you try to help students to intellectualize their methodology in connection with every attempt at reflective problem solving? Why or why not?

4. Draw up a plan for what you would consider an ideal college program for a prospective social-studies teacher. In your plan describe (a) the ideal way in which he might acquire an understanding of essential content of the social sciences and (b) the ideal way in which he might acquire an understanding of educational theory and teaching techniques.

5. Compare the core classes you have observed in operation with the proposals for core stated in Chapter 10. To what extent do they incorporate ideas proposed herein? What are some of the problems involved in making a problem truly problem centered for students? If a core is not problem centered, does it have any advantage over separate subject courses?

6. If a committee were to be selected in your state to develop a social-studies curriculum for state-wide application, what sort of persons would you want on it? What general outlook would you prefer them to have? What fields of scholarly inquiry should be represented?

REFERENCES

The idea that content becomes meaningful only as it functions as the data of reflection is implicit in the psychology of pragmatic philosophy. As good as any references on the subject are Bode, *Conflicting Psychologies of Learning,* cited earlier, and Kelley, *Education for What Is Real,* also cited. The same outlook is expressed in the much more difficult *How We Think* by Dewey.

For material on the continuity of culture and personality, refer to any general text in sociology or anthropology. Recommended is Francis E. Merrill and H. Wentworth Eldredge, *Culture and Society* (Prentice-Hall, 1952). One of the best discussions of the cultural origin of needs is in B. Othanel Smith, William O. Stanley, and J. Harlan Shores, *Fundamentals of Curriculum Development* (World, 1950).

For discussion of new concepts of the curriculum, probably the best reference is Smith, Stanley, and Shores, cited above. Also useful is Virgil E. Herrick and Ralph W. Tyler (eds.), *Toward Improved Curriculum Theory* (University of Chicago Press, 1950). An excellent survey of curriculum problems is Harold J. Alberty, *Reorganizing the High-School Curriculum* (Macmillan, 1953).

Chapter 11

The Closed Areas: Economics

The General State of Economic Thought in Modern America

LIKE other closed areas, economics is characterized by an extensive system of beliefs and attitudes which function very much as do religious dogmas. The fury of present debates over "free enterprise," "socialism," and "creeping socialism" suggests that perhaps Americans take their economic beliefs even more seriously than their religion.

Until recently, the leading economic beliefs of middle- and upper-class Americans reflected (not always consistently) the central ideas of "classical economics." Adam Smith's great book, *An Inquiry into the Nature and Causes of the Wealth of Nations* (1776), offered the first systematic analysis of the nature of economy in what came to be known as the classical pattern. Smith was followed by David Ricardo, Thomas R. Malthus, James Mill, and his son, John Stuart Mill. These men developed and refined a body of doctrine which was to influence economic thought profoundly to the present day.

The core of classical economic thought is the idea of the self-regulating or "laissez-faire" economy—an economy composed of a large number of independent producers in competition with one another. In such a system, supposedly, everyone seeks to do as well as he can—that is, to get as much as he can for what he has to sell and to give as little as he can for what he has to buy. As people followed this pattern, competing and bargaining as individuals, the "self-regulating market" would appear.

This self-regulating market guarantees that resources will be used wisely and that people will get what they want. If demand for a certain product rises without a corresponding increase in supply, the price of that product will rise. The increase in price will reduce the number of customers and increase the number of producers (who rush in to take advantage of rising profits). Thus, through the mechanism of price, balance between demand and supply is restored. If demand for a product drops, prices fall; and demand rises again at the same time that supply falls (because falling prices will have bankrupted or discouraged the less efficient producers). According to this description of economy, supply and demand tend to balance each other, and prices tend to fluctuate about a norm, which over the long run represents the lowest price at which products can be sold without ruining producers. Economists often refer to this picture of the economy as the "competitive model," meaning that it involves a large element of abstraction and simplification but at the same time contains the essential truth of the operation of a competitive economy as seen by classicists.

To understand fully the competitive model it is necessary to comprehend the role of Say's law of markets (introduced by J. B. Say, a French economist writing in 1803). According to Say's law, the act of producing goods automatically creates a market for them. In other words, supply creates its own demand because production of a good creates total income payments (to workers, other firms, landowners, and investors) equal to the market price of the good. Say assumed that all income created would be spent, in purchases of either consumer or capital goods. He assumed no hoarding of income. The classical conception of economy, because of this assumption embodied in Say's law, excluded any possibility of a protracted business depression caused by a failure of purchasing power. It assumed that full employment is the normal state of an economy.

In order for the classical model to work, free competition is always necessary. Central to free competition is free pricing, not merely rivalry over quality of product or service given. Free pricing requires conditions such as these: numerous sellers and buyers, unaffected by any sort of monopolistic collusion; buyers and sellers informed at all times of market conditions; and complete freedom of labor and capital to move to new types of production or new geographic regions.[1]

Classical economic thought fostered a cluster of popular economic beliefs, some of which are as follows:

---

[1] Those who wish to read short but generally competent descriptions of the classical "competitive model" may turn to almost any introductory textbook in economics. Also recommended are Dudley Dillard, *The Economics of John Maynard Keynes*, Prentice-Hall, Inc., 1948, chap. 2, and C. E. Ayres, *The Industrial Economy*, Houghton Mifflin Company, 1952, chaps. 1, 13, and 14.

a. People do (or should) compete economically with each other.

b. Monopoly does not (or should not be permitted to) interfere with free competition.

c. The chief motive to behavior is the hope of economic gain (i.e., desire for money or goods).

d. The economy can operate successfully without central planning, which means government can, and should, keep hands off.

e. The laissez-faire system is harmonious with political democracy, because free competition prevents the emergence of any single individual or group with power over others.

f. Whatever economic problems may arise, they may best be handled by leaving them alone—letting nature take its course. (Business recessions can best be handled this way, for example.)

g. The economic system (if it functions properly) requires the right of private ownership and use of property, and the sanctity of contracts.

h. It is the private businessman, with his willingness to take risks in hope of profit, who supplies the mainspring of the economy.

i. The chief source of discouragement to private businessmen is government interference in their affairs. (Another source of discouragement is labor unions.)

j. Currency is sound only when it is freely exchangeable for gold or other precious metal.

k. Governments should spend as little as possible and try always to operate on a balanced budget.

Probably in no other field of human interest is there a greater gulf between present understanding of experts and that of the lay public. Average citizens have never fully understood the structure and implications of the classical competitive model. They have never understood clearly that competition meant "price competition" nor have they grasped the conditions of price competition and the role of price competition in the market. They have not even understood that the competitive model implies an absence of protective tariffs and all forms of subsidies, and a ruthless disregard for inefficient producers.

To the long-standing confusion of laymen over the nature of a competitive economy a new source of confusion has been added. Academic economists generally, as well as certain business and political leaders, have adopted a new and radically different set of economic beliefs patterned after ideas of the late John Maynard Keynes. This seems to favor large-scale public spending (even deficit spending), to be unconcerned about the size of the national debt, to take very lightly the old injunctions regarding thrift, and to reject the need for a gold-based currency. It calls for economic remedies almost exactly the opposite of what laymen have been taught to accept. In general, laymen understand the new no better than the old—in fact, they often accept both in spite of their apparent contradictions.

It is very difficult in the United States for the federal government to pursue a rational and consistent economic policy because of popular misconceptions about economics. Whatever the government may try, even though it makes sense economically, becomes a subject of widespread and heated debate and an object of "movements" to change it. But more often policies which make the most economic sense are never tried because of opposition to them. In commenting on the fate of the Brannan Plan, J. K. Galbraith, an economist who is anything but socialistic, has observed:

The most recent suggestion was that put forward by Secretary Brannan after the 1948 elections: prices of *perishable* farm products would simply be allowed to find whatever level in the market that would insure their use. The government would then make up the difference between the price actually realized and the guaranteed price with a direct subsidy. It would do no buying of perishables at all. Few ideas in American history have had a more unfortunate fate than the Brannan Plan, *and not the least of its misfortunes was in being dubbed a Plan.* In its essentials Mr. Brannan's recommendation was conservative: prices would be determined by the free play of supply and demand, the government would refrain from rigging markets even as Adam Smith would have wished. Were this plan now being applied to butter, Secretary Benson would be totally relieved of his unwelcome obligation to buy, on occasion, several million pounds a day; prices of butter would be nearer those of margarine; and dairymen would not be watching a steady and perhaps permanent disappearance of their customers. The eventual cost to government would not, in principle, be greater, nor would the income of dairymen be less. But in a notable triumph of semantics over sober debate, the Brannan Plan became solidly identified with socialism and for reasons that would be mystifying to any Socialist. In the last four years, Republicans and Democrats alike have mentioned it only to proclaim their total lack of interest in the idea.[2]

The Brannan Plan was defeated by groups reluctant to accept any governmental control or subsidy which encourages consumption. The same groups accept—with apparent but not always genuine reluctance—subsidies and controls which restrict production and therefore consumption. This conflict between the desire of little consumers and the desire of big,

[2] J. K. Galbraith, "Why Be Secretary of Agriculture?" *Harper's Magazine*, July, 1953, p. 86. Italics are the authors'.

monopoly-minded producers was the basic issue of the Brannan Plan. It was not debated openly and intelligently because of semantic tricks employed on all sides. Proponents called the plan "a restoration of the free market"; opponents called it "socialistic." The plan may not have been an adequate solution to agricultural difficulties, but the adequacy of an idea can never be determined by a frenzy of name calling. An overwhelming majority of American people do not have a grounded opinion of the Brannan Plan. Most of them, as a consequence of semantic difficulties, do not even know what it is. Regardless of whether it is any good, its rejection was accompanied by untrustworthy intellectual methods.

The failure of large numbers of Americans to think critically in the area of economics is in part a failure of the public schools. Statistics given in *Offerings and Enrollments in High School Subjects* [3] show that no more than half the students who graduate from high school have had any contact at all with the content of formal economics. Lack of emphasis on the subject matter of economics is less serious than the fact that what economic education there is in the schools focuses largely on noncontroversial content. Confusion over the meaning of free enterprise and socialism is an inevitable result of economic education which avoids controversial content.

The remainder of this chapter describes a few typical contradictions, confusions, and controversies of American economic life. It is not our purpose to supply answers to the problems posed, and the order in which contradictions are presented does not imply order of importance. Treatment of each contradiction includes a list of questions which may stimulate student reflection and lead to a better understanding of the contradiction.

Contradictions and Confusions in Economic Thought and Practice

1. *Spending and prosperity: It is believed that any prosperity resulting from large-scale government spending is false prosperity and cannot last; but it is also believed that a reduction in spending is likely to plunge the nation into a recession or depression which would be much worse than false prosperity.*

During the first administration of Franklin D. Roosevelt a deliberate effort was made to reduce unemployment through federal spending. Judged

[3] Biennial Survey of Education in the United States, 1948–50, U.S. Government Printing Office, 1951, chap. 5. Students commonly encounter incidental economic content in history, civics, and geography courses; the course in problems of democracy is typically about one-third economics; and at any given time about 5 percent of secondary-school students are enrolled in a course called economics.

by modern experience, government expenditures of these years were puny, though at the time they seemed gigantic. The economic effect of fiscal policy during these years is still debated. Some economists attribute the drift toward recovery between 1933 and 1939 to government spending and to bolster their case point out that a cut in spending in 1936 was followed by a sharp recession in 1937. But because recovery was so slow during all those years many conservative businessmen, who had always taken a dim view of government spending, began to say, "You can't spend your way out of a depression."

The quick recovery of 1941–42 seemed so obviously a result of huge sums poured into the war effort that many more persons than before began to associate large-scale public spending with high-level prosperity. Thus, the belief "You can spend your way out of a depression, and the war experience proves it," came to oppose the belief "You can't spend your way out of a depression." The view now gained acceptance that a reason the government failed to achieve prosperity through spending during the 1930's was that not enough had been spent; if deficits of $20 or $30 billion or more a year had been incurred, prosperity would have returned in a hurry.

This conflict has probably been resolved on one level. Hardly anyone any longer doubts that government spending can bring prosperity. In this respect it is no different from any other kind of spending. The issue now is over the long-term effects of using this method to achieve prosperity. It is now widely held that any prosperity so reached is "false" or "phony" and can lead only to disaster. The nature of the disaster is not usually defined operationally but often the term *national bankruptcy* is used. No one knows how soon bankruptcy will strike, or exactly what happens when a nation becomes bankrupt.

Even its critics, however, seem to enjoy the prosperity resulting from government spending. They can hardly escape the fact that the nation's productive capacity is expanding and the efficiency of labor is increasing; that living standards are rising; that businessmen are making money; and that most people seem happy. In fact, phony prosperity looks so good to its critics compared to what they remember of the depression of the 1930's that the prospect of its coming to an end badly frightens them.

A conflict is usually felt by all those who are worried by the phoniness of the prosperity they are enjoying as soon as it becomes feasible for the government to reduce expenditures and balance the budget. This is what they say they want, but they fear that actual reduction of expenditures will throw the country into recession. Many persons are put in the position one moment of praising attempts to cut government expenditures and the next moment of gloomily forecasting a business recession as a result of reduced spending. In 1953 this sort of schizophrenic thinking appeared in almost every business journal and in statements of many prominent business leaders.

Fear that a cut in spending will prove disastrous exists alongside a fear that continuation of spending will also prove disastrous. It is believed that no prosperity which is "false" can last indefinitely, that sooner or later the deluge must come. But every period of prosperity in our history, and in the history of other capitalistic nations, has come to an end—often with a financial panic and severe depression. Does this mean that every period of prosperity has been "false"? But all previous depressions have come to an end too, so, if impermanence is a mark of unsoundness, our depressions have also been phony. When one tries to pursue our national beliefs about prosperity and depression, spending and saving, it is easy to become entrapped in a web of circular reasoning.

1.1 What is false prosperity? What characteristics mark it as false? During such prosperity are new houses and factories being built, better machines designed, our productive plant expanded? Are people at work producing needed goods? Do these things add to the wealth of the nation? Will the new buildings and machines still be there when the prosperity ends?

1.2 If government spending is accompanied by prosperity, and if prosperity is accompanied by increases in productivity and wealth, why do many persons believe such spending will bankrupt the nation? What is bankruptcy? What happens when a business goes bankrupt? What happens when a nation goes bankrupt?

1.3 Which do you believe the American people are more willing to accept: deficit financing in order to maintain national defense, or deficit financing in order to build houses, hospitals, highways, and schools? Is one type of spending more likely to produce prosperity than the other? Is one type more likely to produce "false" prosperity? Why were some Americans in the 1930's reluctant to have the government spend money on public works of permanent value?

1.4 Under what conditions, if any, could the American people experience both full employment and a balanced budget? Under what conditions, if any, could the American people have prosperity without having the government spend more than it receives in taxes?

2. *Foreign aid and a favorable balance of trade: It is believed that giving a bottle of milk to every Hottentot is a form of globaloney; but it is also*

believed that we can help maintain full employment and prosperity in this country if we export more than we import.

Foreign-aid programs have been criticized on the ground that the United States cannot afford to strengthen economically the so-called backward nations. It would be to our advantage, financially and otherwise, to consume the goods ourselves rather than give them away to foreigners. Although some mitigation of conditions abroad is necessary and desirable for both military and humane reasons, there is a limit to the burden we can afford to assume, a burden carried by American taxpayers. Probably most Americans look forward to a day when foreign aid can be ended; they expect to live better as a consequence because taxes will be lower and goods more abundant.

But even more ingrained than a distaste for "giveaway" programs is the belief that it is good business for the United States to export more than it imports. Such a practice produces "a favorable balance of trade"—favorable because other nations find themselves in debt to us rather than we to them. However, close analysis of what happens when a nation exports more than it imports reveals a "giveaway" essentially no different from the foreign aid we customarily denounce.

The United States expects to be paid the amount by which its exports exceed its imports, and paid in gold or dollars. Payment in gold is largely impossible because most of the world's supply of monetary gold is already in this country. At present it is just as difficult for importing nations to pay us in dollars.

There are a limited number of ways by which they can acquire dollars. They may, of course, get dollars from the spending of American tourists. Another possible source is sale of services (shipping goods for other countries, for example). But our debtors need many more dollars than they can get in this way in order to finance our gigantic net export surplus.

The chief alternative to these measures would be to open our domestic market to foreign-made goods. If our debtors could sell their goods in America, they could easily acquire the gold or dollars with which to pay for goods received in the past. However, we oppose this method because we believe foreign goods would compete with our own manufactures. If the competition were successful, the increased sale of foreign-made goods would obliterate the net export surplus, without which there would be no favorable balance of trade. We usually try to extricate ourselves and our debtors from this dilemma by lending them the dollars. This is exactly the policy followed by this country throughout the 1920's, when we eagerly exported more than we imported and with equal eagerness provided foreigners with the necessary credit. Much of this credit assumed the form of private investments—that is, investors in the United States bought bonds issued by foreign governments and corporations. The total amount of foreign capital investments floated in this country from 1920 to 1931 is estimated at over $11.6 billion. This device only deferred the day of reckoning, since nations and corporations to whom money had been loaned still have to find a way to pay it back. Whenever they were unable to do so, which was often the case, they defaulted on their bonds, which meant that we had literally given away the difference between our imports and our exports. At the end of 1935, bonds still unpaid had a face value of more than $5.3 billion, and defaulted interest exceeded $1.7 billion.[4]

Year after year we have justified to ourselves a giveaway program hidden beneath the guise of a favorable balance of trade. If we can justify such a policy with the belief that it supplies jobs, maintains prosperity, and protects American industry, we can justify with the same arguments other giveaway programs. If Point Four is globaloney, so is a net export surplus (another name for the same thing). If we cannot afford to give milk to the Hottentots, neither can we afford to export more than we import.

In recent years it has not been unusual for our exports to exceed imports by $5 billion a year. The total discrepancy between exports and imports of merchandise for the period 1916 to 1950 was $86.3 billion.[5] These goods represent debts to be paid. The easiest way to pay this kind of debt is through an increase in exports on the part of debtor nations. Much of this nation's net export surplus has been due to various forms of foreign aid and there is considerable significance to the fact that the British, as well as some people in this country, have been advocating "more trade and less aid." The British are beginning to regard aid from America as a burden, and a greater export trade as a necessity. Those Americans who believe that any increase in British exports will jeopardize American prosperity will oppose "more trade and less aid." But, if they believe that foreign-aid programs threaten to bankrupt the American nation, they will also welcome this proposal. They cannot logically resist and welcome a policy, yet this is what they are likely to do, provided they continue to compartmentalize

[4] Thurman Arnold, *The Folklore of Capitalism,* Yale University Press, 1937, pp. 273–274.

[5] W. Nelson Peach and Walter Krause, *Basic Data of the American Economy,* Richard D. Irwin, 1950, p. 121.

their beliefs, and to remain confused in their understanding of foreign trade.

2.1 A debtor nation is one which owes other nations for goods and services received. The United States was a debtor nation for most of its history prior to the First World War. Would a high protective tariff and similar restraints on imports help or hinder a debtor nation in its efforts to pay off its debts to other nations? How would a tariff and similar measures affect a creditor nation? When and how did the United States become a creditor nation? Did we change our tariff policy when we became a creditor nation?

2.2 How do you explain the fact that the European nations who were our allies in the First World War eventually defaulted on the debts they incurred with us during that war? What was the attitude of the American people during the 1920's toward (a) collecting the war debts and (b) reducing our tariff? Were these attitudes consistent with each other?

2.3 Why has the United States never made a serious attempt to collect on goods and services supplied to our allies under Lend-Lease during the Second World War? What is a possible economic explanation which would also explain our lack of interest in exacting reparations from Germany and Japan?

3. *Taxes and government spending: It is believed that spending by government is a burden on the economy which must be borne by taxpayers; but it is also believed that spending by private corporations is not a burden and that private corporations never tax the public.*

Americans dislike taxes to a point where tax evasion is a fine and widely practiced art. They always assume that taxes are too high, and that purchasing power and standard of living are lowered by the amount of the tax. Government expenditures are thought to be essentially nonproductive, even when not inflated by graft and inefficiency.

On the other hand, it is generally assumed that corporations charge for their services but never tax. When a corporation receives a price for its product, a customer gets full value in return (if not, it is his own fault). He has parted with his money, but he has received something tangible in return. So, what corporations spend—unlike the expenditures of government —is productive and not a burden to anyone.

Those are the beliefs. Actually, a tax *per se* is never a burden. The government, in spending tax revenue, may channel some of our productive effort in directions which do not directly raise our material standard of living. For example, if tax money is used to pay for national defense, taxpayers get nothing material in return. If tax money is used to improve the national parks, taxpayers may get back only spiritual uplift. But if the government spends for public works of lasting economic value, then such expenditures increase our material standard of living and are productive in exactly the same sense that building a new steel mill is productive. Also, taxes are not likely to detract from the total dollar income of taxpayers. When the government spends tax money (and it always does!) it becomes income, directly or indirectly, for American taxpayers. Tax money is always returned to the economy—even if it goes through the hands of foreign nations first.

Like government, private corporations may make expenditures which do not increase our standard of living. In this category, perhaps, are some kinds of advertising, padded expense accounts, unnecessarily high remuneration for executives, and the production of goods of dubious value. Some corporations—such as holding companies in certain situations—may never in any way contribute to our total production of needed goods and services. And people are wrong to assume that a corporation never spends other than its "own" money. Actually, the money always comes from the people in one way or another and the *function of this money is not unlike that of any tax.* Corporations usually give their "taxpayers" (i.e., their customers and stockholders) something worth while, but occasionally they may not:

Take the example of Paramount Publix. Here fifty thousand so-called investors contributed to the greatest public works project ever known in the amusement field. In this project there was a maximum of what in government would be called graft, but which in finance is recognized as legitimate tribute. Thus the directors voted themselves and the higher executive officers huge bonuses in order to encourage each other. The president of this principality took a salary and stock bonuses of more than a million and a half in 1930. The company lawyer got $75,000 a year and his assistants from $35,000 to $45,000. Kuhn, Loeb & Company, the bankers, received a huge present of stock simply out of gratitude. A list of relatives received fanciful sums for services of doubtful value.[6]

Another aspect of confusion over taxation is a general failure to understand the ways in which taxes can be used to produce greater economic stability. In periods of severe inflation, for example, certain kinds of taxes are among the most effective weapons available to bring prices down. Inflation presents people with a choice between higher prices and higher taxes, and often it would be to their advantage to take the latter. There is also much misunderstanding concerning the role of the graduated income tax—which cuts more deeply into high incomes than low. When our national

[6] Thurman Arnold, *op. cit.,* pp. 302–303.

income is rising, such a tax *automatically* increases the tax rate and when the national income is falling the rate is *automatically* lowered. This helps to dampen the effect of both inflation and deflation. Galbraith says of the graduated income tax, "It is doubtful . . . if any single device has done so much to secure the future of capitalism as this tax. . . . It works silently and automatically on the side of economic stability. Conservatives should build a statue to it and to its inspired progenitor, President William Howard Taft." [7]

3.1 What do people receive in return for the taxes they pay? What does the government do with tax moneys? What kinds of government expenditures tend to build up the productive capacity of the economy? Do these expenditures increase the living standard of the average American?

3.2 Do all expenditures by corporations tend to build up the productive capacity of the economy? Are corporation expenditures ever wasteful? Who pays the bill for wasteful or extravagant expenditures by corporations? How does the long-range economic effect of corporation expenditures differ from that of government expenditures?

3.3 In what way may it be said that taxes are a burden? Are taxes ever an economic burden, or is it only wasteful ways of using productive resources that can be burdensome?

4. *Monopoly and free competition: It is believed that American business-men like the idea of free competition and that most American industry is freely competitive; but it is also believed that much American industry is monopolistic, or tending in that direction, and that only by the vigilant enforcement of antitrust laws can we preserve free competition.*

Most Americans, without bothering to define precisely what it is, believe they have a competitive economy. At the same time, large numbers of Americans curse "the monopolies." They seem to believe that much of United States industry is monopolized, or tending in that direction. And the United States is one of the few countries in the world where the people have shown enough awareness of the economic implications of monopoly to insist on antitrust legislation.

When monopoly is discussed as a problem, confusion, inconsistency, and irrationality triumph over logic. The difference between competition and monopoly is rarely understood. One person may insist that an industry is competitive but another, with much the same knowledge of the industry, may insist that it is monopolistic. Further, many people compartmentalize

[7] John Kenneth Galbraith, *American Capitalism: The Theory of Countervailing Power,* Houghton Mifflin Company, 1952, p. 188.

their beliefs to a point that they easily believe (a) that most prices are fixed by supply and demand and (b) that most prices are higher than they should be because of collusion among businessmen.

When price competition exists, prices are set by the market, and no individual producer has measurable control over the prices he may charge. This situation can hold only where the number of sellers is so great that each one's share of the total market is negligible. According to classical theory, the market of a self-regulating (laissez-faire) economy is governed by price competition. A twentieth-century advocate of laissez-faire says, "The price system will fulfill [its] function only if competition prevails, that is, if the individual producer has to adapt himself to price changes and can not control them." [8]

What is the situation in most of American industry today? The greater part of mining, transport, and manufacturing industry does not practice competition in the classical sense. Control rests with a few gigantic firms having power over the market instead of being governed by it. In most cases, the leading three or four firms in an industry are responsible for more than two-thirds of the industry's production and sales. This sort of industrial structure is known technically as "oligopoly." Where oligopoly exists, any single firm can by its own decisions affect market price for the entire industry. Price competition in the classical sense is found only in a few American industries, and even in these it is adulterated with administrative decision.

Under oligopoly it is common for one firm in an industry to become a "price leader." As long as its decisions seem advantageous to the whole industry, other firms copy its prices. In industries with product differentiation there may be some variation in prices—as between a Ford and a Chevrolet—but it is never extreme. When products are so similar that buyers have no strong preference for one over another, a price cut by one firm must be met by other firms. Thus a price cutter gains only temporary advantage. There is, therefore, a strong incentive under oligopoly not to practice price competition. In most American industries a convention against price competition exists, and habits of this kind cannot be prosecuted under the antitrust laws.

4.1 If American business were competitive in the classical sense, would you

[8] Alfred Hayek, quoted in Galbraith, *American Capitalism: The Theory of Countervailing Power*, p. 15.

expect prices to be higher or lower than now? Would you expect depressions to be more or less severe? Would you expect business to be more or less efficient?

4.2   It is generally accepted among economists that American industry is more efficient each year. How do you explain this in light of the fact that American industry steadily becomes less competitive?

4.3   Which of the following do you believe to be destructive of competition: The closed shop? The quota system by which professions limit the number of new members? Fair-trade laws? Refusal of union plumbers to use pipe threaded at the factory? Destruction of fruit by farmers' marketing associations? Parity prices in agriculture?

4.4   Do you think businessmen generally prefer free competition? Why do they say that they do in their magazine ads? Does any group in our society prefer competition to a sure thing? What are the economic implications of the unpopularity of price competition?

5. *Free enterprise and socialism: It is believed that free enterprise is the best possible economic system, and the only system compatible with polit-ical democracy; but it is also believed that under modern conditions gov-ernment must play an increasingly larger role in the economy, and that as time goes on the economy will almost certainly become more "socialistic."*

We can explore only a few of the many facets to this conflict. In one aspect, there is an issue over the "workability" of capitalism (free enter-prise) and socialism. Socialism, it is argued, simply cannot work. Propo-nents of capitalism argue that socialism centralizes decisions in the hands of "bureaucrats." The meaning is not clear, but presumably a bureaucrat is an incapable political appointee who issues unreasonable manifestoes from behind a large desk in Washington. The economy is stifled when economic decisions are rendered by persons not competent to make them. Another aspect of this argument makes "human nature" a culprit: human beings are innately selfish and individualistic; their chief desire is for self-gain. A competitive system in which each person works for his own self-interest is the only economic arrangement compatible with human nature. If socialism requires a high level of selflessness and coöperation, it is bound to fail.

Another argument is that socialism is inconsistent with democracy. So-cialism means great power concentrated in planning boards, and a central government with enough power to enforce its plans is undemocratic. De-cisions which should be made by individuals become a function of the socialist state. The right to own and operate a business without petty inter-ference, the right to accumulate as much property as one can, the right to choose an occupation and place of residence—all these are said to be usurped by a socialist state. It is foolhardy to try socialism even in small doses as an experiment because mild socialism inevitably leads to extreme socialism, which leads to communism. There is only one direction in which socialism can creep. The process is as irreversible as pregnancy. Socialism and dictatorship are thus identified in the public mind.

In spite of the vigor with which these views are held, there is probably no issue on which Americans are more ambivalent. They have accepted gladly, for the most part, many types of government economic activity which were unknown a century and a half ago, although some were not uncommon during the earlier mercantile period. Certain national controls over business were accepted as early as 1890 (Interstate Commerce and Sherman Antitrust acts). By the time of World War I, legislation designed to protect women and children in industry had been passed. The great era of regulative legislation was, of course, in the 1930's, when it became widely accepted that the federal government may properly lend money, manufacture fertilizer and electric power, control the operations of the stock exchange, specify minimum wages and maximum hours, and provide social security. Not only are most of these practices approved, but it is generally assumed that the government should (and will) use its immense fiscal powers to underwrite prosperity. Any business recession of severity or duration will be met with prompt government action—action as extreme, presumably, as the situation demands.

Historically, each of these moves has been opposed by conservatives and branded socialistic. Furthermore, the brand is not inappropriate. Socialist parties have been the first to advocate these steps. Virtually every proposal (except nationalization of heavy industry) offered by American socialists prior to World War I has been adopted and is now regarded as part of "the American Way." Americans generally are frightened by socialism but approve much that socialism historically has advocated.

5.1 Which of the following countries have (or had) a free-enterprise system: pre-Communist China, India, Iran, Egypt, pre-Hitler Germany (Weimar Republic), Mexico, Canada, Sweden? Which of these are or were democracies? Do you find that only democracies have a free-enterprise economy?

5.2 Look up the Socialist platform for the national elections of 1912. How many of the proposed measures have not yet been enacted into law in this country? Why did the Socialist party in the United States die as a political force during the 1930's?

5.3 Would the law of supply and demand be allowed to operate in a socialist system? How could one be sure under socialism that the goods most desired and needed by the people would be produced? What means could be used to determine the price of goods under socialism? The wages of labor? It has been argued tellingly that a socialist economy must necessarily "allocate" labor to various industries, and that this allocation would lead to "forced labor." Do you agree or disagree with this argument?

5.4 How do you explain the apparent fact that the British Labor party has abandoned a large part of its once extensive plan to socialize British heavy industry?

DISCUSSION QUESTIONS AND EXERCISES

1. What periods or events in American history, or world history, are appropriately related to the study of current economic problems and issues?
2. Do you favor a required course in economics for every high-school student? Why or why not?
3. If you answer Question 2 in the affirmative, what kind of course would you favor?
   a. A course in economic problems.
   b. A course in economic theory.
   c. A course in economic history.
   d. A course in economic institutions.
   e. A course in business organization.
   Give reasons for your answer.
4. Which of the above courses would be among the best for a study of the kinds of economic conflicts described in this chapter? Which would be among the poorest for this purpose?
5. If your students studied each of the economic conflicts described in this chapter, what difficulties would you expect to encounter?
6. What do you believe is the most crucial economic problem facing the American people today? Do you believe that the study of this problem should be incorporated in the high-school social-studies curriculum?
7. Have any of your economic beliefs been clarified by your reading of this chapter? If so, which ones, and in what way?
8. Make a list of economic data, sharply negative in form and quality, which you could use in order to cast doubt upon some of the economic beliefs discussed in this chapter.

REFERENCES

There are several books which explain the theory and practice of Keynesian economics. H. Gordon Hayes, *Spending, Saving, and Employment* (Knopf, 1945) is systematic, complete, and easy to understand. The first four chapters are notable for the paradoxes exposed. A great deal less systematic is Kenneth Boulding, *The Economics of Peace* (Prentice-Hall, 1946). The chapters on the unemployment problem are the best, and every student of Keynes should be familiar with Boulding's Bathtub Theorem and Adjustable Taxation Plan. Clarence Ayres, *The*

Industrial Economy (Houghton Mifflin, 1952) constitutes an interesting fusion of Veblen, Dewey, and Keynes.

George Soule, *Ideas of the Great Economists* (Viking Press, 1952) is a brief and popular history of economic theory. The chapters on the classicists and mercantilists are authentic and to the point. William Van Til, *Economic Roads for American Democracy* (McGraw-Hill, 1947) is a high-school text which gives the pros and cons of five different proposed solutions to our major economic problem, unemployment and depression.

Stuart Chase has a series of books dealing with postwar economic problems which belong in every high school library. All published by Twentieth Century Fund, the titles are: *Goals for America*, 1946; *Road We Are Traveling*, 1942; *Tomorrow's Trade*, 1945; and *Where's the Money Coming From?*, 1945.

An interesting book for teachers which examines what the author believes to be the new social order implicit in our mass production organization is Peter E. Drucker, *The New Society* (Harper, 1950). This book challenges the assumptions of both laissez-faire capitalists and Marxian socialists. An equally disturbing book which is likely to receive brickbats from both right and left is John K. Galbraith's *American Capitalism: The Theory of Countervailing Power* (Houghton Mifflin, 1952).

Elton Mayo, *The Social Problems of an Industrial Civilization* (Harvard University Press, 1945) was the first of several studies to throw doubt on the incentives of workers as viewed by classical economists.

Chapter 12

The Closed Areas: Race and Minority-Group Relations

The Problem of Prejudice in the United States

AFTER making the most exhaustive study which had yet been undertaken of relations between whites and Negroes in the United States, Gunnar Myrdal and associates concluded that the "Negro problem" is primarily moral as experienced by both whites and Negroes.[1] The Negro problem, as well as most problems related to intergroup relations, comprises a large measure of intrapersonal conflict with attendant feelings of personal inadequacy and frustration. Intrapersonal conflicts in the area of group relations result from contradiction between democratic and religious ideals and specific beliefs, attitudes, and behaviors which violate these ideals.

Most Americans are in some way involved in problems of intergroup relations. Studies suggest that at least four out of five white Americans have prejudices directed at some minority group.[2] High-school students may first become involved when, after a life in contact with ideals such as the brotherhood of man, the dignity and worth of every individual, and equality before the law, they become aware that prejudice and discrimination are typical of most adults.

Beliefs and attitudes held by a majority toward a minority are commonly referred to as *prejudices*. Defined strictly from derivation, a prejudice is a

[1] Gunnar Myrdal, Richard Sterner, and Arnold Rose, *An American Dilemma: The Negro Problem and Modern Democracy,* Harper & Brothers, 1944.
[2] David Krech and Richard S. Crutchfield, *Theory and Problems of Social Psychology,* McGraw-Hill Book Company, 1948, p. 475.

prejudgment—i.e., a judgment made before examination of evidence. Now it is not unusual for social scientists to use the term in a more popular sense, as "attitudes and beliefs which serve to place the objects of the attitudes and beliefs at an advantage or disadvantage." [3]

Prejudice may involve beliefs and attitudes of which the holder is barely conscious. It may be incidental and peripheral, and not integrated with a person's central cognitive structure. Prejudiced beliefs and attitudes are usually inconsistent and poorly understood, many prejudiced persons acting according to one belief or attitude in one situation and contradictory ones in other situations. Prejudices may be held so lightly that their holder reacts against members of a minority only by avoiding their company; in some cases he may strongly reject openly discriminatory behavior.

Because the structure of prejudice in individuals is ordinarily rather haphazard, and because of a tendency to turn prejudices on and off according to the situation, it is hardly correct to say that most prejudiced persons have an ideology of prejudice. It is difficult, for example, to identify in the area of race a core of beliefs, widely and popularly held, which compare with the ideology of laissez-faire capitalism described in Chapter 11.

Some persons (known as *racists*) do intellectualize their prejudices to the point of developing a conscious and often elaborate philosophy (*racism*) regarding racial and ethnic groups, and using this philosophy to justify some overt action against the groups in question. Beliefs of racists almost always correspond to widely held beliefs in the culture, but they are held with greater-than-average intensity and are likely to be integrated with the racists' core of beliefs. Racists *value* their prejudices; they are not passive products of a culture pattern.

All human groups appear to think in terms of ethnocentrism. That is, each group accepts its own way of life as best and assumes that ways of other groups are inferior. Although ethnocentrism was common in ancient times, it was not then based upon racial considerations. Ancient Greeks, for example, considered all outsiders culturally inferior, and worthy of the name *barbarian.* But it was the *culture or way of life which was thought inferior, and not people as biological organisms.* It is rare to find in the ancient world examples of discrimination based upon the idea that some people are inferior because of heredity. [4]

[3] *Ibid.,* p. 444.
[4] Material presented here on history of prejudice draws heavily from Ruth F. Benedict, *Race: Science and Politics,* The Viking Press, 1945, Part II.

With expansion of Europe in the sixteenth and seventeenth centuries, Europeans first began to have widespread contact with peoples of other cultures. Although Europeans usually thought them inferior, it was not because of their racial origin but because of their paganism. Conversion brought a pagan inside the fold of humanity, gave him, at least in principle, the rights and privileges of non-pagans. During the earliest period of colonization by Christian powers, for example, it was common to free those slaves who accepted Christianity. Spanish, Portuguese, and French explorers, traders, and colonists regularly married converted native women. The English were an exception.

As colonialism developed, the practice of freeing slaves merely because they became Christians ceased to be good business. Although keeping slaves in spite of their conversion became the rule, actual practice with respect to freeing slaves and their status after manumission varied from place to place depending upon the traditions of the colonial power. In Spain and Portugal there was a tradition of slave law, resulting from the practice of slavery prior to the period of overseas colonization. Persons enslaved in Spain, for instance, included Negroes, Moors, Jews, and Spaniards. Both Spanish and Portuguese slave law was based upon the Justinian Code, which assumed that slavery was a condition of legal bondage unrelated to any imagined biological or moral inferiority of slaves. A slave was seen as a human being reduced by misfortune to a condition of servitude. Upon manumission, he became in principle a person with all the rights of his former master.

The situation in English colonies was quite different. By 1500 the Anglo-Saxon world had lost all vestiges of slavery and slave law. There was no legal provision for slavery, and no tradition for handling slavery on a legal basis. Planters of the southeastern United States found themselves in a legal vacuum and as the ruling class of the region were free to innovate legal definitions and rules as they pleased. It is not surprising that they chose to define slaves as *chattels* and not as persons, and made no provision for reinstatement of slaves to the position of free men.

If human beings are defined as chattels, legally comparable to mules and bales of cotton, it is difficult later to recognize freed slaves as fully human and moral beings. The idea grew, furthermore, that only Negroes could be slaves, as they were the only slaves Americans knew. If Negroes alone are slaves one may logically justify this condition by assuming that they are subhuman and incapable of fully responsible and moral behavior. In the

United States, Negroes came to be regarded as biologically inferior to whites. In countries which began as colonies of Spain or Portugal, Negroes are not regarded as biologically inferior, little prejudice is directed toward them by whites, and intermarriage is common.[5]

Racism was given its modern and classical form by European and American writers between 1853 and 1930.[6] According to one racist of the period, there are three different races of mankind (white, yellow, and black), which differ from one another in physical, intellectual, and moral qualities. Only the white race has "reflective energy," "perseverance," "instinct for order," "love of liberty," and "honor." The only example of a truly white race is the blond "Aryan." Europeans as a whole are a hybridized lot, Alpine types being of "yellow extraction" and Mediterranean types of "black extraction." Aryans are the natural aristocracy of Europe, and the group best fitted to rule.[7]

Near the beginning of the twentieth century the idea of race became attached to nationality. It became popular to speak about the "English race," the "German race," and the "French race." Although the French and Germans appeared to make it more of an issue, each nationality more or less assumed it was superior to the rest. When nationality became equivalent with race, it was necessary to define race other than by surface physical characteristics. Obviously the German nation included persons of many different physical types. A solution was found in a concept of race which was based almost exclusively upon "inner qualities." Thus, all Germans were said to have certain innate moral qualities which, irrespective of physical appearance, mark them as Germans. Under Hitler this notion was developed to the point where a person could be a German without having been born in Germany and without ever having lived there—"a German soul in a non-German body."[8]

Racist literature in the United States during the last half of the nineteenth century and the early twentieth followed European racism and was

[5] The interpretation given here of why there is a "Negro problem" in the United States and none in countries such as Brazil and Cuba follows Frank Tannenbaum, *Slave and Citizen: The Negro in the Americas*, Alfred A. Knopf, Inc., 1947.

[6] The year 1853 marks the first publication of an influential work which was to inspire later racists, Count de Gobineau's *Essay on the Inequality of Human Races*.

[7] Gobineau, quoted in Benedict, *op. cit.*, pp. 115–118.

[8] Among writers who claimed that a nationality may correspond to a race, one of the most influential was Houston S. Chamberlain, *Foundations of the Nineteenth Century*, London, 1911. Chamberlain became a German by adoption. He advanced the theory that Teutons are the chosen people, and that in Germans Teutonic blood is to be found in its purest form.

aimed chiefly at "inferior" southern Europeans who were flocking to the United States in great numbers.[9]

Today popular beliefs in the United States about the meaning of race and proper relationships between different races and ethnic groups reflect the above history of racism. However, persistence of racial prejudice on a wide scale, and of racism among certain groups, cannot be explained wholly in terms of historical developments. Much prejudice today appears too strongly motivated to be simply a result of hereditary belief. Ethnocentric feelings now have a pathological quality, and inherited beliefs are useful chiefly in justifying discrimination which would have been practiced anyway.

Social scientists have identified a number of possible motives of prejudice.[10] It may be a characteristic response by most persons to the existence of out-groups; i.e., ethnocentric behavior involving prejudice may typify normal human relationships. Racial prejudice may be a means of helping a person to identify with his group, and thus to feel accepted and wanted. In some cases, adoption of prejudiced beliefs may be in response to a need to find an understandable interpretation of some social situation. For example, one who lacks an understanding of war and its causes may clarify the problem to his own satisfaction by accepting the idea that "international Jews" promote war for their own profit. The motive in this case is the need common to everyone to make sense of his world. In still other cases, economic or other forms of competition may explain prejudice. If there is not enough of some wanted thing to go around, then an individual may reason, "Unless I assert my own strength, *they* will take what I want."

Although such motives may help to explain the persistence of prejudice from one historical period to another, they are not adequate to explain the pathological level of prejudice typical at certain times and among certain groups. A more promising hypothesis which has a great deal of presumptive evidence in its favor treats this pathological level of prejudice as a *personality disorder*. It is now believed by many social scientists that a highly prejudiced person is to some degree mentally ill. Such persons may be normal at most times, but occasionally, victimized by temporarily frustrating circumstances which generate intense aggressive impulses, they

[9] American racists include Madison Grant (*The Passing of the Great Race*, 1916), Clinton S. Burr (*America's Race Heritage*, 1922), and Lothrop Stoddard (*The Revolt Against Civilization: the Menace of the Under Man*, 1922).

[10] For a summary of motives which have been found to operate in connection with racial prejudice, see Krech and Crutchfield, *op. cit.*, pp. 447 ff.

direct their aggression at minorities. Other persons may have deep frustrations of a more permanent nature stemming from parental rejection, repressed needs, or other causes. The result is a personality structure which includes a "need" for "inferior persons" who can serve as objects of aggression.

It is now customary to call the type of individual who has a deep and permanent need to persecute weaker persons the *authoritarian* personality type.[11] A tendency toward prejudiced belief is not the only conspicuous trait of this type; it is one trait among many which together comprise a distinctive pattern. One had best be cautious in use of this concept since many persons who are basically democratic may occasionally exhibit authoritarian traits, and relatively few authoritarian individuals have all the traits associated with the type. Furthermore, some persons who exhibit many authoritarian traits show them only to a mild degree. With these cautions in mind, the authoritarian personality structure is believed to have such traits as the following:

1. Hierarchical orientation, which leads to an admiration of, and submissiveness toward, persons who are strong (strong in the sense of having political, economic, or social status), and contempt for weak persons. The authoritarian tends to exploit and manipulate the weak, often in cruel and callous fashion. Because he sees society as a hierarchy, he is often a ruthless social climber given to fawning on superiors and abusing inferiors.

2. Conventionality and pseudo conservatism. To gain respect in his community, he is likely to want his wife to dress modestly, to stay at home, and to send the children to Sunday School (although not everyone who does these things is an authoritarian). His political and economic beliefs are best described as pseudo conservative because he admires the power of big business and strong but reactionary political leaders and accepts violence and expediency as necessary means for preserving his "one hundred percent Americanism." As Adorno observes, he is characterized by "conventionality and authoritarian submissiveness on the ego level, with violence, anarchic impulses, and chaotic destructiveness in the unconscious sphere." [12]

[11] For one of the best treatments of this subject, see Erich Fromm, *Escape from Freedom,* Farrar & Rinehart, 1941. Perhaps the most ambitious studies of the authoritarian personality were sponsored by the American Jewish Committee and published under the general title *Studies in Prejudice.* Among the volumes published, the one most pertinent to our thesis is T. W. Adorno and others, *The Authoritarian Personality,* Harper & Brothers, 1950. Discussion on following pages draws heavily from this source.

[12] Adorno, *op. cit.,* p. 675.

3. Tendency to view other persons as means. The authoritarian tends toward an exploitive-manipulative type of power orientation." He sees others as tools for furthering his ends. He regards marriage, for example, as a way to gain wealth, status, and respectability. He judges his wife and children according to how they make him look in the community.

4. Repression of instinctual tendencies. An authoritarian is seldom able to enjoy the erotic or sensual. He may be cold and prudish, or he may pursue a crude, compulsive kind of promiscuity lacking in any real satisfaction, or he may lead a dual life, exhibiting great conventionality on the surface but pursuing numerous extramarital affairs.[13] Male authoritarians tend to idealize women on an abstract level ("American motherhood," for example) but be incapable of establishing warm and affectionate relations with them.

5. Exaggerated ethnocentrism, which may lead to fear of, and hostility toward, all groups which are "different." The authoritarian tends to see every group as an out-group except his own inner circle and the power groups with which he identifies. A conspicuous aspect of his ethnocentrism, contrasted with more normal ethnocentrism, is the *generality* with which he rejects others. Levinson points out that to the ethnocentric or authoritarian type "The social world . . . is arranged like a series of concentric circles around a bull's eye. Each circle represents an ingroup-outgroup distinction; each line serves as a barrier to exclude all outside groups from the center, and each group is in turn excluded by a slightly narrower one. A sample 'map' illustrating the ever-narrowing ingroup would be the following: Whites, Americans, native-born Americans, Christians, Protestants, Californians, my family, and finally—I." [14]

6. Mental rigidity and tendency to think in stereotypes. The authoritarian often rejects science as a method, and in view of his frequent rejection of cultural interests he may be called anti-intellectual as well. Although exhibiting a closed mind most of the time, he may be gullible and suggestible when under the influence of persons or groups of superior power. He rejects critical analysis of any sort, particularly self-criticism. For this reason, the typical authoritarian is usually more ignorant and confused about social affairs than most other persons. He tends to generalize on the basis of

---

[13] *Ibid.*, pp. 393–397. Studies by Frenkel-Brunswik and Sanford of a group of college coeds indicate a significant correlation between anti-Semitism and sexual repression. See "Some Personality Factors in Anti-Semitism," *Journal of Psychology*, 20: 271–291, 1945.

[14] Adorno, *op. cit.*, pp. 147–148.

scanty or nonexistent evidence. A result of this habit is stereotypy, in which he attributes certain traits to "all Jews," "all Armenians," "all socialists," or "all professors."

7. Self-glorification and projection. The authoritarian male typically boasts of obstacles which he has overcome (in Horatio Alger pattern), and of possessing all the most admired traits of a virile American male. He may boast of his morality, of his sexual conquests, of his conservatism, and of his associations with the "right people." At the same time, he usually blames his failures on others. He projects his difficulties on whatever scapegoat is convenient, and often his anger is focused on a minority group.

The authoritarian is a person of deep frustrations, who finds little pleasure in life. Typically, the adult authoritarian was reared in a home where love and mutuality were lacking, where the father was an autocrat, where conventional mores were enforced with an iron hand. As a rule, some aspect of his adult life is also highly unsatisfactory. He may be a member of a depressed group, as a white sharecropper in the South; or a clerical worker who finds it impossible to rise from a routine and unrewarding job; or a businessman frustrated by an inability to keep up with the Joneses. Authoritarians are usually rootless, unintegrated with the culture around them, lacking in a sense of purpose, and facing obstacles which are too great for them to surmount. They are fodder for any sort of "movement" which gives them adventure and a feeling of importance.

Any cure to the problem of prejudice must include cognitive reorganization of the prejudiced person—no easy task. Strong psychological motives push people in an ethnocentric direction. A certain proportion of youth have undoubtedly developed these motivations to a point where they are impervious to teachers and their attempts at reëducation. On the other hand, millions of Americans, both youth and adults, have exhibited open-mindedness and a willingness to study intergroup problems.

The studies of authoritarian personalities indicate that solutions to the problem of intergroup prejudice will necessarily include serious attention to the emotional atmosphere within which intellectual reorganization is to be undertaken. Group-leadership techniques, as described in Chapter 7, can help create this atmosphere. Several studies have suggested that children's attitudes become more democratic when teachers are sensitive to the social-emotional needs of children—the needs for belonging, achievement, and love.

Contradictions and Confusions in Social Thought and Practice

1. *Racial differences and human similarity: It is believed that there are distinct races of mankind which differ from one another physically, intellectually, and morally; but it is also believed that race is only skin deep and that all men are brothers.*

The assumption that there are different races of mankind which differ in physical, mental, and moral characteristics has already been described. There is value, however, in reviewing some widely held associated beliefs. Many persons, for example, assume that all persons speaking a particular language, or languages of a related group, are of the same race. An example is use of the term *Aryan* to designate a race. Originally this term referred to a group of languages which included Sanskrit of ancient India and languages of ancient Persia. Later it came to designate a large language group which included the above and also German, English, Latin, Greek, Armenian, and Slavic. These are the Indo-European languages. According to one belief, persons whose ancestors spoke any of these languages are members of the "Aryan race."

It is also widely believed that race and nationality are the same. This notion is related to identification of language and race, since most nationalities have a distinctive language. Another common belief is that race and culture are related—that is, persons of a particular race show certain cultural preferences because "it is in them" to be that way. Conversely, when persons show certain cultural characteristics, these are supposed to represent hereditary differences attributable to "racial influences." The popular belief in a Jewish race is rooted in assumptions such as these. Persons who believe in racial differences of an innate sort ordinarily believe also that some races are superior to others.

In contrast to a belief in fundamental biological differences which separate men into races composed of superior and inferior beings is a belief that all men are essentially alike, that race is "only skin deep." This equalitarian idea sometimes has a religious basis. Many believe that the human race sprang from Adam and Eve, and so all people have common ancestors. Closely related is the belief that, since all human beings have souls, and all souls are composed of the same primal stuff (the universal soul-substance), human beings are necessarily alike in their most important characteristics. The belief that all races are essentially alike is also rooted in (a) eighteenth-century liberalism, which furnished background for Jefferson's proposition

258

in the Declaration of Independence, "All men are created equal," and (b) a scientific-naturalistic outlook which makes no reference to religion or the ideals of the Age of Enlightenment.

There is evidently considerable popular confusion over the meaning of the term *race*. Most persons probably have a nebulous conception of race, and their actual opinions in this area undoubtedly shift a great deal from one occasion to another. A general understanding of what science knows to be true of race would not in itself eliminate patterns of discrimination, but it would be a necessary step in that direction and would certainly reduce ambiguity in the popular conceptions of race. The following are some of the scientific facts.

It is clear to all scientists that all men belong to a single species. There are no divisions within mankind such as divide the different species of animals. Compared to their similarities, differences between races are insignificant. Yet men do differ; a Norwegian and an Australian bushman are clearly distinguishable one from the other.

However, attempts to classify human beings into races have always encountered difficulty. It is possible to compile a list of widely shared characteristics for a given group, such as skin or eye color, hair texture, or head shape, and to describe generally a "typical" individual of that group. But very few, if any, members of a given race correspond in all respects to the average type. Each individual in a given race has unique characteristics. Many individuals of a given race show traits which are more to be expected in some other racial grouping. There are some grounds for saying that every individual belongs to a race of his own; but it would not be helpful to define race in this way.[15]

Modern knowledge about heredity helps one to understand better the problem of defining race. It was believed once (and still is in some places) that blood carries hereditary characteristics. Now we know that hereditary characteristics are carried by genes. Genes retain their identities for countless generations, and this is one of their most significant features. For example, a gene which produces a particular shade of brown in eyes will continue to do so for an unknown number of generations. Genes may change as a result of mutation; but in the absence of mutation they are remarkably durable. Another significant feature of genes is that they vary independently. Genes which produce tall stature may occur in persons who

[15] L. C. Dunn and Theodosius Dobzhansky, *Heredity, Race, and Society,* The New American Library, 1952, p. 114.

carry genes for black or white skin, narrow or broad nose, blond or dark hair, blue or brown eyes. Thus, *any hereditary physical or mental trait may appear in conjunction with any other trait.*

This principle gives meaning to the following definition of race: "Races are populations which differ in the relative commonness of some of their genes." [16] Thus, in a particular race a given trait, such as tallness, may occur more often than in some other race. A particular shade of skin may be more common in one group than in another. This does not mean that genes capable of producing traits quite different from the usual ones are absent from a race. Rather there are "majority traits" which are sufficiently common to make most members of a race look different from most members of another race.

Even this definition presents difficulties. A problem remains of deciding which traits to use in defining a particular race. Obviously, combination of characteristics is called for. If we use only one characteristic, such as dark skin color, and assume that everyone with this characteristic belongs to a "black race," we must include peoples who differ markedly from one another in other characteristics (e.g., Indians, Melanesians, and Africans). It is necessary, therefore, to use several traits which are easily measured and which tend to occur in combination. Anthropologists have used skin color, hair color and texture, eye color, head shape, and stature. Such classificatory schemes usually produce several hundred distinct races (e.g., Nordic, Alpine, Mediterranean, Armenoid, and Hindi). Anthropologists have also identified primary races (sometimes called stocks). Primary races are usually limited to three: Caucasoid, Negroid, and Mongoloid.

Students are likely to forget, however, that it would be just as logical to classify persons according to traits not now commonly used. Distribution of blood types in a population is one such trait, as is distribution of color blindness, or ability to taste phenyl-thio-carbamide.[17] Yet if any of these clearly hereditary and easily measurable traits were used, present classifications would be completely changed. It is correct to say, therefore, that the present scheme for classifying people into races is arbitrary. Dunn and Dobzhansky also believe that it has only limited usefulness: "When we say that two populations are racially different we are not saying very much." [18]

1.1 What meanings have been given to the term *race?* What is the scientific

[16] *Ibid.,* p. 125.
[17] *Ibid.,* pp. 121–122.
[18] *Ibid.,* p. 125.

meaning? How many races are there? Does race, scientifically speaking, relate in any way to cultural achievement, or nationality?

1.2 How does science account for the fact that some whites have darker skins than some Negroes, that some Swedes are brunet and short, that some Chinese do not have high cheekbones?

1.3 In countries which were once colonies of Spain persons of mixed white and Negro ancestry are commonly regarded as white but in the United States they are usually classified as Negro. How do you explain this inconsistency in racial classification?

2. *Negro inferiority and Negro capacity: It is believed that of all races the Negro is lowest on the evolutionary scale and least capable of a high order of civilized living; but it is also believed that all human beings should have equal rights and opportunities, and that Negroes have been treated more unfairly than any other minority.*

The anti-Negro ideology of American whites places the Negro in a *caste*. A caste is a group permanently set apart in that it is not allowed the right of intermarriage or of full social intercourse with the majority group. A *class*, in contrast, represents a status position which is not necessarily permanent, since members of one class may move with some freedom into another, and classes may intermarry without serious affront to the mores.

The basis of a Negro caste in America is assumed biological inferiority. Negroes are believed to be unassimilable because their ancestry is different from that of whites and inferior to it. One of the cruder beliefs holds that Negro blood infects the white race, and intermarriage will weaken the white race. Miscegenation is a threat to "racial purity" and "contrary to nature." [19]

An anti-Negro ideology exists on both sides of the Mason-Dixon line but there are some differences between North and South. Although many citizens of the South are more democratic than some of their Northern neighbors, in the South one is more likely to find die-hard acceptance of the belief that amalgamation of races will forever remain intolerable. Northerners may deplore the possibility of intermarriage, but their resistance to it is seldom fanatical. Northerners and Southerners share many beliefs about the traits of Negroes but Northerners are more likely to attribute these traits to environmental influences, Southerners to biological inheritance.

The South commonly believes that Negroes are less intelligent than whites, and more ignorant and superstitious; that Negroes are lazy and,

---

[19] Myrdal, *op. cit.*, p. 55.

when they do work, do so more slowly and casually than whites; that Negroes are happy-go-lucky, childish, and irresponsible, more emotional, less stable, and more inclined to behave impulsively. There is a pretty general assumption that Negroes are more susceptible to disease, and that they have a distinctive, ineradicable odor. The notion that Negroes are subject to congenital physical weakness applies with special force to mulattoes, who are believed often to be sterile, inharmoniously proportioned, and more susceptible to disease than are full-blooded Negroes. Oddly, the achievement of successful mulattoes is usually attributed to their white ancestors. It is also thought that Negroes are endowed with a more powerful sexual drive than are whites and possess greater sexual capacity and skill. Negroes are said to be loose in their morals, and frequently to become criminals. It is even believed that they cannot learn to speak clear and correct English.[20]

Northern whites are more likely to feel that Negroes are entitled to the same rights and the same justice as other citizens, but the differences between North and South can be, and usually are, exaggerated. Most Northerners are willing to extend certain rights to Negroes provided "equal rights are not abused" or "carried too far." Schermerhorn summarizes the beliefs of Northern whites by saying, "With regard to results, the northern ideology accents subordination while it minimizes segregation. Internally it is composed of moral idealism with a touch of complacency, indifference unless circumstances force the issue, withdrawal to prevent occasions that might test a real concern, and practical ignorance of the Negro as a human being or of his culture. . . ."[21]

Another group of popular beliefs attributes especially desirable traits to Negroes: they are gifted in music, art, dancing, and acting; they are superior to whites in handling animals, or, sometimes, children; they make loyal and reliable servants; they are happier, more relaxed, and more free from tensions; they are capable of more emotional warmth and can take sorrows and disappointments more easily than whites; they are more religious.[22] These more favorable beliefs do not imply unqualified admiration of Negroes and neither do they imply that they are "as good as whites." Their function seems to be to define a Negro's "place" since one of the most general beliefs of all is that "Negroes are all right in their place."

[20] *Ibid.*, pp. 106–108.
[21] R. A. Schermerhorn, *These Our People*, D. C. Heath & Company, 1949, p. 137.
[22] Myrdal, *op. cit.*, p. 108.

The chief moral conflict of whites is undoubtedly as follows: Whites feel that Negroes—more than other minority groups—are innately inferior to whites and forever incapable of living as whites do. But they are entitled to better treatment. Undoubtedly, many persons who in their idealistic moments want more opportunities extended fear the imagined consequences. They are afraid that Negroes will not profit by it, that they will take advantage of whites, that "easing up" may promote an increase in tension and violence. In spite of these fears, they continue to feel that an extension of greater equality is "the only Christian thing to do."

There are numerous inconsistencies and contradictions within the mental outlook of most whites, and while these do not always produce moral conflicts they do make it difficult for whites to perceive clearly the consequences of equality; and it is the inability to anticipate consequences with accuracy which accounts for many of their imagined fears. For example, it is believed that Negroes are lazy and incompetent but at the same time that, if given full economic equality, they would take jobs from whites. It is also felt that Negroes are satisfied with their lot (except when stirred up by damnyankees) but that unless forcibly kept in their place they would soon get out of hand. Another contradiction says that Negroes are submissive and docile and prefer paternal treatment but that they are, unless kept in their place, overly independent and aggressive. Again, Negroes are particularly repugnant because of a supposedly greater sexuality but, as our folklore, literature, and advertising indicate, Americans admire and envy sexuality to the point of making a fetish of it. Sexual relations between Negro males and white females is regarded as an offense so serious as to be punishable by death of the male, but relations between white males and Negro females have been common in the United States, and in some localities are still fairly so. The whole issue of miscegenation shows a degree of inconsistency and irrationality quite puzzling to foreign observers. The very whites who have in greatest numbers practiced *illicit* miscegenation are often the ones most bitterly opposed to *legal* miscegenation.

2.1 How do you explain that in the United States anyone with a Negro ancestor is considered a Negro, but offspring of white-Indian marriages are thought to be white? If a person with Negro ancestry who "looks white" is able to "cross the color line" and is freely accepted as white by whites, is he still a Negro? If he marries a white, would his children be Negroes?

2.2 Is it possible to combine segregation and equality of treatment? Is segregation in itself a form of discrimination? If an employer provided separate rest rooms for Negroes and whites, and if those for Negroes were the cleaner and

more modern, would you say that anti-Negro discrimination was being practiced? Anti-white discrimination?

2.3 It is argued that Negroes like paternalism (i.e., kindly domination by
whites). It is also argued that Negroes must be kept in their place. If Negroes
like paternalism, why would it be necessary to take special pains to keep them
in their place?

3. *Jewish greed and Jewish radicalism: It is believed that Jews control
most industry and money in the United States; but it is also believed that
most Jews tend to be radical and communistic in their political philosophy.*

This contradiction is only one of many central to anti-Semitism in America. Anti-Semitism is probably as common here as in countries of western
Europe. It appears to be stronger in rural areas than in cities, and stronger
among middle- than among upper- or lower-class persons. It correlates with
ultraconservative political and economic beliefs; reactionaries, unless they
are Jews, are usually anti-Semites. Beliefs about Jews which are widespread
among Christians include the following: [23]

a. There is a Jewish race, easily identifiable by certain physical characteristics: a prominent hooked nose, a dark and oily skin, black—often wavy
—hair, and a narrow jaw.

b. Jews are grasping and greedy. Their chief aim in life is to make
money, and they will resort to the most unethical business practices in order
to do so.

c. Jews are aggressive and power-seeking. They have too much power,
especially in the economy, and will gain more as they can.

d. Jews adopt radicalism and intellectualism (which are thought to be
the same). They lean toward all kinds of radical doctrine. They tend to be
atheists, to believe in moral relativism, and to approve modern art and
music.

e. Jews are morally impure, are sensual, and often practice perversions.

f. Jews control most industry in the nation. Through their control of
banks they also control the money supply. Jewish international bankers
control the world economy.

g. Jews are industrious and intelligent, but their intelligence is characterized by a shrewdness and craftiness unappealing to decent persons.

h. Jews are clannish; they do not welcome non-Jews into their circle and
make no attempt to adopt customs of people around them.

It is unlikely that anti-Semitism creates in the minds of Americans the

[23] For data on the ideology of anti-Semitism, see Schermerhorn, *op. cit.*, pp. 31–32,
and Adorno, *op. cit.*, pp. 94–100.

same dilemma as does discrimination against Negroes. Discrimination against Jews is less conspicuous than that against Negroes. Jews are refused lodging at many resorts and hotels, yet a Jew can go almost anywhere in the United States and secure first-class hotel lodging and restaurant service—a possibility regularly denied to Negroes. Jews may be admitted to universities according to quota, but there are few institutions of higher learning which exclude them altogether. Jews are discriminated against in employment, yet many of them manage to attain high positions in business and the professions. Anti-Jewish discrimination is—much of the time—a quiet, "gentlemen's agreement" sort. Therefore, Americans do not sense a "Jewish problem," nor do many of them feel moral qualms about present treatment of Jews.

Anti-Semitism dates at least as far back as the pre-Christian era, when Jews were persecuted for political and cultural reasons. It increased during the late Roman and medieval period, when it was largely based upon religious differences, and began to function as a political weapon in the latter half of the nineteenth century. The only country prior to Nazi Germany to use anti-Semitism as a state policy was czarist Russia.

In the United States restrictions were first placed upon Jews in the 1870's. Anti-Semitism developed gradually in this country until the 1920's, when it received stimulus from the Ku Klux Klan and the anti-Semitism of prominent figures, among them Henry Ford. By the late 1920's Americans were generally familiar with the idea that the Christian world was under the power of Jews, and that Jews were radical and dangerous.

Because it has a long history and is prevalent in almost every Western country, anti-Semitism is a special kind of problem in prejudice. It cannot be explained in exactly the same way as prejudice against Negroes, Japanese, and Chinese. Jews, more than any other minority, are economic competitors of those who mold public opinion. However, this fact does not explain all anti-Semitism. A psychoanalytic explanation has been offered, and it seems to be winning acceptance among social scientists. For a review of some of its chief points, see pp. 254 ff. above.[24]

3.1 A *Fortune* survey showed that among anti-Semites in the poll sample 45 percent belong to the lower-middle class. How do you explain this? Are middle-class persons more frustrated than other groups? Why would resentment be di-

---

[24] Typical of the psychoanalytic explanations is Nathan W. Ackerman and Marie Jahoda, *Anti-Semitism and Emotional Disorder*, Harper & Brothers, 1950. See also Adorno, *op. cit.*

rected against Jews? Are lower-middle-class persons upwardly mobile? Would there be any tendency for the lower-middle class to regard Jews as competitors?

3.2   It is easy to find facts to refute the belief that our economic system is controlled by Jews. Why are these facts not distributed more generally? Why is it that one who criticizes a Jewish capitalist is never called a communist, but those who criticize non-Jewish capitalists are likely to be so labeled?

3.3   Negroes are criticized for stupidity and laziness. Jews are criticized for shrewdness and industry. How do you explain this difference, and what is its significance?

4. *Catholic menace and Catholic influence: It is believed that the Catholic Church in the United States is loyal to the Vatican rather than to the United States and is seeking to extend its power over the American people; but it is also believed that the loyalty of Catholics to their church is admirable, and that Catholics have the right idea about a number of things.*

It is clear that among American Protestants there is considerable prejudice about Catholicism, and much hostility toward the Church, and that discrimination of a sort is widely practiced. However, anti-Catholicism is not as widespread as anti-Semitism.[25] An understanding of anti-Catholicism involves distinguishing two kinds of hostility: one kind against individual Catholics merely because they are Catholics; the other primarily against the Church, or its hierarchy, sometimes entirely by-passing Catholic laymen. Persons who are hostile to the Church may be very friendly toward Catholics generally, and may even sympathize with them since the Church is regarded by them as an exploiting agency. Hostility toward Catholic laymen probably reached its height in the United States in the period of heavy immigration of the nineteenth and twentieth centuries. The Know-Nothing party, organized nationally in 1856, was a political expression of this antagonism, and anti-Catholicism was promoted vigorously by the Ku Klux Klan during the 1920's.

Present hostility seems to be shifting from laymen to the Church.[26] Whether or not this hostility is prejudice depends on how well grounded the criticisms are.

Anti-Catholicism is unlike the prejudice directed at Jews, Negroes, and foreigners. Whereas the latter is often highly emotional, and an expression

[25] This conclusion is based upon results of a public-opinion poll reported in *Fortune*, October, 1947.

[26] There are no studies available to support this point. It is suggested by an apparent increase in anti-Catholic articles in Protestant magazines and the extraordinary sales of certain anti-Church books (e.g., *American Freedom and Catholic Power* by Paul Blanshard, The Beacon Press, 1949).

of aggressive impulses, anti-Catholicism is often exhibited by naturalistic-humanistic liberals who show no evidence of prejudice toward other minority groups. It is based upon intellectual grounds rather than upon a need for a scapegoat and is seldom directed against individuals because they are Catholics.

Common beliefs directed against Catholics are as follows: Catholics give their first allegiance to the Church, and only a secondary allegiance to democratic institutions and government in the United States. The Vatican seeks spiritual conquest of the world, and indirectly, political conquest. Organized along the lines of a totalitarian state, the Church uses many of the same opportunistic methods which totalitarian political movements use. It tries to place its representatives in key posts of government, business, and various community organizations for the purpose of undermining the American system of democracy—particularly the public-school system (in favor of parochialism) and the democratic principles of free speech and thought embodied in the Bill of Rights. The Church is an exploiting institution which thrives on the ignorance and poverty of its congregations. So go the naturalistic-humanistic criticisms of the Church.

Many Protestants who hold anti-Catholic prejudices may also admire certain aspects of Catholicism: [27] the loyalty of Catholics toward their church and the faithfulness with which they adhere to tenets of their religion. These people often strongly approve Catholic moral ideas and the penchant of the Church for censorship. Motion-picture censorship largely follows the dictates of the Catholic Church; the industry's production code was written by a Jesuit, Father Daniel Lord, and the Production Administrator, Joseph I. Breen, is a Catholic. Furthermore, the Legion of Decency, which either approves or disapproves all movies shown in the United States, is a Catholic organization. Apparently most Protestants are content to have the Church serve as their watchdog of the movie industry, although some may not know what the Church is doing. It also appears that censorship of books, magazines, and newspapers, which is sometimes attempted by Catholic officials, meets with favorable response among most Protestants. Those who fear the power of the Catholic Church and who also approve the exercise of that power are clearly ambivalent in their attitudes.

Protestants may also find themselves in a dilemma in their attitudes toward the anticommunism of the Catholic Church, admiring, because it is

[27] There are no studies on this point; therefore, it should be treated as a hypothesis.

267

anticommunist, an organization which they believe to be undemocratic and power-seeking.

4.1 Catholics include persons of all racial origins and nationalities. What effect, if any, might this fact have on the pattern of anti-Catholic prejudice in the United States?

4.2 American Catholic soldiers fought against Italy in World War II. At the same time, an accord existed between the Vatican and the Italian government. Thus American Catholics were fighting troops of a government which was recognized and approved by their own church. What does this suggest concerning the loyalty of American Catholics to the United States?

4.3 Do you believe that the intellectual studies of the Catholic Church which have been made by American liberals (the one by Paul Blanshard is just one example) could feed the fires of religious bigotry?

DISCUSSION QUESTIONS AND EXERCISES

1. Most studies of attitude change indicate that high-school students, over a four-year period, change very little in their prejudices. The same results have been found among college students over a four-year period. How do you explain this almost complete failure of higher education to develop more democratic attitudes?
2. Some teachers will not encourage a class to discuss problems of racial prejudice if the class includes both white and Negro students. Why do you suppose they do this? Is this practice sound?
3. Which do you believe is the most significant difference to be taken into account when a couple are contemplating marriage? A religious difference between them; a social-class difference; a racial difference; a difference over whether they want children.
4. The teachers in an elementary school learned how to recognize and meet some of the emotional needs of their pupils: the need for belonging, for achievement, for affection, and for sharing in decisions. It was found that these children became less prejudiced toward minorities as they became more and more secure. At no time did the teachers promote among the children an intellectual examination of racial attitudes and beliefs. Why did these children become more democratic? Does this experiment question the value of a reflective approach to racial prejudice among children? Would you expect the same results with high-school students?
5. Would you expect a straight factual course on racial characteristics and differences to produce changes in racial attitudes? Why, or why not?

REFERENCES

For brief treatments of the nature, origins, and extent of prejudice in the United States, see David Krech and Richard S. Crutchfield, *Theory and Problems of Social Psychology* (McGraw-Hill, 1948), Chapters 12–14, and R. A. Schermerhorn,

These Our People (Heath, 1949). For fuller treatment of the motivation of prejudice, see Erich Fromm's excellent *Escape From Freedom* (Farrar & Rinehart, 1941) and T. W. Adorno and others, *The Authoritarian Personality* (Harper, 1949). A pioneering work in the same tradition is John Dollard, *Frustration and Aggression* (Yale University Press, 1945).

On the subject of the meaning of race and problems involved in defining race, a very good reference is L. C. Dunn and Theodosius Dobzhansky, *Heredity, Race, and Society* (New American Library, 1952). Also see Ruth F. Benedict, *Race: Science and Politics* (Viking Press, 1945).

Perhaps the best study of Negro-white relations as a social problem is Gunnar Myrdal and others, *An American Dilemma: The Negro Problem and Modern Democracy* (Harper, 1944). Other worth-while books on the Negro "problem" include: Otto Klineberg, *Characteristics of the American Negro* (Harper, 1948); Melville J. Herskovits, *The American Negro: A Study in Racial Crossing* (Knopf, 1930) and by the same author, *The Myth of the Negro Past* (Harper, 1941). On the subject of anti-Semitism, see James Parkes, *An Enemy of the People: Anti-Semitism* (Penguin Books, 1940). The general problem of discrimination in this country is treated in Charles Wilson, *To Secure These Rights: The Report of the President's Commission on Civil Rights* (United States Government Printing Office, 1947).

Chapter 13

The Closed Areas: Social Class

Social Class as an Area of Contradictory and Irrational Belief

Problematic aspects of social-class behavior may best be understood against the backdrop of the American creed of equality, described briefly in Chapter 12.[1] When asked about their class affiliation or that of their acquaintances, many people say, "We have no classes here. In this community everyone is equal." The average American, especially of a small town or rural area, regards class as something alien and undemocratic. He is loath to admit that classes exist in his community.

One reason for this attitude is popular identification of class with the social structure of Europe and England. Probably most Americans think of a class system as having sharply delineated status levels, from which it is virtually impossible to move. They associate class with hereditary position. When conceived in these terms, the idea of class seems so contradictory to American ideals of democracy that to many persons it is highly unpalatable, if not actually menacing.

Nevertheless, Americans behave daily as if classes exist. Fortunately, research conducted by W. Lloyd Warner, Allison Davis, John Dollard, Robert J. Havighurst, and many others has told us a great deal about the class structure of the United States, and about thinking and behavior related to class membership.

A social class is an aggregation of persons having a given social ranking in a community. Membership in a social class represents one form of status,

[1] For a summary statement of the American Creed, see Gunnar Myrdal and others, *An American Dilemma: The Negro Problem and Modern Democracy*, Harper & Brothers, 1944, pp. 8–12.

but there may be bases of status other than class—sex and age, for example. The definition of class most commonly used among social scientists is largely objective; that is, it assumes that a person's rank depends not on what *he* thinks it is but on what *others* think it is. It is possible to develop objective criteria for ranking persons which will assign them with great accuracy to the class to which most other members of the community assign them.[2] Social classes tend to differ in income level and occupation, manners and customs, beliefs and attitudes. No sharp lines can be drawn between classes, however, since they shade into one another at their upper and lower borders.

In old communities in the United States, particularly in the East and South, it is possible to identify six classes, as follows:

Upper-upper class
Lower-upper class
Upper-middle class
Lower-middle class
Upper-lower class
Lower-lower class

In younger communities class structure may be less complex; for example, communities of the Middle West and West often lack an upper-upper class.

Where six identifiable classes exist, the upper class divides into two groups, according to age of family: an "old" and a "new" aristocracy. Very often lower uppers have more money, but they cannot boast the ancestral lineage of upper uppers. They are the *nouveaux riches*. The upper-middle class consists of solid community citizens, persons successful in business and professions, who are prosperous but not wealthy. The lower-middle class is chiefly made up of persons with white-collar jobs who do not make much money: clerks, salespeople, stenographers, and farmers of moderate means. The upper lowers are mainly skilled and semiskilled workmen, persons who work in overalls but are thought respectable. There is a marked range of income within this group, and many upper lowers have higher

---

[2] Warner and associates recently have used two fundamental methods of "placing" individuals classwise. One is known as the Index of Status Characteristics, and assigns scores to individuals according to their occupations, sources of income, house types, and dwelling areas. Each of these criteria is weighted and a total score derived for each person. Class membership is determined according to a score table. The second method is the method of Evaluated Participation; it consists of techniques which expose a person's rank by getting at what other community members think of him and how they behave toward him. See W. Lloyd Warner, *American Life: Dream and Reality*, University of Chicago Press, 1953, pp. 60–66.

incomes than most lower middles. The lower-lower class consists of unskilled or semiskilled workers who are thought by others to be ignorant, dirty, and sometimes immoral. Warner and associates refer to the upper-middle and upper classes as the "level above the common man," the lower-middle and upper-lower classes as the "common man level," and the lower-lower class as the "level below the common man."

In communities studied, from 3 to 4.2 percent of the population are upper class, approximately half of them upper uppers, except in communities where there is no upper-upper group. The upper-middle class may include from 10 to 22 percent of the population, lower middles from 28 to 35 percent, upper lowers from 28 to 41 percent, and lower lowers from 10 to 25 percent. The "level above the common man" includes from about 13 to 26 percent of the population, depending upon the community. The "common man level" comprises from 60 to 70 percent.[3]

Although class has been defined objectively, classes exist in an identifiable form only on the basis of what people *believe* about class. That is, Americans hold a complex pattern of beliefs which assume that classes exist and which tend to call forth overt class-oriented behavior. Both ideology and behavior are in direct contradiction (much of the time) to professed beliefs in equality.

Persons may, and often do, experience moral conflict in the area of class behavior, as will be shown later in this chapter. Warner points out that "It is clear to those of us who have made studies in many parts of the United States that the primary and most important fact about the American social system is that it is composed of two basic, but antithetical principles: the first, the principle of equality; the second, the principle of unequal status and of superior and inferior rank."[4] Although antithetical, these two principles are not considered by Warner to be necessarily inconsistent if properly balanced; on the other hand, Warner and others recognize that class phenomena may produce frequent and serious conflicts for individuals. Because most persons believe and behave in contradictory ways where class is concerned, because for the most part they are unaware of these contradictions, and because these contradictions often lead to irrational and confused behavior, social class is properly included in our list of closed areas.

The existence of class-related beliefs complicates the problem of describing ideologies in other closed areas. Classes vary considerably in their

[3] *Ibid.*, pp. 58–59.
[4] *Ibid.*, p. 104.

beliefs about sex, economic matters, religion, politics, nationalism and patriotism, and manners. As a result, we do not have on most of these matters *an American ideology*, but several ideologies which are different in important respects.

However, belief patterns are less chaotic than they seem at first glance. There is a general American culture which cuts across class lines. This includes not only the American creed of equality and liberty but also a number of almost universally accepted beliefs—that it is proper to wear clothes, that murder is undesirable, that monogamy is the best form of marriage, etc. And, although each social class has its own characteristic beliefs about a number of matters, it is not improper to refer to the United States as a "middle-class nation." Although the lower class outnumbers the middle class in many communities, the middle class tends to set the ideological standards of the culture. For example, upper-lower-class persons tend to emulate middle-class standards, presumably because they hope to rise some day to middle-class status. Lower-upper persons typically accept many middle-class beliefs and attitudes, partly because most of them rose from the ranks of the middle class, partly because they wish to be "democratic," and partly because upper uppers, whom they are trying to imitate, also share many traditional middle-class thought patterns. Although media of mass communication sometimes express upper-class sentiments, they generally promote a middle-class outlook.[5]

Here are a few of the middle-class beliefs which so profoundly affect American life: Economic beliefs are typically conservative. They follow the free-enterprise ideology described in Chapter 11. They emphasize "getting ahead," which means getting better jobs, making more money, and living more comfortably than previous generations. Although the middle class places more emphasis upon thrift and prudent management than does either upper or lower class, middle-class persons usually try to "keep up with the Joneses," which requires compromise in the valuing of thrift.

Standards of sex behavior are rather puritanical. A strong taboo against pre- and extra-marital sexual contacts exists. Children are usually protected from sexual knowledge and experimentation as far as possible.

Parents tend to supervise their children closely, commonly restricting their play activities and choice of associates. They often nag their children in an effort to keep them physically and morally clean, safe, and in good company. They insist on early toilet training and on early learning of re-

[5] *Ibid.*, chap. 10. See particularly the analysis of a "soap opera," pp. 216–234.

spectable language and manners. They are also willing to make major sacrifices for their children.

Church membership and attendance looms high, and patriotic organizations and ceremonies receive support. Honesty, fair play and sportsmanship characterize all relationships where a strong person is dealing with a weaker (as expressed in the saying, "Never kick a man when he's down").

One might summarize the dominant middle-class beliefs and attitudes by saying that they strongly uphold "success," "respectability," and "morality," all defined in a traditional and essentially Calvinist sense.

Although middle-class ideology tends to dominate American thinking, beliefs and attitudes of both upper and lower classes do differ sharply at certain points. For example, both upper- and lower-class persons tend to be less puritanical and inhibited where sex is concerned. A fairly large proportion of lower-class persons, especially those of the lower-lower class, are frankly irreligious and unpatriotic. Upper-class persons usually belong to a church but seldom attend, and often hold very liberal religious views; they are also usually cold to patriotic ceremonies. Lower-class persons often do not take seriously middle-class beliefs about fair play, honesty, cleanliness, and respectability. Both upper- and lower-class persons often regard middle-class persons as stuffy and hypocritical.

Because of these differences, members of each class except the lower lower look down upon and in various ways discriminate against members of inferior classes. Discrimination may take the form merely of avoidance. It may go farther and involve actual manipulation of persons for class ends, as when an upper-lower employee is fired to make room for the son of an upper-middle acquaintance of the boss, or when a lower-class girl is ousted as drum majorette because of pressures put upon a principal by upper-class parents.

Social-class problems are basically problems in intercultural or intergroup relations. Since each class tends to have its own characteristic beliefs, it is reasonable to view classes as *subcultures* within the broader framework imposed by the "American creed" and other nationally held beliefs and attitudes. Prejudiced beliefs, and discrimination directed toward an inferior class are not unlike those directed at an ethnic minority (except where caste behavior is involved).

Class discrimination is felt very sharply in most American public schools. At least 94 percent of public-school teachers identify themselves with the middle class and may be judged to be middle class according to objective criteria. But about 60 percent of the student body of a typical school is lower class.[6] Probably many problems experienced by lower-class children in school arise from the fact that schools prize middle-class culture and penalize manifestations of lower-class culture wherever these happen to deviate markedly. Curriculums and activities are arranged, for the most part, to favor middle- and upper-class children. This is not to suggest that there are not many programs available for the lower-class child; the point is, the highest awards from the standpoint of prestige, honors, and privileges almost invariably go to middle- or upper-class children. Discrimination may be so obvious as to embitter lower-class children who are objects of it.[7]

Children experience conflicts when they observe that their own behavior does not square with American ideals of equality and liberty. Children of lower ranks experience conflict when they try to conform to middle-class standards pressed upon them by the school, since such conformity often means violating the standards of their home and neighborhood. Conflicts arise also when children reject friends of their own class in order to take advantage of friendships offered them by children of a higher class.

Contradiction and Confusion in Belief and Behavior

1. *Rank in a classless society: It is believed that there are no social classes in America; but it is also believed that some persons are better than others and entitled to more of the rewards of life.*

First in our equalitarian ideology is the belief that "All men are created equal," sometimes stated, "All men are equal in the sight of God." We may identify a cluster of beliefs which support or logically follow from this basic proposition: All occupations are to be respected, even the most lowly. Honest toil, earning one's bread by "the sweat of one's brow," is honorable and respectable. The poor have special virtues seldom found among the rich (we may sometimes identify a kind of doctrine of inverted status—hard-working laborers are thought the true aristocracy, and the rich regarded as parasitical, profligate, and immoral). A social climber—anyone who "puts on airs"—is contemptible, and to be shunned rather than admired. It is only the "cheap" and the "small-minded" who "lord it" over

[6] *Ibid.*, p. 177.

[7] For an interesting account of discrimination among high-school students see W. Lloyd Warner and associates, *Democracy in Jonesville*, Harper & Brothers, 1949, chap. 6.

those who are less fortunate. Such persons put on a "false front" by living in ways they "cannot really afford."

We shall comment on but one other example of our equalitarian ideology. A rich man who behaves like a common man, who has the language and manners of a plain person, who is willing to associate with plain persons, is much admired. He is a "regular guy," as "common as an old shoe." Persons who are socially inferior report glowingly on their "democratic" associations with the great man. Similarly, when young Mr. Van Swank marries Sadie O'Leary from the other side of the railroad tracks, he is much admired by middle- and lower-class persons. Such a marriage proves, it is thought, that America has a truly classless society.

Alongside the foregoing beliefs are an equal or greater number which assume that classes exist, or ought to exist. These are less widely held by lower-class than by middle-class and upper-class persons; but even members of the lower-lower group may accept some of them. Foremost is the notion that some persons and some families are better than others. One constantly encounters statements such as, "He comes from a fine family," "She is a nice girl, but her family doesn't rate," "I wonder why Jack and Ted run around together—Jack is such a well-bred young man," "The trouble with joining the club is that some of the people in it you would want to associate with, and some you wouldn't." Occasionally one hears statements which suggest that superiority-inferiority is a function of heredity, and blood is the carrier of hereditary qualities. "Blood will tell" communicates this idea. One also hears the expressions "blue blood" and "fine-blooded family." The saying "You can't make a silk purse out of a sow's ear" probably assumes a hereditary basis for upper-class status. Expressions referring to inherited superiorities occur more often among upper-class than among middle- or lower-class persons.

It is commonly believed that some behaviors are "vulgar," "coarse," "crude," "awkward," or "unrefined." By contrast, other behaviors are "correct," "polished," "stylish," "well bred," or "proper." Whenever behaviors are so labeled, persons using them are likely to be categorized as either "high type" or "low type," which is equivalent to assigning class rank.

Some jobs, some clubs, some schools, and some churches [8] are thought better than others—not objectively, according to money earned, physical facilities, or usefulness, but in terms of greater "social respectability."

[8] In Jonesville, for example, churches rank socially from high to low as follows: Federated (Congregational and Presbyterian), Methodist, Lutheran, Catholic, Baptist, Free Methodist, and Gospel Tabernacle. *Ibid.*, p. 153.

The Closed Areas: Social Class

Since most individuals accept to some degree both the American creed of equality, with all that it implies with respect to social class, and a class-accepting group of beliefs, it is obvious that in the area of social class there is much inconsistent and compartmentalized thinking. For example: Persons who dislike to think of our culture as class structured work very hard at acquiring and displaying symbols of status. A wife of an equalitarian professor is likely to prefer that her children not associate with children who display lower-class traits, such as "smutty" talk or use of the word "ain't." Even though she regularly denounces upper-class persons as snobs, a middle-class housewife is likely to be very pleased to be invited to a tea given by an upper-class woman. Even though there may be plenty of food and a vacant place at the table, a middle-class person of equalitarian philosophy is still not likely to invite into the house for a meal a laborer who comes to tend the lawn.

Persons who are most class conscious are most likely to become entangled in inconsistencies of the above sort. Certain groups, identifiable by sex, status, or occupation, usually take class more seriously than do other groups. Women tend to be much more class conscious than men. Newspaper society pages are read chiefly by women, it is primarily women who organize social functions in which symbols of class are conspicuously displayed, and women are more prone than men to snub or ostracize persons of a lower class. In contrast, men of all class levels are often able to associate harmoniously in a veterans' organization, church, or club. Probably class consciousness increases among both sexes as one moves upward in the class hierarchy, upper uppers being the most aware of class distinctions although sometimes exhibiting more outward democracy in their behavior than lower uppers.

Certain occupational groups seem largely to escape class entanglements and discriminations; they are "outside" the class system, so to speak. Examples are artistic and scholarly professions and government service. Small children are not at first class conscious, but evidence suggests that they steadily become so as they mature, and over two-thirds of sixth-grade children are able to rate other children in terms of conventional symbols of social class.[9]

1.1 How do you define social class? How does a class differ from a caste? Are social classes necessary?

[9] For an interesting study on class attitudes of children see Celia Burns Stendler, *Children of Brasstown*, University of Illinois Press, 1949.

1.2 What would a classless society be like? Would any of the following have a role in such a society: stylish clothes, correct English, proper etiquette, formal teas, tuxedos, sororities, finishing schools?

1.3 Is it possible to have equality and social class at the same time? How would each have to be defined in order for them to coexist without conflict?

2. *Earned success and fortuitous success: It is believed that the United States is a land of opportunity and that anyone can get ahead if he tries hard enough; but it is also believed that a person cannot move upward nowadays unless he gets lucky breaks or knows the right people.*

The first belief has such a long tradition and such wide currency that it needs but little comment. It perhaps reached its zenith in popular acceptance in the late nineteenth century, when "success novels" achieved a circulation of millions of copies.[10] The belief is accompanied by a cluster of optimistic notions of the following sort: America is a classless society. Since ancestry and childhood circumstances are irrelevant to success, it is no real handicap to be born poor or on the wrong side of the railroad tracks. Anyone can move upward if he has what it takes. If a person is of high character, works hard and conscientiously, and saves his money, reaching the top is virtually guaranteed. If he fails to reach the top it is because he did not try hard enough, or showed moral weakness, or did not have what it takes. The life of Abraham Lincoln has come to symbolize the dream of American opportunity, with the result that Lincoln is perhaps the greatest of all American folk heroes.

A belief in equal opportunity may be associated—as demonstrated by some of the beliefs just mentioned—with a belief in the essential equality of individuals. If one assumes that everyone is created equal, then success becomes a matter of *effort*. On the other hand, a belief in equal opportunity may be associated with a belief in the essential *in*equality of individuals: Social status and success are a manifestation of "survival of the fittest." Persons who feel that those who get to the top do so because of superior biological endowment, and that those who fail do so because they are biological weaklings, properly eliminated through natural selection, are ideological descendants of the "social Darwinists" of the nineteenth century.[11]

Whether one's philosophy of opportunity assumes that people begin the

[10] Horatio Alger wrote more than one hundred novels on the "rags-to-riches" theme, most of which were widely read in the late nineteenth and early twentieth centuries.

[11] This group, writing between about 1860 and World War I, included such names as Herbert Spencer, Walter Bagehot, and Francis Galton.

278

race as equals or as unequals, it usually maintains that everyone should try to rise as far as he can, should make maximum use of his powers.

Countering ideas such as those above is the more cynical notion that America is no longer a land of opportunity except for a fortunate few, and that one joins their ranks chiefly as a result of "lucky breaks" or "knowing the right people." Warner reports that a considerable, and in his opinion a growing, proportion of people feel that opportunity for the average person is declining in the United States.[12] This opinion is widely held by industrial workers, most of whom are in the upper-lower class; but it is probably also held by a considerable number of lower-middle-class white-collar workers. America's success ideology presumably has a stronger hold during periods of business prosperity when opportunity is greater.

Our success ideology produces a number of contradictions and conflicts in thought and behavior. People are likely to believe, on an abstract level, in the prevalence of opportunity, and in the obligation and possibility of "making good." These same people may in concrete situations attribute success to lucky breaks, as when they say, "No wonder Jones made foreman —his and the boss' kids were in the same outfit during the war." Upper-class persons tend to attribute their success to biological superiority; lower-class persons, on the other hand, who are less successful, often attribute success to lucky breaks.

A belief checklist administered by one of the authors to a group of college sophomores seemed to indicate that a number of students attributed membership in the upper class to biological superiority, and membership in the lower class to faulty environment. Gorer sensed the same discrepancy in the thinking of American adults.[13] If this inconsistency is widespread, it represents an interesting amalgamation of "social Darwinism" and modern sociology.

Another contradiction is apparent when persons, who preach the doctrine of success to their children and to adults less successful than they, criticize their former equals who have managed to outdistance them in the race. Since getting ahead usually means moving into a higher social class, and since this almost inevitably means the abandonment of old friends, persons

---

[12] For example, see W. Lloyd Warner and associates, *Democracy in Jonesville*, chap. 6. The Lynds also reported this trend in the second of their Middletown studies (Robert S. and Helen Merrill Lynd, *Middletown in Transition*, Harcourt, Brace & Company, 1937). See also Richard Centers, *The Psychology of Social Class*, Princeton University Press, 1949, p. 147.

[13] Geoffrey Gorer, *The American People*, W. W. Norton & Company, p. 168.

who get ahead are likely to be accused by their former friends of "getting a swelled head" or "getting uppity." In short, "getting ahead" is often advocated by the same persons who feel that social climbers are contemptible.

Probably the chief conflict is that between the ideals of success and social reality. Although we believe that everyone should try to be successful, and that failure is a result of personal inadequacy, it does not require much thought to see that everyone cannot reach the top. The upper class comprises no more than 3 or 4 percent of the population, and the upper-middle class comprises from one-tenth to one-fifth of the population. Many persons would be satisfied to move upward only a notch or two—let us say, from upper-lower to lower-middle status. But evidence indicates that even this kind of jump is more difficult now than it was a few generations ago. Upward mobility (although the evidence is not conclusive) seems to be declining because the structure and demands of American industry are changing. Executives—from top foremen to corporation presidents—are now likely to be college-trained specialists and increasingly are recruited from upper and middle classes rather than from the ranks of labor. Business leaders are drawn more and more from among the sons of the previous generation of businessmen, with the result that we are gradually developing occupational inheritance as an outstanding culture trait.[14]

2.1 Take a poll to find what proportion of your classmates hopes to enter professions or become business owners or executives. Then try to find statistics on what proportion of the population is in these occupations. Do you think that most of your classmates can achieve their occupational goals?

2.2 What determines the level which each individual reaches in life, heredity or environment or both? What data do you need in order to answer this question?

2.3 How do you explain the tendency to explain success as a result of inherited superiority, and failure as a result of poor environment? Is it consistent for one to explain success and failure in these terms?

3. *Success and happiness: It is believed that everyone should try to be a success; but it is also believed that the happiest persons are those who learn to relax and take it easy.*

Although in special situations "success" may be defined as formation of good character, it is usually correlated with occupational and social advancement. Success is a relative concept; at the very least it means achieving wealth and status beyond what a person was born into, but for many it is always just out of reach because it is defined as a step higher than pres-

14 W. Lloyd Warner, *American Life,* p. 111.

ent attainment, whatever the latter may be. Thus, a member of the lower-middle class by birth who becomes a member of the *nouveaux riches* may feel deep frustration because he cannot expect to become a member of the *anciens riches* during his lifetime. In our culture a person is expected never to feel satisfied with present attainment; he should strive always for a higher place.

At the same time, those who are struggling up the ladder of success may sincerely envy those who are, by conventional standards, failures. One often hears statements such as "Old Joe never made anything of himself, but he is a lot happier than some top executives I know," or "The Scrogginses never had a cent ahead, but look how content they are." In more general form, the belief is expressed as "Lower-class people are usually happier than the rich." Envy for the unsuccessful who at the same time appear to enjoy life issues from an ambivalence of motives which is apparently very common among those who are working to improve themselves. This ambivalence is expressed, on the one hand, in a craving for the self-esteem which accompanies occupational and social advancement and, on the other, in a craving for stability, relaxation, and freedom from excessive responsibility.

The literature of psychiatry frequently offers the opinion that the conflict most often observed in patients is that produced by a desire for "success," on the one hand, and a desire for stability and security, on the other. Social realities tend to make impossible the achievement of both goals; yet many persons find it emotionally difficult deliberately to choose one to the exclusion of the other. An eminent psychiatrist, Franz Alexander, describes this conflict as follows:

The [explanation] . . . is to be found in the culturally determined internal inconsistency of our social standards; the traditional one-sided worship of individual success in a complex and interdependent society and the exaggerated emphasis on independence in times of great insecurity. . . . The prestige attached to independent achievement on the one hand and the longing for security, love, and belonging to somebody or some group on the other are the two poles between which patients are torn in a futile struggle. . . .

. . . The analyst sees his patients . . . engaged in a Marathon race, their eager faces distorted by the strain, their eyes focused not upon their goal, but upon each other with a mixture of hate, envy, and admiration. They would all like to stop but dare not as long as the others are running. . . . If one of them finally stops and begins leisurely to whistle a tune or watch a passing cloud or pick up a stone and with childish curiosity turns it around in his hand, they all look upon him at first with astonishment and then with contempt and disgust. They call him names, a dreamer or a parasite, a theoretician or a schizophrenic. . . . They not only do not understand him—they not only despise him but "they hate him as their own sin." All of them would like to stop . . . [but] they do not dare . . . lest they lose their self respect, because they know only one value—that of running for its own sake.[15]

In Alexander's opinion the chief dread of the American male is that he will not make the grade in life, that he will not be "a success." Alexander believes this anxiety to be the most common cause of mental breakdown and neurosis among men in the United States.[16]

3.1 How does a person determine whether he is a success? What are your criteria for success? Is a person successful if he is merely happy? Is a lower-class person a success if he is happy? Is it possible for a person to be happy if he is a thief? A tramp? A prostitute? Is it possible for a person to be both a success and a failure?

3.2 Would it be a good idea to quit teaching children that "everyone should try to get ahead"? What alternatives are there to the goal of "getting ahead"? What would be the effects upon our nation if people generally ceased to pursue wealth and social position?

3.3 What has been the effect upon the United States of the "gospel of success"? What has been the effect of the "gospel of democracy"? Are these two gospels in any way conflicting?

4. *Liberal versus vocational education: It is believed that children of the upper class should have a liberal education and that children of the lower class should have a vocational education; but it is also believed that all children should have an equal opportunity for an education which fits them for citizenship and cultured living.*

According to the first belief, the best place for an upper-class child to get an education is a private liberal-arts college, preferably one which is old enough to have traditions. Many upper-middle-class parents include their own children among those deserving of a liberal-arts education. Prerequisite to this kind of education is a college-preparatory course in a public high school, or in a private secondary school.

Those who hold this view of what is proper education for upper-class children usually believe that a liberal education is beyond the capacity of lower-class children, and that furthermore they have no practical use for philosophy, literature, music, and the fine arts. Acquaintance with these fields might even make them unhappy and dissatisfied. A much better education for lower-class children is one which emphasizes vocational training.

[15] Franz Alexander, *Our Age of Unreason: A Study of the Irrational Forces in Social Life*, J. B. Lippincott Company, 1942, pp. 309–310.
[16] *Ibid.*, pp. 307–308.

These beliefs date from the ancient world. They are explicitly stated in Plato's *Republic* and characterize the educational thought of many Greek philosophers. They have had wide currency in Europe to the present day and were generally accepted in colonial America. They are still held by a considerable number of persons in all walks of life but have been reinterpreted in the modern world so that their meaning is different from Plato's. Whereas Plato meant that the recipients of liberal education were to be an "aristocracy of brains" and not an aristocracy of wealth, it is assumed today that an aristocracy of wealth is an aristocracy of brains. In fact, the modern tendency is to judge a man's intelligence by how much money he has been able to accumulate.

The notion that liberal education should be reserved for upper-class children is part of an aristocratic tradition. It is a logical corollary of the assumptions that some individuals are intellectually superior by virtue of heredity, that these persons are destined to become a governing class, and that a liberal education is the best means for equipping our natural leaders. It develops the mind, and those who are to rule should achieve the greatest possible mental development, while those who are to follow need only enough to understand what their leaders require.

Since a liberal education has been historically associated with high social position and superior intelligence, middle- or upper-lower-class children are often encouraged by parents, or they desire independently, to pursue in high school a college-preparatory course, the nearest thing to a liberal education which one can get in a secondary school. Parents of moderate status may also encourage their children to attend a liberal-arts college or to take a liberal-arts course at a state university.

In contrast to these ideas is a belief that all children should have essentially the same education. In a democratic society, it is held, all children are citizens and as adults will share in political control. Therefore all need the same basic education for citizenship and have an equal right to the benefits of cultured living, usually taken to include acquaintance with good books, music, and art, and development of a variety of intellectual interests.

This idea may stem from basically different philosophical outlooks. For example, a contemporary group of liberal-arts professors in the United States, often called humanists, feel that "true education" requires the same subject matter in every situation, and that all educable children should receive the same kind of education. This group would not limit a liberal education to the wealthy; they feel that it is good for everyone. If there are those who are incapable of learning the liberal arts, it is because they are ineducable. In opposition to the humanists are various branches of another philosophical tradition which advocate a core of common learnings. Within this general framework are at least two groups—followers and interpreters of Bode and Dewey, and followers and interpreters of Kilpatrick. Although the two groups may have divergent views concerning what the core of common learnings should be and how it should be taught, they agree that the traditional liberal-arts curriculum, and its high-school counterpart, has not succeeded very well in liberating human intelligence.

Emotional conflict arises when upper-class children who are not academically inclined are pressed by parents and school authorities to complete a college-preparatory program in high school or a liberal-arts program in college. Parents may believe that a vocational program would be more practical, or that its pursuit would make children more happy and useful, but they dare not dishonor the family name by letting a child take such a program. A lack of interest in, or an inability to master, the content of a liberal-arts course (as traditionally organized and taught) is not evidence of stupidity in a child except for those parents who have been victimized by an aristocratic tradition, in which case both child and parent suffer. Very frequently parents fail to recognize that it is social status they want rather than education of their children.[17]

Teachers become entangled in the patterns just described. Being aware that somehow a college-preparatory program is more "respectable" than other programs, they tend to favor college-preparatory students and often in subtle ways discriminate against vocational students. It is easy to assume that the latter are less bright and less gifted than the former. Teachers may vacillate between the attitude expressed in "If only those dumb kids who ought to be in the shops full time were not in my history class, teaching would be a pleasure" and the attitude reflected in "Some of my students don't learn much history, but they *need* it just as much as anyone else so I'll teach them all I can."

4.1 Is it true that some students are incapable of profiting very much from a liberal-arts course? If so, why? Can a liberal-arts course be redesigned in both content and method so as to benefit more fully greater numbers of students? Can this be done without "watering down" its traditional content?

4.2 What revisions, if any, in a liberal-arts course would increase its value to

---

[17] It must be recognized, however, that while not displeased by the status-conferring qualities of a liberal-arts education, many parents do value genuinely the kind of education which a liberal-arts program is capable of giving.

lower-class students? If such revisions were carried out, would the program still be "liberal arts"?

4.3 Are liberal-arts subjects maintained in their present form *because* only a minority of students do well in them? Would they lose their prestige value if most students did well in them? Is there any possible value to an education that the children of all the classes are interested in, are capable of mastering, and find useful?

DISCUSSION QUESTIONS AND EXERCISES

1. What current beliefs about social class could be studied in connection with each of the following topics and periods in American history?
   a. American Revolution.
   b. Sectional conflicts between North and South.
   c. Rise of big business.
   d. Growth of organized labor.
   e. The New Deal.
   f. Tariffs.
   g. Populism, free silver, and progressivism.
2. Charles Beard is known for his economic interpretation of history. Browse through his *An Economic Interpretation of the Constitution of the United States* (Macmillan, 1914) and note his use of social class as a tool in interpretation. Does his interpretation strike you as fair, accurate, and sufficiently restrained? Is it overdrawn? If it is, in what ways and at what points?
3. Which of the following social-science subjects can be most appropriately adapted to the study and discussion of social class? Why?
   a. Sociology.
   b. Geography.
   c. History, World.
   d. History, American.
   e. Economics.
   f. Problems of democracy.
   g. Civics.
   h. Common learnings.
4. If you focused your teaching of American history upon the study of social class, what do you believe would be the most likely result, and why?
   a. Much of the content in American history would be slighted and given only the most cursory treatment.
   b. American history would become more interesting.
   c. American history would help students understand the present.
   d. American history would have its meaning distorted and given a one-sided interpretation.
5. In order to help students understand social class, which of the following do you favor, and why?

   a. A six-weeks' unit on social class in a common-learnings group, or in a course such as problems of democracy.

   b. A strong course in straight sociology.

   c. Touching on social class in all the social-science courses whenever possible.

   d. Individual counseling on personal problems.

   e. Studying the behavior of sororities and fraternities.

   f. Making a community study which focuses on problems and tensions in the community.

6. As a student in teacher training, you have had many opportunities to participate in and to observe campus life. In your opinion, how does social class manifest itself on a college campus?

REFERENCES

The number and variety of class structure studies is suggested by the following references: John Dollard, *Caste and Class in a Southern Town* (Yale University Press, 1937); Allison Davis, Burleigh B. Gardner, and Mary B. Gardner, *Deep South* (University of Chicago Press, 1941); August B. Hollingshead, *Elmtown's Youth* (Wiley, 1949); W. Lloyd Warner and Paul S. Lunt, *The Social Life of a Modern Community* (Yale University Press, 1941); W. Lloyd Warner and associates, *Democracy in Jonesville* (Harper, 1949); W. Lloyd Warner, *American Life: Dream and Reality* (University of Chicago Press, 1953); and Carl Withers (James West, pseud.), *Plainville, U. S. A.* (Columbia University Press, 1945).

The impact of social class upon learning is treated in the following: Allison Davis, *Social Class Influences upon Learning* (Harvard University Press, 1948); John Dollard, *Children of Bondage* (American Youth Commission, 1940); W. Lloyd Warner, Buford Junker, and Walter A. Adams, *Color and Human Nature* (American Council on Education, 1941); and W. Lloyd Warner, Robert J. Havighurst, and Martin B. Loeb, *Who Shall Be Educated?* (Harper, 1944). The latter is the best factual study so far on the extent to which social class erodes equality of educational opportunity, but its recommended solution leaves much to be desired.

A provocative but by now somewhat outdated study of conflict between personal and property rights is Alfred Winslow Jones, *Life, Liberty, and Property* (Lippincott, 1941). For more up-to-date handling of class differences in economic ideology see Richard Centers, *The Psychology of Social Class* (Princeton University Press, 1949).

Chapter 14

The Closed Areas: Sex, Courtship, and Marriage

American Sexual Ethics and Their Implications for Education

ALTHOUGH millions of American adults apparently believe that sex education is desirable, it is one of the most neglected subjects of study in the secondary-school curriculum. Neglect of sex education may be attributed to lack of preparation (both emotional and informational) among teachers, and to a belief among many parents that what sex education is needed is better given in the home. However, demand for sex education in the schools appears to be growing, stimulated probably by a belief that, however good their intentions, many parents fail to give children the help they need in this area. Growth of concern is facilitated by the introduction in many schools of a common-learnings, or broad-fields, approach to curriculum organization, which is sufficiently flexible to allow treatment of any problem area of widespread interest.

Present sex education typically has two emphases: (1) dissemination of facts concerning the physiology of reproduction and (2) attempted inculcation of traditional middle-class attitudes toward sex. The first is usually a responsibility of biology or health-education teachers, or boys' and girls' counselors. The second task may be performed by health, physical-education, home-economics, and social-studies teachers, or by counselors.

In the opinion of many persons sex education, even where most fully developed, remains grossly inadequate. Dissemination of physiologic facts may be reasonably satisfactory but ordinarily an attempt is made to inculcate traditional sexual ethics in uncritical and authoritarian fashion. This

287

approach does not help students to resolve conflicts they may have developed in the area of sex. As in other problem areas, teaching of this sort is likely to intensify conflicts and make them less manageable than would instruction emphasizing reflection and clarification.

If one knows the origins of traditional middle-class sexual ethics, he is likely to understand them better. Some present-day notions have been in the Western culture stream since the development of early Mediterranean civilizations. For example, certain attitudes toward sexual practices are expressed in the Egyptian Book of the Dead, the Code of Hammurabi, the Talmud, and the Old Testament, and most of them continue to be held by large sections of the American population.

Since Hebrew and Christian scriptures are the most important sources of our traditional sexual ethic, it is helpful to examine their pronouncements regarding sex. Premarital coitus is severely condemned in the Old Testament, as are also adultery and homosexuality. The Old Testament condemns every type of sexual experience except marital intercourse, and decrees the harshest of punishments for those who transgress.

Extreme asceticism, however, was not associated with ancient Hebrew culture. It remained for early Christianity to develop the ideal of asceticism, and in so doing it borrowed heavily from oriental paganism. For St. Paul existence was a struggle of desires of the spirit against desires of the flesh; victory of spirit could come only as demands of the flesh were subdued: "It is good for a man not to touch a woman. . . . I say therefore to the unmarried and widows, It is good for them if they abide even as I. . . . But if they cannot contain, let them marry: for it is better to marry than to burn." [1]

By the fourth century A.D., asceticism had become an ideal to most Christians. The monastic system translated the ideal of celibacy into a way of life. The notion that sexual desire and fulfillment are intrinsically evil, and that the surest road to salvation is denial of the flesh, thus became instated during the Middle Ages.

One finds in the ancient and medieval world the origin of contemporary beliefs such as these:

a. Virginity is to be prized above all else. A virgin is nearer spiritual perfection than any non-virgin can hope to be.

b. Sexual relations, although regrettable under any circumstances, are

[1] Corinthians 7:1, 2, 7, 8, 9.

permissible only between man and wife. The chief end of sexual relations should be procreation and not recreation.

c. Adultery is a mortal sin, deserving of severe punishment. But it is worse for a woman to commit adultery than for a man.

d. Since sex is evil, everyone should avoid experiences which arouse sexual desire. It is best for people not to talk or think about sex any more than necessary, and children should be protected from knowledge of sex.

e. Any type of sex experience except marital intercourse is a mortal sin. Perversions are abominable.

Certain other beliefs may be traced straight to ancient times. The paternalistic culture of Judea, Greece, and Rome gave rise to beliefs that a husband should be head of his household, that wives and children should be submissive and obedient, and that woman's place is in the home.

The influence of Hebrew and Christian ideas upon sex, marriage, and the family has fluctuated from time to time and place to place. With the rise of Puritanism in England and its spread to the New World, the Christian sexual ethic was pursued with intense vigor. In Puritan England, fornication was once classified a felony, punishable by death. In Puritan New England, adultery was punishable by death, and fornication by fine and corporal punishment. Later, adultery was punished by requiring an offender to wear a letter *A* sewn on the outside of his upper garments, or, as in Connecticut, by having a letter *A* branded on his forehead with a hot iron.[2] The Puritan code was relaxed in the eighteenth century but underwent a powerful resurgence in the late nineteenth.

Today the traditional sex ethic is under attack from many directions and on many grounds. A new sexual ethic is struggling for emergence, one which is vastly less restricting and which tends to regard pleasures of the flesh as natural and wholesome, and as necessary to full mental and physical health. The changes taking place in our traditional sexual ethic probably stem from a series of specific events within a framework of *growing secularization of society*. This is not to say that Americans are necessarily any "less religious" than a century ago. But they have liberalized their religious beliefs; they no longer regard as law every dictate of Old Testament prophets or early Christian fathers. In addition to development of contraceptives, more effective treatment of venereal disease, invention of the automobile, economic emancipation of women, development of Freudian psychology, and changing patterns of courtship, there is no doubt that war

---

[2] Morris Ploscowe, *Sex and the Law*, Prentice-Hall, Inc., 1951, pp. 143–144.

has had an eroding effect upon the old morality. Almost all investigators have discovered a sharp break in sexual beliefs and practices occurring about the time of World War I.

Persons who believe sincerely in the old ideal of chastity outside marriage do not regard the new conventions with complacency. A counterattack on modern beliefs is being waged by religious leaders, authors, and newspaper columnists, all of whom deplore our "eroding sexual morality." Most mass media of communication stanchly uphold tradition while at the same time expressing enough liberalism to give encouragement to those who are critical of the older pattern. In one study of sexual attitudes as expressed in books, newspapers, magazines, radio and television programs, stage plays, and motion pictures the investigator concluded that humor and men's magazines express a preponderance of liberal sexual attitudes, while stage plays, newspapers, and scientific journals express liberal attitudes as often as conservative. Furthermore, salacious material seems to be increasingly tolerated, if not demanded, by the American public.[3] This represents a drastic modification of the state of affairs a half-century ago.

Ambivalence of attitudes expressed by our mass media resembles the ambivalence in the attitudes of average American youth and adults. Summarizing a number of studies including their own, Burgess and Wallin state that engaged couples form three clearly defined groups: a minority who do not question and scrupulously follow traditional Christian sexual morality; a minority who, without guilt feelings, have abandoned the old ethic completely for a more liberalized one; and a majority who waver somewhere between these two extremes. It is among this majority that serious emotional conflicts arise. Individual couples may adopt liberal sex practices but feel guilty; or they may remain chaste but seriously wonder whether they should. These unfortunates have incorporated cultural ambivalence and inconsistency into their own personalities until they are unable to move wholeheartedly in any direction without misgivings.[4]

Whatever the outcome of present confusion and inconsistency, one trend seems clear: sex is no longer as closed an area as it once was. Traditional taboos on discussion of sexual issues have evaporated to a remarkable degree since World War I. It is now common to find articles treating any of several aspects of sex in women's and family magazines and in newspapers,

[3] Albert Ellis, *The Folklore of Sex*, Charles Boni, 1951, pp. 261–263.
[4] Ernest W. Burgess and Paul Wallin, *Engagement and Marriage*, J. B. Lippincott Company, 1953, p. 387.

or to see notices of lectures on this subject. Fiction and nonfiction alike deal more frankly with sex now than ever before in American history (this is not true of moving pictures). It is exceptional for engaged couples not to talk rather freely of sex. Parents increasingly expect schools to give sex education to children. College classes in sociology and psychology study problems of sex and marriage more freely than ever before. However, discussion of certain aspects of sex remains largely taboo, and attempts at censorship are vigorous and often successful. In spite of this, sex is steadily opening as a field of reflective inquiry.

Contradiction and Confusion in Sexual Beliefs and Attitudes

1. *Purity versus experience: It is believed that sexual experiences before marriage are always sinful; but it is also believed that sexual experience is good preparation for marriage.*

The religious origins of the first belief are well known. Some specific and supporting beliefs include the following: Men prefer to marry virgins. Men lose respect for any girl who submits to them. Persons who have premarital intercourse are likely to develop a taste for it which will lead to adultery in marriage. Any sort of love-making which arouses sexual passion should be avoided. It is the girl's responsibility to see that things don't go too far on a date. Continence is neither physically nor psychologically harmful. Persons who enter marriage as virgins are more likely to have a happy and successful marriage. The best preparation for the sexual relationship of marriage is complete avoidance of it until the wedding night. One premarital sexual experience is decisive—an unchaste woman is a fallen woman, even though she succumbs to temptation but once (or as a minister expressed it to one of the authors, "You never saw a girl who was only halfway a sinner, did you?"). [5]

Even among relatively conservative persons there is one situation which allows some exception to the general stand expressed above. If a couple are desperately in love, and if they are engaged and soon to be married, sexual liberties are considered a little more tolerable. Although such liberties are not to be encouraged, they will be understood and condemned only mildly. Marriage will "cleanse the couple of sin."

[5] For traditional arguments against premarital experience see Gladys D. Shultz, *Letters to Jane*, J. B. Lippincott Company, 1947. For arguments offered by subjects of one scientific study, see Burgess and Wallin, *op. cit.*, pp. 380–384; for a compilation of arguments from other sources, see Alfred C. Kinsey and Associates, *Sexual Behavior in the Human Female*, W. B. Saunders Co., 1953, p. 308.

The second of our dichotomous beliefs takes more than one form. In its older form it referred to males only and was thus an expression of a double standard. Sometimes it was stated as "Men who sow their wild oats before marriage make the best husbands." One ground for this belief was a common opinion that men are naturally unsatisfied with one woman, that all men want experiences with as many women as possible. It was believed by many women that it is better for a man to work the edge off his polygamous instincts through premarital affairs than to establish adulterous connections later. Another possible ground for this notion may be a belief that an experienced male is a better lover, that he will be able to afford his wife more physical satisfaction in the bedroom than will an inexperienced man.

The double standard in sexual belief and behavior is disappearing. Those who believe that premarital intercourse is desirable now commonly feel that if it is good for a male it is also good for a female. Some reasons cited for premarital coitus include these: Sexual experiences bring lovers closer together and make them love each other more. Sexual relations before marriage prove sexual compatibility; if compatibility is absent, it is better to find out before marriage. Tension produced by long-enforced continence among lovers is damaging to their physical and mental health; release of tension is healthful. In reducing tensions and bringing lovers closer together, sexual relations also reduce friction and quarreling.[6]

There is a tendency for many persons to vacillate between liberal and conservative positions. Ellis, generalizing from his analysis of attitudes expressed in mass media of communication, says:

> . . . Twentieth-century attitudes toward fornication are certainly disapproving enough if we are to believe some of the most authoritative and widely read, seen, and heard sources of the day; but at the same time these identical sources leave ample room for the inclusion of attitudes that are often frankly, insinuatingly, sophisticatedly or romantically pro-fornicative.
>
> To confuse the issue still further, a considerable portion of the published and broadcast literature of today seems to have accomplished the noteworthy feat of, in precisely one and the same breath, accepting *and* rejecting premarital sex relations.[7]

This ambivalence is reflected in actual behavior. Almost everyone is verbally opposed to fornication and strongly in favor of chastity. Yet studies

[6] These reasons follow closely those given by persons who have engaged in premarital coitus, as reported by Burgess and Wallin, *op. cit.*, pp. 373–374. See also Kinsey, *op. cit.*, pp. 308–309.

[7] Ellis, *op. cit.*, p. 32.

by Kinsey and others show that virginity at marriage is not as widespread as verbal endorsement would lead us to expect. Among predominantly middle-class samples, about 85 percent of married males and 50 percent of married females had premarital intercourse. These percentages would probably have been much higher had the samples studied contained a normal proportion of lower-class persons.[8]

1.1 Considering the nature of American society, what are some advantages of remaining chaste until marriage? Is a person more comfortable if he confines his behavior to what is socially approved? Or does one have more fun, and is there more zest to living, when conventions are flouted?

1.2 Are there any satisfactory substitutes for premarital sexual intercourse? Are any of the following acceptable substitutes? Masturbation, necking, petting? What do we know about the effects of each? Would complete continence be better than any of these substitutes?

1.4 How do you explain the fact that in the area of sex what we do does not always conform with what we say? Is inconsistency between behavior and belief a sign that sex codes are changing? Is such inconsistency typical of any period of transition?

2. *Chastity and peer-group status: It is believed that premarital sexual relations are immoral; but it is also believed by many youth that demonstrations of seductive ability and capacity as a lover are among the best means for gaining status and popularity among peers.*

These beliefs are perhaps as widely accepted among middle-class high-school youth as any others which might be named. Of the first one, Havighurst and Taba report that the sexual ideology of typical high-school students in Prairie City is conventionally middle class.[9] Gorer comments on a tendency of American girls to lead a man on only to refuse intercourse (presumably because of commitment to the ideal of chastity).[10] Margaret Mead maintains that most middle-class girls of high-school age, and possibly a majority of boys, value chastity and manage to maintain it in spite of behavior which appears on the surface to reject it.[11]

Despite conservative pressures and considerable conformity to them, American middle-class youth, both male and female, have strong motives to prove maturity by demonstrating sexual prowess. It is thought to be manly

[8] For conflicting data on the consequences of premarital sexual relations, see Burgess and Wallin, *op. cit.*, pp. 366, 324, and Kinsey, *op. cit.*, pp. 386–387, 316–319.

[9] Robert J. Havighurst and Hilda Taba, *Adolescent Character and Personality*, John Wiley & Sons, 1949, p. 36.

[10] Geoffrey Gorer, *The American People*, W. W. Norton & Company, 1948, pp. 116–117.

[11] Margaret Mead, *Male and Female*, William Morrow & Company, 1949, p. 285.

to have a girl and to try to seduce her—although attempted seduction is often a game, indulged in for the sake of appearances and not seriously intended to lead to sexual intercourse as its climax. It is considered womanly to dress and behave seductively, to seem sexually experienced and sophisticated. A high-school girl is thought most mature who emphasizes her sexual characteristics in her dress, speech, and manner—although obviously this can be overdone to the point where she is regarded as a real hussy instead of merely a girl trying to look and act like a hussy. An immediate aim of adult-appearing behavior is not adult status but peer-group status. In describing the American dating pattern, Margaret Mead has this to say:

> . . . Growing-up does not mean to the American boy taking on the responsibilities and the trials of full sexual behavior. Growing-up means wearing long pants like his elder brother, driving a car, earning money, having a job, being his own boss, and taking a girl to the movies. A little petting, certainly, a lot of petting maybe . . . but no one expects the imitations of adult behavior that are involved in dating to have results, either in lifelong union or in pregnancy. Instead it is just part of the competitive game in which boys and girls demonstrate their popularity by being seen with popular members of the other sex. . . .
> . . . The boy who longs for a date is not longing for a girl. He is longing to be in a situation, mainly public, where he will be seen by others to have a girl, and the right kind of girl, who dresses well and pays attention. He takes her out as he takes out his new car, but more impersonally, because the car is his for good but the girl is his only for the evening.
> . . . Yet the game is cast in highly sexual terms; breasts and legs are emphasized for girls, all sorts of trappings of maleness are emphasized for boys. An accentuation of one's sex membership is phrased as a counter in the game, and sex becomes a secondary thing. . . .[12]

That this pattern places youth in a difficult situation scarcely needs stressing. The sexual drive of males soars at adolescence and reaches its peak during high-school years. The sexual drive of females seems to develop more slowly, if we are to accept Kinsey's evidence, yet perhaps in large part because of inhibitions imposed by middle-class notions of what is proper behavior for a girl. Freedom which is accorded modern youth tends to undermine these inhibitions. It is certain that practically all high-school boys and a substantial proportion of high-school girls are erotically aroused, as a result of their dating practices, and feel strong impulses toward fulfillment. Although the apparent contradiction between the notion that sex should be deëmphasized among youth (as stated in the traditional middle-

[12] *Ibid.,* pp. 284–288.

class ideology) and the notion that sex should be openly displayed as a means of seeking peer approval (which is believed by many high-school youth) is sharp enough, and a probable cause of friction between youth and their parents, there is a more irreconcilable conflict at a much deeper level. Margaret Mead describes this conflict:

> . . . As a culture, we have given up chaperonage. We permit and even encourage situations in which young people can indulge in any sort of sex behavior that they elect. At the same time we have not relaxed one whit our disapproval of the girl who becomes pregnant, nor simplified the problems of the unmarried mother. . . . We disapprove of abortion and adequate and available birth-control information is almost impossible to obtain. . . . We actually place our young people in a virtually intolerable situation, giving them the entire setting for behavior for which we then punish them whenever it occurs.[13]

Contradictions in the sexual ethic, as it applies to high-school youth, produce conflicts with a high emotional component; a youth wants to be loyal to the beliefs of his parents, but he wants his dating behavior to confer maximum prestige and acceptance among his peer group. In specific dating situations he feels loyal to the parental dictum, "No sex before marriage," and to the peer-group ideology which says, "Don't go all the way." When dating, he is pulled emotionally in three ways—by adult standards, by peer-group standards, and by primal impulses.

Lower-class youth are more likely to indulge their sexual appetites without qualms—although they may be persecuted by teachers and school authorities for doing so. Middle-class youth appear to rely heavily on two devices for resolving conflict between impulse and moral restraint. One of these is masturbation, engaged in almost universally by teen-age boys but more intensively by middle-class boys, since they commonly have no other sexual outlet. Masturbation is also widely practiced among teen-age girls, although not as frequently as among boys. A second device is petting. Petting is probably practiced more here than in any foreign nation. In the United States it is a substitute for the premarital coitus which many other cultures allow. Needless to say, these devices do not relieve tension without at the same time producing feelings of guilt.

2.1　What are some of the bases of popularity among high-school students? Is sophistication and acting grown up one of them? What does "acting grown up" mean in the sexual area?

2.2　Why do high-school students "pet"? Is this a method for getting popu-

[13] *Ibid.*, p. 290.

larity? Does "petting," since it is accompanied by unchaste thoughts, violate the chastity ideal? Is "petting" good or bad preparation for marriage?

2.3   Why are people strongly motivated to behave as their associates do? Do most high-school students "go along with the crowd"? To what extent should high-school students conform to peer-group behavior if it violates parental teachings?

3. *Mental cleanliness and natural interests: It is believed that interest in sex should be discouraged as much as possible (by not talking or thinking about it, by deëmphasizing it in mass media of communication); but it is also believed that it is natural and proper for people to be interested in sex much of the time.*

We have noted the ancient origins of the belief that sex is unclean, something to be tolerated grudgingly only because it perpetuates the human species. A good many people continue to believe that sexual impulses, interests, and desires are essentially evil. Jokes with a sexual motif are called "dirty" or "smutty." If a person shows an inordinate interest in sex, someone is likely to suggest that he "get his mind out of the gutter." Literature with a sexual theme is often termed "obscene" or "indecent." Numerous words are taboo in polite society because they make direct reference to sexual organs or behavior. A "clean-minded" individual is one who lacks interest in sex. The term *pure* also denotes mental processes uncontaminated by carnal interests. It is thought especially bad for women and children to show interest in sex. In summary, sex is supposedly corrupting; the best thing to do is to keep it out of sight and out of mind.

However, as the study by Ellis makes clear, it would be difficult to find an area of American culture in which attitudes are more inconsistent. Ellis analyzed a wide range of mass media of communication in an effort to discover the frequency with which attitudes toward sex were expressed, whether attitudes were "conservative" or "liberal," and the extent to which sexual matters were portrayed in salacious terms (i.e., in a way designed to arouse sexual desire). Although his study is open to certain criticisms, his major findings are well supported. He found that most of the time most mass media express conservative views toward sex but they also accord it a prominent place. Although illicit expression of sexual impulses is decried, much space is given to material which has the effect of arousing sexual impulses. Ellis concluded that a majority of the references to sex in books, magazines, movies, plays, and newspapers were salacious in effect if not in intent.[14]

[14] Ellis, *op. cit.*, p. 263.

Nor is this constant diet of sex which is fed to the American public unwelcome. Interests run heavily to sex in some form. Seldom do a group of men get together for any length of time without an exchange of "dirty" jokes, or references to sexual behavior of some sort. They may boast of previous conquests, of "naughty" women they have known, or speculate on whether a certain lady can be "made." Women are much less likely to discuss sex openly, but the heavily sex-laden content of women's magazines, and of movie and radio programs beamed at women, suggests that abundant interest is there even though repressed or subdued in many social situations.

It is significant that the one thing certain to make a book or movie a moneymaking success is trouble with censors. The advertising industry in America relies more heavily on a sexual motif than on any other; apparently beer, cigarettes, and soap cannot be sold successfully without advertisements featuring curvaceous females. Even religious movies produced by Hollywood are salted with a liberal sprinkling of sex.[15]

A typical American expresses ambivalence in his sexual attitudes whenever he regards sex as intrinsically evil but at the same time thrilling, exciting, and emotionally enriching. He may swing from one attitude to another, or he may attempt to operate with both at the same time. Ellis concludes that "American attitudes toward human sex behavior, as expressed in our popular types of mass media, are amazingly diverse, conflicting, ambivalent, and confused." [16]

3.1 What is the basis for the belief that sexual expression is sinful? What is the basis for the belief that sexual expression is natural and good? Do you know anyone who seems to believe one and practices the other?

3.2 Sometimes a painting or a book is banned because it is believed to be "obscene." Art and literature are frequently censored on this ground. What is "obscenity"? Who in society should have the final say as to whether a work of art or literature is obscene? Music is seldom attacked for its obscenity (although words to a song often are). Is it possible for music to be obscene? What do you think of the idea that "obscenity is all in the imagination"?

3.3 Are there books which young people should not read, paintings they should not see, and movies they should not enjoy? How does one determine what is suitable for young minds? Who should determine this matter? When is a person "too young" or "old enough" to have experiences reserved for adults?

4. *The nice girl versus the good sport: It is believed that women should*

---

[15] A nonreligious film, *The French Line,* has had difficulty with censors but a religious film, *The Robe,* which is not without salacious content, has not.

[16] Ellis, *op. cit.,* p. 261.

not be interested in sex as men are, that their minds and behavior should remain on a higher and cleaner plane; but it is also believed that women should have the same right as men to enjoy life, and that men dislike prudish women.

The double standard which decrees that what is proper for a male is improper or sinful for a female may be found originally in ancient Hebraic law, where it is ordered that women should be punished more harshly than men for certain immoralities. The following notions express or uphold a double standard between the sexes: There is, first of all, the concept of the "nice girl" or "good woman," sired by man's desire to idealize womanhood and to attribute to women traits which are more refined, more delicate, more gentle, and more spiritual than those of males.

A nice girl (or good woman) does not have very much interest in sex except for procreative purposes. She never really desires sexual experiences, does not consider sex a proper source of pleasure. If a man makes an indecent suggestion, she blushes, and perhaps even forcefully slaps his face. If a nice girl falls in love and becomes engaged, she resists suggested intimacies, but if she and her fiancé engage in intimacy at all she is extremely reluctant and guilt ridden. Her surrender is not supposed to represent any desire for sex, but only a service or gift to the man because she "loves him very much" or "feels sorry for him." However, a nice girl who weakens under these circumstances will probably lose the respect of her fiancé, and he will probably break the engagement.

A nice girl is always refined in her behavior. If she does discuss sex, it is discreetly with members of her own sex. In such conversation she persistently avoids words of one syllable, preferring instead to use approved medical terms. But a really nice girl—unless forced to—will not discuss sex at all. She never tells dirty jokes, and if one is told in her presence, she shows embarrassment or, if she is extremely nice and the joke very dirty, indicates that she has been insulted. When a nice girl gets married, it is thought proper that her husband initiate their sexual relations with as much tact as possible. She is to wait passively, submit passively, and make no show of pleasure—always remembering that a lustful woman is a depraved woman. So go the cultural beliefs about the nice girl.

A double standard assumes that a female will be a virgin at marriage, but no such assumption is made for the male. It is much worse for a wife to commit adultery than for a husband to do so. A double standard applies also to children. Small girls should be protected from sex to a greater degree than small boys. A small girl who innocently shows an interest in her genitals, or in any kind of sexual experience, is shamed or punished more severely than a small boy.

Recent years have seen a growing assumption of equality in all respects between the sexes. The twentieth century has brought the emergence of a new philosophy which grants to women rights and privileges traditionally reserved for men. If a man is to "sow wild oats," then an equal privilege should be accorded a woman. If woman is to remain chaste until marriage, then so is man.

With the rise of a single standard has developed a concept of the woman who is a "good sport." A good sport is not shocked by earthy language in men; she uses it herself on occasion. She understands a dirty joke, laughs at it, and then tells a better one. She fits in at a poker party, knows how to act at a bar, and will accompany a male friend to a burlesque show. She reads the novels banned in Boston; she can talk about sex intelligently and without embarrassment. She may smoke and drink; she is not always modest in attire; and she does not blush every time she leaves for the powder room. A good sport pets, but not necessarily indiscriminately. She may even indulge in premarital sexual intercourse as a means of releasing sexual tension.

A mid-twentieth-century good sport would have been considered a fallen woman in the nineteenth century—and indeed still is by many persons. Yet she is usually not promiscuous; she may have a strong sense of responsibility in accepting consequences; she may be honest, generous, and selfless. She is, in short, an emancipated woman who is behaving as many males have behaved for generations. In her values and conduct she is very similar to the men with whom she associates so freely.

An increasing number of men not only accept a "good sport" but prefer her to the nice girl, as indicated above. Many boys of today may actually criticize their girl friends, including girls they regard as nice, for not being better sports. Many husbands are critical of wives for being too prudish and inhibited. The proportion of men who demand that their wives be virgins at marriage is probably decreasing although the data on this matter are inadequate.[17] Despite the fact that a double standard is still very much alive for many persons and still has legal sanction, its erosion is obvious; for a large segment of our population it has practically ceased to exist.

[17] Kinsey, *op. cit.*, p. 323, referring to his studies of American males, says that over 50 percent do not insist that their wives be virgins at marriage. From what is known of attitudes fifty years ago, this represents a marked shift.

That this kind of change could occur as rapidly as it has without the generation of moral conflict is very unlikely. Many men are uncertain in their attitudes toward women. They cannot decide whether they want their women to be old-fashioned or modern. Many of them indulge their desire for a "good sport" through associations with women who are not their wives —secretaries, girl friends, prostitutes. They may feed their desire for "naughty women" by reading salacious literature or patronizing risqué shows. Women also are ambivalent. They want to be "good sports" for the fun of it, but they find it difficult to do so without developing feelings of guilt. Moreover, they are not sure whether men really want them to assume this role. Apparently many women receive vicarious pleasure from reading sexy fiction and listening to radio soap opera (or looking at the same thing on television), most of which includes at least one woman who is a "good sport."

4.1 Are there any good reasons why women should not follow the same moral standards as men? Are women more likely than men to be harmed by smoking and drinking? Is a woman more likely than a man to want to "go too far" in petting? Is a woman more likely than a man to abuse the practice of premarital intercourse?

4.2 What are the origins of the double standard? Was the double standard developed by a patriarchal, by a matriarchal, or by an equalitarian society? Do you think we would have a double standard if women had been in a position to make the rules? Why do men wish to deny to women privileges which they regularly claim for themselves?

4.3 Since World War I an increasing proportion of American women appear to conform to the "good sport" pattern. Do you think they are more likely than the "old-fashioned" girls to fail as wives? Is the rise of modern woman responsible for the increase in divorce rate which has occurred since World War I? Are American women going to the dogs?

5. *Modesty and sex appeal: It is believed that lack of modesty is shameful and immoral; but it is also believed that an attractive woman would be a fool if she did not reveal some of her charms, and that clothes should be designed for comfort and healthful living rather than for concealment.*

The first belief is as old as Genesis, in which it is told how Adam and Eve were made ashamed of their nakedness. A belief in modesty is logically related to a belief that things of the flesh are "unclean" and "indecent." In the United States, a belief that the human body is shameful, and that sexual organs are the most shameful part of all, dates from colonial Puritanism. It continues to be widely believed that the body, except for the extremities, should remain clothed at all times. A person who exposes himself is considered either unbalanced mentally or depraved morally. West reports that in Plainville many married adults have never seen the nude body of their spouses.[18] The law regularly punishes night-club artists who strip to the raw. Nude bathing is prohibited on public beaches, and many states outlaw sun-bathing societies. Anyone who appears unclothed in public is arrested, and in many places Bikini bathing suits are illegal. Hollywood, television, and the stage have strict rules concerning the extent of undress permitted.

There are certain qualifications to the taboo on exposure of the human body. Nakedness is permitted in small infants, although many believe that it is best to keep a nude infant belly-down. Nude modeling is permitted under properly controlled conditions. It is considered proper for a trained nurse or physician to see nude bodies of patients of the opposite sex. A few states permit sun-bathing societies to operate legally.

Americans are amusingly, and at times tragically, inconsistent in their attitudes toward modesty and nudity. They consider the human body in full view somewhat indecent but at the same time they strive to see as much of it as possible. Seminudity has become a fetish. Nudity carried as far as the law allows is practiced on beaches, in night clubs, on the stage, in popular magazine art, and even in fashions and styles. Although it is considered decent to conceal tabooed parts of the body with clothing, or some type of adornment, it is also proper, and even socially necessary, to wear clothing and adornment which *calls attention to and exaggerates the sexual characteristics of the body*. Thus, although female breasts are considered so indecent as to warrant concealment in public, women often exaggerate their size, and improve their shape, through the use of falsies. Exaggeration of the female bust has, in fact, become a cult in the United States, and a flat-chested girl is an object of pity or scorn.[19] In addition to artificial busts, American women exploit their curves through use of plunging necklines, clinging, form-fitting dresses, and foundation garments designed to emphasize feminine characteristics. Some males likewise pad the shoulders of their coats and wear girdles with the intent of achieving a more masculine shape. Ambivalent attitudes expressed in American behavior regarding modesty seem but another example of our cultural schizophrenia wherever matters of sex are concerned.

[18] James West, *Plainville, U.S.A.*, Columbia University Press, 1945, p. 177.

[19] Although the large bust is now an object of worship and is displayed in almost every visual medium of communication, some quirk of the American mind has decreed that the once respectable practice of nursing infants in public is now improper if not indecent.

Taboos with respect to modesty obviously create confusion, inconsistent behavior, and moral conflict. Enjoyment of seminudity—as practiced in night clubs, theaters, and the public press—may be accompanied by guilt feelings. Among couples engaging in petting or sexual relations exposure of the body may be painful and a source of later remorse. Within families, attempts to enforce severely the traditional taboos regarding modesty may lead children to regard their own bodies as indecent and make it difficult for them, as adults, to adjust to normal sexual relationships. Conflicts may also result from differences between lower-middle and upper-class attitudes toward nudity. Probably lower-class persons are most prudish about nudity, middle-class persons somewhat less so, and upper-class persons least of all.

Whereas taboos on exposure of the body may produce embarrassments of various kinds, as well as feelings of guilt, the American cult of exposing as much of the body as possible and insisting that exposed portions be "alluring" also creates conflicts. A small, flat-chested male may have trouble getting a girl, though not as much as a thin, flat-chested girl will have in getting a boy. A "glamour-girl" pattern is firmly established in the culture, and woe betide a girl who cannot in at least small ways measure up. In order to gain popularity, a girl who lacks glamour may feel obligated to engage in intimacies of which she disapproves.

5.1 How do you explain the American craze for partial nudity, coupled with firm insistence that nudity not be complete? Is there any difference in morality in the night-club entertainer who strips completely to the waist and an entertainer who wears tiny bits of cloth over each breast? Would the law punish one and not the other? Is the law rational?

5.2 How do you explain the fact that it is possible to publish reproductions of the most revealing paintings and statues, and that photographs of relatively if not completely nude women of so-called primitive tribes or cultures can also be published, but it is not permissible to publish photos of nude white women? Is this kind of code consistent? What is its basis?

5.3 American legal codes, as well as popular attitudes, assume that the human body is essentially "indecent," "unclean," and "evil." What is the origin of these attitudes? Are they widely shared by other peoples of the world? What do some other cultures believe about modesty?

5.4 What is "sex appeal" and how important is it? To whom and for what is it important? Is it a means of gaining social status? To what extent is "sex appeal," its manufacture and sale, a profitable American industry? How much does an average American girl or woman spend on items designed to enhance "sex appeal"? How much profit is made by American merchants and manufacturers on sale of such items? Is the "glamour-girl" idea publicized in American advertising for mercenary purposes?

The Closed Areas: Sex, Courtship, and Marriage

DISCUSSION QUESTIONS AND EXERCISES

1. Certain aspects of sex education in the public schools are offered on a segregated basis—girls in one class, boys in another. Do you believe conflicts such as are described in Chapter 14 can or cannot be discussed in mixed groups? Why or why not?

2. The conflicts described in this chapter are not the only ones relating to sex, courtship, and family which young persons are likely to have. Nor are they necessarily the most important ones. What are some other problems which might be an appropriate part of education in this general area?

3. How will a person's religious and social-class background influence the kind and degree of his sexual conflicts? Can a teacher who is deeply religious and steeped in middle-class values help youth understand their sexual conflicts? Can a teacher who has serious conflicts over sex help youth with sex problems?

4. Not everyone who is exposed to the conflicts and contradictions of America's sexual ideology incorporates these inconsistencies into his personality. Why?

5. Procure as many teaching materials as you can relevant to the general topic of sex, courtship, and the family. (Movies and filmstrips, pamphlets, and books are available.) Evaluate these materials in terms of their usefulness in a situation of reflective learning.

REFERENCES

In spite of legitimate criticisms concerning sampling procedure, probably the most useful studies of sexual behavior in the United States are those of Alfred Kinsey and associates, *Sexual Behavior in the Human Male* (Saunders, 1948) and *Sexual Behavior in the Human Female* (Saunders, 1953). Also of value are the following commentaries: Albert Deutsch (ed.), *Sex Habits of American Men: A Symposium on the Kinsey Report* (Prentice-Hall, 1948), and Morris L. Ernst and David G. Loth, *American Sexual Behavior and the Kinsey Report* (Greystone, 1948).

The Kinsey studies focus on behavior rather than ideology. Readers wishing treatments of sexual beliefs of Americans are referred to the following: Albert Ellis, *The Folklore of Sex* (Boni, 1951); Margaret Mead, *Male and Female* Morrow, 1949), especially Part 4; Geoffrey Gorer, *The American People* (Norton, 1948), Chapter 4; and August B. Hollingshead, *Elmtown's Youth* (Wiley, 1949), Chapters 9 and 12. For an excellent treatment of the American sexual ideology as reflected in legislation, see Morris Ploscowe, *Sex and the Law* (Prentice-Hall, 1951).

Two rewarding studies of comparative sexual mores and practices are Clellan S. Ford and Frank A. Beach, *Patterns of Sexual Behavior* (Harper, 1951) and Georgene H. Seward, *Sex and the Social Order* (McGraw-Hill, 1946). For studies of sex in primitive societies, see also Margaret Mead, *From the South Seas* (Morrow, 1939), which includes three earlier titles by Mead, *Coming of Age in Samoa,*

Growing Up in New Guinea, and *Sex and Temperament in Three Primitive Societies.* These titles are available singly in Mentor Book editions.

Most books on the ethics of sex attempt to promote conventional Christian attitudes, but with varying degrees of stringency. Sylvanus M. Duvall, *Men, Women and Morals* (Association Press, 1952) is a guide to Christian ethics, but written from a relatively liberal point of view. Gladys Shultz, *Letters to Jane* (Lippincott, 1948) presents the orthodox arguments in a form intended for reading by youth. A wider range of viewpoints may be found in Simon Doniger (ed.), *Sex and Religion Today* (Association Press, 1954). Those wishing an objective sociological analysis of problems of sexual behavior can probably do no better than read the pertinent chapters in Ernest W. Burgess and Paul Wallin, *Engagement and Marriage* (Lippincott, 1953). The classic work in the field of sexual ethics is undoubtedly Bertrand Russell, *Marriage and Morals* (Liveright, 1929). Although not an indiscriminate attack on the conventions, it reflects a decidedly liberal point of view. Also offering an outlook opposed to traditional sex mores is the readable historical treatment of sexual ideas given by Gordon R. Taylor in *Sex in History* (Vanguard, 1954).

Chapter 15

The Closed Areas: Religion and Morality

Religion and Morality in Modern American Society

THE situation with respect to moral education in our public schools was reviewed in Chapter 5.[1] Public schools have tended to ignore those moral issues in which youth are most vitally concerned. When moral issues have been treated, they have been most commonly handled on an unreflective level.

Many people feel that religious and moral instruction cannot be separated. For this reason they urge that religious instruction be installed in public schools. Although some probably favor some sort of sectarian instruction, it is generally conceded that this is impractical and that religious instruction, if it is to be inaugurated at all, must be nonsectarian to avoid offending any religious element in a community.

There is already a considerable amount of religious education in the public-school curriculum. Although virtually all the states have laws which prohibit teaching sectarianism, and few communities have devised acceptable schemes of nonsectarian religious instruction, nearly all public schools offer some instruction *about* religion. This kind of instruction is legal, and it does not conflict in any way with the constitutional barriers separating church and state. World-history courses always deal with the history of Judaism and Christianity; some include a comparative treatment of the

---

[1] The issues we have considered in each of the closed areas are moral in their nature. Unfortunately, most citizens do not see them as moral. In this chapter we are concerned with exploring some of the more traditional conceptions of morality. Morality in the lay sense usually points to issues involving alcohol, card playing, gambling, sex, and church attendance. In this chapter sex will not be treated, since it was given rather full attention in Chapter 14.

world's great religions. Courses in United States history normally include some treatment of the history of religion in this country. Senior problems and problems-of-democracy courses ordinarily have a unit on religion. Units of this kind usually stress aspects of the psychology and sociology of religion and may include a brief review of church history in the United States. All these types of religious instruction are now the almost exclusive responsibility of social-studies teachers.

There can be little doubt that the study of morals and religion deserves a much larger place in the public-school curriculum. If increased study is to be effective in changing attitudes and behavior, it will be necessary to approach religious and moral issues more reflectively. Whether reflection has a function in the religious and moral area is itself an issue. Many argue that religion is a matter of faith, and that reflective thought tends to undermine faith. This argument implies that faith is "believing what you know ain't true." It also implies that someone has to determine the substantive content of a religious faith, and the common man's duty is to accept this content uncritically. In any case, given the present state of religious thought in the United States, adolescent youth are very likely to develop religious conflicts whether or not a study of religion is included in the curriculum. Only through reflective analysis can they be resolved democratically. It is true that such reflection may undermine particular beliefs; but it is equally true that many religious and moral beliefs will be sustained by reflection, and a given faith will be better understood and more likely to influence behavior.

Another argument against reflective study of religious beliefs claims that they include metaphysical assumptions not susceptible to scientific verification. For example, how is one to test the assertion that "The Devil is the cause of all evil"? We have discussed in Chapter 5 the question of whether the reflective method can function in the area of moral judgment. In most cases beliefs of the so-called metaphysical kind can be analyzed according to the rules developed in that chapter.

Contemporary religious thought in the United States is profoundly affected by early Judaism and Christianity. One of the leading contributions of the ancient Hebrews was their conception of God. They came to believe that there was only one true God, Yahweh. Yahweh was regarded as a tribal god, in the sense that the Hebrews believed themselves to be his "chosen people." The important point for our purposes is the conception of the character of Yahweh which developed, since this has colored our thinking about God to the present day. First, the Hebrew God was anthropomorphic —that is, described in essentially human terms; even though just and righteous, he was also capable of great anger and harsh vengeance. Second, God was much concerned with the moral behavior of men. He was the source of ethical principles which man was expected to follow. Third, although God was the source of everything in nature, he governed and manifested himself directly rather than through natural law. God was thus thought to talk to persons directly, to inflict droughts or plagues as punishment, to raise the dead and smite the wicked, and to perform various other miracles. Man's relation to God furnished the theme of the Old Testament.

Although Christ was a Jew and sympathetic to many aspects of Hebrew religion, he introduced a new group of insights which distinguish early Christianity from the Hebrew religion which preceded it.[2] Like the Hebrews, Christ taught that God was a sovereign moral personality, ruling the universe with perfect justice and righteousness. But Christ, much more than earlier Hebrews, emphasized the loving and forgiving nature of God. According to Christ, God has no favorites. He is the God of rich and poor, and of all races and nationalities. No person, said Jesus, is natively unworthy of God's grace or man's fellowship. Men are to live religiously oriented toward God as sons toward a father, and toward each other as brothers. Christianity thus implies both equality and brotherly love as guides to social living. Christian teaching softened the sternness of God and introduced greater tolerance and sympathy into moral codes.

Further changes in religious belief occurred during the first three centuries A.D., chief of which was adoption among church fathers of asceticism as an ideal of life on earth. Asceticism as an ideal developed from a growing belief in dualism of matter and spirit. Whereas Jesus had "apparently accepted the body as functionally integrated with the mind and spirit in a working unity,"[3] by the time of Augustine it was believed that the soul was in bondage to the flesh, which was thought corrupt. The only way the spirit could be freed from lusts of the flesh was through self-denial. Some authorities feel that the ascetic ideal was a perversion of Christ's teaching. For example, Noss states "[Jesus] . . . was no ascetic. He enjoyed wedding feasts and banquets. He never suggested that the body is inherently corrupting and defiling, or that the soul is foully imprisoned in the flesh."[4]

---

[2] Some Bible scholars doubt that Christ intended to establish a new religion called Christianity. They attribute this achievement to St. Paul.
[3] John B. Noss, *Man's Religions,* The Macmillan Company, 1949, p. 587.
[4] *Ibid.,* p. 587.

The idea that the body is vile seems to have been borrowed from pagan belief systems of the Middle East. For example, Augustine was greatly influenced by a Persian philosophical system known as Manichaeism, which combined elements of Zoroastrianism, Buddhism, Judaism, Gnosticism, and Christianity. Manichaeists stressed the dualism of light and dark, good and evil, spirit and matter.[5] Augustinian thinking also stressed mystical experience and blind reliance upon faith, with a result that intelligence was all but excluded as a guiding force in life.

Medieval religious thought was influenced strongly by Greek philosophy. Thomas Aquinas adopted virtually all of Aristotle's thought except where it conflicted irreconcilably with beliefs central to Christianity. Aristotle had advocated substitution of reason for blind faith, and use of sense observation to establish the truth of propositions. He had urged that man learn all he could through intellectual inquiry. Aquinas tried to reconcile and synthesize the uncritical reliance on faith which characterized Augustine and the appeal to reason which characterized Aristotle.

By the time of the Reformation, Christianity had thus come to combine aspects of the thought of Greece and the Middle East, and of Old and New Testament teachings. This amalgam was distilled and bolstered by authority of the Church. The religious system which developed constituted a world-outlook. Stripped of minor and incidental aspects, the Christian world-outlook embraced three major ideas, as follows:

Belief in a personal God of stern but loving character, who created man and the universe and who governs them according to his will.

Belief in a purposeful universe. It was thought that the universe and every thing and event in it are part of a divine plan—consequently man and nature are moving inexorably toward an end already determined by God.

Belief in moral order—that is, belief that moral ideals exist in the universe as absolutes, universal and unchanging. Man's duty is to ascertain these moral values and try to follow them.

Protestantism arose as a protest against the means by which the medieval Church had asserted that individuals may gain religious understanding and salvation. Both Catholics and Protestants assume that early prophets and apostles were instruments of divine revelation. Catholics believe it is a role of the pope and bishops to interpret this revelation to men and a duty of

[5] *Ibid.*, p. 633 n.

men to accept submissively their authority. Protestants strongly reject the Catholic attitude toward this role of the Church. They assume that all guidance necessary for man's salvation is provided in Holy Writ. They assume that men can directly approach God without mediation by church or priesthood. Contrary to Catholicism, Protestantism came to advocate individualism and personal freedom in religious affairs. Early Protestantism also rejected the Thomist attitude toward natural reason and adopted an extreme Augustinianism which denied competence to human reason and relied upon faith alone. Although this was Luther's position, Calvin modified it somewhat to allow a place for natural theology. To this day, orthodox Protestants place faith or mystical experience above reason as a means of knowing God and interpreting his will.[6]

During the past generation we have come to refer to orthodox or traditional Protestantism as fundamentalism. Although Calvin's *Institutes of the Christian Religion* (1536) remains perhaps the outstanding systematic formulation of Protestant orthodoxy, present-day fundamentalists have in various ways modified the strict tenets of Calvinism. For example, many fundamentalists have abandoned Calvin's doctrine of predestination. Yet fundamentalists continue to share a strict core of belief which includes the following: [7]

1. God is sovereign in the universe, and although his will may sometimes seem inscrutable, his character is righteous and his decisions just.

2. Man is possessed of a certain natural knowledge of God, but this understanding is dimmed by innate depravity and he needs the aid of revelation of the Scriptures.

3. Man is subject to a hereditary corruption which makes him obnoxious to God. The original source of man's defilement was Adam's sin.

4. In spite of his predilection for sin, man can gain salvation through God's grace. He needs only to repent his sins and accept Christ as his savior.

5. On Judgment Day, Christ shall return to earth and the dead shall be resurrected. The saved shall enjoy eternal bliss in heaven and the damned eternal torment in hell.

Beliefs such as these led to formulation of a distinctive social and moral code and encouraged development of particular economic and political

[6] *Ibid.*, p. 144.

[7] For an excellent description of the leading tenets of Calvinism, see Noss, *op. cit.*, pp. 668–669. The first three items in the following list follow Noss closely.

doctrines. As we have seen, Protestant religion implied a belief in freedom of mind and conscience. Although early Protestantism was highly intolerant, gradually it came to recognize that freedom of individuals to interpret the Bible according to conscience leads to considerable diversity in belief—a diversity to be not only expected but tolerated. Furthermore, Calvin insisted that the first allegiance of man is to conscience rather than to any temporal ruler. Protestantism thus led not only to religious individualism but also to republican political institutions. And Calvin's emphasis on faithful pursuit of one's calling elevated thrift, hard work, and enterprise to the status of cherished values. Hence, Protestantism was a stimulus to rising capitalist institutions. Historically, it has defended virtually unlimited freedom for businessmen, even being charged with allying itself with predatory business interests and against laborers. Protestantism has also advocated strong national states and overseas imperialism because in this way the interests of business could best be served, but at the same time it has emphasized softer and more humane values of family loyalty, charity, and personal integrity.

Although intellectual freedom and religious tolerance became a part of the Protestant heritage, moral tolerance did not. A literal interpretation of the Bible, combined with a tendency to construe as sinful many acts not clearly condemned in the scriptures, has produced an elaborate and rigid moral code which makes a life free from sin practically impossible. Orthodox Protestants tend to define sin in Old Testament terms, and to denounce vigorously persons who deviate from traditional sexual codes, or who drink, gamble, and carouse.[8]

On many basic questions Catholics, orthodox Jews, and Protestant fundamentalists are in agreement. All three subscribe wholeheartedly to the three central elements of medieval religious philosophy: God the Father, a purposeful universe, and an eternal moral order. These three groups accept as literally true the moral injunctions of the Bible and add their own interpretations of sinfulness to behavior not specifically condemned in scripture.

Differences between Protestant fundamentalists, orthodox Jews, and Catholics are much less significant than differences between any orthodox faith and any naturalistic philosophy. Naturalism denies the existence of supernatural forces of any kind. It substitutes the reign of natural law for rule by a personal God, natural causation for teleological explanations. The

[8] See Burtt, *op. cit.*, chap. 4, for an excellent description of Protestant thought since the Reformation.

belief that moral law is made by man is substituted for the belief that moral ideals are suprahuman and eternal. Naturalism as an outlook originated in ancient Greece. It all but disappeared during the medieval period but emerged more strongly than ever in the seventeenth and eighteenth centuries.

The rise of modern science between the sixteenth and nineteenth centuries provided a renewed impetus to naturalistic philosophy. It is by now common knowledge that certain scientific discoveries have tended to undermine orthodox religious interpretations. Yet none of these specific discoveries is as important as the growing acceptance of a naturalistic world-view. Stace puts the issue when he says:

> While it cannot be doubted that these shocks have had a powerful effect in the way of undermining religious faith, it must be pointed out that this is on the whole a very superficial account of the conflict between religion and science. The real antagonism lies much deeper. It is not between particular discoveries of science and particular dogmas of religion at all. It is rather that certain very general assumptions which are implicit in the scientific view of the world conflict with basic assumptions of the religious view—any religious view, not merely the Christian view—of the world.[9]

The assumptions of the scientific (or naturalistic) view of the world, if they did not exclude God altogether, produced a feeling of the remoteness of God. God was now seen, if at all, only as a first cause, who ruled the universe quite impersonally through natural law. This was a central belief of the deism of the late 1700's. As a result of this trend, interest in religious affairs waned. In America, for example, many prominent persons were deists, and the masses likewise lost interest in religion. One writer says, "It was not uncommon for missionaries to report . . . that a whole region [of the frontier] was destitute of religion. . . ."[10]

Among established churches, liberalizing influences appeared. Although a reaction to the forward march of a scientific world-view occurred in the nineteenth century, a scientific view seems to have established itself solidly in the twentieth. "Modernism," a religious movement developed in the twentieth century, makes numerous concessions to it. Whereas Protestant fundamentalists maintain that religious truth is independent of science, and authoritative over it, modernists generally assume that scientific method is the most reliable—and perhaps the only—means of ascertaining truth. Some

[9] W. T. Stace, *Religion and the Modern Mind*, J. B. Lippincott Company, 1952, p. 53.
[10] William Warren Sweet, *Religion in the Development of American Culture, 1765–1840*, Charles Scribner's Sons, 1952, p. 211.

modernists explicitly renounce belief in the supernatural. Although the same tendencies which have produced Protestant modernism have been apparent within Catholicism, Pope Pius X condemned the movement and it was suppressed among Catholics early in the century. Among Jews, modernist tendencies have also produced a retreat from orthodoxy. Primarily, however, modernism is a phenomenon of Protestantism.[11]

What do modernists believe? Although modernism is a tendency rather than a position, it is possible to identify a group of beliefs commonly a part of it. Modernism places scientific methodology above faith, intuition, and authority. It employs scientific procedures in Biblical criticism and as a result rejects belief in the literal truth of the Bible. On social issues many modernists are politically liberal. They believe in social reform, international coöperation, social-welfare programs, and a morality which is congenial to fundamental human impulses. They tend to favor relatively easy divorce, liberalization of sexual codes, practice of birth control, and a frank acceptance of sexual relationships between man and wife as contributing toward higher values of love and friendly harmony. They seem to be moving toward a morality more pragmatic than that which has characterized earlier religious outlooks.

Many persons believe that modernism has gone too far, but others feel that it has not gone far enough. In this conflicting moral and religious climate children, youth, and adults are pulled in more than one direction.

Specific Points of Conflict and Confusion in American Moral and Religious Ideology

1. *Religious belief and practice: It is believed that persons should take their religion seriously and try to understand and believe its teachings in order to practice them in daily living; but it is also believed that anyone who tried seriously to practice the philosophy of Jesus would not get very far in today's world, and besides, extremely pious individuals are usually a little queer.*

The first belief above is so widely held in America that anyone who openly derides it is likely to be rebuked. Most Americans verbally uphold such purportedly Christian values as honesty, love and kindness, forgiveness, charity, generosity, and humility. If asked, most Americans assert that they are Christians and accept as true the central teachings of Jesus. Furthermore, most Americans feel, at least most of the time, that they practice

[11] One of the best short treatments of modernism is in Burtt, *op. cit.*, chap. 8.

a Christian philosophy in daily life. When they admit lapses, they are usually quick to say, "But I try to be a good Christian."

On the other hand, many beliefs and practices which contradict the philosophy of Jesus are prevalent. For example, "Business is business" seems to mean, in some situations, that anything goes in business—"Let the buyer beware." A businessman must learn to buy cheap and sell dear, to use whatever advertising and selling techniques will sell the most goods, to cover his hand when competitors or customers become too curious. Another principle with unChristian implications is expressed in the general rule "Don't let others shove you around." As a nation, we are ready at a moment's notice to defend national honor by fighting "aggressive foreigners." Carrying a chip on the shoulder is widely condoned, even though it is inconsistent with turning the other cheek. Under another popular belief, "People should get what's coming to them," we condone punishment for wrongdoers and try to adjust punishment to fit an offense. If a wrongdoer escapes the law but loses his fortune or becomes ill, we say, "It is good enough for him." This general point of view is scarcely in harmony with Jesus' espousal of sympathy and forgiveness.

These and other unChristian points of view are upheld so insistently that it is easy to understand why many persons agree that "Anyone who tried seriously to practice the philosophy of Jesus would not get very far in today's world." A result is that many attend church on Sunday and verbally espouse Christian doctrine but relegate these ideas to the background on weekdays and behave not as Christians but as hard-headed, practical Americans.

A standard device for reducing conflict is reinterpretation of Christian teaching to fit the needs of a situation. We say, "I don't think Christ really meant what he seems to have said. He must be taken for what he meant, not literally." Nowhere is this approach better illustrated than in the writings of Paul Elmer More (1864–1937). More was sharply critical of equalitarianism and humanitarianism. He wished to teach respect for authority, the past, the elite, and the institutions of private capitalism. The teachings of Christ, he maintained, supported this position. More said one part of Christianity has a purely spiritual phase, and this is what is expressed in the terms *faith, hope,* and *love.* "But faith, hope, and love, in this spiritual sense, have no direct bearing on the social question we are here considering. . . . They are of the spirit and not of this world. Even love, which at

313

first might seem corroborative of humanitarian equality and is no doubt so interpreted, is in this spiritual sense *a state of mind, not a rule of action.*" [12]

The ability of many Americans consciously to violate Christian ethics because they are "impractical," or to reinterpret them to suit a situation, is an indication of how lightly they take religion. That ours is basically a secular society is borne out by a fairly common belief that an extremely devout person is a "crackpot," "odd," or "crazy over religion." Devout laymen are likely to try to conceal their true attitudes because of this notion.

Confusion and conflict are widespread as Americans vacillate between expected piety and expected impiety. Adolescent youth, more than others, often become confused and puzzled. Adolescence is usually a period of high idealism and religious awareness. Religious conversion is common. Certainly many youth, wanting to take religion seriously but faced with a practical necessity of not taking it too seriously, need whatever guidance and other assistance a teacher can give.

1.1   Do you consider any of the following practices unChristian? Fraudulent advertising, reckless driving, cheating on tests, petting, drinking, snubbing a lower-class acquaintance, selling shoddy goods? Why or why not?

1.2   What do you consider to be the essence of Christ's teachings? Are the central ideas applicable in the modern world? Could they be applied if people were willing to try? How many persons do you know who regularly apply them?

2. *Science and religion: It is believed that although this is an age of science many problems cannot be handled scientifically and require a return to faith; but it is also believed that all problems, including moral ones, can be studied scientifically.*

ALSO

It is believed that science and religion often conflict; but it is also believed that there is no conflict between science and religion because the former deals with means and the latter with ends.

In popular thought, the leading issues involving religion stem from the relationship between science and religion. Two common ones are stated above. Both involve the question of proper spheres of religion and science. Many persons assume that science is a legitimate tool for the study of nature, including all animals below man, but always fails when applied to a study of human affairs. The willfulness of man makes prediction of human behavior impossible. Furthermore, they posit an eternal and univer-

[12] Shelburne Essays, quoted in *American Issues* (Willard Thorp, Merle Curti, and Carlos Baker, eds.), J. B. Lippincott Company, 1944, p. 885. (Italics the authors'.)

sal moral law; the truths embodied in such law, once discovered through divine revelation, need only to be followed. It would be senseless and sinful to seek through science for better behavior.

The naturalistic tradition, in sharp contrast, assumes that any problem is potentially susceptible to scientific solution, or that it is unreasonable to reject science until it has been given a fair trial. If science does not work in certain areas, its failure may be due to lack of human knowledge. The studies of sexual behavior by Alfred Kinsey and his associates are examples of investigations consistent with a naturalistic tradition. Although Kinsey tries to avoid conclusions concerning what is "right" and "wrong," the studies are evidently conducted in hope that their findings will provide more adequate bases for making moral decisions. It would be hard to justify them on any other ground. Nevertheless, many persons oppose the studies because they believe not only that science lacks competence in the field of sexual values but also that traditional values are of divine origin and thus eternal.

A variation of this conflict is expressed by those who believe that the discoveries of science conflict with established religious truths. For example, science's theory of the creation of the universe and man, although not claiming to explain "first causes," differs fundamentally from the story of Genesis. Another example is the belief that historical criticism casts serious doubt upon the literal truth of the Bible. Some persons also believe that science can produce no evidence that God has ever willfully interfered with natural law in order to answer prayer (as would be the case if God, in response to prayer, caused rain to fall at some unscheduled time).

There is a school of thought which believes that all controversy of this kind can be avoided. It assumes that means and ends are separable, that science deals exclusively with means and religion exclusively with ends, or the purposes, of life. Accordingly, one seeks ends in life by turning to the Scriptures or consulting a priest; once ends are determined, it is appropriate to use scientific means to achieve them. If this position is to be tenable, religious dogma must confine its remarks to statements of value and avoid attempts at description of man and the universe, or at least insure that any such descriptions conform to the findings of science. A common solution denies to religion any competence to describe the natural universe, which in turn means a rejection of the Scriptures as a source of literal truth. Modernists often hold to this view, and for them religion becomes a search for social ideals.

Confusion is enhanced by a tendency to mix and blend these various positions: "There is really no conflict between religion and science, but if they do conflict, religion must take precedence over science," or, less commonly, "In case of conflict, science must take precedence." It is highly confusing for anyone to take the position that "There is no conflict, but if there is, then . . . !"

Whether there is a necessary conflict between religion and science—and this is a difficult question, depending in part on how the major terms are defined—many persons experience a conflict which is real to them and can involve genuine emotional pain. Children reared in fundamentalist homes may wish to accept the Bible as a source of literal truth but find it necessary to accept, as they pursue their education, scientific interpretations which are inconsistent with certain interpretations of the Scriptures. Children who have been taught by their parents that science should not tamper with certain types of problems are upset when required to study and understand certain scientific investigations. Hollingshead describes vividly such conflicts among fundamentalist Lutheran youth in Elmtown.[13]

2.1 Can you name any problems which an American might have to face but which cannot be solved or understood if studied scientifically?

2.2 How do you explain church groups who appear to accept a religious world-view but who also encourage scientific research? Are such church groups consistent or inconsistent? Give reasons for your answer.

2.3 Is it consistent for a church group to oppose historical criticism of the Bible and at the same time insist that youth learn the facts of history?

2.4 Are most scientists in the United States religious persons? If so, what kind of religion would you expect them to hold?

3. *High pleasures and low pleasures: It is believed that the highest and most desirable satisfactions result from subordinating sensual to spiritual pleasures; but it is also believed that life is short and that we should live fully while we can.*

Prominent among religious beliefs is the notion that pleasures of soul, or mind, are "higher" than pleasures which involve physical sensations alone. "Higher" in this case probably means "more pleasing in the sight of God." It may also imply that a person who experiences spiritual pleasures feels a greater 'rapture, or receives more lasting satisfaction, than he would feel from any sort of pleasurable sense stimulation. This general position stems from dualisms assumed by early Church fathers—particularly the idea that

[13] August B. Hollingshead, *Elmtown's Youth: The Impact of Social Classes on Adolescents,* John Wiley & Sons, 1949, chaps. 10, 12.

man consists of two discrete parts, flesh and spirit, and flesh is evil whereas spirit is pure and good, or can be made so.

Beliefs about pleasure include the following: The fullest ecstasy known to man occurs during deeply religious experiences, as when the soul establishes communication with the eternal. Prayer and religious meditation provide deep spiritual satisfaction. A source of great pleasure is any service performed for the Lord—such as missionary service, ministering to the sick, or giving alms. Next in satisfaction to purely religious experience is meditation, contemplation, speculation—in short, any sort of "philosophizing." An existence which emphasizes such experiences is called a "life of the mind." High pleasures also include enjoyment of art, literature, and music. One is more likely to experience high pleasures if he subordinates to them all pleasures of the flesh. Poverty, chastity, and physical discomfort are often viewed as necessary or helpful means for experiencing high pleasures.

In contrast to "high" pleasures, many "low" or "vulgar" pleasures are enjoyed by those who lack spiritual perspicacity. Although low pleasures may involve mental satisfactions, most of them indulge only the physical senses. The more they indulge the senses the lower they are. Thus, copulation performed solely for erotic delight is the lowest pleasure of all. Drug addiction is low for similar reasons. The use of tobacco and alcohol is also suspect— these substances "dull the spiritual sensibilities." High living of any sort is condemned. Attending horse races, visiting taverns, watching burlesque, playing poker, using perfumes and cosmetics, and eating exotic foods are all objectionable. Plain loafing—"sleeping in the sun"—is criticized if practiced habitually. Low pleasures are not thought to be lasting, genuine, or deep. Habituation to them conditions one against the enjoyment of higher pleasures and is likely to make a person self-centered, brutish, and unable to commune with God.

Despite such beliefs about vulgar pleasures, a growing number of people are embracing a frankly hedonistic outlook. They argue that man has but one life to live, and it behooves him to live it well. "High living" is enjoyed by most persons who can afford it and some who cannot. The poor must be content with cheap liquor, roll-your-own cigarettes, and low-stake crap or poker games. But on all social levels there is a search for adventure, variety, and spice. Commercialized recreation has blossomed. Night clubs, race tracks, amusement parks, and liquor stores flourish, and on Sundays highways are crowded with persons pleasure bent. Occasionally someone pauses long enough to remark that "Americans are too materialistic," but this comment seldom engenders in its speaker or anyone else a serious yearning for a monastic existence.

Acceptance of the idea that pleasures can be classified as high or low, along with acceptance of the idea that "You only live once" can produce inconsistency, confusion, and conflict. Often the ideal of spiritual pleasure is accepted only on an abstract and verbal level. Gestures are made during seasons of fast to revoke a few—but never all—worldly pleasures. Hardly anyone really denies himself. Fundamentalist ministers continue to inveigh against card playing, alcohol, sex, gambling, tobacco, and cosmetics; but the influence of such persons is usually slight and temporary. It is often difficult to decide which pleasures are proper, and many people feel guilty for practicing a condemned activity. High-school youth are likely to develop emotional conflict as they try to decide whether they should smoke, drink, gamble, visit taverns, or drive recklessly. Parents, although enjoying some of these recreations, usually wish to deny them to sons and daughters as long as possible. Therefore, conflicts develop between adults and youth, particularly during adolescence, when youth have a strong desire to "grow up" and to seem adult.

Other emotional conflicts result from the fact that certain "low pleasures" are status symbols in American culture. For example, it is a symbol of status to serve martinis before dinner, to eat exotic foods, to use good perfumes, to smoke good cigars, to attend horse races, and to visit night clubs. Another type of inconsistency arises when hedonistic upper- or upper-middle-class persons urge simplicity and moderation upon the poor, in the belief, no doubt, that if the poor are more content with their station in life they will make less trouble for their social superiors.

3.1 The following behaviors have been variously described as morally harmful, damaging to health, or sinful: drinking, smoking, card playing, gambling. Which do you consider immoral, which sinful, and which physically harmful? Is there a difference between immorality and sin? How can one determine whether an act is immoral? Whether it is sinful?

3.2 Do you believe there is a divine law which rates pleasures as "high" or "low," and "respectable" or "unrespectable"? How does one determine what this law decrees? Does the Bible have anything to say about the use of alcohol? About smoking? Gambling? Petting? Use of cosmetics? Visiting night clubs? Have ministers ever made claims about sin which could not be substantiated with Scripture?

3.3 Is it possible that a person might achieve what is usually considered a "high pleasure" through indulgence in a "low pleasure"? Could a person experience religious ecstasy while under influence of alcohol or drugs? Could a person develop a feeling of love and kinship toward mankind while drunk? Could a person meditate and philosophize in a tavern?

4. *Democracy and religion: It is believed that Christian religion is the basis of democracy and that democracy cannot function successfully except among a people who are deeply devout; but it is also believed that democracy is a secular philosophy and that some well-known democrats have been irreligious.*

The first position has it that Jesus laid the foundation for democracy when he affirmed that all men are equal in the sight of God and all men are brothers on earth as well as in heaven.

But the equalitarianism taught by Jesus is not thought the chief reason that Christianity is essential to democracy. It is usually assumed that democracy cannot survive without widespread and voluntary acceptance of certain Christian moral ideals—for example, the golden rule. It is further assumed that acceptance of this or any other moral ideal is improbable without religion. The source of moral ideals is thought to be an eternal moral order, established by God and interpreted for man by Jesus. Survival of democracy is therefore commonly linked with Christianity and vice versa.

On the other hand, some persons argue that democracy is a secular and not a religious philosophy, and that its origins are to be found in motives which are strictly human. Modern democracy is an outgrowth of a long historical process associated with emergence of a middle class in Europe and its colonies. The struggle of merchants and manufacturers for freedom from feudal controls could be won only through establishment of representative forms of government. The divine rights of kings, a thoroughly Christian concept at the time, was one barrier to the achievement of representative government. Those who argue that representative government entered the world scene at the same time as free enterprise (except for a few isolated and temporary experiments with republicanism, as in ancient Greece) do not deny that certain religious ideas, especially those associated with Protestantism, have helped greatly in establishing representative government. Protestantism, in defending individual freedom, property ownership, and a money economy, undoubtedly gave the rising capitalist class an invaluable assist. But the primary motives behind the attack on feudalism and aristocracy, these persons contend, were *economic*, and availability of religious ideas consistent with political liberty was a fortuitous circumstance, not a decisive cause.

319

It is pointed out that democracy as a social ideal became widely understood and accepted only after the scientific world-view reached ascendancy among intellectual leaders. Exponents of political-intellectual liberty in the eighteenth century were, for the most part, either "supernatural rationalists" or deists. The former included Descartes, Newton, and Locke; the latter Diderot, Voltaire, and Hume. Locke was a leading exponent of constitutional government, and his ideas, supplemented by those of Montesquieu, were appropriated by such American revolutionary leaders as Thomas Jefferson, John Hancock, and Thomas Paine (all deists). However, it should be remembered that democracy, in its modern sense, was not popular even in revolutionary France and America except among a small group of intellectuals and lower-class persons whose opinions were not influential. But many people believe that it was the eighteenth-century intellectual, usually unorthodox in his religion, who established the groundwork for modern democracy and whose theories continue to form its ideological underpinning. For example, Randall suggests that modern ideas of democracy can be traced to Locke, Rousseau, and Jefferson.[14]

In 20th-century America, while a large number of spokesmen for democracy are Christian or Jewish theists, many are philosophic naturalists. It would be indefensible to say that one group is more sincerely and effectively democratic than the other. The issue, as stated at the head of this section, is such that many individuals will find intrapersonal conflict to some degree inescapable. If one's minister asserts that no atheist can be a sincere democrat, and one then becomes acquainted with an atheist who is also sincerely democratic confusion is likely to result. On the other hand, a person reared in a naturalistic tradition, who has been taught that democracy is a secular philosophy and that all religions are to some extent authoritarian in outlook, may also be troubled when he meets a devout individual who seems honestly dedicated to the cause of democracy. A further problem may arise when a person who has been taught to believe that only Christians can be sincere democrats finds that some non-Christians can be more democratic than some Christians.

4.1   It is assumed that any social ideal, including democracy, must have a moral basis. Is it possible to defend any moral system except in religious terms? Can a person be a moral individual and still be irreligious? Would abandonment of traditional Christianity lead to moral deterioration?

4.2   What sort of moral ideals are consistent with democracy? How does a

[15] John Herman Randall, Jr., *The Making of the Modern Mind,* Houghton Mifflin Company, 1940, pp. 349–357.

democratic person behave? Does democracy imply a whole way of life? Does the idea of democracy apply to operation of a school? Are parochial schools generally more democratic than public schools?

4.3 Does democracy apply to running a home? To associations with one's friends? If so, what are the basic moral principles involved?

DISCUSSION QUESTIONS AND EXERCISES

1. Some who favor religious instruction in public schools believe that clergy rather than public-school teachers should give this instruction. Without regard to questions of constitutionality, analyze this argument and locate relevant assumptions in educational philosophy and learning theory.
2. Is it possible to study ideas in the closed areas of sex and economics without also studying certain ideas in religion? Some have argued that critical thinking in economics is desirable but that such analysis in religion is unfair. How could one limit his critical thinking to economics so that it would not tread upon religion? What would be the consequences of such limitation? How would one's understanding of economics be affected?
3. One man's meat is another man's poison. Likewise, one man's religion is another man's superstition. Is there any rational and objective basis for distinguishing between religion and superstition?
4. Some states have statutes which require a teacher to begin the school day by reading without comment a short passage from any part of the Bible. What do you believe to be the purpose of such statutes? What would be the effect of enforcing them? Is this religious instruction?
5. What is a theocracy? Can a theocracy be democratic? Do religious fundamentalists desire a theocracy in America?
6. There are those who fear that democracy as a social philosophy will replace traditional Christianity as a primary source of moral ideals. Is this change likely to occur? What would be the consequences of such a change?

REFERENCES

Contemporary conflicts in religious ideology cannot be understood apart from their historical origins. The following all treat religion historically. Especially readable is Joseph Gaer, *How the Great Religions Began* (McBride, 1929; also New American Library edition, 1954). See also Sir James G. Fraser, *The Golden Bough* (Macmillan, 1923, abridged one volume edition); Herbert J. Muller, *The Uses of the Past* (Oxford University Press, 1953); and Arnold J. Toynbee, *A Study of History* (Oxford University Press, 1947, one volume abridgement by D. C. Somerville). Religious history as viewed by a naturalistic philosopher and critic is presented in Homer Smith, *Man and His Gods* (Little, Brown, 1952).

Religious development in the United States is treated ably in William W. Sweet, *Religion in the Development of American Culture* (Scribner, 1952). See also Henry F. May, *Protestant Churches and Industrial America* (Harper, 1949) and Anson P. Stoke's exhaustive study of the relation between government and religion, *Church and State in the United States* (Harper, 1950).

A standard reference in comparative religious philosophy is Edwin A. Burtt, *Types of Religious Philosophy* (Harper, 1939). Also helpful is J. Donald Butler, *Four Philosophies and Their Practice in Education and Religion* (Harper, 1951). A readable and provocative examination of whether there is a place for religion in our modern scientific age is W. T. Stace, *Religion and the Modern Mind* (Lippincott, 1952).

A student of religion should be familiar with some of the polemical literature on present-day religious outlooks. Richard Boynton, *Beyond Mythology: A Challenge to Dogmatism in Religion* (Doubleday, 1951) is critical of conventional religions and advocates an emphasis upon Christian values which would be consistent with the realities of a scientific age. Paul Blanshard's two volumes, *American Freedom and Catholic Power* (Beacon, 1949) and *Communism, Democracy and Catholic Power* (Beacon, 1951) indict many official policies of the Catholic Church. James M. O'Neill answers Blanshard in *Catholicism and American Freedom* (Harper, 1952). Theodore Maynard, *Catholic Way* (Appleton-Century-Crofts, 1953) affords a sympathetic treatment of the general position of modern Catholicism. Protestant fundamentalism is energetically defended in William ("Billy") Graham, *Peace With God* (Doubleday, 1953).

For studies in the psychology of religion, William James, *The Varieties of Religious Experience: A Study in Human Nature* (Longmans, Green, 1923), remains a classic. The most significant recent book in this area is probably Gordon Allport, *The Individual and His Religion* (Macmillan, 1952). A proposal for the religious education of children is developed by Sophia Fahs in *Today's Children and Yesterday's Heritage: A Philosophy of Creative Religious Development* (Beacon, 1952). The author attempts to outline an indoctrination-free program of religious education.

Students wishing to study scriptures are referred to: Robert O. Ballou (ed.), *Portable World Bible: Sacred Scriptures of the Eight Basic Religions* (Viking Portable Library, 1944); *Bible* (Westminster study edition, an authorized King James version, Westminster Press, 1948); and *Bible* (Revised Standard Version, T. Nelson, 1952). The latter edition represents an attempt to modernize the Bible by bringing its phraseology into line with modern usage.

Chapter 16

The Closed Areas: Nationalism, Patriotism, and National Institutions

---

Nationalism and Patriotism in American Life

THE teaching of patriotism has always been one of the functions of public schools in the United States. This instruction traditionally has taken the form of acquainting students with the lives of national heroes, with heroic national deeds, and with patriotic ceremonies (such as the flag salute, singing the national anthem, and rituals of Memorial Day, Veterans' Day, and Fourth of July). However, there are different conceptions of patriotism, and many teachers and parents maintain that traditional instruction fails to build the kind of loyalty essential to a modern democratic society.

Although critics of traditional instruction in patriotism do not claim that schools have failed entirely to teach democratic patriotism, they argue that adult Americans who have completed a public-school education behave in ways which, from the standpoint of citizenship, leave much to be desired. Many American soldiers during World War II and the war in Korea appeared to lack an intelligent understanding of the meaning of democracy, or of the genuine differences between democracy, fascism, and communism. Many did not seem to know what the fighting was intended to preserve, nor did they understand how political warfare could function to aid democratic causes.

Inability to understand democracy also manifests itself within the United States. Most high-school students and a considerable number of college undergraduates cannot give an intelligible definition of democracy or identify the practical implications of democratic ideals. This lack of understanding is revealed among adults by their favorable reaction to the undemocratic behavior of many public officials. Demagogues seem able to arouse as much mass support now as at any time in our past history. Under their spell, millions of Americans readily come to accept the belief that such essential features of democracy as civil liberties, academic freedom, and racial equality are communist inventions. Without knowing better, millions of Americans who believe in democracy apparently would subvert its very foundations.

In similar vein, many Americans give tacit, if not direct, support to the doctrine "A good end justifies any means." Although Abraham Lincoln suspended the right of habeas corpus, and other great leaders of democracy have on occasion abandoned democratic methods in order to achieve some cherished end, this principle is not characteristic of democracy, and it is not likely that democracy could survive its general application.

All too often the kind of patriotism taught in our public schools has been blind and mechanical. Students have been taught habits which are unintelligent and undemocratic in nature. This kind of patriotism contains definite dangers. The only kind of patriotism which a democratic civilization can afford is reasoned commitment to democratic ideals. The chief burden for teaching intelligent patriotism rests upon our social-studies teachers.

Those beliefs, attitudes, and practices which we label nationalism appeared in Europe toward the close of the Middle Ages and marked the beginning of what we regard as "modern Europe." The appearance of nationalism was hastened by the erosion of feudalism and a Christendom united under the international authority of one church. It was accompanied by formation of national states with strong central rulers, by development of national languages, and by a surging interest in commerce and industry. A motive for formation of national states was the need of the rising commercial and manufacturing interests for stable currencies, strong governments, and strong armies.

The Reformation was a potent stimulus to nationalism. Both Luther and Calvin turned to national states as bulwarks of Protestantism against the internationalism of the Catholic Church. Luther trusted to the state power to decide what was in accordance with the gospel, but Calvin insisted on supremacy of church over state. However, Calvin believed churches should be organized on a national, not an international, basis. The Protestant Church, organized along state lines and appealing strongly to the middle class, thus had immeasurable influence in uniting populations under the rule of a single monarch and in inducing them to think in national rather than international terms.

As Randall puts it, the concept of nationalism contained an acceptance of—if not hearty belief in—the growth of "independent, irresponsible, absolutely sovereign territorial states, the avowed sanction of whose acts is power." A chauvinistic and commercial patriotism developed which emphasized the slogans "For king and country," "For the glory of France," and "My country, right or wrong." [1]

Counterforces arose in the eighteenth century. Intellectuals, imbued with the spirit of the Age of Enlightenment, looked upon nationalism as irrational, unnatural, and harmful to human welfare. They condemned war and advocated unity of all mankind. In addition, the commercial groups had by now recognized that their interests were not served by mercantilistic nationalism. Businessmen began to favor international free trade, and this attitude had a corrosive effect upon nationalist sentiments.

The nineteenth century tells a different story. Sparked by a resurgence of nationalism which accompanied the French Revolution and the rule of Napoleon, the nineteenth century retreated from the humanitarian and internationalist thinking of the eighteenth. Nationalism became popular in Britain, France, Germany, and the United States. Randall tries to express the spirit of the age:

> What, after all, is my country? Is she a group of discordant little men who have agreed to live together to serve their own selfish interests? Is she founded on an artificial contract, on a man-made and written constitution? A thousand times No! She is My Country! She is something sacred, something living, something one and eternal, the central source of my life, my aspirations. She is greater than any man, than all men now living, than all generations of men: she is an organic whole, one and indivisible, a past, a tradition.[2]

Patriotism became correlated with a blind, unreasoning love of country and obedience to national rulers. It came to have a mystical quality, to resemble a religion. One expressed his patriotism by undergoing appropriate rites, such as saluting his national flag, displaying it in respectful ways, and standing at grave attention when the national anthem was sung.[3] Another common feature of patriotism was its tendency toward intolerance

---

[1] John Herman Randall, Jr., *The Making of the Modern Mind*, Houghton Mifflin Company, 1940, p. 172.

[2] *Ibid.*, p. 433–434.

[3] Of course, these practices are not in themselves undemocratic and are not inconsistent with a reasoned commitment to democratic ideals.

and ethnocentrism. All other countries were thought inferior to the fatherland. In some cases, every country but one's own was an object of contempt and hatred. Anyone within the fatherland who disregarded customary patriotic rites, or who advocated a philosophy of internationalism, was considered ignorant, depraved, or traitorous.

Nationalism and patriotism have continued as major forces into the twentieth century. Nationalistic feeling appears to rise during war and to remain at fever pitch for several years thereafter. These waves of ultranationalism are usually accompanied by conservative reactions in political, economic, and social thought, and by attacks on traditional ideals of free speech and right of dissent.

In the United States today, the following beliefs reflect our nationalistic outlook:

1. One's first loyalty should be to his country.
2. One should love his country more than life.
3. One should respect the symbols of national power and greatness (the flag, national heroes, the national anthem, patriotic documents, and the uniforms of our armed forces).
4. Peace without national honor is worse than war.
5. A nation's greatness is measured by its military strength and success.
6. The worst of all crimes is treason.
7. The United States is the greatest nation in the world and must always remain so.

A contrasting point of view, modifying or rejecting the ultranationalism just described, is essentially internationalist, anti-chauvinist, and critical of national institutions. Associated with the ideology of democratic liberalism, it has deep roots in the history of Western civilization. As we have seen, this viewpoint was introduced most conspicuously in the eighteenth century and lay largely quiescent in the nineteenth. A number of recent developments have contributed to its resurgence in the twentieth. One of these was "muckraking," which fostered a more critical attitude toward American heroes and institutions. Although muckraking represented a somewhat cynical manifestation of "scientific history," it approached that kind of historical research which stresses publication of unvarnished truth no matter whom or how much it hurts.

The liberalism of Populism and Progressivism was not internationalist in outlook; the former was largely unconcerned with the issue, and the latter, particularly as interpreted by Theodore Roosevelt, was frankly chauvinist.

But these movements did help to prepare the soil for Wilson's New Freedom and the popularization of his brand of internationalism. World War II and the years following, in spite of a resurrection of extreme nationalism, were accompanied by a considerable movement which was internationalist in outlook and definitely hostile toward older nationalistic outlooks and saber-rattling patriotism.

A distinctive form of nationalism is "isolationism." Contributing to this movement was the debunking of World War I myths, performed with incisive skill by persons such as Sidney B. Fay and Harry Elmer Barnes and presented in popular version by Walter Millis. World War I was shown by these scholars not to have had the simple origins once supposed. Germans were shown not to be the ogres which American folklore had portrayed. Blame was placed upon the heads of Americans and the Allies as well as upon the Germans.

These interpretations, coupled with the unhappy aftermath of the war in Europe, led to development of an American pacifist and isolationist movement of major proportions. Whatever else this movement may have contributed, it did make millions of Americans more skeptical of government-sponsored propaganda and more critical of the point of view expressed in "My country, right or wrong." The more liberal among isolationists seem to have switched in recent years to an internationalist outlook, and the more conservative have gravitated toward a position which combines an "America first" with a "go-it-alone" attitude.

Most of the liberal tendencies in American history were captured and synthesized under the spiritual and intellectual leadership of Franklin Roosevelt during the New Deal era. The New Deal was broadly internationalist in outlook, critical of many of the old nationalist myths, yet willing to fight when the threat of fascist military victory in Europe became too compelling to ignore. It is notable that World War II was fought in a much more restrained emotional atmosphere than was World War I. Although feeling ran high against the enemy, especially the Japanese, there was a minimum of hysteria. Evidence of the new outlook was furnished by the enthusiastic part played by the United States in the founding of the United Nations and its accessory agencies, and the continued support of this organization by an apparent majority of Americans.

Although pressure is now being applied on historians and writers of history and civics textbooks to rewrite their subjects in more conservative and ethnocentric vein, history books remain far more objective than they were in the decade following World War I. However, a few professional historians would like to see American history rewritten or reinterpreted so as to depict businessmen and materialist values in a more favorable light. As this is written, a leading exponent of a "new look" in American history is Professor Allan Nevins.[4]

As in other closed areas, it is possible to identify sharply opposed points of view with reference to nationalism, patriotism, and national institutions. One is the traditional conservative outlook, in this case favoring old-fashioned nationalism, imperialism, conventional forms of patriotic expression, and worship of the American past. The other is the modern liberal-democratic viewpoint, favoring international coöperation and some form of world order, aid to foreigners without exploitation, and a calm and reasoned patriotism which pays as much attention to thoughtful understanding and appreciation of the democratic tradition as to ritualistic symbols.

Many Americans vacillate between support and rejection of aid to American allies, the United Nations, and programs such as NATO. They do not understand the implications of nationalism and internationalism in today's world. They want positive steps to be taken in the struggle against world communism, but they fear both the sacrifice and the dangers of possible military entanglement.

Points of Confusion and Contradiction in American Beliefs about Nationalism, Patriotism, and National Institutions

1. *Nationalism and internationalism: It is believed treasonable to favor any step which would undermine the sovereignty of the United States; but it is also believed that responsible participation by the United States in some form of world organization is essential to maintenance of world peace.*

According to the first view, a nation (by implication the United States) should be completely independent of all other nations. Under no circumstances should it make commitments or sign treaties which would curtail its right of unilateral action. The idea of world government is particularly disturbing to those who hold that our government is entitled to rights of unilateral action and unrestricted sovereignty.

This general outlook subsumes two other viewpoints. One has been called "nationalistic imperialism." So long as the United States remains dominant

[4] See Arthur Schlesinger, Jr., "The History of Business and Vice Versa," *The Reporter,* March 30, 1954, pp. 38–40.

in the world, it is thought proper for us to take an interest in world affairs and to have relationships with other nations. It is also permissible for the United States to have allies and attempt to achieve national objectives through them. But the allies should know their place and stay in it; they should grant deferential treatment to, and accept orders from, the United States. This general attitude, very similar to that espoused by "big-stick" nationalists early in this century, is often characterized by a marked jingoism, which in recent years has taken the form of urging "preventive wars."

Another variant of the nationalist outlook is "isolationism." According to this view, the United States should remain militarily strong and strictly independent, pursuing a "go-it-alone" policy. It is assumed that the United States can remain self-contained. However, most isolationists favor national independence and preëminence so strongly that wherever they are forced to concede the necessity of dealing with other nations they fall into the imperialistic position described in the preceding paragraph.

Extreme nationalists identify any form of internationalism with alien ideologies. At present internationalism is called "communistic," and the extremists believe that the United Nations was born in the Kremlin with Stalin as midwife. Persons who support treaties which look upon America and her allies as equals, who support the United Nations and associated organizations, or who uphold schemes of world government are traitors. According to a report in a national magazine, a congressional investigating committee announced its intention to investigate a number of organizations to find whether they support "internationalist," among other, causes. Such support was to be construed as evidence of a conspiracy to promote communism and socialism.[5]

In contrast to attitudes of the above variety, many persons believe in "internationalism." They hold that the long-range security of the United States depends upon close and equalitarian alliances with other peace-loving nations; that the United States has neither the industrial capacity, the resources, nor the military strength for a "go-it-alone" policy; that security agreements among nations must be mutually satisfactory; and that the United States does not have a God-given right to dominate other nations, even those that depend upon us for aid and protection.

Most internationalists seem to favor a network of agreements and mutual-aid pacts, or some other means by which nations can work closely together. Virtually all internationalists support the United Nations, or something like

[5] *Newsweek,* August 10, 1953.

it, and many support some one of various schemes for world government. They believe that no international pact, organization, or government can be successful unless each participating party agrees to give up rights of unilateral action and to relinquish some part of its sovereignty. Some internationalists would prefer to say that mutuality of agreement and responsibility is essential to any national sovereignty which may be said to exist in an interdependent world. Many internationalists deplore the veto power in the Security Council of the United Nations because they believe it represents an attempt to retain rights of unilateral action.

Much of the support for an effective United Nations or world federation is generated by fear of war. Revulsion against war as an instrument of national policy has grown since World War I, nourished by a variety of developments and changing viewpoints: First, it has become apparent that the United States can no longer avoid participation in a major war once war begins; consequently, the only possible way to stay out of war is to prevent its outbreak. Second, development of highly destructive weapons has created a fear that another war would obliterate the human race. Third, civilians can no longer hope to escape the effects of battle. With long-range guided missiles carrying atomic warheads, the concept of "noncombatant" ceases to have meaning. Fourth, the cost of preparation for war is becoming so oppressive that there is question whether the economic systems of even the wealthiest nations can endure indefinite continuation of an armaments race. These four beliefs are popularly summarized in "No one wins a war any more." Nevertheless, the old notions of national sovereignty and national independence continue to thrive, and many Americans are enmeshed in varying degrees of ambivalence and indecision.

1.1 Does membership in any organization require a person to relinquish some of his "personal sovereignty"? When you join a club, do you curtail in some ways your rights of unilateral action? Does the same follow when you join a church? Coöperate as a member of a family group? Become a partner in a business firm? Join a labor union? If your individual freedom is curtailed by membership in such groups, why do you join them?

1.2 Did the thirteen colonies lose their sovereignty when they ratified the Constitution in 1789? Could the nations of the world ratify a world constitution which would leave their sovereignty untouched? What kind of constitution would this be? Would it be worth ratification?

1.3 Discuss the following in order to clarify your thinking about the conflict between unilateral action and international coöperation: State rights, Articles of Confederation, Constitution of the United States, Hartford Convention, Virginia and Kentucky Resolutions, doctrines of nullification and secession, the Civil War, and the Bricker Amendment.

1.4 How does our membership in the United Nations affect our national sovereignty? Is there anything the United States is not free to do because it is a member? Is there anything which the United States can do because it is a member of the United Nations? Have gains in freedom made up for losses in national sovereignty?

2. *National security and civil liberties: It is believed that as a nation we cannot protect ourselves adequately from subversion as long as we are hampered by due process of law; but it is also believed that a loss of traditional liberties would be equivalent to destruction of democracy itself.*

Beliefs associated with the first position include the following: If Reds are dealt with by extraconstitutional methods, they are only getting a dose of their own medicine. If they were in control, their first action would be to suspend traditional civil liberties. Rats do not deserve a fair trial. A democracy should take vigorous steps to defend itself. It is necessary to fight fire with fire. The above beliefs are substantively contained in the proposition that "A democratic end may be achieved through undemocratic means." It is clear that a sizeable minority of Americans now accepts this position and is very vocal in proclaiming it.[6]

In contrast, it is believed that constitutional rights should be extended to all citizens, no matter how unpopular their opinions may be. Many persons believe that an accused should know the charges against him, that he should be allowed to face his accusers, that he is entitled to legal counsel, that he should be allowed to subpoena witnesses, that his counsel should be free to cross-examine those who testify against him, and that he is entitled to trial by jury. Many believe that liberty is indivisible; that as soon as we deny to some persons protection of constitutional rights the liberty of all will be in jeopardy. Many believe that no one should be persecuted for his convictions; that a person is a menace to democracy only if his actions constitute a "clear and present danger" to democratic institutions. These beliefs reject any theory of "guilt by association." There is a widespread assumption that it is almost always impossible to achieve good results with bad methods.

At present writing, inconsistent sets of proposals are before the American

[6] No accurate quantitative data are available on this point. Informed guesses place the proportion of American citizens who reject the basic tenets of the Bill of Rights at from one-fifth to one-third of the adult population. See Bernard De Voto, "The Easy Chair," *Harper's Magazine*, April, 1954.

people. One set would "clean up" the procedures of congressional committees, and make them conform to the Constitution. But another set would legalize the use of evidence acquired through wiretapping, and would also make it possible to require a witness to testify against himself without fear of prosecution from the national government. The latter proposal would evade the Fifth Amendment without the tedious procedure of amending the Constitution.

The above dichotomy of belief produces intrapersonal conflict of the following order: Many persons who accept verbally the traditional Anglo-Saxon liberties reject them in practice. We have seen in Chapter 12 how persistently traditional codes of fair play are violated in relations between whites and Negroes. Although this situation continues, a more conspicuous example is now furnished by treatment of allegedly subversive persons. Hundreds of individuals, both in and out of government, have been discharged, suspended, or asked to resign from their jobs, and often the accusations are made publicly without any regard for traditional legal practice. The tendency to call certain rights "privileges" and to maintain that they may properly be revoked at the whim of prosecutors is a form of question begging.

In fighting communism it is necessary to preserve what the communists seek to destroy. But many who have made anticommunism a pretension have adopted methods identical with those habitually used by communists when in power. Many Americans have missed the significance of this point. They divorce ends from means. They assume that once an end is established any means—even the most primitive, reckless, and undemocratic—serves as well as any other. They may deplore methods used by some legislators but will nevertheless support these legislators because they feel that the *end* is laudable.

2.1 Some persons who have been asked to testify before congressional committees interested in the study of subversive activity have refused to answer some questions by invoking the Fifth Amendment to the United States Constitution. What does "invoking the Fifth Amendment" mean in such a case? Does it mean that the person is guilty and does not wish to testify against himself? Would an innocent person ever find it necessary or wise to invoke the Fifth Amendment? Why did many of the political leaders in America insist upon this and other amendments before they would agree to work for the ratification of the Constitution?

2.2 Would you favor changing the Constitution so that persons investigated by congressional committees could not invoke the Fifth Amendment? How would elimination of this amendment change the relationship between Congress and the people? How can abuse of the Fifth Amendment be avoided without destroying it? How was this amendment used by corporations and business leaders in the late nineteenth century? How was this use different from, or similar to, its present use before congressional committees?

2.3 It is claimed that there are many subversives in America who would be in jail if our courts could use evidence gained through wiretapping. It has been proposed that Congress pass a law which would legalize such evidence. Do you think it is possible for our government to employ wiretapping without turning America into a police state?

3. *Enlightened citizens and ignorant rabble: It is believed that citizens of the United States are better educated, more enlightened, and more capable of governing themselves than is any other citizenry; but it is also believed that the American masses are ignorant, easily confused, and likely to vote according to passions of the moment.*

One view has it that because they are a generally enlightened people, citizens of the United States have a decisive advantage in self-government. Anyone who wishes can get all the facts he needs in order to decide important political issues through reading newspapers, magazines, and books, or by listening to radio and watching television. Our mass media of communication are the most reliable in the world. Likewise, the American school system is something to be proud of and, on the average, American youth stay in school longer than do youth elsewhere.

Not only are Americans believed to be better informed than citizens elsewhere, but they are also said to have an innate gift for self-government which is rare in the human race. When a cabinet falls in Europe, or when a revolution explodes somewhere in Latin America, someone is likely to observe that democratic institutions cannot be expected to thrive abroad as they do in this country. Although foreigners may some day be ready for American-style democracy, most of them have not yet reached such a state of enlightenment and emotional maturity.

The foregoing optimistic view is accompanied by considerable skepticism as to the intelligence and common sense of the common man. Typical arguments made by political campaigners, as anyone may verify by reading political speeches, assume that voters are ill informed, illogical, and weak in their capacity to understand issues.

Radio and television soap operas are said to base their offerings on the premise that an average adult has an eighth-grade mentality. Many magazine editors have been sold a "readability formula" designed to help writers keep articles and stories on a junior-high-school intellectual level. It is also a practice among mass media to withhold many facts, or to select carefully those facts which citizens "need" in order to reach "correct" conclusions. Rarely does an owner of a mass medium supply impartially all the available facts and then wait for citizens to make up their minds. There is always the editorial and the expert interpretation to "guide" thought into the right channels.

In summary, there are two contrasting assumptions at work in the American culture. One holds that ordinary persons are capable of governing themselves, and the other that they need an intelligent minority to help them govern. One outlook assumes that a capacity for genuine reflection is widely distributed among human beings, and that whether or not they are now habitually disposed to reflect they can learn such disposition. The other outlook assumes that opinions and attitudes are products of conditioning and that *someone must do the conditioning.*

Every political scientist is aware that informed opinion concerning human capacity to be politically rational has fluctuated with the spirit of the times and the type of available research evidence. The concept of man as a rational political animal reached a peak in the eighteenth century, since when it has been under steady attack. The nineteenth century witnessed the emergence of intuition theory, instinct theory, belief in man's animal origins, and belief in basic hereditary inequality among men. Psychologists of the twentieth century have produced mountains of evidence to support the belief that human beings tend to behave emotionally and irrationally much of the time. Carried to extreme limits, the reaction against eighteenth-century rationalism can amount to a rejection of democracy and its premises.

Human behavior is probably much less simple than either extreme in interpretation implies. Certainly, man is not a thinking machine who makes every decision on the basis of rational calculation. Nor is he exclusively a victim of blind emotion or instinctual compulsion. Nor is there any evidence that persons in high social positions are less emotional or more rational in their decisions than is the so-called common man. Rather the weight of evidence is in the direction of saying that, provided necessary data are available, all persons of normal mentality can acquire attitudes and skills necessary to resolve issues reflectively. Such learning is not easy, and in most cases it can be achieved only with skilled group leadership and personal guidance. Emotional repression must be overcome, biases identified, and inadequacy of data openly recognized. In light of the foregoing, it is reasonable to assume that in the future man can learn to be more rational in his problem solving and decision making.

3.1 Studies show that Americans typically vote against incumbents when economic conditions are unfavorable and for incumbents when conditions are favorable. Is this a sign of intelligent behavior? To what extent, if any, is it intelligent to refer to "Hoover depression" and "Eisenhower recession"?

3.2 Is there reason to believe that the American electorate is more rational in its voting and other political behavior than it was 25, 50, or 100 years ago? How does the extent of hysteria during the great "Red scare" of the post-World War II era compare with the extent of hysteria in previous "Red scare" periods?

3.3 How does behavior of an average person now compare in rationality with that of an average person in the fifteenth century? Was there more superstition, emotionalism, and hysteria then than now? Has the rise of science been a factor in bringing about more rational behavior? Has science affected equally all areas of behavior?

4. *Democratic ideals and need for practicality: It is believed that democracy is the finest system of human relationships ever invented and should be practiced in all situations; but it is also believed that, if not actually dangerous, democracy is often impractical, and besides, the United States is a republic and not a democracy.*

Although its implications are not fully understood, the idea of "democracy as a way of life" has taken root in America. Democracy is no longer restricted to government. It is conceived suitable for families, schools, clubs, churches, relationships between ethnic and racial groups, and even for interpersonal relations within business corporations. Within families wives should have the same rights and privileges as husbands, and the same "say" in decision making; children should be heard and their opinions respected. In school, children should receive equal treatment from teachers and principals and they should be permitted a voice in school policies. Clubs should elect their officers democratically, and individual members should not be discriminated against for any reason. Modernists in religion feel that church policy should result from collective decisions of congregations. Ministers try to behave in such a way that they will appear to be one of the people. Industrial workers consider that bosses should not be arbitrary, that they should treat employees equally and fairly, and that workers should be consulted whenever their interests are involved or at stake.

Opposed to this view of society is the widespread feeling that, no matter how fine democracy may be in theory, it is fundamentally impractical in many situations. The more crucial and critical the circumstances the less practical democracy is said to be. When the going gets rough, it is best to find strong leaders and to follow their bent and wish.

According to this view, many day-to-day circumstances cannot be handled democratically. A family actually cannot be run democratically; the principle that "the husband should be head of the family" is as sound as ever. Schools can very easily become too democratic; the children can be treated "too well" and will become unruly in consequence. A club gets more done when led by a few capable persons. And no business would ever make money were it run according to popular vote of workers and other interested individuals; if a firm is to be efficient and remain strong competitively, employees must be told what to do and disciplined for misbehavior.

Inconsistency of behavior and emotional conflict result from simultaneous acceptance and rejection of democracy as a social principle. A "democratic" husband orders his wife and children to do thus-and-so. Students are allowed what is called "self-government," but most student councils are carefully controlled by seasoned adults. Clubs may elect officers in an ostensibly democratic manner but the results may be predetermined through clever and concealed "string pulling." Churches which appear democratic may cling to authoritarian theological tenets. Industrial workers may be allowed to drop complaints into a "gripe box" but it remains the board of directors and the top executives who rule the firm, often in ways unknown to employees and stockholders.

Departures from democratic practice in government are sometimes excused with the observation that the United States is a republic, not a democracy. This rationalization deserves our consideration. Conservatives generally prefer the term *republic* to the term *democracy* when describing the American way of life, and social-studies teachers would be wise to explore the motivations behind this preference. With a few exceptions, the founders of this nation were republicans, not democrats. They feared any system which permitted direct rule by the masses. Voting was restricted to persons of "substance." The Constitution provided for selection of legislators and administrators by processes a step or two removed from "passions of the mob"—indirect election of senators and the electoral college. These early founders intended to establish an aristocracy, and such was the meaning of republic to them.

Little by little we have moved toward more direct election of government officials. But this development is no more significant than the increased base of the electorate, and a great deal less significant than the introduction into human relations of a democratic ideal which transcends mere political behavior. The general application of this ideal does not necessarily require further movement toward direct political rule, or even as much direct political rule as we now have. In short, a republic *is* a democracy if its citizens generally accept democratic principles as a guide to human relations; a republic is *not* a democracy if it rejects these principles.

Apparently, some citizens who promote the idea that the United States is a republic *rather* than a democracy would like to dispense altogether with democratic human relationships and return to an aristocratic conception which would extend even to government. Some persons even seem to prefer a form of government in which businessmen would constitute an elite with extraordinary power over human affairs.

4.1   To be thoroughly and consistently democratic, tell how you think each of the following would need to be organized and operated: A home, a school, a church, a business corporation. Is it foolish to try to apply democracy to any of these?

4.2   Give as many examples as you can of false or pseudo democracy—that is, practices which appear democratic on the surface but are really not.

4.3   Is the preservation of a republican form of government essential to the preservation of democratic freedom? How would you appraise the belief that our form of government is republican but our society is democratic? Can a nation be democratic without being a republic? Can it be a republic without being democratic? Can it be a republic though democratic?

DISCUSSION QUESTIONS AND EXERCISES

1. What is the social function of such patriotic ceremonies as saluting the flag, pledging allegiance to the flag, singing the national anthem, and holding memorial services for the war dead? Do these ceremonies make citizens more patriotic? More democratic?
2. Is loyalty to the United Nations incompatible with loyalty to the United States? Why, or why not?
3. Should public-school teachers teach American youth to support the United Nations? Or should they merely teach *about* the United Nations? Should public-school teachers teach American youth to support the Constitution of the United States? Or should they merely teach *about* the Constitution of the United States?
4. To what extent, if any, should the teaching of history have as one of its purposes the building of patriotic sentiments? Can one teach patriotism at the same time that he teaches the truth about his country?
5. Every nation has a body of myth or legend concerning its past. One of the

purposes of historical research is to determine the relative amounts of truth and falsity incorporated in any nation's myth and legend. What attitude toward myth and legend should a history teacher foster? Is it possible to teach patriotism without teaching that certain myths and legends are true?

6. Is the myth and legend approach to teaching patriotism essentially different from the ritual approach? If so, what is the difference? Do these two approaches have anything in common?

7. What program for teaching patriotism is suggested by this chapter? Be specific. Is this proposal patriotic? Would most Americans consider it patriotic or unpatriotic?

REFERENCES

On the general subject of nationalism, Carlton J. H. Hayes, *The Historical Evolution of Nationalism* (Smith, 1931) is one of the best treatments of the history of nationalist ideas. Hans Kohn, *The Idea of Nationalism; A Study of Its Origin and Background* (Macmillan, 1945) traces the development of nationalism up to the French revolution. A sociological study is presented in Karl W. Deutsch, *Nationalism and Social Communication* (Wiley, 1953).

Since nationalism has stressed national sovereignty and independence, students should be familiar with arguments relating to international organization. The following are recommended: Sir William Beveridge, *The Price of Peace* (Norton, 1945); Francis Biddle, *The World's Best Hope* (University of Chicago Press, 1949); Vernon Nash, *The World Must Be Governed* (Harper, 1949); Emery Reves, *The Anatomy of Peace* (Harper, 1945). In *Foreign Policy Without Fear* (McGraw-Hill, 1953), Vera M. Dean tries to expose ambiguities and contradictions in American foreign policy. One of the best descriptions and analyses of the United Nations is Herbert V. Evatt, *The United Nations* (Harvard University Press, 1948).

If in the United States patriotism is best expressed through an understanding of the democratic ideal and its implications for social life, teachers should be familiar with books such as the following: Boyd H. Bode, *Democracy as a Way of Life* (Macmillan, 1937) and John Dewey, *Freedom and Culture* (Putnam, 1939) provide excellent philosophical treatments. Classics with which everyone should be familiar are James Bryce, *The American Commonwealth* (Macmillan, 1906) and Alexis de Tocqueville, *Democracy in America* (Knopf, 1954). Recent pocket books on the subject are David C. Coyle, *The United States Political System and How It Works* (Signet Books, 1954) and T. V. Smith and E. C. Lindeman, *The Democratic Way of Life* (Mentor Books, rev. ed., 1951).

Problems of loyalty, security, and subversion are treated in the following: Alan Barth, *The Loyalty of Free Men* (Viking, 1951); Francis Biddle, *The Fear of Freedom* (Doubleday, 1952); Henry Steele Commager, *Freedom, Loyalty, and Dissent* (Oxford University Press, 1954); Elmer Davis, *But We Were Born Free* (Bobbs, Merrill, 1954); Walter Gellhorn, *Security, Loyalty and Science* (Cornell University Press, 1950).

Nationalism, Patriotism, and National Institutions

The American government, its functioning and structure, is treated analytically and sometimes critically in books such as the following: Thomas K. Finletter, *Can Representative Government Do the Job?* (Reynal and Hitchcock, 1945) traces the conflict between executive and legislative branches. James M. Burns, *Congress on Trial: The Politics of Modern Law-Making* (Harper, 1949) argues the need for Congressional reform. A historical study which attempts some debunking of political figures is Richard Hofstadter, *The American Political Tradition and the Men Who Made It* (Knopf, 1948). Problems of state governments are treated in readable and provocative fashion in Richard Neuberger, *Adventures in Politics* (Oxford University Press, 1954). For an excellent study of the functioning of our legal institutions, see Jerome Frank, *Courts on Trial* (Princeton University Press, 1949). A good short treatment of pressure groups and lobbying is Stuart Chase, *Democracy Under Pressure: Social Interests vs. the Public Welfare* (Twentieth Century Fund, 1945).

PART THREE

Special Problems

Chapter 17

Adapting Reflective Method to the Standard Social-Studies Subjects

---

THE function of the present chapter is to show concretely how a teacher may operate within a conventional school to produce maximum reflection among students. We shall discuss first the general use of textbooks, then ways of coping with administratively imposed ground-covering requirements, and finally, instruction in the three most commonly taught social-studies subjects: history, civics, and geography. Discussion of other subjects is omitted because of limitations of space and because essentially the same principles and procedures which make for good teaching in these apply equally in all the secondary social studies.

Textbooks as Aids to Conceptualization

High-school textbooks usually survey a particular subject field, treating, in so far as possible, all the topics considered important by specialists in that field. In most social-studies textbooks hundreds if not thousands of different topics are mentioned in a general way, but seldom is any topic developed with thoroughness. World-history books particularly illustrate such generality.

This kind of treatment does not induce much conceptualization. A student left to himself to get whatever he could from a textbook would probably acquire little more than a collection of memorized associations, the deeper meaning of which would largely escape him. A teacher can help students acquire memorized associations, or he can help students delve more deeply into the meaning of textbook content. If he does the latter, it is necessary for him to "dig in" at appropriate places and develop topics in sufficient detail to make them meaningful.

USING TEXTBOOK PASSAGES AS SPRINGBOARDS

A textbook offers a succession of "jumping-off places," or springboards. A springboard is a place in a text which is thought-provoking, or can be made so, and the study of which can lead to conceptualization about some problem of importance. The exploitation of a textbook springboard may in some cases combine study and research in such a way as to form a comprehensive unit of work. As a teacher moves through a book, he should be watchful for such places and should encourage his students to do likewise.

There are at least three general types of springboards which we may identify. One kind of springboard consists of a group of descriptive but related facts. For example: "Small quantities of American manufactured products gradually began to go from one colony to another, to the West Indies and to England. In this way, they came into competition with goods made in England. When this happened, English manufacturers complained, and Parliament passed laws intended to limit the colonists to the production of raw materials." [1]

Without trying to demonstrate at this point how such a passage could be made to serve as a springboard, let us examine another potentially provocative collection of facts, which is shown in the accompanying table.

Decline in Prices and Production from 1929 to 1932

	Percent Drop in Prices	Percent Drop in Production
Agricultural implements	6	80
Motor vehicles	16	80
Cement	18	65
Iron and steel products	20	83
Tires	33	70
Textiles	45	30
Food products	49	14
Leather	50	20
Petroleum	56	20
Agricultural commodities	63	6

From Ruth Wood Gavian, A. A. Gray, and Ernest R. Groves, *Our Changing Social Order*, D. C. Héath & Company, 1953, p. 385.

[1] Ruth Wood Gavian and William A. Hamm, *The American Story*, D. C. Heath & Company, 1951, p. 20.

A second type of springboard is a generalization, or general idea. Some examples, all taken from history texts, follow:

". . . A great general may be a babe in politics." [2]

"The business of the United States is business" (the philosophy attributed to Harding, Coolidge, and Hoover).[3]

"Inflation injures everybody. . . ." [4]

"A protective tariff creates prosperity. . . ." [5]

"Riches may bring evil as well as good. Too much wealth may lead to waste and neglect." [6]

"Paper money is not real money." [7]

If a generalization seems outrageous to a class, so much the better. They may be provoked into trying to find out exactly what is wrong with it (if indeed it turns out to have anything wrong with it). What seems at first to be an acceptable generalization can still serve as a springboard if the teacher asks provocative questions about it.

A third kind of springboard is comprised of facts or ideas which seem mutually contradictory. Textbook writers do contradict themselves with surprising frequency, and such contradictions—if properly exploited—may make a book more teachable (other things being equal) than if it were perfectly consistent. In a study of the economic content of selected high-school textbooks no less than twenty-one instances were uncovered in which, if one takes literally what was said, authors appeared flatly to contradict themselves.[8] Here are a few examples:

Money can never be created, but, says the same author, over 90 percent of American business is done with "checkbook money."

Business is almost always conducted in an enlightened, strictly honest way, but, says the same author, consumers in the United States had better beware or they will surely be taken advantage of.

A capitalist economy is inherently peaceful, but, says the same author, most major wars have resulted from competition for markets and sources of raw materials between capitalist nations.

[2] *Ibid.,* p. 328.

[3] *Ibid.,* p. 531.

[4] Ralph V. Harlow, *Story of America,* Henry Holt & Company, 1947, p. 354.

[5] *Ibid.,* p. 630 (quoting Representative Hawley).

[6] Harold U. Faulkner, Tyler Kepner, and Victor E. Pitkin, *USA,* Harper & Brothers, 1948, p. 225.

[7] Gertrude Hartman, Charles C. Ball, and Allan Nevins, *America, Land of Freedom,* D. C. Heath & Company, 1952, p. 215.

[8] Maurice P. Hunt, "The Teaching of Economics in the American High School," unpublished doctoral dissertation, The Ohio State University, 1948, pp. 247–249. The statements given here are not literal quotations.

Because human nature is what it is, business cycles are inevitable, but, says the same author, there are no business cycles under communism.

Economic affairs are governed by natural laws which are beyond the power of men to influence, but, says the same author, the best way to cure a poorly functioning economy is for each individual to apply the Ten Commandments in his economic life.

TECHNIQUES FOR EXPLOITING SPRINGBOARDS

Whether any of the above examples of springboards would actually lead to fruitful conceptualization depends on whether their content conforms to criteria for the selection of content which we have suggested previously (e.g., potentially problematical, within experiential range of students, and pedagogically manageable) and also on the techniques used to exploit it.

The development of a springboard involves, first, having students read together the textbook material, and second, asking questions about it, or about ideas suggested by it, such as will cause students to question some one or more of their present beliefs. If, after the most skillful questioning possible, a teacher is unable to "strike fire," in the sense of inducing interested discussion, he can either abandon the springboard on the assumption that its ideas are too mature for his group or begin over on a lower level of experience and try to give students insights which will enable them to comprehend the significance of the text material. The latter course is usually taken when a teacher feels that the ideas involved are too important socially to omit.

The following statement from a high-school history textbook represents a springboard from which a class might be introduced to discussion of the nature and function of money. "When there is no gold or silver in the national treasury, paper money is of no more value than the paper it is printed on." [9]

This generalization has become almost a cliché in our society; this means that its meaning has not been carefully examined by very many people. The following questions might result in reflection on the meaning of money:

1. Does our paper money today have gold behind it? Can you exchange your paper money for gold? Does the amount of gold in the national treasury limit how much paper money the government could print?

2. What limits the number of Federal Reserve notes? United States Treasury

[9] Hartman, Ball, and Nevins, *op. cit.*, p. 215. Discussion questions which follow are our own.

notes? Silver certificates? Checks? How much would the metal in a fifty-cent piece be worth if it were melted down?

3. How does a general rise in prices affect the value of money? Does the amount of gold in the national treasury affect the general price level? What factors account for a general inflation? Was the German mark any good during the 1930's? Did German currency of that period permit economic growth in that country? How much gold did the German mark of that period have behind it?

4. What gives paper money its value? Is it the gold behind it? The confidence that people have in the honesty and stability of government? Why are people willing to accept checks in payment for a debt? Is paper money valuable for the same or different reasons that checks are valuable?

5. What determines the soundness of money? How did devaluation of the currency in 1933 affect its soundness? Did this devaluation cause an upsurge in prices? What do prices have to do with the soundness of money?

Some of these questions may cause students to become uncertain about the meaning of the textbook generalization. If this happens, the textbook generalization becomes a hypothesis. The testing of this and alternative hypotheses can result in development of a more adequate concept of money. In addition to the generalization in the textbook, students should examine alternative generalizations such as: "The value of money is not primarily determined by the amount of gold or silver backing it has" and "The value of paper money is largely a result of the ratio between the quantity and velocity of money in circulation and the value of goods and services for sale." The role of the Federal Reserve System in regulating the supply of money should also be introduced.

Using Textbook Aids

A textbook for high schools would be considered incomplete and unsalable if it lacked chapter-end helps—usually questions and suggested activities. One textbook, which may be taken as fairly typical, includes at the end of each of its chapters these categories of exercises:

To CHECK YOUR READING . . . . Answer these questions:
To ADD TO YOUR VOCABULARY . . . . . . Give the meaning of these terms:
To STIMULATE YOUR THINKING . . . . . Give your views on these statements:
FOR INTERESTING SIDELIGHTS . . . . . . Follow these suggestions:[10]

Another book organizes its chapter-end helps this way:

CORRECT THESE STATEMENTS
QUESTIONS FOR DISCUSSION

[10] Ernest B. Fincher, John H. Ferguson, and Dean E. McHenry, *American Government Today*, McGraw-Hill Book Company, 1951.

Chapter-end helps range from being potentially very useful to almost completely useless as instigators of reflection. All too often one encounters factual-recall questions of the most routine sort. When facts are needed in order to test a hypothesis, it is appropriate for a teacher to ask pertinent factual-recall questions because the answers facilitate progression of thought. However, factual-recall questions usually function in a classroom to promote memorization-level learning, and most chapter-end helps appear designed only for that purpose.

Many of the projects suggested by textbook writers are equally sterile for purposes of serious reflection. The following suggestions show the kind of busywork which could take the place of reflection:

Color on an outline map the area of North America claimed by England in 1754.
List some of the songs which were popular during the Civil War period.
Draw on a map some of the major transcontinental rail and air lines.
Prepare a table which will show the approximate north-south and east-west dimensions of states west of the Rocky Mountains.
Make a list of the canned sea food for sale in your neighborhood market. Where were these sea foods canned?
Make a list of the spices which your mother uses in cooking.

From time to time, one does find chapter-end questions or projects which could effectively promote thought.

If every country in the world stopped using gold as the standard for its national currency, do you think gold would have any value? [12]
You have doubtless seen or heard the slogan "Buy American." The purpose of this slogan was to influence you to buy only American-made goods. What would you think of the slogan "Eat American"? Do you think such a program would be best for our country? for the world? [13]
Give your views on this statement: The Federal Bureau of Investigation could become a threat to our civil liberties. [14]
Account for the election of a Democrat, Grover Cleveland, after 24 years of Republican presidents. [15]
How did American tariff policy interfere with payment of the war debts? [16]

[11] John H. Bradley, *World Geography*, Ginn & Company, 1948.
[12] Lawrence V. Roth, Stillman M. Hobbs, and Walter J. Greenleaf, *Living in the Peoples' World*, Laidlaw Brothers, 1949, p. 216.
[13] *Ibid.*, p. 188.
[14] Fincher, Ferguson, and McHenry, *op. cit.*, p. 342.
[15] Faulkner, Kepner, and Pitkin, *op. cit.*, p. 409.
[16] Gavian and Hamm, *op. cit.*, p. 572.

Appoint three or four members of the class to search recent magazines for articles dealing with American ideals. Ask each committee member to prepare a written analysis of one article. Read and discuss each analysis in class. What is the central point made by each writer? Do you detect any fallacies in his reasoning? Does he betray prejudices? [17]

The spotty quality of chapter-end helps means that a teacher who is interested in the promotion of conceptual learning will have to be selective. In the case of some textbooks, a wise teacher would make no use at all of chapter-end helps.

In any case, chapter-end helps cannot take the place of teaching. One satisfactory way to use chapter-end helps is to select a limited number which appear provocative and use them as leads to class discussion or other teacher-directed activities. A usable chapter-end help ought to be handled like a springboard.

Workbooks are an extension of chapter-end helps. They include questions to be answered, projects to complete, charts and maps to interpret, and sometimes tests to take. The routine completion of the exercises can consume so much of the students' time that a teacher need not teach; use of workbooks may—and undoubtedly often does—become a substitute for teaching. A competent and professional teacher will use the better workbook exercises as springboards for developing problem-solving discussion.

Dealing with the "Ground-Covering Fetish"

Part and parcel of instruction in the standard social-studies subjects is the concern of many teachers with covering a specified amount of content according to a predetermined time schedule. This outlook may be forced upon teachers by administrators or it may result from the training and philosophy of teachers themselves.

All schools are not afflicted with the ground-covering disease. But usually the tendency is to bring uniformity into the curriculum, and uniformity requires an emphasis on ground covering. One manifestation of the drive toward uniformity is the growing reliance on central-office experts to tell teachers what they should teach and how much time they should spend on each topic. In some states curriculum planning has become a function of a state department of instruction. State legislatures occasionally prescribe parts of the curriculum. Consultants from universities and teachers' colleges

[17] Edward Everett Walker, Walter Greenwood Beach, and Olis Glen Jamison, *The Government of the United States*, Charles Scribner's Sons, 1948, p. 91.

sometimes urge on public schools ideas of curriculum organization which require uniformity.

But these influences are perhaps not so significant as the apparent fact that many teachers enjoy highly routinized teaching situations, which, by their nature, require exact and rigid scheduling of time. Or teachers may prefer to avoid the day-by-day planning required by more flexible schedules. Or, if it is assumed that students achieve fruitful learning when they memorize textbook content, and that one item of content is as important as any other, then ground covering will appear necessary to achieve the maximum amount of learning possible.

MEANINGFUL LEARNING PREVENTED BY FIXATION ON GROUND COVERING

The chief criticism of ground covering is its incompatibility with meaningful learning. *The amount of conceptualization achieved by a student bears little relationship to the quantity of facts he has encountered.* A class might spend an entire semester on one or two topics and achieve more useful conceptualization (i.e., a greater quantity of functional generalizations) than if it covered superficially a hundred topics. The total quantity of transferable learning acquired depends on the amount and depth of reflection. The complete picture of a subject which a student is expected to acquire from a survey of the subject is often very blurred and obscure. An expert may logically be expected to know all that is embraced in his field, but even this kind of knowing does not depend upon survey courses for its attainment. The aim of general education for a high-school student is mastery of *those parts of a field of inquiry which can function evidentially for him in solving problems that concern him.* Sound pedagogy requires the thorough study of some parts of a textbook and omission of other parts.

Rejection of the ground-covering fetish does not mean that students are to be freed from requirements and prerequisites. No doubt there are many concepts which every high-school student in the United States should learn (because of their relevance to personal and social problems) and it behooves the profession to create a workable answer to this necessity. The demands of citizenship are so great that we can no longer afford the luxury of citizens who lack basic understandings in areas of cultural confusion and irrationality. Ground covering which requires study in depth of certain critical issues is the only kind of ground covering which belongs in a twentieth-century high school, and it would be catastrophic to our civilization to omit it.

How to Live with Administratively Imposed Ground Covering

There are two situations in which a good teacher may have to compromise with necessity and accept conventional ground covering at least as a peripheral aim. State or local school administrators may (1) stipulate as a condition of employment that a teacher must use and "cover" a particular textbook or course of study, or (2) require a teacher to give standardized tests over a subject.[18] Teachers usually believe, with or without warrant, that these tests will be used by administrators to judge the "progress" of students (whatever progress may mean in this context) and, by implication, the quality of instruction.

One possible compromise for either situation is to allocate a definite time for ground covering and another equally definite time for reflective learning. For example, during a six-weeks grading period the first five weeks could be scheduled flexibly and every opportunity for conceptualization be thoroughly exploited. The last week could be frankly devoted to drill designed to fix in students' minds the "facts" designated to be "covered" during the period. Similarly, the last two weeks of each semester could be devoted to intensive drill designed to prepare students for the semester examinations. If a class is required to take a standardized achievement test, the two weeks preceding the test might be devoted exclusively to memorization of material which the test is expected to cover. The above time allotments are merely suggestive. More or less time might be necessary for intensive drill prior to examinations, depending on the importance which administrative officers assign to examination results, the capacities of the class, and the degree to which experiences in problem solving may have prepared the class to take routine factual-recall examinations.

If a teacher who recognizes the ground-covering fetish for what it is deliberately schedules time for intensive drill for examination purposes, he should also recognize that it is rote learning he is pursuing during the drill period and that he may legitimately use the most efficient means of achieving it.

Rote learning is usually motivated by a system of rewards and punish-

[18] A standardized test typically consists of items requiring students to recall facts ordinarily included in a course when it is "fully covered." A standardized test in American history, for example, will include some items from every period of American history, and the items will correspond to events typically included in high-school textbooks.

ments. In the situation we have been discussing, the reward for successful memorization of more or less meaningless statements is the opportunity to continue devoting most of the course time to reflective study of vital and interesting issues. A teacher can make it plain to students that unless test results show that the prescribed ground has been adequately covered they will no longer be free to spend time digging into challenging problems. There is probably no reason why a teacher should not put the case in these honest and straightforward terms. If they understand the purpose of drill, students are more likely to coöperate during drill periods.

Drill can be made more palatable by use of specialized techniques. Variations of the old-fashioned spelldown can be adapted to factual content in the social studies. Quiz games patterned after radio and television programs can be devised. It may even be profitable to use flash-card drill. Teaching students to outline and to summarize a chapter in a textbook can be immensely helpful. Most of the standard how-to-study pamphlets emphasize memorization of verbal associations and provide hints on how to cover ground efficiently.

Test results are usually improved if students take several preliminary tests which follow as closely as possible the pattern of the final official one. Even though a standardized test is to be given, a teacher may create tests which anticipate its content. Students could score their own tests and spend the remaining time in intensive drill over the most frequently missed items.

The Teaching of History

More secondary students are enrolled in history than in any other social study. Junior-high-school students usually are required to study United States history, often in eighth grade; senior-high-school students take it in eleventh or twelfth grade. In most high schools world history is an elective in ninth or tenth grade, and large urban schools frequently offer as electives Latin American and European history. Several states in the United States require all students to take a course in the history of their state.

History as a Pedagogical Problem

Whether one prefers to blame teachers for inadequacy, students for stupidity, or the subject itself, retention of historical knowledge is generally poor, and its significance for current living is but dimly grasped. Students tend to emerge from a study of history pretty much unscathed. It is true that history is not the only offender on this score. But it is uniquely a problem subject in the sense that students spend a relatively large amount of time on it and much is expected from it—yet in probably no other subject are the results obtained so out of line with the pedagogical importance assigned it.

INHERENT WEAKNESS OF CONVENTIONAL SURVEY COURSES IN HISTORY

We take the position that the failure of most instruction in history to make much difference in the lives of students is to be explained by qualities inherent in the subject matter itself. *As traditionally organized*, the school subject of history could not possibly have much effect on the beliefs or lives of a majority of students.

In Chapter 9 we suggested that history, taken alone, and as conventionally pursued, is not a science. History confines itself to facts of the past. Historians do not attempt as a rule to develop social theory (i.e., if-then-always generalizations). Even the few historians who do attempt it often find their generalizations open to criticism from members of the nonhistorical social sciences. More often than not, historians are relatively naïve about the nature and implications of research in the nonhistorical sciences. It is inevitable that when a department of history begins dealing with the broad current problems of mankind it will run afoul of other university departments which consider themselves better equipped to do the same thing and assume, as a result of a long-standing convention, that historians have no business exploring the present. Hence the penchant of most historians, and particularly the writers of textbooks, for "objective" history. But objective history is not scientific history unless it rises to the level of theorization; and when it does, nonhistorical social scientists immediately charge that it is presumptuous. However popular historical books or the school subject of history may be among laymen, the professional field of history faces a methodological dilemma.

The tendency of history textbooks to be "objective," in the sense of confining themselves to *descriptive narrative of traditionally selected past events*, causes much of their content to be irrelevant to the contemporary thought-needs of students. When students set about learning "history," they are trying to learn facts outside the context of problems. Thus the facts of history fail to achieve the status of data. For many students the facts remain lifeless, and courses in history seem pointless. Learning of irrelevant or isolated facts is possible on a memorization level if extrinsic goals are strong enough (see pages 37–38). But abundant research, plus the experience of almost every social-studies teacher, confirms the belief that facts learned in this way are quickly forgotten and seldom become a basis for conceptualization. Such learning is unlikely to have transfer value; it is therefore unlikely to affect basic beliefs and behaviors.

A Way Out

Every human problem, when subjected to scientific study, requires a look at history—the history of man's struggle with that problem. Apparently all scientific fields find it necessary to make use of both historical and contemporary data. Without experience—which, in a broad sense, is history— human behavior could never be intelligent. Historical knowledge, then, is absolutely essential.

But we are not here talking about the content of conventional school textbooks in history. We are talking, rather, about carefully selected historical data—those facts which are relevant to problems which we wish to study. And these are not problems of the past but present contradictions and confusions in the minds of individuals—the problems of today. Historical knowledge as it bears on such problems is indispensable; and historical knowledge which is irrelevant to them is pointless. Nor can we assume that most persons can memorize and retain historical knowledge outside of problematic situations and at some future time employ it in conceptualization. This is the "background fallacy" discussed in Chapter 2, and it violates most of what we know about the nature of learning.

The implications for the teaching of history seem clear. Ideally, there would probably be advantages in abandoning entirely conventional survey courses in history. From a strictly pedagogical standpoint, it would always be preferable to teach history *through* the study of contemporary issues (*not* current events as popularly defined), during which procedure all pertinent facts would be utilized, whether gleaned from some past century or from experimentation of the present moment. In a pedagogy which takes maximum advantage of the theory of learning presented in Chapter 2, reflective study of problems is what is sought; to survey the facts of a field of inquiry is meaningless unless a substantial number of them are clearly relevant to problems of learners. The content of reflection is always highly selective and pointed; and this suggests what is wrong with survey courses in history. No survey course is likely to provide much content for conceptualization. Of history courses now being taught, those which make the most sense pedagogically are upper-division and graduate courses which are "focused"—which treat intensively a particular idea, problem, or issue.

In schools with flexible curriculums, where teachers are free to innovate (as they *should* be in *every* school), the above considerations suggest directions in which to move. Courses labeled history may perhaps be abandoned entirely and courses which focus on contemporary issues and problems substituted. History will be taught as needed to illuminate the issues and problems studied. Students will not learn fewer historical facts than now; they might learn a great many more. But this is not the primary point. Our first interest in any subject is that students achieve a maximum amount of generalized insight.

On the college level, where variety of offerings makes it possible, it might be wise to add a number of specialized courses (particularly courses which illuminate the historical origins of contemporary ideological conflicts) and to abandon the usual survey-course prerequisites to such offerings. If surveys are to be used at all, they could be better justified pedagogically during the senior year as a conclusion rather than as a beginning to historical study.

We would be unrealistic to suppose that surveys in history will soon yield to courses organized more in accord with how students learn. Probably survey courses in history are a permanent feature of the American educational landscape. If the liberal-arts tradition does not guarantee this, community pressures and legislative fiat do. Therefore we need to explore ways in which a teacher can work with maximum effectiveness in a survey course.

A Recommended Approach for Teaching Survey Courses in History

High-school students who study history can increase their understanding of the present only to the extent to which they can be led to hypothesize about the present meaning of past events. Hypotheses may be suggested by a passage in a history text or by content from nonhistorical social sciences which seems to have some bearing on a passage in a history text. The testing of such hypotheses would utilize data from both history and the nonhistorical social sciences. There are several ways in which teachers may stimulate such hypothesization.

One approach begins with a descriptive passage in a textbook. A teacher then asks questions which encourage students to interpret the passage in terms of its contemporary significance. The questioning seeks to relate the passage evidentially to a live issue of the present or to some currently held social theory or belief which in turn may be related to a live issue. In any case, study of the implications of the passage should lead students to formulate one or more generalizations of potential future usefulness.

A basically similar approach begins not with a descriptive passage in a text but with a theoretical passage, which does occasionally turn up (see examples on page 345). Attempts to theorize usually pertain to past events (past-tense, as contrasted to if-then-always, generalizations). However, it is sometimes implied that such ideas might well be true today too.

Theoretical passages in a textbook may be handled by raising questions designed to inquire into their validity. Students may question the assertion that lack of business confidence causes business recessions and depressions, for example, when they learn that the worst depression in American history began under a political administration in which business was given every reason to have confidence. The noting of this fact may stimulate a search for other explanations of business declines, including nonpsychological theories of the business cycle. Effective learning will have occurred when students gain some grasp of theoretical explanations of the business cycle which can be applied to contemporary business fluctuations. If the generalization encountered in the text is about past behaviors or situations (a past-tense generalization), questioning should be designed, first, to explore whether such general statement has continuing validity, and if it is agreed that it has, to try to determine its accuracy.

Both these approaches to a reflective method of teaching history use textbook passages as springboards for problem-solving discussion. It is the steady, persistent, and varied use of this technique which makes the school subject of history an accessory in the building of social theory. Of course, the amount of accurate social theory now available to social scientists is limited by the immaturity of their own subject fields, and the most effective teaching techniques will not enable high-school students to theorize more effectively and more richly than social scientists have been able to do. But it is necessary for high-school students themselves to theorize if they are to understand and use theoretical generalizations. The springboard technique can lead to such theorizing.

Using the Springboard Technique in Teaching History

If teacher and class are moving forward through a textbook, they may watch for promising spots (springboards) from which to leap to an intensive study of an issue. If the springboard is a descriptive passage, the event described should be one which supports, or casts doubt upon, some one or more generalizations, and the generalizations in turn should bear an evidential relationship to a contemporary issue, or problem.

The questions raised by a teacher should expose the relevant issue. In the process of developing it, and identifying the problem, students state and test general ideas through problem-solving discussion and more formal research activities.

The character of a problem-solving discussion in history is the same as in any other social-studies class. Discussion focuses on ideas or issues of contemporary significance, and not on those of historical importance only. This point cannot be overstressed. It would be irrelevant to our purposes, for example, to discuss whether John D. Rockefeller formed the Standard Oil Trust as a service to mankind or as a means of indulging a personal lust for power and money. But it might be worth while to discuss whether monopolies are *generally* formed in order to raise or lower prices. The Rockefeller case history could then be introduced as one item of evidence.

An illustration of how a springboard in a history text might be developed follows:

Spain forbade English traders to enter Spanish waters. But the treasure ships from America were a great temptation to the skillful sailors of England. Attacks upon foreign commerce in distant waters were regarded as piracy rather than war and English sea captains did not hesitate to seize any Spanish ship which was not well defended. John Hawkins and Francis Drake were only two of the many who sold slaves in Spanish colonies, sold goods in violation of Spanish laws, and captured Spanish ships.[19]

Questions for instigating reflection:

1. Were Hawkins and Drake guilty of violating the laws of Spain? Were they guilty of theft? What did the Spanish think of Hawkins and Drake? Were their deeds criminal by modern standards?

2. Did the British regard Hawkins and Drake as lawbreakers and thieves? What did the British people think of Hawkins and Drake? Did the British admire these men? Were they regarded as criminals or heroes?

3. Are persons who are regarded as criminals by one country sometimes regarded as heroes by another? Can you think of any modern examples? Is it common for a people to use different standards in judging a person of their own nationality and in judging someone of another nationality?

[19] Dwight L. Dumond and others, *History of the United States,* D. C. Heath & Company, 1948, p. 12. Discussion questions following quote are our own.

Generalizations to be considered:

A person may be called a criminal by one nation and a hero by another.
People of any given nationality are likely to use a double standard in judging themselves and foreigners.

Some students, perhaps, will have been doing the latter without being aware of it; study of the idea may thus appear as a challenge and motivate them to serious reflection.

SPRINGBOARDS AND ATOMIZATION

It might be charged that the development of springboards, as proposed here, will atomize history; that if teachers select successive focal points which may be several pages apart in a textbook students will acquire fragments of historical knowledge without awareness of continuity or relationship in historical events. On the contrary, a skillful teacher can probably use the springboard technique to *unify* history. At the beginning of a course, springboards may be single passages, but as the course progresses the generalizations formulated will tie the passages which first suggested them to other passages. By the end of a course, students may be able to identify twenty or thirty events (as described in the textbook) which support or question a single generalization. In other words, all these events are seen as having the same meaning. *Because they are seen as data supporting or refuting a single generalization, they possess unity.* Furthermore, groups of events supporting single generalizations tend to fall together under increasingly more inclusive generalizations, until large parts of man's history are seen as illustrating certain general ideas.

There are many generalizations which can be illustrated time and again from United States history; once they are understood they unify many items of descriptive content. The following are examples of such social theory (see also the propositions listed at the end of the section).

People tend to cling to many customs and beliefs long after the causes which gave rise to them have disappeared.
From generation to generation, people to some degree change their moral standards and their fundamental beliefs about most matters.
Americans tend to accept technological innovations more readily than they accept social or ideological innovations.
Technological innovations tend to produce social tensions which can be eased only by appropriate social innovations.
People commonly violate in behavior ideals to which they verbally subscribe.
To some degree, political parties represent economic interests and groupings

(i.e., the Republican party tends to be more popular with propertied people, the Democratic party with working-class people).

War is a stimulus to certain kinds of economic expansion and overall prosperity.

LIMITATIONS TO THE USE OF HISTORICAL SPRINGBOARDS

Many, and perhaps most, theoretical generalizations suggested by events in history cannot readily be tested with any degree of finality by high-school students. It is very easy to create a generalization, to find two or three events which seem to support it, and then to conclude that it is accurate, a suitable guide to behavior. The cure for this superficiality is not to be found in instruction which discourages any attempt to generalize. Unless generalization occurs, no transferable learning has taken place and instruction has been futile. Furthermore, bright students in any class will make some generalizations—and often superficial ones—no matter how hard a teacher tries to avoid theorization.

If a teacher deliberately entices his students to generalize, he can watch for over-generalization, and he can teach his students how to distinguish between good and poor generalizations. One aim of high-school teaching of history should be an increased capacity to generalize. Moreover, students can be taught to regard every conclusion as a starting point for additional inquiry. Although there are certainly some generalizations for which a great deal of historical support can be gathered, many student conclusions deserve considerable suspicion and reëxamination. Nevertheless, these weakly grounded principles are often better guides to action than the prejudices which typically govern much of American life.

Perhaps the chief weakness against which to guard is a teacher's tendency to rationalize—to help students find historical support for the teacher's beliefs. If he knows that he has a preference for a particular interpretation of history, he should consciously strive to create doubt in his students concerning the validity of such an interpretation when it is presented by a textbook author.

EXAMPLES OF SOME CURRENT ISSUES WHICH CAN BE ILLUMINATED
WITH HISTORICAL DATA

To be understood, any social issue must be studied in the light of historical as well as current data. But many contemporary issues do not have deep historical roots. Other issues do have deep historical roots, but standard history textbooks omit any consideration of them, and other relevant materials may not be available. Consequently, a teacher must select issues which can be studied *profitably* in history classes through materials which are available (sometimes only a textbook).

The following propositions are a brief sample (meant only to be illustrative) of the hundreds potentially suitable for study in a history class. Each proposition is controversial and, with its converse, reflects an issue which might exist in some American community. One cannot determine outside a particular teaching situation whether students could be made to feel some of these issues as problems. Nevertheless, they are likely to be appropriate to many high-school history classes. No attempt is made to list types of evidence which a typical history textbook would provide; probably an adequate analysis of most propositions listed would require gathering evidence from additional sources.

1. In order for a nation to make economic progress, it must eventually retire its national debt.

2. A capitalist nation makes its greatest economic progress when taxes and controls imposed on business are kept at a minimum.

3. New machines create more jobs than they destroy.

4. The immigration of foreigners into the United States causes unemployment among American workmen.

5. The adoption of a socialist economy inevitably leads to a loss of political freedom.

6. Professional soldiers make successful Presidents in the United States.

7. Businessmen in the United States always support freedom and democracy.

8. The mixing of races through intermarriage produces inferior and degenerate offspring.

9. Atheists tend to be maladjusted and often immoral.

10. The nonwhite races are inferior to whites in business and financial acumen.

11. The class structure in America represents a natural ranking based upon mental, moral, and physiological differences.

12. There are no social classes in America.

Teaching of Civics

Civics is second to history in overall enrollment. One or two semesters of civics, dealing primarily with American government, are commonly required in eleventh or twelfth grade. Community civics, which treats local government and the nature of community life, is usually offered in seventh, eighth, or ninth grade.

The chief weakness of instruction in the field of civics is precisely the same as in history. Much civics instruction seeks to feed a student's mind with facts straight from a text and leaves the student, unless he is very bright, largely untouched and unstimulated. He sees little relationship between the content of civics and the content of issues significant to himself and his community. Moreover, ideas which are treated in a civics course, particularly in junior high school, are often too difficult for students. For instance, under the most favorable circumstances eighth-graders have difficulty understanding the abstract ideas of government on which the Constitution is founded. Under average conditions, most eighth-grade students will be able to do little more than recite a number of meaningless word combinations. Some states, however, require students to pass an examination on the Constitution before they finish eighth grade.

Use of Textbook Springboards in Civics

Springboards in civics are fundamentally the same as in history. A teacher watches the textbook for appropriate descriptive passages or other collections of data, or theoretical generalizations, or contradictions or discrepancies. He then tries to promote discussion by asking questions which reveal inadequacy in students' beliefs.

Following a quotation from the Declaration of Independence, one textbook reads: "With these bold words our forefathers founded this nation—the United States of America. This faith in individualism, in freedom, in equality, which gave it birth, has made it the greatest nation on earth." [20] And a few pages later appears: "We have defined the American heritage as a faith in individualism, in freedom, in equality." [21] These statements may be used to develop more fully the idea of individualism, and to contrast this idea with that of brotherhood and mutual help. A teacher could start a discussion of individualism by asking:

1. What is meant by individualism? Does it mean that everyone is free to do as he pleases? Does it mean that each person tries to be independent? Does independence mean working without outside help and direction? Does individualism mean a willingness to take risks, and to compete for the good things of life?

2. Does individualism mean a minimum of governmental interference with business? Is individualism the same as laissez-faire capitalism? As free enterprise? Do you accept the idea of individualism?

Following this discussion a teacher might call the attention of students

[20] Quoted in Frank A. Magruder (as revised by William A. McClenaghan), Allyn and Bacon, Inc., 1953, p. 1. Questions following quotations are our own.
[21] *Ibid.*, p. 5.

to the section in the textbook entitled "Government As Servant." The gist of this section may be gathered from the following:

Centuries ago the chief task of government was felt to be that of defending the people against foreign invasion and domestic violence . . . but gradually through the years government has assumed a much broader role. Especially in democratic countries, such as the United States, it has become the *servant* as well as the protector of our people. . . .

All through life the citizen is served by his local, State, and National governments. The food that he eats is inspected to guarantee its purity and protect his health. He may receive much of his education at public expense. The hours and conditions under which he works, the quality of the clothing he wears, and the home he lives in, all are protected in one way or another by governmental regulations meant for his safety and well-being.[22]

There is an apparent conflict between these passages and the earlier praise of individualism. In examining this apparent contradiction many students may also examine their own confusions:

1. Do these paragraphs mean we are increasingly trying to protect individuals against the hazards of life? What is the attitude today toward helping the unfortunate? Is the social security idea a part of this attitude? Do the practices described above reflect an attempt to apply a philosophy of brotherhood? Do you like the idea of helping and protecting the unfortunate?

2. Is the idea of social insurance and government regulations consistent with the idea of individualism? How can a person learn to stand on his own feet if he is protected from the major risks of life? How could you practice individualism and mutual help at one and the same time? What meaning do you assign to the expression: "The best place to find security is in jail"?

3. Do you believe that individualism is basic to the American way of life? Do you feel the same about the idea of mutual aid and coöperation? If you believe that we should practice both individualism and brotherly sharing, which spheres of living would you reserve to each?

ISSUES APPROPRIATE TO STUDY IN HIGH-SCHOOL CIVICS

Some important political issues are perhaps too complicated for most high-school students to understand, and many cannot be studied fruitfully in high school with the sparse data available. But there is a limited number of controversial propositions pertinent to the field of government which can be tested with evidence generally available to high-school students. For example:

1. Americans believe in and practice democracy as a way of life.

[22] *Ibid.,* pp. 6–7, 16.

2. The nation faces bankruptcy unless the federal budget is balanced.

3. The national debt must be paid out of taxes and is a burden on future generations.

4. Federal expenditures could be greatly reduced by eliminating waste and inefficiency in the government or by curtailing unnecessary expenditures of a "socialistic" nature.

5. A general lowering of tariffs would be disastrous to this country.

6. The problem of war can be solved only as individual nations are willing to relinquish sovereignty to an international police force.

7. The American court system dispenses justice equally to the rich and the poor, and to all political and religious creeds.

8. American citizens are the most enlightened the world has ever known.

9. The federal government could not operate basic industries as efficiently as can private corporations.

10. The Republican party is the party of big business.

Teaching of Geography

If one lumps together all geography taught between grades seven and twelve, in overall enrollment it is the third most popular secondary-school social study. Economic or commercial geography deals with industries, products, and trade by regions or nations. World, or global, geography treats physical features and human culture of regions or nations. In addition to these senior-high-school courses, world or American geography is widely offered as a required subject in seventh or eighth grade.

Textbooks in geography describe contemporary conditions, and a geography teacher, like a teacher of civics, does not have the problem of "bringing the past into the present." Even so, it is not easy to use geographic textbook content in reflectively examining ideas. One source of difficulty is that much content of geography textbooks is physical science rather than social science and belongs logically in a general-science course rather than a social-studies curriculum. Most teachers of social studies are not adequately trained to work with concepts from the natural sciences, and unless geography can be related to a study of social issues they hardly know what to do with its content.

Even "human geography" is handled rather badly by most present geography texts. Its relevance to social problems is seldom made apparent, especially in textbooks on economic or commercial geography, which often describe in considerable detail occupations, industries, and volume of trade between nations. Generalizations on a theoretical level are comparatively rare and the descriptive content given is seldom directly or even potentially relevant to social theory. An exception in a few texts is inclusion of trade theory which considers the advantages of geographic specialization, effects of tariffs, and necessity for long-term balance of trade.

Generally these books, dealing with effects of physical environment on economic life, products of agriculture and industry, and trade within and between nations, stress mechanical and technical aspects. In a sense, this content could be described as "engineering data" simplified for junior- and senior-high-school students.

Because in most of the available texts it is virtually impossible to find spots from which one can move from descriptive material to study of controversial issues to formulation of social theory, geography is more difficult to teach as a social science than is history or civics. But geography texts do vary in quality and some are much better than others.

The sterility of most geography texts places an extra burden on teachers. They must help students find meaning where none appears to exist. A teacher should be on the alert for springboards, even though most of those which are found require considerable ingenuity to develop.

USE OF THE SPRINGBOARD IN GEOGRAPHY

In one geography text we read:

The great number of storms in Mexican political history have been closely related to the small number of storms in Mexican climate. Much of Mexico is semiarid steppe land, where water is scarce. Very soon after the Spaniards conquered Mexico, a few men got control of the well-watered places. Large cattle ranches (haciendas) grew up on those places, some of them hundreds of thousands—and a few of them millions—of acres in extent. On these ranches the white owners lived very well on the proceeds of their great herds. The Indians and half-breed peons who worked for them lived little better than the cattle.

The modern history of Mexico has been largely an attempt to distribute more justly the meager blessings of a semiarid climate. The monstrous private haciendas have been broken up by the government and distributed among the poor. Irrigated farm lands have been created in many places where once only grazing was possible.[23]

The following questions might arouse reflection concerning implications of the foregoing passage:

1. Is it common for people, if allowed to do as they please, to acquire as much property as they can? Does your answer apply particularly to land? What has been the history of land acquisition in the United States?

[23] John H. Bradley, *World Geography*, Ginn & Company, 1948, p. 104. This is one of the most teachable of the geography texts examined by the authors.

2. Does control of a large amount of land always mean that the owner controls people? Does such ownership increase his control of government?

3. What were the economic results of the hacienda system? Did the haciendas promote economic progress? Did they contribute to stability in government? Do extremes of wealth and poverty strengthen a nation?

4. Did the Mexican government have the right to take the haciendas from the owners and divide them among the peons? Did it have the right to seize the properties of United States petroleum corporations? What effects have wealthy persons in the United States had on government in Mexico? Have they been generally in favor of the social revolution in Mexico?

Ideas for examination which may emerge from a discussion of these questions are as follows:

When free to do so, men will acquire as much land as they can.

The men who can seize the essential natural resources of a nation usually have great power over the lives of other persons.

When wealth in a nation is very unequally divided, government is likely to lack stability.

The purpose of government is to prevent the strong from exploiting the weak.

A nation will be stronger if everyone is free to acquire all the property he can and use it as he wishes.

ISSUES APPROPRIATE FOR STUDY IN GEOGRAPHY

Although most geography texts illuminate current social issues only slightly, there are a number of propositions the study of which can be adapted to a conventional geography course. Below is an illustrative sample:

1. A nation's natural resources can best be exploited in the interests of all the people only as long as private individuals and corporations are free from hampering governmental restraint.

2. Most foreign peoples are inferior to Americans intellectually, morally, and physically.

3. Much of the discontent of common people in the world can be attributed to unequal distribution of wealth, particularly farm land.

4. The federal government could operate railroads and air lines more efficiently than could private corporations.

5. Without governmental regulation, monopolies will charge the highest prices the market will bear.

6. The government must subsidize large segments of American industry if it is to remain profitable to its owners.

7. The United States is more prosperous when it exports more than it imports.

8. The lowering of tariffs would injure or destroy a large part of American industry.

9. If people are to enjoy the highest standard of living which modern technology makes possible, it will be necessary to reduce the world's population.

10. The full development of power resources can be carried out more rapidly and efficiently by building hydroelectric projects at government expense.

11. A mixture of diverse nationalities, races, and religions can learn to live together in peace.

DISCUSSION QUESTIONS AND EXERCISES

1. When a teacher insists that it is necessary to "cover" a textbook or course of study in a specified length of time, what assumptions is he making about (a) the learning process, (b) the content of learning, and (c) the purposes of social-studies education?

2. State one or more hypotheses which might explain why many social-studies teachers require students to devote most of their time in class to individual work on chapter-end exercises or workbooks. What assumptions are such teachers making about (a) the learning process, (b) the content of learning, and (c) the purposes of social-studies education?

3. Chapter 17 is critical of conventional survey courses in history. What might be said on the other side? Do history surveys perform a function which no other approach could perform so well? If survey courses do not usually produce the outcomes expected of them, can you suggest any ways of organizing such courses (without departing from the survey principle) which would make them more fruitful?

4. Edgar Wesley has said, "An ancient history text may be of greater contemporary significance than one in modern history" (*Teaching Social Studies in High Schools*, p. 163). What do you think is the reasoning behind this statement? Do you agree or disagree?

5. Select a few widely used social-studies textbooks and read at least one chapter in each in a search for possible "springboards." Show how, as a teacher, you might try to exploit some of these. (Be sure to include at least one history textbook on your list.)

6. See how many generalizations you can add to the list on page 360 of generalizations which can be supported or refuted by events in United States history. See how many you can think of which might be supported or refuted by events of (a) ancient history, (b) modern European history, and (c) the history of Asia.

7. Explore ways in which a course in world geography might be used as an instrument for examining issues in one or more of the six closed areas treated in Chapters 11–16.

REFERENCES

Although not usually reflecting a point of view such as is expressed in Chapter 17, certain texts in the teaching of the social studies do include suggestions for improving the use of textbooks. Students may wish to read Ernest Horn, *Methods of Instruction in the Social Studies* (Scribner, 1937), Chapter 6, Arthur C. and David H. Bining, *Teaching the Social Studies in Secondary Schools* (McGraw-Hill, 1952), Chapter 4, and Edgar Wesley, *Teaching Social Studies in High Schools* (Heath, 1950), Chapter 24.

The following references treat the teaching of history specifically: Henry Johnson, *Teaching of History* (Macmillan, 1915); National Council for the Social Studies, *The Study and Teaching of American History*, Seventeenth Yearbook, 1947, and *Improving the Teaching of World History*, Twentieth Yearbook, 1949; Maurice P. Moffatt, *Social Studies Instruction* (Prentice-Hall, 1950), Chapter 7.

A useful reference on the teaching of civics is John J. Mahoney, *For Us the Living: An Approach to Civic Education* (Harper, 1945). See also National Council for the Social Studies, *Citizens for a New World*, Fourteenth Yearbook, 1944, and *Education for Democratic Citizenship*, Twenty-Second Yearbook, 1951. Both the latter titles apply equally to all social-studies subjects.

Students interested particularly in geography may read the Nineteenth Yearbook of the National Council, *Geographic Approaches to Social Education* (1948), Roderick Peattie, *The Teaching of Geography* (Appleton-Century-Crofts, 1950), and Chapter 8 of Moffatt, cited above.

The Eleventh Yearbook of the National Council, *Economic Education* (1940), treats the teaching of economics. See also Frank D. Graham's excellent essay, "The Role of Economics," in *Education for Citizen Responsibilities* (Franklin L. Burdette, ed.), published by Princeton University Press, 1942. Chapter 9 of Moffatt deals with the teaching of economics and sociology. The Joint Council on Economic Education, 444 Madison Avenue, New York 22, New York, will furnish teachers with a number of useful teaching materials in this area.

Chapter 18

Materials of Instruction in the Social Studies

IT HAS been common in the past for educationists to recommend materials in accordance with criteria such as difficulty level, capacity to arouse interest, attractiveness, and variety. Recently less attention has been given to symbolic materials and proportionately more to direct experience and manipulative and pictorial materials. This trend has been considered "progressive" and is often indulged for its own sake rather than with any clear pedagogical justification. Suggested criteria usually do not reflect a theory of teaching such as we pose in the present book. They are generally peripheral, if at all related, to the central problem of inducing sustained reflection on critical social issues. Therefore, we shall suggest criteria for selection which appear to be in line with our educational philosophy.

Suggested Criteria for Selecting Materials

According to the theoretical definition of content given in Chapter 10, the psychological content of learning consists of the data of individual acts of thought. The content of learning is therefore not to be regarded as systematically organized bodies of knowledge, fixedly established prior to learning. It is always in the process of emerging, according to the thought-needs of a situation. As was indicated in Chapter 10, this definition of content does not exclude the possibility of gathering and organizing potential content (that is, materials of instruction) prior to a given act of learning. It is only necessary that writers of textbooks and other persons who prepare teaching materials select content with a high probability of being relevant to problems in which students can be involved.

In short, the usefulness of instructional materials varies according to how well they supply food for thought. If a given item of material furnishes data for one or more steps of an act of reflective thought, it is worth while. If it does not, its use would be pointless. But, since it is often impossible to determine in advance whether a given item of material will strike students as relevant, an experimental approach to the use of materials is always indicated. A teacher tries one thing and another. Materials of instruction which we shall list in the present chapter are to be viewed only as *potential* bearers of learning content; it remains for individual teachers in each case to judge whether a given item is likely to be useful.

If our criterion for selection is valid, it is evident that certain widely held beliefs about the selection and use of materials are of questionable worth. A few of these questionable notions are listed and briefly evaluated below.

1. "A teacher should make use of as great a variety of materials as possible." Variety, in itself, is not a satisfactory criterion. A teacher might use great ingenuity in introducing a great variety of teaching materials all irrelevant to the thought-needs of students. In connection with a given problem, a single book might provide all pertinent evidence which is then available. Attempts to use a wide variety of materials may only confuse students.

2. "A teacher should make every use possible of pictorial materials." Obviously, pictorial materials can play an important role in reflective learning; but whether they do depends on their relevance. There is nothing virtuous about motion pictures, slides, or pictures *per se*.

3. "Materials of instruction should be selected to add interest, novelty, color, and excitement to a learning situation." This criterion stems from what might be labeled "the entertainment theory of education." This outlook seems to press the point that, above all else, experiences in school should be fun. Although not denying that if learning is accompanied by a certain amount of fun it may be more attractive, we take it that reflective study of serious issues is the first aim of learning. Materials introduced primarily for the purpose of adding color are likely to divert attention from sober learning. Nor are they needed for motivation; if social-studies education focuses on the types of issues described in Part II of the present book, there is certain to be motivation aplenty.

4. "Materials should be selected to make learning easier and less time consuming for students." Two separate but related ideas are involved here:

(a) materials should provide simplification; (b) materials should add efficiency to learning. These, again, are peripheral ends and may or may not have anything to do with reflective problem solving. Pictures or charts may help make a point clear; and they may speed learning. The question always is, What quality of insights is being achieved? Materials may have the effect of speeding memorization-level learning only. Or they may be selected primarily for the purpose of instigating and guiding reflective problem solving.

Materials for Use of Teachers and Students

We shall describe materials as belonging to two broad categories: subject-matter materials for use by teachers and students and professional materials for teachers. The first classification includes basic references, books of current social significance (fiction and nonfiction), books of historical interpretation, magazines and newspapers, pamphlet series, and a variety of free and low-cost pamphlet and pictorial materials. The second classification includes materials which pertain almost exclusively to problems of teaching and the professional self-study of teachers.

In the first group (materials for teachers and students) no attempt will be made to distinguish between "teacher materials" and "student materials." Very few, if any, materials listed are beyond the understanding of the more talented high-school students, and even the easiest of the materials listed may be useful sources of data for the self-education of teachers. Furthermore, among relatively difficult books teachers will be able to find particular chapters or passages which the average student can read meaningfully; and even where the most significant ideas of a difficult book cannot be understood through direct reading by students, a teacher through lecture or discussion can present the ideas in language which will make them comprehensible to students. It seems apparent, therefore, that the most important considerations are the *relevance* of an item and the *provocativeness of its ideas,* rather than its difficulty.

TEXTBOOKS

The content of textbooks designed for use in high-school social-studies classes was discussed in Chapter 9, where we suggested that such content tends to be relatively standardized and to be selected with reference to what has been included traditionally within each of the social-science fields. It was also suggested that, as judged against the aim of social-studies instruction stated in the present book, such content tends toward irrelevance. We recognize, however, that most courses in social studies will continue to be organized more or less around a textbook.

Criteria for selection of textbooks have already been implied; it remains to make them explicit.

1. A textbook should contain a relatively large amount of content bearing on critical controversial issues of the culture. Such content should include, or be pertinent to, possible general ideas (if-then-always generalizations, as defined in Chapter 2), and should also include abundant factual detail which is directly relevant to such ideas.

2. A textbook should be provocative. That is, it should suggest ideas (with supporting factual data) which challenge conventional beliefs in areas of controversy.

3. A textbook should be honest. Although a good textbook is likely to be written from a particular point of view, and in this sense will reflect the outlook of its author, it can and should also reflect integrity. That is, it should not attempt to distort or conceal facts. Nor should it try to hide or gloss over seamy aspects of American life past or present.

4. A textbook should be scholarly. Although a textbook which contains inconsistencies or inaccuracies may be teachable (as indicated in the previous chapter), it is likely to prove, if not a menace, at least an inconvenience.

5. A textbook should communicate to the average student who will be using it. A great deal of nonsense has been written about the subject of making textbooks readable. The problem is not solved by attractive format, abundant pictures, or limiting vocabulary to two-syllable words. We suggest that the first task in writing a textbook which communicates is to write about subjects concerning which students want to read. If it entrances him, a mediocre student can read relatively difficult material. A second requirement is that a text be well written. By this we mean it should have stylistic quality, one aspect of which is lucidity.

At present, there do not appear to be many textbooks written for the high-school social studies which conform to these standards. But some conform better than others, and a teacher faced with the necessity of selecting a text may need to remember that "Half a loaf is better than none."

Although the basic technique for using a text is the development of "springboards" (see Chapter 17), a textbook may play a variety of roles in a given course, depending on how central the book is to the course. A course may be built around a single text or around two or more texts. Or it may be built around a course of study or outline unrelated to any particular book and make use of textbooks when needed as references.[1]

Books in this general category vary greatly both in usefulness and in price. The following list is not intended to be exhaustive.

Social-science teachers will find useful any good general encyclopedia, such as *Britannica* or *Americana*. One general encyclopedia, *Worldbook,* is designed particularly for junior- and senior-high-school students. Of special value in the field, however, is *The Encyclopedia of the Social Sciences* (Macmillan, 8 vols.). Of possible use are the *Dictionary of American History* (Scribner, 4 vols. plus index) and the *Encyclopedia of World History* (Houghton Mifflin, 1 vol.). Of less value is the *Cyclopedia of American Government,* now outdated. A biographical dictionary is of occasional usefulness, and the standard set in this field is the *Dictionary of American Biography* (Scribner, 21 vols.).

A good general atlas is an essential for classes in social studies. The *Encyclopaedia Britannica World Atlas* (Hammond) and Rand McNally's *Cosmopolitan World Atlas* are comprehensive volumes, but probably not much more useful than the smaller and much cheaper *Goode's School Atlas* (Rand McNally). The latter is excellently done and inexpensive enough so that most schools can supply one to each social-studies classroom. Historical atlases are sometimes needed. One such is Lord and Lord's *Historical Atlas of the United States* (Holt, 1944).

There are several useful fact books. One of the most widely used is *The World Almanac and Book of Facts,* published annually by the New York World-Telegram. Somewhat on the same order is the *Information Please Almanac,* published by The Macmillan Company and revised annually. Both books contain large quantities of factual data on many aspects of American life—legal, political, economic, recreational, and cultural. Another useful reference is the *Statistical Abstract of the United States,* published annually by the Bureau of the Census. This volume includes data for every aspect of American life about which the federal government gathers statistics—population, economic development, climatic conditions, crime and delinquency, vital statistics, and the like. *The Economic Almanac,* published

[1] Readers may find of value the six "levels of textbook teaching" given by Edgar Wesley in *Teaching Social Studies in High Schools,* D. C. Heath & Company, 1950, pp. 448–450.

by the Conference Board, 247 Park Avenue, New York 17, contains a large quantity of basic economic data.

Every school should own a copy of the *Educational Film Guide* and the *Filmstrip Guide*. Both are published by the H. W. Wilson Company and revised annually. Regular supplements are also issued. The former volume lists 11,000 16 mm. motion-picture films and gives basic data about them, including quality ratings where they are available. The latter lists most of the filmstrips which are currently available in the United States. Another useful volume is the *Educators Guide to Free Films,* available from Educators Progress Service, Randolph, Wisconsin.

Nonfiction Books of Social Analysis and Interpretation

Books listed in this group are written by trained social scientists, journalists, foreign correspondents, and other supposedly skilled observers of the social scene. These books express a variety of outlooks, from conservative to liberal—and sometimes outlooks which cannot be classified as either. In selecting titles we have tried to apply criteria such as social importance of subjects treated, depth and incisiveness of analysis, and lucidity of treatment. However, we recognize that some books in the following list cannot be read with understanding by any except the most gifted high-school students. Books of this general type are "must" reading for teachers, however, and often teachers will find it possible to communicate to students the insights gained thereby.

Many titles which might appropriately be listed here have already been given in footnotes or in chapter-end references earlier in the book. Particularly, consult the bibliographies at the ends of Chapters 11–16. To procure additional titles teachers may wish to consult *Good Reading* of the Mentor Books series, published by New American Library, or a critical summary such as Asa D. Dickinson, *The World's Best Books* (Wilson, 1953). However, both of the foregoing omit many good titles, and for current titles teachers are advised to follow the book-review sections of magazines such as *Harper's* or *The Nation,* or to read the *New York Times Book Review* section or the *Saturday Review.*

The following list is only a brief sampling of the many excellent titles available. It is to be regarded as suggestive rather than definitive.

1. Benedict, Ruth, *Patterns of Culture* (Mentor, 1948)
2. Brown, Harrison, *The Challenge of Man's Future* (Viking, 1954)
3. Childs, Marquis, *Sweden, the Middle Way* (Yale University Press, 1947)

4. Commager, Henry Steele, *Freedom, Loyalty, Dissent* (Oxford University Press, 1954)
5. Davis, Elmer, *But We Were Born Free* (Bobbs-Merrill, 1954)
6. Ernst, Morris, *The First Freedom* (Macmillan, 1946)
7. Federal Council of Churches (Department of the Church and Economic Life), *The Ethics and Economics of Society* (Harper). A series by prominent authors on ethics and economic life
8. Frank, Jerome, *Courts on Trial* (Princeton University Press, 1949)
9. Fromm, Erich, *Escape from Freedom* (Rinehart, 1941)
10. Fromm, Erich, *Man for Himself* (Rinehart, 1947)
11. Gunther, John, *Inside U.S.A.* (Harper, 1951)
12. *Hoover Institute Studies: World Revolution of Our Time,* Stanford University Press. A series of paper-bound, low-cost volumes in three groups, "General Studies," "Elite Studies," and "Symbol Studies"
13. Horney, Karen, *The Neurotic Personality of Our Time* (Norton, 1937)
14. Jacoby, Annalee, and White, Theodore, *Thunder Out of China* (Sloan, 1946)
15. Lilienthal, David E., *TVA—Democracy on the March* (Harper, 1944)
16. Lynd, Robert S., *Knowledge for What?* (Princeton University Press, 1940)
17. Myrdal, Gunnar, *An American Dilemma* (Harper, 1944)
18. Northrop, F. S. C., *Meeting of East and West* (Macmillan, 1946)
19. Powdermaker, Hortense, *Hollywood, the Dream Factory* (Little, Brown, 1950)
20. *Problems in American Civilization* (Heath). The famous "Amherst Series" of inexpensive volumes of social analysis
21. Schumpeter, Joseph, *Capitalism, Socialism, and Democracy* (Harper, 1950)
22. Seldes, Gilbert, *The Great Audience* (Viking, 1950)
23. *Short Studies in Political Science, Sociology, and Psychology* (Doubleday, Doran). A series of paper-bound, low-cost volumes
24. Sternberg, Fritz, *Living with Crisis* (John Day, 1950)
25. Veblen, Thorstein, *The Engineers and the Price System* (Viking, 1921)
26. Veblen, Thorstein, *Theory of the Leisure Class* (Vanguard, 1926)
27. Willkie, Wendell, *One World* (Simon & Schuster, 1943)

FICTION OF SOCIAL SIGNIFICANCE

In its ability to expose and clarify social issues and problems, or to describe situations of conflict, fiction may be just as "true" as nonfiction. In fact, some authors of novels and short stories probably have achieved more incisive and accurate analyses of the social scene than are contained in many supposedly scientific works of economic or sociological analysis.

Novels may be read by students, or teachers may read excerpts or paraphrase incidents described. Novels also provide teachers with valuable illustrative materials for use in lectures and discussions. The following list includes novels of varying levels of maturity and reading difficulty, on the assumption that a teacher can best determine what books to use.

Space does not permit more than a sampling of socially significant fiction. We have deliberately included only books which in one way or another appear to expose and illuminate contradictions and problems in American life—books usually classed as "realistic." Many of them are critical of beliefs and behaviors common in the United States, but at the same time virtually all of the authors represented express a deep sympathy for and commitment to democratic ideals.

One of the most convenient sources of fiction titles is Otis W. Coan and Richard G. Lillard, *America in Fiction* (Stanford University Press, 1949). This is an annotated bibliography of American fiction, classified according to several broad headings. Also useful is *Good Reading,* cited earlier, and Edward Wagenknecht's *Cavalcade of the American Novel* (Holt, 1952). Teachers wishing to use historical novels will want to consult a volume such as Ernest E. Leisy, *The American Historical Novel* (University of Oklahoma Press, 1950).

1. Anderson, Sherwood, *Winesburg, Ohio* (Modern Library, 1919)
2. Asch, Sholem, *East River* (Putnam, 1946)
3. Bellamann, Henry, *King's Row* (Simon & Schuster, 1940)
4. Caldwell, Erskine, *Kneel to the Rising Sun* (Viking, 1935)
5. Churchill, Winston, *The Inside of the Cup* (Macmillan, 1912)
6. Davenport, Marcia, *The Valley of Decision* (Scribner, 1942)
7. Dos Passos, John, *U.S.A.* (Harcourt, Brace, 1937)
8. Dreiser, Theodore, *An American Tragedy* (World, 1925)
9. Dreiser, Theodore, *The Financier* (World, 1912)
10. Farrell, James T., *Studs Lonigan: A Triology* (Vanguard, 1937)
11. Fitzgerald, F. Scott, *The Great Gatsby* (Scribner, 1925)
12. Gellhorn, Martha, *The Wine of Astonishment* (Scribner, 1948)
13. Green, Paul, *This Body the Earth* (Harper, 1935)
14. Hemingway, Ernest, *For Whom the Bell Tolls* (Scribner, 1940)
15. Hobson, Laura A., *Gentleman's Agreement* (Simon & Schuster, 1947)
16. Huxley, Aldous, *Brave New World* (Harper, 1932)
17. Lewis, Sinclair, *Babbitt* (Harcourt, Brace, 1922)
18. Lewis, Sinclair, *It Can't Happen Here* (Doubleday, 1935)
19. Lewis, Sinclair, *Kingsblood Royal* (Random House, 1947)
20. London, Jack, *The Iron Heel* (Regent, 1907)
21. McCullers, Carson, *The Heart Is a Lonely Hunter* (Houghton Mifflin, 1940)
22. McKenney, Ruth, *Industrial Valley* (Harcourt, Brace, 1939)
23. Morley, Christopher, *Kitty Foyle* (Lippincott, 1939)
24. Norris, Frank, *The Octopus* (Doubleday, 1901)

25. Norris, Frank, *The Pit* (Doubleday, 1903)
26. Orwell, George, *Nineteen Eighty-Four* (Harcourt, Brace, 1949)
27. Sandoz, Mari, *Capital City* (Little, Brown, 1939)
28. Sheldon, Charles M., *In His Steps* (Advance, 1897)
29. Sinclair, Upton, *The Jungle* (Harper, 1951)
30. Sinclair, Upton, *Oil!* (Boni, 1927)
31. Smith, Lillian, *Strange Fruit* (Reynal & Hitchcock, 1944)
32. Steinbeck, John, *The Grapes of Wrath* (Viking, 1939)
33. Stribling, Thomas S., *The Sound Wagon* (Doubleday, 1935)
34. Warren, Robert P., *All the King's Men* (Harcourt, Brace, 1946)
35. Wright, Richard, *Native Son* (Harper, 1940)

HISTORY: INTERPRETIVE STUDIES, HISTORY OF IDEAS, SELECTIONS OF DOCUMENTS

Before listing titles of some interpretive studies of history, we should note a few well-known series which have proved of value to many history teachers. The "Chronicles of America" series, edited by Allen Johnson (Yale University Press, 1918–21), includes fifty short volumes on different periods and events in United States history. The "Pageant of America" series, edited by R. N. Gabriel (Yale University Press, 1925–29), includes fifteen volumes of pictorial material. Of continuing usefulness is the "American Nation" series, edited by Albert B. Hart (Harper, 1904–18). In progress is a "New American Nation" series, edited by Henry Steele Commager and Richard B. Morris, published by Harper & Brothers. Titles available to date are: Lawrence Henry Gipson, *The Coming of the Revolution: 1763–1775;* Wallace Notestein, *The English People on the Eve of Colonization: 1606–1630;* John Richard Alden, *The American Revolution: 1775–1783;* and Arthur S. Link, *Woodrow Wilson and the Progressive Era: 1910–1917.* A *History of American Life,* edited by Arthur M. Schlesinger and Dixon R. Fox (Macmillan, 1929–33), includes twelve volumes and emphasizes sociological aspects of history.

The following list is a sampling of what is available to history teachers in addition to the usual textbook surveys. On the whole, special interpretive studies of the sort listed here contain more material relevant to contemporary issues than do the standard surveys. Teachers should gain familiarity with as many such books as possible and, to the extent that situations permit, encourage their use by students.

1. Allen, Frederick Lewis, *The Big Change: 1900–1950* (Harper, 1952)
2. Allen, Frederick Lewis, *Only Yesterday* (Harper, 1931)

3. Beard, Charles A., *An Economic Interpretation of the Constitution of the United States* (Macmillan, 1913)
4. Beard, Charles A., and Beard, Mary, *The Rise of American Civilization* (Macmillan, 1927)
5. Beard, Charles A., and Beard, Mary, *America in Midpassage* (Macmillan, 1939)
6. Brinton, Crane, *The Anatomy of Revolution* (Prentice-Hall, 1952)
7. Bury, John B., *A History of Freedom of Thought* (Holt, 1913)
8. Bury, John B., *The Idea of Progress* (Macmillan, 1928)
9. Clough, Shepard B., *The Rise and Fall of Civilization* (McGraw-Hill, 1951)
10. Cochran, Thomas C., and Miller, William, *The Age of Enterprise* (Macmillan, 1942)
11. Dulles, Foster Rhea, *America Learns to Play: A History of Popular Recreation* (Appleton-Century-Crofts, 1940)
12. Evans, Bergen, *The Natural History of Nonsense* (Knopf, 1946)
13. Faulkner, Harold U., and Starr, Mark, *Labor in America* (McGraw-Hill, 1949)
14. Muller, Herbert J., *The Uses of the Past* (Oxford University Press, 1952)
15. Myers, Gustavus, *History of Great American Fortunes* (Modern Library, 1937)
16. Polanyi, Karl, *The Great Transformation* (Farrar, 1944)
17. Robertson, Archibald, *Morals in World History* (London, Watts, 1947)
18. Schlesinger, A. M., *Learning How to Behave; A Historical Study of American Etiquette Books* (Macmillan, 1946)
19. Schlesinger, A. M., *New Viewpoints in American History* (Macmillan, 1926)
20. Sullivan, Mark, *Our Times* (Scribner, 1926–35, six vols.)
21. Toynbee, Arnold, *Study of History* (Oxford University Press, 1947). For student use, one-volume abridgment by D. C. Somervell recommended.
22. Toynbee, Arnold, *The World and the West* (Oxford University Press, 1953)
23. Turner, Frederick J., *The Frontier in American History* (Holt, 1920)
24. Walworth, Arthur, *School Histories at War* (Harvard University Press, 1938)
25. Wells, H. G., *The Outline of History* (Macmillan, 1921)

Excluded from the above group of books are those which deal primarily with the history of ideas. To some degree, most books in the list treat intellectual history, and any attempt to categorize books as history of thought or history of something else is bound to be arbitrary. However, the following books deal pointedly and exclusively with intellectual history. Books in this category are among a teacher's most useful tools in exposing and analyzing present ideological patterns.

1. Barnes, Harry Elmer, and Becker, Howard, *Social Thought from Lore to Science* (Harren, 1952)
2. Brinton, Crane, *Ideas and Men* (Prentice-Hall, 1950). The second half of

this work bears the title *The Shaping of the Modern Mind* (Mentor Book Edition)

3. Commager, Henry Steele, *The American Mind* (Yale University Press, 1950)
4. Commager, Henry Steele, *Living Ideas in America* (Harper, 1951)
5. Curti, Merle, *The Growth of American Thought* (Harper, 1951)
6. Heilbroner, Robert L., *The Worldly Philosophers* (Simon & Schuster, 1953)
7. Lerner, Max, *Ideas Are Weapons* (Viking, 1939)
8. Parrington, Vernon L., *Main Currents in American Thought* (Harcourt, Brace, 1930)
9. Randall, John Herman, Jr., *The Making of the Modern Mind* (Houghton Mifflin, 1940)
10. Robinson, James Harvey, *Mind in the Making* (Harper, 1921)
11. Stevers, Martin D., *Mind Through the Ages* (Doubleday, 1941)
12. White, Morton G., *Social Thought in America* (Viking, 1949)
13. Wish, Harvey, *Society and Thought in Modern America* (Longmans, Green, 1952)

A teacher of social studies finds it necessary from time to time to consult documentary sources. In the area of history, document collections usually include state papers, excerpts of treaties and court decisions, speeches, and letters. A number of such compilations have been made, a few of which are listed below:

1. Commager, Henry Steele (ed.), *Documents of American History* (Appleton-Century-Crofts, 1949)
2. Harley, John Eugene, *Documentary Textbook on the United Nations* (Los Angeles, Center for International Understanding, 1950)
3. Knoles, George H., and Snyder, Rixford K., *Readings in Western Civilization* (Lippincott, 1951)
4. Robinson, James Harvey, *Readings in European History* (Ginn, 1906)
5. Setton, Kenneth M., and Winkler, Henry R., *Great Problems in European Civilization* (Prentice-Hall, 1954)
6. Stearns, Raymond P., *Pageant of Europe: Sources and Collections from the Renaissance to the Present Day* (Harcourt, Brace, 1947)
7. Thorp, Willard, Curti, Merle, and Baker, Carlos, *American Issues* (Lippincott, 1944). Vol. I, "The Social Record" is the more useful.

MAGAZINES AND NEWSPAPERS

Not only are magazines and newspapers good sources of information for problem-centered study, but guided use of them in the classroom may have the worth-while effect of improving students' reading tastes. At present, periodical reading habits of the American public are badly in need of improvement. Most Americans are almost completely unfamiliar with quality magazines and the best newspapers. In the list below we have deliberately excluded the national "slicks," such as *Time, Life, Newsweek, Collier's,* and the *Saturday Evening Post.* These are too well known to require listing here. They are also "overread," in the sense that most people place inordinate dependence on them as sources of news and opinion, to the exclusion of magazines which express more provocative insights.

The following list includes most of the magazines and periodical news sheets which regularly contain material useful to social-studies teachers. Many of these can be read understandingly by average high-school students. Some are of use chiefly to teachers and exceptionally mature students.

1. *American Civil Liberties Union News.* The news organ of the Civil Liberties Union. Reports threats to civil rights as they arise.
2. *The American Federationist.* A monthly magazine published by the American Federation of Labor. Reports news of labor, government, and business. Strong prolabor bias.
3. *Américas.* A magazine published monthly by the Pan American Union. Carries news and commentary on all the Americas. Popularly written, available in English, Spanish, or Portuguese editions.
4. *Atlantic Monthly.* Articles, short stories, essays, and book reviews on many subjects. Prints material ranging in outlook from conservative to liberal.
5. *Business Week.* A weekly magazine of business and economic affairs, published by McGraw-Hill Publishing Company. Conservative in general outlook, the magazine contains relatively objective and often very perceptive reporting.
6. *CIO News.* Official weekly news sheet of the Congress of Industrial Organizations. Reports news of labor, government, and business. Strong prolabor slant. Excellent for reading concurrently with a magazine like *Business Week.*
7. *Consumer Reports.* Monthly magazine of Consumers' Union, Inc. In addition to ratings of consumer goods, it contains articles on general economic conditions and reports regulatory activities of the federal government. A generally liberal slant.
8. *Current History.* A monthly magazine which contains articles on political and economic affairs. Strong coverage of the international scene. Relatively scholarly and objective, and written in semipopular style.
9. *The Economist.* Published weekly in London, England. Considered by many to be the world's best periodical devoted to economic problems and affairs. Mildly conservative in outlook. Too difficult for any but most able students.
10. *Foreign Policy Bulletin.* Published twice monthly by the Foreign Policy Association. Honest, unbiased reporting and liberal commentary. One of best sources of information about foreign affairs and United States foreign policy.
11. *Fortune.* A magazine written primarily for the more sophisticated business-

man. Although displaying a strong probusiness slant, reporting is objective and many of the interpretive articles are excellent.

12. *Harper's.* Monthly magazine containing articles, essays, short stories, and book reviews. Prints material both liberal and conservative in outlook. An excellent source of social interpretation and commentary.

13. *The Nation.* One of America's oldest liberal weeklies. Devoted to news interpretation and articles of social analysis and interpretation. Good book reviews. Should be read with *Time* or *Newsweek* to help one gain perspective.

14. *National Geographic Magazine.* Useful articles and pictorial material on foreign nations and states and regions of the United States. It is unfortunate that the editors strive so hard (and so successfully) to exclude all controversial content from articles.

15. *New Republic.* A liberal weekly, companion to *The Nation.* Every social-studies teacher should have access to one of these magazines.

16. *New York Times Book Review* and *Magazine* sections. An excellent weekly source of book reviews and articles on political, economic, and social affairs. The *Times* is as impartial and honest as it seems possible for a newspaper to be. Its articles reflect many shades of opinion.

17. *The Reporter.* Weekly magazine of news interpretation, social analysis, and commentary. Has a generally liberal slant, but prints many articles by conservatives and middle-of-the-roaders. Brilliantly edited, vigorous, and entertaining. One of the most useful magazines for social-studies teachers and students.

18. *Saturday Review.* Book reviews and literary criticism, also articles on a variety of socially important subjects. Middle-of-the-road editorial policy.

19. *Survey of Current Business.* Published monthly by the United States Department of Commerce. Subscription includes a weekly statistical supplement. This magazine is one of a teacher's best sources of current data on the economy, but requires some ability to interpret statistics.

In addition to local papers, every social-studies teacher should read a quality newspaper and should try to have such a paper available to students. Of course, many local newspapers may be regarded as of relatively high quality. However, certain papers are widely known for their excellence. These have a national circulation, and at least some of them are to be found in most larger public libraries. The reading program of teachers and students is not complete unless it includes at least one of the following papers (or papers of equal quality):

New York Times
St. Louis Post-Dispatch
Christian Science Monitor
New York Herald Tribune

Louisville Courier-Journal
Washington Post
Baltimore Sun
Kansas City Star
Milwaukee Journal
Cleveland Plain Dealer

Any list of the world's great newspapers would undoubtedly include the *Manchester Guardian* (published in England). The *Guardian* may be obtained in an air-mail weekly edition.

SOME USEFUL PAMPHLET SERIES

There are hundreds of sources of pamphlets, a number of which are given in the section below on free and low-cost materials. Here we shall list a few series which may be subscribed to at low cost, or obtained free, and which many social-studies teachers have found useful.

1. *American Nation Series.* Pan American Union, Nineteenth Street and Constitution Avenue, N.W., Washington 6. Also series on Commodities, Capital Cities and other subjects. Ten cents each.
2. *America's Town Meeting of the Air.* Town Hall, Inc., 123 W. 43rd Street, New York 36. Printed copies of broadcast programs. Fifteen cents each, $5.00 a year.
3. *Economic Series.* Joint Council on Economic Education, 444 Madison Avenue, New York 22. Twenty cents each.
4. *Fact Booklet Series.* Distributed by Better Business Bureaus; consult local office. A number of titles, mostly on fraudulent business practices. Ten cents each.
5. *Freedom Pamphlets.* Anti-Defamation League, 11 Pryor Street, S.W., Atlanta 3, Georgia. Deal with intercultural relations. Twenty-five cents each.
6. *Headline Series.* Foreign Policy Association, Inc., 22 E. 38th Street, New York 16. Thirty-five cents each, $2.00 for six issues.
7. *National Park Series.* National Park Service, U.S. Department of the Interior, Washington. Free.
8. *Problems in American Life.* National Council for the Social Studies, 1201 Sixteenth Street, N.W., Washington. Thirty cents each. Designed especially for use by social-studies classes.
9. *Public Affairs Pamphlets.* Public Affairs Committee, 22 E. 38th Street, New York 16. Over 200 titles have been published. Twenty-five cents each.
10. *What the United Nations Is Doing.* International Documents Service, Columbia University Press. Free.

FREE AND LOW-COST MATERIALS

It is possible to obtain an abundance of teaching materials free or at very nominal cost. These materials consist mainly of pamphlets, leaflets, pictures, posters, maps, and charts. One aspect of fact-gathering projects of students may be the procuring of such pertinent materials.

Free and low-cost materials are supplied by business corporations and businessmen's associations, labor unions, veterans' associations, religious and fraternal organizations, departments of the federal and state governments, farm organizations, and numerous other groups. As a general rule, they are slanted in favor of some particular philosophy or program of action. In some cases their propaganda motif obtrudes rather glaringly. One would hardly expect, for example, that free pamphlets distributed by the National Association of Manufacturers would depict the CIO in a favorable light; or that those distributed by the CIO would shower brotherly love on the NAM. Even publications of agencies of the federal government express a point of view (for example, see pamphlets distributed by the Tennessee Valley Authority or Central Valley Project).

Thus, most free and low-cost materials must be used with awareness of their possible propaganda motives. This does not destroy their usefulness. They are a valuable source of opinion; study of them helps us understand areas of controversy in the United States. Many of these materials, however slanted their interpretations may be, contain facts from reliable sources.

A teacher may be helped to discover sources of free and low-cost materials by some of the directories and bibliographies on this subject now available. The Division of Surveys and Field Service, George Peabody College for Teachers, Nashville, Tennessee, publishes a list entitled *Free and Inexpensive Learning Materials* ($1.00). Most public libraries have a copy of the *Educators Index of Free Materials*, edited by John Guy Fowlkes. Perhaps the most steadily helpful sources of information on free and low-cost materials are the regular departments dealing with this subject in professional magazines such as *Social Education, The Social Studies,* and the *NEA Journal.*

However, there is no substitute for a teacher's striking out on his own. Most source lists on free and low-cost materials are obsolescent within a few months after publication. Materials are available which seldom get listed in either the source lists or magazine departments. We suggest that as teachers have time—perhaps with student help—they compile lists of promising places to which to write for free teaching materials. For names of organizations which might be able to supply teaching materials, the following publications are helpful:

1. *The World Almanac* (published annually by the New York *World-Telegram,*

125 Barclay Street, New York 15). See section entitled "Associations and Societies in the United States" and look for trade associations, scientific and professional organizations, labor unions, fraternal societies, business, religious, patriotic and veterans' associations, and information offices of foreign nations. Many organizations of this type publish educational materials.

2. *Information Services and Embassies in the United States of Members of the United Nations* (available free from the Department of Public Information, United Nations, New York, New York). This is a mimeographed list of embassies and information offices, almost all of which will supply pamphlets, reprints, posters, and maps to teachers upon request.

3. *United States Government Manual* (distributed by the Superintendent of Documents, Washington). This booklet lists all government departments, bureaus, and agencies and provides a variety of information about them. A number of government agencies publish free and low-cost materials of value to teachers. Write to all those which you suspect might supply teaching aids.

4. *National Associations of the United States*, by C. J. Judkins (distributed by the Superintendent of Documents, Washington). This book lists 3000 trade and professional associations of the United States, many of which are good prospects for your mailing list.

5. *Thomas Register of American Manufacturers* (Thomas Publishing Company, New York). This volume lists manufacturing corporations in the United States, giving their addresses and other pertinent information. Most of the large manufacturing corporations have a public relations department which distributes free educational materials.

6. *Moody's Industrials* (Moody's Investors' Service, 65 Broadway, New York 6). This reference lists business corporations in the United States, giving addresses and other information. It is a more complete source than *Thomas' Register* because it lists nonmanufacturing corporations. If neither of these sources is available, a teacher can compile a list of leading business corporations by drawing from magazine advertising. Magazine ads commonly do not give street addresses, but they often give the city in which the major office of the company is located, and a letter addressed to that city will reach the corporation.

Below is a list of organizations, governmental and otherwise, which are ordinarily able to supply free and low-cost materials to teachers. It is, of course, only a sampling. For convenience we have classified the sources under general subject headings.

AGRICULTURE

1. Office of Information, U.S. Department of Agriculture, Washington. Lists of USDA films and slide-films, and of free and low-cost pamphlets; also information about the Rural Library Service.

2. The American Farm Bureau Federation, 221 N. LaSalle Street, Chicago 1.

Leaflets describing the work of the FB, articles and bylaws of the FB, and miscellaneous mimeo and leaflet materials.

3. The National Grange, 744 Jackson Place, N.W., Washington 6. Booklets describing the work of the Grange, copies of the annual reports, a short history of the Grange, and reprints of magazine articles on the Grange.

CIVIL LIBERTIES

1. The American Civil Liberties Union, 170 Fifth Avenue, New York 10. Leaflets describing the work of the ACLU, a list of the ACLU's publications, and other leaflets.

CONSERVATION

1. The American Forestry Association, 919 Seventeenth Street, N.W., Washington 6. Reprints on problems of deforestation, overgrazing, and water conservation.

2. The Bureau of Reclamation, Department of the Interior, Washington 25. Many useful materials—lists of government publications, illustrated booklets, colored wall maps, and illustrated folders on projects such as Hoover Dam, the Columbia Basin Project, and Central Valley Project.

3. The National Parks Association, 1214 Sixteenth St., N.W., Washington 6. A number of reprints and mimeographed leaflets.

4. The Director of Information, Tennessee Valley Authority, Knoxville, Tenn. Charts, reprints, and pamphlets, including an excellent survey entitled *Progress in the Valley;* also a film list.

5. Wildlife Management Institute, 709 Wire Bldg., Washington 5. Well-done illustrated brochures on game-bird propagation and management.

6. Soil Conservation Service, U.S. Department of Agriculture, Washington. Pamphlets on soil conservation.

CRIME AND DELINQUENCY

1. The National Probation Association, 1790 Broadway, New York 19. Miscellaneous leaflets and pamphlets, and a bibliography on delinquency.

ECONOMICS AND BUSINESS

1. Association of Better Business Bureaus, 723 Chrysler Bldg., New York 17. Leaflets and pamphlets on the functions of the BBB. Some free, some from three cents to ten cents.

2. The National Association of Manufacturers, 14 W. 49th Street, New York 20. A large variety of teaching materials available free in quantity lots, including pamphlet series for high-school students. Write for catalogue of teachers' materials.

3. The Chamber of Commerce of the United States, 1615 H Street, N.W., Washington 6. (Order from Economic Research Department.) A number of pamphlets on current economic issues, some bearing a nominal charge.

4. League for Industrial Democracy, 112 E. 19th Street, New York 3. Distributes an extensive series of pamphlets, bearing prices from ten cents to twenty-five cents. Send for price list.

5. The Cooperative League of the U.S.A., 343 S. Dearborn Street, Chicago 4. Catalogue of films, recordings, and literature on the coöperative movement.

6. The National Council of Farmer Cooperatives, 744 Jackson Place, N.W., Washington 6. Free and low-cost pamphlets and leaflets on the farmers' cooperative movement.

7. Tennessee Valley Authority, Knoxville, Tenn. A packet of pamphlets and chart materials for teachers. Free. Also free from U.S. Printing Office, *TVA: Its Work and Accomplishments.*

8. Public Affairs Institute, 312 Pennsylvania Avenue, S.E., Washington. A number of excellent pamphlets on economic and other subjects.

GEOGRAPHY

1. U.S. Weather Bureau, U.S. Department of Commerce, Washington. A wall chart on cloud forms, leaflets on weather forecasting, the function of the Weather Bureau, and sample "Daily Weather Maps."

2. Australian News and Information Bureau, 639 Fifth Avenue, New York 20. Free maps, posters, picture books, and pamphlets.

3. Union of South Africa Government Information Office, 500 Fifth Avenue, New York 18. A large packet of free material.

4. The Belgian Government Information Center, 639 Fifth Avenue, New York 20. A large packet of free materials, dealing with almost all aspects of the government, economy, and culture of Belgium and including large colored travel posters.

5. The Netherlands Information Bureau, 10 Rockefeller Plaza, New York 20. A map of the Low Countries, travel posters, and sample copies of the *Netherlands News Letter.*

6. Government of India Information Services, 2111 Massachusetts Avenue, N.W., Washington 8. A large packet of material covering many aspects of Indian life, and including a large colored map.

7. New Zealand Embassy, 19 Observatory Circle, N.W., Washington 8. (Or write New Zealand Government Tourist Bureau, 606 S. Hill Street, Los Angeles, Calif.) Travel guide, film list, and colored posters.

8. Royal Norwegian Information Services, Rm. 1826, 30 Rockefeller Plaza, New York 20. (Or write Consul General of Norway's Office, 244 California Street, San Francisco, Calif.) Beautifully illustrated travel brochure, *Norway Today,* and *The Youth of Norway Today* (with parallel French and English text), leaflets and booklets on the labor movement, social legislation, school system, government of Norway, and other materials.

9. Scandinavian National Travel Commission, Suite 1515, Rockefeller Plaza, New York 20. Materials on all Scandinavian countries.

10. Swedish Travel Information Bureau, Inc., 630 Fifth Avenue, New York 20. Travel posters and folders, and catalogue of low-cost materials on Sweden.

GOVERNMENT

1. National Civil Service League, 40 E. 40th Street, New York 16. Reprints and low-cost pamphlets on the subject of political reform.
2. National Municipal League, 299 Broadway, New York 17. A large number of materials prepared for teacher and students, e.g., *Model City Charter, Model State Constitution,* and *Model Election Administration System.* Write for sample copies and price list.
3. League of Women Voters of the United States, 1026 Seventeenth Street, N.W., Washington. Miscellaneous materials on civic affairs.

HEALTH AND MENTAL HYGIENE

1. American Medical Association, 535 N. Dearborn Street, Chicago 10. Free reprints on health education topics, also a series of sex education pamphlets at twenty-five cents each.
2. American Social Hygiene Association, 1790 Broadway, New York 19 Pamphlets on venereal disease, sex and health education, and community hygiene; also films. Send for price list.
3. The National Committee for Mental Health, Inc., 1790 Broadway, New York 19. Low-cost pamphlets and free leaflets and reprints; also books and films.
4. Alcohol Education, 1730 Chicago Avenue, Evanston, Ill. A packet of free and low-cost materials for teachers.
5. The Temperance League of America, 131 B Street, S.E., Washington 3. Three free periodical services—*Alcohol Lesson Leaflet, Alcohol Statistics Letters,* and *Temperance League of America Research Service.*
6. Metropolitan Life Insurance Company, New York. *Health Heroes* pamphlet series. Free.

INDUSTRIES

1. The National Dairy Council, Chicago 6. Illustrated pamphlets and booklets on the dairy industry and health education; also booklet entitled *Hello South America.* Free.
2. American Forest Products Industries, 1319 Eighteenth Street, N.W., Washington 6. Teaching units and instruction manual on lumbering industry, colored wall posters, a cartoon book on forest fires, and numerous other free leaflets, pamphlets, and booklets.
3. Bureau of Mines, U.S. Department of the Interior, Washington. Film list and other materials on mining.
4. Department of Information, American Petroleum Institute, 50 W. 50th Street, New York 20. A large number of free illustrated leaflets, pamphlets, and booklets, and a wall chart. Also free monthly newsletter on petroleum industry.
5. National Association of Broadcasters, 1760 N Street, N.W., Washington 6. Numerous free reprints, leaflets, and pamphlets.

6. Association of American Railroads, Transportation Bldg., Washington 6. A variety of free materials, including a Teachers' Kit.
7. National Federation of American Shipping, 1809 G Street, N.W., Washingon. Free leaflets, pamphlets, and booklets on U.S. merchant marine.
8. American Iron and Steel Institute, 350 Fifth Avenue, New York. A number of free teaching materials, including an illustrated book entitled *The Picture Story of Steel*.
9. The National Association of Wool Manufacturers, 386 Fourth Avenue, New York 16. An illustrated brochure entitled *Wool in the United States*, free and available in quantity.
10. Automobile Manufacturers Association, New Center Bldg., Detroit 2. Free educational publications including *Automobile Facts and Figures, Motor Truck Facts*, and *From Horses to Horsepower*. One booklet, *A Car-Traveling People*, treats some of the social effects of the use of the auto.
11. Transportation Association of America, 130 N. Wells Street, Chicago 6. Leaflets and pamphlets including *Quiz on Railroads and Railroading; 450 Questions and Answers*.
12. Educational Division, Institute of Life Insurance, 488 Madison Avenue, New York 22. Pamphlets, posters, comic books, a teachers' unit on life insurance, and list of teaching aids on insurance.

INTERNATIONAL RELATIONS

1. World Peace Foundation, 40 Mt. Vernon St., Boston 8. A free list of publications. The International Friendship League (same address) conducts a pen club for school children. It can supply names and addresses and other necessary information to assist school children in corresponding with children in foreign lands.
2. Department of Public Information, United Nations, New York, N.Y. Free materials including bibliographies, informational leaflets on the United Nations and its divisions, a list of volunteer United Nations educational centers in the U.S., and a list of information services and embassies maintained by foreign nations in the U.S. Also a variety of low-cost pamphlets.
3. Carnegie Endowment for International Peace, 405 W. 117th Street, New York 27. A 40-page bibliography of pamphlet material on the United Nations and international relations, twenty-five cents.
4. Public Affairs Institute, 312 Pennsylvania Avenue, S.E., Washington 3. A group of pamphlets, nominally priced.
5. International Document Service, Columbia University Press, 2960 Broadway, New York 27.

LABOR

1. Department of Research and Education, Congress of Industrial Organizations, 718 Jackson Place, N.W., Washington 6. Pamphlets and poster materials on labor and economics. Most materials carry a nominal charge, but teachers can get sample copies free.

2. American Federation of Labor, A.F. of L. Bldg., Washington 1. Numerous pamphlet materials.
3. National Women's Trade Union League of America, 317 Machinists Bldg., Washington 1. Several pamphlets and leaflets, including monthly periodicals, *Life and Labor Bulletin*.
4. The American Federation of Teachers, 28 E. Jackson Boulevard, Chicago 4. Pamphlets, leaflets, and reports of the national conventions.
5. The National Child Labor Committee, 419 Fourth Avenue, New York 16. A number of useful reprints and pamphlets, most of which are free to teachers.

MINORITY GROUPS

1. American Council on Race Relations, 32 W. Randolph Street, Chicago 1. Several printed and mimeographed leaflets and booklets.
2. Division of Youth Services, The American Jewish Committee, 386 Fourth Avenue, New York 16. Pamphlets, filmstrips, materials for exhibits, recordings, radio scripts, plays, comic books, etc. Also an annotated bibliography, *About 100 Books*.
3. Anti-Defamation League of B'nai B'rith, 212 Fifth Avenue, New York 10. Perhaps a teacher's most prolific source of materials on intergroup education. Most materials free of charge to teachers.
4. Bureau of Intercultural Education, 1697 Broadway, New York 19. Write for a list of publications.
5. National Association for the Advancement of Colored People, 20 W. 40th Street, New York 18. A variety of free and low-cost materials.
6. National Citizens' Council on Civil Rights, Wilkie Memorial Bldg., 20 W. 40th Street, New York 18. Several pamphlets and reprints.
7. National Conference of Christians and Jews, 381 Fourth Avenue, New York 16. A number of free reprints, a bibliography, and some low-priced pamphlets.
8. National Urban League, 1133 Broadway, New York 10. Several free and low-cost materials.
9. Association on American Indian Affairs, Inc., 48 E. 86th Street, New York 28. A number of free reprints.
10. Indian Rights Association, Inc., 1505 Race Street, Philadelphia 2. Free reprints.

MORALS

1. National Legion of Decency, 453 Madison Avenue, New York 22. Reprints, leaflets, and pamphlet materials dealing with alleged indecency on the screen. Includes a copy of the motion picture *Production Code* and a pamphlet entitled *How to Judge the Morality of Motion Pictures*.

RELIGION AND THE CHURCH

1. The National Council of Churches of Christ in the U.S.A., 297 Fourth Ave-

nue, New York 10. A variety of pamphlet materials at low cost (samples free).

SEX

1. The American Institute of Family Relations, 5287 Sunset Boulevard, Los Angeles 27, Calif. Low-cost pamphlets.
2. The Association for Family Living, 28 E. Jackson Boulevard, Chicago 4. Pamphlets on sex education, preparation for marriage, and family life.
3. Science Research Associates, Inc., 57 W. Grand Avenue, Chicago 10. Life Adjustment Booklets on Sex.

THE USE OF COMMUNITY RESOURCES

Traditionally, schools have been cultural islands in the sea of community life. Materials of instruction usually have been confined to symbolic and pictorial materials which could be introduced within classrooms. Only in recent years have we come to recognize the degree to which local communities are important potential sources of content for reflective learning. As with current events and audio-visual aids, use of community resources may add much of value to social-studies education or it may degenerate into busywork. Like other kinds of learning materials, community resources must function as data in the reflective study of problems or they will mean little to students.

Direct contact with a community problem may involve students more deeply than contact with the same problem via printed or pictorial materials. Aspects of community life may thus be used to inaugurate study of a given issue. They may also suggest hypotheses or become sources of needed data.

Suggested community resources are as follows:

1. Trips or excursions
2. Guest speakers who come to classroom
3. Interviews with persons in community who can supply needed data
4. Use of documentary and audio-visual materials from community, which include:
   a. Records of state and municipal agencies
   b. Local newspaper files
   c. Materials published by community groups: labor unions, businessmen, citizens' groups, veterans' organizations, and the like
   d. U.S. Census reports
   e. Diaries and memoirs
   f. Publications of historical societies
   g. Published findings of community surveys

    h. City directories and telephone books
    i. Recordings of local radio programs
    j. Locally produced motion-picture films or pictures
5. Community surveys made by students. Objects of study might include:
    a. Occupations
    b. Industries
    c. Housing
    d. Attitudes and beliefs of community residents
    e. Transportation and communication facilities
    f. Public and private welfare agencies and work
    g. Income distribution
    h. Business practices
    i. Taxation

Students may utilize community resources on three levels: (1) They may observe, study, and think. (2) They may participate actively in community activities and institutions, such as bond drives, union meetings, elections, and part-time work in industry. (3) They may contribute to community welfare by suggesting and pushing some reform. Of course, the more controversial the reform, the more difficult the latter is likely to be. As a general rule, such activities are difficult because they encounter sharp opposition which a public agency such as a school is in no position to buck. Even so, in most communities certain possible reforms may be identified which no one is willing openly to oppose—for example, increasing the percentage of the electorate which votes or contributing to public information about some issue of general concern.

If community resources are to be used with maximum effectiveness, it is necessary for teachers and students to survey and catalogue available resources. In larger communities, this task can be managed successfully only if schools gain coöperation of community leaders and agencies: public libraries, councils of social agencies, planning and coördinating councils, service clubs, chambers of commerce, and departments of city government. The catalogue may take the form of a mimeographed directory, a card file, or a folder of information on each resource. Such records should include the types of information which might be secured from each resource and just how it may be used (the mechanics).

Community resources, like textbooks or classroom motion pictures, are *tools* and not learning ends in themselves. They are aids to conceptualization and are of no educational value unless they help a student reach useful generalizations. Forgetting this fact is one of the common weaknesses of modern education. A field trip or listening to a community speaker tends to degenerate into "something to do." If a community resource is to be of maximum value, it must become a part of intellectual processes which are being nourished through classroom discussion and study. Ordinarily, a community resource is to be used only after problem-solving discussions in which the need for community data has become clearly evident. Contact with the resource will always be followed by further problem-solving discussion—discussion which explores the meaning of information gained. It must also be remembered that, in connection with many problems under study, community resources which are available have nothing to contribute, or less to contribute than printed materials available for classroom use.

Recognizing the potential pedagogical value of school-community contacts, many studies have been made and several movements inaugurated to bring schools into a closer relationship with their communities. One of the most impressive programs of this sort has been conducted since 1949 by the Citizenship Education Project, operating out of Teachers College, Columbia University, and financed by grants from the Carnegie Corporation which at this writing total over one and one-half million dollars. The CEP is primarily a service—not a research—project. It aims to provide leadership and materials for in-service training programs. It has worked with schools over the nation in the local improvement of citizenship education.

The key idea of the CEP is to get students into their communities, to give them practical experiences in a variety of activities which have significance in the learning of good citizenship. In an attempt to prevent community activities from becoming busywork, the CEP has constantly stressed the need for classroom intellectualization of the meaning of whatever activities are undertaken. Chief among the materials developed by the CEP is a list of more than 130 "laboratory practices" (community activities) and a "materials card file" which includes about 1300 reading references. These materials are organized according to themes which correspond to a list of the "Premises of American Liberty" as defined by CEP staff consultants. These and other materials are sold at cost but may not be purchased by teachers directly from Teachers College. To insure that effective use is made of the materials, school persons who are to be responsible for their use are first required to attend a workshop conducted by CEP staff members or other specially trained individuals.[2] A large number of local and regional workshops have been held.

[2] A booklet entitled *Improving Citizenship Education* describes the history of CEP, what it is trying to do, and the materials which have been developed.

Professional Materials for Teachers

The professional magazines designed for teachers of social studies are valuable sources of ideas regarding techniques and of subject matter; they have regular departments which describe and evaluate currently available motion-picture films, filmstrips, slides, picture series, recordings, and pamphlet materials; and they publish book reviews. Professional journals of national circulation include the following:

1. *Journal of Geography,* published monthly by A. J. Nystrom and Company, 3333 Elston Avenue, Chicago 18. This is the official journal of the National Council of Geography Teachers. Annual dues of $4.00 include a subscription to the journal.
2. *Social Education,* published monthly by the National Council for the Social Studies in collaboration with the American Historical Association, executive offices at 1201 Sixteenth Street, N.W., Washington 6. Annual dues of $5.00 include the journal, yearbook, and occasional publications.
3. *Social Studies,* published monthly by McKinley Publishing Company, 809–11 N. Nineteenth Street, Philadelphia 30. Annual subscription, $3.00.

In addition, a teacher of the social studies will find useful a magazine on audio-visual education, such as *Educational Screen,* published at 64 E. Lake Street, Chicago 1, costing $4.00 a year.

Social-studies teachers should be familiar with the technical and semi-technical journals in the various social-science fields. These are valuable sources of data on frontier thinking and research in social science. The following list is a sampling of the more valuable:

1. *American Anthropologist,* published six times annually by the American Anthropological Association, executive offices at the University of Chicago. Annual membership fee of $8.50 includes journal.
2. *American Economic Review,* published quarterly by the American Economic Association, at 450 Ahnaip Street, Menasha, Wis. Annual membership fee of $6.00 includes journal.
3. *American Historical Review,* published quarterly by The Macmillan Company. Official journal of the American Historical Association. Membership dues of $7.50 include journal.
4. *The American Journal of Economics and Sociology,* published quarterly at 50 E. 69th Street, New York 21. Subscription, $3.00 a year. Aims at synthesis of the social sciences. Generally more provocative than some of the more specialized journals.
5. *The American Political Science Review,* published quarterly by the American Political Science Association, 1785 Massachusetts Avenue, N.W., Washington 6. Membership fee of $10.00 a year includes journal.

6. *American Sociological Review,* published twelve times annually by the American Sociological Society, executive offices at New York University, Washington Square, New York 3. Annual membership fee of $10.00 includes journal.

7. *Human Relations,* published quarterly by Tavistock Institute and the Research Center for Group Dynamics. Annual subscription, $6.00. Order from Research Center for Group Dynamics, University of Michigan, Ann Arbor. Devoted to the integration of the social sciences; one of the more significant of present journals.

8. *Journal of the History of Ideas,* published quarterly at the City College of New York, New York 31. Perhaps the most valuable of the professional journals for teachers who are interested in how present-day ideological patterns developed. Subscription, $5.00 a year.

9. *The Journal of Political Economy,* published twelve times annually by the University of Chicago. Subscription, $6.00 for twelve issues. Order from University of Chicago Press. The field of political economy synthesizes economics and political science.

10. *Journal of Social Psychology,* published quarterly by the Journal Press, Provincetown, Mass. Subscription, $14.00 a year. For teachers interested in patterns of value and belief in contemporary culture, and who can afford the relatively high price.

There are a number of books which, in one fashion or another, treat the teaching of the social studies. Most of the general methods textbooks have been cited earlier. Here we shall name only a few which have not been cited elsewhere, or which deserve emphasis because of excellence. Ernest Horn's *Methods of Instruction in the Social Studies* (Scribner, 1937) remains one of the best general texts in this field. Henry Johnson's *Teaching of History* (Macmillan, 1940) comes nearer treating techniques in relation to a philosophy of teaching than most methods textbooks. In the opinion of many, nothing better has been written on the teaching of history. Some students prefer the earlier editions of Johnson's book because of their fuller treatment of historical method. Students interested in the teaching of history should also find valuable Herbert J. Muller's *Uses of the Past* (Oxford University Press, 1952), a brilliantly provocative treatment of ways in which earlier patterns of civilization have current significance.

Although not directly concerned with the teaching of the social studies, several of the writings of James Harvey Robinson are steadily pertinent. Particularly recommended are *The Humanizing of Knowledge* (Doran, 1926), *The New History* (Macmillan, 1912), and *The Mind in the Making* (Harper, 1921). Probably no one else has written with as deep insight as has Robinson about ways in which study of history can assist individuals to test outworn prejudices and adjust their beliefs to the needs of the twentieth century.

Literature for Human Understanding by Hilda Taba and others (American Council on Education, 1948) attempts to show how teachers can use literature to suggest insights about many of the common problems of life, including those which fall in areas of irrationality and controversy (closed areas, as we use the term).

There are few books on the teaching of geography intended for secondary teachers. Of some use is the Nineteenth Yearbook of the National Council for the Social Studies, *Geographic Approaches to Social Education* (1948), and Roderick Peattie's little book *The Teaching of Geography; A Dynamic Approach* (Appleton-Century-Crofts, 1950).

Social-studies teachers may profit from possession of the various bibliographies prepared by the United States Office of Education, Division of Secondary Education, Washington 25, D.C. Since new materials are being prepared continuously, what is available changes. The Office of Education has supplied lists of books for a social-studies teacher's professional library, lists of sources of current teaching materials for social-studies classes, and bibliographies of periodical materials for use in the social studies. In addition, the Office occasionally prepares bibliographies on special subjects of instruction, such as conservation. Teachers may also be interested in *Sources of Materials Dealing with Reading Difficulties,* which is designed to help junior- and senior-high-school teachers who have students with reading difficulties.

All social-studies teachers should be familiar with the best of the books which discuss the nature and role of the social sciences in American civilization. Knowledge of this sort is necessary if a teacher is to understand the potential values as well as problems of the subjects he is teaching. Robert S. Lynd's *Knowledge for What?* (Princeton University Press, 1940) remains the classic statement of what the social sciences are about and fruitful directions in which they might move. Teachers will also find useful Stuart Chase, *The Proper Study of Mankind* (Harper, 1948), and Clyde Kluckhohn, *Mirror for Man* (McGraw-Hill, 1949). Both of these books may also be read with profit by able high-school students. More technical is a group of studies, *The Policy Sciences,* edited by Daniel Lerner and Harold D. Lasswell and published by Stanford University Press. These are Hoover Institute studies, and treat all the social sciences.

DISCUSSION QUESTIONS AND EXERCISES

1. Evaluate a sample group of social-studies textbooks in terms of criteria given on page 371, or any other set of criteria which make sense to you.
2. How might social-studies teachers go about getting better textbooks and other teaching materials written? Could they work through teachers' associations? Professional associations such as the American Historical Association or the American Economic Association?
3. Make a study of paper-bound books in the 25–75 cent price range with a view to locating titles which would be useful as references or collateral reading in social-studies classes. Keep a record on cards of promising titles. What possibility do you see of teachers' developing low-cost classroom libraries from such sources?
4. What sort of collateral reading plan (if any) would you establish for each of the following courses? United States history, world history, civics, geography, economics, sociology, problems of democracy, core.
5. What sort of social-studies program (reading or otherwise) would you establish for (a) students who read with poor comprehension and (b) students who read with unusually high comprehension?
6. Compile your own list of sources of free and low-cost teaching materials. Send for a sampling of such materials, analyze, and rate according to potential usefulness. Perhaps you will want to begin a card file, to be expanded later as you teach. Some suggested categories of materials to write for are (a) materials representing the general outlook of labor, as from the CIO; (b) materials representing the general outlook of business and management, as from the NAM; (c) materials advocating some particular reform or social program, as materials on temperance, film censorship, or race relations.

REFERENCES

All of the general methods textbooks in social studies, as cited at the end of Chapter 17, contain chapters on materials of instruction. See also the yearbooks cited of the National Council for the Social Studies.

Teachers may also find of some usefulness J. W. Baldwin, *The Social Studies Laboratory* (Teachers College, Columbia University, 1929).

Chapter 19

Evaluating the Results of Reflectively Oriented Teaching

WE HAVE proposed that the foremost purpose of social-studies instruction should be to promote reflective analysis of closed areas of American culture. This purpose has been defended by indicating the chief consequences of its achievement. The role of evaluation is to measure the extent to which consequences predicted from a theory of teaching actually follow. If evaluation is to be successful, it is necessary to define these anticipated consequences concretely (i.e., operationally).

Although they represent two sides of the same coin, we may say that consequences of any approach to teaching fall into two broad categories: (1) social consequences and (2) individual consequences. Social consequences refer to what happens to a social group as a result of its educational practices and are reflected in the functioning of institutions of government, economics, and social life. If our schools were to achieve greater success in promoting reflective study of areas of irrational belief and behavior, we may infer that eventually this would be reflected in social phenomena such as more general acceptance of the democratic core values of the culture, greater social cohesion and stability, enhanced ability of society to solve its problems, and closer correspondence between the professed ideals and behavior of society. Social consequences of an approach to teaching are hard to measure reliably. It is always difficult to determine the role of formal education in producing a given social condition—for example, if Americans should vote a fascist or communist into the presidency, what part of this behavior could be attributed to the kind of teaching which they have experienced? In any case, the attempt to evaluate the success or failure of education in terms of social consequences is a long-range procedure. Today's teaching may not begin to show observable social effects for half a century.

Because of such difficulties, evaluation of teaching must, for the most part, confine itself to more or less immediate consequences as reflected in the thinking and behavior of individual students. But if this kind of evaluation is to show results, anticipated outcomes must be defined with great care. We assume that consequences such as the following may be expected from teaching which emphasizes the reflective analysis of social issues and personal beliefs:

1. Learning of meaningful generalizations (concepts, ideas, theory) in relation to critical areas of controversy; and learning of relevant facts as data—i.e., in their evidential relationships to ideas.
2. Achieving generalizations and supporting data which tend (a) to be internally consistent and (b) to reflect all available and obtainable evidence, both experiential and experimental. The foregoing may be referred to as the tests of harmony and adequacy.
3. Acquiring an understanding of the nature and implications of reflective methodology, and forming the habit of a reflective approach when faced with a problem.

For a social-studies teacher pursuing a reflective approach to teaching, evaluation takes the form of trying to determine how well students are achieving beliefs and behaviors in line with predicted consequences such as those given above. Such a teacher will try to determine the degree to which students are conceptualizing (in contrast to memorizing isolated facts), achieving more consistent and better-grounded beliefs, and learning habitually to tackle problems reflectively.

Evaluation also tries to expose reasons for achievement or lack of achievement of goals. This is its *diagnostic* function. Evaluation therefore employs two basic types of tests, achievement and diagnostic. However, many tests perform both functions with considerable adequacy. In the present chapter we shall be concerned with techniques which have been developed for measuring achievement in situations dominated by reflective teaching; in general, the same techniques can serve valuable diagnostic functions.

Unfortunately, techniques of evaluation so far devised for the purposes we have in mind are not entirely adequate. Although we have tests designed to measure conceptualization, consistency in attitudes, and ability to use reflective processes, their accuracy is open to doubt. Some tests make different assumptions from those we have made about the nature of concepts and conceptualization. Many tests designed for use in social-studies classes bear but lightly on critical social issues as exemplified in the closed areas of culture.

The Measurement of Understanding

In Chapter 2 we dealt generally with the nature of concepts and tried to show how they differ from arbitrary associations. From that discussion it should be apparent that a student who is able to say that "an income tax accords with the principle of ability-to-pay" does not necessarily understand an income tax. If we want to know whether he has achieved worthwhile conceptualization, we shall have to ascertain more about his thought processes than merely whether he can state a textbook definition. This does not mean that recall is never involved in the measurement of conceptual learning; but recall alone is not evidence of conceptualization. We do have evidence of conceptualization when a student demonstrates ability to *use* something he has learned in a novel situation: when he generalizes from data, when he makes inferences, and when he applies principles fruitfully in new confronting situations. These same operations may also be taken as evidence of the presence of thinking. In other words, thinking rather than mere recall during a testing situation is the kind of behavior most likely to be taken as evidence of conceptual learning.

We shall discuss later various tests for measuring thinking processes of students. These instruments are intended to measure a certain kind of concept—that is, the extent to which a student has conceptualized the thinking process.

In the present section we want to find out how a teacher may measure the learning of many other concepts. An instrument which measures a student's understanding of events in American history requires a student to think. But it does not measure only how well he thinks. It measures, too, the conceptual results of his thinking. It tells us how well he has thought about the significance of certain events in American history.

As indicated above, techniques for measuring the amount and quality of conceptualization achieved in particular subject areas remain primitive when compared with techniques used to measure mere recall of arbitrary associations. Much of the progress which has been made consists of refining objective or short-answer types of examination so that they will have fewer clues which enable a student to guess or merely to recall a correct answer. Less progress has been made in devising new instruments. We shall first survey some of the refinements made in standard testing items such as true-false, multiple-choice, and matching questions.

IMPROVEMENTS OF TRUE-FALSE EXAMINATIONS

Various studies have shown that true-false examinations have contained specific determiners which provide a test-wise student with a basis for guessing the correct answers. Hawkes, Lindquist, and Mann have summarized these studies as follows: "Four out of five statements containing 'all' were false. Four out of five statements containing 'none' were true. Nine out of ten statements containing 'only' were false. Three out of four statements containing 'generally' were true. Four out of five 'enumeration' statements were true. Two out of three 'reason' or 'because' statements were false. Three out of four statements containing 'always' were false. The longer the statement, the more likely it is to be true." [1]

These results were based on studies of examinations actually constructed and used by teachers. The point is not that teachers should avoid statements including the use of "all" and other terms indicated above but rather that, in a given examination, at least half the statements using a particular "cue term" should be false and half should be true. This kind of reform would not guarantee the measurement of understanding but it would reduce the chances that a student could guess the correct answer.

In addition to this reform a teacher would have to test for interpretive and inferential, as well as purely descriptive, facts. True-false items may indicate various degrees of understanding, including understanding of descriptive facts, interpretive facts, and inferential facts. The following three items represent these three levels of understanding:

T F The United States makes use of protective tariffs. (descriptive) (true)

T F A rise in the cost of living reduces the gold backing of a dollar. (interpretive) (false)

T F During World War II the inflationary spiral was characterized by a series of wage increases. Each wage increase was followed by a price increase. It has been argued that labor unions were largely responsible for wartime inflation. Is it true or false that this argument assumes that there would

[1] Herbert E. Hawkes, E. F. Lindquist, and C. R. Mann, *The Construction and Use of Achievement Examinations,* Houghton Mifflin Company, 1936, p. 72.

have been very little inflation had the government frozen wages? (inferential) (true)

The validity of a true-false item is reduced when it is subject to two conflicting interpretations, the more obvious one being keyed as correct. Inferior students are more likely to respond to the obvious meaning of such an item, and mark it accordingly, whereas students with greater depth of understanding may respond to the hidden meaning. As a result, a student who has thought carefully about the subject may get a lower score on a true-false examination than a mediocre student. If it is depth of understanding which we are trying to measure, then tests of this sort violate the purpose of evaluation. To a large degree, careful phrasing of items will eliminate this problem.[2]

Another common error in the construction of true-false items is the practice of burying a minor false item in a statement the major elements of which are correct. The following, taken from Hawkes, Lindquist, and Mann, are examples of good and poor items:

Bad   T F 1. The Sherman Anti-Trust Act, passed in 1870, declared combinations in restraint of trade illegal.

Better T F 2. The Sherman Anti-Trust Act, which declared combinations in restraint of trade illegal, was passed in 1870.[3]

Experience with items of this kind indicates that students, whether they are inferior or superior in depth of understanding, tend to mark the first example true since the major elements are true. This first example is a "catch" question; such questions, contrary to opinion, are unlikely to measure understanding. One does not measure depth of insight by deliberately distracting a student's attention from the crucial elements in an examination question. As Hawkes, Lindquist, and Mann have explained: "They [statements of this kind] tend to trip up the student whose knowledge is sound but who naturally ignores what should logically be minor or unimportant elements in the statement and who interprets a statement in the straightforward fashion characteristic of ordinary reading. Statements of this kind tend to test for the student's mental alertness or "test-wiseness" rather than for his knowledge or understanding of the subject matter involved." [4]

The same kind of reasoning applies to the construction of true-false items which contain a "reason" or a "because" element. The false element, if there

2 *Ibid.*, p. 55.
3 *Ibid.*, p. 156.
4 *Ibid.*, p. 157.

is one, should be in the "reason." The following is an example of good and bad practice:

Bad   T F 1. Grant's administration was marked by very little political scandal, because his own honesty was an incentive to those holding political offices.

Better T F 2. Grant's administration was marked by serious political scandal because . . . (either correct or incorrect reason may be provided).[5]

The second item is better than the first because the false element, if there is one, is left until the last. If the first part of such an item were false, and the last part true, some students—and not necessarily those with the least knowledge or understanding—would be "caught" by the item.

Even the most careful construction of true-false items leaves much to be desired. Test makers have steadily lost confidence in the technique because of the difficulty of eliminating ambiguity and reducing guessing. Hawkes, Lindquist, and Mann are of the opinion that much of the ambiguity of true-false items is inherent in the technique. It also seems probable that frequent use of this technique encourages students to do "either-or" thinking.

Despite the inadequacies of the true-false technique, Hawkes, Lindquist, and Mann suggest two circumstances in which true-false items may be justified:

> The true-false test appears to be particularly well adapted to those situations in which one wishes to test for the persistence of popular misconceptions or superstitious beliefs, where the suggestion of a correct response will make a multiple-choice item too obvious. It is also well adapted to the situation in which it is impossible or extremely difficult to find enough plausible alternate responses to make a multiple-choice item, or in which there are only two *possible* responses, as in the following item: "In a lead-zinc cell, the lead plate is *positively* charged." Here there are obviously only two possible forms of the statement—"is positively charged" and . . . "is negatively charged"—and the construction of a multiple-choice item would be impossible.[6]

IMPROVEMENT OF MULTIPLE-CHOICE ITEMS

The multiple-choice technique has grown in popularity and there is no doubt that it is generally superior to the true-false scheme when one's purpose is the testing of certain kinds of understanding. It is, however, subject to misuse, and there is nothing in the technique itself which guarantees

[5] *Ibid.*, p. 156.
[6] *Ibid.*, p. 154.

measurement of understanding. If it is used largely for the asking of *who, what, when,* and *where* questions, it is no better than the true-false technique. On the other hand, it may ask *how, why, with what consequences,* or *of what significance* questions, which require students to interpret events, institutions, and personalities. True-false items are generally ill adapted to asking the latter type of question.

Hawkes, Lindquist, and Mann feel that multiple-choice items are better than any other short-answer form for the measuring of inferential reasoning, reasoned understanding, and judgment or discrimination. However, unusual care is required in their construction.

An example of the direct-question multiple-choice item is the following:

Which of the following U.S. industries is characterized by relatively free price competition?

       1. steel
       2. petroleum
       3. non-supported agriculture
       4. farm machinery manufacturing

An example of the incomplete-sentence form is as follows:

Labor in the U.S. is generally more productive than labor in foreign countries because

       1. American workmen have higher IQ's than foreign workmen.
       2. American factories use more capital per worker.
       3. American laborers work more strenuously than foreign laborers.
       4. Americans are more inventive and ingenious than foreigners.

The direct-question form is generally thought superior to the incomplete-sentence form because it is less likely to be ambiguous and to contain clues which give away the answers. (The foregoing example, however, is of a type which could just as well be handled through true-false items.) If the incomplete-sentence form uses an initial statement which is the equivalent of a direct question, then these weaknesses may be eliminated. To be avoided is the type of incomplete-sentence item which is essentially a collection of true-false items, each beginning with the same phrase, as in the following example taken from Hawkes, Lindquist, and Mann: "The Declaration of Independence (1) was drafted by Thomas Jefferson, (2) was signed in 1778, (3) contained an indictment of the English king, (4) was signed by all the members of the First Continental Congress." [7]

As with other types of short-answer questions, multiple-choice items must

[7] *Ibid.,* p. 140.

be phrased so they will not contain irrelevant clues to the correct response. For example, it is advisable to avoid the use of textbook language or pat questions and answers; unfamiliar phrasing is more likely to insure that questions will be answered in terms of underlying meanings rather than simple recall. If stereotyped phrasing is used, it should be used in the incorrect responses. Such practice can mislead rote learners and reveal their lack of understanding. Another type of clue is the tendency of teachers to make the correct response consistently longer or shorter than incorrect responses. When this is done regularly, students soon "catch on."

Inclusion in the correct response of the same word, words, or phrases as are contained in the question or introductory statement forms another irrelevant clue. Because of its phraseology, a student with no understanding of government regulatory agencies should be able to answer the following item.

Railroad companies and other companies carrying on interstate commerce are now regulated by a commission appointed by the President of the United States. This commission is called

...... the Civil Service Commission
...... the National Chamber of Commerce
...... the Interstate Commerce Commission [8]

Of similar nature is the error of making one or all incorrect responses grammatically inconsistent with the introductory question or statement. For example, the verb of an introductory statement might call for a plural noun in any correct choice but the test maker might inadvertently use singular nouns in some of the wrong choices.

One further irrelevant clue is the tendency habitually to place the correct choice in a particular position with reference to other choices. For example, a test maker is likely to think of the correct choice first, and unless he guards against it, he may place a predominant number of correct choices at the beginning of the group of choices. Students soon sense any uniformity in placement of correct answers.

An important rule for the construction of any multiple-choice item is that all choices be made to sound plausible. Any choice which is obviously incorrect is eliminated on sight by students taking the test, and therefore should not be included in the first place. The following item illustrates this error:

[8] *Ibid.*, p. 70.

According to most labor economists, what is the central aim of organized labor in the United States today?

...... 1. to achieve basic social reforms, such as elimination of slums
...... 2. to improve wages and conditions of employment
...... 3. to elect government officials who are sympathetic to labor
...... 4. to destroy the American economic system

To any normally bright student the last choice will appear so far-fetched that his thought will immediately focus on the first three. In effect, the foregoing item is a three-choice one. Occasionally a multiple-choice item is so constructed that all but the correct choice seem implausible. Such an item measures nothing except the ability of a student to read. A teacher must be careful, however, not to make wrong choices so plausible that an item is negatively discriminating, in which case it will be checked incorrectly more often by good than by poor students.

An item may discriminate negatively for several reasons. In the following example, students who selected choice number 1 were on the average superior in achievement to students who selected choice number 4, the correct answer.

What was one of the immediate results of the War of 1812?

(1) the introduction of a period of intense sectionalism
(2) the destruction of the United States Bank
(3) the defeat of the Jeffersonian Party
(4) the final collapse of the Federalist Party [9]

Hawkes, Lindquist, and Mann explain this response as follows:

. . . The pupils selecting the first and incorrect response apparently did so because of positive but insufficient learning. They knew that a period of intense sectionalism did set in before the middle of the century, and therefore chose the first response. Apparently, they did not know, or failed to recall, that a short period of intense nationalism was an immediate result of the Second War with Great Britain, and that this war, therefore, could not be considered as "introducing" an era of sectional strife. Other pupils, with less knowledge in general, were able to select the correct response since they were not attracted to the first response by a certain knowledge that intense sectionalism did develop in the nineteenth century. . . .[10]

Negative discrimination may sometimes result from misinformation on the part of a test maker. The following item illustrates this effect:

In the second half of the fifteenth century the Portuguese were searching for an all-water route to India because:

[9] *Ibid.,* p. 59.
[10] *Ibid.,* p. 60.

(1) They wished to rediscover the route traveled by Marco Polo.
(2) The Turks had closed the old routes.
(3) The Spanish had proved that it was possible to reach the east by sailing westward.
(4) An all-water route would make possible greater profits.[11]

A superior student might reject the answer keyed as correct (number 2) because of acquaintance with recent historical research, which regards the second response as insufficient explanation of Portuguese attempts to round Africa.

A similar result may be obtained when an item deals with a controversial subject for which the authoritative answer is at variance with popular opinion. The following item discriminated negatively because its keyed answer (number 3) conflicts with the popularly held belief—also expressed in some textbooks—that altruistic motives were primarily responsible for our entry into World War I:

America's entry into the World War was largely caused by the
(1) fear that the defeat of the Allies would lead to the overthrow of republican government in France.
(2) violation of Belgian neutrality.
(3) fear of losses by the moneyed interests if the Allies were defeated.
(4) declaration of war by Italy.[12]

The foregoing examples illustrate the fact that a multiple-choice item may fail to measure what it is intended to measure. The fundamental problem is stated by Hawkes, Lindquist, and Mann: "In a general achievement test intended for a given group . . . an item testing for a high level of understanding will function effectively only if there is in the group a significant proportion of students who have actually attained that high level. If the group tested does not include a reasonable number of such students, the item not only will fail to discriminate as it should but may discriminate in the wrong direction." [13]

The kind of invalidity discussed above will be reduced to the extent that a teacher makes successful use of the reflective method. Such a teacher need not construct items pitched at a low level of understanding. He can test for a level of conceptual learning which the commercial publisher of standardized tests cannot, for the latter must take into account the generally low level of understanding which is characteristic of his mass market.

[11] *Ibid.*, p. 63.
[12] *Ibid.*, p. 64.
[13] *Ibid.*, p. 61.

The Improvement of Matching Items

A matching item is fundamentally a variation of a multiple-choice item, just as the latter is a variation of a true-false item. Matching items are not as well adapted to the testing of understanding as are multiple-choice items. The chief use of matching items is testing for descriptive information. However, some measuring of understanding may be achieved when one column consists of principles or laws, and the second column consists of situations which can be explained when they are matched with the appropriate principle or law.

A matching item is more susceptible to technical imperfections than is even a multiple-choice item. One of the most common sources of difficulty is the use of incomplete sentences, which makes it possible for a student to respond correctly by looking for grammatical consistency. The following example illustrates this bad practice:

...... 1. Most normally green-plants lose their color when   a. through their stomata

...... 2. The common characteristic of flowering plants is   b. contracts into a rounded mass

...... 3. Almost all plants which form coal   c. grown in the dark

...... 4. When an expanded amoeba is strongly stimulated it   d. are now extinct

    e. the formation of a reproductive body [14]

Another kind of clue is offered when a matching item lacks homogeneity. When an item possesses heterogeneity, alternate responses lack the plausibility they should have in order for the item to be valid. Since a matching item is really a multiple-choice item which employs the same responses several times, the ideal exercise is one in which each particle in one of the columns is a plausible answer for all particles in the other column. The following are examples of wrong and right practice respectively:

...... The law that forbade slavery north of the Ohio   1. Mason and Dixon line

...... A boundary between two colonies, that later became famous as the division between slave and free states   2. Dred Scott Decision

    3. Spanish Armada

...... The fleet whose defeat in 1588 gave England control of the Atlantic   4. Ordinance of 1787

    5. Missouri Compromise [15]

[14] *Ibid.*, p. 69.
[15] *Ibid.*, p. 172.

. . . . . . A boundary between two colonies, that later became famous as the division between free and slave states	1. Mason and Dixon line
	2. Missouri River
. . . . . Marked the northern boundary of slave territory in the area immediately west of the Alleghenies	3. Ohio River
. . . . . Was intended to be the boundary between free and slave territory in the Louisiana Purchase	4. 49°
	5. 36° 30' [16]

The second item will have more discriminating power than the first because students will be unable to guess the correct responses so easily. Both items have the advantage of listing more particles in one column than in the other, which reduces the chances that students will reach a correct answer by elimination.

Essay Examinations

Some educators believe that essay examinations are superior to any short-answer technique for the testing of understanding. They deplore the tendency of teachers to use short-answer examinations virtually to the exclusion of oral or written examinations which require students to organize and express ideas. Opposition to declining use of essay examinations is probably greatest among college and university faculties. High-school teachers by contrast have made what seems to them a necessary compromise with the exigencies of student overload. A high-school teacher who teaches five classes a day, each with thirty or more students, feels he does not have time to read carefully answers to essay examinations.

This compromise does not appear as a solution when one remembers that the time saved in grading short-answer examinations would be more than canceled if the teacher were to exercise proper care in their construction. It takes hours of reflection to build a good short-answer test, and further hours of labor to keep it up to date. If teachers are to justify the displacement of the essay examination, they will need a more convincing argument than the claim that they are too busy to read essay examinations.

Any proper assessment of essay examinations must take into account the different kinds of questions which may be asked on them. Some common kinds of questions could be asked just as well on a short-answer examination. It would be better to ask such questions via a short-answer examination and thus make possible the asking of more questions and consequently

[16] *Ibid.*, p. 173.

the covering of a larger sample of understandings or facts. A question such as "Describe the chief features of the Treaty of Versailles" calls for a highly factual response which could be covered more effectively in a short-answer test. It is important to remember that one of the criticisms of essay examinations has been the unreliability of scoring. If a factual outcome in learning can be covered in a short-answer test, which is reliably and objectively scored, a teacher gains nothing by asking the same question on an essay examination, which is more difficult to score objectively.

Sims [17] has made a study of the kinds of questions asked on essay examinations, and most of them do not require a thoughtful handling of materials in answering. He found three types of essay questions: (1) simple-recall, (2) short-answer, and (3) discussion. Obviously, the first two do not require a student to manipulate ideas creatively. They ask him *who, what, where,* or *when* questions, or they ask him to *list, state, name,* or *find.* The descriptive material covered in such items could be covered more objectively and more fully in a short-answer examination. Questions which ask students to *discuss, explain, describe, compare,* or *outline* are more likely to reveal the extent and quality of conceptualization, but even this would depend on how a teacher and his students interpreted the questions. For example, for some persons the term *explain* can have a meaning which amounts to recall rather than reflection. When asked to explain an event some students will simply list three causes from the textbook. Others will carry on a discussion comparable to a scientist's attempt to explain in laboratory terms. It is undoubtedly more difficult to control a student's mode of response in an essay than in a short-answer examination.

Apparently the worth of an essay examination depends very much on what kinds of questions are asked and how a student interprets them. Also important is the manner in which students are accustomed to approach examinations. Although an essay question may be designed to evoke a reflective response, few students may respond in this way because of contrary habits. If one is accustomed to parroting a textbook, or to displays of empty rhetoric, an essay question may reveal little more about his depth of understanding than will a short-answer question. Also, students who are unable to express themselves on paper may fail to reveal the actual conceptualization which they have achieved. Limitations of time may handicap slow writers and prevent their answers from reflecting fully the quality of their thought.

[17] Verner Martin Sims, "Essay Examination Questions Classified on the Basis of Objectivity," *School and Society,* January 16, 1932, pp. 100–102.

Evaluating the Results of Reflectively Oriented Teaching

A recommended reform has been the "open book" examination, which may even be taken outside the classroom and at a more leisurely pace. It is possible to ask questions which cannot be answered straight from a book but only after a student has reflected upon ideas in a book. An even more promising procedure may be the assignment of a short research paper. This paper can be written as leisurely and reflectively as an "open book" examination. Either short research papers or "open book" examinations are probably preferable to traditional essay examinations.

If one views the short research paper as a superior form of essay examination, there is no issue between short-answer and essay examinations. Both can be used for reflective and conceptual ends if the intent and skill of a teacher permit. The only advantage that a short-answer examination would have would be in the objectivity of its scoring and the greater scope of its coverage. Useful techniques have been developed for objectifying the scoring of essay examinations,[18] and some of these could just as well be applied to the grading of a short research paper. What a short-answer examination contributes in scope of coverage a short research paper can contribute in depth of treatment. These techniques can be used effectively in combination for measurement of conceptual understanding.

The Measurement of Attitudes

For practical purposes of measurement there is no difference between an attitude and a value. In Chapter 2 we defined an attitude as a persistent feeling tone with reference to some object or process in the environment. We defined a value as an attitude which has been intellectualized or clarified as a result of reflective scrutiny. When a person thinks about an attitude, so that he is fully aware of it and of its implications, we say that he has acquired a value. However, a statement of preference (value judgment) may reflect either an attitude or a value.

We assume that it is possible to discover attitudes (or values) of a student by requiring him to respond to a series of preference statements (i.e., value judgments). For example, suppose a student is confronted with the statement "The United States made a big mistake when it joined the United Nations" and says he agrees. Assuming he understands the thought expressed in the statement, and that his answer is sincere, we may infer that he has a negative attitude toward membership in the United Nations.

[18] See Verner Martin Sims, "The Objectivity, Reliability, and Validity of an Essay Examination Graded by Rating," *Journal of Educational Research*, October, 1931, pp. 216–223. Also see Hawkes, Lindquist, and Mann, *op. cit.*, pp. 207–209.

To date, measurement of attitudes has commonly taken the form of asking students to respond to series of statements of the general type indicated above. Although several weaknesses of this procedure have been identified, probably the greatest obstacle to overcome is lack of sincerity on the part of students. Because teaching is so often authoritarian (even when teachers do not intend it to be), students come to feel it expedient to respond to attitude tests in what they see as "respectable" ways. When confronted with a value judgment, they are likely first to decide what response would be most pleasing to the teacher or other adults who might learn of the test results. Attitudes thus remain concealed.

To acquaint readers more fully with what has been done in the field of attitude testing, and to indicate more specifically what some of the problems are, we shall review some of the attitude scales which have been developed in the United States.

SCALE OF BELIEFS 4.21 AND 4.31

This instrument was developed by the Evaluation Staff of the Eight Year Study. It is intended to gather evidence on the liberalism, conservatism, uncertainty, and consistency of student attitudes in areas such as democracy, economic relations, labor and unemployment, race, nationalism, and militarism. There are a number of items for each area on each of the two forms, 4.21 and 4.31. The six areas mentioned above were considered among the most controversial at the time the test was developed. No doubt a similar instrument constructed now would include areas not covered in the original scale.

In this test a liberal point of view is revealed when students subscribe to statements which endorse "freedom of speech; democratic processes in government; responsibility of the government for promoting the welfare of all groups in society with respect to health, security for old age, and the protection of consumers; and reinterpretation of the Constitution and other basic laws in keeping with present-day social and economic demands." [19] A conservative cluster of attitudes is revealed when students "approve restrictions on freedom of speech," [20] and when they say it is all right "to limit the responsibilities of government for social welfare, and to favor a strict inter-

[19] For a fuller treatment of this problem as well as for a more complete discussion of Scale of Beliefs 4.21 and 4.31, see Eugene Smith and Ralph Tyler, *Appraising and Recording Student Progress,* Harper & Brothers, 1942, p. 217.
[20] *Ibid.*

410

pretation of the Constitution." [21] These are the definitions of liberalism and conservatism for the first part of the test, which deals with democracy and its interpretations. There are similar definitions of liberalism and conservatism for each of the other five parts of the test.

Each form of the test, 4.21 and 4.31, has 100 statements. Students are asked to indicate whether they agree with, disagree with, or are uncertain about each statement. Agreement with certain items along with disagreement with certain other items indicates liberal attitudes. Likewise, there are items with which agreement or disagreement indicates conservatism.

The uncertain responses, although easy to count, are difficult to interpret. A student may mark a particular statement "uncertain" for one or more of three reasons: He may not understand the statement; he may understand it but be uncertain of his attitude toward it; or he may be afraid to reveal his position to the teacher.

Consistency is measured by comparing the responses on 4.21 with the responses on 4.31. For example, statement 97 on 4.21 reads "It is all right for Negroes to be paid lower wages than whites for similar kinds of work" while statement 192 on 4.31 reads "The same wages should be paid to Negroes as to whites for work which requires the same ability and training." If a student agrees with both statements, or disagrees with both, or agrees or disagrees with either statement when he is uncertain about the other one, such response is taken as evidence of inconsistency. A consistency score is easier to interpret than an inconsistency score because of the difficulties posed by the uncertainty response. Obviously, agreement-uncertainty as a paired response is not the same degree and perhaps not the same kind of inconsistency as agreement-agreement.

Consistency is counted as a percentage of the total items on either form. A consistency score can be derived for each of the six areas as well as for the whole scale. The least consistent areas are the ones within which students need the most clarification. However, any growth toward greater consistency must be interpreted with considerable care. It is customary to administer the two forms at the beginning and end of a school year (at the beginning and end of a unit of work is not good practice since the span of time covered by a unit is usually too short for significant change in attitudes). A higher consistency score cannot always be taken as evidence that reflective clarification of attitudes has occurred. The internal structure of the test is such that a student who becomes more liberal or more conserva-

[21] *Ibid.*

tive will also become more consistent. If a student has been thoroughly indoctrinated by a conservative or a liberal teacher, his responses to the test at the end of the school year may be more certain and more consistent even though he has not reflected very much on his attitudes.

It has been many years since the Scale of Beliefs was constructed, and rather than use the original form teachers should build new forms based upon the original structure and capable of sampling attitudes in closed areas. In constructing any scale of this kind certain precautions are necessary. The definition of democracy implied by the scale should be explicitly recognized by the teacher when he formulates items. In the attempt to measure consistency a teacher should not make contradictions too apparent. The statements "Negroes should not be paid as much as whites" and "Negroes should be paid as much as whites" present a contradiction which is too easy because it is too sharp. The example given earlier is more illustrative of correct phrasing and a desirable degree of contradiction.

Thurstone Scales for the Measurement of Social Attitudes [22]

These scales consist of weighted items and therefore are intended to measure the depth of an attitude. Each scale has a list of statements dealing with the same general topic. There are usually twenty or more statements, each with a point value assigned to it by a jury of adults. The higher the point value the more unfavorable the attitude expressed by those who check the statement. The scale for measuring the attitude toward war is typical of Thurstone's technique. The following is an excerpt from this scale:

(2.7) 1. The benefits of war outweigh its attendant evils.
(7.8) 6. The misery and suffering of war are not worth its benefits.
(9.4) 16. It is difficult to imagine any situation in which we should be justified in sanctioning or participating in another war.
(10.6) 20. He who refuses to fight is a true hero.
(10.7) 22. It is the moral duty of the individual to refuse to participate in any way in any war, no matter what the cause. [23]

The numbers in parentheses indicate the point value assigned the statements by the jury. The student checks the statements with which he agrees, and his score is the median point value for all the statements he checks. The scale for measuring a student's attitude toward war is indirectly a

[22] L. L. Thurstone and E. J. Chase, *The Measurement of Attitudes,* University of Chicago Press, 1929.
[23] L. L. Thurstone, *Attitude Scales, Attitude Toward War,* Form A, University of Chicago.

measure of his pacifism. The higher his score the more pacifistic he is. The directions tell students that there is no right answer to the test.

In addition to this scale Thurstone also has scales on God, Church, Negro, Treatment of Criminals, Constitution, Birth Control, Chinese, Germans, Sunday Observance, Law, Censorship, Evolution, and Capital Punishment, all constructed in roughly the same way.[24]

REMMERS ATTITUDE SCALES

These scales, like the ones developed by Thurstone, consist of weighted items. Both Remmers and Thurstone make use of the technique of equal-appearing intervals. The construction of a scale based upon equal-appearing intervals follows steps analogous to certain practices in psycho-physics. First, a large number of statements of opinion concerning some attitude-object are formulated. Second, these statements are given to a jury, or group of judges, who are asked to rate each statement on an eleven-point scale. The neutral statements are sorted into the mid-point of the scale. The very favorable statements are placed at one end of the scale at varying distances from the mid-point of neutrality. The unfavorable statements are distributed from the center to the other end of the scale. If there are 100 judges, there is likely to be some disagreement over the weighting of each statement. The average weight assigned to each statement is taken as the correct weight. Some of the statements may be given radically different weightings, and these are discarded. The third step is the arrangement of acceptable statements on the attitude scale. Remmers arranges his statements according to decreasing favorableness, i.e., the first statement is the most favorable one. Thurstone prefers a random arrangement of statements.[25] Research with the two scales indicates no particular advantage for either arrangement.

The Remmers scales are more general than those by Thurstone and are advertised as Master Attitude Scales. They purport to measure attitudes toward attitude-objects such as Any Disciplinary Procedure, Any Proposed Social Action, Any Teacher, or Any Racial or National Group. Students are

---

[24] For a good discussion of these scales, the difficulties involved in their construction, and criticisms of their validity see Marie Jahoda, Morton Deutsch, and Stewart W. Cook, *Research Methods in Social Relations, Part I: Basic Processes,* Dryden Press, 1951, pp. 190–194.

[25] For a much fuller discussion of how to construct an attitude scale based upon equal-appearing intervals see H. H. Remmers and N. L. Gage, *Educational Measurement and Evaluation,* Harper & Brothers, 1943, pp. 390–392. For a fairly complete list of both Remmers and Thurstone scales see the same work, pp. 392–393.

told to write in the name of the teacher, the social action, or the racial group toward which they have been asked to respond.

The following excerpt from *A Scale for Measuring Attitudes Toward Any Proposed Social Action, Form A*,[26] illustrates the nature of the Remmers approach:

(10.9)   1. Is the best thing that can ever come into existence.
 (9.3)   7. Is greatly needed.
 (8.5) 15. Is sure to be effective.
 (6.1) 30. Cannot do any serious harm.
 (3.8) 40. Dodges the real issue.
 (2.8) 44. Is based upon an unsound principle.
 (1.2) 50. Is perfectly absurd.

THE LIKERT SCALE

This scale is also intended to measure the intensity of an attitude. Students are presented with a list of statements and indicate the extent to which they agree or disagree with each one. They are usually instructed to mark each statement as follows: agree strongly, agree somewhat, uncertain, disagree somewhat, or disagree strongly. The Likert Scale is undergoing something of a boom in popularity at present. It is easier to construct than the Thurstone or Remmers scales as it does not require the cumbersome use of a jury. Sometimes an evaluator will use some variation of the Likert Scale, with a six-point rather than a five-point rating scale. The following excerpt from the F Scale used in a study of the authoritarian personality is illustrative of one variation:

Mark each statement in the left margin according to how much you agree or disagree with it. *Please mark every one.* Write in $+1$, $+2$, $+3$, or -1, -2, -3 depending on how you feel in each case.

1. I AGREE A LITTLE	1. I DISAGREE A LITTLE
2. I AGREE PRETTY MUCH	2. I DISAGREE PRETTY MUCH
3. I AGREE VERY MUCH	3. I DISAGREE VERY MUCH

 1. Human nature being what it is, there will always be war and conflict.
 4. It is up to the government to make sure that everyone has a secure job and a good standard of living.
11. When a person has a problem or worry, it is best for him not to think about it, but to keep busy with more cheerful things.

[26] H. H. Remmers, Division of Educational Reference, Purdue University, Lafayette, Indiana.

16. Men like Henry Ford, or J. P. Morgan, who overcame all competition on the road to success, are models for all young people to admire and imitate.[27]

Unlike Remmers and Thurstone, Likert has not prepared attitude scales for commercial distribution. His chief contribution has been the idea of a five- or six-point rating scale for each statement in an attitude test. Ideally, the rating scale is repeated after each statement instead of being presented once at the beginning of the test as we gave it above. In common with the Remmers and Thurstone scales, the Likert Scale attempts to measure intensity without trying to measure consistency. At present there is no attitude scale which measures both intensity and consistency.

VALUE ANALYSIS

Attitude scales are sometimes criticized for the rigidity of their structure. Some authorities believe that students are more likely to reveal their attitudes in an unstructured situation. Actually, no testing situation is completely unstructured; what these authorities probably want is a situation which is structured so that individuals are relatively free to express attitudes in their own manner. Value analysis as it has been developed by Louis E. Raths and Newton Hodgson may be an answer to the need for a more valid measure of attitudes.

This technique involves placing students in some kind of situation to which they are asked to react by writing answers to certain questions. They may be placed in the situation by teacher assignment, or they may help determine the situation through teacher-pupil planning. Possible situations would be visiting a public housing project, observing a legislative committee at work, taking part in a cleanup campaign, trying to get signatures on a petition. The situations selected are supposed to be ones likely to elicit attitude expressions from students. Students are asked to write answers to questions such as the following:

1. What did you like or approve in the situation?
2. What did you dislike or disapprove in the situation?
3. What recommendations do you have for improving the situation?

A teacher may vary the questions, but he always tries to get evidence on students' feelings of approval and disapproval and recommendations for change. This method may be criticized on the ground that it does not yield

[27] T. W. Adorno, E. Frenkel-Brunswik, D. J. Levinson, and R. N. Sanford, *The Authoritarian Personality*, Harper & Brothers, 1950.

a neat quantitative score susceptible to several kinds of pretty statistical juggling. However, it is not entirely free from quantitative features. It is possible, for example, to count the number of things which the writer of a certain response is against as compared to the number of things toward which he is favorable. It is even possible to combine certain responses to form categories. Certain responses when placed together may be taken as evidence of a person's attitude toward government, human nature, and a variety of other objects or processes.

A few observers of this technique have argued that it has the virtue of taking its categories from the free responses of students rather than forcing students to respond to certain predetermined categories, as they are obliged to do on attitude scales. However, any teacher can take the free responses of a student and force them into certain categories which are just as predetermined as the ones implicit in the attitude scale. But the fact that the "forcing" is done after the student has responded rather than before can mean that the student has felt more free to express his attitudes and therefore that the teacher has more valid data in his predetermined categories.

Almost any student paper or report can be value-analyzed provided it deals with some problem or issue about which its writer has some strong feeling and genuine interest. The technique may also be used with movies or recordings. After viewing a movie, a group may be asked to write answers to questions like the following:

1. Some incidents in the movie are more important than others. Which incidents or scenes seem to you to be the most important? (Do not name more than *three*.)
2. Why do you think these incidents are important? What makes them significant as far as you are concerned?
3. How could each situation be improved so as to contribute to the growth of everyone in the situation?

The Measurement of Thinking

As we have seen, there is a difference between thinking about the subject matter of the social sciences and thinking about thinking. It is necessary that students think about thinking if they are to acquire more effective habits of thinking. Those who examine reflectively beliefs in closed areas will not necessarily acquire thereby a complete and rounded conception of the thinking process. Whether they do or not will depend on the extent to which teachers promote examination of the process by which they reach conclusions. A teacher who promotes reflection about reflection will want to know whether his students are improving the quality of their thinking. In other words, he will want to use tests which measure achievement in reflective thinking.

The following tests require a student to apply what he knows about thinking just as the tests described earlier require him to make some application of his social-science knowledge. However, it is impossible to divorce tests of conceptual achievement and tests of how well reflection itself is understood. Most of the tests described in the present section, for example, not only test a student's understanding of thinking but also measure his understanding of certain social-science concepts.

Prior to the Eight Year Study not much was known about the evaluation of thinking. The Evaluation Staff was interested in getting evidence on achievement of the more intangible outcomes of education. Improved thinking was one of these outcomes. The staff took the position that they could not measure progress toward any educational objective unless that objective was given an operational definition. That is, they believed it would clarify what they were trying to evaluate if they could identify the overt behavior which could be taken as evidence for the presence or absence of thinking.

In their judgment a person who thinks conducts operations such as interpreting data, using principles of logic, identifying assumptions in an argument, recognizing evidence and seeing its relationship to a hypothesis, making hypotheses and inferences, and applying principles to new situations. They devised instruments for measuring many of these behaviors. An understanding of these instruments not only is basic to an understanding of the Eight Year Study but helps to clarify the nature of thinking; it also helps the more creative teachers to devise better means of getting evidence on these and other aspects of thinking.

INTERPRETATION OF DATA 2.51 AND 2.52

This instrument was developed by the Evaluation Staff of the Eight Year Study for the measurement of a student's ability to interpret data. Intended for use with high-school students in grades 9 through 12, it has also been used with freshmen in college, and some high-school teachers have developed forms for use with junior-high students. At present the high-school forms, 2.51 and 2.52, can be purchased from the Cooperative Testing Service of New York.

Each form of the test consists of ten exercises. Each exercise presents a set of data in the form of a table, a graph, a chart, or a prose description and accompanied by fifteen statements, each of which represents a possible interpretation of the data. Students are directed to mark each statement according to whether it is true, probably true, false, probably false, or unsupported by sufficient data, limiting their judgment of each statement to the data given them in the test item—that is, not intruding any other data which may be known to them. In other words, this test tries to discover whether a student can determine the limits of the data supplied to him.

A student who takes an interpretation of data test receives four different scores—a general accuracy score, an overcaution score, a going-beyond-the-data score, and a crude error score. The general accuracy score indicates the extent to which the responses of a student agree with the test key. The other scores are diagnostic, as they indicate the nature of errors made. The most frequent error of students who took this test in the Eight Year Study was a tendency to go beyond the data. Most students found it tempting to infer a meaning which was not justified by the data they were asked to interpret.

High-school students were at their best when they had to distinguish between true and false interpretations. They were weakest in distinguishing between the true and the probably true, the false and the probably false. One may infer that high-school students are not learning adequately to distinguish different degrees of probability. Their tendency to think in terms of either-or categories presents serious difficulties in understanding today's world.[28]

The following is an example of an exercise from an interpretation of data test constructed by one of the authors for use in a high-school social-studies class. The example is keyed and each item is followed in parentheses by an explanation of the principle being tested by the item:

Study the given facts carefully. Read each statement carefully. In answering each statement, *stick to the given facts*. Refer to the facts each time and place a number in front of the statement:

Mark it 1 if the facts given make the statement true.

Mark it 2 if the facts given make it probably true.

Mark it 3 if the facts given do not make it possible to judge the statement one way or another.

Mark it 4 if the facts given make it probably false.

Mark it 5 if the facts given make the statement false.

[28] Smith and Tyler, *op. cit.*, pp. 38–76.

Evaluating the Results of Reflectively Oriented Teaching

Statement of Facts: The following table represents the relationship between yearly income of certain families and the medical attention they receive.

Family Income	Percent of Family Members Who Received No Medical Attention During the Year
$1,200 to $3,000	40%
$3,000 to $5,000	33%
$5,000 to $10,000	24%

Interpretations:

(3) 1. Many family members do not receive medical care because they cannot afford it. (Assuming Cause)

(3) 2. The members of wealthy families require less medical care than the members of other families because they are well-fed and well-housed. (Assuming Cause)

(2) 3. At least 70 percent of the members of families with incomes of $11,000 a year receive some medical care during the year. (Extrapolation)

(2) 4. The members of families with incomes of $1,500 a year receive less medical care than members of families with annual incomes of $3,500. (Interpolation)

(5) 5. The lower the family income, the greater is the percent of family members who receive medical care. (Recognition of a Trend)

(3) 6. If those families with incomes under $3,000 a year would double their income, fewer of their family members would go without medical care. (Assigning Effect)

(2) 7. A smaller percent of members of families with incomes of $10,000 to $15,000 a year received no medical attention than did members of families receiving $1,200 to $3,000 a year. (Extrapolation)

(3) 8. The government should give free medical care to families with low incomes in order to improve the health of the nation. (Value Judgment)

(3) 9. John's father makes $1,500 a year while Jim's father makes $3,000 a year. Jim receives medical attention more often than John. (Sampling)

(4) 10. Families with incomes of $8,000 a year had a greater percentage of family members who went without medical care than did the members of families with incomes of $4,000 a year. (Interpolation.) [29]

[29] The Ohio Thinking Check-Up, issued by Bureau of Educational Research, The Ohio State University, 1945. Constructed by Lawrence E. Metcalf and Louis E. Raths.

Sometimes a teacher who uses an exercise like the one above is tempted to review the test, item by item, with his students. If he succumbs to this temptation, he may teach his students how to take the test instead of how to interpret data. In teaching students how to take a test a teacher destroys the future usefulness of the test and tests similar to it. An alternative to going over a test is to teach students principles of interpretation which they have a chance to apply when they take almost any kind of thinking test.

Application of Some Principles of Logical Reasoning Test, Form 5.12

This test, developed by the Evaluation Staff of the Eight Year Study, tests a student's ability to apply certain principles of logic and to take note of relationships between assumptions and conclusions. It does not examine students on all principles of logic but is restricted to the following five:

1. Do students recognize the necessity for defining precisely certain key words and phrases?

2. Do students understand the conditions necessary to the soundness of an indirect argument?

3. Do students understand the invalidity of name calling?

4. Do students see the relationship between premises and conclusions when they are asked to assess an example of if-then reasoning?

5. Do students understand the necessity of determining whether a sample is representative of a larger population about which they are trying to reach a conclusion?

The student is given a series of exercises toward which he is asked to react logically. In the total test he deals with ten different exercises, two for each of the five principles of logic. Each exercise has three possible conclusions and twelve possible reasons. The reasons consist of: (1) general or abtract statements of the logical principle involved, (2) specific statements of the logical principle involved, and (3) general or specific statements of logical principles which are irrelevant to the conclusion selected. A general accuracy score is obtained by computing twice the number of correct responses (both conclusions and reasons) minus the total number of wrong responses (both conclusions and reasons).[30]

Form 5.12 is no longer available for distribution, but in 1950 the Educational Testing Service published a Logical Reasoning Test which follows the pattern of the original instrument. The following is an example taken from the Logical Reasoning Test, Form A, Test Number 282-42-1:

[30] This test is discussed by Smith and Tyler, *op. cit.*, pp. 111–126.

Evaluating the Results of Reflectively Oriented Teaching

Problem III

John L. Lewis, head of the United Mine Workers, once described the results of a conference on unemployment which a union delegation had with Frances Perkins, who was then Secretary of Labor. Secretary Perkins had assured the delegation that the unemployment situation was less critical than they had believed and that the government was taking steps to solve the problem.

"After three hours," Lewis related, "the delegation went away woozy in the head, just like the good woman who is Secretary of Labor." Lewis remarked that he believed Miss Perkins would "make a good housekeeper" but he added, "I don't think she knows any more about the economic problems of this country than a Hottentot does about the moral law."

Directions:

Examine the conclusions that follow. Accept as true the charges made by Mr. Lewis, and choose the conclusion which you believe is justified.

Conclusions:

X The charges made by Mr. Lewis proved that the statements made by Secretary Perkins to the union delegation were wrong.

Y The charges made by Mr. Lewis did *not* prove that the statements made by Secretary Perkins to the union delegation were wrong.

Z More information is needed to decide whether or not the charges made by Mr. Lewis proved that the statements made by Secretary Perkins to the union delegation were wrong.

Mark in Column:

A: Statements which explain why your conclusion is logical.
B: Statements which do not explain why your conclusion is logical.
C: Statements about which you are unable to decide.

Statements:

1. Since we assume that the Secretary of Labor was really as incompetent as Mr. Lewis implied, we must conclude that her statements to the union delegation were wrong.
2. When Secretary Perkins assured the union delegation that the unemployment situation was less critical than they believed, she was obviously wrong.
3. Before we can decide whether or not Mr. Lewis proved his point, we must know what he meant by such terms as "woozy," "Hottentot," and "moral law."
4. To make a sound argument, Mr. Lewis would have to consider Miss Perkins' knowledge of all the other possibilities including social problems.
5. Even if Miss Perkins were shown to be ignorant of economics, this would not prove that the particular statements which she made to the union delegation were wrong.
6. An attack upon certain aspects of a person or institution, even though justified, is not enough to prove the lack of all merit in that person or institution.

7. The soundness of an indirect argument depends upon whether all the possibilities have been considered.
8. A changed definition may lead to a changed conclusion even though the argument from each definition is logical.
9. In order to prove a point, one must direct his argument to the point and not attempt to discredit those who think otherwise.
10. The statements quoted give only a sample from Mr. Lewis' remarks, and so no logical conclusion can be drawn.
11. A sample does not necessarily represent all of the data which may apply to a situation.
12. Whether or not Mr. Lewis' accusations are true, they do not apply directly to the issue of whether the statements made by Miss Perkins to the union delegation were right or wrong.[31]

In the above example the correct conclusion is Y, and the correct reasons are 5, 6, 9, and 12. This exercise tests a student's ability to resist name calling as a method by which to reach a conclusion. The list of reasons in the exercise includes all five of the principles of logic used in the test so that a student has an opportunity to distinguish among them.

NATURE OF PROOF, 5.21 AND 5.22

Understanding the nature of a proof has been an educational objective in the teaching of geometry for a great many years. However, restricting the teaching of the nature of proof to geometry classes appears unreasonable to teachers who recognize that their students are exposed every day to a variety of arguments, all of which try to prove something to students and hence induce them to act in certain ways. Newspaper editorials, public speeches, advertisements, books, magazines, movies, radio and television programs—all make such appeals. These appeals are not equally sound in their intellectual content. No doubt there are many persons "taken in" every day by unsound arguments because they lack ability to analyze the nature of the proof which is offered them. This ability can be acquired from a study of various examples of proof.

Schools which participated in the Eight Year Study tried to develop in their students improved ability to analyze arguments and proofs. The Evaluation Staff developed some instruments for evaluating understanding of proofs. Prominent among them were Nature of Proof, 5.21 and 5.22.

[31] Logical Reasoning Test, Form A, *Cooperative Test Division, Educational Testing Service,* Princeton, New Jersey, and Los Angeles, California, Copyright 1950, pp. 6–8. This test is no longer available for distribution, but rights to reproduce it may be obtained for some purposes. It is very desirable that teachers study this test in order to learn how to build their own tests of logical thinking.

Evaluating the Results of Reflectively Oriented Teaching

In Nature of Proof, 5.21, students are presented with a series of exercises each of which includes a conclusion which they are asked to accept. This statement of problem and conclusion is followed by a list of fourteen statements. In Part I of the exercise students are directed to mark each statement as follows:

1. With an *A* those statements which either support or contradict the conclusion. These are the relevant statements.
2. With a *B* those statements under *A* which support the conclusion.
3. With a *C* those statements under *B* which students do not consider satisfactorily established by whatever general knowledge they have but which must be included in their argument if the conclusion is to be acceptable.

In Part II students are directed to indicate whether they are inclined to accept the conclusion, to reject it, or to be uncertain. They also indicate on their answer sheet which of the statements marked with a *C* in Part I might cause them to reconsider their decision if more information were made known to them. These statements are marked with a *D*. Statements marked with a *D* represent what a student believes to be the crucial assumptions, the truth of which he is willing to question.

The following excerpt is from Nature of Proof, 5.21:

Problem IX

In a radio broadcast the following story was told: "The people in a little mining town in Pennsylvania get all their water without purification from a clear, swift-running mountain stream. In a cabin on the bank of the stream about half a mile above the town a worker was very sick with typhoid fever during the first part of December. During his illness his waste materials were thrown on the snow. About the middle of March the snow melted rapidly and ran into the stream. Approximately two weeks later typhoid fever struck the town. Many of the people became sick and 114 died." The speaker then said that this story showed how the *sickness of this man caused widespread illness, and the death of over one hundred people.*

Statements:

ABCD 1. Typhoid fever organisms can survive for at least three months at temperatures near the freezing point.

2. Good doctors should be available when an epidemic hits a small town.

ABCD 3. Typhoid fever germs are active after being carried for about half a mile in clear, swift-running water.

A 4. There may have been other sources of contamination by waste materials containing typhoid fever germs along the stream or at some other point in the water supply of the town.

AB   5. The waste materials of a person who has a severe case of typhoid fever contain active typhoid organisms.

AB   6. Typhoid fever is contracted by taking typhoid organisms into the body by way of the mouth.

        7. Only a few people in this town had developed an immunity to typhoid fever.

A   8. Typhoid organisms are usually killed if subjected to temperatures near the freezing point for a period of several months.

        9. Sickness and death usually result in a great economic loss to a small town.

ABCD 10. The only typhoid organisms with which the people in the town came in contact were in the water supply.

       11. Vaccination should be compulsory in communities which have no means of purifying their water.

ABCD 12. The worker's waste materials were the only source of contamination along the stream.

A   13. There may have been other sources of typhoid fever germs in the town such as milk or food contaminated by some other person.

AB   14. The symptoms of typhoid fever usually appear about two weeks after contact with typhoid germs.[32]

Statements 2, 7, 9, and 11 are irrelevant to the conclusion. If a student marks any of these with an *A*, he has failed to relate assumptions to a conclusion. A general accuracy score on this test does not mean very much. Separate scores which get at separate behaviors have more meaning. One such score indicates the extent to which students recognize the relevant aspects of an argument. The above form of the Nature of Proof Test is so constructed that the total performance depends on how well a student does on the early parts. A later revision of this test, Form 5.22, takes care of this difficulty so that each part of the test can be scored separately.[33]

The data yielded by nature-of-proof tests supply answers to questions such as the following:

1. To what extent does a student recognize relevant phases of an argument and distinguish between considerations which support and ones which contradict a stated hypothesis or conclusion?

2. To what extent does a student challenge the assumptions underlying an argument and distinguish between assumptions which, from the point of view of a committee of adults, should and should not be challenged?

3. How do the conclusions reached by a student compare with those reached by a committee who made the test?

[32] Smith and Tyler, *op. cit.*, pp. 133–134.
[33] For a full discussion of nature-of-proof tests see *ibid.*, pp. 126–156.

4. To what extent does a student recognize the relevance of proposals for the further study of a problem?

5. To what extent does a student judge the relevant activities as practicable, i.e., distinguish between activities which, from the point of view of a committee of adults, are and are not practicable? [34]

The fourth and fifth questions above are not treated in Form 5.21. Teachers who are interested in these two questions should consult and study a sample exercise from Form 5.22.[35]

Both 5.21 and 5.22 emphasize the subject matter of the physical sciences, but many of the exercises also recognize social aspects. Teachers of the social studies may be more directly interested in a special form of the nature-of-proof tests called Analysis of Controversial Writing (Form 5.31).[36] This test is designed to show whether students can make logical analyses of propaganda materials. The behaviors on which the test focuses are:

a. Recognition of the purposes of authors of propaganda—that is, ability to make more discriminating judgments as to the points of view which it is intended a consumer should accept or reject. (In a broad sense, this refers to the generally accepted concept of "reading comprehension.")
b. Identification of the forms of argument used in selected statements of propaganda. (This refers to reading comprehension in a different sense.)
c. Recognition of forms of argument which are considered intellectually acceptable and which are not employed in certain statements.
d. Critical reaction to the forms of argument which represent typical devices employed in propaganda.
e. Ability to analyze argument in terms of established principles of proof.
f. Recognition of the relation of propaganda to the social forces which breed it.
g. Knowledge of the psychological mechanisms involved in the susceptibility of people to certain language symbols.[37]

APPLICATION OF PRINCIPLES TEST, FORM 1.5

Students who can think effectively and who have conceptualized their learning are able to apply principles (i.e., generalizations) in a variety of new situations. The Application of Principles Test measures two related kinds of achievement: logic of thinking and understanding of social principles, or social theory. This test, constructed by the Evaluation Staff of the Eight Year Study, overlaps somewhat the Nature of Proof Test and the

[34] *Ibid.*, p. 143.
[35] *Ibid.*, pp. 136–139.
[36] Discussion and sample exercises may be found in *ibid.*, pp. 148–154.
[37] *Ibid.*, pp. 149–150.

Application of Some Principles of Logic Test, but it differs in its emphasis upon measuring understanding of certain social principles. Smith and Tyler state the purpose of the test when they say:

The analysis of the objective resulted in the following list of important types of behavior to be evaluated: (1) *The ability to see the logical relations* between general principles and specific information on the one hand and the issues involved in a given social problem on the other; i.e., to see whether a statement supports, contradicts, or is irrelevant to a conclusion. (2) *The ability to evaluate arguments* presented in discussing a specific social problem, and in particular, to discriminate between statements of verifiable fact, statements of opinion and common misconceptions. (3) *The ability to judge the consistency of social policies with social goals;* i.e., to judge the appropriateness of certain policies for achieving certain social aims.[38]

The following sample taken from Application of Principles Test, Form 1.5, illustrates how the test measures achievement of the above objectives:

Problem:

Housing is one of the problems of concern today. Many schemes have been suggested as a means of improving housing conditions. In general there are two major ways in which government can aid in solving this problem: (1) by setting standards for and regulating the construction of private housing, and (2) by building houses at public expense, contributing either part or all of the funds necessary. Nevertheless, many people believe that the *government should build houses at public expense to rent to those sections of the population with the lowest incomes.*

1. Directions:

For each of the following statements, place a check mark in one of the columns labeled Part I. Place the check mark opposite the number which corresponds to the number of the statement in:

Column A if the statement *may logically be used* to support *the underlined* conclusion.

Column B if the statement *may logically be used* to contradict *the underlined* conclusion.

Column C if the statement neither supports nor contradicts *the underlined* conclusion.

Check each item in only one column. In case of doubt, give the answer which seems most nearly right.

In this part of the exercise, assume that each statement is true.

[38] *Ibid.*, pp. 197–198.

Evaluating the Results of Reflectively Oriented Teaching

Supports   1. Whenever houses are not available to the public, society
Assumption   should assume the responsibility for making it possible for
                  everyone to have a decent place to live.

Contradicts   3. Government-built houses are more expensive to construct
Misconception   than comparable houses built by private companies.

Supports   11. It has been demonstrated that the federal government can
Misconception   build adequate houses for the lowest income group cheaply
                  enough so that they can be paid for out of income from rent.

Contradicts   14. Individuals who have heavy investments in slum property
Accurate   would probably suffer heavy losses if a broad program of
                  federal housing went into effect.

Contradicts   17. The system of private initiative in business should not be
Assumption   jeopardized by the socialization of any of the fundamental
                  industries.

Supports   20. Under present conditions, at least 50 per cent of the people
Accurate   cannot easily afford to own a decent home; at least one-third
                  of the population cannot afford to rent decent homes.

Irrelevant   22. Comparable houses can frequently be rented in the suburbs
Accurate   for somewhat lower rentals than in the city.

II. Directions:

Go back over the statements. In the columns labeled Part II place a check mark opposite the number which corresponds to the number of the statement in:
Column D if you believe the statement can be proved to be true.
Column E if you believe the statement can be proved to be false.
Column F if you believe the statement cannot be proved either true or false.

Check each item in only one column. In case of doubt, give what seems to you to be the one best answer.
When you have finished Part II, go on to Part III.

III. Directions:

In the column labeled Part III opposite the number which corresponds to the number of the statement, write: *A plus sign if it expresses a type of action which you think* would improve the housing conditions of that third of the population with the lowest incomes. *A zero sign if it does not express a type of action which you think* would improve the housing conditions of that third of the population with the lowest incomes.

1. New buildings should be required to measure up to higher minimum standards for construction.
2. Credit for housing should be supplied in larger quantities and at lower rates of interest.
3. All city land should be reassessed.
4. Laws should be passed requiring the destruction of all slum areas.

5. The government should subsidize housing for lower income groups.[39]

[39] *Ibid.*, pp. 199–202.

This excerpt does not represent a complete exercise from the Application of Principles Test, but it indicates the nature of the test. The comments to the left of the statements in Part I represent the key for that part of the test and for Part II. Part III, which consists of true-false items, is also keyed. This is an old test and some of the statements contain obsolete statistics. Nevertheless, teachers may profitably study it for ideas in constructing their own versions.

In constructing this test it is necessary to exercise certain cautions. If the material used in the test is not new, students may be able to respond correctly on the basis of memory rather than application and interpretation. If the situations in the test are too novel, students may not be able to make application at all. Ideally, a teacher should have several forms, each testing at a somewhat higher level. From the use of different forms he can get some notion of how deep and complete is students' understanding of certain principles.

In order to interpret test results it is helpful to know something about the factual background of students. If they do not know the relevant facts on the housing problem, they may fail to apply a principle even though they have studied it in connection with some other social problem for which they have factual background.

Besides ability to apply social facts and social generalizations to a social problem teachers are concerned with the application of social values. Social Problems, Form 1.41 and Form 1.42, is an attempt to measure ability to apply social values to social problems. The following is an illustrative excerpt:

Cotton Picker. Cotton has been picked by hand which is a slow and expensive process. Recently, the Rust brothers invented a machine to do this work. It would pick in 7½ hours as much cotton as one hand picker could pick over a whole season of eleven weeks. The cost of production of cotton could be reduced from $14.52 to $3.00 per bale. To date, this machine has not been placed on the market. What should be done with this machine?

Solutions: (Check one or more which you think are desirable)

...... A. The machine should be placed on the commercial market for immediate manufacture and sale.
...... B. The machine should be made available under some form of public control and provisions made for establishing in other jobs the cotton pickers who are thrown out of work.
...... C. The machine should not be put to use at the present time.

Evaluating the Results of Reflectively Oriented Teaching

Directions:

Write in the space below the reasons which you would use to support the solution or solutions you have checked. Be sure to write all the reasons you can think of.[40]

TEACHER-MADE TESTS OF THINKING

Tests developed as part of the Eight Year Study are no longer available. Even if they were, it is doubtful if public-school teachers could make much use of them because many of the data contained in them are now obsolete. Nevertheless, familiarity with these tests should be of value to teachers. They represent the profession's most mature achievement to date in evaluating thinking and incorporate the most adequate operational definitions of thinking yet reached.

Even though a teacher may feel that he lacks technical competence necessary to construct formal tests of thinking, the Eight Year Study tests can show him what to look for when he attempts to make informal judgments about his students' thinking. Informal judgment ought always to accompany the use of formal instruments. The following are some of the things to look for when one is interested in analyzing student thinking:

1. Are students confusing values with facts?

2. Are students attributing purpose, cause, or effect when the data do not warrant their doing so?

3. Are students able to distinguish between that which is true and that which may be true? Between that which is true and that which is probably true? Between that which is probably true and that which may be true?

4. Are students able to see the relationship between a conclusion and related assumptions?

5. Are students able to use simple principles of logic in reaching a conclusion? Are they familiar with the simple rules of evidence and the characteristics of a hypothesis?

6. Do they know what a theory is and how it is different from a hypothesis? Do they ever confuse the theoretical with the ideal?

7. Are students given to believing what they want to believe even when the data are contrary?

8. Do students have tenable reasons for the policies they recommend?

9. Are students able to apply their values in ways which lead to goals implied in the values?

[40] *Ibid.*, p. 178.

10. Are students relatively free from rationalization?

It does no good, of course, to ask these questions if instructional procedures are such that the answers cannot appear. A teacher who uses the reflective method of teaching the social studies will find, however, that the answers do tend to appear, particularly when reflection is focused on beliefs in the closed areas.

DISCUSSION QUESTIONS AND EXERCISES

1. Why is the measurement of understanding more difficult than the measurement of arbitrary associations?
2. Summarize what you have learned from this chapter about the measurement of understanding. Measurement of thinking. Measurement of attitudes.
3. What relationship exists between the validity of the attitude tests described in this chapter and the classroom atmosphere within which the tests are administered?
4. How could results obtained from administering the Scale of Beliefs be used by a social-studies teacher who is preplanning what to teach?
5. What use could be made of results obtained from the Interpretation of Data Test?
6. What should be the aim of a teacher in the area of attitude education?
7. To what extent should a teacher depend upon pencil-and-paper instruments as a means for getting evidence on the effectiveness of the reflective method? To what extent upon techniques of a more casual nature—such as teacher observation?
8. How is the teaching of history different from the teaching of thinking? Can both be taught in the same course and at the same time?
9. Can thinking be taught? Can thinking be evaluated? Should we teach that which we cannot measure or evaluate? Should we teach only that for which we have adequate evaluative techniques?
10. What is the difference, if any, between measurement and evaluation?

REFERENCES

For assistance in the construction of achievement tests, teachers will find the following useful: Ralph W. Tyler, *Constructing Achievement Tests* (Ohio State University, 1935); Herbert E. Hawkes, E. F. Lindquist, and C. R. Mann, *The Construction and Use of Achievement Examinations* (Houghton Mifflin, 1936).

A good reference on situational examinations is *Assessment of Men* (Rinehart, 1948). The Office of Strategic Services is usually credited with authorship of this volume.

The best single reference on the PEA tests of the Eight Year Study is Eugene R. Smith and Ralph W. Tyler, *Appraising and Recording Student Progress* (Harper, 1942).

Chapter 20

Building and Maintaining Academic Freedom in the High School

DESPITE the theoretical soundness of a reflective approach to teaching social studies, many teachers do not feel free to use this method. It is frequently claimed that communities would fire teachers who provoked thinking in their students. Although some teachers are probably excessively timid and tend to underestimate the amount of freedom in their possession, there is doubtless much opposition to provocative types of teaching, particularly in the closed areas. Some of this condemnation originates with powerfully organized interest groups who oppose in high schools an objective study of controversial issues.[1]

A major part of the opposition to reflection in schools originates, however, with a public opinion which simply misunderstands what teachers are trying to do. Since the public controls the schools, there can be no more academic freedom than the public is able to appreciate. Building and maintaining academic freedom in the high schools involves education of the public. It also involves the effective organization of teachers so that they can deal with minority attacks upon academic freedom. No matter how committed to academic freedom a majority of persons may be, there is likely always to be an antagonistic minority. The tasks of this chapter are (1) to indicate the public-relations job necessary to build mass appreciation of academic freedom and (2) to discuss minority attacks on freedom of learning in schools and indicate how, through organization of teachers, these

[1] Robert Maynard Hutchins has observed that all issues are controversial, and that effective opposition to a study of controversial issues would mean no study of any issue.

431

attacks may be countered. The public-relations job is actually a problem in adult education and should not be regarded as a soap-selling chore.

What to Teach About Academic Freedom

Four points of misunderstanding constitute threats to freedom of teaching in schools: (1) failure to appreciate the values of academic freedom; (2) failure to see the relationship between reflection and democratic freedom; (3) failure to understand the reflective process itself; (4) misconception concerning the meaning of academic freedom. All four misunderstandings can be clarified by a program in adult education, and such clarification would nurture freedom of learning in schools.

VALUES OF ACADEMIC FREEDOM

A statement on "The Right to Intellectual Freedom" as developed by the Philosophy of Education Society helps to put before us the case for academic freedom in any educational system. Although this statement was developed by college professors for consumption in universities, its content is appropriate to those who teach social studies in high school.

A vigorous democracy continuously builds upon the faith that in matters of public policy the people can decide what is best for them as a result of open discussion. A democratic people puts its trust in procedures that provide a hearing for contending beliefs and the weighing of differing ideas. Anything which prevents or restricts the process of public inquiry and the free communication of ideas interferes with the process by which the people decide what is good in every aspect of their common life. In this manner, they seek to improve the institutions which serve them.

We have a distinguished tradition which affirms the right to engage in free and open inquiry into problems of public concern. Our Founding Fathers, knowing the free exchange of ideas to be indispensable to the progress of a free people, provided that "Congress shall make no law . . . abridging the freedom of Speech." Throughout our history we have attained, even in perilous times, a vital and abiding faith in the free expression and examination of ideas. Jefferson affirmed clearly this deeply held value. "If there be any among us who would wish to dissolve the Union or to change its republican form, let them stand undisturbed as monuments of the safety with which error of opinion may be tolerated where reason is left free to combat it." This tradition has been the keystone of this country's greatness.

When ideas are not freely exchanged and judged on their merits, decisions and judgments are controlled by the arbitrary authorities of the moment. Then, to hold a belief at variance with the views of those who hold arbitrary power is to risk suppression, perhaps by an official police power. Tyranny, rooted in the effort to control the thoughts of men, may gradually come upon us if in timidity or thoughtlessness we fail to practice our tradition of speaking, hearing, thinking and choosing.

Mature minds cannot be developed where ideas deemed dangerous are kept out of our common life. We must provide, therefore, those conditions which make the full range of alternatives freely available for public inspection. To the degree that the conditions of open inquiry and communication are established we need have no fear but that our citizens will choose policies that advance the common good. Failure to accept this responsibility is to deny the very basis of self-government and thereby to surrender to tyranny.

Consequently, the freedom to inquire is a public necessity. Our society will be renewed not by those who know no other way to live but only by those who, knowing others, prefer the democratic way. Thus, the rights to inquire, to hear, to speak, are not rights we hold privately, but rights we share in common through our citizenship.

It thus becomes the duty of thoughtful citizens to protest the suppression of freedom of thought, inquiry, and communication wherever it may occur. In each instance, where the rights to hear and study and explore ideas are infringed, there is a present danger to our way of life and to the freedom of each of us. These rights should be exercised, to be sure, in a thoughtful manner, with full regard for the obligations of personal sincerity and integrity and a commitment to the ways of a free society. Yet responsible inquiry and expression are best safeguarded and nourished when intellectual freedom is held so dear that we protect the right of individuals to express even the most unwelcome ideas.

In the light of these considerations we affirm that the indispensable condition for the preservation and enrichment of our democratic heritage is the full and free examination of ideas. A living danger to a free society exists whenever a particular interested group appropriates for itself the right to censure ideas, to determine what others may hear. This course, though pursued in the name of democracy, can lead only to the subversion of our way of life. It is the obligation of a democratic community to provide the maximum opportunity for the full, free, and responsible exchange of ideas on matters of public concern.[2]

This statement puts academic freedom within the broader context of a free society. When we defend academic freedom we are defending a total way of life. Teachers who promote reflection in closed areas need make no apologies for their patriotism. They are acting in the spirit of America's most democratic traditions. The fact, however, that this kind of teaching is sometimes attacked by well-meaning Americans simply means that the issue of reflection has not been understood by everyone who is interested in our

---

[2] This statement was prepared by the Committee on Freedom of Inquiry of the Philosophy of Education Society. The committee consisted of Professors George E. Axtelle, H. Gordon Hullfish, Kent Pillsbury, B. Othanel Smith, and A. Stafford Clayton. Professor Clayton was chairman of the committee.

public schools. Indeed, those who misunderstand reflective types of teaching include substantial numbers of teachers, so that the problem involves educating not only the lay public but the profession as well.

Although the profession and large segments of the public often agree on the wisdom of reflection, this agreement is likely to vanish at the level of concrete action. Proposals for implementing a reflective study of alternative ways of life encounter a multitude of objections—one of the most common in the form of an allegation that such teaching is "communistic." Since the leading Communist state in the world has successfully eliminated such teaching from its educational institutions, the reasoning behind this allegation is not easy to follow. A most practical question facing the teaching profession in the area of academic freedom is whether it can prove to itself and to its public supporters that reflection is necessary to the preservation of democratic values, and that a lack of reflective teaching constitutes subversion by default.

Since the public schools belong to and are controlled by the public, however nebulous the thinking of that public may be, no attempt to promote reflection in the closed areas can succeed without widespread public support and appreciation. It can be assumed that most Americans prefer democracy to any other way of life, and that a reflective study of the closed areas would deepen and enrich this preference. But one cannot assume that many Americans understand democracy well enough to defend it. It is particularly true that high-school students, their parents, and teachers are not always aware of the place that reflection has in democratic citizenship.

REFLECTION AND DEMOCRATIC FREEDOM

In a democratic society or group, individual members are free to participate in making decisions which affect them. Since these decisions include judgments of value as well as judgments of fact, a democratic citizen has a voice in shaping both the ends and the means of group living. No one has the right to determine for anyone else what his purposes shall be or how his purposes may best be attained. Democratic freedom means freedom to choose. It means freedom to participate in shaping the beliefs and values of associated living.

The Bill of Rights is intended to protect individuals from governmental restraint in the area of beliefs and values. But the absence of this kind of restraint does not guarantee to any individual that his choices will be effective, wise, or intelligent, or even that his choices will be freely given. Whether he can participate freely, wisely, intelligently, and effectively in

making choices depends in no small part on the extent to which his education frees him from the dictates of cultural determinism. A citizen who does not have "all his buttons" or who goes to the polls under the influence of intoxicating liquor can hardly be described as free. Likewise, a citizen who is the unreflective victim of cultural conditioning lacks the capacities of freedom.

As pointed out earlier, individuals begin in infancy to acquire beliefs and values from the surrounding culture, an acquisition that, by the very nature of circumstances, has to be unreflective. This unreflective content can dictate to an individual what his choices will be, in which case, he does not choose at all. He does whatever his background suggests as desirable and proper. The person who votes as his family votes, or who embraces the religion of his parents can hardly be said to choose a political party or a religion. If he should reflect upon the choices of his parents, he might acquire the freedom to choose. Exercise of this freedom might result in agreement with his parents, but it could also result in disagreement. Many parents who want their children to think also want them to follow the religion and politics of the parents. However, no one can predict that every thinking child will perceive wisdom in all the choices of his parents. The issue is thus clear enough: Do parents want freedom of choice developed in their offspring, or do they prefer a particular pattern of belief and value more than they prefer freedom of choice? A rejection of freedom of choice amounts to a rejection of democracy. It is not wise for children to attempt choices before they possess the requisite maturity, but a complete absence of reflection in the education of children will mean indefinite prolongation of their immaturity.

For students in high school the problem of democratic freedom is not merely a problem in parental conflict. Most high-school students have fixed beliefs and values, almost all of which were unreflectively acquired, and therefore they find it difficult to reflect upon certain matters. If they cannot free themselves from their preconceptions, they will lack freedom to choose. A law which would extend to eighteen-year-olds the right of suffrage might remove a barrier to the exercise of democratic freedom, but a student who had never reflected upon his political preferences would still be lacking in democratic freedom. His votes would be dictated by his cultural background.

A person cannot choose until he has choices to make. That is, the presence of alternatives is essential to any freedom to choose; in the absence of alternatives a choice is neither necessary nor possible. The citizens of the

Soviet Union have no freedom of choice in an election because there is only one slate of candidates. Likewise, a citizen in America who has never reflected upon political issues may have only one slate of candidates before him even though both major parties place candidates on the ballot.

Public Misunderstanding of the Reflective Process

It is a teacher's attempt to create alternatives that is most likely to produce public suspicion of his motives. The teacher realizes, if he is well trained, that freedom of choice for students depends upon whether they can entertain alternatives in beliefs and values. Students who have been conditioned by a culture cannot accept or reject any part of that culture except as they examine reflectively the consequences of any choice they may follow. But examination of consequences involves the weighing of alternatives, which will not take place in a student who takes for granted his cultural environment.

For example, a teacher who wishes to promote a consideration of the consequences of racial segregation must, in some instances, induce a doubting of segregation in order to promote an understanding of it. A well-grounded theory of conceptual learning implies reflection as the basis for understanding, and doubt as the usual basis for reflection. However, a teacher who fosters doubt will often appear to the lay public in the same light as the subversive agitator who seeks to undermine our freedom. At the point of fostering doubt there is no observable difference between a loyal teacher and a subversive agitator. But there is a fundamental and clearly observable difference at other points in the reflective process.

A widespread public understanding of the reflective process would protect loyal teachers from charges of subversion. The really disloyal teachers are those who fail to promote reflection when they are free to do so. More teachers would be free to promote reflection if more citizens realized that a provoking of doubt usually accompanies effective teaching. Educational process is a closed area for many adults, and few public-school leaders are helping them acquire any understanding of it.

Myths About the Nature of Academic Freedom

There are at least three major misconceptions concerning academic freedom, each one shared to some degree by the teaching profession and lay public.

1. Academic freedom is for teachers alone. To many persons academic

freedom means that a teacher is free to teach as he pleases, and it is easy to see why few are willing to grant him any such license.

The teaching profession should make it plain that academic freedom does not mean the freedom to impose upon youth the prejudices of any teacher. An enlightened citizenry will value in teachers a freedom to promote learning in students, and on this ground academic freedom can rest its strongest defense. Even an organized interest group as conservative as the National Association of Manufacturers has publicly endorsed an academic freedom which protects a student's right to learn while wisely refusing to permit victimization of any student: "Every teacher in America should have the unquestioned right to impart knowledge objectively. . . . Teachers of . . . any of the social sciences should discuss without hesitation the theories, practices, and histories of all systems of government including the government of collectivist states. . . . But neither freedom of speech nor freedom of academic inquiry and instruction gives a teacher the right to a captive audience of impressionable young people. . . ." [3]

Unfortunately, many of the defenses of academic freedom have tended to emphasize freedom of teachers without relating it to a student's freedom to learn. Consequently, students and their parents are not always in the forefront of efforts to preserve or to create academic freedom; one cannot expect them to feel a stake in the defense of a freedom which is interpreted only as a privilege of the teacher. Until freedom to teach *in certain ways* is defended as the only means by which students can learn to understand the world in which they live, this freedom will lack widespread public support.

If teachers are negligent in their promotion of learning, an additional difficulty will exist for those who desire a public valuing of academic freedom. A prominent educator gives an example of a kind of teaching which makes it difficult to build a case for academic freedom:

Even granting, however, that the vast majority of teachers *intend* to assist their pupils toward independent judgments, it is by no means certain that they can live up to this intention. The writer vividly recalls observing a teacher who avowed as her sole aim the development of independent thinking among her pupils. The class had embarked upon the discussion of such current events as happened to be treated in the weekly paper to which they subscribed for this purpose. The lead story was on the then-current coal strike. A boy in the class delivered himself of the idea, "If miners would be sensible with their money, instead of throwing it all away on whiskey, they'd find that their wages were more than they need."

[3] *Newsweek*, March 1, 1954, p. 71.

The teacher moved in fast. Under a barrage of well-placed questions, the lad admitted that (1) he had no idea how much a miner was paid; (2) he had no firsthand knowledge of the personal habits of miners; (3) his sole source for the view he had announced was a muttered reaction of his father's at the breakfast table; (4) he doubted if his father had any actual information on either of the relevant points; (5) he recognized that one ought not to make such a drastic or sweeping generalization unless he had facts to back it up. So far, so good.

The next reaction came from a girl who remarked with deep feeling that whenever men strike they lose money, and that this fact so disturbs wives as to upset their home life very seriously. "So," she concluded, "I think that whenever men strike they must be in the right, or they wouldn't do a thing that's going to be so unpleasant for them." The writer's eyes were on the teacher as he waited for this avowed foe of the facile generalization to swing into action. All that the teacher did, however, was to beam and announce solemnly, "Helen, that's what I call a very nice insight." [4]

In this anecdote, a teacher who claims to value reflection makes use of the process only when she disagrees with a view expressed by a student. The students with whom she agrees do not have their beliefs challenged, and their powers of judgment are not developed. The reflective process becomes in her unprofessional hands a tool by which to purvey her private, and occasionally prejudiced, judgments. There is no gainsaying the fact that substantial segments of the public believe, or suspect, that academic freedom would protect, and perhaps even establish and nurture, this kind of teaching.

When a teacher challenges conservative beliefs while neglecting to challenge liberal beliefs, two consequences follow. First, the suspicion of communism is aroused in that segment of the public which makes no distinction between liberalism and communism, and it becomes more and more difficult to make any distinction. Certainly a teacher of liberal beliefs who fails to challenge any but the most conservative beliefs in his students is engaging in an indirect kind of indoctrination the results of which are not much different from the more direct indoctrination of the communist propagandist. A kind of teaching which blurs the differences between liberalism and communism makes it almost impossible to defend the schools against externally imposed regimentation.

Second, there can be no doubt that such externally imposed disciplinary measures as the loyalty oath and the legislative investigation have had some public support. A profession which fails to discipline itself invites discipli-

[4] Alan Griffin, "The Teacher as Citizen," *Educational Leadership*, October, 1952, p. 7.

nary measures from nonprofessional sources, or from an administrator who claims to act as an agent of the public.

There is a simple solution to this problem of nonprofessional discipline. Every profession must define the conditions of membership in the profession. For the teaching profession a minimum condition of membership ought to be a demonstrated mastery of the reflective process. The public could soon learn that it has nothing to fear from the teacher who has mastered this process and is committed to its use. Teachers of this kind would then be granted freely the right to teach as they please for it would be apparent that such teaching is democratic in every sense. The profession would do well to refuse to protect any teacher who violated the canons of reflection.

2. Academic freedom requires a teacher to be neutral. Those who believe that teachers should be free to promote a study of controversial issues sometimes insist upon neutrality in teachers. Teacher objectivity is defined as teacher neutrality. A neutral teacher is defined as one who either has no opinions on the issues to be studied or conceals from students the exact nature of his opinions. Since teachers are almost certain to have opinions, it is concealment which is usually implied by those favoring neutrality.

There is some ground for the belief that teachers should conceal their opinions on controversial issues. It is feared that students will agree with teachers because it would be academically risky for them to disagree. Since teachers largely determine their grades, students will try to curry favor by agreeing with them, which is far from engaging in a reflective study of issues.

There are serious weaknesses in this argument. An effective enforcement of the ban on expression of opinion by teachers would seriously limit their civic freedom. In fact, it would probably put them in the role of second-class citizens. A first-class citizen is allowed full, free, and public expression of personal opinion—usually considered a duty as well as a right. We constantly insist that citizens "stand up and be counted" on important civic issues. Participation in politics is one of the ways by which citizens publicize their opinions. In a small community a teacher who takes an active part in politics cannot possibly conceal from his students the nature of some of his beliefs. Even in a large metropolitan area a teacher cannot achieve concealment if he gains any kind of civic prominence. If we are serious in our demand that teachers be neutral, we shall have to be equally serious in insisting that they relinquish many of their civic responsibilities. A teacher of social studies who relinquishes these responsibilities sets a bad example for his students.

A second flaw in the argument for teacher neutrality is the relative difficulty if not impossibility of concealment. The opinions of a teacher are often revealed in his assignments and his questions, even in his tone of voice. Most students are able to "figure out" where their teachers stand. Since a chuckle in the throat or a twinkle in the eyes can speak volumes, a teacher would have to maintain a wooden face and a monotonous voice in order to be a neutral personality. There is, too, a sense in which a teacher reveals something about himself no matter what he does. If he runs for public office, everyone who reads newspapers will know the nature of his political preferences. If he does not run for public office and avoids, in general, all kinds of political activity, his students may infer that he is not interested in this aspect of citizenship. If he joins a union, his preference for collective bargaining is publicized. If he joins a classroom teachers' association rather than a union, his students may make different inferences—provided they know the difference between a union and an association.

A third objection to the rule of concealment is that one of the purposes of a social-studies curriculum based upon the method of reflection is teaching students to be critical of an idea irrespective of its origin. Unfortunately, too many of our citizens are more interested in the source of an idea than in its truth or falsity. Ideas emanating from certain sources are assumed to be true; those from other sources are assumed to be false. One cannot imagine a scientist using source as a test of truth. Truthful ideas sometimes originate with the most disreputable sources. Although some sources have been more truthful than others, none is infallible. There is no single political party which one can always trust, no single newspaper which always prints the whole truth. High-school students must learn to use evidence rather than source as a basis for belief. If they are to learn to be critical of an idea when it comes from a teacher, they must criticize ideas which they know to be held by the teacher.

The assumption that expression of opinion by a teacher will always discourage students from thinking is not consistent with what is known about the thinking process. Thinking occurs when students feel a problem; it is a teacher's failure to create problems which accounts for the absence of thinking in a classroom. True, expression of opinion by a teacher may sometimes have the effect of "solving" a problem. Whenever a teacher senses that this would be the probable effect, he will, of course, refrain from expressing an

440

opinion. However, his attention should focus upon reflective teaching rather than upon caginess and reticence.

Moreover, a teacher who actively seeks to promote thinking is not neutral. He reveals in his teaching a preference for the values of objectivity, a preference for democracy. He values differences, dissent, controversy—and opinions based on evidence. There would be no point in concealing his preference for objectivity. He will try to teach his students what objectivity is, and what values it implies. If he is successful, his students will develop an ability to recognize objectivity when it is present. They will note it when it appears in their own thinking and will learn to recognize when others have failed to exhibit it. This kind of instruction aims to develop the habit of judging an idea not in terms of its origins but in terms of evidence related to it. It aims to make students critical of ideas—even ideas of teachers.

The tendency of any student to agree or disagree with a teacher as a matter of regular habit may be taken as evidence that the teacher is failing to develop objectivity in that student. Teachers will have to express opinions occasionally in order to find out whether students are learning to be objective in their appraisal of a teacher's opinion. Students who are urged to be objective will want an occasional sample of the kind of opinion proffered by a teacher who urges objectivity. There will be times, of course, when a teacher will not express a certain opinion with a certain group of students because he suspects that they will not be able to criticize it. And in some communities it may not be safe for a teacher ever to express certain opinions. But a blanket refusal to reveal any opinions would be as foolish as the habit of always making one's position known.

Although it may be desirable with some groups for a teacher to introduce his opinion as though it belonged to someone else, such concealment should be tactical rather than strategic in nature. Otherwise he will have to become 100 percent effective in his defense against student curiosity, which is naturally accentuated by teacher efforts to be cagey. Students who feel that they are captives of a teacher—and in the modern high school characterized by some kind of marking system they sometimes feel so—can expend much energy in trying to "figure out" their teachers. This activity may become more important intellectually than attempts to determine the reasonableness of beliefs. Not only does a teacher's reticence encourage this unintellectual tendency but also the slightest revelation of opinion by a teacher is given undue significance by students. How much better it would be if permissiveness in a classroom meant that (a) teachers were permitted to have opinions and (b) students were encouraged to be critical of such opinions.

3. Academic freedom is justified only if teachers promote the right beliefs. This notion is contrary to the one that teachers should be neutral. A typical application is to say that it is all right for a teacher to teach the pros and cons of any subject provided he always emphasizes the wrongness of certain practices and beliefs. Persons who hold this belief are not always aware that they are advocating card stacking—although they are quick to recognize biases different from theirs. They usually feel that anyone who thinks is bound to agree with them. This faith, however, is not so strong that they are willing to take the risks of objective teaching; it is a teacher's duty to perpetuate things as they are. In contrast, an objective teacher is more interested in propagation of truth and perpetuation of democratic values.

Objective teachers do not take the position that there are no "right answers," but rather that the rightness of an answer depends upon the evidence and logic which support it. Some traditional beliefs and social practices may lack such support, and it would be unprofessional for a teacher to conceal evidence which refutes or undermines any belief. Objective teachers are not social reformers, do-gooders, or welfare statesmen, but neither are they stand-patters, die-hards, or backers of normalcy. They are not committed to change for the sake of change, but neither are they committed to perpetuation of everything as it is. They instigate reflection and let the chips fall where they may. In controversial areas where the evidence is inconclusive they prefer to leave a student in doubt rather than to inculcate a security-giving belief which is unwarranted by available data.

The pressure to conform which society sometimes exerts upon a teacher who is striving for objectivity has been described by Robert S. Lynd. His comments on the demands placed upon the research worker in social science apply also to teachers of social studies: ". . . He lives in a world which, by and large, is not asking, 'Is Smith trying to get at the facts? Is he trying to be fair and constructive at the same time that he is unwilling to pull his punch?' but which asks, 'Are you for us, or against us?' . . ." [5]

These pressures may take the form of loyalty oaths and textbook censorship, which are usually presented as if they would be innocuous to loyal teachers. It is argued that only disloyal teachers need worry about the effects of such measures. It is even implied that a teacher who opposes them is of questionable character. Professional organizations have, never-

[5] Robert S. Lynd, *Knowledge for What?* Princeton University Press, 1940, p. 10.

theless, opposed them on the ground that they represent thought control rather than attempts to weed out subversive elements. On this ground the measures are as subversive as their alleged target.

A disquieting note in this whole business is the vague language of the typical loyalty oath. Teachers are never sure about the meaning of their asseverations. This vagueness exposes a teacher to the dangers of ex post facto interpretation. One proposed oath, for example, required teachers to swear "that I do not directly or indirectly teach or advocate the overthrow of the government of the United States or of this State or any unlawful change in the form of governments thereof by force or any unlawful means." It would be possible under this vaguely worded oath to charge a teacher with indirectly advocating overthrow of the government should he teach his students the Declaration of Independence. Almost all loyalty oaths have this feature of vagueness.

The following attempt at textbook censorship is further illustration of the problems teachers face in this field:

Recommendations for the adoption of textbooks and workbooks shall be made by the Superintendent. Before recommending the adoption of a textbook or supplementary workbook for general use, the Superintendent shall require of the teacher who is to use the book, a written statement certifying that the book does not advocate the support of a foreign power nor of a doctrine inimical to the principles of government established by the Constitution of the United States of America and the Constitution of the State of ———, and further that it does not advocate a principle or doctrine inimical to the American system of free enterprise.

Teacher organizations which opposed and defeated this proposal argued that attempts to teach an understanding of the United Nations might be taken as evidence that a teacher was supporting a foreign power. Such interpretation of the oath is not unlikely since the groups which support such oaths usually feel that the United Nations is a foreign nation with its capital located in New York City. Another argument against an oath as vague as this one is that an objective treatment of the Tennessee Valley Authority might be interpreted as advocacy of doctrines inimical to free enterprise.

These interpretations are not fantastic conjecture when one considers the frenetic temperament of the groups which ordinarily advocate textbook censorship and loyalty oaths. The lengths to which such groups may go is indicated in another measure intended as a sister proposal to the one described above and offered as an answer to the argument that the first would prevent teachers from teaching *about* communism. That is, since it was recognized that there was some virtue in "knowing your enemy," the patriots tried to construct an offering which would permit a teacher to "explain" the evils of communism to his students. The proposal was careful to avoid putting any great trust in a teacher's objectivity:

Whenever as a necessary step in the teaching process, a teacher desires to lecture, use printed material or other devices to explain, for purposes of comparison, doctrines which are contrary to the principles of government of the United States, the teacher shall submit to the Superintendent the plan of procedure, together with requests for purchase of necessary textbooks and other teacher materials and shall sign the following statement:

It is my desire to present to my class in ———— instruction in principles of government which are contrary to the principles of government of the United States as follows: (give description of plan with reasons)

In doing this I certify that I shall inform the students that this doctrine is contrary to the established principles of government in the United States, and I shall stress with the students the superiority of the principles of government of the United States and of the American way of life. In order to accomplish this instruction I desire the purchase of the following materials:

Materials which are purchased for use in classroom activities as described in this paragraph are not to be placed on open library shelves nor distributed indiscriminately among students. If they are used in elementary schools, they shall be kept in the principal's office and released for use upon special requisition of teachers who use the foregoing statement; if in junior and senior high schools, they shall be kept in the libraries where the librarian shall store them in locations which do not have open access to students. They shall be catalogued in a separate file.

In general, it is suggested that classroom teachers in this school system avoid topics in teaching, except for purposes of illustrating wrong practices, which tend to undermine and destroy the highest standards of American family life, the importance of religion in a person's individual life, or deviations from traditional standards of honesty, truthfulness and moral conduct. Indeed it is urged that wherever possible teachers avail themselves of every opportunity to strengthen the attitudes of students toward family life, religion, honesty, truthfulness and moral conduct.

The dangers to democratic teaching contained in the vague wording of this measure are not softened by a specific exhortation to advocate honesty, truthfulness, filial duty, and spirituality, probably inserted in order to cast in a poor light any teacher who would "quibble" with the more dangerous content of the proposal. "What decent teacher," it could be asked, "would refuse to honor such proposals as these?" It is plain from the general nature of this proposal that the sponsoring groups do not believe in an academic freedom which treats American institutions objectively.

4. There are minor myths about academic freedom. We have discussed the major misunderstandings, which a program in adult education should aim to correct. At least four others are sufficiently prevalent to warrant our attention.

First, there is a failure to distinguish between civic freedom and academic freedom. As pointed out in our discussion of teacher neutrality, any requirement that teachers conceal their opinions from students implies some restriction on their behavior as citizens. When community sentiment prohibits a teacher from running for political office, he is restricted in his civic freedom. This is not the same as being restricted in his academic freedom. A teacher who is not free to run for political office is not necessarily lacking in the freedom to teach his students to reflect. Professional organizations will want to protect both civic and academic freedoms, and, although the two are related, the defense of one does not necessarily include defense of the other.

The existence of academic freedom in our schools is a factor working against totalitarianism in the surrounding culture, but it is possible to have academic freedom without civic freedom. In the Middle Ages the universities possessed academic freedom even though the surrounding society was authoritarian. But we have never had a free society which did not also honor freedom of inquiry in its schools. It is possible to have academic freedom without civic freedom but civic freedom is impossible without academic freedom.

Second, some teachers confuse personal with academic freedom. Many communities restrict the private lives of teachers. They may be expected to teach a Sunday School class. There may be objections to their smoking and drinking. They may be urged to live in the community which employs them as teachers. There is usually a preference for teachers who marry and have families, and divorces among teachers are severely condemned. Whatever one may believe about these restrictions, they are not restrictions upon academic freedom but upon personal freedom, and their only relationship to academic freedom is their possible effect upon teacher efficiency.

No doubt some of the common restrictions on personal freedom are damaging to mental health. A teacher who lacks mental health cannot always promote learning.[6] He may have highly cynical attitudes which are com-

---

[6] Nevertheless the most stimulating teachers in our schools are not always well-balanced, well-adjusted middle-of-the-roaders.

municated to his students. He may be so frustrated by community mores that he is extremely sarcastic toward students, with the result that permissiveness in his classroom is nonexistent. When permissiveness is absent, reflection is largely absent too. Another effect of these restrictions is that teachers leave the profession rather than lose their mental health. Those who remain can make the most effective use of the reflective process in communities which permit them a private, autonomous existence. The use of the reflective process requires a highly skilled teacher who feels wanted and accepted by the community.

Third, academic freedom is thought to be for colleges and universities but not for public schools. When it is discussed in professional education courses teacher trainees often respond as if it were a college or university problem. They apparently believe that teachers back home have no such freedom and they act as if teachers were not supposed to have it. Furthermore, teachers have tended to use the word *tenure* to refer to many of the same things that a professor means when he speaks of academic freedom, and neglect of intellectual inquiry in the public schools has caused them to have greater use for tenure than for academic freedom. A teacher who limits his instruction to recitation would not know what to do with academic freedom. As teachers come to see the significance of reflection in a democratic society they are likely also to see the need for academic freedom in all grades of the public school as well as in colleges and universities.

Fourth, it is thought that academic freedom means no more than the consideration of both sides of an issue. This belief appears on first sight to be sound. Its weakness is not only in the assumption that there are only two sides to every question but also in the implication that there are always at least two sides. There is a large body of facts in social science, yet large numbers of people sometimes dissent from these facts. For example, the belief that Jews are not a race is not a controversial issue among social scientists but it is among some lay persons. If a teacher allows both sides to be heard on this issue, when it becomes an issue rather than a fact, and then says to students, "Now you have heard both sides. Make up your own mind," he is failing to do all that he could to insure full examination of the issue. It is not the business of a teacher to determine which side is right, but to teach students to recognize the difference between fact and ignorant opinion. Since the gap between the knowledge of social science and the beliefs of laymen continues to widen, many matters of fact will probably

446

be treated as issues in many communities. Teachers can use their academic freedom to help evidence and logic prevail in these communities.

It would be an equally serious mistake for a teacher to identify his own prejudices as facts, and this is likely to happen, too, since many teachers find it difficult to keep abreast of developments in social science. The best cure is a thorough grounding in the subjects they teach. This knowledge can then be married to teaching techniques which enable students to determine whether there is more evidence on one side of an issue than on any other. The neutral listing of arguments, pro and con, is, on the other hand, a poor substitute for objective study of an issue. The neutrality of a teacher should never go so far that any student is encouraged to embrace a conclusion which lacks reasonable ground. A belief in examining both sides of an issue is sound enough only when "examination" is interpreted as use of reflection. When it is interpreted as neutrality—even neutrality toward facts—it is far from sound pedagogy and can mean that academic freedom is given an interpretation which retards conceptual development of students.

Education of the Public

The above discussion has analyzed seven myths concerning the nature of academic freedom. Commitment of any powerful segment of the public to any of these myths bodes ill for teachers who foster reflective thinking in the closed areas. A type of adult education which would submit these myths to examination would support the cause of academic freedom. Such examination should not imply that there is only one proper meaning for academic freedom. It is possible that our labeling certain beliefs *mythical* has prejudiced their examination. It was intended, however, merely to imply that certain meanings of academic freedom would be inconsistent with certain meanings given to democracy, and that reflection in the closed area of education would reveal these inconsistencies.

OUR NUMEROUS PUBLICS

In the opinion of many sociologists, the well-knit community of the nineteenth century has been replaced by a conglomeration of interest groups. Each interest group not only has a somewhat different ax to grind but identifies its own interests with the public interest—and not necessarily insincerely or hypocritically. Many business leaders honestly believe that what is good for business is also good for the community, just as many

447

leaders of organized labor believe that any measure which benefits labor also promotes the general welfare.

Thus, public welfare consists of a number of welfares which are roughly equal to the number of "publics" in the community. Since many organized interest groups conflict in their purposes and perceptions, it is almost impossible to find on certain issues enough consensus to warrant the belief that there is a public opinion. Rather there are many opinions all of which are public in their expression.

The kind of community typical of this country in the first half of the nineteenth century possessed value consensus as its leading characteristic. Conflicts were largely over how to achieve certain purposes, almost never over purposes. The good life and the good society were clearly defined by the community. The purposes of education were not in doubt. In contrast, today's community possesses value conflict rather than value consensus. It fails to provide its public schools with any clear directive. They are likely to drift from purpose to purpose according to which interest group has momentarily the most influence.

In this modern community, which many social scientists believe is not a true community at all, personal character is shaped largely by one's membership in organized interest groups. A businessman who belongs to a trade association, for example, may have more purposes and values in common with businessmen in other communities than with consumers in his own immediate community. He may agree with other businessmen on the purposes of education while disagreeing on this same matter with some of his nearest neighbors. A further complication arises if the businessman who has derived certain purposes for education from his associations in business has learned to value quite different purposes from some of his other associations. In the modern community, then, schools are exposed to conflicting pressures. Occasionally teachers and administrators have mistakenly interpreted the loudest voice in a community as the voice of the public. But the fact that a few are vocal in their objections to reflective thinking does not usually mean that a majority of citizens are opposed to such teaching.

An alternative to a policy of drift or a policy of responding to the loudest voice is leadership by the teaching profession in community consensus-building. Since the modern community is no longer integrated enough to provide its schools with direction and sense of purpose, schools can no longer afford to play a passive and accepting role.

Leadership by the profession does not mean an attempt to build unanimity of purposes. Some interpretations of the group-process movement have implied that consensus means unanimity. A more democratic concern is the attempt to build a majority opinion based upon logic and evidence, and this is the interpretation here given to consensus. Neither does leadership in consensus-building imply that the teaching profession should determine educational purposes. If it is undemocratic for any organized interest group to determine the purposes of the public schools, it is equally undemocratic for the teaching profession (which is merely another organized interest group) so to do. It is rather for the teaching profession to help citizens in all interest groups think through the problem of purposes.

This approach is sound for it recognizes that the public today consists of many publics and each citizen may belong to more than one. Each citizen, therefore, tends to have intrapersonal conflicts over the role of education, and since the study of education tends to be a neglected, if not a closed, area of inquiry, the criticisms of education made by citizens are likely to be apathetic or frenetic rather than effective.

The purposes pursued by the school in any local community should be consistent with the purposes valued by our broader national community—i.e., with the democratic traditions to which our nation is committed. Most schools today are not giving the attention to reflective learning implied by our commitment to democracy. However, an attempt to introduce into high schools a heavier emphasis upon the reflective study of ideological issues would represent for many communities a fundamental curricular revision. And experience in curriculum planning and curricular revision proves that fundamental changes seldom occur without the support and understanding of teachers and lay persons. This is another reason for building consensus on the purposes of education. When a substantial majority of lay citizens agree on the purposes of education and how they can be achieved, then it can be said that a public opinion about education exists. If the formation of this opinion includes a rational study of the purposes of education in a democracy, an increased valuing of academic freedom and reflective learning is likely to emerge where at present there are only uncertainty and confusion about these two concepts.

ORGANIZING PUBLIC EDUCATION

The study of democratic education—the meaning of academic freedom and reflective learning, together with their justification and the responsibilities of teachers—need not take the form of special classes for adults, although such formal study would be valuable in any community. Fortunately, many agencies already exist which could be turned in this direction.

One such is the lay advisory council. Ideally, the lay council is a cross section of the community and is not loaded with certain interest groups to the exclusion of others. A school administrator can raise with a lay council, as well as with his faculty, certain questions to be discussed and answered on a policy level. A lay council can never do more than recommend certain policies to the board of education, but in order to recommend policy it must occasionally, if not frequently, agree on the purposes of public education in a democracy.

A popularly elected school board usually wants to carry out public wishes, and the lay advisory council can become an instrument by which public opinion is built and passed on to a school board. A school administrator who hesitates to "educate" a school board may work more freely with a lay advisory council. Conclusions reached by the council, as well as recommendations submitted by the superintendent of schools or by teachers and considered by the council, can then be communicated to the board as a sample of what the community wants.

Another agency which can be used for the education of the public is the local PTA. Unfortunately PTA meetings are often poorly attended. Overworked teachers resent any kind of evening activity which extends their workday. Parents have been indifferent or have felt that meetings were rigged by school authorities so as to avoid basic and important topics. A major weakness of the PTA has been its tendency to become a middle-class organization, understandable in view of the fact that the middle class usually has the strongest interest in community improvement.

PTA meetings could be made more interesting and challenging if frank discussions of the educational perplexities and conflicts in a community took place and were accompanied by effective social action. An airing of the differences surrounding the issue of reflection in the schools would contribute to adult understanding at the same time that it increased adult interest in educational problems. If PTA members understand the issue of reflection, they are not likely to be idle when minority organizations seek to subvert academic freedom.

A teacher who is asked to speak before the PTA can use this occasion to advantage by indicating what is known about the values of reflection. The implications of reflection are so far-reaching that almost any topic in public education can be discussed in terms of it. Surprisingly, however, many speakers are able to talk to the PTA without ever mentioning reflection as a basic function of all education.

Teacher reports to parents constitute a third means of promoting adult education. The traditional report card with its letter grades communicates very little and very poorly. Nevertheless, elimination of such report cards would be unwise in most communities. Parents like them because they read into them more than is actually reported. It might, however, be wise to supplement such reports with additional information about a student's learning. Letters to parents, visits in homes, and conferences at school are other means of communication. Encouraging parents to visit classes during a regular rather than a special school day can be a useful channel of communication. Any kind of school-community function offers an opportunity to learn about purposes of education in a democracy. Parents can teach teachers as much as teachers can teach parents.

Another place where teachers and parents can study and learn together is on one of the many committees on curriculum revision found in most school systems. These committees have often neglected such fundamental matters as the nature of reflection, the role of a school in a democracy, and the values of academic freedom. These matters are proper objects of study for any curriculum committee, whatever its specific assignment may be.

Meeting Minority Attacks on Academic Freedom

Even though a majority of persons in a community favor reflective study of issues, there is sometimes a vocal and well-organized minority which does not. Criticism by minorities, organized or not, is a well-established right in a democracy, and protection of academic freedom includes a valuing of minority opinion. Democracy, however, does not mean rule by a minority, and it is necessary to act vigorously against any minority that would thwart the will of a majority. The avoidance of minority rule is more than half solved when a majority of the people in a community know what they want from their schools. It is a modern community, with its conflicts and uncertainties, with its lack of vigorous majority opinion, that is most likely to succumb to attacks of minority organizations. In many communities it falls to the teaching profession to meet and defeat these groups.

Minorities which may oppose reflection in the schools are of several kinds. First, there may be a taxpayers' federation, league, or committee which consists of a few well-heeled property owners who seek to lower the costs of public education. Second, there are various groups which oppose

451

any kind of public education and attack the school no matter what it does. These would like to substitute private schools for the American system of free, public education. Teachers and administrators in private schools seldom have any connections with these groups; they regard their own schools as healthy alternatives rather than substitutes for public education. A third kind of group consists of special pleaders who want the public school to propagate particular doctrines. Fourth, there are the many groups organized by opportunists and charlatans who make their living from criticism of public schools. These include leaders of various lunatic fringes, many of whom have been listed as officers in organizations designated as subversive by the U.S. Attorney-General. This category also includes respectable politicians who sponsor loyalty oaths, textbook-censorship bills, and other measures as vote-getting devices.

Teachers may receive some protection from minority attacks under tenure laws. If a community values reflection, this legislation will protect competent teachers from arbitrary dismissal. If it values non-reflective teaching, however, it will subvert the tenure laws in order to punish those teachers who promote reflection. A common form of such subversion is to refuse promotion to such teachers, or even to demote them. In some school systems teachers who "cause trouble" may be given so many unpleasant assignments that they leave voluntarily. Tenure laws can nevertheless function effectively in communities which support good teaching in their schools. These laws are intended to protect teachers against vicious minorities.

Teacher-tenure laws are a product of efforts of the National Education Association and of the American Federation of Teachers. These organizations have assumed the defense of academic freedom in public schools as one of their main tasks. Among their functions are investigations of breaches of academic freedom, lobbying for improved tenure laws, and provision of legal assistance to teachers who have been arbitrarily dismissed. The American Federation of Teachers through its affiliation with the American Federation of Labor can bring to a teacher's support the weight of an entire labor movement.

Although much of a teacher's acceptance and recognition depends upon his own competence and personality, he needs organization in order to survive professionally in a community comprised of organized interest groups. In urban communities, especially, the general public may be quite indifferent to the school and its program, and a powerful minority can take advantage of this apathy. A strong teachers' organization can arouse the general public when a teacher is attacked by an organized interest group intent on the prevention of reflection. The chief problem for a teacher is to decide which organizations to join. Shall he join the local teachers' association which is affiliated with the National Education Association? Shall he join the local teachers' union, if there is one, which is affiliated with the labor movement? Shall he join both? Some teachers also consider membership in the Progressive Education Association, which tries to educate the profession and general public on the nature of modern education. The teaching profession, unlike medicine and law, does not have a single organization embracing substantially everyone in the profession.

In addition to organization a teacher can rely on his individual resources. In almost any community he will find some opportunities to promote reflection. He may attempt to instigate it first in the least closed of the closed areas. A subject which is closed tightly to rational inquiry in one community may be relatively open in another. Also, some of a teacher's freedom to use the reflective method of teaching depends upon his success with it. He may want to develop his mastery of this method by trying it in the least touchy areas of the community culture. As he experiences success and develops confidence he may grow in boldness and move into more issue-laden areas. The successful use of reflection is one way of placing before the general public the values of the method.

It should not be forgotten that a major factor in support of reflective teaching is the democratic tradition, which is healthy, alive, and kicking in most American communities. True, this tradition has developed within itself serious conflict, but there remains a general attitude which is favorable to reflection, knowledge, and intelligence. It is significant that a minority group with totalitarian values never dares to attack thinking directly but usually does so indirectly by advocating a return to the three R's, or by accusing the school of subversion. It succeeds, therefore, only when the nature of thinking is misunderstood. No one who understands what thinking is will believe that it encourages subversion. Neither will they believe that a reflective curriculum neglects the three R's.

The continued vitality of the democratic tradition (in spite of minorities which reject it) is undoubtedly a teacher's best protection. If he bases his teaching on a thoroughly democratic foundation, and knows what he is doing, there are relatively few communities in which he risks anything by promoting the study of controversial issues. All he must do is unostentatiously help the community to understand what democracy means and his job will be secure.

DISCUSSION QUESTIONS AND EXERCISES

1. Does academic freedom restrict in any way a teacher's expression of opinion?
2. What benefits can students expect from academic freedom? Which do you believe to be the more accurate expression, "a teacher's academic freedom," or "students' academic freedom"? Who gains the most from academic freedom, teachers or students?
3. How do you explain the fact that the general public is seldom aroused by attacks on academic freedom? How do teachers usually react to such attacks?
4. If as a teacher you were asked to speak to a group of parents on the subject "Academic Freedom in the High School," what would you say, and why?
5. It is sometimes argued that our teacher-tenure laws protect the incompetent teachers and fail to protect the competent. Is this true? If it is, why?
6. What, if anything, does the Code of Ethics of the National Education Association have to say about academic freedom? What program does the NEA have for maintaining academic freedom?
7. What is the program of the American Federation of Teachers for maintaining academic freedom? Has the AFT been more effective, or less effective, than the NEA in its efforts to protect academic freedom?
8. In connection with the problem of maintaining academic freedom, what are the pros and cons for each of the following? Is each of the following a desirable means for maintaining academic freedom? Loyalty oaths; teachers' unions; tenure laws; professionally controlled procedures in teacher certification.

REFERENCES

For additional reading on purposes of education in a democracy, see Educational Policies Commission, *The Unique Function of Education in American Democracy* (National Education Association, 1937). For a statement of purposes in the social studies, see American Historical Association, Commission on Social Studies, *Conclusions and Recommendations* (Scribner's, 1934).

At the present time, there is considerable debate over whether it would be a breach of academic freedom to refuse Communists the right to teach in public schools. A powerful case against their employment is made by Sidney Hook, *Heresy, Yes—Conspiracy, No* (John Day, 1953).

For variety of opinion on the teaching of controversial issues, read John S. Brubacher, *Eclectic Philosophy of Education, A Book of Readings* (Prentice-Hall, 1951), Chaps. 19, 20.

For those interested in the history of academic freedom in recent times, and in methods of meeting minority attacks, the following are recommended: Howard K. Beale, *Are American Teachers Free?* (Scribner's, 1936); David Hulburd, *This Happened in Pasadena* (Macmillan, 1951); *Progressive Education,* January, 1952 (entire issue), "Meeting Attacks on Education."

For those interested in the organization and function of lay advisory councils, see Herbert M. Hamlin, *Citizens' Committees in the Public Schools* (Interstate Printers and Publishers, 1952).

INDEXES

INDEXES

Index of Names

Adam and Eve, 300
Adler, Mortimer, 56
Adorno, T. W., 255, 256, 414–415
Alden, John Richard, 376
Alexander, Franz, 281–282
Alger, Horatio, 278 n.
Anderson, G. Lester, 17 n.
Aquinas, St. Thomas, 308, 309
Aristotle, 12, 56–57
Arnold, Thurman, 243
Augustine, St., 307–308, 309

Bagehot, Walter, 278 n.
Bain, Alexander, 12, 16
Ball, Charles C., 345, 346
Barnes, Harry Elmer, 327
Bayles, Ernest E., 36
Beach, Walter Greenwood, 349
Beard, Charles A. and Mary R., 55–56
Beardsley, Monroe C., 79
Bell, B. I., 56
Benson, Ezra Taft, 236
Bode, Boyd H., 14, 15, 20, 21, 31, 284
Bradley, John H., 347–348, 364
Brannan, Charles F., 236–237
Breen, Joseph I., 267
Brown, Thomas, 12
Burgess, Ernest W., 290

Calvin, John, 309, 310, 324
Chamberlain, Houston S., 253 n.
Chase, Stuart, 58, 194, 198–199, 394
Coan, Otis W., 375
Commager, Henry Steele, 376
Coolidge, Calvin, 345
Crutchfield, Richard S., 31–32

Davis, Allison, 270
Descartes, René, 320
Dewey, John, 14, 17, 20, 21, 35, 41–42, 44, 58, 59–60, 284
Dickinson, Asa D., 373
Dickson, W. J., 135–136
Diderot, Denis, 320
Dobzhansky, Theodosius, 260
Dollard, John, 270

Dumond, Dwight L., 357
Dunn, L. C., 260
Eldredge, H. Wentworth, 5–6, 7
Ellis, Albert, 292, 296, 297

Faulkner, Harold U., 54, 345, 348
Fay, Sidney B., 327
Ferguson, John H., 347, 348
Fincher, Ernest B., 347, 348
Ford, Henry, 265
Foulkes, S. H., 134
Fowlkes, John Guy, 382
Fox, Dixon R., 376
Frank, Philipp, 97
Freud, Sigmund, 130, 131, 135, 289
Fromm, Erich, 7

Gabriel, R. N., 376
Galbraith, John Kenneth, 236, 244
Galileo, 57
Galton, Francis, 278 n.
Gavian, Ruth Wood, 344, 345, 348
Gipson, Lawrence Henry, 376
Gorer, Geoffrey, 279, 293
Gray, A. A., 344
Greenleaf, Walter J., 348
Griffin, Alan, 437–438
Groves, Ernest R., 344

Haiman, Franklin S., 135
Hamm, William A., 344, 345, 348
Hancock, John, 320
Hand, Harold C., 226
Harding, Warren G., 345
Harlow, Ralph V., 345
Hart, Albert B., 376
Hartman, Gertrude, 345, 346
Havighurst, Robert J., 95, 270, 293
Hawkes, Herbert E., 399–407
Hawley, Willis C., 345 n.
Hayek, Alfred, 245
Hechinger, Fred, 57
Hitler, Adolf, 253
Hobbs, Nicholas, 134
Hobbs, Stillman M., 348
Hodgson, Newton, 415

457

Index of Names

Hollingshead, August B., 316
Hood, Fred C., 199
Hoover, Herbert C., 345
Horn, Ernest, 124, 205–206, 393
Horney, Karen, 7, 228–229
Hume, David, 320
Hutchins, Robert Maynard, 56, 431 n.

Jackson, Andrew, 54–55
Jamison, Olis Glen, 349
Jefferson, Thomas, 258–259, 320
Jesus Christ, 307, 312–313, 319
Johnson, Allen, 376
Johnson, Henry, 393
Johnson, Wendell, 65, 66, 68
Jones, Alfred Winslow, 229
Judd, Charles H., 33

Kelley, Earl C., 24
Kepner, Tyler, 54, 345, 348
Keynes, John Maynard, 202 n., 235
Kilpatrick, William H., 284
Kinsey, Alfred C., 293, 294, 315
Kluckhohn, Clyde, 394
Krech, David, 31–32

Laski, Harold, 229
Lasswell, Harold D., 394
Leisy, Ernest E., 375
Lenin, Nikolai, 9
Lerner, Daniel, 394
Levinson, D. J., 256
Lewin, Kurt, 15, 40, 110, 132–133, 141,
    144, 147, 148, 150, 195–196
Lillard, Richard G., 375
Lincoln, Abraham, 278, 324
Lindquist, E. F., 399–407
Link, Arthur S., 376
Lippitt, Ronald, 138, 152
Locke, John, 320
Lord, Fr. Daniel, 267
Luther, Martin, 309, 324
Lynd, Robert S., 193, 194, 394, 442

Magruder, Frank A., 361, 362
Malthus, Thomas R., 55, 233
Mann, C. R., 399–407
Marx, Karl, 9, 55
McHenry, Dean E., 347, 348
McKinley, William, 55–56
Mead, Margaret, 90, 293, 294, 295
Mevrill, Francis E., 5–6, 7
Mill, James, 233
Mill, John Stuart, 233
Millis, Walter, 327

Montesquieu, Baron de la Brède et de,
    320
More, Paul Elmer, 313
Muller, Herbert J., 393
Murphy, Gardner, 12, 13, 14, 15–16
Myrdal, Gunnar, 46, 250, 251, 261

Napoleon Bonaparte, 325
Nevins, Allan, 328, 345, 346
Newton, Sir Isaac, 320
Noss, John B., 307
Notestein, Wallace, 376

Paine, Thomas, 320
Paul, St., 288, 307 n.
Pavlov, Ivan Petrovich, 13
Peattie, Roderick, 394
Pitkin, Victor E., 345, 348
Pius X, Pope, 312
Plato, 283

Randall, John Herman, Jr., 320, 325
Rapoport, Anatol, 96–97
Rasey, Marie I., 24
Raths, Louis E., 220–221, 415
Raup, Bruce R., 89, 90, 103
Redl, Fritz, 51, 91–92
Remmers, H. H., 413–414
Ricardo, David, 55, 233
Robinson, James Harvey, 393–394
Rockefeller, John D., 357
Roethlisberger, F. J., 135
Rogers, Carl B., 110, 131–132, 146, 151
Roosevelt, Franklin D., 237, 327
Roosevelt, Theodore, 326
Roth, Lawrence V., 348
Rousseau, Jean Jacques, 320

Say, J. B., 234
Schermerhorn, R. A., 262
Schlesinger, Arthur M., 376
Schutte, T. H., 124
Shatsky, S., 9
Shaw, Marjorie, 141
Sherman, Mandel, 5
Sims, Verner Martin, 408
Slavson, S. R., 134
Smith, Adam, 55, 233, 236
Smith, Eugene, 410–411, 423–429
Spencer, Herbert, 12, 16, 278 n.
Stace, W. T., 311
Stalin, Joseph, 329
Sweet, William Warren, 311

Taba, Hilda, 95, 293, 394

458

Index of Names

Taft, William Howard, 244
Thorndike, Edward Lee, 13
Thurstone, L. L., 412–413
Toro, Alfonso, 54
Tyler, Ralph, 410–411, 423–429

Voltaire, 320

Wagenknecht, Edward, 375
Walker, Edward Everett, 349

Wallin, Paul, 290
Walworth, Arthur, 54
Warner, W. Lloyd, 229, 270, 271 n., 272, 279
Watson, John B., 13
Wattenberg, William, 51, 91–92
Wertheimer, Max, 142–143
West, James, 301
White, Ralph K., 139, 152
Wilson, Woodrow, 327

Index of Subjects

Ability, range of, 209
Abstractions, 37, 70
Academic freedom, 431–432
  and minority attacks, 451–453
  and public education, 447–451
  misconceptions about, 436–447
  reflection and democratic freedom, 434–436
  values of, 432–434
Achievement, sense of, 220
Activities, 126–128, 206, 275
Addiction, drug, 317
Adequacy, 62
Adolescence, and values, 89–93
Adultery, 288, 289, 298
Affection, 220
Aggression, 220, 254–255
Agreement, general, 74
Agriculture, materials on, 383–384
Aimlessness, 18
Ambiguity, 69–70, 165–167
American Creed, 46, 270, 273, 277
American Federation of Teachers, 452
Analysis of Controversial Writing Test, 425
Anarchy, 136
Anthropology, cultural, 192, 193, 194, 222–223, 228
Anti-Catholicism, 266–267
Anti-Semitism, 256 n., 264–265
Antitrust legislation, 244–245, 247
Application of Principles Test, 425–429
Appreciation, 31
Arbitrary statements, 37–39
Area studies, 193
Arguments, 147
Aryanism, 253, 258
Asceticism, 288, 307
Associationism, 12–14, 16, 17–18, 19, 45, 105, 127, 208
Associations, education, 452–453
Assumptions, 420, 424, 425, 429
Atlases, 372
Atomic weapons, 330
Atomization, 358

Attitudes, 30–33, 36, 45, 48
  measurement of, see Evaluation
Audio-visual aids, 121, 122–123, 204–205, 373, 389, 392
Authoritarian personality, 255–257, 414–415
Authoritarianism, 119, 139–140, 150, 152, 157, 445
Authorities, 78–79
  appeal to, 55–56, 62–63
Autocracy, 136

Background fallacy, 38, 354
Balance of trade, 239–242
Bankruptcy, national, 238
Behaviorism, 12–14
Behaviors, 144–145
  and psychotherapy, 132–134
  changing, techniques for, 146–151
  constructive, see Intellectual attack
  unconstructive, 50–52
Beliefs, 8, 36, 45–46, 48, 60, 150, 435
  and academic freedom, 442–445
  and failure of perception, 143–144
  and problem solving, 175–180
  and teacher, 113, 115–116, 123, 124–125
  and topic selection, 172–175
  closed areas of, see Closed areas
  defined, 31–32
Belonging, 220
Bible, 288, 300, 307, 308, 310, 312, 315, 316
Bibliographies, 375, 394
Bill of Rights, 331 n., 434
Biology, 226
Birth control, 312
Blocking, 142–143, 152
Boards of education, 450
Body, exposure of, 300–302
Book of the Dead, 288
Books, fiction, 374–376
  history, see History
  nonfiction, 373–374
  reference, 372–373
  social-studies teaching, 393–394

461

Books (*Continued*)
  textbooks, *see* Textbooks
Brannan Plan, 236–237
Brazil, 253 n.
Breasts, exaggeration of, 301
Buddhism, 308
Budget, balanced, 235
Bureaucracy, 246
Business, materials on, 384–385
Businessman, 235, 245, 280, 313, 325, 448
Busywork, 18, 127, 347, 389

Capitalism, 246–248, 313
Card playing, 305 n., 318
Carnegie Corporation, 391
Caste, 261
Catharsis, 153
Catholic Church, *see* Roman Catholic Church
Celibacy, 288
Censorship, 48, 267, 297, 442–443, 452
Census, Bureau of, 372
Center of interest, 206
Chapter-end helps, 347–349
Charts, 122, 128
Chastity, 290, 291–296
Chattels, 252
Chauvinism, 326
Chicago, Ill., 136
Choice, *see* Moral choice
Christianity, 252, 288, 289, 305–314, 319–320
Citizenship Education Project, 77, 391
Civics, 25, 48, 191, 237 n., 360–361
  issues for study, 362–363
  springboard techniques, 361–362
Civil liberties, 229, 331–332
  materials on, 384
Class, 230
  beliefs about, 270–275
  contradictions and confusions about:
    liberal and vocational education, 282–285.
    rank in classless society, 275–278
    success, 278–280
    success and happiness, 280–282
  structure of, 271–272
Climbers, social, 221, 275
Cliques, 148–149
Closed areas, 6–8, 20, 47, 52, 89, 92, 123, 144, 148, 433
  ·and content, 223–225, 229–231
  class, *see* Class
  economics, *see* Economics

minority groups, *see* Race and minority-group relations
nationalism, *see* Nationalism and patriotism
religion and morality, *see* Religion
sex, *see* Sex
Clothing, 300–301
Clubs, 335, 336
Code of Hammurabi, 288
Colonialism, 252
Columbia Associates in Philosophy, 97, 98, 99
Columbia University, 77, 97, 141, 391
Common sense, 58–59, 63
Communication, facilitating, 165–168
Communism, 6, 247, 323, 324, 329, 331, 332, 434, 438, 443–444
Community, and academic freedom, 445, 447–453
  ideology of, 112–113
  resources of, 389–391
  studies of, 228
Compartmentalizations, 46
Competition, free, 234–235, 244–246
Competitive model, 234, 235
Concealment, overcoming, 167–168
Conceptual change, 146–151
Conceptualization, 11, 21, 76, 185, 350, 351, 408
  and evaluation, 397–398
  and insight, 29, 35, 37, 38, 40–41
  and learning theory, 15–17
  and problem solving, 41–47
  and textbooks, 343–349, 354
Conclusions, 60–61, 117–118, 125, 420, 423–425, 429
  and leadership, 185–187
Concretions, 37
Configurational ˙psychology, 14
Conflicts, and teacher, 113, 114
  resolution of, 8–11, 19–21, 46
    and psychotherapy, 131–134
  types of, *see* Interpersonal conflict; Intrapersonal conflict
Confronting situation, 27, 33–34, 114
Connectionist psychology, 13, 14, 15–16
Consensus, 103, 151
  building of, 10–11, 448–449
Consequences, 98, 102–103
Conservation, materials on, 384
Conservatism, 410–412
Consistency, 46, 61, 410–412, 415
Constitution, Federal, 47–48, 331–332, 336, 361

Index of Subjects

Constructs, 13
Contemporary data, 76, 77–78
Content, 25, 191–192
  and closed areas, *see* Closed areas
  and life problems, 226
  and method, 198–199, 216–217, 218
  and needs, 217–223
  and social analysis, 228–231
  as data of reflection, 214–216
  current-events movement, 205
  history, *see* History
  integration movement, 206–207
  social-science fields, 192–194
  specialization, 196–198
  teaching-aids movement, 204–205
  textbooks, *see* Textbooks
  traditional, 207–211, 225–226
  unit-teaching movement, 205–206
  See also Materials
Controversial issues, 4–5, 6, 20, 48, 113, 123, 223–225, 371
  and academic freedom, 431, 446–447
Conventionality, 46, 255, 256
Cooperative Testing Service, 417
Core curriculum, 207, 227–228
Corporations, 242–243, 280
Courtship, 230
Cortex, 13
Counselors, 110
Courses, *see* Closed areas; Content; Curriculums
Credit, 241
Crime and delinquency, materials on, 384
Critical-mindedness, 169–171
Cuba, 253 n.
Cultural anthropology, 192, 193, 194, 222–223, 228
Culture, and adolescence, 90–92
  and education, 3–8, 19–20
  closed areas, *see* Closed areas
  defined, 3 n.
  democratic, 10–11
  needs of, 219–223
  totalitarian, 8–9
Currency, 235, 346–347
Current-events movement, 205
Curriculums, 4, 56, 90, 275, 349–350, 355, 449, 451
  and reflection, 225–228
  core, 207, 227–228
  See also Content

Darwinists, social, 278, 279
Data of thought, 214–216

Dating, 294
Daydreams, 51
Debtor nations, 240–241
Decisions, group, 148–151
  sharing in, 220
Declaration of Independence, 259, 361, 443
Defensive mechanisms, 221
Definitions, 70
Deflation, 243–244
Deism, 311, 320
Delinquency, materials on, 384
Delusions, 51
Demand, 233–234
Dementia praecox, 92
Democracy, 43, 46, 47
  and academic freedom, 432–436, 451, 453
  and education, 3–11, 20–21
  and nationalism, 323–324, 331–337
  and religion, 319–321, 324, 325, 335
  and socialism, 246
  defined, 136–137
  evaluation of, 410–412
  group-leadership movement, *see* Group leadership
  problems of, course in, 191, 237 n., 306
Demonstration, 123–124
Denial, 51
Depressions, 237–238
Dictatorship, 8–9, 247
Dictionaries, 372
Directed techniques, 119
Directive therapy, 131–132
Discrimination, *see* Class; Race and minority-group relations
Discussion, 150, 151
  and essay questions, 408
  leading, *see* Leadership
  problem-solving, 158–160
  teacher-led, 125–126
  undirected, 126, 157–158, 159
Divine rights of kings, 319
Divorce, 312
Doctrine, totalitarian, 8–9
Documentary evidence, 77
Documentary sources, 377
Dollars, 240–241
Double standard, 292, 298
Drill, 14, 19, 351–352
Drinking, 305 n., 310, 317, 318
Drives, 132
Drug addiction, 317

Economics, 25, 55, 78, 191, 192, 194, 202, 226, 228, 230
  and specialization, 197–198
  contradictions and confusions about:
    foreign aid and favorable trade balance, 239–242
    free enterprise and socialism, 246–248
    monopoly and free competition, 244–246
    spending and prosperity, 237–239
    taxes and government spending, 242–244
  modern beliefs about, 233–237
  teaching materials, 384–385
Education, and needs, 218–223
  and sex, 287–291
  function in democracy, 3–11
  liberal and vocational, 282–285
  moral, 103–106
  philosophy of, 109–110
  U.S. Office of, 394
  See also Content; Learning; Teacher
Educational Testing Service, 420
Effect, world of, 36
Effort, 278
Egypt, 288
Eight Year Study, 410, 417–418, 420, 422, 425, 429
Either-or reasoning, 57, 401
Elmtown study, 316
Emotional climate, 145–146, 153, 162–165
Empirical thinking, 58–59
Encyclopedias, 372
Engagements, 290
England, 136, 241, 252, 270, 289, 325
Enterprise, 206
Epistemology, 108
Equal-appearing intervals, 413
Equality, 259, 270, 273, 275, 277, 313, 319
Essay examinations, 407–409
Ethics, 192
Ethnocentricism, 251, 254, 256, 257, 326
Evaluated Participation, 271 n.
Evaluation, 120–121, 351, 352, 365
  and evidence, 79–87
  and thought, 100–103
  attitude measurement, 409–410
    Likert Scale, 414–415
    Remmers scales, 413–414
    Scale of Beliefs, 410–412
    Thurstone scales, 412–413
    value analysis, 415–416
  essay examination, 407–409
  matching items, 406–407

multiple-choice items, 401–405
  of hypotheses, 182–185
  of insight, 29–30
  role of, 396–399
  thought measurement, 416–417
    Application of Principles Test, 425–429
    Interpretation of Data tests, 417–420
    Logical Reasoning Test, 420–422
    Nature of Proof tests, 422–425
    teacher-made tests, 429–430
  true-false examinations, 399–401
Evidence, 75–79, 332, 429
  deductions, 79–82
  supporting of hypotheses, 82–87
Evil, 94–95
Evolution, 12
Examinations, *see* Evaluation
Exhibits, 122
Experience, remembered, 76–77
  sexual, 291–293
Experiment, 76, 77–78
Experimental test, 30
Expert opinion, 78
Exports, 240–241
Exposure, bodily, 300–302

Fact books, 372–373
Facts, 75–76, 143, 209
  judgments of, 70–75, 101–103, 125, 180–182, 187
Factual-recall questions, 348, 351
Failure, 221
Faith, 306
Falsies, 301
Fantasies, 51
Fascism, 97, 323
Fear, 220
Feeling tones, 31
Feudalism, 324
Fiction, 374–376
Field psychology, 14–18, 20, 143
Field trips, 122
Fifth Amendment, 48, 332
Figurative language, 69
Files, clipping, 120
Films, 122, 123, 204, 267, 297, 373, 392, 416
Filmstrips, 373, 392
First Amendment, 332
Flash cards, 352
Foreign aid, 239–242
Fornication, 289, 292
France, 252, 325
Free competition, 234–235, 244–246

Free enterprise, 246–248, 273
Freedom, 136, 310
  academic, *see* Academic freedom
Frequency, 13
Frustration, 221, 222, 254–255, 257, 281
Fundamentalism, 309–310, 311, 316, 318

Gallup Poll, 228
Gambling, 305 n., 310, 318
General agreement, 74
Generalizations, 37, 38–40, 63, 68, 169, 170, 209, 214, 363, 397, 425, 438
  and evidence, 85–86
  and history, 345–347, 356–359
  See also If-then-always generalizations; If-then statements
Genes, 259–260
Genesis, Book of, 300, 315
Geography, 25, 191, 192, 194, 198, 202, 207, 227–228, 237 n.
  issues for study, 365–366
  springboard techniques, 364–365
  teaching materials, 385
  textbooks, 363–364
Geometry, 422
George Peabody College for Teachers, 382
Germany, 97, 253, 265, 325, 327
Gestalt psychology, 14–16, 21
Glamour, 302
Gnosticism, 308
Goals, 5, 7, 26–27, 34, 38, 39, 42, 45, 50, 131, 353, 429
God, 306–307, 308–309, 310, 315, 317, 319
Gold, 235, 240
Good, 94–95
"Good sport," 297–300
Government, 207, 235, 236–237, 382
  and foreign aid, 239–242
  and monopoly, 244–246
  and nationalism, 336–337
  spending by, 237–239, 242–244
  teaching materials, 386
Graphs, 122, 128
Great Books Movement, 56
Great Britain, *see* England
Greece, 251, 283, 289, 308, 319
Ground covering, 349–352
Group leadership, 135–136, 224, 257, 449
  and failure of perception, 142–146
  and growth, 137–138
  conceptual and behavioral change, techniques for, 146–151
  democratic group, nature of, 136–137
  experiments in, 138–142

teacher in democratic classroom, 151–155
Group psychotherapy, 132–134
Growth, and leadership, 137–138
Guilt feelings, 7, 220, 221

Habeas corpus, 324
Habits, 34
Hammurabi, Code of, 288
Happiness, and success, 280–282
Harmony, 62
Harvard Graduate School of Business, 135
Hawthorne Works, Western Electric Company, 136
Health, materials on, 386
Hebrew law, 288, 289, 298, 306–307
Heredity, 12, 251, 276
Heritage, American, 10
Hierarchical orientation, 255
Historical data, 76–77, 84
History, 25, 39–40, 48, 54–55, 191, 192, 228, 237 n.
  and nationalism, 327–328
  and religion, 305–306
  as content, 194–196, 197, 198, 201, 202, 204–205, 207
  as pedagogical problem, 352–353
  current issues, 359–360
  documentary sources, 378
  ideas, history of, 377–378
  interpretive studies, 376–377
  series titles, 376
  springboard technique, 356–359
  survey courses, 353–356
  textbooks, 343, 345, 346–347, 353, 356, 359–360
Hollywood, 301
Honesty, 95
Hoover Institute, 394
Humanism, 56
Humanitarianism, 313
Hunch, 57
Hypotheses, 28, 35, 57–58, 60, 62, 65, 148, 347, 355, 429
  and evidence, 75–76, 79–86
  and leadership, 180–185
  and moral choice, 98–99, 101–102
  and teacher, 116–117, 125
  as verifiable statements, 68–75

Ideals, 46
Ideas, history of, 377–378
Ideational learning, 13
Ideological issues, 47–48

Ideologies, 90
  of class, 272–276
  of community, 112–113
If-then-always generalizations, 29, 39, 192 n., 194–195, 353, 356, 371
If-then statements, 28–29, 39, 80–82
Imperialism, 328–329
Imports, 240–241
Income tax, 243–244
Inconsistency, 45–46, 61, 62, 115, 145, 230, 411
Index of Status Characteristics, 271 n.
India, 258
Individualism, 361–362
Indo-European languages, 258
Indoctrination, 9
Industrialization, 4
Industry, 244–245, 280, 335, 336
  teaching materials, 386–387
Inflation, 243–244
Inquiry, freedom of, 6
Insights, 14–15, 25–26, 52, 78, 131, 145–146, 346
  and attitudes and values, 32–33
  and continuity of learning, 35–37
  and facts, 37–41
  and transfer, 33–35
  nature and role of, 27–29
  testing of, 29–30
Integration movement, 206–207
Intellectual attack, 52–53
  and reflection, 62–63
  appeal to authority, 55–56, 62–63
  common sense, 58–59, 63
  intuition, 57–58, 63
  rationalization, 53–55, 62
  reasoning, 56–57, 63
Intellectualism, 264
Intensity, 13, 415
Interaction, 133
Intercommunication, 138, 149
Interest groups, 431, 447–449, 452–453
International relations, materials on, 387
Internationalism, 325, 326–331
Interpersonal conflict, 4–5, 9, 97
Interpretation of Data tests, 417–420
Interstate Commerce Act, 247
Intrapersonal conflict, 5–8, 9, 45–48, 97, 250
Intuition, 57–58, 63
Investigation, 120–121
Iowa Child Welfare Research Station, 138, 140
Irrelevancy, 171
Isolationism, 327, 329

Japan, 327
Jews and Judaism, 252, 254, 256 n., 258, 264–266, 305–307, 310, 312
Jingoism, 329
Journals, 392–393
Judea, 289
Judgments, 41
  of fact and value, 70–75, 96–103
Justinian Code, 252

Know-Nothing party, 266
Knowledges, 36
Korea, 323
Ku Klux Klan, 265, 266

Labor, 135–136
  teaching materials, 387–388
  unions, 235
Laissez-faire economy, 233, 235, 245, 251
Laissez-faire leadership, 139–140
Language, 65–66, 258
Lay advisory council, 450
Leadership, 160–161, 448–449
  clarifying and defining problem, 175–180
  communication, facilitating, 165–168
  emotional climate, 162–165
  group, *see* Group leadership
  hypotheses, developing and refining, 180–182
    testing, 182–185
  problem solving, 168–172
  procedural rules, 161–162
  topic selection, 172–175
Learning, and facts, 37–41
  and insight, *see* Insights
  and problem solving, *see* Problem solving
  attitudes and values, 30–33
  continuity of, 35–37
  perceptual basis of, 23–25
  theories of, 11–12
    historical development, 12–14
    present tendencies, 14–20
    uncertainty over, 16–20
Lectures, 121–122, 140–141
Legion of Decency, 267
Liberal education, 282–285
Liberalism, 258, 410–412, 438
Liberties, *see* Civil liberties
Life problems, 226
Likert Scale, 414–415
Logic, 56–57, 65, 193, 422, 429
Logical Reasoning Test, 420–422
Love, 220, 307

Lower class, 271–275, 276, 279, 282, 283, 295, 302
Loyalty, 94–95, 221
Loyalty oath, 438, 442–444, 452
Lutheran Church, 316

Magazines, 378–380
Manichaeism, 308
Manumission, 252
Maps, 122
Markets, 233–234
Marriage, 230, 256, 291
Masturbation, 295
Matching items, 406–407
Materials, community resources, 388–391
  criteria for selection of, 368–370
  fiction, 374–376
  free and low-cost, 381–389
  history, 376–378
  magazines and newspapers, 378–381
  nonfiction, 373–374
  pamphlet series, 381–389
  professional, for teachers, 392–394
  reference books, 372–373
  textbooks, *see* Textbooks
Mathematics, 193
Meaning, 14–15
Memorization, 11, 14, 16, 105, 127–128, 208, 348, 350, 351–352, 370
Mental health, 7, 46–47, 445–446
  teaching materials, 386
  See also Neuroses
Metaphysics, 306
Methodology, 108–110, 111, 151, 168
  and content, 198–199, 215, 216–217, 218
Methods courses, 217
Mexico, 54–55
Middle class, 221, 229, 271–275, 276, 277, 279, 280, 281, 283, 293–295, 302
Middletown study, 228
Minority groups, *see* Race and minority-group relations
Minorities, and academic freedom, 451–453
Miscegenation, 261, 263
Models, 122
Modernism, religious, 311–312, 315, 335
Modesty, 300–302
Monasticism, 288
Money, 235, 346–347
Monopoly, 235, 244–246
Moors, 252
Moral choice, 90–92

method of, 96–103
nature of, 93–96
Moral decisions, 89 n.
Moral education, 103–106
Moral uncertainty, 92–93
Moral values, 210
Morality, 230
  and religion, *see* Religion
  teaching materials, 388
  See also Moral choice; Values
Motion pictures, 122, 123, 204, 267, 297, 373, 392, 416
Motivation, 27, 224
Motor responses, 13, 105
Motor skills, 11, 16, 26
Muckraking, 326
Mulattoes, 262
Multiple-choice items, 401–405

Nakedness, 301–302
Name calling, 422
National Association of Manufacturers, 437
National bankruptcy, 238
National Education Association, 452–453
Nationalism and patriotism, 230–231, 253, 313
  beliefs about, 324–328
  contradictions and confusions about:
    democratic ideals and practicality, 335–337
    enlightenment and ignorance, 333–335
    national security and civil liberties, 331–333
    nationalism and internationalism, 328–331
NATO, 328
Naturalism, 310–311, 315
Nature of Proof tests, 422–425
Nazism, 97, 265
Needs, individual and social, 217–223
Negroes, 250, 252–253, 261–264, 265, 332
Neuroses, 7, 92, 131, 152, 282
  and problem solving, 47, 50–52
Neutrality, teacher, 439–441
New Deal, 327
New Freedom, 327
New Testament, 308
New York University, 220
Newspapers, 380–381
"Nice girl," 297–300
Non-directive therapy, 131–132, 151
Nonfiction, 373–374
Non-threatening climate, 145–146, 153

Note-taking, 120
Nouveaux riches, 271, 281
Novels, 374–376
Nudity, 301–302

Obscenity, 296–297
Observation, 76, 77–78
Occupations, 4
Ohio Thinking Check-Up, 418–419
Old Testament, 288, 300, 307, 308, 310, 316
Oligopoly, 245
Open-book examination, 409
Open-mindedness, 146–148
Operational definition, 70
Opinions, 146–148, 162–163, 439–442
Out-groups, 254

Pacifism, 327
Paganism, 252, 288, 308
Pamphlets, 381–389
Panel, 160
Paranoia, 51
Parent-teacher associations, 450–451
Parents, reports to, 451
Past, psychological, 40
Pathways in nervous system, 13
Patriotism, *see* Nationalism and patriotism
Peace, 326, 328
Peckham Experiment, 136
Peer culture, 91, 95, 150, 293–296
Perception, 23
    failure of, 142–146
Perceptual field, 24–25, 27, 40, 41
Perceptual skills, 11
Periphery, 13
Permissiveness, 104–105, 117, 119, 150, 157, 441–442, 446
    in emotional climate, 145–146, 153, 162–165
Persecution, delusions of, 51
Persia, 258, 308
Personality disorders, 254–257
Petting, 294, 295, 302
Philippine Islands, 55–56
Philosophy, 192, 228, 283
    of education, 109–110
Philosophy of Education Society, 432–433
Pioneer Health Centre, Peckham, England, 136
Plainville study, 301
Pleasures, high and low, 316–319
Point Four program, 241
Policy statements, 72, 186
Political science, 191, 194, 198, 202, 228

Politics, 226, 362–363, 435–436, 439, 452
Polls, public-opinion, 112, 228, 229, 266 n.
Populism, 326
Portugal, 252, 253
Pragmatic psychology, 14, 15
Preconceptions, 185–186
Predestination, 309
Prejudice, 113, 230, 250–255, 447
Pressure groups, 200
Prices, 234
Private ownership, 235
Problem solving, ability in, 11, 15, 16, 17, 20, 138
    and content, 217–218
    and learning, 41–48
    and teacher, 114–118, 206
    intellectual attack in, *see* Intellectual attack
    meaningful statement of problems, 66–68
    reflective method, 59–63
    unconstructive behaviors in, 50–52
Problem-solving discussion, 158–160, 168–172, 357
    steps in, 172–187
Problems and projects, 205–206
Problems of democracy, course in, 191, 237 n., 306
Procedure, rules of, 161–162
Progressive Education Association, 453
Progressive-education movement, 9, 20, 386
Progressivism, 326
Projection, 51, 257
Projects, 126–128, 205–206
Propaganda, 425
Proportional selection, 84
Proposition, 148
Prosperity, and spending, 237–239, 247
Protestantism, 266, 267, 308–312, 319, 324
Pseudo conservatism, 255
Psychiatry, 193, 194, 222–223, 224, 228, 281
Psychological past, 40
Psychology, 226, 228, 291, 306, 334
    educational, 12–21
    social, 193, 194
Psychosomatic illness, 51–52
Psychotherapy, 143, 265
    and cultural needs, 222–223
    directive and non-directive, 131–132, 151–153
    individual and group, 132–134
PTA's, 450–451
Public, and academic freedom, 447–453

Public-opinion polls, 112, 228, 229, 266 n.
Punishments, 13, 14, 351–352
Puritanism, 289, 300
Purity, sexual, 291–293
Purposelessness, 18, 19

Questioning, 124–125
Quiz games, 352

Race, defined, 259–260
Race and minority-group relations, 230, 250–255, 332
    authoritarian personality, 255–257, 414–415
    contradictions and confusions about:
        Catholic menace and influence, 266–268
        Jewish greed and radicalism, 264–266
        Negro inferiority and capacity, 261–264
        racial differences and human similarity, 258–261
    teaching materials, 388
Racism, 251, 253–254
Radicalism, 264
Radio, 122, 128, 300, 333
Random selection, 84
Rank, 275–278
Rationalization, 53–55, 62, 144, 195, 336, 359, 430
Reasoning, 56–57, 63
Recall, 398–399, 408
Recency, 13
Recessions, 235, 237, 239, 247
Recordings, 122, 204, 392, 416
Reference books, 372–373
Reflection, 21
    and academic freedom, *see* Academic freedom
    and content, *see* Content; Materials
    and language, 65–66
    and problem solving, *see* Problem solving
    and values, *see* Moral choice
    evaluation of, *see* Evaluation
    evidence, *see* Evidence
    hypotheses as verifiable statements, 68–75
    techniques, *see* Techniques
Reformation, 324
Regression, 51
Religion, 226, 230, 259, 274, 276, 435
    and morality, 305–312
    contradictions and confusions about:
        belief and practice, 312–314

democracy and religion, 319–321, 324–325
    pleasures, 316–319
    science and religion, 314–316
    teaching materials, 388–389
Remembered experience, 76–77
Remmers scales, 413–414
Repression, 51, 153
Republicanism, 310, 319, 336–337
Research paper, 409
Responsibilities, shared, 138
Revelation, divine, 315
Rewards, 13, 14, 351–352
Roman Catholic Church, 266–268, 309, 310, 312, 324–325
Rome, 265, 289
Rote learning, 351–352
Round table, 160
Russia, 265

Salacity, 290, 296–297
Samoa, 90
Sampling, 83–85
Sanskrit, 258
Say's law of markets, 234
Scale of Beliefs test, 410–412
Scales, *see* Evaluation
Scapegoating, 51, 139
Schizophrenia, 47, 92
School boards, 450
Science, 7–8, 311
    and religion, 314–316
Scientific thinking, *see* Reflection
Sectarianism, 305
Security, 132–133, 220
Seduction, 294
Segregation, 436
Self-glorification, 257
Self-government, 333, 334, 336
Self-regulating market, 233–234
Semantics, 193, 236, 237
Sensory-motor skills, 11
Sex, 6, 91, 93, 229, 230, 256 n., 305 n., 312, 315, 317
    and class, 273, 274
    and education, 287–291
    and minority groups, 262, 263
    contradictions and confusions about:
        chastity and peer-group status, 293–296
        mental cleanliness and natural interests, 296–297
        modesty and sex appeal, 300–302
        nice girl and good sport, 297–300

Index of Subjects

Sex (*Continued*)
    purity and experience, 291–293
    teaching materials, 389
Sherman Antitrust Act, 247
Short-answer questions, 399, 408, 409
Short research paper, 409
Simple-recall questions, 408
Sin, 309, 310
Skills, 11, 16, 21, 26, 30
Slavery, 56, 252
Slides, 392
Social class, *see* Class
Social Darwinists, 278, 279
Social needs, 219–222
Social psychology, 193, 194
Socialism, 229, 230, 233, 236–237, 246–248, 329
Sociology, 25, 191, 192, 193, 194, 223, 228, 279, 291, 306
South, 261–262
Soviet Union, 9, 228, 436
Spain, 252, 253
Special pleaders, 452
Specialization, 196–198
Specimens, 122
Spelldown, 352
Spending, public, 236, 237–239, 242–244
Springboards, 344–347, 371
    civics, 361–362
    geography, 364–365
    history, 356–359
S-R bond, 13
Statements, meaningful, 66–68
    verifiable, 68–75
Status, 270–271, 277
Stereotypes, 46, 256–257
Still pictures, 122
Stimulus-response theory, 13, 14
Subject-matter courses, 216–217
Subject-matter switch, 116
Subsidies, 235, 236
Subversion, 8, 436, 443, 452, 453
Success, 221, 278–280
    and happiness, 280–282
Superficiality, 185
Supply and demand, 233–234
Syllogism, 56
Symposium, 160

Taboos, 61, 225, 230, 290, 301–302
Talmud, 288
Tariffs, 235
Tastes, 11
Taxes, 242–244
Taxpayers' federation, 451

Teacher, and academic freedom, *see* Academic freedom
    and college choice, 284
    and evaluation, *see* Evaluation
    and ground covering, 349–352
    and leadership, *see* Group leadership
    and moral education, 103–106
    and textbooks, *see* Textbooks
    and theories of learning, 18–20
    materials, *see* Materials
    organizations, 440, 452–453
    techniques, *see* Techniques
    tenure, 446, 452
Teachers College, Columbia University, 77, 391
Teachers' colleges, 16
Teaching-aids movement, 204–205
Techniques, 18–19
    and method, 108–110
    classification of, 119
    discussion, 125–126
    investigatory, 120–121
    projects and activities, 126–128
    questioning, 124–125
    teachers' responsibilities and, 111–118
    transmitting or telling, 121–124
Television, 128, 300, 301, 333
Telling techniques, 121–124
Tennessee Valley, 229, 382, 443
Tenure, 446, 452
Terms, value, 72, 73
Tests, *see* Evaluation
Textbooks, 122, 124, 217, 227, 343–344
    and appeal to authority, 55
    censorship of, 442–443, 452
    chapter-end helps, 347–349
    civics, 361–362
    criteria for selection, 370–372
    educational psychology, 16–17
    geography, 363–364
    high school and college, 202-204
    history, *see* History
    modern, 201–202
    springboard techniques, 344-347, 371
    rationalization in, 54–55
    traditional, 199–201
Theorization, 63, 429
Theory building, 195
Therapy, *see* Psychotherapy
Thought, data of, 214–216
    habits, changing of, 163–165
    measurement of, *see* Evaluation
Thought questions, 125
Threat, 145
    reducing, 146–148

Index of Subjects

Thrift, 273
Thurstone scales, 412–413
Tobacco, 317
Topics, 172–175
Totalitarianism, 6, 8–9, 20
Trade, balance of, 239–242
Transfer, 33–35, 354
Transmitting techniques, 121–124
Treason, 326
True-false examinations, 399–401
Two-valued orientation, 57
Tyranny, 432–433

Uncertainty, in beliefs, 410–411
   moral, 92–93
Understanding, 14
Undirected techniques, 119
Unions, labor, 235
   teachers', 440, 452–453
Unit-teaching movement, 205–206
United Nations, 328, 329–330, 443
Universe, 308, 310, 315
Universities, 6
Upper class, 271–272, 274, 276, 277, 279, 280, 282–284, 302

Value terms, 72, 73, 222

Values, 8, 46, 48, 68, 115, 144–145, 210, 435
   analysis of, 415–416
   and adolescence, 89–93
   conflicts in, 122–123
   judgments of, 70–75, 96–103, 125, 180–182, 186–187, 410
   learning of, 30–33
   See also Attitudes; Moral choice
Vatican, 266, 267
Verbal associations, 19, 210
Verifiability, 68
Veto power, 330
Virginity, 288, 291, 293, 298, 299
Vocational education, 282–285

Weasel words, 69
Western Electric Company, 136
Wiretapping, 332
Withdrawal, 51
Workbooks, 349, 443
World War I, 290, 327, 330, 405
World War II, 133, 140, 229, 323, 327

Yahweh, 306
Yankee City study, 228

Zoroastrianism, 308

471